MASTERPLOTS II

DRAMA SERIES
REVISED EDITION

MASTERPLOTS II

DRAMA SERIES
REVISED EDITION

2
Dog–Lia

Editor, Revised Edition
CHRISTIAN H. MOE
Southern Illinois University

Editor, First Edition
FRANK N. MAGILL

SALEM PRESS
Pasadena, California   Hackensack, New Jersey

Editor in Chief: Dawn P. Dawson

Managing Editor: Christina J. Moose   *Assistant Editor:* Andrea E. Miller
Project Editor: R. Kent Rasmussen   *Research Supervisor:* Jeffry Jensen
Production Editor: Joyce I. Buchea   *Acquisitions Editor:* Mark Rehn
Copy Editor: Sarah Hilbert   *Layout:* William Zimmerman

Library of Congress Cataloging-in-Publication Data
Masterplots II : drama series / editor Christian H. Moe. — Rev.
   p.   cm.
   ISBN 1-58765-116-5 (set : alk. paper) — ISBN 1-58765-117-3 (vol. 1 : alk. paper) — ISBN 1-58765-118-1 (vol. 2 : alk. paper) — ISBN 1-58765-119-X (vol. 3 : alk. paper) — ISBN 1-58765-120-3 (vol. 4 : alk. paper)
   1. Drama—20th century—Stories, plots, etc.   I. Moe, Christian Hollis, 1929-
PN6112.5 .M37 2003
809.2′04—dc21

2003012651

Second Printing

TABLE OF CONTENTS

TABLE OF CONTENTS

COMPLETE LIST OF TITLES IN ALL VOLUMES

Volume 1

Volume 2

Volume 3

COMPLETE LIST OF TITLES IN ALL VOLUMES

Volume 4

MASTERPLOTS II

DRAMA SERIES
REVISED EDITION

THE DOG BENEATH THE SKIN
Or, Where Is Francis?

Authors: W. H. Auden (1907-1973) and Christopher Isherwood (1904-1986)
Type of plot: Satire
Time of plot: The mid-1930's
Locale: Mythologized Europe
First produced: 1936, at the Westminster Theatre, London
First published: 1935

> *Principal characters:*
> THE VICAR OF PRESSAN AMBO
> GENERAL HOTHAM
> MRS. HOTHAM, his wife
> MISS IRIS CREWE, of Honeypot Hall
> SIR FRANCIS CREWE (THE DOG), her brother
> ALAN NORMAN, the unassuming protagonist
> FIRST JOURNALIST
> SECOND JOURNALIST

The Play

   The Dog Beneath the Skin opens in the garden of the vicarage at Pressan Ambo; the setting resembles that of a prewar musical comedy. The villagers promenade with several of the principal characters—the Vicar, General Hotham, his wife, and Miss Iris Crewe—who introduce themselves in lilting verse.

   The Vicar explains the fairy tale quest that is to serve as the main structure for the plot. He says that the patriarch of Pressan Ambo, Sir Bingham Crewe, has died, leaving behind two heirs: his son, Sir Francis Crewe, and his daughter, Miss Iris Crewe. Sir Francis Crewe, however, has disappeared; consequently, Sir Bingham's estate is left unsettled. Each year a man is chosen by lottery to find Sir Francis, and, if successful, his reward will be half of the land and Iris Crewe's hand in marriage. So far, eight have tried, and eight have failed. This year, the task falls to Alan Norman, a somewhat unassuming young man whose success seems no more likely than that of his predecessors.

   At this point, the Dog enters and "begins sniffing about." It is apparent that both the Vicar and General Hotham have kept the Dog at one time or another. As the General puts it, he turns up "like the prodigal son," stays one or two weeks, and then is off again, "cool as you please." Alan takes the Dog along as he sets out on his quest.

   After a brief scene in the saloon of a channel steamer, in which Alan meets the First and Second Journalists, the remaining two scenes of the act take place in the kingdom of Ostnia. There he witnesses preparations for the execution of several political prisoners. As the prisoners are led onstage with their wives and mothers, the Master of Ceremonies and the king of Ostnia discuss the matter as if it were itself a bit of show business, critiquing the previous execution and settling plans for the one now under way. Although the king is both apologetic and sympathetic, he carries out the execution with a gold revolver (amid Latin invocations to Zeus and Mars). The ladies of the court serve champagne and cakes as the queen attempts to comfort the bereaved wives and mothers. One of the women shouts "Murderers!!" and is "instantly and politely removed by footmen" as several courtiers "cough and look at the ceiling in pained embarrassment." Alan Norman and the two Journalists enter to enquire after Sir Francis. No one seems to have heard of him, but the king suggests that they try the red light district. They do, but do not find Sir Francis among the prostitutes and drug addicts of Ostnia.

The second act opens in Westland, a highly politicized and militarized lunatic asylum. At the back of the stage, overlooking the lunatics, there is a large portrait of a man in uniform, beneath which "Our Leader" is written. Instead of a face, the Leader of the Lunatics has a loudspeaker. Two medical officers push Alan onstage in a wheelchair and leave him with the lunatics, bound in a straitjacket. The Leader of the Lunatics, through the loudspeaker, makes a blatantly paranoid speech against the threats to the safety of their homeland. Noticing that he does not cheer their leader, various lunatics threaten Alan, but the Journalists and the Dog succeed in rescuing him. Sir Francis Crewe is not to be found among the lunatics of Westland.

During a transitional scene in a railway car, Grubstein, a shady sort of profiteering financier, suggests that they look in Paradise Park. There, the stage is set to resemble "a beautifully-kept lawn," and a number of people are walking about in sports clothes or pushing themselves about in wheelchairs. Paradise Park is the haunt of poets, lovers, and hypochondriacs; they are all too self-involved to know the whereabouts of Sir Francis Crewe.

The third and final act takes place in the Ninevah Hotel, located, as the introductory chorus tells us, in "a center of culture." Alan, the Journalists, and, after some squabbling with the hotel staff, the Dog all make their way to the restaurant. A revue is in progress, representing "all that is mechanical, shallow, silly, hideous and unbearably tragic in the antics of a modern cabaret." When Miss Lou Vipond appears onstage, Alan Norman exclaims, "By Jove, she's a stunner." Despite the warning of the journalists—"she's brought enough good men to their ruin"—Alan immediately forgets Miss Iris Crewe and falls in love with Miss Vipond. He goes off in search of flowers.

In the following scene, the stage is divided in half. To the right is Miss Vipond's bedroom, to the left the corridor outside. When the curtain rises, the corridor is lit, revealing the Dog, off in a corner. The hotel manager and a caravan of waitresses, pages, and chambermaids carry onstage an array of champagne, frocks, and furs for Miss Vipond. The lighting shifts as the scene progresses to the bedroom. Alan is embracing Miss Vipond, who is "a shopwindow dummy, very beautifully dressed." They carry on an amorous conversation. (When Miss Vipond speaks, Alan runs behind her and speaks for her in falsetto.) As Alan begins to undress Miss Vipond, the lights come up on the Dog, who, after a lengthy satiric monologue, takes off his dogskin, lays it aside, and exits as Sir Francis.

At this point, the manager enters and presents Alan with a bill. Alan cannot pay it, and the manager exits to get the police. When Sir Francis slips back onstage to retrieve his disguise, Alan recognizes him as the object of his quest. After a brief moment of elation, he remembers that the Manager is returning with the police. At Sir Francis's suggestion, he dons the dog costume and slips past the Manager and the police.

The final scene takes place once again in Pressan Ambo and the garden of the vicarage. A platform draped with a Union Jack and other flags of the empire occupies the greater portion of the stage. Sir Francis is once again wearing his dog disguise, but he now walks upright wth the costume head draped behind "like a monk's cowl." General Hotham, his wife, and Miss Iris Crewe all take their places on the platform as the Vicar delivers a long, patriotic sermon, recalling the similar speeches by the king of Ostnia and the Leader of the Lunatics. Mildred Luce, rendered hysterical by the speech, exclaims: "My sons were murdered, and they were bigger and handsomer than you'll ever be, any of you!" Reminiscent of the bereaved widow of Ostnia, her outburst makes the "most painful impression on all present."

The finale of the play has undergone some evolution. In the published version, Mrs. Hotham quickly leads Mildred offstage. The General restores order and, before Alan can reveal the success of his quest, announces that Miss Iris Crewe is engaged to be married to a well-known munitions manufacturer; Alan cries out, "Shame." Sir Francis then steps forward to reveal that he had been among them all along, disguised as the Dog. Both the Vicar and the General are dismayed, but Sir Francis condemns them for their hypocrisy and renounces his inheritance. He and Alan go off together with others from the village to join "a unit in the army of the other side," ostensibly the Socialist Party.

In the first production version, however, when Mildred Luce grows distraught at the Vicar's sermon, Sir Francis explains that the loss of her sons is all a neurotic fantasy, the result of poverty and an unsympathetic social system. Mildred, in her hysteria, takes a gun and kills Sir Francis.

Themes and Meanings

Most critics agree that *The Dog Beneath the Skin* reflects the political and social realities of the early to mid-1930's. In the year of the play's first production, Adolf Hitler had been rising in power for three years, the Spanish Civil War had begun, and European civilization seemed to be once again on the brink of general war. A sense of impending cataclysm continues through the play to Mildred Luce's hysterical speech at the end: "It's only play now. But soon they'll give you real rifles. You'll learn to shoot. You'll learn to kill whoever they tell you to. And you'll be trained to let yourselves be killed, too." She provides an explicit warning against the militarization sweeping Europe.

In Westland, the illogical logic of paranoia becomes pointedly a satire of Nazi Germany. "Of recent years," as the First Lunatic puts it, "there have appeared in our midst, masquerading as men of science, certain Jews, obscurantists and Marxist traitors," specifically recalling the Nazi pogroms and purges. The paranoia becomes international in scale as the Leader of the Lunatics directs his fears at socialist Russia, a nation "schooled in military obedience and precision, saluting even in the cradle." The lunatics of Westland, however, with their own militaristic posturing, have become the very image of their own fears.

W. H. Auden and Christopher Isherwood found social inequities to be at the root of the world's impending cataclysm. The people of Ostnia are said to "lead such terrible lives"; indeed, the Ladies of the Court, serving cake and champagne, point to the absurd disparity between the social classes, but little is offered to remedy the situation. "Believe me," the king tells his prisoners, prior to their execution, "I sympathize with your aims from the bottom of my heart. Are we not all socialists nowadays?" However, clearly, his aims are not socialist; they are designed to maintain, by violence, an aristocratic order which perpetuates the disparity between the privileged and the poor.

In the chorus that introduces Ostnia and Westland, the audience is warned not to "comfort yourself with the reflection: 'How very un-English.'" If British "follies are different," the chorus maintains, "it is because you are richer." Alan's inability to pay his bill at the Ninevah Hotel serves as a metaphor for the social and economic conditions of Europe. The narcissistic self-indulgence of the upper classes comes more and more at the expense of the lower. Sir Francis tells us: "As a dog, I learnt with what a mixture of fear, bullying, and condescending kindness you treat those whom you consider your inferiors, but on whom you are dependent for your pleasures. It's an awful shock to start seeing people from underneath."

His message is clear: The upper classes must renounce their self-indulgent pleasures. As one chorus puts it, "the film of poverty is expanding/ And soon it will reach your treasure and your gentlemanly behavior." When Sir Francis goes off to join "a unit in the army of the other side," most critics agree that he refers to the Socialist Party and is enjoining his audience to support Marxist reforms. Indeed, the play ends with the Marxist epithet: "To each his need; from each his power."

Dramatic Devices

At one level, *The Dog Beneath the Skin* is obviously intended to be a bit of satirical fun. Blatantly slapstick in its visual presentation—Sir Francis, for example, in his dog costume—it resembles the musical comedies and revues of its time. The fairy tale quest contains few genuine surprises and serves mainly as a pretext for broad political burlesque and caricature. On the whole, the effectiveness of the play depends largely on the verbal virtuosity of its playwrights and on an audience attuned to the unconscious ironies of naïve or self-indulgent characters.

On another level, however, the choruses which appear between scenes strike an ominously serious and morally didactic tone often quite different from the scenes they introduce. Derek Verschoyle, who reviewed the original production for *The Spectator*, summed it up nicely. It differs from musical comedy, he said, "chiefly in its assumption of a comprehensive moral outlook"; while the choruses "are eloquent and often moving," they are nevertheless difficult to reconcile with the burlesque of the plot. Even those critics who praise the play have felt it necessary to apologize for the work's lack of dramatic unity.

Auden and Isherwood must have themselves felt the difficulty. Indeed, the end of the play was revised not only for the initial production but again for the 1947 production at the Cherry Lane Theater in New York. In 1957, while teaching at Smith College, Auden asked his students to devise yet another closing scene.

Despite the tensions that inevitably arise in the staging of the play, however, most contemporary critics agree that the play is imaginative and ambitious in its attempt to draw together diverse elements. If it is not altogether satisfactory, the language of the play retains vitality, its satire its bite, and the choruses some pathos. As Charles Osborne has suggested, it retains "great energy and pace, and a really imaginative production, with appropriate cuts, would very likely reveal it as still able to entertain audiences in the theater."

Critical Context

Some critics have suggested that the patchwork manner of its composition may well have created many of the difficulties with the dramatic unity of *The Dog Beneath the Skin*. It is the first full-scale collaboration between Auden and Isherwood; in it, they draw together several of their earlier pieces. Several of the choruses, the main structure of the plot, and the Vicar's long sermon near the end come from an earlier, unpublished piece by Auden alone, "The Chase" (wr. 1934). "The Chase," in turn, had borrowed elements from an even earlier Auden and Isherwood collaboration, *The Enemies of the Bishop: Or, Die When I Say When* (1929).

"The Chase" has three interwoven subplots. The first, Alan Norman's search for the missing heir and his distraction by Miss Vipond, survived intact in *The Dog Beneath the Skin*, while incorporating elements of the second, in which two boys escape from a reformatory—one dressed as a dog, the other as a young woman. The third subplot, which rather tenuously links the others, involves a workers' strike at a lead mine. The missing heir, as well as the two escaped boys, had joined the workers' movement.

Faber and Faber had accepted "The Chase" for publication, but, having some misgivings, Auden withdrew it and revised it, following Isherwood's suggestions to eliminate the sexual implications of the young boy dressed as a girl and the political proselytizing centered on the strike. It remained, however, largely the work of Auden. *The Dog Beneath the Skin*, as it evolved from "The Chase," became dramatically more compact and more burlesque in tone, but many of the broader social and psychological concerns were lost.

The trend was reversed somewhat in the next Auden and Isherwood collaboration, *The Ascent of F6* (pb. 1936, pr. 1937). Like *The Dog Beneath the Skin*, it uses a fairy tale quest. The mountain F6 lies between British and Osnian Sudoland, and the first white man to reach its summit will rule both. The interest of the play, however, is sustained not by the specifics of its satire, but rather by the psychology of the characters in their quest for social power. Auden's long, Pulitzer Prize-winning poem *The Age of*

Anxiety: A Baroque Eclogue (1948) focused on man's isolation in a world of crumbling social traditions and beliefs without using the fanciful trappings of *The Dog Beneath the Skin* and *The Ascent of F6.*

Sources for Further Study

Auden, W. H. *In Solitude for Company: W. H. Auden After 1940—Unpublished Prose and Recent Criticism.* Edited by Katherine Bucknell and Nicholas Jenkins. New York: Oxford University Press, 1995.

Buell, Frederick. *W. H. Auden as a Social Poet.* Ithaca, N.Y.: Cornell University Press, 1973.

Carpenter, Humphrey. *W. H. Auden: A Biography.* Boston: Houghton Mifflin, 1981.

Davenport-Hines, Richard. *Auden.* New York: Pantheon Books, 1995.

Duchêne, François. *The Case of the Helmeted Airman: A Study of W. H. Auden's Poetry.* London: Chatto and Windus, 1972.

Fuller, John. *A Reader's Guide to W. H. Auden.* New York: Farrar, Straus, and Giroux, 1970.

Mendelson, Edward. *Early Auden.* New York: Viking, 1981.

Osborne, Charles. *W. H. Auden: The Life of a Poet.* London: Michael O'Mara, 1995.

Christopher L. Picard

DREAM ON MONKEY MOUNTAIN

Author: Derek Walcott (1930-   )
Type of plot: Allegory
Time of plot: The 1960's
Locale: A West Indian island
First produced: 1967, at the Central Library Theatre, Toronto, Canada
First published: 1970, in *Dream on Monkey Mountain and Other Plays*

>   *Principal characters:*
>   TIGRE and
>   SOURIS, two criminals
>   CORPORAL LESTRADE, a mulatto jailkeeper
>   MAKAK, a charcoal burner who becomes a visionary
>   MOUSTIQUE, a crippled friend of Makak

The Play

Dream on Monkey Mountain opens with a prologue set in a West Indian jail where Makak, an old black man, is placed after his arrest on Saturday night for being drunk and disorderly. The mulatto jailer, Corporal Lestrade, tells the two thieves in the other cell, Tigre and Souris, that Makak thinks he is the king of Africa. The three men taunt and mock Makak, who reveals that during a dream an apparition in the form of a beautiful white woman had appeared and ordered him to reclaim his African heritage.

Shifting to Monkey Mountain, where Makak lives, scene 1 re-creates in a flashback the inception of the dream. Early in the morning, Moustique awakens his friend Makak so they can go to the market to sell coal, but Makak insists that they instead begin a journey to Africa, as an apparition appearing before him during the night had commanded. Mounted on a donkey, with a bamboo spear in his hand and Moustique at his side, Makak starts down the hill to set out on his quest. In scene 2, Makak heals a man near death, thereby beginning to establish his fame among the folk. The third scene, still in the dream state, takes place a few days later in the market, where the vendors talk excitedly of Makak's miracles. Then Moustique enters, pretending to be Makak, and takes money and goods from the people, supposedly to finance his African journey; when they discover that he is a fake, they beat him. Makak arrives just as his friend dies.

Part 2 of the play returns to the jail. Scene 1 first recounts in a fairly realistic way the actual exchanges among Makak, the two thieves, and the corporal. It then moves into the dream state once more, acting out Makak's hallucinations, in which he stabs the corporal and escapes with the other two men. Once they have left the stage, the supposedly dead corporal rises, draws the knife out of his chest, and announces that he will track down Makak and the thieves, who are "attempting to escape from the prison of their lives." He goes on to explain: "That's the most dangerous crime. It brings about revolution."

Scene 2 continues the dream that began in the jail. The old black man and his fellow escapees, Tigre and Souris, stop to rest in the forest. Tigre, believing that Makak has money hidden on Monkey Mountain, plays along with the idea of going to Africa in order to pacify the old man; Souris, on the other hand, has started to believe in the vision, telling Makak: "But your dream touch everyone, sir. Even in those burnt-out coals of your eyes, there is still some fire." The corporal enters in pursuit and imitates a British colonial authority, ordering his imaginary native people in phrases like "What-ho, chaps, more lights" and "No fear, lads! Steady on!" Before long, though, the corporal becomes a convert as well. He murders the doubting Tigre and insists that they fulfill Makak's vision, claiming, "We cannot go back. History is in motion. . . . Forward, forward."

Scene 3 completes the dream and is called in the stage directions an "apotheosis," or an exaltation and glorification of an ideal. Makak, now a king in Africa, presides over a court where judgment falls on racial oppression throughout history. At Makak's side stands the corporal, a fanatical adviser who demands that all prisoners and traitors be put to death, including historical figures such as Abraham Lincoln and Cecil Rhodes. Moustique, who died in an earlier dream but has been resurrected, is also condemned—for betraying the vision and arguing that Makak's followers have corrupted his good intentions in order to fulfill their own desire for power and revenge. Finally, the white apparition appears before the court, the corporal demanding her death, explaining, "She is the colour of the law, religion, paper, art, and if you want peace, if you want to discover the beautiful depth of your blackness, nigger, chop off her head." Once Makak beheads the symbol of whiteness, he regains his freedom.

The epilogue, which takes place the next morning in the jail, returns to realism. Sober now, Makak is released, and his friend Moustique comes to take him back to Monkey Mountain. Although he had only dreamed his moment of glory, Makak has experienced a true apotheosis, one in which he discovered his own worth as a human being.

Themes and Meanings

In a production note, Derek Walcott calls *Dream on Monkey Mountain* "illogical, derivative, contradictory" and explains that "its source is metaphor." It should be treated as an allegory, whose themes and meanings emerge on several levels that do not allow for a single, well-defined interpretation.

The play first takes up the theme that has occupied so many Third World writers: revolution. Makak dreams of rejecting the white world and its tattered vestiges of colonialism in order to reclaim his African heritage. He sets out to arouse the people and in his dreaming establishes an African kingdom. However, unlike other revolutionary works, *Dream on Monkey Mountain* goes a step further and depicts the kingdom's ruination at the hands of lieutenants anxious for revenge and power. This apparent contradiction—the need for revolution versus its ultimate failure—sets the work apart from many such plays that call for an end to colonialism and foresee a utopia once the forces of white domination have been banished.

Thus, revolution may only be a metaphor to suggest another kind of change: that which takes place within the individual. On one level, Makak seeks to restore his black identity; on another, he reaches out purely for identity, neither as a black man nor as a white, but as a man. Early in the play, when he is asked his name by the jailer, he replies, "I forget." He has thus far been called only by his nickname Makak, which means monkey and was intended to describe his ugliness. When asked his race, he answers, "I am tired." At the end of the play, though, he says without hesitation, "My name is Felix Hobain." He returns to Monkey Mountain a man who has changed nothing outwardly but whose inner vision has altered dramatically.

These two kinds of revolution—national and personal—make up the major dichotomy that marks a play abounding in opposites. The distinction between dream and reality blurs, as do the lines between purity and corruption, good and evil, ambition and passivity. However "illogical" and "contradictory" the play may be in its treatment of the struggle against colonialism, *Dream on Monkey Mountain* makes it clear that self-realization must precede communal change. Although the work has been interpreted as radically anticolonial, Walcott himself has pointed out in an interview that he held higher aims than political confrontation.

Dramatic Devices

Dream on Monkey Mountain has about it a theatricality that not only forcefully depicts the outward experience of Makak but leads the audience into his interior life as well. This double entry depends in large part on the melding of reality and dream, which is attained through the rich language, the intentionally chaotic plot, the spare but original production techniques, the provision for spectacle, and the abundant symbols, both visual and linguistic.

The dialogue makes effective use of the West Indian dialect and idiom. It also satirizes the bureaucratic language of colonialism. At some points it borrows familiar lines and blends them into the characters' speech, as when Moustique begs and recites the Lord's prayer intermittently:

> And give us this day our daily bread . . . and is that self I want to talk to you about, friend. Whether you could spare a little bread . . . and lead us not into temptation . . . because we are not thieves, stranger . . . but deliver us from evil . . . and we two trespassers but forgive us brother . . . for thine is the kingdom and the power and the glory . . . for our stomach sake, stranger.

Like the language, the plot unfolds the play's action through mixing Western culture and the daily activities of West Indian life. For example, when Makak, riding a donkey and carrying a bamboo spear, and Moustique descend the mountain as they start their quest, the image of Don Quixote and Sancho Panza comes to mind.

Because the production techniques have been freed from the constrictions of realism, the stage becomes as fluid as the landscape of a dream. Action moves from the jail to mountain to marketplace to forest, accompanied by the dimming and raising of lights and the lifting and lowering of suggestive scenic pieces. Although the play might be performed with economy by doubling actors' roles and all but eliminating scenery, it could also take a spectacular turn, especially by accentuating its use of dance, costume, and music. Allegorical in its thematic structure, the play incorporates a wealth of symbols. Some are visual, as in the case of the black and white mask; others emerge from the action, as in the scene where the corporal mocks the British colonial attitude; and some arise from the diversity of the language, which employs the new English of the West Indians.

Critical Context

Although more widely known abroad as a poet, Derek Walcott has been the director and chief playwright of the Trinidad Theatre Workshop since he founded it in 1959. *Dream on Monkey Mountain*, his first play to gain international acclaim, won the Obie Award for a Distinguished Foreign Play when produced in New York in 1971, following its premier in Canada. As well as being staged in various parts of the United States and Europe, it was presented as part of the 1972 Olympics cultural program.

Walcott, in both his poetry and his drama, draws heavily upon his experience in the West Indies. Born in 1930 and descended from two white grandfathers and two black grandmothers, he grew up in a colonial environment on the tiny island of St. Lucia, where his mother was a headmistress in a Methodist grammar school. Walcott addressed this twofold identity in one of his poems, "A Far Cry from Africa":

> Between this Africa and the English tongue I love?
> I who am poisoned with the blood of both,
> Where shall I turn, divided in the vein?
> I who have cursed
> The drunken officer of British rule, how choose
> Between this Africa and the English tongue I love?
> Betray them both, or give back what they give?

Walcott, the 1992 Nobel Prize in Literature recipient, has managed to betray neither, but to meld the two parts of his heritage into a consistently humane expression through his art. *Dream on Monkey Mountain*, with its call for the revolution of self before the political revolution, remains central to an understanding of his work. The play shows that Walcott, although "divided in the vein," has enlarged the colonial experience and given it universal meaning. He is not revolutionary in the mode of the angry, didactic writer; he is instead a revolutionary in the matters that concern the human spirit.

Sources for Further Study

Baer, William, ed. *Conversations with Derek Walcott.* Jackson: University of Mississippi Press, 1996.

Brown, Stewart. *The Art of Derek Walcott.* Chester Springs, Pa.: Dufour, 1991.

Colson, Theodore. "Derek Walcott's Plays: Outrage and Compassion." *World Literature Written in English* 12 (April, 1973): 80-96.

Hamner, Robert D. *Derek Walcott.* Rev. ed. Boston: Twayne, 1993.

_____. "Mythological Aspects of Derek Walcott's Drama." *Ariel* 8 (July, 1977): 35-58.

_____, ed. *Critical Perspectives on Derek Walcott.* Boulder, Colo.: Reinner, 1997.

King, Bruce Alvin. *Derek Wolcott and West Indian Drama—Not Only a Playwright but a Company: The Trinidad Theatre Workshop, 1959-93.* Oxford, England: Clarendon Press, 1995.

Walcott, Derek. "Man of the Theatre." *The New Yorker* 47 (June 26, 1971): 30-31.

Robert L. Ross

A DREAM PLAY

Author: August Strindberg (1849-1912)
Type of plot: Expressionist
Time of plot: The beginning of the twentieth century
Locale: Sweden
First produced: 1907, at the Svenska Teatern, Stockholm, Sweden
First published: Ett drömspel, 1902 (English translation, 1912)

> *Principal characters:*
> INDRA, the Vedic god of war and thunder
> AGNES, Indra's daughter, incarnated as the Glazier's daughter
> THE GLAZIER, a glass-setter
> ALFRED, an officer who waits for Victoria
> THE FATHER, Alfred's father
> THE MOTHER, KRISTINA, Alfred's mother
> VICTORIA
> THE LAWYER, AXEL, who marries Agnes
> THE QUARANTINE MASTER
> THE POET
> HOMELY EDITH, who plays Bach on the piano

The Play

The prologue to *A Dream Play* is set in the firmament. Indra, the Vedic god of war and thunder, is addressing his daughter, who has followed a streak of lightning from the High Ether past the planet Venus and finds herself sinking toward Earth. She is puzzled by the dualities that she observes—stuffiness and beauty, darkness and light, and lamentation and joy. Indra instructs his daughter to visit Earth for the purpose of determining whether the constant complaints of humans are justified. She is then to return and make her findings known to him.

The action begins outside a castle, which is both mineral and vegetable: It is fertilized by stable manure, it grows, and it is crowned by a huge chrysanthemum bud. Indra's daughter is now incarnate as the daughter of a glazier. She tells her father that she is going to free someone who is a prisoner in the castle. The prisoner proves to be Alfred, the officer, who recognizes that the daughter is a child of Heaven and who complains of life's unjust treatment of him.

As the daughter and Alfred converse, their attention is caught by a domestic scene. In this scene the Mother (Kristina) and the Father of Alfred greet their son and the Glazier's daughter, whom they identify as Agnes. Kristina speaks of being about to die and reminds Alfred of his having committed a wrongdoing for which his brother was punished. Alfred, realizing that his mother has been dead for ten years, nevertheless continues his conversation with her and chides her for letting the maid Lena wear the mantilla that his father had given to her as a present. The Father lets his hurt be known; Kristina, concluding that to do good for one person is to hurt another, trims the candle and extinguishes it, leaving the stage in darkness.

Agnes hereupon utters two statements which will be repeated during the play and which will underscore the irony of human existence. The first is "Det är synd om människorna" (humans are to be pitied), an echo of Vergil's "Sunt lacrimae rerum et mentem mortalia tangunt" (there are tears for sufferings, and there is pity for humankind); the second is "Kärleken besegrar allt!" (love conquers all), a literal translation of Vergil's "Omnia vincit amor." She then finds herself in a stage-alley, on the far right of which is a door with an airhole in the shape of a four-leaf clover. She talks with a motherly doorkeeper, whose shawl she borrows, and with a billposter, whose life's wish, a dip net and a green fishing-box, has been realized after a wait of fifty years; later he will confess a gnawing disappointment for his fulfilled wish.

Alfred appears with a bouquet of roses to wait happily for Victoria, whom he is to marry. He calls to her, and she answers, but his wait will go on for years: The roses will wither, he will grow old, and Victoria will never come to him. He expresses his curiosity about what lies behind the door with the cloverleaf hole. A locksmith is summoned to open the door; the Glazier comes instead, but a policeman intervenes to prevent the opening. Alfred decides to consult a lawyer.

The next scene is set in the Lawyer's office. Agnes enters, still wearing the doorkeeper's shawl, with which she intends to gather up all human sufferings. The Lawyer insists that the shawl would be insufficient for the task and catalogs the extent of human sufferings. Agnes places a crown of thorns on his head and wins his consent to be married. During their married life, which is shown in the wretchedness of its poverty and sacrifice, Agnes addresses her husband as Axel. Their maid Kristina pastes strips of paper on the windows to keep out the cold. Alfred enters and Agnes accepts his invitation to go to Fairhaven.

They arrive at Foulstrand instead, a hellish place presided over by the Quarantine Master, who appears in blackface. An old dandy is pushed forth in a wheelchair; at his side are a sixty-year-old flirt and her forty-year-old companion. Alfred recognizes him as "the major, our schoolmate"; the Quarantine Master identifies him as Don Juan. The Poet joins the Quarantine Master, Alfred, and Agnes and points out to Agnes the married drudgery of Lina. The young lovers, He and She, arrive by boat from Fairhaven to spend forty days of quarantine on Foulstrand; they are horrified, and they learn that happiness must be built on agony. Alfred then relives one of his class sessions in school, where his answers are logical but totally wrong. The scene shifts to Fairhaven, where newlyweds learn that happiness is deceptive, the Blind Man bemoans the loss of his son, and Axel appears with information for the Blind Man and Agnes that the worst thing in life is repetition and that life consists of doing the same thing over and over again. As cries of agony from Foulstrand are heard, Axel tells Agnes that a liberator once came but was crucified by all the right-thinking people. Another hellish scene develops as coalheavers on the Italian coast punctuate their misery with explanations of the difference between labor and management.

The Poet and Agnes come to Fingal's Cave, where, again, the beauties of life are seen to be fraught with agony and suffering. The next major scene involves "all the right-thinking people" in the presence of the deans of the university faculties, who speciously argue the merits of their respective disciplines. At the end of this dispute the cloverleaf door is opened, presumably by the Glazier: The secret of life concealed behind it is Nothing. The deans debate the meaning of this and conclude that they have been deceived, but Agnes informs them that they "didn't understand the nothing." The Poet and Agnes muse upon their understanding of human life. The Doorkeeper returns to burn her shawl. Victoria, unseen by Alfred, enters to say, "My beauty, my sorrow"; she is followed by Homely Edith, who says, "My homeliness, my sorrow." The Blind Man puts his hand in the fire. Don Juan, from his wheelchair, urges haste, because "Life is short." Kristina enters, looking for more windows to paste. Finally, Agnes ascends to heaven after stating that the Poet has the best understanding of life, that she knows the agony of what it is to be human, and that she will intercede for humans when she is before the throne of heaven. She accomplishes her ascension by entering the growing castle, which then bursts into flames as its rooftop explodes into a giant chrysanthemum.

Themes and Meanings

A *Dream Play* consists of numerous variations on the theme of the essential unhappiness and meaninglessness of human existence. This is the same theme, in sum, of ancient Greek tragedy and of twentieth century existentialist literature. Indra's Daughter (as Agnes) explains it mythically shortly before her ascension: Brahma, the potential energy of the universe, permitted Maja, the World Mother, to activate him so that there would be complexity; the union of the divine Brahma with the earthly Maja was the Fall. Brahma's consequent descendants must, in order to free themselves from earthly bonds, cultivate asceticism and suffering, but the need to suffer is in conflict with the inherent predisposition toward pleasure and love. Ultimately love finds its greatest pleasure in the greatest suffering; the struggle between the suffering in pleasure and the pleasure in suffering produces the power that sustains the world; peace and rest are to be found only in death. Agnes's explanation, in concert with her understanding of the Nothing behind the cloverleaf door, reads like a passage from the new physics: Matter comes from nothing, from a state of complete entropy (or potential energy); energy's consciousness of itself kineticizes itself, and the material universe with all of its complexity results, but the complexity (the struggle) will eventually wind down as the universe returns to complete simplicity (complete entropy), possibly to be reactivated by its consciousness of itself.

Greek tragedy and existentialist literature both call upon humans to confront the nothingness of universal existence and to find meaning in accepting the responsibility for being what they are. Strindberg's admonition to this effect is implicit in his refrain, "Det är synd om människorna," which, as at least one critic (Evert Sprinchorn) has pointed out, means not only "Humans are to be pitied" but also "Sin is inherent in humans." The first meaning, with its element of pity, is dominant in Agnes's first six utterances of the line. In her seventh utterance of the line, during the Fairhaven-Foulstrand episode, the two meanings are in equipoise. Her subsequent two utterances of the line give dominance to the second meaning, with its element of sin. Agnes learns that humans deserve pity for the imperfections of human existence and that these very imperfections constitute sin.

Strindberg's observation of the paradox of human existence is expressed throughout the play, chiefly in reflections by characters that nothing is ever what one wants it to be. Homely Edith plays beautiful music, but no one will dance with her; her ugliness is her sorrow. Beautiful Victoria has the attractiveness that Edith desires, but Victoria's beauty itself is her sorrow. Humans want absolute or preordained meaning to exist behind the cloverleaf door, but there is nothing there; Strindberg thus reminds his audiences and readers that much of human life consists in fashioning meanings out of nothing.

Dramatic Devices

The actions, stage settings, and stage directions of *A Dream Play* are all calculated to produce the effect of a dream. To this end Strindberg removes the demarcations of logic, space, time, life, death, myth, and reality. While the work was in progress he retained the demarcation of acts: "Act 1" included all the scenes up to and including Agnes and Alfred's decision to marry, "act 2" moved from the wretchedness of the actual marriage through the Coalheavers episode, and "act 3" began with the visit to Fingal's Cave. Subsequently, however, he abandoned the division into acts and all designations of scenes and episodes save for asterisks and white spaces. The dreamlike continuity that he thereby achieved has been deprived of much of its efficacy by editors and translators, who preferred to restore the three-act structure of the draft.

The nebulousness of a dream is created through unobtrusive scene changes—sometimes in brief darkness, sometimes with the addition of a screen or simple backdrop, sometimes by allowing a single prop to serve different functions in different scenes—and by overt characteristics of fantasy. The Father, for example, at one point walks right through a wall. The growing castle combines the worlds of mineral, vegetable, and, given the humans inside it, animal. The living converse with the dead as though the dead were still alive (but not, it is to be noted, as though the dead had been resurrected). The effects of time's passage are discernible, as in the cases of a Lina grown ten years older and the naïve, girlish Agnes having developed wisdom and maturity, but the passage itself is entirely indistinct. Agnes plays a *Kyrie* on the organ, which produces music in the form of women's and children's voices. Later, a ships' buoy issues forth music, again a *Kyrie*, as prelude to a vision of Christ walking on the water. The conclusion of the play—the burning castle and the blooming of the giant chrysanthemum—is consistent in its special effects with the continuum of the phantasmagoria.

The major dramatic device is the use of Vedic deity in the context of incarnation, ascension, and mediation between the human and the divine. Into this context are woven symbols and images of the Christian Messiah. The Lawyer, for example, serves as a repository of human suffering and is accordingly given a crown of thorns by Indra's Daughter; the marriage of the two, as Agnes and Alfred, manifests a conjunction of Eastern and Western religions, the dramatic import of which is both the religious complementarity of male and female and the failure of religion (as a human construct) to provide a meaning for human existence.

Critical Context

Where Henrik Ibsen had hit his stride with realistic drama and then developed a naturalism in his later work, August Strindberg hit his stride with naturalistic drama— for example, *Fadren* (pr., pb. 1887; *The Father*, 1899) and *Fröken Julie* (pb. 1888; *Miss Julie*, 1912)—and turned, after a particularly harrowing period in his life, to expressionist drama. The turning-point period lasted from 1894 through 1897 and is detailed in his autobiographical work, *Inferno* (1897; English translation, 1912). During this period, which followed the divorce from his first wife in 1891 and separation from his second wife in 1894, he existed in a state marked by hallucinations, near madness, and odd pursuits, including occultism and alchemy. His unhappy marriages—he later, in fact, had a third unhappy marriage ending in divorce—contributed to the sense of incompatibility between the sexes that is much in evidence in *A Dream Play*.

The canon of Strindberg's expressionist plays include one early work, *Lycko-Pers resa* (pr., pb. 1883; *Lucky Peter's Travels*, 1912; better known as *Lucky Per's Journey*), a play modeled less on expressionism than on Ibsen's *Peer Gynt* (pb. 1867; English translation, 1892). The others, along with *A Dream Play*, are *Himmelrikets nycklar* (pb. 1892; *The Keys of Heaven*, 1965); *Till Damaskus* (parts 1 and 2, pb. 1898; part 3, pb. 1904; *To Damascus*, 1913), a trilogy which Strindberg considered to be his companion piece to *A Dream Play*; *Spöksonaten* (pb. 1907; *The Ghost Sonata*, 1916); and *Stora landsvägen* (pb. 1909; *The Great Highway*, 1954), Strindberg's last play.

Criticism of *A Dream Play* ranges to extremes; some critics dismiss it as totally incoherent while others see it as Strindberg's greatest play. Against the charge that it lacks characterization, defenders cite the subjective growth of Agnes from her incarnation as an innocent girl to her ascension as a female force of divine wisdom. That Strindberg wanted his characters to serve as generic types is clear from his identifications of them by function (the Mother, the Lawyer, the Poet, and so on) more than by name. Properly produced, *A Dream Play* provides audiences with a lyrically spectacular display of existential insufficiency; carefully and appreciatively read, it offers the satisfactions of poetic drama in the tradition of Johann Wolfgang von Goethe and Percy Bysshe Shelley.

Sources for Further Study

Austin, John. Review of *A Dream Play*. *Theatre Journal* 47 (December, 1995): 553-556.

Carlson, Harry G. *Out of Inferno: Strindberg's Reawakening as an Artist*. Seattle: University of Washington Press, 1996.

Johnson, Walter. "*A Dream Play:* Plans and Fulfillment." *Scandinavia* 10 (1971): 103-111.

_____. "Introduction to *A Dream Play.*" In *A Dream Play and Four Chamber Plays.* Seattle: University of Washington Press, 1973.

Marker, F. J., and Christopher Innes, eds. *Modernism in European Drama.* Toronto, Ont.: University of Toronto Press, 1998.

Meyer, Michael. *Strindberg: A Biography.* London: Secker and Warburg, 1985.

Sprigge, Elizabeth. *The Strange Life of August Strindberg.* New York: Macmillan, 1949.

Sprinchorn, Evert. "The Logic of *A Dream Play.*" In *Strindberg: A Collection of Critical Essays*, edited by Otto Reinert. Englewood Cliffs, N.J.: Prentice-Hall, 1971.

_____. *Strindberg as Dramatist.* New Haven, Conn.: Yale University Press, 1982.

Tornqvist, Egil. *Strindbergian Drama.* Atlantic Highlands, N.J.: Humanities Press, 1982.

Roy Arthur Swanson

THE DRESSER

Author: Ronald Harwood (Ronald Horowitz, 1934-   )
Type of plot: War; tragicomedy
Time of plot: January, 1942
Locale: A small theater in the English provinces
First produced: 1980, at the Royal Exchange Theatre, Manchester, England
First published: 1980

> *Principal characters:*
> NORMAN, a theatrical dresser
> SIR, an actor-manager
> HER LADYSHIP, an actor and Sir's partner
> MADGE, the stage manager

The Play

A two-act play, *The Dresser* is set in the principal dressing room, corridor, and wings of an unspecified provincial theater in England, in January, 1942. Present are Norman, Sir's dresser, and Her Ladyship, Sir's personal and professional partner. They are discussing the bizarre behavior and state of mind of Sir, who is elderly and becoming feeble: Earlier in the day he was out in the local marketplace, in the rain, undressing and crying, and has been taken to hospital. Her Ladyship and Madge want to cancel the performance, but Norman demurs.

Sir walks in, having discharged himself from the hospital. He wants to get ready for the play, though he cannot remember which play. Norman keeps reminding him that it is William Shakespeare's *King Lear.* While Norman attends to his makeup and costume, he also strengthens Sir's resolve to perform by saying that there will be a full house.

At this point, the problems of a small company of players begin to emerge. One actor, Davenport-Scott, has been kept in police custody for homosexual behavior, so the casting will be altered. Another actor, Oxenby, is unhelpful because Sir will not read the play he has written. Sir assures Her Ladyship and Madge that he is fine and will give a good performance as King Lear. Only to Norman does Sir show his doubts, and his bantering relationship with Norman, by turns respectful, worried, insulting, and witty, is demonstrated. Norman projects a degree of confidence in Sir's ability to perform this evening, though he clearly is unsure.

Another problem is that World War II rages around them: German aircraft drop bombs before and during the performance, and the air-raid sirens can be heard at intervals. The lines of the play make frequent reference to the war and its effects.

As he helps Sir with his first lines, Norman swigs brandy. There is some discussion of Sir's autobiography, which he is on the verge of beginning. Norman is very worried at having to make an opening announcement to the audience that the play will continue despite an air-raid warning. It is this announcement that closes the first act and, repeated word for word, opens the second.

The performance of *King Lear* is overheard from the wings, so that the audience sees Norman, Madge, and those waiting to go onstage, though the play itself is set off-stage. However, Sir's mind has seized up again, and he will not stand up and walk on-stage. The line "The King is coming" has to be repeated before he will cooperate. Only a few lines of *King Lear* are heard. It is clear that this is a scaled-back version for a small company, with Her Ladyship, as Cordelia, being the only one of Lear's daugh-ters to appear onstage.

Norman and the others work hard in the wings to create sound effects for the storm, but as Sir comes off for the interval he is unhappy with the lacking sound effects. Her Ladyship and Norman take turns in staying with Sir during the interval, when he needs to rest. Her Ladyship begs Sir to announce his retirement and not tempt fate with more performances. It is revealed through this exchange that not only are they unmarried (he is not divorced from his wife) but he is not really a "sir" and has never been knighted by the monarchy.

Suddenly aware of his own frailty, Sir attempts to give Madge, who has been with him for twenty years, the ring he wears, supposedly once worn by the famous actor Edmund Kean, and he enjoys a physical grope of Irene, the youngest member of the company. Norman, listening to the groping incident, intercepts Irene and interrogates her. When she admits that Sir has lifted her up, Norman laughs and tells her that Sir is only seeking somebody lighter than Her Ladyship for the scene in which he must lift the dead Cordelia.

Just a few lines of the second half of *King Lear* are heard. Sir then makes a short speech to the audience, prompted by Norman, advertising a performance of *Richard III* for the following night and performances in the town of Eastbourne the following week. Yet back in his dressing room, Sir has a word with Norman and two of the ac-tors and then, with little warning, dies. Norman calls Madge and, though he is rude about Sir's ingratitude, makes it clear that he, like her, loved Sir very much.

Themes and Meanings

Chief among the themes and meanings of the play is a loving and respectful por-trait of an actor-manager, a type which was an endangered species in 1942 and later became virtually extinct. The play thus serves on one level as a piece of nostalgia. Ronald Harwood worked as the dresser for Sir Donald Wolfit (an actor-manager who specialized in Shakespearian roles) for almost five years, but, as Harwood points out in a foreword, the play must not be read as autobiographical. Nonetheless, Har-wood's knowledge enables him to construct a plausibly grand and idiosyncratic actor-manager character and provide an accurate portrait of theater life. Some of the actors may be getting too self-important, like Oxenby, while some are willing to take on larger parts, like Geoffrey Thornton. Some commit indiscretions, like Davenport-Scott, necessitating wholesale shuffling of parts. There are always financial problems, with the worry of attracting a sufficient paying audience. The fact that the whole company stays not in hotels but in poor-quality "digs" (boarding-house accommodation) is mentioned only in passing. Sir has problems with himself, not knowing when to retire (though acutely aware of his failing health and memory) and unable to keep his hands off young women. The audience begins to suspect that, despite the loving nicknames Sir and Her Ladyship have for each other, there may be sexual tension between them, perhaps related to Sir's old-age impotence.

The relationship between Sir and Norman is central to the success of the play. Both Norman and Madge have fallen for Sir's charisma. Norman is the major character with the wittiest lines. Sir and Norman can only cooperate in a roller-coaster fashion, with Norman hiding his feelings behind a façade of cynicism and humor, but needing both alcohol and Sir's respect to keep his insecurity in check. Norman's overt campiness is no problem in a theatrical milieu, though he has problems talking about himself and instead claims to have a friend in any apropos situation.

The World War II setting—with frequent references to air raids, bombs, shortages, rationing, Adolf Hitler, the fact that most able-bodied men are in uniform, and a mention of a recuperating airman in the audience—not only adds excitement but also makes the setting more closely resemble the time of war in which King Lear finds himself. In fact, Sir and Norman are fighting their own separate internal and external wars: One is too old for call-up and the other is considered psychologically unfit due to his homosexuality. Sir's external "war" includes his determination not to let the Germans prevent the dissemination of culture, but to continue to present Shakespeare to the English people. Norman's external war (in a subordinate role—he is more of an experienced sergeant, while Sir is definitely officer material) is to help Sir in any way he can.

Harwood uses many period and locale-specific references that may be obscure for American theatergoers. These include references to Dunn's (an old-fashioned chain of gents outfitters), the Kardomah (a chain of cafés, now defunct), the difficulty of obtaining chocolate at the time (even though it was not rationed until later), and Sir telling Norman that he could find work as a steward on a ship, a sly reference to Norman's homosexuality because a steward was a job often sought by gays when their sexuality was still illegal in Britain.

Dramatic Devices

To show a play within a play was a device used by Shakespeare himself, but to have the play's action technically occur offstage while a major Shakespearean work occurs onstage (but out of sight to the audience of *The Dresser*) is a device that might have come from the pen of playwright Tom Stoppard, whose *Rosencrantz and Guildenstern Are Dead* (pr. 1966, pb. 1967) made famous use of it. Apart from this device, *The Dresser* is conventional. It builds up the character of Sir (the most impressive of the cast) before he enters. The same minimal set of Sir's dressing room, the corridor outside it, and the wings can be used throughout the play, with only a change of lighting for emphasis on different areas at different times. This is economic but never boring: The relative lack of physical action is more than compensated for by frequent entrances and exits, by the drama of revelations, and by the tensions of *King Lear* being performed just offstage. Sir's breakdown in the marketplace is only reported, and his death at the end is undramatic, but both work well in context.

Most of the play consists of scenes between two characters. The most successful of these are undoubtedly those between Sir and Norman, due to their love-hate relationship and to Norman's over-the-top performance. The sparkling wit and frequent allusions, particularly in Norman's speeches, make these scenes entertaining and add depth to the characters. There is irony in the fact that Norman is meant to be the best actor in the company, even though he lacks the confidence to appear onstage. The other parts seem to have been deliberately underwritten, and to a certain extent the members of the company represent types that used to be found within a small traveling theater company.

Critical Context

The Dresser is essentially a play about the theater. It was written from a deep understanding of a vanished facet of the English theatrical world and is a warm and loving tribute to that lost world. While the play was written when Harwood was in his forties, its detail comes partly out of his theater work during his twenties, including a spell as a dresser for Sir Donald Wolfit. Harwood has always been interested in theater, studying at the Royal Academy of Dramatic Art in London as a young man and working as a stage actor for seven years. Much of his writing has been for or about the stage, including more than one dozen plays and a biography of Wolfit.

The Dresser is in part a historical play, keeping alive the details, topics of conversation, and prejudices of English life during World War II. Its setting is a time when Harwood was alive but still a boy in South Africa, so the details have been researched, yet are true and vivid; the setting is part of the play and is not forced. Its accurate historical depiction of setting, era, and profession is its most significant feature.

The Dresser was critically acclaimed as a play. There have been many productions of it around the world, and it remains Harwood's best-known play, thanks in large part to its quality and to the success of the 1983 film version with its screenplay by Harwood.

Sources for Further Study

Brustein, Robert. "The Naked and the Dressed." *The New Republic* 185 (December 9, 1981): 21, 24-25.

Harwood, Ronald. *Sir Donald Wolfit, CBE: His Life and Work in the Unfashionable Theatre*. London: Secker & Warburg, 1971.

Rich, Frank. "'Dresser,' a Monarch, and His Loyal Vassal: The Show Must Go On." *New York Times*, November 10, 1981, p. C7.

Chris Morgan

DRIVING MISS DAISY

Author: Alfred Uhry (1936-   )
Type of plot: Social realism
Time of plot: 1948-1973
Locale: In and around Atlanta, Georgia
First produced: 1987, at Playwrights Horizons, New York City
First published: 1988

> *Principal characters:*
> DAISY WERTHAN, an elderly Jewish widow
> HOKE COLEBURN, her somewhat younger chauffeur
> BOOLIE WERTHAN, her son

The Play

   Set in Atlanta during the 1940's through the 1970's, Alfred Uhry's Pulitzer Prize-winning play, *Driving Miss Daisy*, is an engaging drama that captures effectively the blossoming friendship between two unlikely characters—Miss Daisy, a wealthy, elderly Jewish widow, and Hoke, her African American chauffeur. Uhry explores the nuances of their growing personal affinity within the context of Atlanta, historically the locale of economic instability and significant civil rights activity. Proudly self-reliant, independent and sprightly, Miss Daisy is forced by her son, Boolie, to accept Hoke as her chauffeur. Boolie determines that she is incapable of driving herself after she backs her car into the garage of her neighbors, the Pollards. Although initially she is reluctant to accept Hoke's services, Miss Daisy soon perceives that she has more in common with Hoke than she ever imagined. Within the first few days of their encounter, Hoke defines the parameters of their relationship when he says, "Miz Daisy, you needs a chauffeur and Lawd know, I needs a job. Let's jes' leave it at dat." Hoke's observation of their situation echoes Miss Daisy's statement about Idella, her housekeeper: "She's been coming to me three times a week since you [Boolie] were in the eighth grade and we know how to stay out of each other's way."

   Uhry weaves the tapestry of their relationship deftly with incidents like one in which Miss Daisy accuses Hoke of eating her can of salmon without her permission and demands that Boolie have a talk with him but is deeply embarrassed when Hoke returns the next morning with a new can of salmon as replacement. This incident is similar to the morning of the ice storm, years later, when Hoke braves the storm to bring Miss Daisy her morning coffee from Krispy Kreme as he knows that she does not have electricity in her house. Such scenes define the rich texture of their relationship. Another such incident occurs when Hoke and Miss Daisy go to Alabama for her brother Walter's ninetieth birthday. They get delayed after losing their way once, in spite of her meticulous planning, and Hoke has an urgent need to relieve himself. They have just passed a service station, but it is the age of Jim Crow, and "colored" people are not allowed to use this facility, so Hoke stops the car just a few miles short of Mobile, much to the chagrin of Miss Daisy. He leaves the car and takes the key with him. She realizes her dependence on him and he articulates his need for maintaining his dignity.

Along with these "nicks and dents" in the relationship, Uhry provides glimpses of rare intimacy emerging between the two characters. They share their deepest memories uninhibitedly. One such moment occurs when Miss Daisy shares with girlish timidity her first memory of her trip to Mobile, Alabama, and the memory of the salty taste of the ocean waters. When Hoke drives Miss Daisy to the synagogue and learns that the temple has been bombed, he recalls the lynching of his friend's father and the effect it had on him as a young boy while gently reminding Miss Daisy that although she and the world may claim that things are changing, prejudice still lingers. Earlier, during a routine visit to the cemetery, Hoke also discloses to her, with great embarrassment, his inability to read. Miss Daisy teaches him to read and gives him a gift at Christmastime (all the while insisting that it is not a Christmas gift). It is a writing tablet that she used as a teacher. With characteristic sense and keen sensibility, Uhry charts the course of their friendship through everyday incidents.

There are two other characters in the play, Idella, the housekeeper, and her daughter-in-law, Florine, who are so often alluded to, and in such vivid manner, that the audience feels their presence. Uhry shows the bond strengthening between Hoke and Miss Daisy by showing how she gradually takes him into confidence and feels comfortable enough to make derogatory remarks about Florine. When Idella dies, Miss Daisy and Hoke feel her absence, and Miss Daisy remarks that Idella is lucky, thus revealing her innermost fears about her own future. Idella and Florine serve as catalysts in strengthening the bond between Hoke and Miss Daisy.

Near the end of the play, Miss Daisy is in her nineties, slow in her movements, but with her characteristic pride and independence intact. However, she suffers an attack of senile dementia one day, and Hoke encounters a distraught Miss Daisy desperately looking for her students' papers, thinking that she is still a teacher. Hoke warns her assertively that if she does not collect herself together she may end up in an institution. Miss Daisy then admits to Hoke that he is her best friend. Boolie sells the house two years after Miss Daisy's admittance to a nursing home, and the play ends on a very tender note: Affirming their long-lasting friendship, Hoke feeds Miss Daisy her Thanksgiving pie.

Themes and Meanings

Although friendship between two unlikely persons—an elderly, wealthy, white Jewish widow and her black chauffeur—is the predominant theme of the play, race relations, human dignity, integrity, and trust are other important themes in the play. It takes a man of great personal integrity like Hoke to lessen and eventually to eliminate the subconscious prejudice harbored by Miss Daisy. Although Miss Daisy compares African Americans to little children and makes snide remarks about Christians, she asserts to Boolie throughout the play that she is not prejudiced and he knows it. Miss

Daisy's subconscious bigotry is also depicted in her expression of utter displeasure at her daughter-in-law's elaborate Christmas decorations and her socializing with Episcopalians.

Hoke, honest and protective of Miss Daisy but never subservient, is also not free from prejudice. He successfully negotiates a raise with Boolie while at the same time making a disparaging comment about Jeanette Harris, Boolie's cousin's wife, who tried to hire him away from the Werthans as her chauffeur. "Now what you think I am? I ain' studyin' workin' for no trashy somethin' like her." When Miss Daisy extends a backhanded invitation to Hoke for the Martin Luther King Day celebration, the audience can see that her prejudice is ebbing but is still present. Hoke establishes his integrity and personal dignity when he responds to the invitation, "Nevermind baby, next time you ask me someplace, ask me regular." It is only after Hoke cautiously and lovingly talks to her during her lapse into senile dementia that she brings herself to say, "You are my best friend, Hoke."

The personal drama of Miss Daisy and Hoke draws its sustenance from the larger context of changing race relations in Atlanta, Georgia, and throughout the United States. Sporadic allusions to segregated bathrooms, Boolie Werthan's hesitation to attend the Martin Luther King dinner for fear of being branded as "Martin Luther Werthan" behind his back and subsequently losing his business contacts, and Hoke's granddaughter teaching biology at Spelman College are examples of the lack of progression in transforming the racial landscape. It is Uhry's brevity and the suggestion of the possibilities of multicultural friendships that lend the play its full meaning and save it from being a sappy melodrama.

Dramatic Devices

Driving Miss Daisy is a one-act play with scene shifts occurring about twenty-four times throughout the play. The play spans two and one-half decades. The structure of the play is episodic and moves chronologically forward, providing insight into characters' lives through simple events and incidents like a trip to the cemetery or to Alabama to attend a birthday celebration, a Christmas party at Boolie's home, an ice storm, a celebration of Martin Luther King, and a visit to a nursing home. The plot and action are deceptively simple while the dialogue slowly unravels key information about the main characters. When Boolie appraises Hoke of his mother's "highstrung" and independent nature and wonders if Hoke would be able to handle her, Hoke's pithy response is "I use to wrastle hogs to the ground at killin' time, and ain' no hog get away from me yet." Uhry creates a charming lyrical rhythm by using southern dialect punctuated with colloquial expressions. He is a master of understatement, and it is what the play does not say that actually enhances its appeal.

Issues concerning ethnicity and race, conflicts between the young and old, rich and poor, Jew and Gentile are all addressed with subtlety and economy. The exposition, besides introducing the conflict, also imparts necessary information pertaining to the geography, economy, and time through dialogue about cars, insurance, and the churches that people attend. The climax is very restrained and refined, with Miss

Daisy simply saying to Hoke, "You're my best friend." At the heart of the play is the value of human dignity, integrity, and humans' inherent dependence on one another, which becomes the pervasive motif throughout the play. The characters, their actions, and the dialogue highlight this theme. When Boolie insists on hiring Hoke to drive Miss Daisy around, she responds,

> I am seventy-two years old as you so gallantly reminded me and I am a widow, but unless they rewrote the Constitution and didn't tell me, I still have rights. And one of my rights is the right to invite who I want—not who you want—into my house. You do accept the fact that this is my house?

Humor is another significant device that Uhry uses to underscore the personalities of the characters and make them come alive without elaborate descriptions or scene settings. One example is Hoke's summation of his achievement, at the beginning of his tenure as Miss Daisy's chauffeur, driving his reluctant passenger to the local Piggly Wiggly: "Yassuh, only took six days. Same time it take the Lawd to make the worl'."

Critical Context

Alfred Uhry's body of work includes songs, adaptations, librettos, musical works, and film scripts. *Driving Miss Daisy* was originally written for his family members and first staged in a theater that would hold approximately seventy-five people. Uhry has noted that he was surprised at the play's subsequent and overwhelmingly wide appeal. When the play was made into a film, he received an Academy Award for best screenplay adaptation. Composer Robert Waldman, his long-standing collaborator with whom he worked as lyricist and librettist for *The Robber Bridegroom* (pr. 1975, pb. 1978; based on the novella by Eudora Welty), also composed the music for the premiere of *Driving Miss Daisy*. The expertise Uhry gained in his musicals *Here's Where I Belong* (pr. 1968; based on John Steinbeck's *East of Eden*, 1955) and *America's Sweetheart* (pr. 1985), in addition to his career as a teacher of playwriting and lyric writing, provided the technical expertise for *Driving Miss Daisy*, although the characters were modeled after his own relatives and acquaintances. In his preface to the play, he attributes the play's remarkable success to the fact that "I wrote what I knew to be the truth and people have recognized it as such."

Sources for Further Study

Gussow, Mel. "Driving Miss Daisy." *New York Times*, April 16, 1987, p. C22.
Kauffman, Stanley. "Cars and Other Vehicles." *The New Republic* 202 (January 22, 1990): 26-28.
_____. "Southern Comforts." *The New Republic* 208 (April 5, 1993): 30-31.

Kokila Ravi

EACH IN HIS OWN WAY

Author: Luigi Pirandello (1867-1936)
Type of plot: Problem play
Time of plot: The 1920's
Locale: Italy
First produced: 1924, at the Teatro dei Filodrammatici, Milan, Italy
First published: Ciascuno a suo modo, 1924 (English translation, 1923)

> *Principal characters:*
> DELIA MORELLO, a leading lady
> MICHELE ROCCA, her lover, an actor
> DORO PALEGARI, a young man
> FRANCESCO SAVIO, Doro's good friend
> DIEGO CINCI, another of Doro's friends
> AMELIA MORENO, an actor viewing the play
> BARON NUTI, her lover

The Play

The handbill that the audience receives upon entering the theater notes that the evening's performance is based on a true tragedy: the suicide of La Vela, a young artist, whose fiancé, the noted actor Amelia Moreno, had betrayed him through an affair with Baron Nuti, a nobleman engaged to La Vela's own sister. The handbill informs the audience that the number of acts to be performed cannot be stated specifically because of "unpleasant incidents" the management fears may arise during the evening.

The performance opens at the Palegari home, with the report of an argument of the previous evening between Doro Palegari and Francesco Savio concerning the guilt of this unfaithful woman, here played by Delia Morello. Doro had defended her as innocent of any intent to harm the artist by her flirtation, while Francesco had blamed Delia for the young man's suicide. Under probing by his friend Diego Cinci, Doro reverses his position and declares Delia guilty of treacherous deceit. At this point, Francesco arrives to apologize for his angry words to Doro on the previous evening; he too, under questioning by Diego, reverses his opinion, so that he now professes Delia blameless in the affair. Paradoxically, Doro and Francesco again quarrel from their new positions, this time to the point of a duel to take place the following morning at Francesco's home.

At this juncture, Delia herself appears to thank Doro for his brave defense of her character, although she confesses herself deserving of blame for the artist's death since she had gone off with Michele Rocca not out of love but rather merely to spite her young fiancé's family for treating her as unworthy to marry their son. Her admission of such motivation only confuses Doro further. He sees himself now as committed to a duel with a close friend over a sordid affair concerning whose moral truth even the chief precipitator has no clear notion.

The curtain falls on the first act, only to go up again immediately on a replica of the side hall and a corner of the lobby of the theater itself. Here actors mingle as "critics" and "audience" to discuss the events of the first act. Some praise it as a true view of life in which "a single conception may present different phases, according as you look at it"; others condemn it as "just word play! All on the surface!" Suddenly Amelia Moreno appears among them, supposedly from her box in the theater, protesting that she is being maligned by this distorted and thinly veiled presentation of her painful situation. Her friends intervene and lead her off as the actors leave the "lobby" at the warning bell, and the curtain rises on act 2.

The second act opens the following morning at Francesco's home, where preparations are being made for his duel with Doro. Diego arrives, bringing news of Delia's visit to Doro's home on the evening before. He reports her self-condemnation as the cause of the artist's death and her confirmation of Francesco's original opinion of her as guilty of the entire tragic affair. Although Francesco now realizes the baselessness of dueling with his friend when neither of them believes—or can even know—the truth of the situation on which they originally quarreled, he intends to continue with the duel simply because Doro insulted him before his friends. Only moments later, however, he is willing to cancel the duel since Delia herself admits her guilt. On urging from Diego, however, he is just as quickly led around to see that he must duel to defend Delia "against herself, now that she's accused herself before the man who at first tried to defend her."

With this same sort of polemic inversion, Diego continues to manipulate Francesco's view of the truth of Delia's guilt or even her level of self-awareness of her actions. Francesco's friends protest Diego's actions until, turning on them, he shows how each one, including himself, is equally unaware of his true motives in any single action. They are all mannequins, mere masks created out of their own false interpretations of their own and others' words and acts. Discovering the truth within, Diego claims, takes a courage of which humans are seldom capable.

At this moment Delia arrives to speak with Francesco, and he withdraws to meet her. Following his exit, Michele bursts angrily into the room, looking for Delia, whom he has followed to this house. He too is confused about his own motives for running off with her on the night before her marriage, protesting that it was only on a bet with the artist to show him what sort of woman she really was; at the same time, he blames himself for being part of such a treacherous bargain. Once again, Diego as provocateur points out the multiple interpretations that could be made of both Michele's and Delia's actions, suggesting finally that Michele acted out of his own fascination with the beautiful Delia.

When Francesco reenters, he quarrels with Michele concerning Delia and proposes to duel with him instead of with Doro. Delia enters, and immediately she and Michele embrace passionately, revealing finally to themselves and the others their fierce love. They leave in each other's arms as the second act concludes.

Again the curtain rises almost immediately, on the same hallway scene as that of the first interlude. Amelia has again come down from her box and is heard on the stage screaming and fighting with the actor playing Delia. The stage door bursts open, and Amelia is heard complaining of the public insult this play is to her. Rumors spread that she has slapped the face of the leading lady as well as the face of Luigi Pirandello, who is in the audience tonight. The leading lady and other actors refuse to go on with the play, and the audience is in an uproar.

Baron Nuti also appears at the stage door to protest the insult to himself. As he and Amelia meet, they replay the very reconciliation scene that has just been played out at the close of act 2. When they leave the theater together, the stage manager announces there will be no act 3 this evening, and he sends the audience away.

Themes and Meanings

Luigi Pirandello had one philosophical tenet that he proffered throughout his several hundred novellas, novels, and plays: Life is without rational, logical meaning, and humans struggle vainly to impose such meaning on the irrational and capricious events of their destinies. *Each in His Own Way*, written at the height of his career, is a comic expression of that central theme, as well as of the incommunicability of the true inner self because that truth is perhaps not known even to the self.

Diego Cinci, spokesman for Pirandello's underlying polemic, declares that each person exists as an image created by others, that there are as many views of the self as there are viewers. Nothing within the person, neither the deepest affection nor the strongest loathing, remains constant. All of one's ideas, beliefs, and judgments change in the restless turmoil of life, and only at rare moments of cataclysmic insight is one aware of one's true feelings and motives. For the most part, passion dominates reason; each individual hides the truth from himself even more than he does from others, until at last he is forced to cry out as Delia does in her confusion: "What is truth? . . . I should like to see with my eyes, or hear with my ears, or feel with my fingers, one thing . . . just one thing . . . that is true . . . really true . . . in me!"

Pirandello's view of personality as a great tangled massing of lie upon lie, of mask upon mask, points toward a confusion about reality with which all people struggle. It is a struggle in which all each person can do is to offer to others honest compassion and the wisdom to cover the terror of naked and destroying truth with the masking lies of love. Amelia Moreno and Baron Nuti have built for themselves images of fictitious reality as barriers to the unacceptable reality of their mutual love. Their real selves, struggling beneath, are hidden out of guilt by complex life—lies that they present to themselves and to the world as truth.

It is Diego who acts as the great unmasker throughout the play. He alone appreciates the bittersweet comedy of life, the absurd contradictions of the human experience—a basic theme upon which Pirandello built his entire canon. Diego alone realizes that only through laughter can human beings endure, and that this laughter must often be directed at the self. He alone realizes that as people move out from a core of circumstantial suffering—attempting to discover meaning and truth perhaps within the suffering itself—they discover instead the perverse comedy of deception upon deception, mask upon mask, reflected in the distorting mirror of the masks of others about them.

In *Each in His Own Way*, Pirandello proclaims that each person is many persons. Each is like a kaleidoscope, with a substantial self always in flux and ever appearing according to the particular perspective from which it is viewed. As for the others who view the person, it is their part always to mistake the apparent configuration before them as the reality of the person.

Dramatic Devices

Each in His Own Way is one element of Pirandello's so-called theater trilogy, which also includes *Sei personaggi in cerca d'autore* (pr., pb. 1921; *Six Characters in Search of an Author*, 1922) and *Questa sera si recita a soggetto* (pr., pb. 1930; *Tonight We Improvise*, 1932). The central metaphorical structure of each of these works is a play folded within a play. Pirandello viewed life itself as the ultimate drama and strove through this structural device to immerse the audience within the ambience of the theater so deeply that they could realize themselves as an integral part of the action being played out before them, as actors in their own dramatic role of spectators in the theater of life.

Within *Each in His Own Way*, the audience actually experiences the dichotomy of reality and illusion as it views its very self in the two interludes. With an inversion of stage space that brings the lobby into the audience chamber, Pirandello allows the audience to eavesdrop on its own ambiguous feelings concerning the convoluted events of acts 1 and 2. The characters are effectively in the actual audience, the apparent audience is in the play, and all is in turmoil. Pirandello extends the physical and psychological limits of the stage into the dressing room and out into the audience itself; characters, actors, and audience together are the drama. Through this metatheatrical device, Pirandello strives to make the viewer/reader of the play fully aware of the theatricality of the supposed illusion and, as a paradoxical corollary, fully aware of the illusionary nature of its own supposed realities.

Pirandello establishes three levels of reality in *Each in His Own Way:* that of the first act presentation concerning the Delia/Michele conflict, that of the "audience" actors as they discuss the presentation, and that of the apparently real persons whose lives are being shown fictionally. Moreover, there is still a fourth level of reality functioning behind all of these: that of the viewer and reader. Thus Pirandello actually models his thesis that reality is an illusory construction each person creates. Using fluidity of time, place, personality, and action that doubles back and repeats itself in mirror images, he illustrates the ambiguity of interpretation of human motives. That ambiguity, to Pirandello, is an inescapable result of the very human practice of denying in words what one cannot help revealing in actions.

A number of lesser devices work together to convey Pirandello's meaning. These include the use of Diego as a character who in a literal sense speaks for the play. Diego explicates Pirandello's purpose by manipulating Doro, Francesco, their well-meaning though equally blind friends, and finally Michele in seesaw response to what each believes to be the truth. Another means of revealing the contrary faces of reality is the acerbic exchange of comments by the "critics" and "audience members" in the interludes. Here Pirandello holds up a critical mirror to the play itself even as it unfolds—and a cracked mirror it is, reflecting now this bit of truth about the performance and now that.

Critical Context

Luigi Pirandello began his writing career as an essayist and poet. He turned soon to narrative fiction, producing several hundred pieces over a period of forty years. His work in drama began in 1908. Critical assessment of Pirandello's drama has moved between the extremes of the continuum from his own time until the present. He has been vilified as a mere juggler of repetitious words and ideas amassed for their confusing effect and lauded as the greatest theatrical innovator of the early part of the twentieth century. His work in drama has been likened to that of Franz Kafka, Thomas Mann, and James Joyce in short stories and novels, in its presentation of fragmented and contradictory views of the same reality.

Pirandello's plays, and especially those of the theater trilogy, were designed to expose the conventional morality and pretensions of European society in the early years of the twentieth century. His style of drama was identified with the "grotesque school," the *teatro dell'grottesco*. Writers in this style were reacting against the romanticized and bourgeois drama of the first dozen or so years of the twentieth century in the Italian theater. Touched as they were by the new pessimism of a Europe about to fall into internecine war, and inspired by the growing body of psychological speculation about the multiple and shifting nature of human beings, writers such as Pirandello sought means of expressing these deeper currents in their drama. For audiences accustomed to accepting surface trivialities as truth, the whole nexus of illusion and reality had to be rent and rewoven and a new system of truth constructed. In his attempt to discover some device through which to present the truth of the convoluted interiority of human experience, Pirandello turned the theater itself inside out before his audience's eyes. *Each in His Own Way*, significant in the development of modern theater yet difficult to produce since it requires a cast of more than fifty actors, is recognized as an exemplar of this technique.

For Pirandello, the theater was not a place for creating perfect illusion, as it was for the realists; nor was it merely an arena of nonillusionary fantasies as for the *grotteschi*. It was a moment of life removed from both of these, a suspended moment during which controlled disillusion might have the power to dissolve reality, push it back from the audience, distance it through conscious role-playing until the real and the unreal became fused and confused, until the make-believe of the theater became the reality of the moment, only to be shown again as the illusion it was. Pirandello held that life itself strives to give the perfect illusion of reality. Humans are all making believe; that pretense, however, is the reality. That is the horror. Life is no more than the reciprocity of illusion; this is humankind's truth, and it is terrible.

Sources for Further Study

Bassanese, Fiora A. *Understanding Luigi Pirandello*. Columbia: University of South Carolina Press, 1997.

Bishop, Thomas. *Pirandello and the French Theater*. New York: New York University Press, 1960.

Caesar, Ann. *Characters and Authors in Luigi Pirandello*. New York: Clarendon Press, 1998.

Caputi, Anthony. *Pirandello and the Triumph of Modern Consciousness*. Champaign-Urbana: University of Illinois Press, 1988.

Matthaei, Renate. *Luigi Pirandello*. Translated by Simon Young and Erika Young. New York: F. Ungar, 1973.

Paolucci, Anne. *Pirandello's Theater: The Recovery of the Modern Stage for Dramatic Art*. Carbondale: Southern Illinois University Press, 1974.

Starkie, Walter. *Luigi Pirandello, 1867-1936*. 3d rev. ed. Berkeley: University of California Press, 1965.

Gabrielle Rowe

THE ECSTASY OF RITA JOE

Author: George Ryga (1932-1987)
Type of plot: Social realism
Time of plot: The late 1960's
Locale: An unnamed city
First produced: 1967, at the Queen Elizabeth Playhouse, Vancouver, British
  Columbia
First published: 1970

Principal characters:
> RITA JOE, a young American Indian woman
> JAIMIE PAUL, a young American Indian man
> DAVID JOE, Rita's father, an American Indian chief
> THE MAGISTRATE, who presides at Rita's trial
> THE SINGER, who provides musical accompaniment to the play
> MR. HOMER, who runs a social service for Native Americans
> MISS DONAHUE, Rita's former teacher and a witness for the
>   prosecution

The Play

The Ecstasy of Rita Joe begins as a trial. Rita Joe is the defendant, alone and without representation, against a policeman, who acts as witness against her, and the Magistrate, who will decide her fate. As the Magistrate's opening lines demonstrate, he is determined to be stern but fair. Rita Joe's first words, however, undermine the Magistrate's eloquent exposition: She was picked up by undercover policemen who offered her money and then arrested her for prostitution. The Magistrate continues his paean to justice while Rita Joe professes her innocence and the Singer offers up a haunting, melodic verse.

The futile exchange between Rita and the Magistrate continues, setting a pattern for the rest of act 1. As the trial goes on, however, the past begins to interrupt and inform the present at various intervals. Even the Magistrate is haunted by memories: Rita Joe reminds him of a young, poorly dressed girl he saw once standing all alone by the side of the road in the harsh Cariboo country. He would like to extend to her the sympathy that this recollection arouses in him, but his sense of duty finally overwhelms his humanity, and he reverts to being officious. The Magistrate becomes increasingly exasperated as he questions Rita about whether she understands the charges against her, whether she can provide witnesses in her favor, and whether she is a carrier of venereal disease.

For her part, Rita seems neither capable of nor interested in defending herself. There is not much she understands or trusts about the system in which she finds herself caught. Thus, she welcomes those figures from her past who intrude upon the action, disrupting her dialogue with the Magistrate and distracting her from the chronic fatigue, hunger, and sickness from which she suffers. Jaimie Paul, Eileen Joe, the Old Woman, and David Joe are American Indians and appear to Rita alone; white people such as the Priest, Mr. Homer, the Teacher, the Policeman, the School Board Clerk, and various Witnesses (who double as murderers) appear both in Rita's dreams and in the trial.

Like Rita, Jaimie Paul succumbs to the lure of the city. Upon his arrival there, he is exuberant and optimistic: He rents a room, finds a job, and delights in how different life is away from the reserve. His hopes fade quickly, however, and he loses his job, starts to drink, and takes to hanging around with other unemployed young American Indian men. Still, he will not return home; he is proud, impatient, and in disagreement with David Joe about how best to run the reserve. David Joe is troubled and sees his people as caught between the old ways and the new. He urges patience and a return to the land, but neither Rita nor Jaimie will listen. Still, Rita is torn; she loves and misses her father and is disturbed by news from the Old Woman and Eileen Joe that he has been ill. With her sister, Rita reminisces about berry picking during the summer; with her father, Rita recalls their favorite story, about how a man once came out of the bush with an extraordinary offer for him. These moments lighten the drama, alternating with the darker, heavier moments provided by representatives of the white man's world.

The Priest has known Rita from the time she was a child; however, he offers only inadequate, clichéd advice about resisting the allure of the sinful city. Miss Donohue, her former teacher, also reveals herself to have been singularly inappropriate for her job on the reserve; she reappears during the trial as a witness against Rita. The School Board Clerk further attests Rita's lack of scholarly ambition when he says that she never replied to a letter in which he recommended she continue her education through correspondence courses; Rita counters by claiming that she never received his letter. Between the testimony from these upstanding citizens and that of another witness (a former employer who seduced Rita and then paid her for her compliance), Rita's fate is sealed. The Magistrate sentences her to thirty days in prison.

Act 2 opens with Rita behind bars. The Priest comes to visit her in jail, but instead of providing comfort, he leaves Rita angry and defiant and cursing his idea of God. The Singer offers a haunting refrain which will be repeated at intervals throughout the rest of the play:

> Sleepless hours, heavy nights
> Dream your dreams so pretty
> God was gonna have a laugh
> An' gave me a job in the city!

Once Rita serves her term, she links up with her embittered friend, Jaimie. Hungry and impoverished, they eventually end up at Mr. Homer's center for Native Americans. Jaimie proudly refuses the food and clothing he is offered, and Rita reluctantly follows suit. Frustrated, Jaimie taunts and provokes Mr. Homer to the point where the charitable veneer of this socially responsible man drops away: He unjustly lashes out at Rita, calling her a slut and a whore. Rita and Jaimie attack him wildly and are once more brought before the Magistrate, who sentences Jaimie to thirty days. David Joe arrives in the city to find his daughter and take her back to the reserve with him, but out of loyalty to Jaimie she refuses to go. Rita lands in prison again, but not before a final verbal confrontation with the Magistrate in which the clash between their two cultures is clearly delineated.

The final scene is brief and brutal. Once out of prison, Rita and Jaimie plan to go out on the town, but voices from their past rise to a frenzied crescendo, and the Murderers close in around them. Jaimie is beaten and thrown in front of an oncoming train; Rita is raped and dies of her injuries. The play ends with their funeral: The young American Indians are defiant and the Singer's song is exultant, but the final tone is poignant. Eileen Joe recalls that "when Rita Joe first come to the city—she told me . . . The cement made her feet hurt."

Themes and Meanings

The Ecstasy of Rita Joe is widely considered to be a play about the white culture's denial of the American Indian's humanity. In particular, George Ryga points to the inadequacy of those organizations that deal with Indians; according to him, the Church, social services, the schools, and the legal system all dole out humiliation in the guise of charity and fail American Indians because they expect them simply to shed their cultural differences and assume white society's ways. Further, the play shows how adrift the American Indian people are: Life on the reservation holds no future, and the city, while it offers much in the way of material advantages, provides no equality of opportunity. Rita and Jaimie remain caught in the enduring conflicts between generations, between whites and Indians, and between the land and the city.

White people receive unsympathetic treatment in the play, and the institutions in which they place so much faith are condemned. With the possible exception of the Magistrate, all the white people are one-dimensional, unsavory characters. However, even he, despite the fact that Rita's youth and vulnerability unsettle him, is far too identified with his official role to allow his humanity to prevail. Although Rita claims to have been entrapped by the police who arrested her, the Magistrate is unwilling to believe her. His feelings range from fumbling attempts at concern and kindness to disgust at her alleged crimes. Rita remains doomed not only by her racial origins but also by her gender: Except for Miss Donohue, all of her accusers are men, and many of them view her as little more than a sexual object. All the white characters, even the socially conscious ones such as Mr. Homer, are shown to be afraid of American Indians because of their preconceived notions of them as unpredictable, violent, and primitive. Thus, suggests Ryga, white people typically react to Indians with either condescension or disapproval.

For their part, the American Indians in the play are angry, defiant, and proud. They cannot seem to escape the distorted, stereotyped image that white culture has always held of them. Ryga portrays Indians as unsophisticated, even childlike, as far as white culture goes. He also suggests that the distance between the two races is at least partly rooted in their linguistic differences. Much of the American Indians' difficulty in dealing with whites lies in their different attitudes toward language. Words as spoken by the Magistrate are businesslike and fact-oriented; Rita, for whom English is a second language, uses words warily, yet whimsically. Lost in her dream world, Rita at one point remembers aloud that "a train whistle is white, with black lines . . . a sad woman is a room with the curtains shut. . . ." As demonstrated during the trial, Rita and the Magistrate talk past each other: He questions her and lectures her, but Rita is too frightened and mistrustful to answer him directly. White culture interprets this failure to communicate as defiance and an unwillingness to cooperate. Thus, misunderstanding and misinterpretation form the basis of exchanges between the two cultures.

Dramatic Devices

The set for *The Ecstasy of Rita Joe* is minimal, consisting mainly of a circular ramp, which wraps the playing area from front to back and around the sides, and a Magistrate's chair and desk, which dominate stage right and are enclosed within the confines of the ramp. A cyclorama backstage creates a sense of compression of stage into audience, thus eliminating the usual dramatic convention of a fourth wall between artifice and reality. It also serves to confuse the issue of who is on trial. Members of the audience are forced to become jurists, if not defendants. This encircling of both the stage and the theater as a whole symbolizes the vicious cycle which George Ryga suggests relations between whites and American Indians have become. It also symbolizes the American Indian belief in the cyclicity of time. Time is compressed in this play: Past and future frequently interrupt the present. Dialogue is composed in such a way that it reinforces this ideal of cyclic patterns. Characters appear and reappear in the private world of Rita's memories, dreams, and fears, as well as in the public realm of the trial. Their voices combine, fuguelike, to illuminate her past, condemn her present, and foreshadow her future. Repetition is a key element in the structure of the play; some of the Singer's verses are repeated over and over, as is the sound of the train whistle.

Language and music are the main devices by which the play's themes are realized. Ryga attributes very different words to the white man and the American Indian; the Priest, for example, preaches humility and passivity in language borrowed from the Bible, and Miss Donohue teaches concepts so entrenched in white culture that they hold no meaning for Native American children. In contrast, the American Indians express themselves ungrammatically but figuratively. In particular, David Joe speaks carefully and thoughtfully in language that springs directly from his own experience. The play's central image of the dragonfly comes from him: He recalls how he once saw the insect break its shell in order to free its wings and fly toward the sun. Such is the slow, painful metamorphosis Ryga suggests American Indians must face in order to regain their rights and recover their heritage. In his vision, Rita Joe and Jaimie Paul become martyrs to the cause of American Indian rights—a theme reflected in the title of the play. "Ecstasy" suggests the exalted passion of Christ, an innocent who also faced trial and death at the hands of those who feared him. In the light of Rita's eventual rape and death, "ecstasy" becomes a brutally ironic pun.

Finally, the use of music—of an onstage Singer—is an unusual dramatic device. Ryga directs that her songs are to seem "almost accidental"; throughout the play they provide oblique, ironic commentary on the action. Still, the Singer is introduced in Ryga's stage directions as having only a limited understanding of the ethnic dilemma her songs accompany. Like many concerned whites, she is earnest but misguided. Her very presence is ironic.

Critical Context

At the time it was first produced, *The Ecstasy of Rita Joe* was widely discussed, first because there was not much in the way of Canadian drama and second because there was little in any art form that dealt so frankly with American Indian issues. The play was immediately controversial, because of both its thematic content and its deeply accusatory tone. George Ryga confronted his largely white audience with the harsh reality of the lives of American Indians who were living only blocks from the theater in which the play was being performed. His general condemnation of the organizations dealing with American Indian people also caused a storm. However, if his play rankled the white population, it also jolted many American Indians to face the issues that concerned them.

Ryga was an eclectic and prolific writer. Besides plays, he published poetry, novels, and radio and television dramas on a variety of subjects, but it is on his plays that his reputation rests. Ryga's works include *Ballad of a Stone-Picker* (1966), a novel about prairie dirt farmers in the 1940's and 1950's; *Nothing but a Man* (pr., pb. 1966), a play about Federico García Lorca; *Captives of the Faceless Drummer* (pr. 1971), a drama based on the October, 1970, terrorist crisis in the province of Quebec; *Paracelsus and the Hero* (pb. 1974), a play about the sixteenth century Swiss physician and philosopher; and *In the Shadow of the Vulture* (pb. 1985), a novel about Mexican immigrant workers.

Similar themes and techniques run throughout his work. In socially conscious plays such as *Indian* (pr. 1962) and *The Ecstasy of Rita Joe*, Ryga portrays the lives of the poor and the dispossessed and strongly criticizes social service organizations that preach conformity and patronize those who dwell on the margins of society. He was an innovative dramatist, mixing realism and lyricism, manipulating time, and using music to complement and counterpoint his themes. Ryga was particularly interested in reviving the oral, tale-telling aspect of drama, and to that end he included ballads and composed music for many of his plays. He also experimented freely with the audience-performer relationship, even inviting spectators to participate in the action, as in *Grass and Wild Strawberries* (pr. 1969). *The Ecstasy of Rita Joe* has also been produced in French and as a ballet, and it is considered a classic because it marked the beginning of modern, indigenous Canadian drama.

Sources for Further Study

Hoffman, James. *The Ecstasy of Resistance: A Biography of George Ryga.* Toronto, Ont.: ECW, 1995.

Innes, Christopher. *Politics and the Playwright: George Ryga.* Toronto, Ont.: Simon and Pierre, 1985.

Moore, Mavor. *Four Canadian Playwrights: Robertson Davies, Gratien Gelinas, James Reaney, George Ryga.* Toronto, Ont.: Holt, Rinehart, and Winston, 1973.

Parker, Brian. Introduction to *The Ecstasy of Rita Joe and Other Plays.* Toronto, Ont.: New Press, 1971.

Sim, Sheila E. "Tragedy and Ritual in *The Great Hunger* and *The Ecstasy of Rita Joe.*" *Canadian Drama* 1 (Spring, 1975): 27-32.

Susan Whaley

EDEN END

Author: J. B. Priestley (1894-1984)
Type of plot: Naturalistic
Time of plot: October, 1912
Locale: Eden End, in the north of England
First produced: 1934, at the Duchess Theatre, London
First published: 1934

> *Principal characters:*
> DR. KIRBY, an ailing general practitioner
> STELLA KIRBY, his firstborn, an actor
> LILIAN KIRBY, his younger daughter
> WILFRED KIRBY, his youngest child, home on leave from the
>   British West Africa Company
> SARAH, the Kirbys' old north-country nurse
> CHARLES APPLEBY, Stella's estranged husband, an actor
> GEOFFREY FARRANT, Stella's suitor, a former army officer

The Play

At the piano in the well-worn but comfortable Kirby sitting room in a village in the north of England, Wilfred Kirby picks out a tune from a London musical. Sarah, the nurse who tended the Kirby children and has remained a family fixture, informs the bored young man that he does not have the talent his older sister Stella has. Lilian, Dr. Kirby's second child, has an equally low opinion of her younger brother's musical ability and tells him so. Wilfred teases his sister about Geoffrey Farrant, who runs a nearby estate, while Lilian questions Wilfred about the barmaid he keeps trying to ring up on the Kirbys' new telephone. Wilfred admits that he is unhappy wherever he is. He had eagerly anticipated his leave, but now he is beginning to look forward to his return to Nigeria. He is dissatisfied with his work and his life but expects that everything will be better in three or four years. When Sarah shows them the costume, now moth-eaten, that she made for Stella for an amateur performance at the Town Hall, Lilian and Wilfred discuss their sister, an actor whom they have not seen in eight years and have not heard from in three. Against her mother's wishes, Stella had left home to make the stage her career. In the intervening years, Mrs. Kirby died, and Lilian has assumed the running of the house.

As they put a record on the gramophone, they hear a voice through the door. Stella, the prodigal daughter, has returned home, a little the worse for wear—like the tattered costume. She reveals to Sarah what she cannot admit to her brother and sister. Her career is a disappointment and she considers herself a failure. Dr. Kirby, delighted to see his daughter, whom he wrongly believes to be successful, admits to his firstborn what he has never told anyone else: He has envied her determination to follow her dream.

He had the opportunity to make something of himself as a specialist in London, but he gave in to his wife's wishes and settled for a steady but unexciting existence as a hard-working practitioner in Eden End. He is aware that his heart condition is serious and that he will not live long enough to see the better world he feels certain will be dawning in a year or two.

Alone with her sister, Lilian forces Stella to admit that she is married to an actor with whom she had toured in Australia three years earlier. Although they have not divorced, they had remained together only a year. Stella had lost touch with Charlie Appleby, her husband, but she unexpectedly saw him in her agent's office in London shortly before traveling north to Eden End. Geoffrey Farrant arrives to see Lilian but is thrilled to learn that Stella is home; Lilian retires with a headache. The act ends with the rest of the family gathered around the piano. Stella is playing a waltz while Wilfred and Geoffrey look on admiringly, Dr. Kirby beats time to the music, and Sarah smiles in the doorway. What appears to be a cozy, even idyllic, family scene masks the reality of the situation. Stella's sudden return has shattered the family's tranquillity.

In act 2, four days later, Wilfred is still unsuccessfully trying to contact the young lady he fancies. He is startled when a stranger walks into the house out of the rain. It is Charlie Appleby, whose charm and breeding are clearly in evidence, as are signs that he drinks too much. Charlie has been invited to Eden End by Lilian, and Wilfred soon decides that his newly found brother-in-law will be a good companion in the local pubs. When Wilfred shows Charlie to his room, Stella enters with Geoffrey. Unaware of Charlie's existence, Geoffrey tells Stella, who encourages him, that he still loves her. When Geoffrey suggests that the coming years will bring little change, Stella, with curious precognition, suggests that in a few years they may look back on 1912 as belonging to another world, a lost world. Their intimacy is interrupted by Charlie, and Stella is forced to introduce her admirer to her husband; Geoffrey, who is devastated, hastily retreats. Soon after, Stella confronts Lilian and slaps her face, accusing her of bringing Charlie there not because she cares about Stella and her marriage, but because she herself is in love with Geoffrey. When Stella leaves the room to introduce her husband to her father, Lilian, to calm herself, sits down to her accounts but loses control and cries.

In the first scene of the last act, Wilfred and Charlie come home drunk. Charlie, the one character who has come to terms with his own mediocrity, tells his young friend about his conquests among the fair sex and the disappointments in his career. He concludes that those things, however, are of little consequence because life itself is wonderful. Wilfred learns that the girl of his dreams, the barmaid at the White Hart, has made eyes at Charlie and, according to Charlie, flirts with all her customers. He is consequently taken ill and must be put to bed. Lilian is outraged and tells her sister to leave and to take Charlie with her. Dr. Kirby returns from assisting at the birth of a baby, a baby who will grow up, Kirby believes, in a world that will soon sort out its problems. The tired doctor tells his eldest child how proud he is of her. He had made a mistake in settling for less than he had really desired, but she is rectifying that mistake by living the life she has chosen. Stella, aware that her father must learn the truth about her failed career should she remain, announces that she and Charlie have been offered good parts and must leave the next day.

The final scene of the play takes place the next afternoon. A house that has been in upheaval since Stella's arrival is about to return to normal with her departure. Geoffrey comes to say good-bye and announces that he himself will soon be off to New Zealand for a year or two. Stella tells him that over the years Eden End seemed to her a haven free of muddle, but now she knows that the village of her girlhood is as confused and confusing as the rest of the world. She will try to get on with her life, living it as best she can, perhaps with Charlie as her partner in adversity. She no longer expects miracles. Left alone in the house as the others go off to the station, Sarah eyes with suspicion the ringing telephone, a newfangled gadget that she does not understand, and refuses to answer it. The firelight fades, there is silence, and the play ends.

Themes and Meanings

Set two years before the start of a devastating world war, *Eden End* evokes a simpler time in an innocent world. The title itself implies that loss of innocence. J. B. Priestley had lived his formative years in Bradford, a city in Yorkshire. After World War I, in which he was wounded and gassed, he looked back at the prewar world with fondness and affection. It became in retrospect a golden world, too fragile to survive the changes, both social and economic, that would mark the postwar years. It had been a time of optimism, of faith in the values of home and family. Great Britain had ruled an empire, creating jobs and opportunity for young men such as Wilfred Kirby. Those opportunities would disappear, along with the empire, in the years of the Great Depression.

As his characters look to a bright future that will not in fact dawn for them, Priestley suggested to the audience that their present complex time, the 1930's, might be remembered by a later generation with the same nostalgia, the same sense of loss, with which his generation viewed the world before the Great War. As Priestley's own optimism waned, he seemed to sense, as does a disheartened Stella in *Eden End*, that the future could be bleaker still. Like Stella, however, Priestley determined to commence again with the business of living and suggested that his beloved countrymen do so as well. As Charlie tells Wilfred, despite its faults, its disappointments, its moments of pain, life is ultimately a wonderful thing. The telephone will ring, sometimes bringing good news, sometimes bringing bad, but it must be answered. Sarah has lived out her life and can ignore telephones, motor cars, and other signs of so-called progress; the rest of the Kirby family, however, must attempt to cope with the present and to prepare for the future, whatever it brings.

Even if life seemed simpler in the Eden Ends of the past, human nature remains constant, according to Priestley. Men and women frequently love foolishly, fail in their endeavors, and cause one another unnecessary pain. However, Dr. Kirby, aware of his oncoming death, continues to bring new life into a world that has disappointed him. That better world that he expects to dawn in one or two years may be slow in coming—but it will come. Humankind will survive.

Dramatic Devices

Eden End achieves its effect through dramatic irony. The audience knows what lies in store for the Kirbys—and for England—although the Kirbys do not. World War I, not the better life Dr. Kirby anticipates, is only two years away. When Wilfred makes jokes about being victimized with a bayonet, his father tells him that no one need worry about bayonets anymore: The world is more sensible than it used to be . . . and science will enable it to become even better. Whatever bleak thoughts Priestley had in mind as he put that optimistic statement into Dr. Kirby's mouth, he could hardly have foreseen the destructive power of atomic weapons.

In the preface to the collected edition of his plays, Priestley suggests that his audience may consider a play like *Eden End* to be entirely naturalistic because of its setting. However, he believes that, like Anton Chekhov, he moved away from conventional realism as the play progressed to concentrate on dramatic color and shape. Mood and atmosphere may bring out the absurdity and pathos of life far better than a complex plot.

Eden End owes as much to Chekhov for its characterization as for its prevailing mood. The sensible, hard-working Lilian suggests Sonya of *Dyadya Vanya* (pb. 1897; *Uncle Vanya*, 1914) and Varya of *Vishnyovy sad* (pr., pb. 1904; *The Cherry Orchard*, 1908). She even has a brief exchange with Farrant in the third act that is reminiscent of Varya's conversation with Lopakhin, in which two people whom the rest expect to wed can talk only about the weather. Stella calls to mind Nina in *Chayka* (pr. 1896; *The Seagull*, 1909) as well as Madame Ranevsky in *The Cherry Orchard*, whose arrival and departure, like Stella's, frame the play. The world of Eden End is coming to an end just as the world of Chekhov's landed gentry did. His characters, too, had to cope with a new life. Sarah, like Firs in *The Cherry Orchard*, sees the others as children and treats them accordingly; she represents an older generation, too set in its ways to adapt to the modern world.

Despite the play's success in Great Britain, a success that was not repeated abroad, some critics consider that Priestley's language is not as evocative as Chekhov's. The Ranevsky estate may stand for all of Russia; Eden End, however, seems to some to be merely a provincial backwater, not truly representative of Great Britain. These critics point out that to achieve poetic effects Priestley has his characters quote from the poems of Robert Louis Stevenson and William Wordsworth. The characters' own language is often that of prosaic reporting rather than poetic evocation.

Critical Context

In a monograph on the dramatist who most influenced him, *Anton Chekhov* (1970), Priestley noted that there have been many plays that resemble the works of the master, but few of these imitations can actually rival such works as *The Cherry Orchard* or *Tri sestry* (pr., pb. 1901; *Three Sisters*, 1920). *Eden End* is an example of Priestley's Chekhovian style at its best, moving beyond imitation to convey the feel of northern England's country life. His characters struggle for a dignity that they cannot quite achieve, as their hopes for the future are frustrated by the disappointments of the present. Priestley continued to write in a Chekhovian vein in *Cornelius* (pr., pb. 1935), a play about a failing business enterprise, and returned to that style with *The Linden Tree* (pr. 1947), in which a family comes to terms with itself in an England that has survived World War II.

The Chekhovian atmosphere, as well as the dramatic irony so effective in *Eden End*, would also be employed in *Time and the Conways* (pr., pb. 1937). This play's second act takes place in 1937, the year in which it was written, moving the characters eighteen years ahead from the first act, set in 1919. When the third act returns to 1919, the audience knows so much more about the fate of the characters than they themselves can imagine that an almost unbearable poignancy is achieved. Stella's hint of precognition is fully developed in the characters of Alan and Kay in *Time and the Conways*, a play in which Priestley dramatized an intriguing theory of time that he had encountered in the works of J. W. Dunne.

If Priestley's innovative expressionistic plays such as *Music at Night* (pr. 1938) and *Johnson over Jordan* (pr., pb. 1939) did not achieve the success of his more naturalistic dramas, they helped to expand the limits of the once stultifyingly conservative British theater. These plays led to works such as *An Inspector Calls* (pr. 1946), in which Priestley moves his characters from a naturalistic setting into a mystical, supernatural world. *Eden End* (Priestley's own favorite among his plays) suggests what lay ahead in Priestley's drama, the genre of his best works: a significant contribution to world literature that would surpass his considerable achievements in the novel and essay.

Sources for Further Study
Cook, Judith. *Priestley*. London: Bloomsbury, 1997.
De Vitis, A. A., and Albert E. Kalson. *J. B. Priestley*. Boston: Twayne, 1980.
Evans, Gareth Lloyd. *J. B. Priestley: The Dramatist*. London: Heinemann, 1964.
Gray, Dulcie. *J. B. Priestley*. Stroud, England: Sutton, 2000.
Klein, Holger. *J. B. Priestley's Plays*. Basingstoke, England: Macmillan, 1988.
Priestley, J. B. *The Art of the Dramatist*. London: Heinemann, 1957.
Wood, E. R. Introduction to *Eden End*. London: Heinemann, 1974.

Albert E. Kalson

THE EFFECT OF GAMMA RAYS
ON MAN-IN-THE-MOON MARIGOLDS

Author: Paul Zindel (1936-2003)
Type of plot: Melodrama
Time of plot: The 1960's
Locale: Inside the dilapidated Hunsdorfer home
First produced: 1965, at the Alley Theater, Houston, Texas
First published: 1971

Principal characters:
BEATRICE HUNSDORFER, a single mother
RUTH HUNSDORFER, her cynical older daughter
TILLIE HUNSDORFER, her intelligent younger daughter
NANNY, the Hunsdorfers' invalid boarder
JANICE VICKERY, a science fair competitor

The Play

In two acts, *The Effects of Gamma Rays on Man-in-the-Moon Marigolds* juxtaposes the explosive emotional conflicts of the Hunsdorfer family against the ordered, logical pursuits of science to reveal that, like the experimental marigolds, people also mutate in response to external forces. As the play opens, Tillie Hunsdorfer introduces this theme with a voice-over in which she marvels that the atoms in her hand were once contained in different parts of the earth. The scene then shifts to the Hunsdorfer home, formerly a vegetable shop run by Beatrice's father. The audience hears the single mother Beatrice Hunsdorfer speaking on the phone to Mr. Goodman, Tillie's science teacher, about the reasons Tillie has been absent. Although Beatrice speaks in a complimentary fashion, once she hangs up the phone, her duplicity is revealed. She berates Tillie for putting her in the position of having to speak to the school, even though Beatrice is responsible for keeping Tillie home.

Tillie's sister Ruth enters, states that Tillie has become the laughingstock of the school, and adds that the school keeps a file on the family. As Beatrice worries about the contents of the file, the stage goes dark, and Tillie is heard marveling with Mr. Goodman at the fountain of atoms produced in a science experiment. When the lights go back up, Tillie readies boxes of dirt for marigold seeds that have been exposed to cobalt-60 in order to study its effects. Beatrice enters with plans of her own: She wishes to transform the house into a tea shop, and as she imagines the changes she would make, she asks Tillie about her experiment. Tillie explains the idea of radioactive half-life to Beatrice, and the elderly boarder Nanny enters. Beatrice speaks loudly and with artificial sweetness to Nanny but voices spiteful malevolence behind her back. Beatrice sarcastically mocks Nanny's professional daughter, who does not want to be bothered with Nanny's care. Beatrice ends the scene in an exhortation that connects her misery and the fate of the marigolds: She tells Tillie that she considers her life the "original" half-life.

The next scene opens with Beatrice again on the phone to Mr. Goodman, this time worrying about how the radioactive marigolds might affect Tillie. He reassures her, and as the stage goes dark, Ruth screams from her room: She is having a seizure. Beatrice calms Ruth by talking of a happier past, before Beatrice's father became ill. The stage again goes dark, and when the lights come up, an inebriated Beatrice dashes about, tossing around papers and junk as she prepares to open her tea shop. She announces plans to take control of her life: She intends to get rid of Nanny, and she tells Tillie to get rid of her pet rabbit. In the midst of this revelation, Ruth enters and proudly announces that Tillie is a finalist in the science fair. The principal's call follows, but his request that Beatrice attend upsets her. Tillie begins to cry as Beatrice berates her, then stops, as the act ends.

Act 2 begins as Tillie prepares for the science fair. Ruth rails about Janice Vickery, Tillie's primary competitor, and tells Tillie that the teachers at school are anxious to see what "Betty the Loon" (Beatrice) will wear. Tillie gives Ruth the rabbit to silence her. Beatrice enters, and, as Ruth gets her coat, Beatrice reminds her that she must stay home to look after Nanny. In anger, Ruth lashes out at Beatrice, calling her "Betty the Loon." Beatrice is visibly defeated and shouts at Ruth to go with Tillie as the lights go down and she begins to sob.

As the lights come up at the science fair, Janice Vickery gives her presentation involving the darkly comic process of skinning a dead cat. The scene then moves to a drunken Beatrice, who is leaving a message at the school thanking the staff for making her wish she was dead. She calls Nanny's daughter to tell her that she must have Nanny out of the house by tomorrow. Beatrice then spots the rabbit, and the lights fade as she carries the cage, towel, and chloroform upstairs. Back at the science fair, it is Tillie's turn, and her intelligent, optimistic description of the past, present, and future of her marigolds takes the prize. When they return home, the news that Beatrice has killed the rabbit sends Ruth into another seizure. As Nanny shuffles back onstage, Beatrice pathetically whines, "I hate the world," before Tillie closes the play with a final voice-over, pondering the possibilities of science.

Themes and Meanings

The play's intimate look into the lives of the Hunsdorfer family illustrates universal truths about the human struggle for acceptance and self-efficacy but reveals that each person adapts and responds differently to life's harsh uncertainties. The play demonstrates that some people will thrive while others will barely survive under similar adverse conditions, much like the marigolds in the parallel world of science. For Tillie, science generates life and hope amid the despair of Beatrice's self-imposed isolation.

Neither Beatrice, with her cynical withdrawal, nor Tillie, with her naïve optimism, presents a healthy solution for dealing with an imperfect world, yet each represents an authentic, if somewhat extreme, coping mechanism. By choosing to see only the potential good in atomic science, for example, Tillie triumphs over her mother's fear and pessimism but is blind to the dangers of radioactivity. Both Tillie and Beatrice have been mocked and treated as social outcasts, but Tillie, who does not value the opinions of outsiders, cannot be wounded by their disdain. Beatrice and Ruth, on the other hand, place inordinate importance on the opinions of others and thus feel compelled to compensate for this perceived loss of esteem, the result of social rejection, by inflicting cruelty upon Tillie and each other. Beatrice and Ruth allow the negativity of others to defeat them, and it is their attitudes that seal their fate.

The numerous reminders of decay that pervade the Hunsdorfer lives reinforce a related theme, the inevitability of death. Nanny's absence of understanding and physical decline mirror the chaotic disarray and faded spirit of the house. Beatrice takes the life of the rabbit to destroy any hope that manages to survive in her daughters. At times of great stress, Ruth becomes paralyzed by seizures. Amid this erratic dysfunction, science, with its order and insight into the origins of the universe, becomes Tillie's lifeline, connecting her to a larger world from which Beatrice, in fear and bitterness, hides. Only Tillie's marigolds, and through them, Tillie herself, experience vitality and growth. Tillie alone has the courage and stamina to pursue her dreams, and this is the spark that empowers her. This optimism reinforces the central idea of the play, since Tillie's positive outlook lifts her dreams beyond those of Beatrice, whose tea shop will never be achieved. Just as some marigolds, when exposed to the cobalt-60, yield spectacular double-blooms—symbolic of Tillie—others mutate into nonvital organisms, like the forever frustrated Beatrice and the shallow, unkind Ruth.

Dramatic Devices

Mostly confined by setting to the dilapidated front room of the Hunsdorfer home, the play reaches into the outside world from a distance. Beatrice never interacts in person with anyone beyond her front door: She speaks to them by telephone, and her conversations reveal her inability to effectively communicate and her deep sense of insecurity. Likewise Tillie's voice-overs provide insight into her motivations and serve to emphasize how removed she is from her negative-thinking family. Her visionary comments hang suspended in air, beyond the comprehension of Beatrice or Ruth. This lack of communication is further represented by the character of Nanny, who cannot hear or respond to any comments that Beatrice makes to or about her. Tillie's attempts to explain the ideas behind her experiment to Beatrice are answered by surly self-pitying comments and unwarranted criticism.

In this highly symbolic play, Zindel infuses the ordinary with powerful messages. Simple marigolds become the harbinger of a new world of understanding for Tillie. They also suggest the power of modern science as a positive force in a chaotic, doomed world. Mr. Goodman, the science teacher, is nearly godlike in his knowledge, and Tillie, his disciple, triumphs under his tutelage. Science frees Tillie from her family's fear and superstition, and like many who embrace science as the answer, Tillie never stops to ponder the cost of these scientific miracles.

Critical Context

Like so much of Zindel's work, this play is based on personal experience. Zindel's youth was spent in the shadow of an abusive, slightly mad mother, and he stated in interviews that he wanted people to sympathize with his underdog characters and to believe in the power of hope against all odds. After the play opened Off-Broadway, it received a Pulitzer Prize as the best drama in 1971. Actor Paul Newman directed a film adaptation of the play the following year. Zindel was hailed as a promising new playwright, and audiences and critics praised his believable teenage characters. Zindel subsequently published numerous works of fiction for a young-adult audience. He preferred writing books over plays because they provided steadier income and published three new titles in 2002, the year before he died of cancer.

Given the subject matter and the historical atmosphere of the time, perhaps this mixed response may be understood. In the early 1960's, fear of an all-out nuclear war gripped the United States. People built bomb shelters, and schools held nuclear safety drills. Scientific activity sped forward, and, as researchers recognized the power offered by atomic energy, they, like Tillie, often embraced a naïve belief in its power for good alone. Fearful people questioned the safety of nuclear power and its long-term impact on the environment. Thus, the driving symbol of the play, the experiment with marigolds, raises pivotal questions about the responsibility of science to protect living things, even as it advances in its ability to destroy them. Many of these questions remain part of popular debate, and this play's important role in providing the impetus for their discussion continues.

Sources for Further Study

Barnet, Sylvan, Morton Berman, and William Burto, eds. *Types of Drama: Plays and Essays*. New York: Little, Brown, 1972.

Dace, Tish. "Paul Zindel." In *Contemporary Dramatists*, edited by K. A. Berney. 5th ed. New York: St. James Press, 1993.

Haley, Beverly A., and Kenneth L. Donelson. "Pigs and Hamburgers, Cadavers and Gamma Rays: Paul Zindel's Adolescents." *Elementary English* 51 (October, 1974): 940-945.

Oliver, Edith. "Why the Lady Is a Tramp." *The New Yorker*, April 18, 1970, 82, 87-88.

Zindel, Paul. "Interview with Paul Zindel." Interview by Audrey Eaglen. *Top of the News*, Winter, 1978, 178-185.

Kathleen M. Bartlett

EINSTEIN ON THE BEACH
An Opera in Four Acts

Authors: Robert Wilson (1941-   ) and Philip Glass (1937-   )
Type of plot: Musical
Time of plot: The twentieth century
Locale: A railroad platform, a courtroom, a spaceship, and other suggested locations
First produced: 1976, at the Avignon Festival, France
First published: 1976

Principal characters:
ALBERT EINSTEIN, the theoretical physicist
A TWENTY-TWO MEMBER ENSEMBLE, undifferentiated actors

The Play

Despite its title, *Einstein on the Beach* is not a staged biography of the German physicist Albert Einstein, and none of its scenes is set on a beach. Moreover, despite its subtitle, it is neither an opera nor a play in any conventional sense. More accurately, it is a theater piece with music. Its text, a collaboration of Robert Wilson and Philip Glass with contributions by Christopher Knowles, Lucinda Childs, and Samuel M. Johnson, has little meaning without the music, composed by Glass, and without the spectacle, staged by Wilson, which accompany it.

The play is essentially plotless and leaves the creation of this crucial element to those who witness its performance, though it provides suggestive aural and visual guidelines which channel and focus audience perceptions. These perceptions arise through a series of musical, verbal, and visual effects which last the four-hour and forty-minute length of the work. They change almost imperceptibly, the stage ensemble often repeating a single word, phrase, or even syllable for as long as twenty minutes to the accompaniment of a matching figure in the music, but there is always change—even when there seems not to be. At various unexpected points, eye and ear simultaneously perceive marked changes, and it is at these times that radical shifts occur, both within the music and on the stage. Because *Einstein on the Beach* portrays a series of these shifts, and because it does so reductively, through increasingly simple yet ever more suggestive musical and verbal devices, one may consider it an example of serial minimalism, a contemporary technique of composition which has received equal amounts of favorable and unfavorable criticism.

Wilson and Glass have steadfastly resisted the writing of any interpretative program or scenario for their work, believing that the audience must derive individual yet complementary experiences from what it witnesses. A summary of the stage action conveys little of the dynamism which infuses the work and nothing of the spectacle essential for the experience its creators intend. One who wishes to comprehend *Einstein on the Beach* must experience its text, music, and spectacle simultaneously; its effectiveness is diminished if any of these elements is lacking.

Outlined, *Einstein on the Beach* contains five "Knee Plays" (metaphorically suggesting bends, turns, and transitions), which precede and follow each of its four acts. The four acts separately introduce three dominant visual elements—a locomotive, a courtroom, and a spaceship—then prismatically combine elements of each with the next dominant element. Both chorus and orchestra complement this visual fragmentation by segmenting and recombining matching textual and musical motifs.

The first Knee Play is in progress as the audience enters the auditorium. Two women sit at tables; their fingers play across the tabletops as one recites numbers at random while the other converses with some invisible companion. Imperceptibly, almost inaudibly, keyboards play a three-note descending figure which begins the music. These two elements proceed for approximately fifteen minutes and are only slightly altered by the sixteen-member Chorus, each member of which appears individually in the orchestra pit, taking a full two minutes to reach his or her assigned place. The Knee Play ends in a blackout when the last member of the Chorus is in position; the entire segment lasts thirty minutes.

Without pause, the lights come up on a boy standing on a tower. He holds a translucent tube in his outstretched hand. Spotlights converge on the tube and reflect prismatically from it. As the scene proceeds, the boy sails paper airplanes to the stage below. A single female dancer appears, wearing tennis shoes and holding a tobacco pipe in her left hand. As she dances, lights slowly come up on the Chorus, the members all holding pipes and dressed in tennis shoes, white shirts, and baggy slacks with suspenders. They recall photographs of Einstein, similarly dressed. At stage right, a man scribbles invisible equations on an invisible blackboard. As all this proceeds, a locomotive in full scale inches across the stage toward the left. Three times, a strong beam of light segments this scene, followed by a blackout and realignment of the Chorus.

When the lights come up again, three horizontal beams of light form a triangle which segments the stage. There is a huge bed, a clock without hands, and elements of a courtroom (jury box with jurors, court clerks, wigged attorneys, a woman defendant, a judge's bench, and a black woman witness). The witness reads from a book about the "baggy pants" of "Mr. Bojangles" (corresponding to the baggy pants of Einstein). A figure dressed as Einstein plays a violin positioned between the orchestra and stage players throughout. The scene moves slowly as the Chorus takes a coffee break and a black disk covers the clock face, recalling a solar eclipse (and possibly a "black hole" of timelessness).

The light triangle now becomes a square and frames the two women of the first Knee Play as they continue to recite. Photographs of Einstein flash on a screen behind them as the Einstein figure continues to play his violin. This second Knee Play provides the transition into act 2, which begins on a bare stage with a spaceship hovering in the far distance. In the Avignon production, dancers spun like dervishes in trance; in subsequent American productions, dancers have moved with mathematical precision to the orchestral accompaniment. The second scene reintroduces the train image—this time, however, constituted as a gaslit passenger train from the turn of the twentieth century. It passes along the still bare stage as though on a desolate plain. The moon shines on a darkened scene as an elegant Victorian couple emerges from the train and mimes a love duet. This time a lunar eclipse occurs, paralleling the eclipse of the clock face in the earlier trial scene. At the conclusion of the scene, the couple reenters the train, though they separate; the woman pulls a gun from her bag and threatens the man. He raises his hands as the train moves away. A blackout follows, and after a few moments the train appears again, now in the far distance.

A third Knee Play begins immediately, the Chorus making steering motions and chanting numbers and syllables; the two women of the previous Knee Play in their square of light stand before a console of flashing lights. The Chorus suddenly produces toothbrushes and mimes brushing their teeth, then sticks tongues out at the audience (recalling a famous photograph of Einstein). All of this introduces act 3, a combined trial and prison scene. The same defendant appears, then moves to the large bed, writhes as if having a nightmare, and describes her surreal vision of an American supermarket crammed with gaudy merchandise. This speech contains the work's single reference to a beach: "I was reminded [by the supermarket] of the fact that I had been avoiding the beach." Suddenly, she collects several nondescript props and, repeating her speech, emerges as Patricia Hearst pointing a machine gun at the audience. Act 3 closes as the spaceship reappears, this time much closer, as dancers move with it across the stage.

In the fourth Knee Play, the same two women reappear, now prone on glass tables illuminated from beneath. They writhe in a horizontal dance, the only visible colors being white and crystal. Act 4 reintroduces the visual shape of the train; this time the train stands on its end and resembles a building in gray shadow. Einstein appears in one of the windows and scribbles equations as a crowd of people stare at him from the stage. The crowd then slowly moves away and the scene fades to black until the bed image reemerges, also on its end; the defendant reappears, sings a wordless aria, then is apotheosized into the heights and disappears.

Ultimately, flickering lights outline the interior of the spaceship. A glass elevator, a human figure within, slides up and down from a smoking slot in the stage floor. A second glass cubicle, enclosing a reclining figure, slides back and forth along the top of the scene continuously, starting from left to right. The Chorus takes various places within the spaceship as one male dancer makes semaphore signals with two flashlights. Smoke pours out, covering the stage; there is a wild orchestral accompaniment as two women astronauts climb out of two plastic bubbles on the stage floor, then slowly collapse. A curtain falls, ending the scene; it bears Einstein's famous equation $E=mc^2$.

The fifth Knee Play shows the two women, this time on a park bench but still doing the finger pantomime with which the work began. A bus appears, with the same headlights as the trains of acts 1 and 2 and with the train conductor as driver. The driver delivers a speech filled with gentle images of stars, moon, heaven and hell, grains of sand, and infinite love. Words and music stop as the bus moves toward the two women and the curtain falls in silence.

Themes and Meanings

Einstein on the Beach is a visual and verbal panorama of the twentieth century that recognizes the passing of time as relentless but relative. Though time produces noticeable changes, these are essentially superficial. People may wait for a train, a bus, or a spaceship, but they wait nevertheless, and the machines which carry them away all perform the same function, though they differ radically in appearance. Lovers love, then destroy each other; this is true whether they are dressed as Victorians emerging from a gaslit train, as astronauts emerging from a space capsule, or as a pair waiting on a park bench for a bus destined for no certain place. Einstein, who propounded the theory of relativity and whose work in theoretical physics made the atom bomb possible, becomes a symbol of this relative way of considering time. His persona recurs throughout the work, sometimes evoked by the violin-playing actor who portrays him, sometimes multiplied through the Chorus, which adopts his distinctive dress, sometimes recalled by screen projections behind the actors, sometimes merely hinted at through the black-hole eclipse which blots out the handless clock face, or by the enormous bed (possibly recalling Einstein's comment that his best ideas came to him through dreams).

Seemingly topical issues are also timeless when considered from this perspective. The black woman defendant of act 1, scene 2 invokes the name of Will "Bojangles" Robinson, a black dancer whose talent was exploited; his identity and plight become hers and everyone's. His baggy pants even resemble Einstein's. A speech on the oppression of women reflects the oppression of black people, both of which remain strong contemporary concerns. The defendant has a nightmare about the oppressive sameness one finds in an American supermarket (recalling Allen Ginsberg's poem "A Supermarket in California," 1955), then transforms herself into the figure of Patricia Hearst in guerrilla garb, brandishing a machine gun—a symbol of privileged youth in rebellion.

Because time is relative, *Einstein on the Beach* can even project the ultimate horror of a nuclear holocaust, which follows the achievement of interplanetary flight. The same principles of physics allow both, yet even nuclear catastrophe halts neither time nor the universal desire for love. An unusual pair of lovers, both female, boards a bus headed for the unknown future, and life goes forward.

Dramatic Devices

Prismatic multiplication of images, their subsequent fragmentation, and their recombined variations characterize the words, music, and stage action of *Einstein on the Beach*. The mathematical precision the work demands is evident in the solfège syllables spoken in tonic rhythm by the Chorus. Prismatic multiplication and segmentation, a signature motif which plays on the surname of the composer, Glass, is carried through the horizontal and vertical triangulations, squares, and lines of light which at times segment the stage, at times isolate, frame, or spotlight one of its elements. Wordplay on the composer's name continues in the use of glasslike materials in the stage settings: the lighted tube the boy holds in act 1, the globes of light on the judge's bench in the two trial scenes, the headlights of the two trains, the underlit glass tables of the fourth Knee Play, the glass elevator and space capsules of act 4. Reappearance of glasslike or prismatic devices is neither caprice nor vanity, however, for the primary theme of *Einstein on the Beach* is that time's movement is actually easy fragmentation followed by recombined variation. All things are relative, relativity is the only constant, and Einstein is the twentieth century archetype of that constancy.

Because this is so, locomotive, gaslit train, bus, and spaceship as symbols of movement appear diachronically, as though passing through time without effect as far as their essential function. The train's conductor becomes the bus driver; the train's spotlights become the bus's headlight. The locomotive can be upended to serve as a skyscraper, one symbol of chronological progress becoming another. However, at the root of such progress, there is only minimal landscape—symbolized by dialogue, music, the desolate plain of acts 2 and 4, and the horizon implied by the second half of the work's title. Infinite progression, multiplication, fragmentation, and permutation are merely an illusion. Progress is illusory, but freedom, dignity, and love remain.

Critical Context

This collaboration of minimalist composer and minimalist stage designer is the result of Glass's having seen Wilson's *The Life and Times of Joseph Stalin* (pr. 1973), a twelve-hour avant-garde theater piece performed through the night at the Brooklyn Academy of Music. Glass was attracted by Wilson's extraordinary use of light, and the two set about finding a subject for an extended theater piece. Both knew they wanted to comment on the twentieth century, but their principal difficulty lay in finding a mutually agreeable unifying historical figure upon which to focus the work. Wilson rejected Glass's suggestion of Mohandas Gandhi (ultimately realized in Glass's own *Satyagraha*, pr. 1984); Glass rejected Wilson's proposals of Charlie Chaplin and Adolf Hitler. Eventually, Wilson thought of Einstein, and Glass immediately agreed. The two developed a script from Wilson's storyboards and stage diagrams; they were occasionally joined by Christopher Knowles, Samuel M. Johnson, and Lucinda Childs, who wrote several of the speeches which appear in the final script. Both Glass and Wilson disclaim inspiration from Nevil Shute's apocalyptic novel *On the Beach* (1956). The original title of their collaboration was *Einstein on the Beach on Wall Street*, though they shortened the title and added the equally misleading subtitle before the Avignon production.

Glass studied composition with the late Nadia Boulanger, famed teacher of composers Virgil Thomson, Aaron Copeland, and many others. Though experimenting with minimalist techniques during these studies, he never demonstrated them to Boulanger for fear she would reject them. Indeed, both he and Wilson come from conservative and traditional backgrounds, though their innovative productions have won wide popular acceptance. They collaborated on another massive theater piece, *the CIVIL warS*, presented in a Rome Section (pr. 1983) and a Cologne Section (pr. 1984). A major revival of *Einstein on the Beach* was given, with great popular success, at the Brooklyn Academy of Music in 1984.

Sources for Further Study

Brecht, Stefan. *The Theatre of Visions: Robert Wilson*. London: Methuen, 1978.

Croyden, Margaret. *Lunatics, Lovers, and Poets: The Contemporary Experimental Theater*. New York: McGraw-Hill, 1974.

Fairbrother, Trevor J., ed. *Robert Wilson's Vision: An Exhibition of His Works*. Boston: Museum of Fine Arts, 1991.

Glass, Philip. *Music by Philip Glass*. Edited with supplementary material by Robert T. Jones. New York: Harper and Row, 1987.

New York Times Magazine, October 25, 1981, p. 69.

Opera News 46 (October 25, 1981): 17.

Rogoff, Gordon. "Time, Wilson, and What a Play Should Do." *Theater*, Summer/Fall, 1991, 52-53.

Shyer, Lawrence. *Robert Wilson and His Collaborators*. New York: Theater Communications Group, 1989.

Stearns, Robert. *Robert Wilson: The Theater of Images*. 2d ed. New York: Harper, 1987.

Robert J. Forman

THE ELEPHANT MAN

Author: Bernard Pomerance (1940-   )
Type of plot: History; biographical
Time of plot: 1884-1890
Locale: London, with one scene in Belgium
First produced: 1977, at the Hampstead Theatre, London
First published: 1979

> *Principal characters:*
> FREDERICK TREVES, a surgeon and teacher
> CARR GOMM, an administrator at the London Hospital
> JOHN MERRICK, the Elephant Man
> ROSS, the manager of the Elephant Man
> NURSE SANDWICH, Merrick's caretaker at the hospital
> BISHOP WALSHAM HOW, a religious leader
> MRS. KENDAL, an actress

The Play

The Elephant Man depicts the difficult life of Joseph "John" Carey Merrick, a real person who lived from 1862 to 1890. Because of his extreme bodily and facial deformities, he was nicknamed the Elephant Man. Until rescued by the physician Frederick Treves and given a home at the London Hospital in Whitechapel, Merrick earned his living as a freak attraction in a traveling sideshow. The play's twenty-one scenes depict selected episodes from the last six years of Merrick's life and emphasize Merrick's strength of spirit and the hypocrisy of Victorian English society.

The action begins not with Merrick, but with Treves, who considers himself a man blessed with a career, a home, a family, and financial success. The audience can contrast Treves's life with that of Merrick, who is shown trapped at the opposite end of the social scale: Merrick's tumor-ridden face, contorted body, and distorted speech doom him to a life of abuse and ridicule.

Merrick's manager, Ross, who claims to have taken Merrick from the workhouse where he was abandoned at the age of three, robs and beats Merrick and confines him like an animal in darkness. He advertises Merrick to paying customers as a creature whose "physical agony is exceeded only by his mental anguish." Merrick is no less an object of morbid fascination at a medical meeting, where Treves exhibits him while lecturing on Merrick's multiple handicaps.

Ross abandons Merrick, complaining of too little profit from his display. Treves, performing what Bishop Walsham How calls his "Christian duty," persuades the London Hospital's director, Carr Gomm, to give Merrick permanent sanctuary. Charitable contributions from newspaper readers will pay for Merrick's lodging, but living arrangements prove difficult. Although Nurse Sandwich has cared for lepers in the Far East, she is so repulsed by Merrick's countenance that she bolts from his room.

In his new life, Merrick is as much on display as in his old life. The royalty and aristocrats who visit him in the London Hospital offer pleasantries and gifts that inflate their own egos as much as they do that of Merrick. Merrick, ever the innocent, receives their attentions with pleasure and views their noblesse oblige as helping him attain the normality and acceptance he craves. Ross returns, demanding repossession of Merrick because high society has suddenly embraced Merrick, and his moneymaking potential has been enhanced. Merrick rejects his proposals.

Unique among the play's characters is the actress, Mrs. Kendal. She alone responds to Merrick as an equal, and in recognizing and appreciating the repressed sexual side of his nature, she undresses for him in scene 14. "It is the most beautiful sight I have seen," says Merrick, but Treves bans Mrs. Kendal from the hospital and chastises Merrick for unacceptable behavior.

Merrick spends his days reading works by William Shakespeare, conversing with his visitors, and building an intricate model of St. Phillip's Church. Although Merrick's quality of life improves, Treves's quality of life deteriorates, and he finds himself trapped in a crisis of conscience. While teaching Merrick that "the rules" make people happy, Merrick observes that Treves cannot distinguish "between the assertion of authority and the charitable act of giving." Treves is troubled by the pressure for conformity he sees in himself and his society: "I conclude that we have polished him [Merrick] like a mirror, and shout hallelujah when he reflects us to the inch."

Despite his social gains, Merrick's physical limitations continue to plague him. His head is so enlarged and deformed that he must sleep with it on his knees. His health is, in fact, worsening, and Treves predicts Merrick's heart will not long sustain him.

In scene 20, Merrick dies while attempting to sleep in a normal reclining position, the weight of his enormous head crushing his windpipe. The play ends with Gomm composing a "report to investors," an obituary for the *Times* aimed at reconciling the charitable accounts that provided Merrick's support. "He was highly intelligent," Treves says. "He had an acute sensibility . . . and a romantic imagination." However, Treves withdraws his assessment in dismay. "Never mind. I am really not certain of any of it."

Themes and Meanings

The historical Merrick was born with Proteus syndrome (not the inherited disorder neurofibromatosis as has been suggested). Although never named by his doctors or mentioned in the play, the disease is central to Merrick's biography and Bernard Pomerance's drama. Proteus syndrome created the extreme deformities of face and form that gave Merrick his cruel nickname and led to his virtual enslavement as a sideshow curiosity.

Throughout his tenure at the hospital, Merrick builds an elaborate scale model of St. Phillip's Church. The model is the play's dominant symbol, for it represents Merrick's attempt to reconstruct himself in a form that will be seen as beautiful by those he hopes to please. Merrick recognizes himself and others as actors, all playing roles. He plans his social role as carefully as he plans his model. Merrick says of himself and the model: "I did not begin to build at first. Not till I saw what St. Phillip's really was. It is not stone and steel and glass; it is an imitation of grace flying up and up from the mud. So I make my imitation of an imitation."

Another theme, the arbitrary distinction between deviance and normality, is brought home in scene 12, titled "Who Does He Remind You Of?" In this scene, the main characters comment on the character traits they recognize in Merrick. Mrs. Kendal sees him as gentle, feminine, cheerful, honest, a serious artist, "almost like me." Bishop Walsham How proclaims Merrick religious and devout, while Gomm thinks Merrick a practical man, like himself. Treves describes Merrick as curious, compassionate, and concerned about the world, "rather like myself." The scene ends with Merrick adding a piece to his model of St. Phillip's, as if adding another stone to the fragile edifice of normality and acceptance he is building for himself.

Throughout the play, Merrick's inner nature emerges. In sharp contrast to those around him, he is kind, patient, loving, and sympathetic. He is a deep thinker and philosopher, seeing what others cannot and expressing what others dare not. For example, when Gomm fires a hospital porter for staring at Merrick, Merrick considers the punishment harsh, but Treves insists that Gomm is a merciful man. "If your mercy is so cruel," asks Merrick, "what do you have for justice?"

The themes of vulnerability and exploitation pervade the story. Merrick is victimized but escapes the scars of victimization through the strength and beauty of his inner being. Ross, on the other hand, is greed personified. He exploits any person or situation that he can, without concern for the toll his avarice takes on himself or others. Treves, by far the most complex character in the drama, is both exploiter and exploited. While he takes advantage of Merrick, he himself is taken advantage of by a society that rewards those who play by the rules with fame and success, while at the same time stripping them of their integrity and conscience.

On the surface, the play is about Merrick, but the lesson the audience takes home comes from Treves. He despairs that his society is sick with the social "deformities" brought on by "unlimited resources and the ruthlessness of privilege." His own success in such a milieu plagues him, and he is sick at heart. He recognizes that his charity is self-serving and patronizing. His angst makes the audience wonder whether they, like Treves, wear a mask of civility to conceal their own contorted souls.

Dramatic Devices

The Elephant Man is a play with little plot. The story is revealed through snapshots in time. The episodes are brief, stylized, and sometimes complemented by theatrical devices, such as three women "Pinheads." Ostensibly an act from Merrick's freak show, the Pinheads act as the chorus in a Greek tragedy. They comment on the characters and action and perform as agents of fate in shifting Merrick from his upright posture into the recumbent sleep position that kills him.

In most performances, the settings are impressionist, achieved with a minimum of backdrops and props: Pomerance mandates little in the way of stage setting. For example, Ross's sideshow in scene 2 requires nothing more to set the stage than a store-front poster heralding the Elephant Man attraction.

The lead role of Merrick is demanding. While Pomerance advises that no actor should attempt to simulate Merrick's near-unintelligible speech, the role requires sustaining a contorted body posture and skewed facial alignment for the entire performance. The actor must skillfully meld Merrick's outer ugliness and his inner beauty.

Critical Context

Of the four plays that have been written about Joseph Merrick, only Pomerance's has received notable attention from drama historians. Like most of Pomerance's other works, *The Elephant Man* uses historical fact to probe the darkest of human experiences and to uncover the failings of society and its members. His sharply drawn characters and precise staging strip away the social norms that veil the greed, unfettered ambition, and hypocrisy that lie within all humans.

While capturing the ugliness of humanity's basest motives and actions, Pomerance simultaneously offers hope for redemption. His best characters, like Treves in *The Elephant Man*, fight the battle of good and evil with others and, more important, within themselves. They seldom win, but they offer hope that the triumph of truth is possible, if rarely or imperfectly achieved. The distinction between wrong and right is blurred in real life, but Pomerance brings it into focus, forcing his audiences to probe their most carefully concealed sins.

The Elephant Man is the best-known, most honored, and most often performed of Pomerance's plays. The New York Drama Critics Circle voted it the best play of the 1978-1979 season. That same year, *The Elephant Man* received Tony Awards for best play, best actress, and best director. Pomerance's other notable works include the play *Superhighway* (pb. 2001), which delves into the grief of a cancer victim's surviving relatives, and *Quantrill in Lawrence* (pr. 1980, pb. 1981), a Civil War story of corrupt leadership and social disruption. The themes of despair and hopelessness arise again in his prose poem *We Need to Dream All This Again: An Account of Crazy Horse, Custer, and the Battle for the Black Hills* (1987).

Sources for Further Study

Guernsey, Otis L., Jr. *The Burns Mantle Theatre Yearbook: The Best Plays of 1978-1979*. New York: Dodd, Mead, 1979.

Howell, Michael, and Peter Ford. *The True History of "The Elephant Man."* 3d ed. London: Allison and Busby, 2001.

Montagu, Ashley. *"The Elephant Man": A Study in Human Dignity.* Lafayette, La.: Acadian House, 1995.

Treves, Frederick. *"The Elephant Man" and Other Reminiscences.* London: Cassell, 1923.

Faith Hickman Brynie

EMBERS

Author: Samuel Beckett (1906-1989)
Type of plot: Absurdist
Time of plot: The twentieth century
Locale: At the edge of the sea
First produced: 1959, BBC Third Programme, London
First published: 1959, in *Evergreen Review*

Principal characters:
HENRY, the play's solipsistic protagonist
HIS DEAD FATHER
ADA, Henry's wife
ADDIE, their daughter
BOLTON and
HOLLOWAY, characters in a story that Henry tells

The Play

Embers, a radio play, begins not with words but with sounds: the "sea scarcely audible," followed by footsteps in the sand. Only then does the listener hear a human voice speaking a single word, "on," followed by the sea again, followed by the voice—louder and more insistent this time, repeating the same word, as it will say, then repeat as a command, the words "stop" and "down." Each time, Henry obediently yet reluctantly does what the voice (his own) first says, then commands him to do. Thus in a few brief strokes, the dramatic pattern for this brief play is established—an alternating rhythmical dialogue of sounds and words. Whenever the voice pauses, as it frequently does, the sea becomes audible once again. Within this macro-dialogue there exist a number of micro-dialogues involving Henry and the voices he hears, recollects, imagines, or projects. The first is with his father, drowned in the same sea before which Henry sits, the father who is now "back from the dead," Henry says, "to be with me." In dialogue with this silent ghost, whose body has never been recovered, Henry makes plain his ambivalence both toward the sea he fears, yet to which he finds himself drawn, and toward the father he once sought to escape but now conjures up from death to act as his sole audience and chief source of reproach for his wasted life.

Henry's garrulous monologue includes (or metamorphoses into) his retelling a story he began some years before, while in Switzerland, where he had gone to escape the "cursed" sea but which he has never finished. "I never finished anything, everything always went on for ever." The story concerns two old men. As it begins, Bolton, "an old man in great trouble," awaits the arrival of Holloway, a doctor, "fine old chap, very big and strong." Neither Henry nor Bolton ever explains why Holloway has been summoned or made to wait with Bolton in a room in which there are "only the embers, sound of dying, dying glow." The mystery left unresolved and unexplained, Henry's larger narrative suddenly shifts from Bolton and Holloway to Henry and his father (each aged pair comprising the one who summons and the one who is summoned). As soon becomes apparent, causality and explanations are far less important in this strange play than these parallel relationships.

Lingering just long enough to voice his father's condemnation of Henry as a "wash-out," Henry again suddenly shifts his narrative focus—this time from father and son to his wife, Ada, and daughter, Addie (the "horrid little creature" whom Henry holds responsible for turning Ada against him). Unlike the father, who serves as Henry's mute audience, Ada converses with him. (Ada may even be present in what follows, though it seems more consistent with the rest of the play that she too is imagined.) Sitting together on the "brink" of the sea, which Henry imagines as "lips and claws," Henry suggests that he and Ada depart, but she poses questions that imply the hopelessness of Henry's situation: Where would they go, and what would Addie do if she found him gone (as he found his father)?

The scene again shifts, this time to Addie at her music lesson, being chastised by her teacher for making the same mistake over and over. Between this brief interlude and the even briefer one that follows (Addie at her riding lesson), Henry presents himself as his daughter's ineffectual champion against Ada, the villainess who forces Addie to submit to the discipline of learning to play a piano and ride a horse. Against this image of a domineering wife, Henry posits the memory (which may be imagined rather than recollected) of Ada "twenty years earlier, imploring" Henry to do (or not do) something that is never made clear. The image of the imploring younger wife contrasts with the older one, who hectors Henry about his hemorrhoids, his underwear, and his habit of talking to himself.

Although Henry finds the sea's sound intolerable, while Ada thinks it soothing, their differences may not be as great as they seem. Ada gives voice to Henry's own doubts, posing the questions he would prefer not to face. When she suggests that Henry may be mentally imbalanced, he reacts "wildly," picking up two stones, clashing them together, and saying "That's life. . . . Not this . . . sucking!" He refers to the sucking of the sea, the slow diminishment of life that has brought him to this impasse. Henry's "roaring prayers at God and his saints" is his way of silencing the sea—which can be heard only in the silences between Henry's words. All that he had counted on—his love for Ada and hers for him, the birth of the child they waited so long to have, the stories he hoped to tell—has come to nothing.

Lear-like in his situation if not his stature, he cannot bring himself to accept Ada's advice that "there is no sense in trying to drown it [the sea]. . . . It's only on the surface, you know. Underneath all is as quiet as the grave. Not a sound. All day, all night, not a sound." It is not silence Henry craves, nor is it merely relief from his loneliness. "I was trying to be with my father," he tells Ada; "I mean I was trying to get him to be with me." He desires recognition and, despite living in a post-Christian age, forgiveness for his sins and the resurrection of the dead. Although Henry asks for much, he appears to be willing to settle for considerably less—but not for nothing. Claiming to have forgotten whether Ada and his father ever met, he has her recount the meeting, and when she pauses he implores her to "keep it going, Ada, every syllable is a second gained."

Her story over, Henry rapidly scales down his desire: She need not speak, "just listen. Not even. Be with me." By then, however, Ada is already gone, replaced by a series of quick pauses broken only by the same sound of hoofbeats heard earlier in the play.

Alone again, Henry attempts to retell the story Ada began. Failing, he simply switches back to retelling the Bolton-Holloway story, one which Henry now seems to be not so much remembering (as he implied earlier) as composing and revising as he goes. However, even as he moves ahead, he circles back to this description: "Fire out, bitter cold, white world, great trouble, not a sound." In his story, Bolton's silence—his refusal to explain why he has summoned Holloway or to answer any of his questions—continues to disturb Holloway. All Bolton does is implore Holloway first with a word, "please," and then with the expression on his face. Henry too implores— "Ada!" "Father!" "Christ!" he cries out—but for what he, like Bolton, does not or cannot make clear. No one intercedes for them or, for that matter, for the puzzled helpless Holloway. The play ends as unfinished as Henry's story, with Henry back where he started, prodding himself "on," moving through the sand, then pausing, filling the silence by reading through his nearly empty appointments book: There is "nothing" that night but "tomorrow . . . plumber at nine. . . . Ah yes, the waste," and then "Sunday . . . nothing all day. . . . All day all night nothing. . . . Not a sound"—except that of the sea, heard as Henry's speech stops.

Themes and Meanings

Samuel Beckett's plays and prose narratives do not so much possess meaning as provoke responses, often of confusion and dismay. The frustration experienced by the reader or listener of *Embers* derives in large part from Beckett's unwillingness to satisfy conventional dramatic or philosophical expectations. Like Henry, the listener or reader conceives of drama and human life in Aristotelian terms: exciting, representative, and with meaningful action leading to climax, recognition, and resolution— Henry's clashing "thuds." Beckett offers just the opposite. Here, for example, Henry describes putting on his jaegers: "What happened was this, I put them on and then I took them off again and then I put them on again and then I took them off again and then I took [*sic*] them on again and then I"—at which point his wife Ada asks him where his jaegers are now and Henry admits that he does not know.

Henry's existence follows the same structural pattern as Beckett's play: repetition of the same or similar elements ending in ignorance, incompleteness, and above all disappointment (rather than the climax that comes at the end of a causally related sequence of events). As Beckett notes in his early study, *Proust* (1931), "we are disappointed at the nullity of what we are pleased to call attainment." The complexity and diversity of meaning which *Embers* generates derives from Beckett's permutations of the simplest and most basic elements: father and son, past and present, male and female, fiction and fact, fire (embers) and water (sea), time and space, habit and memory. "All my life," one Beckett narrator says, "there were three things, the ability to speak, the ability to be silent, and solitude, that's what I've had to make the best of." That is also what Henry, and Beckett's audience, have to make the best of.

Henry represents the meeting place of these three conflicting human desires: for speech, for solitude (or silence), and for society. He possesses the need to speak and, subsequently, develops the desire to speak to someone "other" who, by listening, will confirm Henry's existence. The failure of this other to respond, or to respond as expected, disappoints Henry, but so does all speech other than his own. Consequently he withdraws into his own solipsistic imagination. Even there, however, Henry continues to conceive of speaking as a seeking—despite the fact that his solitude causes him to project the others to whom he speaks and who speak to him. Thus Henry continues his search for meaning and company by paradoxically withdrawing into a world of his own making, a world of words, which, the play suggests, may be the only real world. Henry has another reason for speaking, as well—to silence the world, whose own silence he finds unbearable, a silence he hears in the sound of the sea.

The human sounds Henry makes or hears or imagines—the voices of his wife, his daughter, and the two characters in his story, Holloway and Bolton—prove an inadequate defense against the sea's meaninglessness. (Henry lives on the very "brink" of the sea, on the brink of death and of unintelligibility.) As Ada says, "The time will come when no one will speak to you at all, not even complete strangers. . . . You will be quite alone with your voice, there will be no other voice in the world but yours." This future may already be Henry's present, and Ada may be the company he imagines to warn him of the fate he cannot avoid because it is already his. Her words may be his own, the last dying embers ineffectually banked against the ever-meaningless and all-consuming sea. Comical as he may at times seem, Henry also stands beyond comedy (and solipsism), a tragic figure in the modern mode, made to expiate by dying the original sin of having been born, bereft of all but his words and knowing that not even these suffice, conscious of his condition but unable to extricate himself from it.

Dramatic Devices

In *Embers* Beckett combines two dramatic modes that he used separately and quite effectively in earlier plays: the monologue, as in *Krapp's Last Tape* (pr., pb. 1958), and radio drama, as in *All That Fall* (pr., pb. 1957). The monologue is particularly well suited to Beckett's needs, for it allows him to focus the audience's attention on the character's existential predicament, his aloneness in the world. However, insofar as this aloneness is less physical than mental or metaphysical—a matter not of place and social relationships but of the void both without and within—the staging of the dramatic monologue poses a significant obstacle to the realization of the existential predicament in that pure and extreme form in which Beckett has conceived it.

Beckett's bleak vision of blind human persistence and progressive detachment and diminishment leads to radio drama (or, taken in a slightly different direction, to mime plays, such as *Acte sans paroles* [pr., pb. 1957; *Act Without Words*, 1958]). *All That Fall*, the first of Beckett's radio plays, is for the most part a play performed on radio, having a rather full cast of eleven more or less "realistic" characters. *Embers*, Beckett's second, exploits the form to far better advantage, for as Enoch Brater has noted, radio drama provides "an ideal medium for the transmission of the interior consciousness" that Beckett has made one of his most characteristic obsessions. For one thing, it enables Beckett to dramatize Carl Jung's theory of the multiplicity of the unconscious self as well as Belgian philosopher Arnold Geulincx's belief that one can hope to exert control only over one's own mind, never over the external world.

Radio thus enables Beckett to focus on interior consciousness in such a way as to call into question the existence of any reality whatsoever lying outside the thoughts of the character, since those thoughts are relayed to the audience only through the character's words. Radio drama also allows Beckett to extend the impersonal and antirealistic features of his art, to minimize plot, to limit setting, to narrow characterization, to dispense with psychological development, and to maximize his more theoretical and abstract concerns, particularly his interest in language as a performative rather than a communicative act. Radio drama permits Beckett to shift the audience's attention from narrative to narration, from the sequence of actions to the act of narrating. In this way the play provides an oblique confirmation of the Beckettian view that all narratives exist autonomously rather than referentially and have less to do with discovering truth than with—as Beckett said of his earlier play *Fin de partie* (pr., pb. 1957; *Endgame*, 1958)—delaying the inevitable end.

Radio drama also provides Beckett with one of the most suitable vehicles for dramatizing humankind's essential nature in the form of a disembodied voice speaking to the impossibly distant, perhaps wholly imagined, ear of some unknown but hoped-for other. Finally, radio drama manifests Beckett's continued effort to create not only a denuded landscape but also a denuded art—stripped bare, whittled away in order to discover what, if anything, its essential nature may be. What works in theory does not necessarily work in practice, however; that is the view of one influential Beckett scholar, Hugh Kenner, who has questioned whether Beckett's obsessive interest in illusion, solipsism, and voice does not, at least in *Embers*, interfere with intelligibility and cause the listener to feel "irritated" rather than "moved."

Critical Context

The situating of *Embers* in the context of theater history, of twentieth century literature, and of Beckett's oeuvre is a task made difficult by the apparent slightness of the work. It is, after all, a work of little length and even less mimetic substance, belonging to a form—radio drama—which has not attracted much critical attention, particularly in the United States. Critics—as well as audiences—have found Beckett's earlier, longer, and slightly more conventional plays for stage, *En attendant Godot* (pb. 1952; *Waiting for Godot*, 1954) and *Endgame*, more appealing. Beckett himself has downplayed the importance of all of his dramatic works, this despite his having been placed in the front rank of absurdist playwrights and his having been awarded the 1969 Nobel Prize in Literature for a "body of work that, in new forms of fiction and the theatre, has transmuted the destitution of modern man into his exultation."

Slight (short) and slighted though it may be, *Embers* is nevertheless both a representative work and an important, innovative one. It shows a typically Beckettian movement away from plot and character toward a divestiture of all that is merely theatrical and seemingly human—toward, that is, the distilled essence of both. This "disintegration of form and content," as Raymond Federman calls it, was Beckett's career-long obsession. "The artistic tendency is not expansive but a contraction," Beckett wrote in 1935. "And art is the apotheosis of solitude." This contractive movement inevitably leads, as in *Embers*, to the isolated character whose existence is not even seen but heard, or implied, perhaps merely imagined. This contraction in turn leads the character to whatever consolations memory can provide.

These consolations prove ambiguous, however, for memory is, as Beckett has defined it, "a clinical laboratory stocked with poison and remedy, stimulant and sedative." Memory relieves the individual of the intolerable burden of existential isolation, but only at the price of making one even more aware of one's predicament, which may be not merely psychological, as in *All That Fall* and *Krapp's Last Tape*, but ontological and epistemological as well, as in *Company* (pr. 1983) and *Rockaby* (pr., pb. 1981). As Beckett's plays and fictions oscillate between past and present, hope and despair, speech and silence, it becomes increasingly difficult to distinguish memory from imagination, recollection from solipsistic projection.

Sources for Further Study

Abbot, H. Porter. *Beckett Writing Beckett: The Author in the Autograph.* Ithaca, N.Y.: Cornell University Press, 1996.

Astro, Alan. *Understanding Samuel Beckett.* Columbia: University of South Carolina Press, 1990.

Cohn, Ruby. *Just Play: Beckett's Theater.* Princeton, N.J.: Princeton University Press, 1980.

Esslin, Martin. "Samuel Beckett and the Art of Broadcasting." *Encounter* 45 (September, 1975): 38-46.

_____. *The Theatre of the Absurd.* 3d ed. London: Methuen, 2001.

Gussow, Mel. *Conversations with and About Beckett.* New York: Grove-Atlantic, 1996.

Homan, Sidney, ed. *Beckett's Theaters: Interpretations for Performance.* Lewisburg, Pa.: Bucknell University Press, 1984.

Kenner, Hugh. *A Reader's Guide to Samuel Beckett.* Syracuse, N.Y.: Syracuse University Press, 1996.

Lyons, Charles R. *Samuel Beckett.* New York: St. Martin's Press, 1983.

McCarthy, Patrick A., ed. *Critical Essays on Samuel Beckett.* Boston: G. K. Hall, 1986.

Worth, Katherine J. "Beckett and the Radio Medium." In *British Radio Drama*, edited by John Drakakis. New York: Cambridge University Press, 1981.

Robert A. Morace

THE ENTERTAINER

Author: John Osborne (1929-1994)
Type of plot: Social realism
Time of plot: The 1950's
Locale: An English coastal town
First produced: 1957, at the Royal Court Theatre, London
First published: 1957

Principal characters:
BILLY RICE, an old man, a former music-hall performer
ARCHIE RICE, his son, a fading music-hall performer
PHOEBE RICE, Archie's second wife
FRANK RICE, their son
JEAN RICE, Archie's daughter by his first marriage
GRAHAM, Jean's boyfriend
OLD BILL, Archie's brother, a barrister

The Play

The Entertainer is set in an English coastal town. Its action centers on the Rice family, and specifically on Archie Rice, the "entertainer" of the title. In scene 1, though, the audience is introduced to the family through Billy Rice, Archie's father, and Jean, Archie's daughter. In a sense these two characters represent a saner past and a more hopeful future: The present, for the Rices, is a run-down, noisy, postwar slum.

Scene 2 (like scenes 4, 7, and 13) consists of a short monologue by Archie, delivered onstage just as it would be in one of his performances: He is a comedian in a music hall, or what Americans might call a burlesque theater, and these scenes represent samples of his professional humor. They are deliberately coarse, cheap, and unattractive; they represent the poor, defiant, and selfish attitudes John Osborne thinks typical of the England of his time.

In scene 3, further characters assemble. Phoebe Rice returns from the cinema, where she spends her spare time watching films that make no impression on her. Jean reveals that she has been to a rally in Trafalgar Square which sparked off a row with her conservative-minded boyfriend, Graham. He shares Billy's view—that women should be kept on a tight rein—and wants Jean to marry him; she, however, is budding into something other than the perfect wife. The talk turns to Frank and Mick (Frank's brother), the former having been imprisoned for refusing the draft, the latter having willingly joined up. Jean, representative of the new generation, admires Frank for saying no and going to jail. Billy and Phoebe seem to think Mick has made the better choice.

This issue is not as casual as it might at first appear. All through scene 5 (after another music-hall monologue by Archie) a telegram waits for Archie to open it. It is bound to be bad news, and in the end the audience discovers that it says Mick has been taken prisoner. Archie avoids this knowledge until the very end, in the same way that he has avoided any commitments or intellectual honesty throughout his life. He is a womanizer; he despises and maltreats his family; he makes a joke of everything—including his father's pride and his daughter's passion. He tries to laugh off even the news of his son's capture, but as the curtain comes down his banter ceases—for the first time—and his chronic insecurity is revealed.

In act 2, the family has heard that Mick is to be repatriated, and the mood is lighter; still, tensions are present. Phoebe, maudlin drunk, brings up many memories of Archie which show him in a worse and worse light. Archie eventually launches into a diatribe, justifying himself by attacking his wife's laziness and lack of passion. As the scene develops, order completely breaks down, with all the characters attacking each other and justifying themselves. The feuding is checked only when Billy is found helping himself to a cake set aside for Mick's homecoming. The Rice family, it is clear, is hopelessly contaminated by selfishness, the same selfishness revealed in Archie's monologues.

Is there any hope for this family? Archie, harassed by the Inland Revenue—he has not paid any tax for twenty years—has various plans: leave the country and go to Canada; leave Phoebe and marry a barmaid; bring his father out of retirement in an attempt to save his own career. None of these, except perhaps the first, seems very plausible, and Archie's advice to Jean—to be more selfish in order to survive—rings hollow. However, it may have some validity after all: At the end of the second act comes the news that Mick, the dutiful child of family and country, has been killed by his captors. Only the antiheroes, it seems, are left alive.

At the start of act 3, Frank sings a protest song about the emptiness of a hero's homecoming once he is dead. Jean emerges from her shell more cynical and disillusioned than anyone. She attacks Archie mercilessly for his ineptitude and his inability to change. She demands to know the purpose of their existence—is it just to please an audience? Her comments, however, make no impression whatsoever. The chatter springs off in all directions, even when Jean tells the family about Archie's plans to remarry. Billy is in fact preoccupied by his imminent return to the stage, engineered by Archie, even though Jean predicts that the strain will kill him—which it does. He dies offstage.

In death, Billy at last gains Archie's respect, but Archie's hypocrisy makes Jean even more determined to remain with Phoebe, reject her father, and leave her fiancé, Graham, from whom she has now grown away. As she and Graham argue, Old Bill, Archie's successful brother, is busy convincing Archie that he must go off to Canada—at Bill's expense. As the alternative is jail, Archie gives in and agrees to go. Jean, meanwhile, states that she has lost any spiritual faith she may have had and must rely only on herself.

The final scene shows Archie, onstage for the last time. He tells a vulgar joke about an ordinary man who finds himself in heaven, which says something about Archie's philosophy. Phoebe is there to help him offstage, the light snaps out, and Archie is gone. The music hall, the audience perceives, has gone with him.

Themes and Meanings

The Entertainer is a play about decadence and decay: the decadence of the Rice family's habits, the decay of propriety and of the music hall as a primary form of entertainment (indeed, as a way of life). It also addresses the hypocrisy of war and the futility of ordinary people—nobodies—trying to be somebodies. The man in Archie's joke at the play's end ironically finds heaven by saying a word whose crudity reflects his low class. Mick's death reveals that obedience only leads one to be fodder for leaders to send to war at their will; by brainwashing young people into the patriotic way of thinking, politicians also remove any potential threat to the established order. Jean represents the new mind, the new woman, who will not settle for life as it traditionally has been. She rejects Archie's phony persona, including his need to flirt, as being as old-fashioned as his pathetic antics onstage. She loves Billy because he has faded from the limelight with a dignity Archie cannot muster. She loves Phoebe for her simplicity and endurance in the face of infidelity, the death of her son, and her miserable past existence—which Archie so cruelly and contemptuously dismisses.

The play is not so much concerned with class as with the effects of time upon tradition. Within two generations, a girl like Jean can shock her female ancestry by doing the simple thing of going to a rally in Trafalgar Square, while Archie can desperately destroy Billy's dignity by putting him back onstage, in a last-ditch attempt to impress a dying audience. Archie himself does not know when to give up. He is arguably the unhappiest character in the play because he is the phoniest. Frank's choice of conscientious objection, set against Mick's willingness to enlist, also shows the contrast between old and new attitudes. Mick dies; Frank lives on.

Is Frank's life, however—as a menial worker in a hospital—worth living? Frank becomes more and more cutting toward Archie as the play proceeds, and his resentment builds up. He has something of the family's musical talent but prefers not to develop it further. His choice, like Jean's, is that of the modern generation— again, the past dies out as the world changes. Politics, for them, may be more important than art; music hall and cinema in a parochial setting are no longer valid forms of entertainment and are certainly not to be taken seriously. Although the audience is not told where Jean has traveled from, nor where she will go, she is obviously mobile and independent, not trapped in the town of her birth or imprisoned by outmoded traditions.

In the end, however, interest centers on the figure of Archie. Clearly, he embodies an era, a tradition, a way of life. All these, one may feel, are associated in Osborne's mind with 1950's England, still clinging grimly to its post-Imperial status in the world, but unable to support it: unable to show dignity (like Billy), unable to break loose (like Jean), ultimately facing only death or futility (like Mick and Frank, respectively). Archie Rice's threadbare comedy is, in the end, not only a satire on British humor; it is also a commentary on British attitudes in general—attitudes that, Osborne implies, lead to an evasion of reality.

Dramatic Devices

John Osborne, in *The Entertainer*, gives precise directions on staging, scenery, and characterization. He carefully describes the town in which the Rice family lives, the lighting, music, particular types of "swaggering" onstage, clothing, and even hair-styles—all of which make the play come alive. There is a determined bid for exact realism. However, at the same time the play is interrupted by continued scenes from the burlesque tradition, which could make an audience feel they were not in the 1950's, but back in the 1930's, the 1910's, or even earlier. The implication is that in the play, as in Archie Rice's life, performance and staging, deliberate acting and real feeling, are all inseparably fused.

Further, Archie's burlesque is juxtaposed to his life at home. He is seen acting professionally, then talking more freely, but his real conversation too often slides toward a kind of patter, as at the end of act 1, where the telegram about his son, finally opened, leads only to an obscene joke—of which, however, the audience never hears the end, as Archie belatedly realizes its inappropriateness and inadequacy.

Conversation is important to the play, when Archie can be elbowed out of the limelight. Its orderly or chaotic nature serves as a barometer of family feelings. It also illustrates how seldom people actually listen to each other. Further points are made by the characters' accents, with Billy's in particular being described by Osborne with some care: It is to be old-fashioned, to use pronunciations now the preserve of the English upper classes only (like rhyming "God" with "Lord"), but at the same time not to sound upper class. Such directions give the play its dimension of history and age.

Finally, note should be taken of the play's use of suspense and of action that occurs offstage. The critical event of the play is the death of Mick, with a clear parallel being the death of Billy. Both are sacrifices, the one to Empire, the other to Archie, and both take place offstage. A related onstage event is Archie's refusal to open his telegram. The implications—regarding Archie's evasive character and essentially futile life—are strong.

Critical Context

John Osborne's first major play (he had written but not published several before it) was *Look Back in Anger*, first produced in London in May, 1956. It made its twenty-six-year-old author a sensation overnight. Osborne became immediately and firmly established as one of the "Angry Young Men" of the 1950's, and perhaps the one with the best right to be angry. Unlike other members of the school, Osborne had received little formal education and little previous theatrical experience. However, he seemed to speak for a generation that was feeling a profound disillusionment—a disillusionment prior to "the Sixties" and Vietnam, and specifically British in its disgust with a class system that refused to die, and with Imperial pretensions—1956 was the year of the British invasion of Suez—which the British ruling classes obstinately refused to give up.

Early success is often regarded as difficult to follow, and in Osborne's case there was some truth to the observation. At times it seemed as if the playwright could only build on his earlier fame by increasing his anger and disgust, by making his picture of his own country even more sleazy. At the same time he seemed to be more and more insidiously taken over by the dramatic establishment. Had Osborne, some wondered, become a "turn," like Archie Rice—a predictable, inconsequential burlesque performer?

The Entertainer, however, must take an honorable place in John Osborne's career. It was Osborne's second play, appearing less than a year after the success of *Look Back in Anger*. Among the major plays produced since then are *The World of Paul Slickey* (pr., pb. 1959), *Luther* (pr., pb. 1961), and *Inadmissible Evidence* (pr. 1964). These plays have consistently provoked English society, prodding their audiences (so Osborne claimed) to feel—the thinking can come later. They are, as has frequently been pointed out, plays of strident rhetoric and overstatement, often with naturalistic subjects, but less often capable (for all the stage directions) of a consistently convincing naturalistic style.

Sources for Further Study

Anderson, Michael. *Anger and Detachment: A Study of Arden, Osborne, and Pinter.* London: Pitman, 1976.

Banham, Martin. *Osborne.* Edinburgh: Oliver & Boyd, 1969.

Brown, John Russell. *Theatre Language: A Study of Arden, Osborne, Pinter, and Wesker.* New York: Taplinger, 1972.

Carter, Alan. *John Osborne.* Edinburgh: Oliver & Boyd, 1973.

Denison, Patricia D., ed. *John Osborne: A Casebook.* New York: Garland, 1997.

Ferrar, Harold. *John Osborne.* New York: Columbia University Press, 1973.

Gilleman, Lu. *The Hideous Honesty of John Osborne: The Politics of Vituperation.* New York: Garland, 2000.

Kennedy, Andrew W. *Six Dramatists in Search of a Language.* London: Cambridge University Press, 1975.

Trussler, Simon. *The Plays of John Osborne: An Assessment.* London: Gollancz, 1969.

T. A. Shippey

ENTERTAINING MR. SLOANE

Author: Joe Orton (1933-1967)
Type of plot: Dark comedy
Time of plot: The 1960's
Locale: England
First produced: 1964, at the New Arts Theatre, London
First published: 1964

> *Principal characters:*
> KATH, a middle-aged woman
> SLOANE, a young man
> KEMP, Kath's elderly father
> ED, Kath's brother

The Play

Entertaining Mr. Sloane opens with Kath showing her prospective new boarder, Mr. Sloane, through her house. Kath is dowdy, middle-aged, and clearly attracted to young Sloane, whose surface show of civility masks an air of insolence and potential danger. Kath tells Sloane that she once had a son who would have been about his age, then confesses that the boy did not die but was born illegitimately and given up for adoption. Sloane confides in return that he is an orphan, reared in a children's home after his parents' death when he was eight. Kath's father, Kemp, arrives and is annoyed to learn that Sloane will be moving into their home. While Kath is out of the room, Kemp tells Sloane the story of his former employer's murder at the hands of a hitchhiker whom Kemp had seen, and then studies the young man's face and announces that he has seen him before—and could still identify him. The two argue, and Kemp stabs Sloane in the leg with a fork.

Kath returns and orders her father from the room, then removes Sloane's pants and seductively treats his wound. She has just sent him upstairs to bed when her brother, Ed, arrives, hoping to obtain his father's signature on what may be a nursing-home admittance form. Although he does not live in the house, Ed is angry about the new lodger and insists that the arrangement will ruin his sister's reputation. When he meets Sloane, however, it becomes clear that he, too, is attracted to the young man; he offers Sloane a job as his chauffeur, which the young man accepts with the understanding that he is to stay well away from Kath. After Ed leaves, Kath and her father argue and Kemp accuses his daughter—with justification—of wanting to put him in a home. When Kemp has gone to bed, Kath dons a flimsy negligee and seduces the willing Sloane on the living room sofa.

Act 2 opens several months later. Sloane is stretched out on the couch while Ed works on the car—Sloane's job—outside. Sloane tells Kath about his evening out the night before with three of his friends, and Kath warns him about the dangers of bad company. Kath also announces that she is pregnant, but Sloane dismisses her sugges- tion that they marry. At Kath's insistence, however, he hands over the locket he wears, a keepsake from his mother. Ed enters and asks Sloane if he had borrowed the car without permission the previous night; Sloane denies the allegation. Kath defends Sloane, and she and Ed argue, with Ed accusing his sister of attempting to corrupt Sloane as she once corrupted his friend, Tommy, the father of Kath's son. Kath leaves, and Ed traps Sloane into admitting he used the car. Ed tells the young man that women are a danger to be avoided and insists that Sloane pack his suitcase and come away with him.

Kemp enters and attempts to tell his son, to whom he has not spoken in many years, that Sloane beats and threatens him and that Kath is pregnant with Sloane's child. Ed confronts Sloane, who convinces him that Kath has forced him to become her lover and that Kemp has provoked his own beatings. Ed leaves, and Sloane and Kemp are alone. When the young man threatens him, Kemp insists he will inform on Sloane, re- laying to the police information concerning Sloane's role in the murder of Kemp's former employer. Act 2 ends as Sloane attacks the old man, beating him nearly sense- less.

As act 3 opens, Ed tells Sloane that Kemp has died and implies that unless the young man cooperates with his wishes, he will turn him over to the police. Sloane quickly adopts the attitude that he knows Ed hopes he will take, telling him that he knows himself to be a young man sorely in need of the proper male companion to set him "on the road to a useful life." Their plan is challenged by Kath, who has discov- ered that Kemp is dead. At first she enters eagerly into the scheme to protect Sloane, but when it becomes apparent that Ed intends to take Sloane with him, she, too, insists that she will tell the truth to the authorities.

Ed and Kath spar verbally over Sloane and at last arrive at an agreement. Sloane will live for six months of the year with Ed and six with Kath—at least until they tire of him—in exchange for their complicity in the matter of their father's death. Sloane waits in the car as the two work out the details of their agreement—Sloane will spend occasional nights with Kath, who would also like him to be present at the birth of their child ("It deepens the relationship if the father is there," she says)—and it becomes apparent that Sloane, who had seemed at first to be a potential predator in their strange triangle, is now at the mercy of this unscrupulous and amoral pair. The play ends as Ed leaves with a cheery "Well, it's been a pleasant morning. See you later."

Themes and Meanings

Entertaining Mr. Sloane is a savagely comic attack on bourgeois values and social hypocrisy. Although the details of its plot may at times seem stark and horrifying, the play itself is blackly humorous; it is a barbed combination of farce and satire that strikes at the heart of middle-class morality. The play's dominant theme is the utter amorality of its characters; personal gain and self-interest are the sole factors motivat- ing their actions. Although Kath and Ed both make an elaborate show of respectability intended to hide their true natures, much of the play's humor arises from the disparity between their actions and their explanations for their behavior. Neither actually believes the rationalizations; it is the pretense that matters.

Kath's seduction of her willing lodger is a case in point. With protestations of motherly solicitude, she approaches Sloane in a sheer negligee, teasingly commenting, "This light is showing me up. I blame it on the manufacturers. They make garments so thin nowadays you'd think they intended to provoke a rape." Ed's justification for his interest in Sloane is equally transparent.

> Why am I interested in your welfare? Why did I give you a job? Why do thinking men everywhere show young boys the strait and narrow? Flash cheque-books when delinquency is mentioned? Support the Scout-movement? Principles, boy, bleeding principles.

The play is at its most acidic in its depiction of Kath and Ed's complete lack of concern for their father's welfare. A scheme to place the old man in a home clearly is afoot before the play begins, and his murder at Sloane's hands is, if truth be told, a convenience to his children. Kath and Ed turn a deaf ear to Kemp's reports of Sloane's brutality, their interest in the young boarder far outweighing their regard for their father. When Sloane admits that he has, indeed, beaten Kemp, Ed responds sympathetically, while Kath's response to her father's death is a plaintive, "Will I have to send his pension book in?"

Sloane himself is from a rougher, working-class background and possesses a streetwise sensibility and penchant for violence that are apparent from the start. The play's surprise, and its central message, is that beneath their bourgeois facade Kath and Ed are every inch as ruthless as the young man they both pursue. The hints throughout the play that Sloane could in fact be Kath's illegitimate son have a symbolic purpose as well; if he is not her child in actuality, he is at least her child in spirit—the logical offspring of middle-class hypocrisy. The play's cheeky, irreverent tone toward the conventions of social respectability lays bare the unsavory—and very comical—reality they are intended to hide.

Dramatic Devices

Behind all the dramatic devices used in *Entertaining Mr. Sloane* is Joe Orton's desire to shock and unsettle his audience with his bitingly satirical send-up of social hypocrisy. The play is cast in the mold of a traditional farce, but the dark tone that underlies its actions lends a savagery to its humor that is several steps beyond the image that the term "farce" implies. The barbs Orton hurls at his characters are intended not merely to prick but to skewer, and the events that shape the story are far more deadly than the roundelay of indiscretions and mishaps that characterize the form.

Satire, too, fails to encompass the true nature of the play, missing the bawdy tone and impudent energy with which Orton infuses his work. The dialogue is peppered with sexual innuendoes, thinly veiled references to the underlying lust that motivates both Kath and Ed. In Orton's hands, lines as apparently innocent as "I wouldn't want to restrict your circulation," or "With me behind you, you'll grow out of it," become sharp double entendres. Indeed, Orton's dialogue bristles with hidden meanings, all couched in the familiar phrases of everyday conversation. The phrasing throughout is distinctly British in its inflections, with the differences in class and character carefully delineated in the dialogue.

Orton also amuses and shocks his audience by playing against conventional dramatic expectations. The play's opening establishes a situation in which it seems likely that a menacing intruder—Mr. Sloane—will wreak havoc in the lives of a middle-class family, victimizing them through their own foibles. Ultimately, however, it is Kath and Ed who emerge as the story's most adroit exploiters, using Sloane's own vicious nature and their father's death to secure his cooperation in their "shared custody" agreement.

Entertaining Mr. Sloane also flies in the face of convention with its outrageously irreverent tone toward subjects that generally receive far more somber treatment. Illegitimacy, homosexuality, and the brutal death of an old man all are treated with a black humor that stunned audiences in the mid-1960's. Kemp's death at Sloane's hands is not unexpected; the event's true shock value lies in the cold-blooded reactions of Kath and Ed, who quickly turn the loss of their father to their own advantage. Homosexuality, too, was an explosive subject at the time the play was written, but Orton, who was himself homosexual, approaches it as a subject for humor, attacking Ed's hypocritical rationalizations as mercilessly as he does Kath's.

Through a combination of wicked wit, clever dramatic plotting, and a crucial willingness to hold nothing sacred, Orton succeeds in lampooning his characters' self-serving amorality in a play that will remain timely for as long as selfishness and hypocrisy remain human traits.

Critical Context

Joe Orton's promising career as one of the freshest and most original British playwrights to emerge during the 1960's was cut short by his brutal murder in 1967. Although he had written a radio play, *The Ruffian on the Stair* (pr. 1964), *Entertaining Mr. Sloane* was Orton's first theatrical production, and it won for its young author both acclaim and a degree of notoriety as audiences and critics responded to its irreverent savaging of suburban morality.

Orton himself delighted in the controversy, having intended from the start to break through traditional notions of propriety in his work and provide his audiences with an entertaining yet scathing view of the foibles of the bourgeoisie. It was an intention he would continue to pursue in *Loot* (pr. 1965) and *What the Butler Saw*, which was produced posthumously in 1969. Both of those plays share *Entertaining Mr. Sloane*'s black humor, boisterous energy, and bracing disregard for the cautious limits of good taste. Orton's work now seems both a shaping force and a natural outgrowth of the social upheavals that characterized the 1960's. It is fitting that one of his unrealized projects was a screenplay for the Beatles, who were revolutionizing pop music in much the same way that Orton was changing the tone of British theater. The road he chose was not an easy one. As he noted in a 1967 interview:

> I'm a success because I've taken a hatchet to them and hacked my way in. I mean it wasn't easy. . . . It's always a fight for an original writer because any original writer will always force the world to see the world his way. The people who don't want to see the world your way will always be angry.

That his plays retain their ability to shock and anger his targets is proof of the truth of Orton's words; that the plays remain true in their aim and entertaining in their execution is proof of his exceptional talent.

Sources for Further Study

Charney, Maurice. *Joe Orton*. London: Macmillan, 1984.
Kaufman, David. "Love and Death." *Horizon* 30 (May, 1987): 38-40.
Lahr, John. Introduction to *Joe Orton: The Complete Plays*. London: Eyre Methuen, 1976.
_____. *Prick Up Your Ears: The Biography of Joe Orton*. New York: Knopf, 1978.
Orton, Joe. *The Orton Diaries*. Edited by John Lahr. London: Methuen, 1986.
Rusinko, Susan. *Joe Orton*. Boston: Twayne, 1995.
Worth, Katharine J. "Form and Style in the Plays of Joe Orton." In *Modern British Dramatists: New Perspectives*, edited by John Russell Brown. Englewood Cliffs, N.J.: Prentice-Hall, 1984.

Janet E. Lorenz

EUNUCHS OF THE FORBIDDEN CITY

Author: Charles Ludlam (1943-1987)
Type of plot: Farce; history
Time of plot: 1900-1920
Locale: The Forbidden City and Shantung, China
First produced: 1971, at Der Reichskabaret, Berlin, Germany
First published: 1972

Principal characters:
ORCHID YEHONALA (later TSU HSI), chosen as the emperor's consort
SAKOTA (later TSU AN), her cousin
CHIEN FENG, the emperor
EMPRESS DOWAGER, his mother
T'UNG CHIH, his son
PERVADING FRAGRANCE, a virgin
WELCOME SPRING, a virgin
PRINCE KUNG, Chien Feng's brother
PRINCE YI, Chien Feng's brother
SU SHUN, the Grand Councillor
AN TE HAI, the chief eunuch
LI LIEN YING, a young eunuch
WU YUNG FOO, a loyal eunuch
A LU TE, a servant girl

The Play

Eunuchs of the Forbidden City is a five-act play, set in China around the time of the Boxer Rebellion of 1900. When the curtain opens, Orchid Yehonala is having a bubble bath, attended by a young eunuch named Li Lien Ying. It seems an idyllic moment, but the restful scene is shattered by the arrival of Orchid's cousin, Sakota (later called Tsu An). Sakota has borne a child to Chien Feng, the emperor of China. Orchid is overjoyed until Sakota tells her cousin that she has borne a girl child and that the emperor is in a deep depression. The Empress Dowager has called for the selection of a new consort for her son in the hope of cheering him up, as well as for the practical purpose of securing the Throne of Heaven for her line of descendants. Sakota informs Orchid that she has submitted her cousin's name as a potential candidate.

Orchid is overwhelmed by this honor, although she does not feel she has a chance of being chosen because of the multitude of beautiful women from which the emperor has to choose. However, Sakota's recommendation is not completely benign. If her cousin is chosen and bears the emperor a son, then Orchid can use her influence to make sure that Sakota's place in the palace will not be lost. As Sakota withdraws, Orchid's eunuch, Li Lien, helps her prepare. Orchid is amazed by Li Lien's directions not only about how to make herself beautiful, but also on how to please the emperor. When asked how he has come by such knowledge, the eunuch reveals how much power the seemingly powerless men have.

In due time, the chief eunuch, An Te Hai (played in the play's debut by Charles Ludlam himself), comes to take Orchid to the Pavilion of Selection. Li Lien teaches his young charge how to bribe officials, knowing that it will come in handy if she is selected. Orchid is brought before the emperor and the Empress Dowager as one of the finalists, along with two other virgins, Pervading Fragrance and Welcome Spring. Chien Feng chooses Orchid as his consort, and she later gives birth to a boy named T'ung Chih. As Chien Feng lies upon his deathbed not long afterward, Orchid, now called Tsu Hsi, is forced to blackmail the dying and stubborn emperor to sign a decree making their son the rightful heir.

Upon his death, the empire is thrown into chaos as warring princes vie for the throne. The Boxers ransack China, forcing everyone to run in panic. Meanwhile, Prince Yi attempts to seize the imperial seal to prove his royal claim, but as Tsu Hsi, Tsu An, and their two young children flee the Winter Palace with loyal Prince Kung and the assistance of Wu Yung Foo, the ever-faithful eunuch, Li Lien, thrusts the royal seal into her hands. When Prince Yi and Su Shun, the Grand Councillor, enter, Li Lien hides and overhears their plot to kill T'ung Chih. However, he has no chance to tell his mistress what he has overheard, for Prince Yi, in an effort to disguise his true intentions, plucks out his own eyeball to show his loyalty to the new heir and Tsu Hsi. Believing Prince Yi's word completely, they retire for the night.

Later, disguised as bandits, Prince Yi and Su Shun enter to kill the young prince T'ung Chih. However, Tsu Hsi orders her cousin to switch the children and the princess is killed instead. In the process, before the eunuchs take away the survivors, Tsu Hsi sees Prince Yi's ring and knows he is a traitor. Tsu Hsi then orders Prince Yi brought before her, and Prince Kung beheads him.

Sixteen years later, Tsu Hsi is still in command as empress. Her spoiled son must be married soon, but he seems to have eyes for one of her servant girls, A Lu Te. Tsu Hsi disapproves. Meanwhile, An Te Hai and Li Lien Ying carry on their own war against each other in order to see who can gain more favor with Tsu Hsi. Li Lien works with Tsu An and Prince Kung and orders An Te Hai's execution. Before he dies, he reveals that he is not truly a eunuch, has had sex with countless women, and may be the father of T'ung Chih and the baby A Lu Te is carrying. In a strange plot twist that ends the play, Tsu Hsi executes Prince Kung and poisons Tsu An.

Themes and Meanings

Eunuchs of the Forbidden City is a complex play. It is historical, taking place during a time of emperors and pageantry. It is epic, taking five acts to span more than twenty years and featuring a cast of royalty and servants. It is sexual, featuring eunuchs servicing empresses, princes, servants, and one another. It is comedic, with much wordplay, double entendres, and anachronistic comments.

The names of the characters are, alone, enough to reveal the comedic nature of this play. Tsu Hsi is pronounced "Susie"; Tsu An is "Sue Ann"; T'ung Chih is "tongue-in-cheek." There is scatological humor when the innkeeper Wu Yung Foo hides food for the infant prince in a chamber pot and then sits on it, claiming to have "loose bowels. That was my plot." Ludlam pokes fun at himself in the next line, when Prince Kung says, "This is a loose plot." A Lu Te sings "Tsu, Tsu, Tsu-Hsi, good-bye," a play on a jazz tune. An Te Hai says "Walk this way" and then walks comically, and the innkeeper mimics him, reminiscent of a gag made famous by Groucho Marx.

The sexual nature of the play also goes from subtle to outright blatant and vulgar. In the beginning, there are veiled references to sexual acts being performed by the eunuchs in their "serving" the royalty. As the story progresses, however, we see An Te Hai performing oral sex and anal insertions upon Tsu Hsi, A Lu Te trying to copulate with T'ung Chih, and An Te Hai as he displays his penis, only to have it cut off by the executioner. The play is amusing, tongue-in-cheek, and irreverent, and yet somehow Ludlam never loses sight of the main story line that he is attempting to convey.

Ludlam's play continues his literary tendency for oddity and irreverence in his body of work. His own "Manifesto" lists "axioms to a theater for ridicule" such as "You are a living mockery of your own ideals. If not, you have set your ideals too low," and his "instructions for use" state:

> This is farce not Sunday school. Illustrate hedonistic calculus. Test out a dangerous idea, a theme that threatens to destroy one's whole value system. Treat the material in a madly farcical manner without losing the seriousness of the theme. Show how paradoxes arrest the mind. Scare yourself a bit along the way.

Given these statements, it is not surprising that Ludlam wrote this odd play. Tish Dace, in her biographical piece on Ludlam, writes that Ludlam "employed all his diverse theatrical skills for one overriding purpose—to make people laugh."

Dramatic Devices

Eunuchs of the Forbidden City is a typical example of Charles Ludlam's Ridiculous Theatre. Ludlam made his New York stage debut as Peeping Tom in Ronald Tavel's *The Life of Lady Godiva* (pr. 1966), which was directed by John Vaccaro at the Play-House of the Ridiculous, so it is not a surprise that his own future works (as well as the name of his own company) were influenced by the farcical works of his first director. In fact, after being summarily fired by Vaccaro during rehearsals for his second play, *Conquest of the Universe* (pr. 1967), he started his own company, the Ridiculous Theatrical Company, and produced his own version of the play called *When Queens Collide* (pr. 1967, pb. 1989).

Farce and humor have always been a central aspect of Ludlam's dramatic devices, often used to reinforce Ludlam's strict moralist standards and, as Tish Dace notes, to indict "the objects of his ridicule for violating his own humanistic standards." Farcical humor is the most obvious dramatic device used in *Eunuchs of the Forbidden City.*

Ludlam's work in this play is no different from some of William Shakespeare's work. It is bawdy, irreverent, shameless, funny, and full of asides to the audience.

Ludlam's use of humor helps free the audience's sense of inhibition, according to Dace, by "moving spectators quickly from incredulity at his daring to joining him in raucous belly laughs. . . ." In doing so, Ludlam "demonstrates outrage at hypocrisy, cruelty, greed, con-games, sycophancy, and other violations of his own moral imperatives."

Critical Context

Eunuchs of the Forbidden City was only the fifth (the sixth, *Edna Brown*, 1964, he destroyed) play Ludlam wrote, preceded by plays that included *When Queens Collide, Big Hotel* (pr. 1966, pb. 1989), and *The Grand Tarot* (pr. 1969, pb. 1989). While most of these "chaotic, nonconformist, often all-night affairs," as Steven Samuels describes them, were epic in style, *Eunuchs of the Forbidden City* would be the Ridiculous Theatrical Company's largest production to that date. Ludlam, in "Manifesto," says:

> We'd been working on it for a year and a half. We had trouble getting it on [stage] because it had such elaborate *mise en scène*. We needed a couple of dozen enormous wigs, gongs, music. It's epic style, and you have to have the palanquins and carts or you can't do it. It has long tirades like in French classical tragedy. . . . It was the most demanding play we'd done.

The play opened in Germany, so Ludlam and his cast were free from the more conservative opinions of New York City critics. In fact, the German critics found the play quite refreshing. Ludlam noted that the German press gave it a good reception and saw Ludlam's style as a welcome alternative to then-dominant Living Theater. As Ludlam said, "Europeans appreciated our extensions of tradition—the habit of mining out, redefining and exploiting traditions rather than merely destroying them."

Most of Ludlam's subsequent works proved to be equally epic and grand theatrical productions, such as *Camille: A Tear-Jerker* (pr. 1973, pb. 1989), based on Alexandre Dumas, *fils*'s *La Dame aux camélias* (pr., pb. 1852; *Camille*, 1856), and his tour de force, *The Mystery of Irma Vep: A Penny Dreadful* (pr. 1984, pb. 1987). Charles Ludlam died at an early age, leaving behind an enormous body of work.

Sources for Further Study

Dace, Tish. "Ludlam, Charles." In *Contemporary Dramatists*. New York: St. James Press, 1972.

Ludlam, Charles. *The Complete Plays of Charles Ludlam*. New York: Harper & Row, 1989.

Samuels, Steven, ed. *Ridiculous Theatre: Scourge of Human Folly—The Essays and Opinions of Charles Ludlam*. New York: Theatre Communications Group, 1992.

Daryl F. Mallett

EXECUTION OF JUSTICE

Author: Emily Mann (1952-   )
Type of plot: Epic theater; history
Time of plot: 1978-1984
Locale: San Francisco, California
First produced: 1984, at the Actors Theatre of Louisville, Kentucky
First published: 1986

Principal characters:

DAN WHITE, the man who killed Mayor George Moscone and
 Supervisor Harvey Milk
COURT, the judge at White's trial
DOUGLAS SCHMIDT, White's defense lawyer
THOMAS NORTON, the prosecuting attorney
SISTER BOOM BOOM, a man dressed as a nun
COP, a right-wing supporter of Dan White
DIANNE FEINSTEIN, a city supervisor, later the mayor of San
 Francisco

The Play

Execution of Justice is a two-act play centered on the 1978 murders of George Moscone, the mayor of San Francisco, and board of supervisors member Harvey Milk, the first openly gay elected official in the United States. Much of the play is set in the courtroom at the first-degree murder trial of Dan White, the man accused of the murders. In the scenes of White's trial, it becomes increasingly clear that justice is being "executed"—not in the sense of being carried out, but in the sense of being destroyed—by the wily defense lawyer and the biased judge.

At the trial, Thomas Norton, attorney for the prosecution of Dan White, seems to think the argument for first-degree murder is so obvious that it is unnecessary for him to make a strong case against the accused. He also fails to anticipate the support for White from those who share his antigay views. Douglas Schmidt, the defense lawyer, virtually wins the case in the jury selection process: He allows no one who is homosexual, an ethnic minority, or liberal-minded to serve on the jury. In his opening remarks to the jury, Schmidt establishes the idea that although White did the shooting, the question the jurors should consider is "Why?" Schmidt repeatedly leads the defense witnesses to say what he wants them to say and undermines the prosecution witnesses by asking if they are gay and belittling their professional expertise. The judge overrules most of Thomas Norton's early objections, and Norton essentially gives up in his role as prosecutor.

Schmidt also tells the jurors that because Dan White's recent diet consisted of nothing but "junk food" such as chips, candy, and Twinkie cream-filled cakes, he was suffering from diminished capacity to make rational decisions. This "Twinkie defense" proves effective for Schmidt. The jury finds White guilty only of the reduced charges of voluntary manslaughter, and the judge imposes a prison sentence of seven years and eight months with the possibility of earlier parole. Once the verdict and sentence are announced, gays and other protesters march and riot, followed immediately by the police responding in San Francisco's historically gay district, the Castro, by clubbing down homosexuals on the street and in gay bars. The multiple connotations of "justice" and "execution" are evident throughout the entire play.

Themes and Meanings

Execution of Justice closely follows the real-life case of Dan White and emphasizes a clear lesson: The lack of respect for, and intolerance toward, others leads to and perpetuates violence. Dan White never explains why he shot the two men and never expresses any remorse in the play, just as he did not in the actual case. White is a war veteran and a former policeman who starred in the police baseball league. His closest acquaintances were policemen who had been his former colleagues and who, like White, deplored the openness accorded to gays in the Castro district. White was also an elected member of the board of supervisors, and the fact that Harvey Milk became a supervisor at the same time made White even more indignant in his intolerance. White resigned from the board but later changed his mind and wanted to return. The fact that Mayor Moscone had already chosen a replacement for the position kindled in White a hatred of the mayor and the openly gay Harvey Milk.

The play accurately depicts the historical facts that White took the gun he had as a policeman, now not even registered, along with extra bullets and went to City Hall. He climbed into the building through a back window to avoid going through the metal detector. He chatted with the secretary while waiting to see the mayor, entered the mayor's office, and fired his gun repeatedly, even after Mayor Moscone was clearly dead. He reloaded his gun at some point and headed for Harvey Milk's office, where he again fired obsessively. Jealousy, misplaced revenge, projecting his failures on others—these emotions, the play suggests, seem more likely causes for White's actions than his Twinkie diet.

The play also suggests that in many ways Dan White symbolizes the effects of society's rigid attitudes. White was not alone in his gay-bashing and his narrow-minded certainty that his views were the only correct ones. Perhaps equally apropos is Sister Boom Boom's view that when someone tries too anxiously to live up to the expectations of society, keeping up that pretense can take a heavy toll.

Another theme of the play concerns healing and the changing of discriminatory attitudes. The play encourages discussion of traumatic events and aims to present a troubling public experience theatrically in order to serve as a vital and meaningful forum to heal the individual and the larger collective society. Theater, the play implies, can be an important part of the process of changing attitudes and thus changing behaviors. To emphasize this purpose, both the published script and the performance programs for the audience include "A San Francisco Chronology," which details the actual historical sequence of events surrounding the Dan White murders and trial, a device to emphasize that Emily Mann did not invent the plot.

Dramatic Devices

Execution of Justice adopts devices of epic theater throughout its performance. There is no house curtain; the scenes are open, fluid, and interspersed; and the themes are didactic and socially relevant. The innovative use of documentary films, slides, and audiotapes, and the incorporation of quotations from the actual trial transcripts, provide a strong sense of realism and convey a powerful message of the damage caused by hatred and intolerance. The openness and fluidity of the scenes create a sense of immediacy, as though the action is going on presently rather than merely in the past.

Much of the play, particularly the courtroom scenes, is told in chronological order, but the script often breaks the linear chronology and repeats symbolic moments. The repeated taped sounds of high heels echoing through hallways, people out of breath, and mumbled Hail Marys become a haunting refrain. Audiotape is first used very early in act 1. In a phone conversation, Dan White told his wife Mary Ann to meet him at the church, where he later tells her that he shot the mayor and Harvey Milk. The same audio is used at later times to punctuate various incongruities between justice and intention, just as the church setting is incongruous with murder and Dan White's apparent lack of repentance. This early scene is immediately followed by an amplified gavel sound and a clerk announcing the opening of the trial, but instead of moving to the trial setting, the Cop, wearing a tee shirt that reads "Free Dan White," delivers a monologue about "dirty homosexuals." Sister Boom Boom, a man dressed as a nun, appears onstage and intersperses "her" monologue with that of the Cop. Sister Boom Boom speaks of the pervasive cycle of brutality and the lack of justice for those whom society considers outcasts.

The play jumps from short scene to short scene and incorporates frequent shifts between stage and video screen. A scene in progress may be overlapped with a switch to a film clip of a news reporter giving a live report of the action. The trial section has longer periods of conventional dialogue, including longer speeches, as when the lawyers give their final summations to the jury. Toward the end of the trial, other voices are heard, even as the jurors are being polled about their verdict. The purpose of these various dramatic devices is twofold: to keep the attention of the audience and to suggest the chaotic flux and uncertainty of the situation in San Francisco as the events unfolded.

Critical Context

Like all of Emily Mann's plays, *Execution of Justice* has a strong message, one which is dramatized rather than specifically stated. Mann often tells other people's stories, particularly those of the voiceless. Her plays tell these stories not as strict documentaries but as multimedia presentations that capture the essence of the events and what the events mean to others.

Mann has virtually redefined the art of writing historical drama, particularly because she chooses events that are still remembered by audience members who lived through those times. Her plays focus on the lives of actual persons in situations that provoke critical connections, and draw important links between the recent past and the present. Her first play, *Annulla: An Autobiography* (pr., pb. 1985), tells the story of Annulla Allen, a Holocaust survivor Mann knew and interviewed extensively. *Still Life* (pr. 1980, pb. 1979), based on three people Mann knew, portrays the Vietnam War from the viewpoint of a veteran soldier and connects the warfare in Southeast Asia with the simultaneous violence of the era in the United States. *Greensboro—A Requiem* (pr. 1996) serves as a memorial to five anti-Ku Klux Klan protesters who were murdered during a march in Greensboro, North Carolina, in 1979.

Two other plays are Mann's adaptations of books. *Having Our Say: The Delaney Sisters' First One Hundred Years* (pr. 1995) dramatizes the lives and wisdom of African American women Sarah and Bessie Delaney, who talk of their long lives and their long struggles against the racial prejudice they encountered. *Meshugah* (pr. 1998) is based on the 1994 novel of the same name by Isaac Bashevis Singer and deals with Jewish survivors of the Holocaust who immigrated to New York City. The subject matter of all Mann's plays correlates with her devout belief that the purpose of theater is to provide a forum for ideas, change attitudes and actions, and build community.

Mann is highly respected as a director as well as a playwright. She has received numerous awards for both roles, including several Obie Awards and a 1994 Tony Award for outstanding regional theater for her work as artistic director at the McCarter Theatre at Princeton University. She made her Broadway debut in 1986 with *Execution of Justice*, for which she received a Helen Hayes Award, a Bay Area Critics award, and a Drama Desk nomination. The play was also a co-winner of the 1984 Great American Play Contest the year it premiered at the Actors Theatre of Louisville.

Mann is an important figure in American drama, devoted to the art of theater in its many aspects. She has translated major plays into English, co-edited drama anthologies, and collaborated on scripts with other playwrights. She has acted onstage herself and is a nationally distinguished director. Her plays have been widely produced because of the enduring quality of their social relevance.

Sources for Further Study

Betsko, Kathleen, and Rachel Koenig. *Interviews with Contemporary Women Playwrights*. New York: Beech Tree Books, 1987.

Bienen, Leigh Buchanan. "Emily Mann." In *Speaking on Stage*, edited by Philip Kolin and Colby Kellman. Tuscaloosa: University of Alabama Press, 1996.

Burke, Sally. *American Feminist Playwrights*. New York: Twayne, 1996.

Savran, David. *In Their Own Words: Contemporary American Playwrights*. New York: Theatre Communications Group, 1988.

Lois A. Marchino

EXIT THE KING

Author: Eugène Ionesco (1909-1994)
Type of plot: Absurdist
Time of plot: Modern era
Locale: Throne room of a king
First produced: 1962, at the Théâtre de l'Alliance Française, Paris
First published: Le Roi se meurt, 1963 (English translation, 1963)

> *Principal characters:*
> BERENGER THE FIRST, the King
> QUEEN MARGUERITE, his older wife
> QUEEN MARIE, his younger wife
> THE DOCTOR, the court surgeon
> JULIETTE, a nurse and domestic servant
> THE GUARD

The Play

To the strains of seventeenth century courtly music, derisively played, the curtain rises on *Exit the King* to reveal a shabby throne room. On either side of the King's throne are two smaller thrones for the two queens, Marguerite (the King's first wife) and Marie (his second, and younger, wife). The room has several windows and doors; one small door leads to the King's apartment. The King, his queens, the Doctor, and Juliette are announced by the Guard, who remains onstage with Queen Marguerite and Juliette, the servant. There is a brief glimpse of King Berenger the First, bedecked with crown and crimson robe, holding a scepter.

All is not well. It is soon apparent from the severe comments of Queen Marguerite that Berenger is losing control—of his court, his kingdom, nature, and himself. The central heating has gone out, there are cigarette butts on the floor, and the sky is overcast; even the sun has refused to cooperate with the orders of the King. The court is awakening to its last day, and as the Guard mentions a new crack in the wall, even Marguerite admits that things are moving more rapidly than she expected.

Queen Marie returns to the stage, eyes red from sobbing over the impending death of the King. Marguerite offers little sympathy: Since death is natural and inevitable, Berenger the First (of all people) should have kept this fact always in view, should have organized his life for a "decent" departure. Marguerite is determined in these last moments "to do what ought to have been done over a period of years."

The universe seems to be folding up as well. The doctor-cum-astronomer reports to the queens that the sun is going out, that Mars and Saturn have collided and exploded, and that time itself is speeding up, with cows giving birth twice a day. However, the King, as he enters at last, slipperless, through one of the doors, is more concerned with his stiff legs and sore ribs, and the strange noises at night that have kept him awake.

When Marguerite tells Berenger that he is going to die, he brushes the message aside; everyone is going to die, he says, and he will too—when he gets around to it. The queen, however, is adamant: "You're going to die in an hour and a half, you're going to die at the end of the show."

Marie urges the King not to abdicate his moral and titular position, but with an act of the will to order his kingdom restored and death put at bay. But the Guard is mysteriously paralyzed, unable to speak or carry out His Majesty's wishes. The King, provoked by Marguerite's announcement, stands up, then falls, over and over again. Stage directions suggest that the scene be played "like a tragic Punch and Judy show." Berenger regains his feet and insists that the kingdom is falling apart only through his own neglect. The Guard does not respond: Marguerite can command him, but the King cannot. Queen Marie begs Berenger to command her, but she, too, can only obey the others.

Time is running out. The Doctor reports that there is "a gap in the sky that used to house the Royal Constellation. In the annals of the universe, his Majesty has been entered as deceased." With this, the King's demeanor abruptly changes. He shouts that he does not want death. Already he has aged fourteen hundred years; the King calls for someone to save him, but Marguerite offers little comfort: Because the King did not prepare for this time, he must do all of his thinking about death in an hour. Berenger's shouts through the window that he is dying produce only an empty echo.

He screams and moans, "Why was I born if it wasn't forever?" and confesses he never had time to think about death. Before, Berenger himself commanded the hand of death, executing his brothers and all his rivals—even Marguerite's own parents. Now it is his turn to face the inevitable, but Marie will allow no reverie. Death is just a word, she tells him, and who knows what it means? Berenger must join the present moment and forget the rest. "It's you, all the life in you, straining to break out. Dive into an endless maze of wonder and surprise, then you too will have no end, and can exist forever. . . . Escape from definitions and you will breathe again!"

Marie's speech is drowned by choking sounds from the King. Marie calls on Berenger to grasp the light within, but instead the King calls on the sun to save him, though he knows it is futile. "I'm dying, you hear, I'm trying to tell you. I'm dying but I can't express it, unless I talk like a book and make literature of it."

Finally Berenger asks to be taught resignation, and stage directions indicate that as the others lead him in an examination of his life, the dialogue becomes almost a chant and the movements of the characters like a ritualistic dance. The King, collapsing into a wheelchair, quizzes Juliette on her life, which is poor and miserable, but Berenger insists that she see life itself as a miracle. The Doctor notes that the King is no longer panic-stricken and that his death (though far from noble) will at least be respectable.

The Guard narrates a history of the world with Berenger himself as the main player: He wrote the works of William Shakespeare and split the atom; he was the master of his kingdom and of all creation. The sound of the King's heart, beating loudly, shakes the room; a wall collapses. The King is able to stand, but more and more he resembles a sleepwalker. He says the name Marie, but without understanding. The King is blind, and Marie (as the stage directions have it) simply disappears. The Guard and Juliette disappear as well, and the Doctor, bowing and scraping mechanically, leaves through one of the doors.

Only Marguerite and the King remain. She orders him to stand motionless as she cuts the invisible cords binding Berenger to this life. The stage directions have her remove an invisible ball and chain, take a sack from his shoulders, and grasp a toolbox and an old saber. She orders the King to walk by himself as she speaks to imaginary wolves and rats not to interfere. She directs Berenger the First to his throne and orders him to sit. Marguerite disappears; the throne room, its doors and windows, have quietly disappeared as well. At last, the King on his throne fades into a gray light, into a mist.

Themes and Meanings

Exit the King is a play not about death itself but about the process of facing one's own disintegration. Offered as a kind of debate on death, the play pits the young and passionate Queen Marie (who begs Berenger to be lost in the now) against the older and wiser Queen Marguerite (who insists that death must always inform one's consciousness). The metaphysical debate is not over the nature of death, which remains mysterious in the play, but over its significance. Science, as represented by the learned Doctor, is powerless to stop the inevitable. The rest of humanity, embodied in the choruslike function of the Guard, is reduced to wooden cliché. For each person death is a unique experience, utterly new, and the most one can hope for is a Marguerite, a "guide" reminiscent of those in the ancient Tibetan Book of the Dead.

Exit the King is not a tragedy, for tragedy implies noble defeat in the context of an ordered universe. Berenger and his court are a microcosm of modern man, ludicrously crowned with self-made authority, having lost any connection with a "higher order." Human finitude thus becomes the object of laughter, even of derision, in its futile attempts to command all creation and give it meaning.

The play might be interpreted solipsistically, with the universe itself fading from existence as the King slips into unconsciousness; yet Marguerite assures the King that "nothing will be forgotten. . . . A grain of salt that dissolves in water doesn't disappear: it makes the water salty." In the modern universe, as the Doctor puts it earlier in the play, Berenger would also be remembered—but only as a page in a book in some vast library, and only until the page decays from age or is destroyed by fire. Rather, as Marguerite tells Berenger, "Life is exile," and he must return to his own land. Solipsism is merely the coward's hope; life may well be a cruel joke, but each modern human being must nevertheless face the prankster Death. The King, immobile, passionless, seated in kingly fashion upon his throne, fades at the end of the play into a mist, not triumphant, not resigned, but already less (or more) than human. Some have written that the play actually helped them face death, but, in his seventy-first year, Eugène Ionesco responded that, "Alas, it does not help me, since I am not reconciled to the idea of death, of man's mortality."

Dramatic Devices

One of the most "literary" of Ionesco's plays, *Exit the King* examines the traditional metaphor in which the king and his kingdom represent the universe and its order, and concludes that in an absurd world (the modern world) such order is a chimera. Using the absurdist techniques of ritualistic action, farce, and stylized and clichéd language, the play distances the audience from Berenger and his entourage: No willing suspension of disbelief is possible. The king himself, reduced to being a clown or puppet, is an object of the audience's derisive laughter. However, the play is less "alien" than some of Ionesco's earlier plays, in which the illogic on the stage served to make words into "things" and to force the audience to look into the face of absurdity. *Exit the King* employs more conventional stage language, with the characters of Berenger and the queens, and even Juliette, being more than mere marionettes.

Berenger the man is only partially realized onstage, and his inner debate with death is manifested, often in ritualistic fashion, in and through the other characters (representing aspects of himself). By the end of the play, speech and movement have been united in a ritual preparation for death. The King's increasing loss of command over the elements is portrayed onstage by the growing powerlessness of his words. They can no longer command his Guard; even Marie responds only to Marguerite's orders. The King's order for a bugle to sound produces only a ringing in his own ear.

Toward the end, the King becomes an invalid, being wheeled around in his blankets and supplied with a hot water bottle by nurse Juliette. Ironically, as the others are celebrating Berenger's great accomplishments and his command of his vast kingdom, the King's fear of loss causes his heart to beat loudly, widening cracks in the wall and creating others. The movement of the play is both temporal and psychological, with its self-referential insistence that Berenger as a man will last only the length of the play. The wordplay, the debate between Marie and Marguerite, and the connection between Berenger's fate and that of the universe (a universe presumably containing the play's audience) serve to sustain *Exit the King* until the universe and the King disappear into a sea of gray.

Critical Context

Exit the King is one of four plays written by Ionesco featuring Berenger as a kind of Everyman. *Tueur sans gages* (pr., pb. 1958; *The Killer*, 1960) pits a man named Berenger against the derisively laughing life-taker, representing the forces of unreason, and Berenger succumbs. In *Rhinocéros* (pr., pb. 1959; *Rhinoceros*, 1959), an Everyman Berenger is the last man on Earth, refusing to capitulate to all the others who have joined the "movement" to become horned beasts; the play is a satire on totalitarianism of both the Left and the Right. In *Le Piéton de l'air* (pr. 1962; *A Stroll in the Air*, 1964) Berenger is a French writer tired of using cliché to mock cliché; he thus eagerly visits another universe but returns, his eyes wild, having witnessed horror and ugliness.

Ionesco's first play, *La Cantatrice chauve* (pr. 1950; *The Bald Soprano*, 1956), inaugurated the genre of the Theater of the Absurd, upending traditional stage conventions and making the rational seem irrational and ironic. With playwrights Jean Genet, Arthur Adamov, Harold Pinter, and Samuel Beckett, Ionesco opened the theater to a new kind of tragicomedy which, in its playfulness and its metaphysical consideration of death and meaning, exemplified the angst, or feeling of abandonment and anxiety, of modern humankind.

Exit the King marked a departure for Ionesco from portrayal of the merely absurd to the use of more rounded, less overtly mechanical language and characters. Subsequently, Ionesco concentrated on the subconscious images of dreams. "Dreams," he told an interviewer, "are reality at its most profound, and what you invent is truth because invention, by its nature, can't be a lie." Though still expressing what amounts to nihilism in some of his plays written after *Exit the King*, in others Ionesco seems to affirm the need of his central characters for some kind of love, as in *La Soif et la faim* (pr. 1964; *Hunger and Thirst*, 1968). The works of Ionesco, especially *Exit the King*, confront the audience with the problem of human finitude in the face of a world that has apparently lost its moorings.

Sources for Further Study

Coe, Richard N. *Ionesco: A Study of His Plays*. Rev. ed. London: Methuen, 1971.

Dobrez, L. A. C., ed. *The Existential and Its Exits: Literary and Philosophical Perspectives on the Works of Beckett, Ionesco, Genet, and Pinter*. London: Athlone, 1986.

Esslin, Martin. *The Theatre of the Absurd*. 3d ed. London: Methuen, 2001.

Hayman, Ronald. *Eugène Ionesco*. London: Heinemann, 1976.

Ionesco, Eugène. *Notes and Counter Notes*. Translated by Donald Watson. New York: Grove Press, 1964.

_____. *Present Past, Past Present: A Personal Memoir*. Cambridge, England: Da Capo, 1998.

Kluback, William, and Michael Finkenthal. *The Clown in the Agora: Conversations About Eugène Ionesco*. New York: Lang, 1998.

Lamont, Rosette C., ed. *Ionesco: A Collection of Critical Essays*. Englewood Cliffs, N.J.: Prentice-Hall, 1973.

Lewis, Allan. *Ionesco*. New York: Twayne, 1972.

Plimpton, George, ed. "Eugène Ionesco." In *Writers at Work: The Paris Review Interviews, Seventh Series*. New York: Viking, 1986.

Dan Barnett

EZRA

Author: Bernard Kops (1926-   )
Type of plot: Expressionist
Time of plot: 1945, with flashbacks to 1943 and 1898 and intimations of the late 1950's
Locale: Italy and Washington, D.C.
First produced: 1981, at the New Half Moon Theatre, London
First published: 1980, in *Adam*

> *Principal characters:*
> EZRA POUND, the twentieth century poet
> ANTONIO VIVALDI, the eighteenth century composer
> BENITO MUSSOLINI "IL DUCE," the fascist dictator of Italy, 1922-1943
> CLARA, Mussolini's mistress
> OLGA, Pound's mistress
> DOROTHY, Pound's wife

The Play

As the ninety-minute, one-act *Ezra* opens, Ezra Pound paces the six-by-six-foot gorilla cage in which American troops have imprisoned him. It is May, 1945, somewhere between Pisa and Viareggio. Under arrest for treason, narrating his own situation, the poet moves from self-pity to a joke about Walt Disney; Ezra then sings a song from the Disney film *Snow White and the Seven Dwarfs* (1937) just as his pants fall down. He soon stops mourning the confiscation of his belt and shoelaces as he conjures up visions of two men he admires, composer Antonio Vivaldi and dictator Benito Mussolini. The former dances with Ezra to "Primavera," the spring section of Vivaldi's *The Four Seasons* (1725). The latter enters belting "Funiculi Funicula."

Both try to cheer him with amusing badinage. "I'm the dead one, remember?" quips Il Duce, who then introduces himself to Vivaldi, joining him in singing a bit of "Me and My Shadow." Mussolini's mistress, Clara, appears long enough to scold these leaders—"Men will be boys"—but shifts in the demented Ezra's mind to his own mistress, Olga. Before she is displaced among Ezra's apparitions by his wife, Dorothy, Mussolini and Vivaldi exchange such barbed remarks as the dictator's thrust, "Never trust a composer. A decomposer now, eh!" and the musician's parry, "Italy had a future in the past."

Ezra's free association prompts his connection of his wife Dorothy's entrance to "the yellow brick road." Moments later, a voice-over of one of his pro-fascist radio broadcasts segues into a prison guard ordering the women to leave and then Ezra's fantasy of the two women living together, united by their desire to protect his books and reputation.

As the action jumps backward and forward across 1945, Ezra faces down his interrogator by singing snatches of "Pennies from Heaven" and "Ten Cents a Dance" to explain his anti-Semitic economic theories; he confesses to having personally bombed Pearl Harbor. At his home, American authorities—represented onstage by a Guard—confiscate his typewriter and seven thousand manuscript pages, including his latest *Cantos* and his translations of Confucius. When asked specifically about his radio broadcasts, Ezra praises Mussolini, Joseph Stalin, and Adolf Hitler. Ezra excuses his views by proclaiming that he is above the law, because "a poet listens to his own voice."

Ezra's digressions grow increasingly bizarre. Rather than discuss events of 1943, he invokes Vergil, rambles into World War I, quotes one of his broadcasts calling upon American troops to desert, and focuses upon the question only when permitted, in the longest coherent stretch of text, a long reenactment of his walk from Rome north into the Tyrol to see his daughter. Then Clara complains that she and Benito are being kept awake, apparently by Ezra's having willed them into his brain. Ezra broadcasts another anti-Semitic tirade, then recounts the occupation of his town, Rapallo, by American soldiers, and his arrest.

Although the caged Ezra increasingly appears more genuinely mad than self-mocking, doctors pronounce him sane, and he is shipped off to Washington, D.C., for trial. There, after reminiscences of his youth, he hears the indictment against him, his attorney's halfhearted plea for his release, and a psychiatrist's testimony regarding his paranoia. Alone in his cell at St. Elizabeth's Hospital for the criminally insane after he has been pronounced of unsound mind, Ezra, seeming more rational than at any other time in the play, reflects upon the other geniuses who have been imprisoned or accused of treason or declared insane.

During this soliloquy, eleven years pass. Ezra hears quoted thereafter the pleas of famous men for his release, interrupting the litany to protest that he is "the patsy, the fall guy" for them because he has said what they only thought and to insist that he had known nothing about the gas chambers; had he known, he would have rescued the Jews. Thirteen years after his incarceration at St. Elizabeth's, a voice dismisses the charges of treason against him.

For a few moments Ezra and Dorothy are upon a ship's deck, bound for his beloved Italy. Then they stroll through the Ghetto Vecchio in Venice, as he calls the names of his Jewish friends. Only the wind replies. Confused at first by the empty houses, he then, too late, acknowledges the error of his anti-Semitism. Now the cage that contains him is the shame of his guilt.

Themes and Meanings

Himself a Socialist and a Jew, Bernard Kops dramatized in *Ezra* the postwar mental processes of American poet Ezra Pound, the fascist and anti-Semite whose radio broadcasts supporting Mussolini and attacking Franklin Delano Roosevelt (whom he dubbed "Jewsevelt") caused his arrest for treason when Allied forces occupied Italy. Kops set out to dramatize the actions of a great poet whose ideas appalled him. An admirer of Pound's beautiful and original poetry, Kops nevertheless was horrified at the virulently anti-Semitic tirades Pound broadcast to American troops during World War II. Kops's attempt to reconcile the poet's genius with the man's reprehensible political views produced the paradox embodied in *Ezra*.

Kops's Ezra is childlike, naïve, unwilling or unable to concentrate on his interrogators' questions or to confront the gravity of the charges against him. Deluded about fascism's intentions and evidently ignorant of its effects—that is, of the Holocaust—Kops's Ezra has attacked the Jews out of muddled ideas about international economics derived in part from the Nazis but as well from an upbringing quite segregated from any Jew who might have prepared him for a more realistic appraisal of anti-Semitic propaganda.

As depicted in the play, in his later years Ezra seems not merely duped but also somewhat demented, a creative artist increasingly living within his own brain. Paradoxically, this man of high IQ and immense erudition exhibits the comprehension of a half-wit. Since Ezra's are the visions to which the audience is exposed, Kops's own opinions necessarily reside implicitly in the action rather than being spelled out in dialogue or placed in the mouth of a *raisonneur*, or authorial spokesman.

Nevertheless, Kops's own ethical viewpoint is clear: He applauds the poetic gifts while disparaging the anti-Semitism, not because it was treasonous but because it was inherently wrong. Respecting fellow writer Pound's right to freedom of speech, deploring the inhumane treatment to which Pound was subjected, even conceiving a Pound for whom such a mammoth error was plausible, Kops finally punishes him by granting him the belated insight of anagnorisis, a recognition scene providing tragic self-knowledge. *Ezra* would not wrench viewers' hearts so profoundly if this pathetic poet did not come ultimately to realize his errors and to articulate, finally, Kops's theme. When Ezra calls to "my Jews" at their houses in Venice's Ghetto Vecchio, only the wind answers. Evidently recognizing his own responsibility for their absence—in death—Ezra laments, "The worst mistake I ever made was that stupid suburban prejudice of anti-semitism, the banality of evil."

Hubris gives way to sophrosyne (the motto of the Delphic oracle, "Know thyself"), as comedy turns to the tragedy of knowledge come too late, to regrets that do no good, for the individual Jews Ezra loved have perished because of racist policies he championed. Recognizing his personal complicity in the Nazis' genocide of six million Jews, Ezra imposes upon himself an internal, mental prison more restrictive than the gorilla cage and repeats a song phrase that expresses his ethical schizophrenia as well as hints at the ghosts of dead Jews. The once-comic bars of musical refrain seem sinister, as the final words echoing from *Ezra* are "me and my shadow."

Dramatic Devices

Despite its numerous—though momentary—geographical settings, *Ezra* is located more in the limbo of Ezra Pound's mind than anywhere on this planet. Employing a chronology as fluid as Ezra's startling mental lapses, Bernard Kops conveys expressionistically the workings of the Imagist poet's fractured mind, which free-associates. As one fragmentary thought shoots off into another, a character related to that new notion may obligingly pop onstage. Since these people are merely figments of Ezra's crazed brain, they are likely to appear just as whimsical and as short in their attention spans as he.

Adopting a presentational style, Kops has Ezra provide his own narrative of these hallucinatory experiences, as the poet conjures up characters who are the products of memory and wishful thinking. Ezra converses with ghosts (Vivaldi and Mussolini), delusions (Olga and Dorothy), and an assortment of others—who are doubled by the four performers other than the lead actor—either recalled from his past or attended to only fleetingly in lucid moments if they appear in some "present" time. Through this nonlinear structure, however, Kops does lead spectators to a conclusion that is both chronologically later than any other portion of the play and clear in its import. Although extremely episodic in its cinematic juxtaposition of disparate times and climes, *Ezra* does not confuse its spectators.

As Ezra chats with the audience and torments his mental phantasms, he jokes, often employing wordplay that seems appropriate for a poet (both Pound himself and author Kops). Marshaling his wit to mock his accusers (and occasionally himself), Ezra evades the questions put to him about his complicity with the enemy and perhaps finds, as well, some solace in his humor. Some of his joshing reflects more serious issues—"God is dead, as Sartre said, and I don't feel so good myself"—while other humor, like that in William Shakespeare's *King Lear* (pr. c. 1605-1606, pb. 1608), achieves poignance. In this vein, Ezra assesses his situation at St. Elizabeth's, concluding that he will be imprisoned there forever: "Please do not disturb. He is disturbed enough already. If only I could be alone. If only I could speak to someone. I am here for the rest of time. Time wounds all heels."

Like Ezra's humor, his continued bursting into renditions of phrases from popular songs expresses his great mind mired in illness or susceptible to the trivialities that masked from him the evil he embraced and its consequences. When Ezra and his imagined cohorts sing "A Tisket, a Tasket," "Sisters," "Let's Face the Music and Dance," "You Always Hurt the One You Love," or "The Hokey Pokey," they entertain their audiences, but they contribute also to the pain the viewer experiences at the spectacle of a shattered genius. Music serves another purpose as well. The sections of Vivaldi's *The Four Seasons* frame and underscore the action, leading inexorably to the chilling conclusion of "Winter."

Critical Context

Ezra contributes to the growing body of work analyzing what Hannah Arendt termed "the banality of evil." Because Bernard Kops's Ezra Pound is a man of charm who combines with his erudition and poetic gifts the products of popular culture— Walt Disney's films, hit songs, *The Wizard of Oz* (1939)—his anti-Semitism takes on a run-of-the-mill or commonplace character seductively acceptable in this grandfatherly man-next-door. That he is clever gives the evil he spouts and espouses a disarming claim to respectability, exactly the sort of attractiveness that can lead to such revolting historical aberrations as the Holocaust.

Since Pound is an actual figure from American history, Kops can, and does, employ the facts of the poet's life as they appear in his biographies. The playwright sets Ezra's peregrinations (or his memories and fancies about them) in the appropriate Italian settings—such locations as Genoa, Bologna, Rapallo, Verona, and Naples. Moreover, culling many of *Ezra*'s lines from the historical record, Kops employs portions of Pound's actual radio broadcasts to American troops as well as remarks made by attorneys and psychiatrists during his trial and the pleas for his release made by other famous men, many of them fellow poets.

Ezra resembles other historical plays or docudramas only in such grounding in fact. Its protagonist brings to mind such classical titans as Ahab or Lear—obsessive, crackbrained old men who unwittingly destroy themselves—far more than he does some dry rendering from a historical tome.

Ezra's imaginative construction, leaping about in time and across geography without so much as a scene break while combining characters from different centuries, is recognizably the product of the author of such futuristic fantasies as *The Dream of Peter Mann* (pr., pb. 1960), *Home Sweet Honeycomb* (1962), and *The Lemmings* (1964). Like the latter two an indictment of fascism, *Ezra* resembles the teleplays *Moss* (1975) and *Rocky Marciano Is Dead* (1976) as well as several of Kops's stage plays and novels in its choice of an aging man as its protagonist. Although *Ezra*'s outlook is bleaker than that of Kops's more joyous, life-affirming work, the zany, colorful central character is vintage Kops, as is the madcap comic extravaganza that eventually shifts to an anguish that may move audiences to tears.

Sources for Further Study

Dace, Tish. "Bernard Kops." In *Contemporary Dramatists.* 5th ed. Chicago: St. James, 1993.

Kops, Bernard. "Ezra." *Half Moon Newspaper,* April/May, 1981, p. 2.

_____. *Shalom Bomb: Scenes from My Life.* London: Oberon, 2000.

Walker, Robert. "Pound: In Other Words." *Half Moon Newspaper,* April/May, 1981, p. 2.

Tish Dace

FAMILY VOICES

Author: Harold Pinter (1930-   )
Type of plot: Psychological
Time of plot: The 1980's
Locale: England
First produced: 1981, at the National Theatre, London
First published: 1981, in *Complete Works: Four*

> *Principal characters:*
> VOICE 1, a young man
> VOICE 2, a woman
> VOICE 3, another man

The Play

Family Voices is a radio play which interweaves the voice of a young man with that of a woman who seems to be his mother. The young man makes fourteen speeches; the mother, twelve. Near the end of the play, a third voice, that of a man who seems to be the young man's father, enters and makes two speeches.

The young man's opening monologue appears to be a letter written to his mother. (It ends: "And so I shall end this letter to you, my dear mother, with my love.") The audience learns that he is enjoying being alone in an "enormous city"; indeed, twice he states, "I am having a very nice time." He reports that his room is "extremely pleasant" and attributes this pleasant atmosphere to his seventy-year-old landlady, Mrs. Withers, "an utterly charming person, of impeccable credentials," with whom he regularly drinks.

In the mother's opening monologue, the playgoers realize that she has not received the young man's letter—nor any communication from him. "Where are you?" she inquires. "Why do you never write? . . . Have you changed your address?" After inquiring if the young man has met any nice boys or girls and cautioning him against mixing with "the other sort," the mother imagines living "happily ever after" with the young man and his future "young wife." She indicates that she wrote him three months before, telling of his father's death, and asks if he received this letter.

The young man's tone has changed in his second monologue. "I'm not at all sure that I like the people in this house, apart from Mrs. Withers and her daughter, Jane," he begins. The young man is wary of an old, bald man who retires early, a woman in a red dress, and a big man with black hair on the backs of his hands. He reports hearing whispers from the other rooms and steps on the stairs, but he dares not investigate these sounds.

In his next four speeches (monologues 3-6), the young man reports his discoveries regarding the three people he has feared. The old, bald man who retires early is Benjamin Withers, probably Mrs. Withers's husband. The woman in the red dress is

Lady Withers. She asks to be called Lally and invites the young man to take tea in an immense room with dark blue walls. During tea, fifteen-year-old Jane Withers sits with her feet in the young man's lap. As buns begin to be consumed rapidly by Lady Withers and languidly by Jane, the young man finds that his bun is "rock solid." When he bites into it, it jumps out of his mouth, and into his lap, where it is caught and expertly juggled by Jane's feet.

He next describes two actions of the big man with the black hair, whose name is Riley. He reports that while he is lying in his bath, Riley enters and says that he has chastised and dismissed two women who knocked at the front door seeking the young man. The young man's response is to wonder why his father did not bother to make the trip with his mother and sister. Riley then comments approvingly on the young man's "well-knit yet slender frame." This encounter is followed by a poignant monologue from the mother, in which she indicates that she knew she would ultimately be left alone, even in her closest moments with her son, when he was a baby.

The young man's seventh monologue, coming halfway through the play, echoes the happiness of the first. He finds the three Withers women seated in a room, smiling at him. He takes a seat and states: "I will never leave it. Oh mother, I have found my home, my family. Little did I ever dream I could know such happiness." In the speech that follows, the mother proposes forgetting all about the son. She thinks of cursing him and spitting on his letters should they ever come.

Again echoing the pattern of the opening, the young man follows his speech of happiness with a monologue expressing fear and anxiety and asks for his mother's advice. He recounts the fantastic words of old Mr. Withers, who calls him into his room and warns him that he is in a "disease ridden land." When the young man looks into the old man's eyes, he says, "It was like looking into a pit of molten lava."

The third voice, presumably that of the young man's father, finally enters, stating that he is not dead, as the mother had written. Then he admits that that is a lie, that he is "as dead as a doornail" and is writing from the grave. After first haranguing the son for wishing him dead, he calls the young man a loving son and tells him to "keep up the good work."

The young man then speaks, reporting that he has been renamed Bobo and is called that by everyone in the house except the old man, who "will die soon." The mother then states that the police are looking for the young man, that she believes he is in the hands of underworld figures who are using him as a male prostitute. She insists that he will be found and will be shown no mercy. This threat is followed by the young man's voice saying that he is coming back, coming to hold his mother in his arms and to clasp his father's shoulder.

In her final speech, the mother says: "I've given you up as a very bad job. Tell me one last thing. Do you think the word love means anything?" In his final speech, the young man says: "I am on my way back to you. . . . What will you say to me?" It is the father, however, who has the last words in the play: "I have so much to say to you. But I am quite dead. What I have to say will never be said."

Themes and Meanings

Because of the rich ambiguity of Harold Pinter's poetic language, *Family Voices* can be interpreted in many ways. On the simplest and most realistic level, the play seems to be about failure of communication within families. Though mother, father, and son speak in the play, they do not hear one another, nor do they ever connect physically. In truth, all three vacillate between expressions of love and yearning for one another and expressions of direct and indirect hostility ("If you are alive you are a monster," says the mother in monologue 4). Perhaps because of these ambivalent emotions, all lie during the play, and all mask their feelings with clichés, which they employ almost as weapons. "Lady Withers asked me about you, mother," the young man says in his fourth monologue. "I said, with absolute conviction, that you were the best mother in the world." Hersh Zeifman has gone so far as to call *Family Voices* a parody of communication.

Others have seen the play as an exploration of the complex way in which a child's family is replaced by surrogates as the young person matures. There are, after all, two families in the play: the son's family, which he has at least overtly escaped, and the new family, the Witherses, in which he places himself. The audience hears the specific words (voices) of all the Witherses—save for Jane, who may be too young to have developed a consistent voice.

Much of the dramatic tension in *Family Voices* lies in the tug-of-war between these two families (Riley, who is a relation "of a sort" to the Witherses, denies the son's true mother and sister access to him) and in the young man's own vacillation between the two.

Indeed, the impossibility of determining the speeches' true form (whether letters, voiced thoughts, or unvoiced thoughts) has led some interpreters to believe that the family voices heard in this play are not those of three people (mother, father, and son) at all, but voices projected only in the young man's mind. In his opening monologue, the young man says, "You see, mother, I am not lonely, because all that has ever happened to me is with me, keeps me company; my childhood, for example, through which you, my mother, and he, my father, guided me." Understood in this way, *Family Voices* becomes a play about a young man seeking—with considerable difficulty—to integrate the various voices of his past into a coherent identity. The play ends without successful integration; indeed, it seems to end in regression and paralysis.

Some critics have seen *Family Voices* as another Pinter dramatization of the Oedipus conflict. Mrs. Withers likes to "cuddle" the young man, recalling his possessive mother. Old Mr. Withers calls the young man "son" and warns him against the "disease ridden land." Also, Mr. Withers is old and will die soon (just like the young man's real father). Furthermore, in his new family the young man is able to divide his possessive mother into three female presences, two of whom (Lady Withers and Jane) are overtly sexual.

However one chooses to interpret *Family Voices*, Pinter's focus is clear: the difficulty of integrating (or escaping) family influences.

Dramatic Devices

Harold Pinter is a master of all four dramatic media: plays for the stage, screen, television, and radio. In one interview, he spoke of the purity he finds in writing for the radio: "It reduces drama to its elemental parts and enforces the sort of restraint, simplicity and economy I strive for anyway." *Family Voices* draws on radio's ability to present sound unencumbered by visual distraction. If these family voices exist only in the young man's mind, they come to exist in the listener's mind as well. Inescapably they resonate with, or evoke, each listener's own "family voices"; thus the radio form itself enhances the voices' movement toward the archetypal.

Pinter's characteristic refusal to offer verifiable facts or to issue simple truths further enhances this movement. In *Family Voices*, the characters are not even called son, mother, and father—although they seem to have this relationship. Instead, Pinter calls them the more indefinite "a young man," "a woman," "a man." The effect of this imprecision, as in all Pinter's plays, is twofold: It simultaneously increases anxiety and dramatic tension (for even the most fundamental relationships are not known) and allows space for listeners to fill in the gaps with their own truths or interpretations. (The original "platform performance" of *Family Voices* achieved this imprecision by placing the three actors in cane chairs before a bleak no-background and lighting them so minimally that they appeared to be near-silhouettes on a screen.)

Besides being a medium particularly suited to direct soundings of the subconscious, the radio play, as Martin Esslin has noted, is the form of drama that comes closest to music and thus serves as a showcase for Pinter's poetic gifts, his acute awareness of the rhythms of words, sounds, and silences. *Family Voices* represents a particularly rich mix of the feints, lies, circumlocutions, bombast, banality, and beauty which Pinter weaves into a verbal fabric at once comic and menacing, poignant and unforgettable.

The language of *Family Voices* can be steeped in sexual nuance, as when the young man speaks of his wish to tutor Jane: "When she turns her eyes upon you you see within her eyes, raw, untutored, unexercised but willing, a deep love of learning." Stilted or clichéd rhetoric often betrays the young man's precarious emotional state, as in his unconvincing "Little did I ever dream I could know such happiness." The language can shift, however, to hint at depths of feeling, as in Riley's progressively qualifying "I could crush a slip of a lad such as you to death, I mean the death that is love, the death I understand love to be." Perhaps more than any other contemporary playwright, Pinter makes his audience aware of the many variations and rhetorical purposes (often hidden and hostile) of human speech.

Critical Context

Family Voices has been seen by many as a summation of many of the themes explored throughout Harold Pinter's career. Indeed, L. A. C. Dobrez argues that the play reviews every phase of Pinter's development, "like a symphonic climax." *Family Voices* recalls Pinter's first play, *The Room* (pr. 1957, pb. 1960), in which the leading character lives away from her family and is torn by longings for it while clearly fleeing it. *The Room* even has a character called Riley. *Family Voices* also contains echoes of another early "room play," *The Birthday Party* (pr. 1958, pb. 1959), in which the young man Stanley is cuddled by his landlady, has his parents turned away at the door, and is subjected to the verbal terrorism of Goldberg and McCann.

Also reprised in *Family Voices* is the Oedipal situation of the radio play *A Night Out* (pr. 1960), the most representative of Pinter's realist plays. Similarly, there is the aggressive family environment of *The Homecoming* (pr., pb. 1965), the work of what Dobrez terms Pinter's "hard-edge phase." In *The Homecoming*, the central character is a woman who escapes a former sterile home life for a presumably more sexually and emotionally fulfilling role in a home with three men (her husband's father and two brothers). As with *The Room*, Pinter seems to have reversed the sexes in *Family Voices*, making his central character a young man who escapes his possessive mother and gruff, absentee father to find a more sexually and emotionally fulfilling role in a home with three women. Finally, in its poetic tones *Family Voices* resembles Pinter's memory plays, from the radio play *Landscape* (pr., pb. 1968) to *Old Times* (pr., pb. 1971).

Pinter has carved his own place in contemporary drama through his original blend of Theater of the Absurd with unnerving psychological realism, expressed in a language rich in poetic texture. He has found a dramatically interesting way of joining the existential and the empirical. The very title *Family Voices* suggests the universality of Pinter's subject matter, and the play raises essential questions regarding dependence and independence, love and estrangement, and individual and family identity. Pinter's plays continued to raise thought-provoking questions in the late twentieth century, among them *Moonlight* (pr., pb. 1993), *Ashes to Ashes* (pb. 1996), and *The Dwarfs and Nine Revue Sketches* (pb. 1999).

Sources for Further Study

Burkman, Katherine H. "*Family Voices* and the Voice of the Family in Pinter's Plays." In *Harold Pinter: Critical Approaches*, edited by Steven H. Gale. Rutherford, N.J.: Fairleigh Dickinson University Press, 1986.

Diamond, Elin. *Pinter's Comic Play*. Lewisburg, Pa.: Bucknell University Press, 1985.

Dobrez, L. A. C., ed. *The Existential and Its Exits: Literary and Philosophical Perspectives on the Works of Beckett, Ionesco, Genet, and Pinter*. London: Athlone, 1986.

Esslin, Martin. "Harold Pinter's Work for Radio." In *Harold Pinter: Critical Approaches*, edited by Steven H. Gale. Rutherford, N.J.: Fairleigh Dickinson University Press, 1986.

Gordon, Lois. *Harold Pinter: A Casebook*. New York: Garland, 1990.

Jenkins, Alan. "No Man's Homecoming." *Times Literary Supplement*, March 27, 1981, p. 336.

Merritt, Susan Hollis. *Pinter in Play: Critical Strategies and the Plays of Harold Pinter*. Durham, N.C.: Duke University Press, 1990.

Morrison, Kristin. "I'll Probably Call It a Day After This Canter." In *Canters and Chronicles: The Use of Narrative in the Plays of Samuel Beckett and Harold Pinter.* Chicago: University of Chicago Press, 1983.

Nightingale, Benedict. "Pinter's New Play Evokes *The Homecoming.*" *New York Times*, March 1, 1981, p. D8.

Peacock, D. Keith. *Harold Pinter and the New British Theatre.* Westport, Conn.: Greenwood Press, 1997.

Zeifman, Hersh. "Ghost Trio: Pinter's *Family Voices.*" *Modern Drama* 27 (December, 1984): 486-493.

Barbara Lounsberry

FASHION
Or, Life in New York

Author: Anna Cora Mowatt (1819-1870)
Type of plot: Farce; satire
Time of plot: The early 1840's
Locale: New York City
First produced: 1845, at the Park Theatre, New York City
First published: 1850

Principal characters:
ADAM TRUEMAN, a vigorous seventy-two-year-old farmer from Catteraugus County
COUNT JOLIMAITRE, a phony French nobleman whom Elizabeth wants Seraphina to marry
COLONEL HOWARD, a young American army officer and Gertrude's suitor
ANTHONY TIFFANY, a New York financier involved in embezzlement
SNOBSON, Anthony's confidential clerk and accomplice, who blackmails him
ELIZABETH TIFFANY, Anthony's wife, a zealous devotee of fashion
PRUDENCE, Elizabeth's gossipy spinster sister, who sees Adam as a potential husband
MILLINETTE, the Tiffanys' French maid
GERTRUDE, the sensible governess to Seraphina and granddaughter of Adam
SERAPHINA TIFFANY, a flighty young belle
T. TENNYSON TWINKLE, a bad poet whom Elizabeth patronizes
AUGUSTUS FOGG, a member of high society

The Play

Act 1 introduces the Tiffany household and demonstrates Elizabeth Tiffany's slavish adherence to fashion. Humor lies in her use of French terms that she cannot pronounce and her attempts to transform her slave Zeke into Adolph, a continental butler. In conversation, Prudence, Elizabeth's sister, reveals their humble origins, but Elizabeth sees herself as "fashionable." She is a patron of T. Tennyson Twinkle, who maintains that a poet's "velocity of composition" is the best measure of excellence. Another "fashionable" visitor is Augustus Fogg, a "drawing room appendage" who is indifferent to any subject mentioned. When Count Jolimaitre arrives, Elizabeth maneuvers him toward Seraphina, her daughter, but her machinations are thwarted by the arrival of Adam Trueman, an old farmer, who is openly contemptuous of everyone's pretensions. Elizabeth considers Adam crude and threatens to throw him out.

In act 2, scene 1, Elizabeth's husband, Anthony, and his clerk, Snobson, discuss their illegal business activities in Anthony's office. Snobson threatens to reveal Anthony's forgeries unless Snobson can marry Seraphina, and Anthony agrees to allow this courtship of his daughter. He indicates, however, his hopes for financial rescue from Adam, his father's friend. When Adam arrives, he comments upon Anthony's changed attitudes and values.

In a series of conversations during scene 2, characters reveal their interrelationships. Seraphina's governess, Gertrude, and her suitor, Colonel Howard, are revealed as honorable characters, and their mutual affection is established. Gertrude's encounter with Jolimaitre clearly demonstrates the contrast between his character and that of Howard. Adam overhears the count's improper advances to Gertrude, and hostility between the two intensifies. Adam attempts to learn whether the Tiffanys' corrupt values have influenced Gertrude. In a comic note, Prudence attempts to ensnare Adam in marriage. Her humorous role as a gossip is also developed as she incorrectly identifies everyone's romantic relationships.

In act 3, scene 1, Anthony explains to Elizabeth that Adam is his only hope for financial rescue. Snobson arrives to court Seraphina, and Anthony is relieved when she seems pleased. Jolimaitre arrives, and the scene becomes a verbal duel between the Tiffanys, each attempting to influence Seraphina's choice. In the next scene, the Tiffanys' maid Millinette and Jolimaitre, alone for the first time, discuss their past. Entering unobserved, Gertrude discovers Jolimaitre is a fraud who intends to trick Seraphina into marriage. Gertrude resolves to expose him.

At a fancy ball given by the Tiffanys during act 4, scene 1, Gertrude manages to have Millinette occupied with guests while she invites Jolimaitre to meet her in the servants' quarters. The gossipy Prudence overhears and reveals the meeting. Scene 2 provides the play's crisis. Before Gertrude can force Jolimaitre to reveal the truth, other characters enter, and they believe Jolimaitre's version of the story. Gertrude seems disgraced: She is fired by Elizabeth, condemned by Adam, and rejected by Howard.

In act 5, while preparing to leave, Gertrude writes a letter of explanation to her guardians. When Adam enters and rebukes her again, she gives him the letter to read. He realizes he has misjudged her, though he still criticizes her devious methods of trying to reveal the truth. Howard arrives to tell Gertrude farewell before he resigns his commission and heads west. As he and Adam engage in a heated argument, Gertrude shows the letter to Howard, who apologizes for doubting her. Prudence bursts in to say Seraphina and Jolimaitre have eloped. When the Tiffanys hear the news, Anthony despairs, believing Snobson will now incriminate him. Elizabeth is delighted that Seraphina will be a countess, though disappointed there will not be a large wedding. Next, Adam reveals that Gertrude is his granddaughter. Millinette tells everyone that Jolimaitre is really Gustave Treadmill, who has been a cook, a barber, and a valet, but never a French count. Seraphina and Jolimaitre, still unmarried, return to collect her jewels.

As the play ends, Adam resolves everyone's problems. Gertrude will marry Howard. Snobson will not incriminate Anthony because Adam threatens to expose Snobson as an accomplice; instead Snobson heads west. Adam will provide money to rescue Anthony, on the condition that he sell all possessions and move his family to a rural area other than Catteraugus County. Jolimaitre will marry Millinette and, with Adam's financial support, begin an honest career as a restaurateur.

In an epilogue, Gertrude insists virtue should be its own reward, then asks the audience's verdict on the play's realistic portrayal of the "just value" of *Fashion*.

Themes and Meanings

Most modern productions of *Fashion* have treated the play strictly as social satire. In this interpretation, Elizabeth Tiffany's slavish adherence to fashion becomes the central element of the play, and a central theme is the contrast between the real and the illusory. Elizabeth, whose sister Prudence reminds her that originally they were milliners, has tried to adopt French fashions that she does not understand. Although she asserts that she has studied a book on French and is quite comfortable with the language, she must rely upon Millinette to explain the customs and provide the vocabulary for everyday objects such as "armchair," which she insists upon calling *fauteuil*, or, as she pronounces it, "fowtool." Nevertheless, Elizabeth believes she is a "real" lady of fashion.

Elizabeth's pretentiousness is not limited to language, however. She is determined that her daughter will marry a French nobleman, though she lacks the wisdom to recognize the falsity of Jolimaitre's credentials. Likewise, she becomes a patron of T. Tennyson Twinkle, primarily because she believes such a patronage "fashionable" but also because she lacks the taste to realize that he is a bad poet. She tolerates the condescension of Augustus Fogg because he is supposedly a member of "fashionable" society, and in general she spends so much money frivolously that her husband becomes an embezzler to pay her expenses.

Elizabeth dislikes Adam in part because he knows that Anthony began his career as a peddler, but primarily because he can see through all the shams and identifies phoniness simply and directly, thus serving as a rebuke to her pretensions. Incapable of recognizing true worth, Elizabeth consistently undervalues Gertrude, Adam, and Howard, the admirable characters in the play. For her, wealth and social position determine merit, and she instills the same values in Seraphina. As a result, both women are silly and frivolous, unable to distinguish between real worth and the illusion of nobility.

A secondary theme is the sturdy American farmer's superiority to the pretensions of Europeans and urban capitalists. In this interpretation, Adam and Gertrude become the center of the play, while Howard reinforces this theme in a supporting role. Although Adam is the age of Anthony's father, he is stronger and more vigorous than the younger man. Perhaps because of his closeness to nature, he is also wise, able to evaluate individual character quickly, state his opinions forcefully, and avoid both financial and romantic snares. He supports his granddaughter in a modest way in order to keep her away from the corrupting power of wealth. As a result, Gertrude has grown up accepting rural values and she too is able to discern the falsity of the Tiffanys' lifestyle. She is never deceived by Jolimaitre's claims of nobility or Twinkle's claims of poetic sensitivity; instead she instinctively recognizes the strength of Howard's character and chooses him as her suitor. He likewise possesses the stalwart American's common sense and appreciates her true value. Finally these agrarian values prove so strong that Jolimaitre embraces them readily and even the Tiffanys must acknowledge the wisdom of returning to their rural roots.

Dramatic Devices

Fashion plays well because it employs elements of farce. Characters overhear key conversations, frequently misunderstanding what they hear and misinterpreting what they see. For example, Prudence hears Gertrude set up a meeting with Jolimaitre and assumes it is an assignation. Adam and Howard find Gertrude alone with Jolimaitre and draw negative conclusions about her virtue. These misunderstandings are resolved by methods typical of farce: truths revealed by coincidental overhearing of a conversation or reading of a letter, strategically timed revelations, and abrupt changes in attitude or behavior. Among the comic characters are several stock characters of farce: the poet or pedant, the fop, the meddling gossip, the desperate spinster, the saucy maid, the socially ambitious matron, the flighty belle, the young man with financial problems, and the wise older man who sets everything and everyone right in the end.

Anna Cora Mowatt also employs conventions from melodrama. Most characters are one-dimensional, their actions governed primarily by plot requirements. Potentially dire consequences are averted by fortuitous coincidences. Adam enters as Gertrude finishes her letter. Seraphina returns still unmarried because she forgot her jewels. Millinette reveals the truth just before Jolimaitre returns. Snobson decides to head west instead of incriminating Anthony. Jolimaitre resolves to become an honest man. The Tiffanys agree to adopt agrarian virtues and lifestyle. Perhaps most melodramatic of all is the epilogue, where Adam, Anthony, and Gertrude discuss the "moral" of *Fashion*, which Gertrude defines as the idea that virtue should be its own reward.

Critical Context

Mowatt's interest in social history and customs dates from her earliest published work, *Pelayo: Or, The Cavern of Covadonga* (1836), a critically panned poetic romance dealing with the Asturias in 718. In the 1840's Mowatt's eyewitness accounts of European social customs appeared in several American periodicals including *The Ladies' Companion* and *Sargent's Magazine*. Detailed portrayal of New York social life appeared in *The Fortune Hunter: Or, The Adventures of a Man About Town, A Novel of New York Society* (1844) and *Evelyn: Or, A Heart Unmasked* (1845), novels published under the pseudonym Helen Berkley. These novels satirized New Yorkers' romantic sentimentalism and pursuit of fashion; they also began Mowatt's lifelong battle in defense of actors' morality, a theme developed more fully in later novels:

Mimic Life: Or, Before and Behind the Curtain, A Series of Narratives (1856), *Twin Roses: A Narrative* (1857), and *The Mute Singer: A Novel* (1866). *Mimic Life* includes several episodes that parallel Mowatt's own experiences as described in *Autobiography of an Actress: Or, Eight Years on the Stage* (1853).

Melodramatic incidents are also a staple of Mowatt's work. In *Gulzara: Or, The Persian Slave* (pr., pb. 1841), when the honorable young heroine is captured by Sultan Suliman's soldiers and thrown in prison, she remains faithful to her true love, Hafed, who actually is Suliman in disguise. Likewise, in *Armand, Or, The Peer and the Peasant* (pr., pb. 1849), Armand defies King Louis XV to defend the virtue of Blanche. In *Evelyn*, the melodrama makes Mowatt's social satire more biting as it leads to tragic results for the Willards.

Fashion, Mowatt's best-known work, combines elements of social satire, melodrama, and farce. In the satiric tradition established by Royall Tyler's comedy *The Contrast* (pr. 1787, pb. 1790), Mowatt clearly demonstrates the superiority of the United States' agrarian values as both plays end with major characters discarding artificial European fashions in favor of simple rural life. First, though, misunderstandings place several characters in jeopardy: Gertrude's virtue is questioned, Anthony may be imprisoned, and Seraphina appears destined to make a disastrous marriage. All problems are resolved, however, by improbable coincidences, expeditious revelations, and the wisdom of the sturdy American farmer.

Sources for Further Study

Abramson, Doris. "'The New Path': Nineteenth Century American Women Playwrights." In *Modern American Drama: The Female Canon*, edited by June Schleuter. Rutherford, N.J.: Fairleigh Dickinson University Press, 1990.

Fowler, Lois Josephs. "Anna Cora Ogden Mowatt, 1819-1870." In *Nineteenth-Century American Women Writers: A Bio-Bibliographical Sourcebook*, edited by Denise D. Knight. Westport, Conn.: Greenwood Press, 1983.

Hutchisson, James M. "Poe, Anna Cora Mowatt, and T. Tennyson Twinkle." *Studies in the American Renaissance* (1993): 245-254.

Ito, Akira. "Early American Drama, III: The Flattering Mirror of an Age." *Language and Culture* 5 (1984): 1-25.

Shaffer-Koros, Carole M. "Edgar Allan Poe and Edith Wharton: The Case of Mrs. Mowatt." *Edith Wharton Review* 17, no. 1 (Spring, 2001): 12-16.

Charmaine Allmon Mosby

FEFU AND HER FRIENDS

Author: Maria Irene Fornes (1930-　　)
Type of plot: Absurdist
Time of plot: Spring, 1935
Locale: A country house in New England
First produced: 1977, at the Relativity Media Lab, New York City
First published: 1980

Principal characters:
STEPANIE "FEFU" BECKMAN, a woman who holds parties at her
　　country house
CINDY,
CHRISTINA,
EMMA,
PAULA,
SUE, and
CECILIA, friends
JULIA, her friend in a wheelchair following a shooting accident

The Play

A three-act play (noted in the script as "parts," not "acts"), *Fefu and Her Friends* is set in a country house in New England, with all the action taking place in one day. Parts 1 and 3 take place in the living room, the first in the morning and the third in the evening. Part 2, which covers the afternoon hours, has four sets: the lawn, the study, the bedroom, and the kitchen.

Fefu's friends Cindy and Christina are already in the living room when the play opens, and the other women arrive at the house by lunchtime, invited there to prepare a presentation for an education group of which they are members. Most of them have been friends for some time, and during the day and evening they collect in pairs or in groups of varying size, talking about themselves, their lives, each other, and especially about Fefu, the central figure who knows them all. Fefu says whatever is on her mind, whether or not it appears appropriate or relevant, often with the apparent intent of shocking the others. It is her house party, and she flamboyantly attracts, and apparently wants to attract, most of the attention.

Another major topic for all the women, again talking in small groups rather than in one big group discussion, concerns Julia. She has been injured in a shooting accident and is confined to a wheelchair, and throughout the day she needs assistance. Exactly what happened to her is unclear. It is a matter of considerable speculation, since even Cindy, who was there when it happened, can only give an account that is illogical. A hunter shot and killed a deer, but at the same time Julia fell, had convulsions, was delirious, and apparently suffered a spinal nerve injury. She still blanks out from time to time and she hallucinates.

The circumstances of the accident are even less clear because Christina suspects Fefu was involved, although Cindy maintains the hunter was a man. Fefu used to hunt, and she and her husband, Philip (talked about but never seen), play a bizarre private game in which they shoot at each other with the shotgun that is prominently displayed on stage when the play opens. It is no surprise that the shotgun will lead to trouble: At the end of the play a shot is heard offstage, Fefu enters with a dead rabbit she has shot, and Julia slumps in her wheelchair, blood gushing from her head.

The play is one of talk more than action, however, and the majority of the talk is bits and pieces about various aspects of the women's lives and relationships, rather than a coherent discussion of any single topic. Often they do not respond directly to what another speaker has just said, but start on some other point. Most of all, they like to talk about one another, especially when the other person is not present.

Themes and Meanings

The women have secrets that remain unrevealed to the others or even to themselves. This suggests two related major themes throughout the play: the alienation of the individual and the impossibility of knowing oneself or others. Fefu maintains that if she did not shoot her husband with blanks she would shoot him with bullets but provides no explanation. She makes wild remarks, such as saying all women are loathsome, and claims this wildness is what makes her friends like her. When Cindy objects and says she would love her even if she were not the way she was, Fefu responds that if she were not the way she was Cindy would not know it was her. A rock, Fefu says, may seem smooth and clean on top, but underneath it may be slimy and crawling with worms. People do not manifest all aspects of themselves to others and may not even recognize their own hidden selves. As a result, they feel cut off from themselves and from others. Emma says that heaven is for those who are divine lovers, but she evidently suspects hell is heavily populated, since human relationships are inevitably strained and intimacy is impossible to sustain even between two people, much less in groups or society at large. Yet embracing isolation provides no solution either, only furthering the sense of alienation.

This stance, commonplace in absurdist theater, is demonstrated throughout the play. Julia feels as though she is perishing alone. She longs to be with others who hallucinate to validate her own reality, but none of the women understands her or even what happened to cause her accident the previous year. Cindy relates a recent dream, but no interpretation is forthcoming. Paula and Cecilia were presumably lovers sometime in the past, but they do not articulate clearly their relationship to each other, much less to the group. Christina admires Fefu for being unconventional but feels confused and endangered because Fefu is not respectful of the world as it exists. Fefu claims that she accepts herself and does not mind being strange, but she complains that she is in constant pain, some obscure pain that is not physical. Certainly none of them, even Fefu, is going to be able to make sense of the final scene, when Fefu shoots and brings into the living room a dead rabbit and finds Julia bleeding, her head fallen back, presumably dead.

A corollary theme to alienation and lack of understanding of oneself or others is the breakdown of communication and language itself. The play is filled with non sequiturs, meanings that do not follow from what has been said before. Often the next speaker simply moves on to her own topic. Conversations are elliptical, fragmented, unfinished. Even when the women are rehearsing their upcoming presentation they say "blah blah blah" instead of the actual content, although they agreed they should all give their speeches so their presentations would not overlap. The only one who gives hers is Emma, who reads a passage from a book by Emma Sheridan Fry concerning the need to achieve individual wholeness and social harmony. However, the passage itself is filled with fanciful metaphors and strained personifications, as though the writer was desperately groping for words to convey a meaning she could not articulate.

Dramatic Devices

The most striking device is the innovative staging of part 2, which confounds the usual expectations and blurs the boundaries of performance space. During the first act, the audience is seated together in a theater auditorium to view the action on stage. However, part 2 is presented outside the main theater area on four sets to represent a lawn, study, bedroom, and kitchen. For this act the audience is divided into four groups and each group is led to one of the spaces. The four scenes are performed simultaneously. When the scenes are finished (as close to the same time as possible), each audience group moves on to the next set to watch the actors there, who repeat the scene they presented to the previous group. This moving is repeated until each group has seen all four scenes. Then the audience is led back into the main auditorium to watch part 3 together, as they did part 1. The audience literally does not see the same play, since they do not see the scenes in part 2 in the same order and since there are inevitable minor differences in the performances that the cast repeats four times.

Another dramatic device is the use of frequent entrances and exits that create different groups on stage from one moment to another. The women come and go and regroup in different combinations in all three acts. Those on stage do not necessarily participate in the scene; sometimes they do not pay attention to each other when there are only two present. During part 2, for example, Christina is in the study practicing French, reading a French textbook aloud but nearly inaudibly. Cindy is reading a magazine. She eventually interrupts Christina by reading aloud herself, but they immediately go back to their individual reading. Then Cindy asks Christina if she likes Fefu. Cindy starts relating a dream she had, which has nothing to do with Fefu. The stage directions say that Fefu's entrance may interrupt Cindy's speech at any point, depending upon how long it takes Fefu to reach the kitchen, where she will be next. Thus the actual content of the play varies according to the timing needs. This is convenient or necessary for part 2, because Fefu appears for a short time in three of the four scenes that are being performed simultaneously, and she must move from one stage set to another. However, this movement and recombining of groups is so prevalent throughout the play that it is a notable contrast when it is not happening, such as during the bedroom scene in part 2, where Julia is alone. Her long monologue as she hallucinates is interrupted only at the very end of the scene, when Sue enters to bring her a bowl of soup and then quickly leaves.

The stage sets are realistic, with a couch, coffee table, chairs, and piano in the living room, for example. The script lists spring, 1935, as the time of the play, but nothing in the stage sets, costuming directions, or props is specific to that historical period. Nothing in the rest of the script indicates that era, and in fact the word choices in many of the speeches and the topics being discussed suggest the 1970's, when the play was written.

Critical Context

Fefu and Her Friends is Maria Irene Fornes's best-known play. Fornes received an Obie Award for playwriting for the script, and numerous productions have been staged since the first performance in 1977. During the 1970's, a period of overt feminist discussion and action, producing an Off-Broadway play by a woman writer and director and having an all-female cast were seen as noteworthy accomplishments. Although the play does not include any Latino roles or issues, Fornes was early hailed as one of the emerging Chicana playwrights. She is often cited as the "godmother" of Chicano drama, especially for her years of conducting a theater workshop that developed and encouraged many Chicana writers.

As writer, director, and teacher, Fornes is a leading figure in contemporary theater. She has written more than two dozen stage plays since her first, *Tango Palace* (pr. 1963, pb. 1971), opened in 1963 (under the title *There! You Died* at the Encore Theatre, San Francisco). The 1999-2000 season at Signature Theatre Company in New York was devoted to plays from her oeuvre, culminating with the premiere of *Letters from Cuba* (pr. 2000), the first play in which Fornes deals with her Cuban American heritage. For that play Fornes received her tenth Obie Award, one of which is for Sustained Achievement in Theater.

Fefu and Her Friends is designed to provoke its audience with an experience that is emotionally challenging and intellectually stimulating. The play first appeared toward the end of an era of "theater of the absurd" by such noted male writers as Samuel Beckett, Eugène Ionesco, and Jean Genet, whose works had accustomed audiences to experimental plays that lacked conventional plots. Fornes's plays were embraced as work coming from previously unheard voices. Absurdist drama typically reflects the writer's thoughts about the irrational and stifling aspects of society and the pressures on the individual. In that tradition, *Fefu and Her Friends* shows women trapped in their lives and their roles, with the unspoken message that those in the audience must be the ones to find solutions.

Sources for Further Study

Austin, Gayle. "The Madwoman in the Spotlight." In *Making a Spectacle*, edited by Lynda Hart. Ann Arbor: University of Michigan Press, 1989.

Chaudhuri, Una. "Maria Irene Fornes." In *Speaking on Stage*, edited by Philip Kolin and Colby Kullman. Tuscaloosa: University of Alabama Press, 1996.

Delgado, Maria M., and Caridad Svich, eds. *Conducting a Life: Reflections on the Theatre of Maria Irene Fornes*. North Stratford, N.H.: Smith and Kraus, 1999.

Kent, Assunta Bartolomucci. *Maria Irene Fornes and Her Critics*. Westport, Conn.: Greenwood Publishing Group, 1996.

Robinson, Mark, ed. *The Theatre of Maria Irene Fornes*. Baltimore: Johns Hopkins University Press, 1999.

Lois A. Marchino

THE FIDDLER'S HOUSE

Author: Padraic Colum (1881-1972)
Type of plot: Naturalistic
Time of plot: The beginning of the twentieth century
Locale: Irish Midlands
First produced: 1907, at the Rotunda, Dublin, Ireland
First published: 1907

> *Principal characters:*
> CONN HOURICAN, a fiddler
> MAIRE HOURICAN, his older daughter
> ANNE HOURICAN, his younger daughter
> BRIAN MACCONNELL, a farmer who loves Maire
> JAMES MOYNIHAN, a farmer's son who loves Anne

The Play

   The action of *The Fiddler's House* takes place in a simple cottage inhabited by a widower, Conn Hourican, and his adult daughters, Maire and Anne. As the first of its three acts begins, the very polite and sensible James Moynihan is courting Anne. After James leaves, Conn enters and expresses his nostalgia for the happy days when he and his late wife traveled around the Irish Midlands so that Conn could play his fiddle in many villages. Anne is glad that their grandmother willed their cottage to Maire and not to their father; this gives Anne and Maire a sense of security, but Conn is tired of such a peaceful existence. Playing his fiddle in Flynn's, the local pub, or perhaps even at the Feis of Ardagh, a regional musical festival, would bring Conn much pleasure: Maire, however, begs Conn not to go to Flynn's lest he become drunk and disgrace them again. She obtains his solemn promise not to enter Flynn's that evening. Although Brian MacConnell (a farmer who loves Maire) knows of Maire's wishes, he persuades Conn to accompany him to Flynn's by appealing to his vanity. He tells him that Shawn Heffernan, a fiddler whom Conn does not hold in high esteem, will perform at Flynn's that evening. Unless Conn plays at Flynn's, the villagers will conclude that Conn is no longer a gifted musician who can compete with younger fiddlers.

   Act 2 begins on the following morning. Maire and Anne regret that Brian and Conn went to Flynn's instead of attending the respectable party given by the Moynihans. Anne wanted Conn to create a favorable impression on James's parents. Maire begins to express serious doubts about Brian, whom she now considers to be fairly irresponsible. Conn enters and tells his daughters that several patrons in Flynn's praised his playing and even referred to him as a "master musician." Maire and Anne come to realize that their father lives for music. Maire reminisces that she and her late mother often tried in vain to make Conn think less of music and more of his family's welfare.

James then enters and discusses a very practical problem with Maire and Anne. He loves Anne and wishes to marry her, but he does not know where they could live together. James's father is not wealthy and must still arrange dowries for James's two sisters. Moreover, the Moynihan house is rather small and could not accommodate a new couple. James is in a quandary.

After James leaves the stage, Conn returns, and Maire convinces him that he is wasting his talents by performing for the drunkards in Flynn's. Conn assumes that she will propose that he display his musical skills to the more sophisticated and demanding listeners at the Feis of Ardagh. Maire, however, insists that he stop playing his fiddle in public and help her and Anne take care of their farm. This request almost crushes Conn's spirit. Maire quickly realizes that she is asking for too great a sacrifice from her father; she never intended to destroy Conn's self-esteem. As act 2 ends, Maire brings her father his fiddle so that he can practice for the Feis at Ardagh. Maire even hints that she may accompany him to this music festival.

Act 3 takes place one week later. As the final act begins, all the characters except Brian are having dinner together in the Hourican cottage. Conn speaks of his need to travel around Ireland. He explains that a true musician should not "remain too long in the one place." Traveling will enrich both his life and his musical talent. Maire generously agrees to deed her farm and cottage to Anne; thus, James and Anne can be married. Believing that Maire may well marry Brian, Conn feels free to resume his life as a wandering fiddler. He is pleased that Anne will marry such a reliable and honest man as James. Anne's fiancé sincerely admires his future father-in-law, whom he calls "a man of art."

Maire, however, begins to question her love for Brian, whose unpredictable behavior disturbs her. She tries to discourage her father from leaving the security of their cottage for the life of a wandering fiddler. Conn tells her, however, that with only two exceptions the inhabitants of their village cannot fully appreciate the traditional folk music he plays. He must travel to those sections of Ireland where traditional Irish music is still valued. Conn asks Maire if she plans to marry the "wild and free-handed" Brian. Although she is physically attracted to Brian, Maire concludes that marriage with him would eventually bring her much heartbreak. She decides that she needs to experience the relative freedom of wandering around Ireland with her father. The ending of *The Fiddler's House* is ambiguous. Although it appears that she will not marry Brian, Maire closes the play with this comment to Anne: "Tell Brian MacConnell that when we meet again maybe we can be kinder to each other."

Themes and Meanings

In a 1906 essay titled "Ibsen and National Drama," Padraic Colum described his efforts to create Irish dramas that could be compared favorably to the works of the influential Norwegian playwright Henrik Ibsen. Perceptive critics such as Zack Bowen and Sanford Sternlicht noted similarities both in the art of dialogue and in the representation of moral conflicts between *The Fiddler's House* and Ibsen's *Et dukkehjem* (pr., pb. 1879; *A Doll's House*, 1880). In both plays, important characters must choose between the security of a comfortable home and their desire to experience a new type of freedom. To varying degrees, the five characters in *The Fiddler's House* all deal with the complex relationship between freedom and social responsibility.

Colum wrote this play shortly after Irish peasants had obtained the legal right to own real estate. Thus, Irish farmers no longer had to work for absentee landlords. The importance Anne and James attach to preserving this newly acquired right must have seemed eminently sensible to Dublin theatergoers in 1907. Anne and James are not materialistic characters; rather, they understand clearly the real danger of their falling into poverty if they do not own their farm. James loves Anne, but he knows that enough food and a warm house are indispensable for a good marriage. The two are sympathetic realists who prefer security over adventure. Brian represents perhaps the opposite extreme. Although he does own his farm and thus is expected to act some-what responsibly, he demonstrates neither common sense nor respect for his neigh-bors. He is basically egotistical. Although he claims to love Maire, he is unwilling or unable to make any sacrifices in order to make her happy. Brian is merely a handsome man who does not understand that freedom and a personal search for happiness should coexist with a concern for others' welfare.

Conn and Maire reveal complex reactions to both the meaning of freedom and their responsibilities toward others. In act 1, Maire tries to convince Conn that drinking in pubs provides only an illusory freedom, whereas working to improve the quality of life on a farm frees one from want. Conn does not disagree, yet they both come to real-ize that his desire to interpret traditional Irish music can enrich them emotionally and aesthetically and also enable them to appreciate more deeply the cultural heritage of Ireland. When Maire and Conn begin to travel around Ireland so that he can play at music festivals, they are acting responsibly. In their own ways, they have made James and Anne happy and cognizant of the cultural values of their homeland. It is no acci-dent that the selfish and thus unsympathetic Brian is the only character who remains alone at the end of this drama. Brian never realizes that true freedom requires some-times that one sacrifice one's own wishes so that others may lead richer and more sat-isfying lives.

Dramatic Devices

Critics have often praised the realistic dialogue in *The Fiddler's House*. The five characters express themselves in a style that is neither exceedingly formal nor pa-tently folksy. There is an artistic spontaneity in Padraic Colum's style. This stylistic realism makes it relatively easy for those who attend performances of *The Fiddler's House* to associate Colum's characters with ordinary people. Like Ibsen, whom he ad-mired greatly, Colum wanted his audiences to identify with his key characters so that they could understand more fully the moral and social significance of the characters' actions.

All three acts in *The Fiddler's House* take place inside the simple cottage inhabited by Conn and his daughters. Colum's stage directions indicate that the scenery remains basically the same throughout this play. The house seems to symbolize the very stability and security from which Maire and Conn will escape and toward which Anne and James are drawn. This house is a place of joy, poetry, and music for all except Brian. On several occasions, Colum stresses that warm sunshine passes through the windows of Maire's house. The external beauty that he and Maire often see from inside their cottage comes to represent for them the freedom that both attracts and frightens them. Conn's fiddle itself is an important stage prop, which Colum utilizes to suggest both the creative urge and the desire for freedom. His fiddle is first seen at the end of act 1, as Conn is carrying it "eagerly" to Flynn's. As the second act ends, Maire brings the fiddle to her father; this act symbolizes her approval of his desire to play music in public. Near the end of the final act, Conn can be heard playing his fiddle for the first time. Colum's stage direction "A fiddle is heard outside" is richly suggestive, because the world outside the cottage represents creativity and freedom for Conn. When he next plays his fiddle, Anne realizes that her father and sister are ready to leave for the music festival at Ardagh.

Critical Context

Padraic Colum wrote *The Fiddler's House* near the beginning of his distinguished literary career, which lasted almost seven decades. He wrote important works in such diverse genres as lyric poetry, the novel, drama, biography, and children's literature. His fame as a dramatist is based largely on three plays, *The Land* (pr., pb. 1905), *The Fiddler's House*, and *Thomas Muskerry* (pr., pb. 1910). Along with such distinguished playwrights as William Butler Yeats, John Millington Synge, and Lady Augusta Gregory, Colum created a new Irish theatrical tradition. As an important member of the movement called the Irish Literary Revival, Colum developed purely Irish characters and situations so artistically that he revealed their universal significance for spectators from any culture. *The Fiddler's House* illustrates the great dignity and humanity of simple Irish peasants, whom Colum describes without sentimentality and with much humor.

The Fiddler's House is not merely a play of historical interest to specialists in modern Irish drama. In 1981, Dublin's Peacock Theatre performed the play in celebration of the centenary of Colum's birth. These performances were very well received, a fact that suggests that Colum's witty and powerful portrayal of human beings' conflicting desires for security and freedom continues to fascinate new generations of theatergoers.

After his emigration to the United States in 1914, Padraic Colum became known largely for his lyric poetry and works of children's literature. His early plays, however, are effective dramas of universal interest, and they do not merit the neglect they suffered in the late twentieth century.

Sources for Further Study

Bowen, Zack. *Padraic Colum: A Biographical-Critical Introduction.* Carbondale: Southern Illinois University Press, 1970.

Boyd, Ernest. *The Contemporary Drama of Ireland*. Boston: Little, Brown, 1917.

Fallis, Richard. *The Irish Renaissance*. Syracuse, N.Y.: Syracuse University Press, 1977.

Gregory, Lady Isabella Augusta. *Our Irish Theater*. Reprint. New York: Capricorn Books, 1965.

Malone, Andrew. *The Irish Drama*. 1929. Reprint. New York: B. Blom, 1965.

Sternlicht, Sanford. *Padraic Colum*. Boston: Twayne, 1985.

Weygandt, Cornelius. *Irish Plays and Playwrights*. 1913. Reprint. Westport, Conn.: Greenwood Press, 1979.

Edmund J. Campion

A FLEA IN HER EAR

Author: Georges Feydeau (1862-1921)
Type of plot: Farce
Time of plot: Summer, in the early twentieth century
Locale: Paris
First produced: 1907, at the Théâtre des Nouveautés, Paris
First published: La Puce à l'oreille, 1909 (English translation, 1966)

Principal characters:
VICTOR-EMMANUEL CHANDEBISE, a bourgeois Frenchman
RAYMONDE, his wife
CAMILLE, his nephew
TOURNEY, a friend of the Chandebise family
DON CARLOS HOMÉNIDÈS DE HISTANGUA, a hot-blooded South American
LUCIENNE, his wife
ÉTIENNE, a male servant
ANTOINETTE, his wife, the cook
FERRAILLON, the manager of Hôtel Minet-Galant
BAPTISTIN, his uncle
POCHE, a drunken porter
RUGBY, a randy Englishman

The Play

The play opens in the comfortable apartment of Chandebise and his wife, Raymonde. Two servants, Étienne and his wife, Antoinette, and Chandebise's nephew, Camille, live with them. Because Camille has a cleft palate, he can pronounce only vowels; household members sometimes understand him, but others cannot.

Raymonde suspects that Chandebise is having an affair: The title of the play derives from her nagging suspicions. He has not been ardent recently, and a pair of suspenders has been sent to him from Hôtel Minet-Galant (the gallant pussycat hotel), a meeting place for adulterers. Even though she is considering having an affair with Tournel, Raymonde is outraged. The audience soon learns she is wrong. Chandebise is temporarily impotent; the suspenders were left at the hotel by Camille when he went there with Antoinette.

Raymonde devises a plot to trap her husband. She will send him a letter from an unknown admirer inviting him to meet her at the hotel. Because Chandebise would recognize her handwriting, Raymonde gets Lucienne to write the letter. Chandebise is flattered by the letter, but because he is a faithful husband, he forwards the assignation to Tournel. When Lucienne's husband, the fierce South American Don Carlos Homénidès de Histangua, sees the letter, he recognizes his wife's handwriting, goes berserk, threatens to shoot everyone, and leaves for the hotel. Camille attempts to warn Tournel but cannot find an artificial palate that makes him understandable. After Tournel leaves, Camille finds the device, inserts it, and speaks comprehensibly.

The second act takes place in the Hôtel Minet-Galant's central hall. The hotel has several staircases and doors leading to many bedrooms, the most visible of which has a special bed. When a button is pushed, the bed and the wall behind it revolve, and an identical bed appears. If a jealous spouse arrives, the lovers need only push a button and their bed is replaced by another bed containing someone else.

Many "Chandebises" appear throughout the act: Camille (whose family name *is* Chandebise), Tournel (who pretends to be Chandebise), and Chandebise himself. Moreover, because Poche, the hotel's drunken porter, is played by the same actor who plays Chandebise, he looks like Chandebise. Throughout the act, a libidinous Englishman named Rugby drags women into his room.

Raymonde arrives to confirm her suspicions, but when she goes to "M. Chandebise's room," she finds Tournel. When Tournel presses Raymonde to submit to his desires, Raymonde rings for help by pushing the button. When Tournel turns his back, the revolving bed sends Raymonde out and the old Baptistin in. Tournel jumps into bed and is horrified to discover whom he has embraced. Soon Raymonde reappears, and when they press the button again, the bed brings in Poche. Thinking he is Chandebise, both Raymonde and Tournel beg his pardon. Poche hits the button, and Baptistin appears. They all flee into different rooms.

Camille and Antoinette panic when they meet the Chandebise-like Poche. Antoinette jumps into Rugby's room, and Camille enters the back room with the revolving bed. Raymonde and Tournel return to their original bedroom and order Baptistin out. When they hit the button by mistake, the bed produces Camille, though they do not recognize him because he speaks clearly. Camille finds Antoinette in Rugby's room, and Rugby hits him in the mouth. The artificial palate falls out, and Camille can speak only vowels again.

Étienne arrives. Antoinette, half undressed, breaks out of Rugby's room, sees her husband, and flees. Rugby beats Étienne, who then runs away to find Antoinette. Lucienne arrives. The real Chandebise finally appears and commiserates with Lucienne for loving him and for angering her husband, who is coming to kill her.

Don Carlos arrives brandishing a revolver and roams about the hotel. Everyone panics. Chandebise returns and runs into his wife and Tournel; she flees. Chandebise is about to strangle Tournel when the hotel manager returns to beat him. Tournel and Chandebise exit quickly. Don Carlos appears. Camille hides in the revolving bedroom. Lucienne runs into Rugby's room and then back out again, Rugby in pursuit. She appeals to Poche for help, thinking he is Chandebise, and they hide. Don Carlos forces his way into the revolving bedroom, finds Camille, shoots wildly, and hits the button. The revolving bed brings in Lucienne and Poche, who Don Carlos thinks is Chandebise, into the room. They flee. Don Carlos shoots again as other characters restrain him.

Act 3 returns to Chandebise's apartment. Raymonde, Tournel, and Lucienne discuss their adventures. Poche arrives dressed as Chandebise, and they think he is crazy. Camille arrives, but nobody understands him. Then Chandebise himself returns home (dressed as Poche) and berates Raymonde and Tournel. The hotel manager, Ferraillon, arrives with Camille's lost palate and tries to drag Chandebise away. Don Carlos bursts in and challenges Chandebise to a duel. Chandebise escapes, but Poche reappears. When Don Carlos threatens him, he jumps out the window. Raymonde and Lucienne explain to Don Carlos how innocent everything really is. Chandebise returns, and Ferraillon, who found Poche outside, comes back and matters are sorted out. Raymonde and Chandebise are reconciled.

Themes and Meanings

A Flea in Her Ear contrasts the bourgeois world (or *monde*) of the Chandebise household and the nightmarish otherworld (or *demimonde*) of Hôtel Minet-Galant. This division underlines the divided nature of the play's major characters. Below the elegant surfaces of their lives, the idle and shallow people of the *belle époque*— France at the beginning of the twentieth century—live in a degree of chaos. They constantly deceive and are deceived. The most innocent man, Chandebise, can be humiliated and driven to near insanity. The sexes do not understand each other; wives are shrews and husbands are impotent; sadists find their masochists; one man suffers from a speech impairment that would be pitiful if the audience were not laughing so hard at him. The basic instincts of these people are primarily the desires for self-gratification and self-preservation. Some want sex and revenge, while several want to preserve their honor. All want to avoid being shot.

However, there is little real evil here, and the play ends with the main characters reconciled and happy. Although this could be said of most comedies, here there is little sense that any particular actions or attitudes bring about the happy ending or that the ending represents the triumph of any particular set of values or virtues. In fact, it is not completely certain that farces have themes and meanings. Farcical characters may behave the way they do because they are situated in a farce rather than because their behavior reflects the irrational real world.

Dramatic Devices

Like most farces, *A Flea in Her Ear* moves at a breakneck speed and provides slapstick humor, often violent slapstick. The hotel manager beats his wife and his servant. The servant eventually jumps out a second-story window. Don Carlos roves about violently, threatens to shoot people (and even fires his revolver), and must be physically restrained. All this action occurs in the context of mistaken identities, deceptions, and other confusions. The bewilderment and surprise these confusions cause the characters are humorous, and the audience (who knows the secrets) is delighted by all the dramatic ironies.

Farce depends on stock characters. For example, in this play, the vixen wife and the impotent husband, the ardent lover and the reluctant beloved, the sadistic master, the stage Spaniard (a stereotype), and the stage Englishman (another stereotype) are all present. Georges Feydeau produces some variations on these stock characters. In this play it is the wife (rather than the husband) who has a double sexual standard, although she seems to think being a mistress does not involve sex. Feydeau invents new kinds of characters as well: Camille may be the only character in drama to suffer a cleft palate for a comic effect.

Two additional dramatic devices serve this play well. The revolving bed in act 2 provides for much hilarity, especially when Tournel jumps in it expecting to find the woman he desires but instead embraces an old man. Another device is to have one actor play two parts, Chandebise and Poche. The two devices collide when the bed revolves again to confront Raymonde and Tournel with Poche, whom they take to be Chandebise. Only in act 3 is this confusion explained: The characters realize that Poche is not Chandebise. Yet, because the audience members know the two roles are played by the same actor, they can enjoy his lightning-fast change of costume and his dramatic skill in presenting two very different characters throughout the play. The audience thus enjoys a rare form of dramatic irony: They know a secret that no character can ever know.

The dramatic development of *A Flea in Her Ear* is carefully contrived. Act 1 sets up the basic deception and the characters. In act 2, the pace accelerates. The action moves to a different place where the consequences of the deception will result in the climax of the play. One basic device of farce is to bring together people who should normally be kept apart. For example, here Chandebise and Raymonde eventually meet at the hotel, and the titillating discoveries begin. Act 3 provides a lengthy denouement. More discoveries are made, and most of the characters are reconciled.

Critical Context

Farce is a much maligned form of drama: Most criticism denigrates it due to its lack of seriousness. Many argue it is only theatrical entertainment, not true literature. Even if this were true, the capacity of the theater to delight is important, and it is undeniable that farce delights. While the thematic vision of farce may be hazy at times, farces arguably have a vision of the world turned upside-down, a world in which civilization is stripped away and the chaos of the ego is revealed.

Georges Feydeau wrote thirty-seven plays, some of them only one act long. Of his full-length plays, most are artfully constructed, fast-paced farces whose plots revolve around marital discord and deception. Their construction puts them in the tradition of seventeenth century French playwright Molière and the "well-made play" (or *pièce bien faít*) devised by nineteenth century playwright Eugène Scribe. The appeal of farces lies more in the hilarity of their action than in the depth of their characters. *A Flea in Her Ear* was one of Feydeau's later works. It was a success when it opened in Paris in 1907 and has been his most popular play in England and the United States. Feydeau's other notable farces include *L'Hôtel du Libre-Change* (pr. 1894, pb. 1928; *Hotel Paradiso*, 1957), *La Dame de chez Maxim* (pr. 1899, pb. 1914; *The Lady from Maxim's*, 1899), and *Occupe-toi d'Amélie* (pr. 1908, pb. 1911; *Keep an Eye on Amélie*, 1958).

Though Feydeau was perhaps the leading writer of farce in the era centering on the *belle époque*, he was not the only one. Farces by such writers as Eugène Labiche, Jacques Prévert, and Victorien Sardou can be read and seen with pleasure today. Feydeau's influence has been great. His plays, though often in an altered form, continue to be performed. His influence has been lasting and can be seen in the works of absurdist dramatists Samuel Beckett and Eugène Ionesco.

Sources for Further Study

Achard, Marcel. "Georges Feydeau." In *"Let's Get a Divorce!" and Other Plays*, edited by Eric Bentley. New York: Hill and Wang, 1958.

Baker, Stuart E. *George Feydeau and the Aesthetics of Farce*. Ann Arbor: University of Michigan Research Press, 1981.

Esteban, Manuel A. *Georges Feydeau*. Boston: Twayne Publishers, 1983.

Feydeau, Georges. *Four Farces by Georges Feydeau*. Translated by Norman R. Shapiro. Chicago: University of Chicago Press, 1970.

Pronko, Leonard C. *Georges Feydeau*. New York: Frederick Ungar, 1975.

George Soule

THE FLOATING WORLD

Author: John Romeril (1945-   )
Type of plot: Political
Time of plot: 1974
Locale: A cruise ship traveling from Melbourne, Australia, to Yokohama, Japan
First produced: 1974, at the Pram Factory, Melbourne, Australia
First published: 1975

> *Principal characters:*
> LES HARDING, a working-class Australian and former prisoner of war (POW) of the Japanese in World War II
> IRENE HARDING, his wife
> HERBERT ROBINSON, retired vice admiral of the British Royal Navy
> THE COMIC, entertainment officer of the cruise ship
> HARRY, the straight man and narrator
> MCLEOD, a war buddy of Les
> WILLIAMS, a passenger whom the deluded Les mistakes for McLeod
> THE WAITER, a Malaysian whom Les occasionally mistakes for a Japanese soldier

The Play

The Floating World opens with a dramatic monologue by Harry, lamenting the sale of Australian rain forests to a Japanese developer. Harry introduces the setting for the following nineteen scenes, a cruise ship sailing to Japan on a package tour arranged by an Australian women's magazine. Suddenly, Les Harding appears on the stage, which is designed like a ship's deck. Seasick, he vomits over the railing and is joined by Herbert Robinson.

Their dialogue introduces their opposing backgrounds. Les is a blue-collar Australian former infantryman captured by the Japanese and forced to slave on the infamous Burma-Thailand railroad. Robinson is a retired vice admiral of the British navy. He was never taken prisoner and comes from the upper class. While the two can bond as men, their social differences ultimately remain too strong a division.

When the Malaysian waiter appears first, he is dressed as an officer of the Imperial Japanese Army, an outfit he will don repeatedly to visualize Les's confusion of past and present. Reading from its badly translated instruction manual, the Waiter sets up the first of his Dippy Birds. These are Japanese toys of the 1970's and represent Japan's postwar economic power.

Irene Harding is introduced while writing a letter home. She is a working-class housewife with a married daughter, and she is somewhat disillusioned with her husband. Irene's intellectually shallow yet socially ambitious and racially paternalistic character is revealed through her conversations with Robinson, whose class and status she clearly admires, and through her interaction with the Waiter, whom she treats as the exotic Other and who enacts his revenge by slyly molesting her.

In the course of the cruise, the Comic and Harry perform numerous raunchy vaudeville acts, just as the initial interaction between Les, Irene, and Robinson provides some situation comedy. Yet the play uses these comic routines to expose lowbrow Australian culture as boorish entertainment, full of jokes based on xenophobia and racial prejudice. Les's many dirty limericks may appear funny but are intended to reveal their misogynist and homophobic origin.

Traveling to Japan on a former troop ship converted into a cruise liner brings Les back to his wartime experiences, with which he clearly has not come to terms. He tells of his hard journey to Singapore to engage the Japanese invaders. Lying hung-over in his bunk bed, he sees his old buddy McLeod, who died in the prison camp. McLeod accuses Les of betrayal for going to Japan and vividly reveals the historically accurate horrors endured by Allied prisoners of Japan.

Les's descent into madness accelerates. He confuses passenger Williams for McLeod, and the Waiter for a Japanese soldier. He begins to relive the past, and all characters but Irene start speaking the lines of officers, fellow prisoners, and Japanese guards during the war.

After Les is given an Australian uniform for the cruise's insipid Talent Night, he attacks the Waiter and expresses his hostilities for the upper-class Robinson. Raving in his cabin, he promises McLeod to avenge his death. Docking in Yokohama, Irene and Robinson express their concern for Les, who has been confined below for trying to knife an Asian.

The play concludes with a long monologue by Les, clad in a straitjacket. He retells stories of his youth and of the horrors of the prison camp. Harry interrupts Les to tell the audience that humanity should not suffer but change the world for the better. Finally, Les reveals that he survived by stealing vitamin B tablets from a brutal Japanese soldier. In his last lines, which contrast to his present situation, Les asserts that the vitamins made him become well again.

Themes and Meanings

The challenge of *The Floating World* is that it seeks to tackle not one but many issues, which for John Romeril clearly are related. One issue involves a criticism of capitalism and consumer culture, especially the specter of Japanese economic dominance. For example, the first monologue denounces the Australians as Judas-like traitors for selling their rain forest, and Japanese consumer goods are mocked in the reading of poorly translated instructions for setting up a Dippy Bird, a toy derided as ludicrous.

There is also the voicing of working-class Australian resentment against upper-class British cultural domination, related to the larger issue of class conflict in general. Les often pokes fun at Robinson, and in his imagination he relives the harsh and sometimes ineffectual ways of his own officers. There is also just the hint at the orthodox Marxist view that capitalist societies cause wars to avoid dealing with their own class conflicts, as evidenced when Les relates his hard life during the Depression in his final monologue.

The Floating World is also savagely sarcastic in the mocking of the loutish, misogynist, and xenophobic aspects of Australian entertainment culture. The many comic routines and Les's jaunty limericks are meant to be understood as an indictment of the culture that gave rise to this kind of humor. This message has often been seen as the play's political thematic core by Australian critics.

Finally, the play tries to argue that the solution to confronting the atrocities of war lies in the idea that war must be opposed, not suffered through. Yet given the harrowing dramatic power of Les's vivid recollection of real Japanese mistreatment of their slave laborers, the answer is in danger of appearing too reductive and failing to give full appreciation of heavy suffering.

Les Harding remains an ambiguous and problematic character. He has suffered at the hands of the Japanese, just like Southeast Asians who were forced to work and die alongside Allied prisoners in building the Japanese railroad. Yet, when Les expresses racist and anti-woman opinions of his own, he changes from victim to perpetrator. When he becomes deluded and tries to knife an Asian man, he is morally repulsive. He is wrong in his thinking and delusion, yet he has also been wronged.

Australian critics have argued that Les's final breakdown comes less from his past tortures and instead from his guilt of having survived the war by stealing and not sharing the vitamin B tablets. In contrast, Makoto Sato's 1995 production decided to play straight Les's final words that he is well again and presented his momentary breakdown as the first step of his healing process.

The play explains its title by Les's final allusion to his feeling like he is living in a floating world, when his theft of the vitamins will reduce his diseased, bloated body to a normal state. Critics have related it to the idea of Australia floating on the waters of the Pacific Ocean. Another, ironic connotation has been overlooked. In Japanese, the floating world refers to life in the pleasure district of a major city, like the Ginza of Tokyo. Since the play takes place aboard a cruise ship, it surprisingly functions as a very Australian version of the Japanese pleasure quarters.

Dramatic Devices

The first production at the Pram Factory in Melbourne, Australia, utilized the small theater space to enclose both the audience and the stage in camouflage-green chicken-wire mesh, to indicate the idea that the play takes place in Les's war-afflicted head. The doubling of the Waiter as a Japanese soldier, who is played by the same actor, is a powerful device to visualize Les's mental confusion. This is echoed by the directive that Williams and McLeod are played by the same actor, and the fact that later in the play, every character but Irene assumes a second identity as a member of Les's memory world.

In order to create alienation among his audience and to discourage them from identifying with the twisted values of the Hardings, the first production by the Australian

Performing Group cast actors against type. Middle-aged Les was played by youthful Bruce Spence, and the Waiter/Japanese soldier was played by white actress Carol Porter. When a more realist cast was used, Australian audiences occasionally over-identified with Les Harding's character, to the disapproval of critics. Sato's 1995 production not only translated the play into Japanese but also used Japanese actors and actress Yumiko Itoh for important roles.

By using *bunraku* puppets for the major supporting roles of Comic, Waiter, and Harry, Sato again moved a step beyond realism in order to give the play a more universal focus. Japanese-style puppets were also used in Andrew Ross's production at the Black Swan/State Theatre Company of South Australia, where they doubled for human players in some scenes. Their use was lauded for making Les's anti-Asian statements more alienating, as some were uttered by himself as a Japanese puppet.

The Dippy Birds were a cultural phenomenon of the mid-1970's, and directors have handled their inclusion or exclusion in the play differently. Feeling that the birds' original symbolism—which alluded to the cheapness of Japanese products—had been superseded by the time of their 1986 Sydney Theatre Company's production, the directors replaced them with three demons drawn from the Japanese Kabuki theater. Sato brought back the Dippy Birds, leaving open the question of their exact meaning.

Critical Context

The Floating World has become an often-performed staple of contemporary Australian theater. Its selection for the 1995 Japan-Australia Cultural Exchange Program saw two major new productions, one in English and one in Japanese, both performed in each country. It is one of the few Australian plays translated into Japanese and has given rise to solid literary criticism.

For John Romeril, *The Floating World* remains a landmark in his prolific life as a playwright. Writing his first plays as an undergraduate in the late 1960's, Romeril gained fame beyond Australia with *The Floating World*. He told a critic how he had thought about the play since 1969, when he wanted to write about the clash of Australian and Japanese culture during World War II. In 1972, on a ship from Singapore to Melbourne, which Romeril credits with providing the model for the cruise liner in the play, he heard a story that he likened to that of Les Harding. Further research of historical accounts of the suffering of Allied prisoners and an active interest in the working-class traditions of Australian vaudeville and popular entertainment gave shape to his play. Romeril personally helped with carpentry for the set design of the first production, committed as he was to the idea of collective theater productions.

Since Romeril won the first Canada-Australia Literary Prize in 1976, interest in *The Floating World* has remained steady. He has written more than forty original plays, screenplays, and adaptations. His plays like *Love Suicides* (pr. 1997), *Black Cargo* (pr. 1991), and *The Kelly Dance* (pr. 1984, pb. 1986) continue to critically examine contemporary Australian culture. His script for the film *One Night the Moon* (2001) won a Gold AWGIE (Australian Writers' Guild) award for its sympathetic treatment of an Aborigine solving a murder mystery.

Sources for Further Study

Gilbert, Helen. "Cultural Frictions: John Romeril's *The Floating World.*" *Theatre Research International* 26, no. 1 (March, 2001): 60-70.

Griffiths, Gareth, ed. *John Romeril*. Atlanta, Ga.: Rodopi, 1993.

Sawada, Keiji. "The Japanese Version of *The Floating World:* A Cross-Cultural Event Between Japan and Australia." *Australasian Drama Studies* 28 (April, 1996): 4-19.

Tompkins, Joanne. "Re-orienting Australian Drama: Staging Theatrical Irony." *Ariel* 25, no. 4 (October, 1994): 117-133.

Wigmore, Lionel. *The Japanese Thrust: Australia in the War of 1939-1945*. Series 1 (Army). Vol. 4. Canberra, Australia: The War Memorial, 1957.

R. C. Lutz

THE FLOWERING PEACH

Author: Clifford Odets (1906-1963)
Type of plot: Allegory
Time of plot: Biblical times
Locale: Near East
First produced: 1954, at the Belasco Theatre, New York City
First published: 1954

>*Principal characters:*
>NOAH, the patriarch
>ESTHER, his wife
>JAPHETH, his youngest son
>SHEM, his oldest son
>HAM, his middle son
>LEAH, Shem's wife
>RACHEL, Ham's wife
>GOLDIE, Japheth's prospective wife

The Play

The *Flowering Peach* is a modern retelling of the biblical story of Noah and the Flood. The play begins just before dawn as a rooster crows and Noah, dazed and half-asleep, enters his living room, becomes agitated, and, sobbing, falls on his knees. When his wife, Esther, enters, Noah tries to pretend that nothing is wrong, but he finally tells her that God has revealed to him in a dream that He will destroy the world, saving only Noah and his family and animals and birds of all species. Incredulous, Esther accuses Noah of being drunk. Japheth, their youngest son, awakened by the noise, enters and Noah tells Japheth to fetch Ham and Shem, Noah's two older sons. Japheth replies that Shem and his wife are harvesting the olive crop and will not want to come. Noah instructs Japheth to say that a building proposition has come up, and he needs Shem to give an estimate.

As Japheth leaves to get his brothers, Noah explains to Esther that they are to build an ark according to God's specifications. Esther reminds him that he has never seen a boat—to which he replies that he has seen one "twiced." (Throughout, the characters' speech is slangy, ungrammatical, and down-to-earth.) She insists that Noah must be sick. When he begins to speak aloud to God, she gives up and leaves to bake the Sabbath bread. Noah, musing, wonders if God actually spoke to him. Complaining that he is too old for such a task and that he will be ridiculed, he prays, "Oh God . . . pass me by. Please." As God's presence is expressed by a musical shimmer, Noah asks God not to give him such a task, pleading that total destruction of the world "is something terrible." The Presence of God fades away into silence, and antiphonal roosters crow as the stage lights dim out.

Scene 2 introduces the rest of the principal characters except for Ham's wife, Rachel, and Goldie, a girl who will be proposed as a wife for Japheth. In his early twenties, Japheth is a "proud, private and thinking young man," slow and shy, with whom Noah unconsciously identifies, believing that "they are two outcasts in the more competent and fluent world." Ham, the middle son, is a restless man in whom "malice and jealousy are frequently masked . . . as humor and good fellowship," but he knows how to charm his older brother, Shem, for whom he works. Shem is sometimes "shrewd to the point of foolishness," and his wife, Leah, "is a fit and sometimes prodding mate" for him. Esther is the practical Jewish mother, bossing her daughter-in-law, chiding her sons for disrespect toward their father, chiding Noah with loving banter, breaking up arguments, and maintaining her sanity by keeping occupied with daily chores. Assembled in Noah's house, they discuss Noah's dream, expressing disbelief, and asking Noah how he will gather all the animals.

Only Japheth believes Noah because such cruel imagining is not in Noah's nature, but Japheth wants to die in the flood "to protest such an avenging, destructive God!" In the midst of the bickering, a mouselike creature, the mythical gitka, appears, runs into Noah's hands, and sings in a wordless, falsetto voice while everyone stands amazed. Japheth returns from outside, telling everyone to look out the windows, where animals and birds of all kinds are gathering. Ham and Shem repent in fear, Noah intones Sabbath prayers, and Japheth stands in awe and horror outside the family circle.

The next three scenes occur on a high hillside where the men are building the ark and Esther and her daughters-in-law are preparing provisions. Esther mistrusts Leah's stubborn smugness but loves the delicate, hesitant Rachel. Esther laments Rachel's unhappy five-year marriage to Ham. Noah and Japheth argue over how to pronounce the word "tiger" and whether to put a rudder on the ark; Noah contends that a rudder is not needed because God will steer the ship. Noah also insists that Japheth find a wife because the new world will need plenty of babies; Japheth, lamenting the "bushels of babies" who will die in the flood, leaves, saying he will not be back.

Later, Noah goes into town to buy seeds, but the townspeople refuse to sell to him, calling him crazy and stoning him to drive him out of town. He returns to the hillside angry and humiliated. Japheth also returns, saying that he has come to help build the ark "for the family, not for God." Japheth brings with him a girl, Goldie, who has saved him from being killed by an angry mob. A tax collector appears, seeking taxes for the sale of Shem's land and orchards. Noah, stating that nothing will be for sale on the ark, commands Shem to hand over the money, but Shem refuses to relinquish his keys. Japheth knocks Shem unconscious and retrieves the keys, and the tax collector goes to get the hoarded money. Noah, exhausted, goes to sleep behind a bush. When Esther hears moaning and thrashing from behind the bush, she seeks to awaken Noah, and, frightened, calls her sons, who take hold of their father, then jump back in awe as Noah emerges, transformed, a young man of fifty, and returns to town to buy seeds.

Several days later, signs point to the imminent flood: A blood-red sun reverses itself and moves from west to east; everyone is rushing to load the ark with the animals.

Esther, concerned because she is now much older than Noah, flirts with him, putting on a fancy hat and asking him if she is pretty. Ham flirts with Goldie, but, near hysterics over the supernatural occurrences, she resists his advances. Rachel and Ham bicker, and Esther, knowing that Rachel and Japheth are in love, tries to persuade Japheth to stay on the ark; he has said that he will not sail. When he appears with his luggage, Rachel asks him to change his mind. They declare their love for each other, but Japheth is determined to leave. Noah orders him to sail on the ark, while Esther pleads with him not to die. Finally, Noah knocks him out and Shem and Ham carry him onto the ark. Lightning flashes, thunder rolls, rain begins to fall, and everyone scrambles aboard the ark. Three old men appear and ask to be taken on board, but Noah refuses. They are left, chanting, with rain dripping from their unbowed heads.

Scene 6 shows the forty-first day on the ark. The rain has stopped, but nothing is going well. Noah and Japheth feud, Shem has given Ham liquor to do his work, Esther and Rachel refuse to sleep with their husbands, and Shem and Leah are threatening to sink the ark by hoarding dried manure bricks to sell to the others for fuel. Noah wants to marry Japheth to Goldie, but Japheth refuses, saying he wants to marry Rachel; Esther takes their part against Noah, saying that Ham wants to marry Goldie. Noah rejoins that the law will not allow this and asks God to strike them down. When God does not comply, Noah, deserted, takes a keg of brandy and gets drunk.

Later, Noah faces the changes that have occurred while he was drunk. Japheth has taken control of the ark and gained new respect from his brothers. He steers the ark with a rudder, to which Noah must acquiesce when Japheth refuses to repair a large hole in the ark unless the rudder stays. Moreover, Esther is now gravely ill, but Noah still refuses to marry the two couples. Estranged from human communication, he talks to the old lion and awaits the return of two doves that he has sent out to find land. Esther comes on deck, where she begs Noah to marry the children "for the sake of happiness in the world" and tells him that the old laws no longer apply. As a dove returns with an olive leaf, Esther dies, and Noah grants her dying wish to marry the children.

In the last scene, the ark is aground and the couples go their separate ways; Noah decides to go with Shem. Symbolizing new life, the three wives are pregnant and a little peach tree is discovered in full bloom. Noah gives the children his blessing and talks once more with God, who gives a rainbow as a symbol that He will not destroy the world again. In awe and thankfulness, Noah declares, "Yes, I hear You, God—now it's in man's hands to make or destroy the world"; the play concludes as he repeats Esther's last words, "I'll tell you a mystery."

Themes and Meanings

The Flowering Peach is a play about the family as an arena of conflict and a source of love and security. Clifford Odets portrays parents and children with ambitions, disappointments, anger, frustrations, arguments, and love in a drama that is a distillation of modern and biblical experience; for example, the Bible does not give the name of Noah's wife, so Odets chose the name of his own aunt, Esther, and based the character upon this real person. Tenderness, love, and humor among the family members, in spite of arguing and disagreements—which Odets often uses to show love as well—are evident throughout the play, as when, after Esther asks Noah if he wants eggs and he annoyingly refuses them, she says, "Tell me . . . why don't I give you away for a good cat?" Later she tells the children: "I took your part—but don't make a mistake children, Noah *is* my favorite boy." Japheth tells Noah, "I may be excitable from time to time, but I love you, Poppa, and I always will." Even though Japheth leaves the family, saying that he will die in the flood to protest what he believes is unjust, he returns to help complete the ark. Noah is devastated when Esther dies and, in the end, each of the sons wants Noah to live with him.

The play also reflects the period in which it was written. The years immediately after World War II—metaphorically, after the Flood—brought the promise of new beginnings, yet also the threat (the atom bomb) of even greater destruction. On a more personal level, the prominence of the marriage-and-divorce theme, to which some critics objected, reflects Odets's own experience and the concerns of postwar American society.

In an allegory, there are many levels of meaning, both conscious and subconscious, and Odets weaves all the threads together in this presentation of the survival of the family in a world fated for destruction. He offers no solutions, but he nevertheless presents a hopeful conclusion that symbolizes the eternal questing of humankind.

Dramatic Devices

Bringing a classic work to the contemporary stage is an enterprise fraught with peril, whether the project in question is a modern production of a classic drama (a Greek tragedy, a Shakespearean play) or, as in the case of *The Flowering Peach*, a fresh adaptation of a nondramatic source. It is the authority of the classic—its claim to enduring significance—that makes it an appealing vehicle in the first place, yet authority can be stifling: The classic work may appear to be distant, stuffy, or simply irrelevant to the concerns of a contemporary audience.

Well aware of this tension, Odets in *The Flowering Peach* employs the device of deliberate anachronism. The male characters appear in modern dress, yet the female characters, Odets indicates, are to wear traditional Oriental costumes. More important, as noted above, the characters' speech is highly colloquial. By violating the stereotype of elevated biblical language, Odets clearly sought to underline the timelessness of the Flood story. (One danger of this approach is evident to the reader who comes to Odets's play several decades after it was written: Slang dates very quickly, and the once-contemporary becomes embarrassingly quaint.)

Odets also employs a variety of physical devices, including "shimmering" music, thunder, and lightning to represent God's presence onstage; other supernatural effects such as the mouselike gitka, which sings before the Flood and when Esther dies; the movement of a blood-red sun from west to east just before the Flood, symbolizing impending destruction; Esther's hat decorated with flowers, fruits, and berries to symbolize youth; and Noah's transformation (an Odets invention) from an old man to a younger man, symbolizing rejuvenation of spirit, energy, and purpose.

Finally, the perpetuation and continuation of life are shown through several symbols: the preservation of the animals, the pregnancy of the three wives at the end of the play, Esther's one-leaf plant that needs sun to grow, the flowering peach tree from which the play takes its title, and the rainbow symbolizing God's promise of hope for world survival—Odets's principal concern in this play.

Critical Context

The Flowering Peach was Odets's last produced play. It is usually accounted a critical success but a commercial failure; it was nominated for the 1955 Pulitzer Prize, but the award went to another play. Some critics said it was his best play, but most, including Odets himself, admitted that the last part was not as well developed as the first and needed some revision. Using the story of Noah from Genesis, Odets treated it in the setting that he knew best, the modern, middle-class Jewish family. Odets's career had begun with *Awake and Sing!* (pr., pb. 1935), about a Jewish family's attempt to deal with the social and economic problems of the 1930's. This play established several stock characters: the ineffectual old man, the outspoken Jewish wife and mother, the wry kibitzer, the young man facing life, the materialistic entrepreneur, the idealist, and the young couple in love. These are found in his other family play, *Paradise Lost* (pr. 1935, pb. 1936), as well as in *The Flowering Peach*, and in varying combinations in Odets's other eight produced plays. All of his plays, except *Till the Day I Die* (pr., pb. 1935), which treats fascism and anti-Semitism, are allegorical and deal with the struggle to keep life from being obliterated by negative circumstances, false values, and loss of self-respect.

Odets's first five plays, including the three mentioned above and *Waiting for Lefty* (pr., pb. 1935), about a strike by New York taxi drivers, and *Golden Boy* (pr., pb. 1937), about a violinist who becomes a boxer to gain financial success, are social protest dramas containing proletarian propaganda and were produced by the Group Theatre, with which Odets acted for several years. *Golden Boy*, Odets's biggest box-office success, was written for the Group after Odets went to Hollywood to write screenplays and television scripts. Three plays treating love and marriage, *Rocket to the Moon* (pr. 1938, pb. 1939), depicting the difficulty of finding love in modern society; *Night Music* (pr., pb. 1940), emphasizing the theme of loneliness in modern society; and *Clash by Night* (pr. 1941, pb. 1942), treating homelessness, adultery, and skepticism, were also written for the Group. All these themes can be found in *The Flowering Peach*, along with those of insecurity, alcoholism, and destruction of values—the principal themes of Odets's remaining two plays, *The Big Knife* (pr., pb. 1949) and *The Country Girl* (pr. 1950, pb. 1951). Thus, Odets's plays form a circle, beginning and ending with the family.

Sources for Further Study

Cantor, Harold C. *Clifford Odets*. 2d ed. Lanham, Md.: Scarecrow, 2000.

Clurman, Harold. "American Playwrights: Clifford Odets, *The Flowering Peach*." In *Lies Like Truth: Theatre Reviews and Essays*. New York: Macmillan, 1958.

Cooperman, Robert. *Clifford Odets: An Annotated Bibliography of Criticism, 1935-1989.* Westport, Conn.: Greenwood Press, 1990.

Demastes, William W. *Clifford Odets.* 2d ed. Westport, Conn.: Greenwood Press, 1990.

Goldstein, Malcolm. "Clifford Odets and the Found Generation." In *American Drama and Its Critics*, edited by Alan S. Downer. Chicago: University of Chicago Press, 1965.

Hayes, Richard. *"The Flowering Peach." Commonweal* 61 (February 11, 1955): 502-503.

Shuman, R. Baird. *Clifford Odets.* New York: Twayne, 1962.

Bettye Choate Kash

THE FREEDOM OF THE CITY

Author: Brian Friel (1929-   )
Type of plot: Social realism
Time of plot: 1970
Locale: Derry City, Northern Ireland
First produced: 1973, at the Abbey Theatre, Dublin, Ireland
First published: 1974

> *Principal characters:*
> LILY, a forty-three-year-old mother of eleven, a cleaning woman
> SKINNER, an unemployed and homeless twenty-one-year-old
> MICHAEL, an unemployed twenty-two-year-old who lives with
>   his parents
> THE PRIEST
> THE JUDGE
> DR. DOBBS, an American sociologist

The Play

The Freedom of the City is based on events that occurred during Roman Catholic civil rights protests in Londonderry ("Derry"), Northern Ireland, in the late 1960's and early 1970's. As the curtain rises, the corpses of the three main characters—Lily, Skinner, and Michael—are lying on a darkened street. The clock in the Guildhall behind them chimes six as each corpse is visited first by a photographer and then by a priest, who administers the last rites. Lights illuminate an English judge taking testimony from an Irish constable as he seeks to discover whether the three dead people had been armed. As the judge questions the constable, soldiers drag each body in turn from the stage. Next, an American sociologist addresses to the audience an informal lecture on the culture of poverty.

The lights go down for a moment, and when they come back the time is obviously different, for Skinner, Lily, and Michael enter, staggering and blinded from the effects of gas. To the accompaniment of explosions and the sound of rubber bullets, they gain the relative calm of the Guildhall interior. These three, who have never met before, do not know where they are, but Skinner soon identifies the room as the Guildhall office of the Lord Mayor of Londonderry.

The rest of act 1 consists of a series of very short scenes. Scenes outside the Guildhall show various groups and individuals seeking to understand what is going on inside, and the time shifts so that some observers comment before the deaths and some after. Soldiers attempt to determine how many "yobos" are inside the Guildhall. A television newsman delivers on-the-spot commentary. A balladeer memorializes the takeover of the Guildhall by "a hundred Irish heroes." The priest who administered the last rites suggests that the three died for their beliefs. Testimony before the judge continues as officers maintain that Lily, Skinner, and Michael were armed and dangerous protesters who came out shooting and were killed when police returned fire. The sociologist continues his lecture, describing the poor as lacking "impulse control" but as often having "a hell of a lot more fun than we have."

Meanwhile, inside the hall, the accidental companions discover a degree of luxury they have never seen before and a series of historical mementos: a ceremonial sword, a stained-glass window, an official portrait, a "distinguished visitors book." Skinner, age twenty-one, unemployed and homeless, has little formal education but can quote William Shakespeare and Rudyard Kipling. Bitter and irreverent, he is scornful of the civil rights movement and was not marching but merely passing by when he was caught up in events. He taps into the mayor's liquor supply, dons the mayor's robe, and parodies that official by conferring on Lily the freedom of the city and making Michael a life peer.

Lily, a forty-three-year-old mother of eleven and a charwoman, frequently goes on marches because "it's the only exercise I get." Instinctively motherly, she insists that Skinner change his clothes (soaked by a water cannon) and observes that the mayor's robes would make a lovely new cover for her settee. Gradually, however, as the liquor takes hold, she matches Skinner's irreverence, donning a robe herself and dancing around the office with him.

Michael, who quotes Mahatma Gandhi and brags that he has been on every march, is attending technical school at night. He is awed by his surroundings, appalled by the levity of the others, and frantic in his efforts to erase the mark Skinner makes stubbing out on the desk a cigar he has borrowed from the mayor's supply. Lily is just about to use the mayor's telephone to call her sister in Australia when a loudspeaker announces that the Guildhall is surrounded. Amid warnings to surrender, the act ends and the clock chimes five—only one hour earlier than the time of the opening scene in which the corpses were revealed.

The second act continues the established pattern of short alternating scenes. When the lights go up, Michael, Lily, and Skinner are barely visible. The balladeer and then the judge continue their evaluations. The balladeer memorializes the patriots; the judge exonerates the soldiers. Later, the priest condemns elements in the movement that have gone too far. The sociologist laments the lack of future for the poor, and the television reporter describes the dignity of the funeral proceedings. Each official version is different from the others, and all differ from what the audience sees.

The interior scenes in this act show the three protesters getting better acquainted. Lily invites Skinner to come to her home for a meal whenever he wishes, and she insists that Michael bring his fiancé to meet her. The three are facing their situation and preparing to leave the hall. Skinner conducts a "council meeting" that mocks civic authorities who ignore the poor. He scatters papers and plunges the ceremonial sword into the official portrait. Lily and Michael attempt to restore the office to its original state. Lily dusts; Michael puts away the papers. Skinner, however, stops the attempt to remove the sword from the portrait, stuffs his pockets with cigarettes, and persuades Lily to sign the distinguished visitors book. They exit the Guildhall with their hands above their heads and a dawning realization that, although unarmed, they will be shot. Michael is astounded that such a mistake could be made. Lily regrets only that she is to die without really having lived. Skinner, his cynicism confirmed by the official actions, dies in his familiar posture of "defensive flippancy." In the final scene of the play, the voices of the television announcer and the judge summarize the situation, while the three protesters, hands well above their heads, step out of the Guildhall into the burst of automatic fire that kills them. The lights go out.

Themes and Meanings

Even for an audience unfamiliar with Irish history, the end of *The Freedom of the City* is evident in its beginning. Because the corpses are present in the opening scene, the audience knows from the start that these three Catholics will die before the combined guns of the British army and the largely Protestant police force. Like a Greek tragedy, this play demands that viewers ask not "what will happen next?" but "what does it all mean?"

Suggested meanings abound. British judicial hearings "prove" that these hapless citizens were armed and dangerous, killed only when a restrained British army found it had no choice. An American sociologist turns events into a depersonalized examination of the culture of poverty. An Irish balladeer simultaneously trivializes and celebrates Michael and Lily and Skinner by transforming them into one hundred Irish patriots who died trying to free their country from British domination. An Irish priest begins by praising their willingness to die for their beliefs and ends by condemning them as part of an excessive fringe element. An Irish telecaster surrounds their funeral with the sticky sweetness of popular sentimentality. Each jargon-studded official voice attempts to confine individual experience within an accepted dogma, and each speaker is literally as well as metaphorically outside the events in the Guildhall.

Balancing these glib efforts to impose order on a chaotic situation are the voices of the protesters. Uneducated, inarticulate, incapable of discerning motive or meaning in their own experiences, these voices nevertheless ring with vigor, authenticity, and individuality. Their view of life is often mocking, cynical, and chaotic, but it is also richly humorous and acutely perceptive, balancing the careful, detached formulations of official wisdom. However, the color of their language and their personalities does not disguise the fact that the mayor's office is an enclosure, a trap as difficult to escape as the larger trap imposed by a fractured and hierarchical society.

If the real lives inside the Guildhall obviate the dry formulations outside, however, *The Freedom of the City* does not impose its own "truth." The play balances the lives and concerns of little people against the sweep of historical events, but it never chooses—or demands that the audience choose—an acceptable version of events. Rather, it avoids ultimate interpretations and discards any pretense of final versions or wisdom. The audience becomes in turn jury, television audience, congregation, sociology class, and drinkers listening to a pub balladeer. Recognizing elements of validity in each version of the "truth," they also recognize the extent to which no version approaches the reality of what has happened. The truth, if there is a truth, hovers somewhere as far beyond the formulations of a playwright as it is beyond the formulations of priest, judge, or newsperson. It is Brian Friel's wisdom as a social commentator to realize that, and he pushes the audience to realize it as well.

Dramatic Devices

Like many of Brian Friel's plays, *The Freedom of the City* utilizes a tightly restricted time period. The events inside the Guildhall take only a few hours, and though the outside commentaries are spread over a longer time, they all focus on the Guildhall events, which are viewed with heightened intensity.

The concentration this unity of time permits is bolstered by the restructuring of the traditional relationship between audience and stage. Viewers are not allowed to be passive spectators at removed events but are drawn into decision making, as character after character directs toward the audience an analysis of events in the Guildhall. By forcing the audience out of its familiar, comfortable relationship with the stage, Friel forces audience members out of their familiar, comfortable views as well, to realize the complexity of events and the interaction of public and private.

Friel bolsters the symbolic enclosure of his stage with several other minor symbols. The shots that kill the three protesters, for example, hit them in appropriate parts of their bodies. Lily is wounded in the lower abdomen, the chest, and the hands—the anatomy of motherhood. Michael is injured primarily in the head and neck—appropriate zones considering his stiff-necked insistence that he understands the movement. Skinner, whose acerbic wit only thinly veils the extent of his agony, has wounds evenly distributed over his entire body. The distinguished visitor's book—and Lily's comment in it that she is "looking forward to a return visit"—suggest that these are indeed the Guildhall's most distinguished visitors. By plunging the sword into the portrait, Skinner comments on official Irish history. Even the place names are revealing. Friel identifies the city as Derry, the name preferred by Catholic nationalists, but characters in the play call it Londonderry, the name used by British loyalists.

Friel varies the time and place on the single set of his play by lighting it imaginatively and often expressionistically. He varies strict realism and believability by occasionally allowing his major characters to understand and articulate their feelings more successfully than is thoroughly believable given their limited education and experience. Skinner movingly summarizes the plight of the poor and the sense of power they gain from realizing their brotherhood of purpose and determination. As they leave the Guildhall to face death, each protester articulates a new awareness of the meaning of the life he or she has lived.

The play swings the audience between passages of rare comedy and parodic wit and passages of deceptively simple, powerful emotion. The audience sees the three main characters for a limited time, in limited circumstances, but Friel manages to create a remarkable depth and richness of character as he examines their entrapment by public events over which they have no control.

Critical Context

The Freedom of the City is one of the most specific uses by Brian Friel of history as a basis for drama that concerns itself with social issues. *Translations* (pr. 1980, pb. 1981) is based on the nineteenth century British effort to destroy the Irish language by renaming places and restructuring schools. In *Volunteers* (pr. 1975, pb. 1979), Dublin construction workers unearth archaeological evidence of Ireland's past. Several Friel plays deal more generally with Irish issues: *The Mundy Scheme* (pr. 1969, pb. 1970) with contemporary Irish commercialism, *The Gentle Island* (pr. 1971, pb. 1973) with the traditional conflict between Dublin and western, Gaelic Ireland, and *The Communication Cord* (pr., pb. 1983) with the modern middle-class fascination with restoring the artifacts of the Irish past.

These plays are very Irish and quite direct in their efforts to open debate about contemporary Irish issues. They are also, however, very human, for they reach well below the local-color surface to touch a deep vein of common humanity. In doing so, they mix social commentary with tragedy and comedy, often stretching the audience between emotional extremes. Friel's language can be rich and varied. His world is one of bawdy good humor and of aching human sorrow; it defies easy categorization or formulation. Friel often deals with the efforts of individuals to shape their experiences into stories for better understanding, always recognizing, with Manus in *The Gentle Island*, that "every story has seven faces."

As he has sought new understanding of old pains, Friel has experimented with dramatic devices that break actors and audiences out of their familiar, unthinking roles. Though the technical experimentation of *The Freedom of the City* is less radical than that which he uses elsewhere, it nevertheless provides clear evidence of his concern to break out of conventional patterns and through to new comprehension.

Sources for Further Study

Birker, Klaus. "The Relationship Between the Stage and the Audience in Brian Friel's *The Freedom of the City*." In *The Irish Writer and the City*, edited by Maurice Harmon. Totowa, N.J.: Barnes and Noble, 1984.

Dantanus, Ulf. *Brian Friel: The Growth of an Irish Dramatist*. Atlantic Highlands, N.J.: Humanities Press, 1985.

Grene, Nicholas. "Distancing Drama: Sean O'Casey to Brian Friel." In *Irish Writers and the Theater*, edited by Masaru Sekine. Totowa, N.J.: Barnes and Noble, 1986.

Kennedy-Andrews, Elmer. *The Art of Brian Friel: Neither Reality nor Dreams*. New York: St. Martin's Press, 1995.

Kerwin, William, ed. *Brian Friel: A Casebook*. New York: Garland, 1997.

McGrath, F. C. *Brian Friel's (Post)Colonial Drama: Language, Illusion, Politics.* Syracuse, N.Y.: Syracuse University Press, 1999.

Maxwell, D. E. S. *Brian Friel*. Lewisburg, Pa.: Bucknell University Press, 1973.

_____. "The Honor of Naming: Samuel Beckett and Brian Friel." In *A Critical History of Modern Irish Drama, 1891-1980*. New York: Cambridge University Press, 1984.

O'Brien, George. *Brian Friel*. Boston: Twayne, 1990.

Helen Lojek

FRENCH WITHOUT TEARS

Author: Terence Rattigan (1911-1977)
Type of plot: Comedy
Time of plot: The 1930's
Locale: South of France
First produced: 1936, at the Criterion Theatre, London
First published: 1937

> *Principal characters:*
> KENNETH LAKE and
> KIT NEILAN, young Englishmen studying to enter the diplomatic
>   corps
> BRIAN CURTIS, a young businessman
> ALAN HOWARD, a would-be novelist, about twenty-three
> MONSIEUR MAINGOT, a French tutor
> COMMANDER ROGERS, a British army officer, about thirty-five
> DIANA LAKE, Kenneth's sister, about twenty-five
> JACQUELINE MAINGOT, the daughter of Maingot, in love with Kit

The Play

French Without Tears opens in the living room of a seaside villa in the South of France. It is summer. Kenneth is preparing a French lesson when he is joined by Brian. They discuss career prospects: Kenneth fears he will not pass the French exam required for a diplomatic post he seeks; Brian tells him that Alan is the likely one to win the job. Alan enters and suggests that he might not want the job at all: It is his parents' wish that he become a diplomat. He jokes with the others about his prospects as a novelist, admitting that he has not yet had a manuscript accepted. The conversation turns to the arrival, the previous evening, of a new visitor, Commander Rogers. Maingot enters and reminds the men that their conversation should be in French. He then reads his newspaper, exclaiming on the doings of Adolf Hitler, before leaving with Kenneth for a French lesson.

Rogers enters. He has come to the establishment to study for an interpretership exam. He and Alan are quickly at odds: Rogers resents Alan's joking and sarcasm, and Alan dislikes Rogers's military demeanor. Alan warns him about Diana, Kenneth's "fast" sister, who is currently pursuing Kit. Diana enters in a bathing suit, followed by Kit. Alan and Diana insult each other politely, but when the others leave the room their insults take on a more gentle and romantic tone. Alan insists that she should stop toying with Kit and not make a new conquest of Rogers. After he exits, Rogers walks in looking for a phrase book. Diana flirts with him, telling him to ignore Alan's warnings, since he is really in love with her. She and Rogers agree to go walking.

Act 2 opens a fortnight later, as the household is finishing lunch. Maingot reminds the group that the Bastille Day celebrations—a costume ball and battle of flowers—

take place that evening. Kit asks Diana for a game of billiards, but she has already agreed to play with Rogers. Kit announces that he is taking Jacqueline to the ball and that Diana is going with Rogers. He tells Jacqueline that he likes her and hardly thinks of her as a woman. Alan enters, and he and Kit argue over Diana, with Kit insisting that Diana really loves him, not Rogers. Diana and Rogers enter, and the others leave. Rogers asks Diana why she will not tell Kit that she does not love him. She insists that she is trying to spare Kit's feelings. She finally promises to tell Kit; at this moment Jacqueline enters and overhears. The others wander in, and Alan discovers that his novel has been rejected again. He describes the plot of his novel: Two conscientious objectors go to Africa when war breaks out, but they end up fighting over a woman and, realizing that they cannot achieve their ideals, go back to fight in the war. The subject of competition over a woman causes a fight between Rogers and Kit. A general brawl quickly breaks out among the men, which ceases abruptly as Maingot enters and begins the day's lecture on the Near East.

The next scene begins six hours later, with preparations for the evening out. Diana is seated in the living room; Jacqueline enters in a Bavarian costume. Diana offers to fix a piece of loose braid on the dress, and as she does so the two women begin to argue over Kit. Diana insists that she wants both Rogers and Kit. Having men fall in love with her, she says, is her "one gift," whereas Jacqueline is intelligent and likable. The arrival the next day of another prospect, a Lord Heybrook, is discussed. Diana states that she does not intend to go to the ball after all. Kit enters, half-dressed in a Greek costume. He tells Jacqueline that he, too, would rather stay home; he has asked Kenneth to take her to the ball. Jacqueline quickly leaves. Kit asks Diana to tell Rogers that she does not love him, but loves Kit. Diana, repeating her words to Rogers in the previous scene, claims that she feels sorry for Rogers and does not want to hurt his feelings. Rogers enters as Kit is kissing Diana. Just as a fight is about to begin, Maingot enters in a Scottish Highland costume. He leaves for the ball, followed by Jacqueline and Kenneth. Alan, Brian, and Diana go out for a drink, leaving Kit and Rogers. The two men prepare to fight, but instead begin to laugh at Kit's costume. They agree to discuss the matter rationally. In their discussion they realize that Diana has said exactly the same words to each of them and made fools of both of them. Alan enters, and the three men decide to go into town to get drunk.

Act 3 opens a few hours later, after the three men have returned from the local casino. They drunkenly discuss their problems with women, then the conversation turns to Alan's career: He would like to go back to England and become a writer. It is then agreed that all the men must face Diana together. When Diana enters, Alan tells her that Kit and Rogers demand to know who it is she really loves, and he prevents her from leaving until she answers. After a pause, Diana announces that she loves Alan, then departs. Alan becomes suddenly fearful and asks the other men to protect him from Diana; in particular, they must never leave him alone with her. He goes on to reveal that Jacqueline is in love with Kit.

Maingot and Jacqueline soon return, still in costume. Kit and Jacqueline are left alone, and he tries to kiss her. Alan returns, confessing that he has told Kit of Jacqueline's feelings. She is angry with both of them, but forgives them. Alan is left alone, and Diana enters. She tries to convince him that she does indeed love him, but he keeps attempting to flee the room. Finally, they kiss, and Alan admits that he loves her. Brian enters as Diana leaves, telling Alan of a failed pass he made at Diana and of a new prostitute he has discovered in town. Alan decides that Brian's is the right and sensible approach to women and sex, and he resolves that he will ask Diana bluntly for sex; if she refuses he will return to England. Alan exits, a door slams upstairs, and Alan returns to say that he is going to England.

The final scene opens the next morning, after breakfast; Alan's departure is being discussed. Jacqueline reminds Diana that Lord Heybrook is arriving that morning. Alan enters, guarded by Rogers, who refuses to leave. Diana tries to convince Alan that she is sincere, and Alan tells Rogers to go. Rogers reminds Alan to be rational, and they both leave together, with Diana throwing books after them. Diana goes out for a swim. As Jacqueline gives Kit his French lesson, they circle the subject of a possible romance, and, half-jokingly, half-seriously, they kiss again. Gradually the household assembles to await the arrival of Lord Heybrook, with Diana entering at the last moment. Lord Heybrook enters: He is a boy of fifteen. Everyone laughs but Diana, who announces her intention of going to London. The play ends with Alan's cry, "Stop laughing, you idiots. It isn't funny. It's a bloody tragedy."

Themes and Meanings

French Without Tears is a light—perhaps very light—comedy, and an analysis of its meaning should be approached with caution. It is precisely this resistance to meaning, however, that is at the heart of the play. Terence Rattigan's expert manipulation of pace, rhythm, entrances, exits, and plot turns is often noted; indeed, Rattigan is usually seen as one of the last practitioners of the well-made play, which relied for its effect on a rather machinelike construction. In Britain the well-made play had been firmly tied to the social drama and "problem play" created by such dramatists as George Bernard Shaw, Henry Arthur Jones, and Arthur Wing Pinero. In Rattigan's piece, however, the plot twists and the realignment of relationships among the characters defy any such social or philosophical interpretation.

Early in the play, for example, professional and romantic rivalries seem to be established: Kenneth, Kit, and Alan are preparing for an entrance exam which only one of them is likely to pass; ironically, that person is Alan, who least wants the job. Kit and Rogers quickly become rivals for Diana's affections, along with the again reluctant Alan. Unexpectedly, any tension is quickly dispelled: The impending exam does not become a feature of the plot, and the rivalry among the men is transformed into camaraderie in response to Diana's machinations.

It becomes apparent that Rattigan, while creating a play that is surprisingly plotless, has taken care that numerous opportunities for plot development are raised, only to be let dangle after being shown to be insignificant. Alan, who would seem to be the central character, offers what might be a crucial idea when he outlines the plot of his much-rejected novel. In the story of two conscientious objectors who refuse to fight, and flee to Africa only to fight over a woman, Alan asserts the importance of an ideal, even one that cannot be achieved: "In a hundred years' time men may be able to live up to our ideals even if they can't live up to their own." The necessity of the ideal appears again in Alan's description of the perfect woman and in the comical play on reason and emotion that takes place among the men. The ideal, however, is without power in this play. Its value is posited in the pages of a rejected manuscript—by a man at the mercy of the most unideal of women. While bearing the marks of the well-made play, *French Without Tears* derives its comedy from a denial of the "problem" or "idea" traditionally at the heart of such plays.

Dramatic Devices

In *French Without Tears* Rattigan emphasizes the unfixed quality of the characters and action by subverting anticipated dramatic conventions. The well-made play attached specific meaning to objects and used clear-cut distinctions in type and characterization. In *French Without Tears* such objects as clothing, money, and books feature prominently in the action, but it is noteworthy that they finally have no decisive role in the play and are used interchangeably by the characters. The altered nature of ownership and allegiance is of central interest, and this continuous shifting in the nature of the characters and action extends to friendships, romantic relationships, language, and nationality. One source of the play's comedy is the inept use of French by the students at the villa; for the Bastille Day celebration, French characters don kilts and Bavarian costume, and English characters wear Greek and German costume.

The dialogue in the play is self-consciously dramatic. In act 2 Diana has love scenes with both Rogers and Kit. In each scene the dialogue is nearly identical: The effect is to deny both the distinctions between characters and the connection between character and language. In the last act, Kit and Jacqueline begin their romance by describing what they would say if they were in love, in terms that are deliberately theatrical and trite: "I've loved you all the time without knowing it," says Kit. Again, the comedy is in the insistence upon artificiality at the expense of naturalism.

If the characters come close to being mere props in this play, and the language persistently appears "dramatic," the setting of the play seems no wider than the stage itself. There is little specific social or political background to the play, and this lack points up another contrast with Rattigan's precursors in the British theater. Again, the appropriate possibilities are raised: Hitler is explicitly mentioned, Maingot's history lessons are a running joke, war is central to the plot of Alan's failed novel, and the characters are mainly upper-class men seeking careers in diplomacy. Maingot's history lessons provide a clue to the relevance of this political "background," since most of the characters have no idea what he is saying, and the audience is led to believe that he is a weak teacher with no great understanding of his subject. Rattigan has written a play which blithely denies the importance of the social and political context which it does indeed contain. It is a carefully constructed theatrical piece whose humor is based on escape from the heavy significance of its dramatic precursors.

Critical Context

French Without Tears was Rattigan's first success on the stage, running for more than one thousand performances. The popularity of this play would establish Rattigan as an adept craftsman in the drama: His reputation would remain that of a talented wielder of theatrical devices who persistently avoided the emphasis on ideas evident in such contemporary playwrights as J. B. Priestley. Rattigan's career was a long one: His last West End success was *Cause Célèbre* (pr. 1977, pb. 1978), produced in the year of his death. Rattigan followed *French Without Tears* with such comic pieces as *While the Sun Shines* (pr. 1943, pb. 1944) and *Love in Idleness* (pr. 1944, pb. 1945); both of these rely for humorous effect on the persistent spurning of ideas or "problems," a technique much in evidence in the earlier play.

It was after World War II that Rattigan began to produce "serious" plays, most notably *The Winslow Boy* (pr., pb. 1946), which offers a more thoughtful analysis of the function of the ideal than is found in *French Without Tears*. Nevertheless, certain continuities are evident between this early play and the later drama. The character of Diana is the earliest of Rattigan's "dangerous women," whose obsessive need for love (and its inevitable frustration) leads to chaos. The tragic possibilities in such a character are explored frequently in Ratigan's serious drama, in such plays as *The Deep Blue Sea* (pr., pb. 1952), *The Browning Version* (pr. 1948), and *Separate Tables: Table by the Window and Table Number Seven* (pr. 1954, pb. 1955).

By the end of his career, Rattigan suffered from an identification of his plays with the older, conventional "problem play" of the late Victorian and Edwardian years. In Rattigan's work, however, one can see—even in this early play—a rejection of many of the qualities of the older drama. Rattigan would explore the vitality of specific dramatic forms and devices while rejecting their traditional uses and context. Thus a play such as *The Winslow Boy* clearly relies on such legal dramas as Henry Arthur Jones's *Mrs. Dane's Defense* (pr. 1900), and *French Without Tears* on such Shavian comedies as *Man and Superman* (pr. 1903); both Rattigan plays, however, make a point of denying the specific social or political concerns of their models, and their characters are more ciphers than symbols.

Sources for Further Study

Darlow, Michael, and Gillian Hodson. *Terence Rattigan: The Man and His Work.* New York: Quartet Books, 1979.

Foulkes, Richard. "Terence Rattigan's Variations on a Theme." *Modern Drama* 22 (December, 1979): 375-381.

Rusinko, Susan. *Terence Rattigan.* Boston: Twayne, 1983.

Wainsell, Geoffrey. *Terence Rattigan: A Biography.* New York: St. Martin's Press, 1997.

Young, Bertram A. *The Rattigan Version: Sir Terence Rattigan and the Theatre of Character.* New York: Atheneum, 1988.

Heidi J. Holder

FUNNYHOUSE OF A NEGRO

Author: Adrienne Kennedy (1931-   )
Type of plot: Surrealist
Time of plot: The 1960's
Locale: An apartment in New York City
First produced: 1962, at the Circle-in-the-Square Theater, New York City
First published: 1969

> *Principal characters:*
> NEGRO-SARAH
> DUCHESS OF HAPSBURG, one of her selves
> QUEEN VICTORIA REGINA, one of her selves
> JESUS, one of her selves
> PATRICE LUMUMBA, one of her selves
> SARAH'S LANDLADY, a funnyhouse lady
> RAYMOND, a funnyhouse man
> THE MOTHER

The Play

   Funnyhouse of a Negro is a highly stylized theatrical piece. The setting of the play is the Negro-Sarah's room. The space is dominated by dusty books, photographs, and relics. The other locales—the queen's chamber, Raymond's room, and the jungle—are all part of Sarah's nightmare/fantasy. These are suggested environments, spaces created by lighting. The characters all represent facets of the Negro-Sarah's fantasies.

   Funnyhouse of a Negro begins with the stage in darkness. In front of a closed white curtain, a woman crosses the stage. She is wearing a white nightgown and carries a bald head. Her hair is "wild, straight, and black, and falls to her waist." She is mumbling inaudibly. She crosses the stage and exits, and the curtain opens.

   Queen Victoria Regina and the Duchess of Hapsburg are sitting in their chamber with their backs to the audience. They are dressed in the same ghastly white material as the curtain. Both have wild, frizzy hair and are missing patches of hair on the crowns of their heads. Their faces are white and immobile masks. A loud knocking is heard throughout the scene. They discuss their father, a Negro—the darkest of them all. He has come through the jungle to find them; he is knocking. He is dead, but he keeps returning. The lights black out.

   The woman crosses the stage again, speaking about the black man whom she should never have let rape her. She is the mother. The lights come up again on the Negro-Sarah. She is very dark and faceless. She wears a hangman's noose around her neck and is missing a patch of hair from her head. In a monologue, she reveals details of her life. She is a student and a writer, absorbed with writing in the style of Europeans. She lives in a brownstone in the West Nineties, and her boyfriend Raymond is a white man. Sarah must surround herself with whiteness, avoiding the reality of her blackness. Her only outstanding negroid feature is her hair. Sometimes she is herself, and sometimes she is Victoria Regina. The lights come up on the white Landlady in another area of the stage. She says that Sarah hides in her room, talks to herself, and thinks of herself as someone else. The lights go out.

The next scene takes place in Raymond's room, which appears to be above the Negro-Sarah's room. His room contains a bed and window blinds; the blinds cover a mirror. Raymond is talking with the partially disrobed Duchess of Hapsburg. The Duchess needs to hide from her father, who comes from Africa and pursues her. Throughout the scene, Raymond opens and closes the blinds and laughs. The Duchess is losing her hair, which resembles her mother's hair. Her mother was of very light complexion, her father very dark; she is in between. She embraces Raymond "wildly" as the lights go out. A knocking is heard again in the distance.

The lights come up on a dark, faceless man carrying an ebony mask. He is Patrice Lumumba. He too is losing his hair; he dreams of his bald mother. After she was married, she became insane and her hair fell out. The lights black out. The lights come up in the queen's chamber. In a dumb show, Queen Victoria awakens and discovers that her hair is falling out. The Duchess enters carrying a red paper bag; she removes hair from the bag and attempts to replace her own hair. Patrice Lumumba returns and delivers a monologue detailing his life. He is a student; his friends and surroundings all need to be white; he is losing his hair. A bald head on a string, and a wall are lowered onto the set.

The Negro-Sarah appears and speaks to the audience. Her mother worshiped her father; she wanted him to be Christ and save the race. This worship ended with the rape of her mother, who was committed to an asylum. Sarah says that she was in love with the light skin of her mother and rejected her father because of his dark skin. Her father hanged himself in a Harlem hotel.

The next scene is between the Duchess of Hapsburg and Jesus. In a dumb show, both discover that they are losing their hair, so they comb each other's hair to hide their baldness. The Landlady appears and tells her version of the relationship between Sarah and her father: He came to see Sarah in New York, to beg her forgiveness, but she refused to talk with him. Jesus returns to tell the audience that he has tried to escape being black. He is going to Africa to kill Patrice Lumumba.

The scene changes to the jungle. The characters all appear wearing nimbuses. They talk together in overlapping speech about their father, who is the darkest of them all. He was supposed to be the savior. He was bludgeoned to death with an ebony mask, but he keeps returning. The speeches are first delivered very slowly, and then very quickly.

Another wall descends. The Negro-Sarah is in her room. A faceless dark figure comes to her. The lights black out; when the lights come up again, Sarah is hanging. The final scene is a conversation between Raymond and the Landlady. They talk about what a funny little liar Sarah was. Raymond points out that her father, still alive, is a doctor who lives in very elegant rooms and is married to a white whore.

Themes and Meanings

The struggle of the individual with internalized social and cultural forces is the focal point of most of Adrienne Kennedy's plays. In particular, she focuses on the internal conflict of the African American, whose existence is a result of the violent blending of European and African cultures. This conflict is imaged in the Negro-Sarah's idolatrous love of her fair-skinned mother and rejection of her black father. The mother's whiteness has driven her insane; the father's darkness has tied him to revolution and bloodshed. Sarah's eventual escape is suicide.

The play is set in Sarah's space. The characters in the play are views of herself, or they are inspired by the objects in her room. The space is filled with relics of European civilization: dusty books, pictures of castles and monarchs, the bust of Queen Victoria. Sarah's occupation is writing, the geometric placement of words on white paper. The space is also a coffin; the white material of the curtain looks as though it has been "gnawed by rats." Throughout the play the space becomes more confining as the walls drop down. Eventually it becomes the jungle, overgrown and wild. In the context of the play's imagery of death, the jungle represents the earth's reclamation of the body.

On another level, the play is set within a "funnyhouse," an "amusement park house of horrors." Raymond and the Landlady are representations of the two grinning minstrel faces outside the funnyhouse. They are white society mocking the Negro's confusion. The bald heads and dropping walls are cheap effects designed to create confusion and fear; the mirrors in Raymond's room conceal true reflections, as distorted funnyhouse mirrors do.

Kennedy is also a woman writer, and the play makes a statement about the roles of black women and white women in society. The mother was light-skinned and beautiful by European standards. There was no destiny for her in society except madness: To be a light-skinned woman is to invite the rape of black men. Sarah is dating a white man, and this seems to give her some power in the scene with Raymond when she is the Duchess of Hapsburg. It is Raymond, however, who is asking the questions and who has control over the environment. Even the white female characters in the play who represent powerful figures are victims of hair loss; they too are unable to escape the dark man who pursues them.

In the playwright's view, the world is a disturbing place. The lure of power is held out to women, when in fact they are powerless. For the African American, to be assimilated into white society is to go mad or self-destruct.

Dramatic Devices

Funnyhouse of a Negro invites the viewer into the mind of a very confused young black woman. The characters of the play are identified as facets of herself. She sees herself as omnipotent (Jesus), powerful (Queen Victoria, the Duchess of Hapsburg), and revolutionary (Patrice Lumumba). According to the dream logic of the play, these diverse characters all suffer from the conflict between their father, a black man, and their mother, a light-complexioned black woman who was raped and driven to insanity. The characters evoke the era of European colonialism, the zealotry of Christian missionaries, and the subsequent search for liberation by the peoples of Africa.

The strongest facet of the play is its use of language. The playwright has the characters repeat images, phrases, and in some instances entire speeches. One speech is performed by all the characters in unison at varying speeds. The language takes on a weight of its own through the sheer force of repetition. The characters speak of horrible acts—rape, patricide, and suicide—with words that have the force of blows.

Another strong element of the play is its vivid visual imagery. The contrast between light and dark, repeated in many different forms, contributes to the ritualistic quality of the action. The Duchess and Queen Victoria are both very white and expressionless. Jesus is a hunchbacked, yellow-skinned dwarf, dressed in white rags and sandals. Patrice Lumumba is a black man whose face appears split and who carries an ebony mask. Raymond and the Landlady, who are white, are dressed in black; Raymond's attire suggests that he is an artist, and the Landlady wears a black and red hat. The Negro-Sarah is a faceless, dark character with a rope around her neck. The repeated blackouts between scenes reinforce the contrast between light and darkness.

The play is filled with bird imagery (a recurring motif in Kennedy's work). There are ravens, great dark birds that fly through the queen's chambers. Lumumba recalls his early relationship with his mother as a time when doves flew. The birds are a symbol of freedom.

The device of mirroring is integral to the play's structure and action. All the characters are reflections of the Negro-Sarah. They are all losing their hair; they all perform the same activities. The scenes are similar, mirroring each other; the placement of characters onstage is often similar. The white characters, moreover, provide an alternate reflection of the information given by the black characters.

Critical Context

Adrienne Kennedy is a significant playwright largely because of her pioneering work in nonnaturalistic drama. Her scripts are confusing and difficult to read; in performance, however, there is a clear sense of the playwright probing the workings of the subconscious mind. Her plays are dreamscapes. As in *Funnyhouse of a Negro*, a character may see herself as more than one persona. In *The Owl Answers* (pr. 1963, pb. 1969), for example, the central character is Clara Passmore, "who is the Virgin Mary who is the Bastard who is the Owl." This play also uses repetition of lines or fragments of lines to establish the character as a collage of people. Confusions of identity and inner conflicts are often imaged in Kennedy's work in figures who are part human, part animal, as in *A Rat's Mass* (pr. 1966, pb. 1968) and *A Lesson in Dead Language* (pr., pb. 1968).

Kennedy has refused to create the kind of simplistic, didactic writing about the African American experience that gained widespread attention in the 1960's. Her plays instead treat the black experience in America on a variety of levels: intellectual, sexual, symbolic, and visceral. Her work has pushed other African American dramatists to explore alternative methods of expressing their common concerns. Similarly, as a woman writer, Kennedy has repeatedly raised issues about the tyranny of patriarchal culture, particularly as represented by the Church. She has made a significant contribution to the development of feminist theater in the United States.

Kennedy's achievements as an innovator in dramatic form were acknowledged in 1964 when she received an Obie Award for *Funnyhouse of a Negro*. She has also been awarded several Rockefeller grants, a National Endowment for the Arts grant in 1993, and an American Academy of Arts and Letters Award in 1994.

She has continued to write to the African American experience and women's experience; she has also written for children. Her autobiographical book *People Who Led to My Plays* (1987) gives an interesting account of the many influences on her work, and critics have noted that her 1992 collection *The Alexander Plays*, which encompasses a quartet of plays exploring the life of a woman named Suzanne Alexander, is likely a fictionalized version of Kennedy's own life.

Sources for Further Study

Betsko, Kathleen, and Rachel Koenig, eds. *Interviews with Contemporary Women Playwrights*. New York: Beech Tree Books, 1987.

Bryant-Jackson, Paul K., and Lois More Overbeck, eds. *Insecting Boundaries: The Theater of Adrienne Kennedy*. Minneapolis: University of Minnesota Press, 1992.

Cohn, Ruby. "Black on Black: Baraka, Bullins, Kennedy." In *New American Dramatists*. 2d ed. New York: St. Martin's Press, 1982.

Diamond, Elm. "Adrienne Kennedy." In *Contemporary Dramatists*. 4th ed. Chicago: St. James Press, 1988.

Harrison, Paul Carter. "The Drama of Nommo." In *The Drama of Nommo*. New York: Grove Press, 1972.

Kennedy, Adrienne. *Adrienne Kennedy in One Act*. Minneapolis: University of Minnesota Press, 1988.

_____. *People Who Led to My Plays*. New York: Knopf, 1987.

Keyssar, Helene. "A Network of Playwrights." In *Feminist Theatre: An Introduction to Plays of Contemporary British and American Women*. New York: Grove Press, 1985.

Tener, Robert L. "Theatre of Identity: Adrienne Kennedy's Portrait of the Black Woman." *Studies in Black Literature* 6 (Summer, 1975): 1-5.

Kathryn Ervin Williams

THE GARDEN OF EARTHLY DELIGHTS

Author: Martha Clarke (1944-   )
Type of plot: Surrealist
Time of plot: The age of biblical creation and the fifteenth century
Locale: Hieronymus Bosch landscape from his triptych, *The Garden of Delights* (c. 1500)
First produced: 1984, at St. Clement's Church, New York City

> *Principal characters:*
> ADAM and
> EVE,
> THE SERPENT,
> ANGELS,
> DEMONS, and
> COARSE PEASANTS, all portrayed by an ensemble of seven dancer/
> actors and three musicians

The Play

The Garden of Earthly Delights is a series of pictorial vignettes performed without text or scenery. There are four distinct sections, dramatizing in turn Eden, the Garden of Earthly Delights, the Seven Deadly Sins, and Hell.

Part 1 begins when a smoky mist fills the blackened stage to the low sound of whistling wind. A trumpet blares as blue light illuminates a thicket of leafless tree branches held overhead by a man who trudges slowly to center stage. Six figures enter from the darkness of stage left, walking on their hands and feet, looking like animals cautiously exploring a new world. One falls over and instantly becomes the prey of the others, who pounce on it and devour it. The first musical motif begins on cello and recorder as light spreads across the stage to reveal the figures of Adam and Eve, dressed in skin-colored body suits and standing side-by-side.

The two begin a gentle, fluid movement sequence to the sweet melody of the cello. Eve gradually moves away from Adam, signifying her emergence from his rib. The two move gracefully to the floor as two merry angels piping on penny whistles fly in above them. Adam strokes Eve's hair and then tenderly pulls her from the floor by it. Their brief moment of innocent wonder ends as they are met by the serpent, who pulls an apple from between her thighs, symbolizing the end of innocence in the Garden of Eden. Adam and Eve fold over into the animal shapes of the earlier creatures, and like them exit slowly on all fours, heads bent. The tree-man stalks off, accompanied by stringed instruments playing a dirge.

The second section of the piece is set in the Garden of Earthly Delights. A musical change signals this transition; a more percussive score begins with a knocking sound on the side of a drum underscoring a flute. The musicians enter the empty stage in small groups with the dancers. From stage left, the cellist enters, accompanied by a crawling woman. When he stops upstage left, she stretches out at his feet. From up-stage center another dancer enters with a man playing a lyre. She then nestles against him downstage, holding the lyre while he plucks the strings. A trio enters from stage right, led by the flute player. Two women walk closely behind him, holding the instru-ment as he plays, at right center. The musicians finish this soothing song, then move to the edges of the stage. One woman exits, while the three who remain begin a move-ment sequence which begins on the floor and eventually carries them offstage.

A collage of vivid images ensues. The low, eerie sounds of a tuba accompany the entrance of a grotesque beast. Three men roll toward center stage; a woman balances on each one with a staff for support. One man becomes a boat; the woman on his back calmly guides her stick-oar through unseen water. The other two men swim away. The remaining women kneel and wave their sticks across the floor as if conjuring. The mu-sic grows more animated. A woman in a chiffon robe flies above the heads of five fig-ures, who have replaced the kneeling women. They watch her before dividing into a trio and duet, beginning a movement sequence characterized by contact and acrobatics. The two conjurers reenter, swinging switches like long whips. The sound of the whips and the staccato plucking of violin strings become strident. Two more women join in, with tree branches held overhead. A man enters wearing bells and using a tree limb for a guide stick. Another man enters carrying a mask on the end of a long branch.

The lights fade, leaving only the musicians in a dull, blue-gray light. The music is severe and threatening; the cello and the chimes and the slow, steady beating of the bass drum grow louder. Four figures are seen in the spill light adding layers of cloth-ing over their body suits. Bright light illuminates seven men and women dressed in medieval peasant costumes. The third section of the piece is a broad pantomime of the Seven Deadly Sins. The accompanying music is light and awkward, like carnival mu-sic. The events that follow happen in close succession, some overlapping. A man holding a burlap sack walks to center stage and dumps potatoes onto the floor. A sec-ond adds to this pile, then puts the bucket on his head. The sound of snoring emanates from the bucket. A woman in a wimple lifts her hem and potatoes drop onto the floor. A man urinates into a bucket. A man sits in the pile of potatoes and stuffs them in his mouth as fast as he can; the others gather to watch him.

Three women sit on the floor. The two on the right and left appear to be involved in an argument, while the one in the middle watches them. They strangle her. A man drags her to the side and sexually abuses her body, then the others roll her offstage. All join hands and begin a slow circle dance accompanied by a repeated musical phrase from the cello. Four crawl off, leaving one man and one woman alone onstage. A drum beats, and a pool of light focuses on the potatoes. The woman kneels in the light and begins to gather them around her. The man stands to the side as the lights grow dimmer. The drumbeat is replaced by the rhythm of a man's ax striking a tree. The lights go out. In very low light a woman seems to be flying above the lights, holding her head. Blue light comes up on a man holding tree branches. The flying woman sud-denly begins spinning downward over the potatoes. She is finally dropped to the ground, then hung upside down. The stage goes black.

In the darkness, soft piano music can be heard. As the lights come up, a woman hanging from the catwalk plunges down, then dangles. A high, piercing whistle screams over the piano, announcing the transition into Hell. As in the painting, musical instruments are transformed into instruments of torture, and musicians dominate this section. One man rolls another under a bass drum, beating it as he eventually crushes him beneath the drum. Meanwhile two figures fly and tumble through space; another floats down to meet them as they all begin turning backward somersaults in the air. Below, two men fight, one playing a violin and using the bow like a stick, pushing it into the other's mouth. Two women use drumsticks to beat on the men on whose backs they slowly ride across the stage. A large set of chimes is rolled onstage by three men who seem to be trying to kill one another. These three finally drop exhausted to the floor. A xylophonist's head is pounded into his keyboard. An explosion of sirens, whistles, and drums produces a dissonant cacophony, which combines with the steady beating of a man's head between a bass drum and a cymbal throughout.

Suddenly, it becomes very quiet. A stiff-limbed man with his head thrown back plunks out a simple melody on a toy piano. The other men and women plod noisily off like animals, leaving the cellist alone onstage. The cellist recapitulates the sweet melody from Eden. A young woman crawls to his side and tries to distort the music, pulling the cellist's arm, tugging at the bow, and plucking the strings. They struggle over the bow until she pulls it from his grasp. She lies seductively before him on the floor. He lifts the cello and impales her on its spike. Then he calmly continues to play, plucking out the rest of the melody. She writhes quietly beneath him, and he pulls the cello spike out. Meanwhile, a wan man on tree stump stilts limps into a white light to survey the desolation. It is nearly dark onstage. A flute plays softly in the final moments of light. In the approaching darkness, a woman's lifeless body spins in space.

Themes and Meanings

Martha Clarke's *The Garden of Earthly Delights* is a theatrical interpretation of Hieronymus Bosch's *The Garden of Delights*, a vision of Paradise, humankind's fall from grace, and its subsequent damnation. The original canvas is a densely populated triptych portraying beautiful, humorous, and grotesque images from the Garden of Eden, the Garden of Earthly Delights, and Hell. Clarke's performance piece is similarly structured, but includes the insertion of a section illustrating the Seven Deadly Sins, which is based on another Bosch painting. Like Bosch, Clarke deals with the great, familiar themes of Western religious art.

Clarke's version of events is impressionistic, stressing the blithe innocence rather than the material sinfulness of earthly pleasures, yet she focuses on the relentless horrors of punishment. As in Bosch's painting, no possible redemption is offered to the damned. Bosch's images of humankind's fate seem alarmingly modern when viewed as metaphors for the present condition of humanity.

In the opening section, Adam and Eve move innocently through Paradise as angels swing merrily over their heads. The beauty of Bosch's Paradise landscape remains with them as they move out of Eden into the Garden of Earthly Delights. Darker, more ominous images gradually filter into the dramatic world, but the charm of Eden lingers. The movement is lyrical and the music soothing as couples swim in pools of pleasure or are transformed into boats and sail away. Even though sublime happiness has endured outside the Garden of Eden, however, the habits of civilization eventually produce a coarseness in attitude.

Thus, Clarke inserts the Seven Deadly Sins section as a bridge between the Garden of Earthly Delights and Hell. She implies that natural pleasure is not itself the cause of humankind's fall into Hell, but rather that it is led to its destruction by the excessiveness of its pursuit. The peasants in the Seven Deadly Sins section have grown away from the abstract beauty of Eden. Clarke's depiction of bodily functions, gluttony, rape, and murder illustrates the depravity that leads humans down the inevitable path to damnation. Clarke's infernal setting is a complex nightmare of pungent images: Her angels tumble headfirst toward Hell. Musical instruments become implements of torture; the musical score itself becomes dissonant and deafening.

Clarke seems to accept the premise of Bosch's vision, including its moral perspective, and she strives to restore a vivid, immediate impression of his themes. The primary difference between their expressions surfaces in the mechanisms of performance. In Bosch, the illusion is particular and concrete, completely convincing without emphasizing the technique of painting. In Clarke's case, the use of the ensemble, the visible presence of devices like the lights, the flying harnesses, and the modern dance clothes of the mythic performers suggest that Hell is as much a production of humankind as it is a natural epilogue to his experiences.

Dramatic Devices

The Garden of Earthly Delights is distinguished from much contemporary performance art by the dominance of the expressive use of the human body, replacing all spoken text. Clarke's approach to developing material and directing the action is primarily choreographic. The images of Bosch's paintings are brought to life by the performer's bodies, transmuted into human and animal characters. Clarke is able to evoke a range of beautiful and horrible images by her use of movement motifs which are initially suggested in the paintings and subsequently expanded to extend the ideas of the painting in time and space. The characters are choreographed in the air as well as on the ground, making the entire theater an animated canvas.

The most striking mechanical device used throughout the piece is the flight of actors and musicians, accomplished by means of harnesses and wires. Angels float and soar above the stage and damned souls hurdle toward Hell or hang lifelessly in darkness. The careful blending of dance and aerial movement, mime, acrobatics, music, and lighting effects with a minimum of props exhausts the formal possibilities of expression without surrendering to the demands of specific textual themes.

In the Seven Deadly Sins section, Gluttony, Anger, Envy, Lust, Pride, Sloth, and Covetousness are personified by a band of medieval peasants in a quick series of cartoonlike scenes. These scenes are the most humorous in the piece, but in an unquestionably cruel way. While the peasants' actions are broadly drawn and sometimes clownish, the implications of their coarse behavior are frightening.

By employing actors who constantly transform from one role to another, good to evil, male to female to natural object or animal, Clarke suggests that the range of actions and feeling suggested by the piece are somehow abiding elements within all human beings.

Critical Context

Martha Clarke's use of the paintings of Hieronymus Bosch has been anticipated in various ways in the work of a number of modern artists; she shares, for example, the grotesque physical quality that distinguishes the Rabelaisian pantomimes of Jacques le Coq. *The Garden of Earthly Delights* is most distinctly similar to the works of Michel de Ghelderode, a twentieth century Flemish playwright who frequently reworked painted images and specialized in the use of a grotesque landscape he called Brueghelland. In plays such as *Le Massacre des innocents* (pb. 1929; the slaughter of the innocents), Ghelderode dramatized Brueghel's historical translation of biblical events to the Low Country, duplicating their detailed violence in the context of his Pauline conviction that sin deforms the body. These sacred events, simultaneously being revived by surrealist painters such as Salvador Dalí and Yves Tanguy, were treated by Ghelderode in a meditative but intense symbolist style, not formally complex but self-consciously spiritual. Clarke's theatrical work is clearly a new step in this ongoing reception of the religious imagination in pre-Renaissance northern Europe.

The theatrical genre closest to Clarke's work is the theater of images, a genre which includes the contemporary work of directors Robert Wilson, Peter Brook, Ping Chong, and Meredith Monk. These artists synthesize music, text, gesture, and visual environment to achieve richly textured and thematically complex works of performance art. Clarke's work is distinguished by her detailed articulation of the human body to communicate actions and emotional states, and her collaborative approach to each project. Her work has also been compared to that of the contemporary German artist Pina Bausch, who similarly transforms movement, music, and setting into the choreographed interplay of images and ideas that characterize her work with Tanztheater.

The Garden of Earthly Delights, the first of Clarke's large performance artworks, shows the choreographic influence of her seven years as a performer with the Pilobolus Dance Theater. With Pilobolus, Clarke practiced organizing movement material into a dramatic logic in such dances as *Monkshood's Farewell* (pr. 1974) and *Untitled* (pr. 1975). The acrobatic and distorted use of the human body, a Pilobolus trademark, is employed in *The Garden of Earthly Delights* more than in any of Clarke's later works; the director thinks of it as a last salute to Pilobolus. Subsequent Clarke pieces such as *Vienna: Lusthaus* (pr. 1986) and *The Hunger Artist* (pr. 1987) similarly combine dance, gesture, music, and design elements but add spoken text. Later, in *Miracolo d'Amore* (pr. 1988), song is added to the blend, bringing her work close to opera.

Sources for Further Study

Clarke, Martha. "Images from the Id." Interview by Arthur Barton. *American Theater* 5 (June, 1988): 10-17, 55-57.

_____. Interview by Elizabeth Kendall and Don Daniels. *Ballet Review* 12 (Winter, 1985): 15-25.

Copeland, Roger. "Master of the Body." *American Theater* 5 (June, 1988): 14-15.

Gussow, Mel. "Clarke Work." *New York Times Magazine*, January 18, 1987, pp. 30-34.

Sadler, Geoff. "Martha Clarke." In *Contemporary Dramatists*. 6th ed. Detroit: St. James, 1999.

Smith, Amanda. "Inside the Fellini-esque World of Martha Clarke." *Dance Magazine* 60 (April, 1986): 70-74.

Zimmer, Elizabeth. Review of *The Garden of Earthly Delights*. *Dance Magazine* 58 (September, 1984): 85-88.

Diane Quinn

THE GARDEN PARTY

Author: Václav Havel (1936-   )
Type of plot: Social realism
Time of plot: The 1960's
Locale: Czechoslovakia
First produced: 1963, at the Divadlo na zábradlí (Balustrade Theater), Prague, Czechoslovakia
First published: Zahradní slavnost, 1963 (English translation, 1969)

Principal characters:
HUGO PLUDEK
PLUDEK, his father
MRS. PLUDEK, his mother
PETER PLUDEK, his brother
AMANDA, a messenger
MAXY FALK, an "inaugurator"
CLERK, an employee of the Liquidation Office
SECRETARY, an employee of the Liquidation Office
DIRECTOR OF THE INAUGURATION SERVICE

The Play

The Garden Party begins in the Pludeks' flat; the family members are present while Hugo plays chess with himself. The parents send Peter downstairs so that an expected visitor, Kalabis, will not see that he "looks like a bourgeois intellectual." They then ask Hugo if he has considered his future, the father spouting nonsensical clichés. The conversation is circular and bears no relation to real time. Finally Hugo is told of Kalabis's planned visit, at the same moment that he checkmates himself. Pludek is inspired to discourse on the Japanese and the middle class in history. The doorbell finally rings, after several false alarms; Peter, who has reentered, is hurriedly sent to the pantry. Instead of Kalabis, however, a young messenger named Amanda enters. She reads a telegram explaining that Kalabis will not come; he is going to the Liquidation Office garden party. Mrs. Pludek decides to send Hugo to the garden party. Amanda lingers, and she is told by Mrs. Pludek not to worry: She had small parts in plays, too, when she was younger. After Amanda exits, her possibilities for Hugo are discussed. Hugo wants to play another game of chess, but when his mother explains that life, too, is a chessboard, he resolves to go to the party. Hugo exits to a mixture of quotations and cliché bits of song from his parents. Peter enters simultaneously, then also exits without a word; the parents are still caught up in their inane vision of future happiness as the scene ends.

Act 2 begins at the entrance to the Liquidation Office garden party. A male clerk and a female secretary review guests at a table; Hugo enters and asks them about

Kalabis. They explain to him the organizational structure of the garden party, which is quite complicated in an exaggerated, bureaucratic way. Hugo points to some mistakes in their planning, then says "Check!" The clerks evade his criticism but are interrupted by Maxy Falk. He gives an extended greeting that includes lines which parody Terence's famous pronouncement on playwriting, which reads, in its new form, "Nothing foreign is human to me." After Falk's exit, a brief personal conversation is once again diverted by the officials into petty bureaucratic double-talk. Hugo offers another critique (as a chess move), and Falk returns, explaining his status as an "inaugurator." The two officials encourage Falk to describe his work and publications, which are on an inflated interpretation of garden parties. After his speech regresses into a series of slogans, Falk leaves. The officials speak briefly about nature before returning to the problems of the party. Hugo offers a third criticism, which is rejected, as Falk returns wearing a papier-mâché nose. This time Falk's discourse wanders even more, as Hugo and the others begin to repeat his catchphrases. Hugo slowly absorbs the jargon, and after Falk erupts in a fit of temper that scares away the bickering officials, he speaks.

Hugo's statement begins with a series of rhetorical questions, then evolves into a new, seemingly original combination of the words and phrases he has just heard. Falk, dumbstruck, exchanges identification cards with Hugo, then begins a long conversation in which Falk gradually assumes that Hugo is a liquidator who is planning to abolish the Inauguration Service. Hugo quotes Falk's patronizing lines from the first part of the act and leaves, shouting "Check!" Falk, in despair, is approached by the contrite officials, who explain how they made up their differences in a very personal way. Falk cares nothing for them, announcing that the Inauguration Service is to be liquidated and stalking off. The secretary notices that the clerk has lost interest in her and begins to weep. He begins planning the liquidation as Falk runs onstage and sticks out his tongue at them to end the scene.

Act 3 takes place in the head office of the Liquidation Service, where a secretary stamps and sorts files taken by the director from his desk. They work while conversing; he propositions her, but the topic shifts back to the process of liquidation—as the clothes of the director are gradually taken, stamped, and sorted into the enormous file baskets until he is left in his underwear. The secretary sobs as she remembers famous speeches of inauguration, then exits as the director collapses with weariness. Hugo enters, waking the director, and begins a conversation about the history and meaning of inauguration with the director. Their conversation suggests a filial relationship, and Mrs. Pludek suddenly enters, interrupting the scene, only to be sent off. Hugo and the director then try to decide how to inaugurate the liquidation, working through several variations of the problem's logical contradictions. Their language begins to merge, then lapses into unison until Hugo begins to speak so quickly that the director merely adds phrases to his extended bureaucratic discourse. Hugo emerges as the master, sending the terrorized director out for coffee. The clerk enters; he and Hugo repeat a condensed version of the preceding scene, ending with Hugo storming out on a self-righteous mission to protest the whole procedure.

Hugo returns and asks the director who might be in charge of the liquidation, so that he can protest the contradiction of liquidators continuing to work when they are themselves the ones supposedly being liquidated. The director answers that "Hugo Pludek" is in charge, and Hugo, recognizing neither his name nor his function, goes out to look for himself. The secretary enters again, looking for the clerk. The director repeats his proposition, and the secretary storms out. The director then climbs into one of the enormous file baskets to take a nap. The secretary returns, finds the director, and climbs in too, closing the lid on the basket just as the act ends.

The scene returns to the Pludek home for act 4. The parents converse about Hugo, Japan, and a noise in the pantry. Pludek walks to the pantry and discovers Amanda and Peter, each dressed only in "a hastily arranged overcoat." Amanda gives the parents a telegram, which was sent from Kalabis to report on Hugo's important new work. As the parents rejoice, Amanda and Peter exit in opposite directions. Peter's future is briefly considered, but Hugo returns home wearing a party nose. His parents greet him, but in the following dialogue both the son and his parents talk about "Hugo" in the third person; neither he nor they recognize him since his bureaucratic transformation. The dangers and contradictions of Hugo's new position are considered by the three, until they are interrupted by Amanda and Peter. Amanda reads a telegram, inserting between lines her usual measure of non sequiturs, which reveals that Hugo is also in charge of liquidating the Inauguration Service. The parents rejoice, then ask Amanda and Peter about their future plans. The two lovers then leave, again in opposite directions, while the parents discuss the politics of Hugo's situation—he himself cannot get a word in edgewise.

Finally a third telegram is delivered by Amanda and Peter, this one announcing that Hugo has been given the job of reconstructing the two bureaus into a new "Central Commission for Inauguration and Liquidation." The parents rejoice. Peter and Amanda declare their love and leave holding hands; they decide that they will live together. The parents discuss their children, then stop; they have noticed Hugo and want to know who he is. Hugo replies in his longest, most complicated, most reflexive and nonsensical speech of the play, concluding a declaration of his own erasure with the final move of the game, his "Checkmate!" As Hugo exits, the parents approve of his words, finding in them the patriotic spirit of the Bohemian middle class. Mrs. Pludek predicts that the "hellhound" of Japan may overrun them, a dog howls from the cupboard, and Falk enters—striding down to the footlights to tell the audience to go home.

Themes and Meanings

The principal theme of *The Garden Party* is its criticism of the bureaucratic system of communist government. The institutions are arranged not for any type of normal government service but for the administration of the bureaus themselves. The Office of Inauguration does not introduce new ideas or policies so much as it creates busywork for its employees, much in the same way that Hugo provides a career for himself by suggesting its destruction. The Office of Liquidation does not, in fact, become liquidated; instead, it becomes part of a larger, more complex, more centralized ministry, which will doubtless be even more unwieldy and inefficient than its predecessors. The entire action takes place in such an atmosphere of paranoia and influence peddling as to suggest virtually no hope for the system of order. In a political absurdist play, it is above all else the political structure that is empty, arbitrary, dispiriting.

The second theme of the play distinguishes Václav Havel's work from that of other Eastern bloc satirists. *The Garden Party* provides a brilliant example of the failure of language to communicate human meanings. In this early play, Havel uses cliché and repetition, to provide his commentary. The clichés relate to government and ideal values, and they are expressed without conviction in an atmosphere of careerism. These clichés reveal their power in repetition, as characters hear and absorb the sayings that the prevailing ideology and its language system produce. Hugo enters the garden party as a talented but naïve young man; his exposure to the language and logic of bureaucracy hardens him into the unrecognizable "official" of the final act. Rather than men producing language, in *The Garden Party* language produces men.

The final theme of note is the self-conscious theatricality of the play. Hugo begins the play at the chessboard, and it is this game that provides the prevailing metaphor for his subsequent actions. The bureaucratic system is an arbitrarily structured creation, like a chess game, which Hugo learns to play against itself—as he played both sides of the chessboard. When the game is over, the player, Hugo, ceases to exist as such. Havel also provides a number of other self-conscious gestures to reinforce the themes, such as Amanda's discomfiture in her role, the third act intrusion of Mrs. Pludek, and the party-nose disguises of the second act. Havel regularly disrupts the illusion, turning the play back onto itself in a gesture of erasure that completes the critical indictment of a self-conscious, bureaucratic society.

Dramatic Devices

The most inventive dramatic devices in the play are in the structure and style of the dialogue. The characters repeat one another and vary the combinations of the words to the point that the play becomes a comic fugue of weirdly inappropriate observations. Many speeches and conversations also include complete non sequiturs, often amusing in their own right, which then enter the system of repetition to reappear in new, more bizarre forms. Amanda's telegrams, for example, alternate between terse messages and a series of longer lines that sound like one end of a phone conversation. Falk's ruminations in act 2 are even more like free association. Hugo, in turn, submits these language themes to a kind of inexorable logic that sounds even more convincing as it grows more peculiar.

The language structure produces characters that are exaggerated and grotesque. The parents are a parody of the normal family, unable to express genuine concern or affection for their children while worrying abstractly about their career chances. The bureaucrats seem distant in official situations, but manage to achieve a certain kind of humanity through physical intimacy; it is love, too, that promises eventually to free Peter, the incipient bourgeois intellectual, from his family's machinations—unless love is yet another cliché. Hugo, the hero as Mr. Zero, remains unattached to the end, even severing his familiar connections. He becomes the Soviet version of the anonymous company man.

The dramatic action is rigidly structured, with overriding patterns and symmetrical developments. Falk's visits to the greeting table in act 2 and Amanda's deliveries in act 4 segment those scenes into spirals of increasing complexity and dramatic effect. The play begins and ends at the family home, describing a circular structure that suggests the reflexive principle of the whole work. In the final line Falk presents the audience with a wholly arbitrary gesture, which in turn asks them to view their visit to the theater in terms of the behavioral patterns satirized by the play.

Critical Context

The social context of *The Garden Party* was the gradually developing thaw in Czech society leading up to the Prague Spring of 1968. There is nothing particularly bitter about Havel's critique; the flaws of socialist government are presented as an established, conventional joke, so familiar as to produce the delights of recognition as well as the pleasures of comic surprises for his liberal audiences. Political satire has a long tradition in Czech theater, and *The Garden Party* provided a society hopeful of change with a strong example of the need for sensible reform.

In the course of Havel's career, *The Garden Party* marks the beginning of his first phase of mature work, the political absurdist plays of the 1960's. In two earlier plays Havel had collaborated with others to produce works that promoted audience activity. *The Garden Party* marks his move to a more conservative, but more complex, mature, and malleable dramatic form. The devices of repetition and bureaucratic absurdity became hallmarks of Havel's dramatic style, and have appeared in works written more than two decades later, such as his *Pokoušení* (pr., pb. 1986; *Temptation*, 1988). In this play Havel creates a more serious impression; in *The Garden Party*, a certain comic enthusiasm pervades the text and spills over into sympathetic roles. Havel has matured, developing a more sober but more profound style of writing.

In its literary context, *The Garden Party* is perhaps the first masterpiece of postwar Czech drama, and it provides an early example of the political absurdism that also characterized the work of writers such as Sławomir Mrożek in Poland and Aleksandr Zinoviev in the Soviet Union, as well as Czechs such as Pavel Kohout and Ludvik Vaculík. Havel's play has a firm place in this body of work, yet it retains its distinctness through his use of characteristic devices and his close attention to the formal complexities of language. Havel requires that the accepted meanings, sounds, and visual forms of language be appreciated, so that the failure of language can be attributed not to a failure of idealism but to a failure of common sense in its social uses. In Havel's plays, such as *The Garden Party*, there always seems to be a human ground on which genuine communication could be constructed, if only people would make a commitment to mean what they say, and to care enough to listen to one another. They rarely do so in *The Garden Party*, but the disjunctures are less a cause for real concern than a source of delight.

Sources for Further Study

Goetz-Stankiewicz, Markéta. *The Silenced Theatre: Czech Playwrights Without a Stage.* Buffalo, N.Y.: University of Toronto Press, 1979.

_____, ed. *The Vanek Plays: Four Authors, One Character.* Vancouver: University of British Columbia Press, 1987.

Havel, Václav. *Letters to Olga: June 1979-September 1982.* Translated by Paul Wilson. New York: Knopf, 1988.

Kriseova, Eda. *Václav Havel: The Authorized Biography.* Collingdale, Pa.: Diane, 1998.

Trensky, Paul. *Czech Drama Since World War II.* White Plains, N.Y.: M. E. Sharpe, 1978.

Vladislav, Jan, ed. *Václav Havel: Or, Living in Truth.* London: Faber, 1987.

Michael L. Quinn

GEMINI

Author: Albert Innaurato (1948-   )
Type of plot: Comedy
Time of plot: The 1970's
Locale: South Philadelphia's Italian section
First produced: 1976, at the Playwrights Horizon, New York City
First published: 1977

> *Principal characters:*
> FRAN GEMINIANI, an overweight, forty-five-year-old working-
> class single father
> FRANCIS GEMINIANI, his overweight and insecure son, a senior at
> Harvard University
> LUCILLE POMPI, his lady friend
> BUNNY WEINBERGER, his blowsy, heavy drinking neighbor
> HERSCHEL WEINBERGER, her overweight teenage son
> JUDITH HASTINGS, Francis's beautiful Harvard classmate
> RANDY HASTINGS, Judith's brother, a Harvard freshman

The Play

This two-act comedy is set in the adjoining backyards of two dysfunctional South Philadelphia families. Young Francis Geminiani is at home during his last summer before beginning his senior year at Harvard. An overweight outsider who has never had a deep relationship with anyone, he is alienated from his lower-class father and their environment and appears to find solace only in his collection of opera recordings, which he plays for escape.

Classmates from Harvard, Judith and Randy Hastings, arrive over the backyard fence to pay Francis a surprise visit. The brother and sister set up a tent in the Geminianis' backyard so they can help Francis celebrate his coming of age on his twenty-first birthday. The attractive Hastings siblings are from a well-off Boston family, and Francis is embarrassed by his lower-class Italian American environment. Coupled with this awkwardness, Francis fears that he is becoming infatuated with Randy rather than Judith, who is in love with him.

The personal equation is made more complicated by the addition of a sixteen-year-old Jewish neighbor from next door, Herschel Weinberger. Herschel is a younger, exaggerated version of Francis, echoing the overweight Francis's awkwardness but having an obsession with the subway system instead of opera. Herschel is also smitten with Randy because the Harvard freshman has shown a modicum of interest in his extensive collection of subway transfers. Bunny, Herschel's drunken widow mother, is not above throwing herself at Francis's father, Fran. Despite having had a fling with Bunny, Fran is now having a relationship with Lucille Pompi, an Italian woman who lives in the neighborhood.

The Hastings have ostensibly come to learn whether Francis has lost his feelings for Judith. Francis is at a critical point in his development, as he stands on the cusp of manhood. He loathes himself and wants nothing more than to be left alone with his opera recordings. The body of this seriocomic play is structured around echoing themes rather than traditional plot development. In one of its subplots, the pathetic boozer Bunny tries in vain to rekindle the flame Fran had for her in the past. When he refuses to respond, she attempts suicide in a manner reminiscent of Anton Chekhov's most ineffectual characters by climbing a telephone pole and threatening to jump. The poignancy of the scene is amplified by Herschel's desperate attempt to talk her down from the pole. He pathetically promises to stop having seizures, to take gym class, to burn his subway transfer collection, and to give up his love of the subway.

Fran's own character frailties are revealed through his health problems. The overweight father has emphysema and a persistent rash that he continuously scratches. His most surprising trait is the unusually high regard he has for his first wife. Even though years earlier she abandoned him and her son, Fran does not appear to harbor any ill feeling toward her. He recalls that she "had enough of both of us" and took off for the South, "like a bird [who] had too much of winter. Met a nice Southern man." The kind of legacy that Fran is passing on to his son becomes clear when he continues, "Francis and me, well we stand out. Don't wanna, understand, but we talk too loud, cough, scratch ourselves, get rashes, are kinda big. You have to notice us. Don' have to like us but you gotta see us." The emotionally damaged but well-meaning Fran continues to warp his son's vision of morality by offering a piece of advice he

> learned from the army, from dealin' wit your mother and from twenty years in the Printers' Union: Take wit both hands, both feet and your mouth too. If your ass is flexible enough take wit that, use your knees and your elbows, train your balls and take! *Prend'-cabisce?* Somebody offers you somethin', you take it, then run. . . .

Additional character eccentricities are revealed in the manner in which Lucille refuses to use a supper plate during a meal. She does, however, hover over all the guests, using her fork to eat off other's plates and generally making a nuisance of herself.

After considerable indecision, Francis finally appears to make up his mind to have a sexual experience with Randy. When Randy fails to respond positively, they are left in an awkward situation that is made even more painful when Judith discovers them embracing as she returns to the backyard unannounced. This odd mix of emotions is exactly what Innaurato wanted to depict for his characters. Judith could not be more befuddled as she discovers herself cuckolded by her brother and lover.

Francis's birthday celebration comes to a climax when the deeply confused young man sarcastically thanks everyone for their contributions to his emotional quandary. He thanks his father for teaching him "how to dance and sing and cough and fart and scratch and above all how to treat a rash once it becomes visible." He thanks Bunny "for demonstrating once and for all that motherhood ought to be abolished"; Randy, "for providing us with living proof of the vacuity of American Higher Education";

and Judith, for reciting "in her main-line Italian all the nonsense syllables of her up-bringing and her recent reading." Francis ends his verbal assault with a physical attack on the birthday cake, hurling it at all the celebrants and running offstage.

After the Hastingses have left for the train station, Francis seems to summon up his courage while listening to opera music and prepares to follow them to Boston. When the brother and sister make a rather fortuitous return, Francis embraces Judith, having made his major life choice without fully sharing his reasoning with the audience.

Themes and Meanings

Gemini, as the title (the constellation representing the twins Castor and Pollux) suggests, is constructed around a continuous set of dualities. Whether one examines the play in its entirety or in subtle nuances, it is clear that Innaurato contrasts a world of opposites. The play emphasizes an environment of the grotesque, albeit one with counterpoints from the sublime. Not only are most of the people relatively unattractive, but also the setting is an undecorated backyard of lower-class America. In contrast to this world, Innaurato introduces two attractive people: Judith is described as "intimidatingly beautiful" and Randy as "a very handsome WASP." Innaurato also uses Francis's opera recordings to underscore scenes and contrast the beauty of the opera world with the tawdry environment of South Philadelphia.

Gemini's meaning is capable of many interpretations. In an afterword to a published version of the play, Innaurato states that although some people question the play's ending, he sees it neither as a "cop out" nor as "affirming heterosexuality as a lifestyle chosen by the hero at the ninth hour." Moreover, he adds that he does not mean the reverse as true, either, "nor is the ending meant to be ironic, or to parody affirmative endings." He goes on to argue that the meaning of the play's ending "is transparent: a young man who is in the main heterosexual . . . but who has had some self-doubts . . . elects to continue a more or less successful relationship with a girl to whom he is well suited, and who is well suited to him." He sees the ending as happy because "Francis chooses to work with a realistic situation, despite possible problems, rather than chasing off after a potentially destructive fantasy."

To many critics, however, *Gemini*'s ending feels contrived, and they regard it as the creation of a savvy playwright who wants his play to be popular and commercially successful.

Dramatic Devices

One of the most important devices in *Gemini* is its use of a backyard environment for its setting. The play not only uses the back stoops of neighboring houses, but it also sets some of its action inside the Geminianis' kitchen and bedrooms. How much audiences actually see inside the house is a matter for individual directors and scene designers to determine; however, certain actions must be seen as happening within the privacy of the house.

Innaurato faces the difficult problem of trying to manipulate seven characters somewhat realistically in and out of his multifocal environment. The setting is further complicated with the erection of a tent by the visiting Hastingses. Not only does the tent sit in the middle of the backyard, but also it provides a hiding place for the sexual experimentation of the characters. Other critical moments are partially hidden from view as the audience voyeuristically looks through the window of Francis's bedroom.

At one dramatic moment, Bunny threatens suicide by climbing up a telephone pole and leaping from the back wall to the ground. The semipublic nature of this backyard setting is perfect for allowing two different families the opportunity realistically to intermingle and interact. Moreover, the setting's ability to provide a logical cross-roads for fast-moving disparate actions contributes to the play's success. Whether the characters are eating meals, celebrating a birthday, or experimenting with sex, the Geminianis' backyard is an effective place for the action to unfold.

Critical Context

It is generally agreed that Innaurato's two best plays are *Gemini* and *The Transfiguration of Benno Blimpie* (pr. 1973, pb. 1976). They were his first plays produced in New York City, and both won Obie Awards in 1977. Like *Gemini*, the latter play is built around an overweight and insecure Italian American character, who narrates his story while seated on a stool apart from the main acting area. Many critics agree that Innaurato has a gift for drawing vividly grotesque characters and placing them in theatrical environments. However, there is also broad agreement that he has not grown beyond his early promise. Moreover, many gay critics have found his work overly ambiguous in its presentation of sexuality.

Innaurato's later plays have not enjoyed the popularity with audiences or critical success of his earlier work, and he had no significant productions during the 1990's. Nevertheless, he continues to be remembered for his first two New York productions, which established his place as an important contemporary dramatist.

Sources for Further Study

Freedman, Samuel G. "Reshaping a Play to Reveal Its True Nature." *New York Times*, February 24, 1985, p. B1.

Innaurato, Albert. "An Interview with Albert Innaurato." Interview by John Louis DiGaetani. *Studies in American Drama, 1945-Present* 2 (1987): 87-95.

_____. Introduction to *Bizarre Behavior: Six Plays*. New York: Avon Books, 1980.

Lester, Elenore. "Innaurato: His Passion for Outcasts Is Finding a Place on Stage." *New York Times*, May 27, 1977, p. B4.

Ventimiglia, Peter James. "Recent Trends in American Drama: Michael Cristofer, David Mamet, and Albert Innaurato." *Journal of American Culture* 1 (Spring, 1978): 195-204.

Mike Barton

GEOGRAPHY OF A HORSE DREAMER
A Mystery in Two Acts

Author: Sam Shepard (Samuel Shepard Rogers, 1943-   )
Type of plot: Suspense
Time of plot: The 1970's
Locale: England
First produced: 1974, at the Royal Court Theatre Upstairs, London
First published: 1974

> *Principal characters:*
> CODY, a clairvoyant
> SANTEE and
> BEAUJO, small-time criminals
> FINGERS, their boss, a gambler
> THE DOCTOR, his lieutenant

The Play

    Geography of a Horse Dreamer begins in darkness. The audience hears the sound of galloping horses, at first faint, then growing stronger. A slow-motion color film of a horse race, gradually brought into focus, is projected on the rear wall; as the picture sharpens, the sound becomes louder. There is a yell, the film stops, and the lights come up, revealing a run-down hotel room. Against the rear wall, Cody, dressed in jeans and a cowboy shirt and wearing dark glasses, lies on his back in a bed, handcuffed to the bedposts; it was he who yelled. Santee, in dark coat and gangster-style hat, sits in a chair perusing the Racing Form, a pistol in his lap. Beaujo, wearing a wrinkled pinstriped suit from the 1940's, practices pool shots on the floor, equipped with a cue and three balls. By their dress and manner, Santee and Beaujo appear to be gangsters.

    Cody is gifted with a peculiar form of precognition. In his dreams he is able to "see" horse races before they actually happen; in his trancelike state he is the first to speak, calling out the results of a race in the manner of a trackside announcer. Later the audience learns that Cody was kidnapped by gamblers from his native Wyoming some time before the action of the play begins, and that for a while he was able to predict a steady succession of winners. By the time the play starts, however, he is mired in a long losing streak.

    The first act, "The Slump," is animated by a conflict between Cody's keepers. Santee, who blames Cody for their fallen fortunes, has no sympathy for Cody's pleas to be released from his handcuffs; he fears that Cody will try to escape, as he almost did once before, thereby depriving his abductors of their gold mine. Santee regards Cody as a dream machine, mocking his requests for time off by calling him "Mr. Artistic," "Mr. Sensitive." This resentment increases when the boss, Fingers, hands down orders (by means of an offstage telephone call) that Cody must start dreaming dog races instead of horse races—an order that Santee regards as the ultimate humiliation. Beaujo, on the other hand, is inclined to listen sympathetically to Cody's requests, even if he is afraid to grant them. Cody vainly pleads, for example, to be allowed to play his record: "It's a source of inspiration, Beaujo."

Above all, Cody insists that he needs to know where he is if he is to create the imaginative space needed for his dreaming. During this slump, his dreams have been dominated by the "Great Nature" and Great Plains of his native Wyoming. At Fingers's orders, Cody has been kept isolated, ignorant of his surroundings; he does not even know in what country he is. The turning point of the first act occurs when Beaujo gives him a few clues as to their location. Not long afterward, Cody's gift returns, and the first act concludes with the voice-over of an announcer calling an actual race that vindicates Cody's prediction.

Act 2, "The Hump," opens in darkness with another film clip, this time of a dog race. Again, the lights come up as Cody yells, revealing a fancy hotel room with the furniture arranged as it was in the first act. The characters are dressed as they were before, but their clothes are neat and new. Cody is back to picking winners, now dogs, and Santee and Beaujo's fortunes have risen with his. The strain of the dreaming is telling on Cody, however: He speaks with a slight Irish accent and talks to imaginary puppies as he leads them through a training routine.

The three of them are visited by Fingers and his lieutenant, the Doctor, complete with black bag. The ominous aspect of Fingers, the unseen boss of the first act, is undercut by the figure that appears onstage: Fingers is "tall, thin, and rather effete," according to the stage directions, and he affects a ludicrously poetic idiom: Upon seeing Cody, he exclaims, "I should have known he'd have the look of eagles," and he characterizes the momentous meeting as that of "the tail and head of a great dragon." Clearly, he wants others to regard him as a sensitive, cultivated, perhaps artistic fellow. The Doctor—who, Shepard stipulates, should look like the rotund "heavy" Sydney Greenstreet—is a caricature of the bad scientist. Ruthless, diabolical, he obviously has the upper hand.

Like the first act, act 2 turns on a conflict between two of Cody's keepers; here, the Doctor and Fingers. When Fingers becomes aware of Cody's disturbed condition, he announces that he will personally escort the dreamer back to Wyoming and seems to relish the prospect of returning to the great West as much as Cody did in act 1. The Doctor, who has been staring at a television with the sound turned down, responds with a blood-curdling yell and throws Fingers across the room; Cody yelps like a wounded animal. The Doctor tells Santee to fetch his bag.

Some of the dreamer's power, the Doctor explains to Santee and Beaujo, accumulates in a bone in the back of the neck. He has in his bag a collection of such bones, the efficacy of which can be restored by the addition of a fresh bone from the right dreamer. With Santee's help, the Doctor is just slicing into Cody's neck with his scalpel when the playwright's *deus ex machina* comes to the rescue in the form of Cody's strapping cowboy brothers, Jasper and Jason, never so much as mentioned before their dramatic entrance. They kill the Doctor and Santee and the hapless Beaujo with their shotgun blasts. After they leave with Cody, a waiter (summoned earlier) enters to discover the carnage. At Fingers's request, the waiter puts Cody's mysterious record on the turntable. Here the stage directions specify a particular track from a particular recording by the Zydeco artist Clifton Chenier. With that, the play ends, and "the music continues as the audience leaves."

Themes and Meanings

Geography of a Horse Dreamer is a play about the making of art and the problems of the artist. In many respects Cody fits the familiar model of the Romantic artist: a genius, a seer. He possesses a gift that sets him apart from others, and the exercise of that gift, once a matter of effortless inspiration, now requires conscious labor.

On one level, the entire play—the stage space, the action, the characters—can be seen as a metaphor for the artist's mind. The parallels that Sam Shepard draws between particular characters and various aspects of the process of making and selling art ("separate from each other and yet connected," as the Doctor says) correspond to the conflicts experienced by artists who make a living by their art, especially the playwright, who is paid to put his or her dreams onstage and under public scrutiny. Cody is both misunderstood and exploited; much of the play is given to sketching the spectrum of responses an artist can expect to encounter, from Santee's contempt to Beaujo's clumsy faith to the clinical, businesslike analysis of the Doctor, who may be the playwright's image of the typical drama critic. Fingers's curious connection with Cody—his artistic affectations, his sympathy for the dreamer, his regret that he did not anticipate Cody's disintegration and do something about it long ago, and his attempt to return with Cody to the great outdoors—suggests the divisive effect of these conflicts. Understood as a dream, a "mindscape" or the "geography of a horse dreamer," Shepard's play, especially with its deliberately contrived ending, points to itself as a work of art about the "work" of art.

Such portraits of the artist and the process of art-making are vulnerable to narcissism and self-pity. Shepard largely avoids these pitfalls by presenting Cody in a decidedly unheroic light: It is a long way from the frescoes of the Sistine Chapel to Cody's dreams of dog races, and Cody himself is essentially a passive figure. The play's humor, too, especially the strong element of parody, helps to keep pretentiousness at bay; this humor, along with the suspense and mystery surrounding first Fingers and then the Doctor, sustains audience interest and makes the play work as straight entertainment. Still, it is important to note that Shepard does not ultimately debunk the Romantic image of the artist; on the contrary, he endorses it. This commitment to the visionary power of art distinguishes *Geography of a Horse Dreamer* from most products of the contemporary theater.

Dramatic Devices

Geography of a Horse Dreamer directs the playgoer's attention to the interior experience of the artist through a variety of dramatic devices that invite metaphoric as well as literal interpretation by the audience. At the beginning of the play, for example, the film clip of the horse race is Cody's dream, which becomes evident to the audience as soon as Cody yells, the film goes off, and the lights onstage "bang up." Having established a connection between Cody's mind, on one hand, and the "external" stage setting (and the characters that populate that setting), on the other, Shepard has linked the play's "geography" with that of the artist's mind—both Cody the dreamer's and Shepard the playwright's.

This correlation is immediately sustained and strengthened by the focus of the first act's dialogue—Cody's need to know where he is and his keepers' refusal to inform him—undergirded by metaphors of place that objectify the artist's interior experience: Cody says that he needs a "better situation," that Fingers does not understand "the area I have to dream in," that Fingers fails to consider his "position." Beaujo, after hinting where they are, fears that he has "overstepped his bounds" and later accounts for his sympathetic treatment of Cody: "I keep putting myself in his place." The Doctor notes that "the territory [Cody] travels in" allows him to live "in several worlds at the same time." The pervasiveness of this imagery makes it difficult to overlook, but at the same time it is never heavy-handed: Shepard's procedure is to use idiomatic metaphors that custom has robbed of their force and take them literally, without detracting from the drama's realism. It is customary, for example, to speak of poetic "inspiration"—that is, a kind of spirit possession. Shepard revives this dead metaphor in the second act: As Cody's gift returns, the stage directions specify, he "talks with another voice; slightly Irish, as though he's been inhabited by a spirit."

The geography motif repeats itself in the play's symmetrical structure: Each act mirrors the other, down to the film openings, stage settings, and costuming. There is only one significant difference: In the second act, the furnishings are luxurious and the clothes are new. As a result, the second act seems to occur in the same "place" as the first act, and in fact it does, both metaphorically (in the dreamer's mind) and, from the playwright's perspective, literally (on the stage). The exact geographical location of the events remains as much a mystery to the audience as it is to Cody, and is correspondingly insignificant.

Equally effective is Shepard's oblique humor: Just as he objectifies the metaphors of place, so he takes the artist's plight so literally that potential tragedy is undercut by comedy. "Taking literally" is one of comedy's most reliable devices. The whole conception of Cody-the-artist is so literal that it is comic. Here the nature of theater as performance is vital. Thematically, the opening tableau shows the powerless artist as a victim. As a theater image, however—Cody handcuffed to the bed in a cruciform position—it is comically exaggerated. This tension between theme and image, which runs throughout *Geography of a Horse Dreamer*, keeps the audience entertained. Without it, the play would be an exercise in self-absorbed didacticism.

Critical Context

Geography of a Horse Dreamer is one of many plays in which Shepard makes use of the conventions of genre fiction and their cinematic counterparts. In *Geography of a Horse Dreamer* the plot and the characters are largely drawn from the crime thriller, while the climactic rescue of Cody is straight from the Western. *The Tooth of Crime* (pr. 1972, pb. 1974), Shepard's first play to receive major critical acclaim, is a verbal duel between an aging rock star and his challenger; this tour de force incorporates many elements of the classic Western showdown, but it also features a futuristic setting and other trappings of science fiction. An earlier play, *The Unseen Hand* (pr., pb. 1969), brings together an improbably named alien, Willie, and the outlaw Morphan brothers, resurrected from the Old West's Jameses and Daltons. In *Back Bog Beast Bait* (pr., pb. 1971), a pair of bounty hunters tangle with the occult, another of Shepard's favorite sources for motifs. *Suicide in B Flat* (pr. 1976, pb. 1979) could be described as an off-the-rails police procedural that draws on occult or horror fiction and the espionage genre.

Shepard's use of these popular genres is distinctive and many-sided. They provide a loose structure that permits him to pursue dreamlike associations without lapsing into incoherence. Often, as in *Geography of a Horse Dreamer*, they create a mood of humorous incongruity, evidence that the playwright does not take himself too seriously. *Suicide in B Flat*, for example, is, like *Geography of a Horse Dreamer*, a play about a tortured artist; it is also very amusing. These conventions serve Shepard and his audience as a common language; they are the stuff of his homemade American mythology, the equivalent of the classical myths and stories that sustained centuries of European drama. What is most impressive, however, is the brazen assurance of Shepard's raids on popular art. Rarely does he restrict himself in a given play to borrowing from a single genre; he often combines elements from wildly disparate sources (science fiction and the Western, for example) with an imaginative exuberance that belies the generally grim messages of his plays.

In his work since the late 1970's, Shepard has taken a new direction. In plays such as *Buried Child* (pr. 1978, pb. 1979), for which he received a Pulitzer Prize, *True West* (pr. 1980, pb. 1981), *Fool for Love* (pr., pb. 1983), and *A Lie of the Mind* (pr. 1985, pb. 1986), he has explored the dynamics of family life: the grotesque but unavoidable spiritual deformations, but also the redeeming power of love. Some critics have applauded this shift toward domestic realism, seeing it as evidence of a maturing engagement with perennial human concerns; others see a loss of the qualities that made his earlier work so memorable. There is general agreement, however, that Shepard—who is a much-praised actor, screenwriter, and film director as well—is one of the leading playwrights of his generation.

Sources for Further Study

Bigsby, C. W. E. "Sam Shepard." In *Beyond Broadway*. Vol. 3 in *A Critical Introduction to Twentieth-Century American Drama*. New York: Cambridge University Press, 1985.

Brustein, Robert. "The Shepard Enigma." *The New Republic* 194 (January 27, 1986): 25-28.

DeRose, David J. *Sam Shepard*. New York: Twayne, 1992.

Herman, William. "Geography of a Play Dreamer: Sam Shepard." In *Understanding Contemporary American Drama*. Columbia: University of South Carolina Press, 1987.

King, Kimball. *Sam Shepard: A Casebook*. New York: Garland, 1988.

Marranca, Bonnie, ed. *American Dreams: The Imagination of Sam Shepard*. New York: Performing Arts Journal, 1981.

Sessums, Kevin. "Sam Shepard: *Geography of a Horse Dreamer*." *Interview* 18 (September, 1988): 70-79.

Wilcox, Leonard. *Rereading Shepard*. Basingstoke, England: MacMillan, 1993.

John Wilson

GETTING OUT

Author: Marsha Norman (Marsha Williams, 1947-   )
Type of plot: Psychological
Time of plot: The late 1970's, with flashbacks to the previous twenty years
Locale: Louisville, Kentucky, and places in Arlene's memory
First produced: 1977, at the Actors Theatre of Louisville, Louisville, Kentucky
First published: 1979

> *Principal characters:*
> ARLENE, a recent parolee in her late twenties
> ARLIE, Arlene at various times earlier in her life
> BENNIE, a prison guard
> MOTHER, Arlene's mother
> CARL, Arlene's former pimp
> RUBY, Arlene's upstairs neighbor, an ex-convict

The Play

After serving an eight-year prison sentence for second-degree murder, Arlene enters a dingy apartment in Louisville, Kentucky, to begin her first twenty-four hours on parole. In the course of her first day home, she is visited by four people: Bennie, her sentimental former jailer, who tries to convince Arlene that she needs his help to adjust to life outside prison; her mother, blind to her daughter's struggle to put the past behind her; Carl, a pimp and former partner in numerous crimes, who tries to entice Arlene back to the streets; and Ruby, an ex-convict, who helps Arlene cope with her new life without demanding anything in return.

Arlene's most persistent visitor is her memory of Arlie, her raging younger self, played by a different actor. Arlie's appearance is triggered by the people who come to visit and remind Arlene of the person she once was. The past and the present move forward on two simultaneous tracks: Arlene's struggle through her first day home and Arlie's transformation from a young hellion to a desperate inmate praying for a way out of confinement.

When act 1 begins, Bennie has driven Arlene from the Alabama prison to Louisville, and he plans to settle in town. As Arlene's jailer, he has watched her for eight years, and now he tries to convince her that she needs his help. Arlene, however, distances herself from Bennie, because he is a reminder of the past she is trying to forget. Bennie's visit triggers Arlene's first memory of Arlie, who appears in a series of short interwoven scenes. The audience witnesses Arlie picking up a soldier in a bar, defying a policeman after an apparent burglary, demanding that a prison guard clean up the dinner she threw on the floor, and setting her blouse on fire in her prison cell.

When her mother comes to visit, Arlene reluctantly admits her. As her mother begins to clean the apartment, Arlene presses her for information about her son Joey, asks if she can come for Sunday dinner, and repeatedly has to remind her mother that she is "Arlene," not Arlie, now. The mother recoils from her daughter's attempts to reach out to her and blames her for the trouble she has caused. When the mother finds a man's hat under the bed, she accuses Arlene of returning to prostitution and walks out on her. Her mother spurs Arlene's memory, and Arlie appears. She defends her abusive father and pleads with her mother to believe that it was really a fall from her bike that hurt her.

Carl is the next visitor. When Arlene refuses to open the door for him, he breaks it down. Carl tries to entice Arlene into resuming their former alliance, and she struggles to resist him. Bennie returns with dinner and forces Carl to retreat. Carl leaves with a warning that he will return. Arlene tells Bennie of her hopes for her son, Joey. This triggers the appearance of Arlie, alone in her cell, where she talks to an imaginary child and promises to protect him. Bennie offers to stay the night. When Arlene resists his advances, he attempts to overpower her. She forces him to confront the fact that he is trying to rape her. Denying that he is a rapist, Bennie backs down. Arlene tells Bennie that Arlie would have killed him.

Act 2 begins the next morning, in Arlene's apartment; she is asleep. Simultaneously, the lights come up on Arlie in a maximum security cell, venting her rage at an unseen officer. Back in the apartment, a loud siren wakes Arlene with a start. She begins her morning activities and struggles to put the past behind her. Ruby, the upstairs neighbor, bangs on the door and demands money owed her by the previous tenant. Arlene explains that her sister vacated the apartment and left nothing behind. Ruby, herself an ex-con, understands Arlene's predicament. She tells a story of her first days of freedom. In frustration, she heaved a gallon of milk out the window. When it bounced, it gave her hope.

Ruby encourages Arlene to apply for a job as a dishwasher and invites her upstairs for a game of cards. After Arlene resists both ideas, Ruby returns to her apartment and Arlene leaves for the grocery store. Ruby's show of kindness triggers Arlene's memory of Doris Creech, an inmate who tried to molest her. In a short scene Arlie threatens Doris and attacks an unseen authority for not seeing what Doris was trying to do to her.

Arlene returns from the store and spills all the groceries. Upset, she throws the pickle loaf to the floor; it does not bounce. Her frustration ignites the memory of Arlie in maximum security. Arlie reads the Bible that the prison chaplain gave her and cries out in desperation. When no one responds, her spirit breaks.

Carl returns to Arlene's apartment. He promises easy money, leisure, and Joey's respect. (Carl does not know that Joey is his son.) Arlene tries to make him see that she has changed, but he denigrates her efforts to improve herself. She tells Carl that she does not want to return to prison. Throughout this scene, Arlie is seen praying in her cell—a memory that gives Arlene strength. When Ruby enters, Carl backs off. He leaves after handing Arlene a matchbox with the name of a bar written on it, expecting her to meet him there. She tries to resist the pull that Carl still has on her. Ruby points out to her that in a straight job, "when you make your two nickels, you can keep both of 'em."

Arlene is overcome with the memory of her final period of time in prison, and Arlie appears. When she learns that the chaplain will not be coming back, she cries out for his return. Arlene explains to Ruby that the chaplain was an inspiration to her. He helped her to believe that she could be freed of the vicious part of herself and be loved by God. Arlene describes her attempted suicide. She implores Ruby to understand that in her desperation it was the only way that she could be free of the hateful part of herself still raging within. Arlene breaks down and begs forgiveness. Ruby, understanding Arlene's need to reconcile herself with the person she was, comforts her.

Bennie, bearing plants as a peace offering, returns to the apartment. He restates his desire to help Arlene and leaves a phone number scratched on a piece of paper. When he leaves, Arlene tries to decide between Carl's matchbook and Bennie's piece of paper. She throws the matchbook away. Before Ruby leaves, Arlene accepts her offer of a game of cards.

Arlene is left alone in the apartment. Arlie appears, telling a story of revenge on her mother. In a shared moment of delight, Arlie and Arlene imitate their mother, and Arlene smiles at the memory. The stage goes black except for a light on Arlene's face. Arlie laughs once again.

Themes and Meanings

Getting Out is a play about the difficulty of shedding the past and beginning a new life. The fluidity with which the play moves in and out of memory reinforces the omnipotence of the past. The past is felt both in the progress of Arlie's transformation while still in prison and in Arlene's struggle for self-determination during her first day home. Arlie is the embodiment of Arlene's past, a permanent reminder of the part of her that she has tried so hard to tame.

Arlene's memory is dramatized to give understanding to the present. The seeds of her rage are introduced in act 1: She is molested by her father, neglected by her mother, and pronounced hopeless by the school principal. She is bullied and betrayed by peers, denigrated and threatened by prison officials. Arlie fights back, brutally and without remorse.

The audience witnesses a change in Arlie in act 2. The birth of her son Joey gives Arlie the desire to seek a way out of prison life. A prison chaplain, the first to call her Arlene, gives her the belief that change is possible. When the prison authorities take Joey away from her and she is told that the chaplain will no longer be coming back, her desire to find a way out of confinement intensifies. Furthermore, getting out no longer means simply getting out of jail—Arlie now associates "getting out" with gaining freedom from the hateful part of herself.

Arlene looks to the Bible for a means of redemption. When no one responds to her cries for help, her spirit breaks. She attempts suicide in order to exorcise the violent part of her. Arlene remembers a change after recuperating from her suicide attempt. People were nicer to her. She accepted responsibility. She changed her name to Arlene.

Her rehabilitation has been fragile. In her first twenty-four hours out of prison, the memory of the person she once was still haunts her. The people who visit Arlene know her as Arlie, and they behave as though nothing has happened. She repeatedly has to remind Bennie, her mother, and Carl that she is different, that she is Arlene now. Arlene is a victim—of a criminal family, her own crimes, and the brutal environment of the state institutions where she was confined. Both her mother and Carl believe her incapable of change, and both are coldly indifferent to her desire to improve herself.

Ruby tries to help Arlene cope with her new life: She encourages Arlene to reject Carl, come to terms with her attempted suicide, and reconcile her past with her present. As an ex-con, Ruby knows that prisons are everywhere, and she urges Arlene to accept the impossibility of absolute freedom. In *Getting Out*, prison life is a metaphor for a past that will not go away. At the end of the play, however, as Arlene and Arlie smile at the same story, reconciliation with the past seems possible.

Dramatic Devices

Getting Out incorporates a variety of dramatic devices to dramatize the interior struggle of a woman trying to reconcile her past and present. Arlene's past life is enacted by a second actor who appears in a chain of flashbacks throughout the play. Arlie is "the violent kid Arlene was until her last stretch in prison." Arlie makes it possible to move the play forward and backward in time to reveal the sources of Arlie's rage and her desperate need for change.

The author's specifications for the setting create a present permanently surrounded by the past. A prison cell, a catwalk, and other playing areas that represent the past surround Arlene's "dingy one-room apartment." As the author notes, "the apartment must seem imprisoned." The bars in Arlene's apartment window and the bars in Arlie's prison cell visually link past to present. The set never changes. Arlie's movement throughout the set allows the audience to see the ease with which the past intrudes upon the present. The specifications for lighting in the script suggest that the simultaneous existence of Arlie and Arlene should be sharply focused.

Sometimes the past follows the present sequentially. At the beginning of the play Bennie is carrying Arlene's luggage up the steps to her apartment. He shouts "Arlie!" to Arlene on the stairs above, and in an instant the light comes up on Arlie as a violent kid telling the story of her revenge on the boy next door. In other scenes, past and present are interwoven. In a moment when Arlene is trying to convince Carl of her commitment to get "real work," Arlie appears again and revives Arlene's fears of a life of prostitution.

The language of *Getting Out* draws the audience into the world of the play. Set in the playwright's own hometown of Louisville, Kentucky, the play is written with an authoritative sense of color and authenticity. The regional dialect is subtly suggested in the dialogue, and it is specified that both Arlie and Arlene speak with a country twang. The playwright's use of dark humor not only helps support the characters and the setting but also helps to relieve the harsh brutality that surrounds them.

The use of disembodied sound effectively creates a mood of isolation and terror. Both acts open with a prison loudspeaker droning announcements of the day's activities; the loudspeaker depicts the depersonalization and the relentless regimentation of prison life. The siren that awakens Arlene in act 2 and the loud knocking of the people who come to see her heighten the sense that the world outside is threatening. The climax of the play is Arlie's attempted suicide, which is not shown but told. Telling the story encourages the audience to focus less on the event itself than on its impact on Arlene now that she is out on parole.

The denouement brings past and present together. Only the faces of Arlie and Arlene are seen. When Arlie tells the story of her revenge on her mother and Arlene smiles at the memory, the audience sees that Arlene is now able to gain strength from the rebellious spirit that she was not able to kill. Arlene can at last make peace with Arlie, if only on a moment-by-moment basis.

Critical Context

Getting Out anticipated many of the themes that would characterize Marsha Norman's later plays. In the years immediately following the success of *Getting Out*, she wrote *Third and Oak* (pr. 1978, pb. 1985), about two women in a Laundromat and two men in the pool hall next door who are forced to shed their illusions about the people they love, and *The Hold-up* (pr. 1980, pb. 1987), which charts the liberation of a young farmworker who finds a way to break free of his northern New Mexico home.

'night, Mother is Marsha Norman's best-known play. It was her first to be performed on Broadway (in 1982), and it won the Pulitzer Prize in 1983. Like Arlene in *Getting Out*, Jessie in *'night, Mother* must sever her ties with the past in order to assert her right to self-determination. Unlike Arlene, Jessie can only take control of her life by ending it. *Getting Out* reflects the growing influence of women playwrights as they tackle controversial subjects. The support of regional theaters, national and private foundations, and the feminist movement did much to nurture women writers in the late 1970's and the 1980's, both in New York and in regional theaters around the country.

Getting Out received national recognition rare for a first play. It was co-winner of the Actors Theatre of Louisville Great American Play contest for 1977 and won the Oppenheimer/Newsday Award. It also won the Outer Critics Circle's John Gassner Playwriting Medallion, and the American Theatre Critics Association cited it as the outstanding new play produced outside New York during the 1977-1978 season. In 1979, *The Burns Mantle Theatre Yearbook* featured it as one of the best plays of the New York season.

Sources for Further Study

Brown, Linda Ginter, ed. *Marsha Norman: A Casebook*. New York: Garland, 1996.
Chinoy, Helen Krich, and Linda Walsh Jenkins. "Where Are the Women Playwrights?" In *Women in American Theater*, edited by Helen Krich Chinoy and Linda Walsh Jenkins. New York: Theatre Communications Group, 1987.
Gussow, Mel. "Women Playwrights: New Voices in the Theatre." *New York Times Magazine*, May 1, 1983, pp. 22-34.

Murray, Timothy. "Patriarchal Panopticism: Or, The Seduction of a Bad Joke— *Getting Out* in Theory." *Theatre Journal* 35 (October, 1983): 376-388.

Rubik, Margaret. "A Sisterhood of Women: Marsha Norman's *Getting Out* and *The Laundromat.*" *Gramma: Journal of Theory and Criticism*, 1994, 141-147.

Savran, Bruce. "Marsha Norman." In *In Their Own Words: Contemporary American Playwrights*. New York: Theatre Communications Group, 1988.

Schroeder, Patricia R. "Locked Behind the Proscenium: Feminist Strategies in *Getting Out* and *My Sister in This House.*" *Feminist Theatre and Theory*. New York: St. Martin's Press, 1996.

Weales, Gerald. "*Getting Out:* A New American Playwright." *Commonweal* 106 (October 12, 1979): 559-560.

Marilyn Plotkins

THE GOAT
Or, Who Is Sylvia?

Author: Edward Albee (1928-   )
Type of plot: Absurdist
Time of plot: The early twenty-first century
Locale: Inside an American suburban home and a farm in the Midwest
First produced: 2002, at the John Golden Theatre, New York City
First published: 2002

> *Principal characters:*
> MARTIN, an architect
> STEVIE, his wife
> BILLY, their son
> ROSS, a family friend and television journalist

The Play

The play *The Goat* begins during the week in which Martin, a successful architect who is happily married and the father of a college-age son, turns fifty. In the same week, the audience learns, Martin has also received the equivalent of the Pulitzer Prize in architecture, the Pritzger Prize, and, in addition, he has just been commissioned to design a multibillion-dollar city of the future to be erected in the fields of the Midwest. Martin's oldest friend Ross, a television journalist, is about to tape an at-home interview with Martin in his tasteful abode. Before the taping, Martin appears nervous and forgetful; he cannot recall the names of friends or the origins of the business cards he finds in his coat pocket. He chats with his wife, Stevie, and in casual conversation lets slip the comment that he is having an affair with a goat. She laughs, assuming he is making a jest, and responds that she will stop by the feed store on her way home.

Stevie leaves for a hair appointment and the taping begins, but the interview quickly becomes a futile endeavor; Martin is distracted and uncooperative. Once the camera is turned off, however, Ross and Martin talk as intimate friends, and the cause of Martin's behavior is revealed. Martin tells Ross that he and Stevie have bought a farm, a second home to enhance their stable, wonderful, long-term marriage, one in which there has been no desire to be unfaithful on either side in the nearly twenty-five years they have been together. However, Martin tells Ross, on this farm there is a goat, a goat with eyes that have captivated Martin and evoked in him a passion that has led to his first extra-marital love affair, one that has been going on for nearly six months.

Ross is understandably appalled by this revelation, and, on the surface at least, believing he is helping his friend, writes a note to Stevie. The climactic confrontation that follows forces Martin to confess, both to Stevie and to their son Billy, who is gay, that, indeed, the romance with the goat named Sylvia is no joke. Martin tries to ex-

plain, and Stevie tries to understand. Martin offers in his defense that this is his first affair and that he is still happily married, but there is his love for Sylvia to be dealt with.
Stevie's rage crackles in the air as she tries to process this strange confession. She
screams, throws a vase, upends furniture, and even destroys a painting in frustration,
and her emotionally intense, often sarcastic, dialogue reveals that she, unlike Martin,
fully recognizes the devastation of both her marriage and their life together that Martin's actions have wrought.

After initial outrage, anger, and resentment, Billy, with whom Martin has had a
good relationship despite the fact that he never understood Billy's sexual orientation,
manages to find understanding and forgiveness for his father's odd infidelity. In the
play's final scene, Ross appears to witness a moment of complex intimacy between
father and son, as Edward Albee dares to probe even more deeply into the confusing
intersections of love and sexuality. However, the audience is left to infer that Stevie is
a woman of action, and in tragic Greek fashion, this breaking of taboo demands a ritual sacrifice. The actual death of Sylvia is not shown on stage, but the horrifying result, and Martin's lonely cries at his total loss, linger as the audience is left to draw its
own conclusions about the fate of Martin and his family.

Themes and Meanings

Albee's version of the emotional ties within a family and the behavior of Ross,
Martin's "best" friend, suggest a bleak outlook for a society that reverts to primal instincts when threatened. Could any marriage withstand the test to which Martin puts
his? *The Goat* returns to the theme of the problems within a marriage that were brutally explored in Albee's play *Who's Afraid of Virginia Woolf?* (pr., pb. 1962), but it
makes the gender warfare between the warring couples in the earlier play seem like a
mere game.

Martin, the epitome of a good man, successful in every sense of the word, has ven-
tured somehow into a place where the morals he has lived by do not matter, and he
does not seem to understand why he should care. His "things happen" philosophy be-
speaks a moral indifference, and, in his view, he just cannot be held accountable for
his feelings or his actions in regard to Sylvia, the goat. This passion beyond reason
that Martin feels for Sylvia calls into question many aspects of the life that he has been
living, undermining its authenticity and creating the never-answered question of what
propelled him into this carnal compensation in the first place. Acceptance of this paradox is beyond the purview of any wife, the play suggests, and, despite Martin's previously good track record as a husband and provider, the marriage is irrevocably destroyed.

Elsewhere in this provocative play, Albee touches on familiar themes, such as the
myth of the American Dream and the hypocrisy of the striving American establishment, and on issues such as homophobia and disillusionment with people in power.
The fact that Martin's gay son Billy is able to empathize with his father's misplaced
passion suggests a certain commonality in their like-father, like-son rejection of a traditional heterosexual relationship. In addition, the duplicity of Martin's personality

suggests that identity is a fluid, rather than fixed, entity, one that can shift inexplicably, without discernible cause. *The Goat* is a puzzle not meant to be solved, but to provoke, challenge, and shock audiences into confronting social norms that constrain human behavior and define family relationships. At the same time, open-minded viewers might also find the absurdity of the situation quite amusing.

Dramatic Devices

As one might expect in an absurdist play, the premise and its outcome defy convention and break social taboos, yet simultaneously Albee manages to combine classical elements of both tragedy and comedy into this unlikely story. By taking human behavior to seldom-explored extremes, Albee moves questions relating to human passion and family bonds to what might be called logical absurdity. Martin's life is above reproach, yet he has fallen in love with a goat. His perversity is beyond controversy or debate, but at the same time, he is presented as a sympathetic character. In this manner, Martin portrays the most classic of tragic heroes, one whose tragic flaw, his inability to accept responsibility for his own actions, results in his fatal undoing. He cannot see the justice in the devastation that his affair brings to his life and to his family, and he fails to comprehend that he is a man who has lost his way.

The play moves from its opening scene of domestic comedy, one in which Martin might be considered to be dealing with a midlife crisis, to a black comedy, where Ross's betrayal of Martin's trust creates the pivotal climax, to the suburban American version of the Greek tragedy, complete with ritual sacrifice, a suggestion of incest, and uncertain outcome. Throughout the entire play, a not-too-subtle irony lurks in the background. For example, until the final scene, Sylvia the goat never appears onstage, but her existence, and Martin's love for her, drives the entire drama. Ironically, too, the setting, that of an immaculately decorated, perfectly maintained, upper-middle-class suburban home, the ideal for which most American couples strive, is not sufficient to sustain Martin or his marriage; he seems to find more meaning in his affair with the goat. In the classical city-versus-country dichotomy constructed by Albee, Martin wants both, but this duality of passion is impossible to sustain.

Critical Context

Most critics are quick to compare *The Goat* to Albee's renowned work *Who's Afraid of Virginia Woolf?*, but the points of reference are diverse. In both works, Albee deconstructs the American Dream, from Martin's ideal marriage to his highly successful career, but in *The Goat* the real source of that dissolution remains unclear. As Martin's world splinters, he is rejected by his family and betrayed by his best friend; this much is a typical Albee event. That Martin's genuine love for Sylvia, a goat, is tragically tainted, however, is atypical and nearly impossible to reconcile.

The dialogue in *The Goat* is crisp, witty, smart, and well considered, a classic characteristic of Albee's oeuvre, just one degree more articulate than actual conversation, even in the midst of Martin and Stevie's intense marital battles. It is the nature of an Albee play to be dense and not quite knowable, and *The Goat* presents an audience with one of his most profound conundrums. Moving from a comedy-of-manners opening capable of evoking laughter to a tragically poignant climax and a starkly horrific conclusion, the play has earned both lavish praise and vehement condemnation.

Given that Albee is a gay writer and that some of his works, such as *The Play About the Baby* (pr. 1998, pb. 2002), explore the philosophy that heterosexual relationships are necessarily suspect, some critics have observed that this theme may be a subtext of *The Goat*. While there is no overt suggestion in the play that latent homosexuality is behind Martin's now dysfunctional marriage, it is perhaps significant that Billy, the gay son, is the only one who can relate to Martin's dilemma. In addition, the veiled suggestion that Martin and Billy (as in billy goat) may have had some sort of incestuous episode in the past is alluded to near the end of the play.

In addition, the fact that Martin's male best friend Ross provides the note that ultimately brings the marriage to an end might also complicate the nature of their relationship and muddy the already dark waters of motivation in this work. If, in this plot situation, another man is substituted for the goat, the parallels to the experiences of many gay people in Albee's scenarios are precise. It does not take much imagination to carry the parallel further, to interracial or interfaith marriages, for example, in communities that do not tolerate these unions. By choosing an extreme situation to drive this play, Albee calls into question all social restraints on the individual expression of love.

Sources for Further Study
Bloom, Harold, ed. *Edward Albee*. New York: Chelsea House, 1987.
Davis, J. Madison, and Philip C. Kolin, eds. *Critical Essays on Edward Albee*. Boston: G. K. Hall, 1986.
Gussow, Mel. *Edward Albee, a Singular Journey: A Biography*. New York: Simon & Schuster, 1999.
Paolucci, Anne. *From Tension to Tonic: The Plays of Edward Albee*. Wilmington, Del.: Griffon House Press, 2000.
Roudane, Matthew C. "Communication as Therapy in the Theater of Edward Albee." *Journal of Evolutionary Psychology* 6, nos. 3/4 (August, 1985): 302-314.
Solomon, Rakesh H. "Crafting Script into Performance: Edward Albee in Rehearsal." *American Drama* 2, no. 2 (Spring, 1993).

Kathleen M. Bartlett

THE GOOD WOMAN OF SETZUAN

Author: Bertolt Brecht (1898-1956)
Type of plot: Epic theater
Time of plot: Between World War I and World War II
Locale: Fictive province of Setzuan, China
First produced: 1943, at the Zurich Schauspielhaus, Zurich, Switzerland
First published: Der gute Mensch von Sezuan, 1953 (English translation, 1948)

> *Principal characters:*
> WANG, a water seller
> THE THREE GODS, who are searching for a good person
> SHEN TE, a woman of Setzuan
> SHUI TA, Shen Te disguised as a ruthless businessman
> YANG SUN, an unemployed flier
> MRS. YANG, his mother
> SHU FU, a wealthy barber
> MRS. MI TZU, the house owner
> LIN TO, a carpenter and father of four

The Play

The plot of *The Good Woman of Setzuan* winds through a prologue, ten scenes with numerous interludes separating them, and an epilogue. The action centers on the desire of Shen Te to be good and the impossibility of living up to that standard in society as it is presently configured. She has a small amount of money, which she must use to help herself and those around her to a better life if she is to be good. She discovers very quickly, however, that in order to survive she must invent a tough cousin, a formidable businessman, to protect her interests. Thus throughout the play she alternates between two roles: As herself, she is the gentle, generous, sweet Shen Te, but when she must meet business crises head-on, she assumes the identity of a man, the harsh and sometimes vicious Shui Ta.

In the prologue, Wang, the water seller, speaks directly to the audience, explaining that he is waiting to greet the gods, who are secretly searching for a good person to help end the horrible poverty and the intense drought that plague the province. Wang easily recognizes the gods—they are well fed and well dressed compared to the poor citizens of Setzuan. Wang hopes to find lodging for the gods but is turned away from the homes of all the wealthy. He shelters them in the home of Shen Te, a prostitute. In the morning, as they prepare to depart, certain that they have found a good person in Shen Te, the gods give her one thousand silver dollars, with the proviso that she must remain good. Shen Te uses the gift of the gods to buy a tobacco shop, turning away from her previous profession. However, as claim after claim is made on her food, shelter, and money, she recognizes that she will be able to save no one if she herself does not survive.

As the second scene begins, Shui Ta introduces himself as Shen Te's cousin. He makes friends with the local police, rids the shop of a family of eight who have moved in, cheats the carpenter of his shelves, and rents the shop space on less stringent terms than those proposed by Mrs. Mi Tzu in the first scene. With a tough business approach, it seems, the shop and Shen Te will survive.

As scene 3 begins, Shen Te hurries to a teahouse to meet a rich man who might marry her at Shui Ta's request. She interrupts Yang Sun's attempt to hang himself out of despair over not being able to ply his trade as an airplane pilot. She falls in love with Sun and forgets the meeting with the old man in the teahouse who could save her shop.

In a dream, Wang sees the gods. Shen Te is as good as ever, but Shui Ta's cheating of the carpenter besmirches her reputation; the gods are discouraged by this imperfection. Their physical condition is deteriorating. Their search is leading them to more contact with the misery of the human condition.

Outside Shen Te's shop at dawn, the hungry people who depend on her rice await her return. There is an altercation between Wang and the wealthy barber, Shu Fu. The barber breaks Wang's hand. Shen Te arrives, glowing with the joy of her night's encounter with Yang Sun and happy to give rice to the hungry. The carpet dealer and his wife recognize the look of one in love. They ask if she met the man at the teahouse. Shen Te realizes that she has forgotten about paying the rent in the flush of romantic love. The old couple happily loan her all they have, two hundred silver dollars, to pay her rent. Moments later, Shen Te impulsively and lovingly turns this money over to Yang Sun's mother to help him get a pilot's job. She also promises to testify for Wang that she saw Shu Fu break his hand.

In an interlude, Shen Te appears, carrying the clothing and mask of Shui Ta. Before the eyes of the audience, she becomes Shui Ta. Yang Sun meets Shui Ta in the fifth scene. Sun reveals that he is not in love with Shen Te but is only using her. Mrs. Mi Tzu arrives to collect the rent. Sun, who needs three hundred dollars more to get the pilot's job in Peking, offers to sell Shen Te's shop to Mrs. Mi Tzu for that amount. The deal will be sealed in two days. Wang enters to have Shen Te help him file his suit against Shu Fu, but Shui Ta refuses to let Shen Te perjure herself. Shu Fu offers to allow Shen Te to continue her good deeds through marriage to him; he will make his houses behind the cattle yard available to her to shelter the poor. Yang Sun returns. Shen Te appears and chooses Sun, rather than accept Shu Fu's offer.

On the way to her wedding, Shen Te tells the audience that the wife of the carpet dealer needs the two hundred silver dollars back because her husband is gravely ill. The wedding never takes place, because Yang Sun first wants possession of the three hundred silver dollars. Shui Ta never brings the money.

As scene 7 begins, Shen Te is preparing to move away in ruin. Shu Fu brings her a blank check to save her business. However, owing to her love for Yang Sun, she refuses to take advantage of Shu Fu's generosity. She also discovers that she is carrying Sun's child. Reversing herself, Shen Te commits herself to Shu Fu by promising to find shelter for the whole Lin family in his houses. She gives all of her possessions to

Wang so that he can receive medical care for his hand. Members of the family of eight show up with three bales of tobacco, which they ask Shen Te to hide for them. Shen Te realizes that she must save her own unborn child, so she calls upon Shui Ta once again. He uses Shu Fu's blank check and commandeers the bales of tobacco. He announces that only those who work will be fed, and that the barber's houses are not available for living because they will become the location of a tobacco factory.

The gods appear to Wang in the interlude. They are suffering terribly from their earthly sojourn. Wang tells them of a dream of seeing Shen Te almost drowning as she tries to cross a river with a heavy load of moral precepts on her back.

Scene 8 is set in Shui Ta's tobacco factory. Mrs. Yang narrates the rise of Yang Sun in Shui Ta's business. He ingratiates himself to owner Shui Ta and rises to become foreman in just a few months by cheating and brutalizing his fellow workers.

By scene 9, Shui Ta has grown fat. The neighbors think that it is caused by prosperity and complacency, but the audience knows that it is Shen Te's pregnancy. Wang the water seller stops outside the shop and cries out for Shen Te and her goodness. Sun hears from Wang that Shen Te is pregnant and assumes that it is his child. Sun also hears weeping from the back room, yet only Shui Ta emerges. The police are called, Shen Te's clothes are found, and Shui Ta is arrested for the murder of his kind cousin.

The gods are almost finished as they appear to Wang in the interlude. They recognize that their moral precepts may make it impossible for people to live. They vanish quickly. The final scene of the play is the trial of Shui Ta for the murder of his cousin. The gods will serve as judges. Shui Ta promises to make a confession if the courtroom is cleared. He strips off his costume and Shen Te stands before the judges. She explains that she could not be good and still survive, especially when she had to think about the future of her unborn child. The gods shut off her discussion of the predicament of humankind. They are overjoyed to have found their good person again and quickly depart for heaven now that their work is done. As they leave on their pink cloud, they ignore her cries for help.

The epilogue is a kind of tongue-in-cheek summary of the action. The audience is challenged to find a solution to Shen Te's dilemma in spite of the contradiction between the way society is structured and the domination of the moral precepts of the gods.

Themes and Meanings

The Good Woman of Setzuan raises the question of morality in Western culture by enacting a dilemma of goodness versus survival. The issues are encompassed in the play in two basic philosophies: The Chinese yin/yang and Marxist dialectical materialism. The highly contrasting behaviors of Shen Te and Shui Ta illustrate the Asian philosophy of the yin/yang that says two sides of nature—the passive woman and the active man—make up the whole. The constant opposition between Shen Te and Shui Ta and their desperate need for one another, as well as the economic questions that their disparate behaviors raise, point to the Marxist underpinnings of this play. Out of Shen Te's need to survive despite her goodness and generosity comes the constructive manner in which Shui Ta uses the resources at Shen Te's disposal to multiply the wealth and thus create more for distribution. On the other hand, Shui Ta's tight-fistedness and cruelty creates a need for more of the human warmth and aid that Shen Te brings to people in misery in the slums of Setzuan.

Both the yin/yang and Marxist philosophies are poetically realized through water imagery and are dramatically stated in terms of the economic situation in Setzuan. The poverty and drought which serve as the backdrop for this play unite the two sets of ideas. The gods do not bring water to everyone; they only bring a small amount of money to Shen Te. They frequently appear to Wang, the water seller, in his night's lodgings of a dry culvert. Wang dreams that the weight of the gods' moral precepts will drown Shen Te. Her shop, which she considers a gift from the gods, is an economic lifeboat. However, it may sink, because too many drowning hands reach out for it. The name Shen Te, in Chinese, connotes gentle rain. The name Shui Ta suggests the rushing waters of a flood tide. The generous Shen Te rains her small gifts on those around her; Shui Ta, the unrelenting capitalist who washes away restraints in his rush to succeed in business, emphasizes the relationship between water and the economics of Setzuan, and between the yin/yang and the Marxist dialectic.

With the firm connection between water and economics poetically embedded in the text, Bertolt Brecht goes a step further for the philosophical education of his audience. Instead of creating a play steeped in Chinese tradition, he uses a fictive Chinese setting and Chinese names, exotic gods who become less so as the play progresses, and a sprinkling of tales to divorce the play from the everyday realities of his intended Western audiences. If the play had a less exotic setting, the audience could simply accept the problems and conditions as those of their society, too long ingrained to be solved, or even willed by God as the natural order of things. The critical distance that the Chinese setting provides is designed to let the audience recognize that human action is responsible for the conditions of poverty and can be marshalled to solve those problems.

Dramatic Devices

The Good Woman of Setzuan has an episodic structure that allows the playwright to establish the problems of poverty and generosity and then depict them in different ways. Each restatement of the problems is accompanied by a raising of the stakes—first it is just a night's business Shen Te will lose, then her shop, then someone else's shop, then the future of her child. Each time, Shui Ta finds some solution to save Shen Te through cold-hearted business tactics. The loose episodes, with the counterbalancing effects of the two sides of the character, lead to an alternation between the scenes of Shen Te and Shui Ta, until in scene 10 they both make appearances.

The episodic structure also allows for the interludes, which interrupt the development of the plot. In one, the audience sees Shen Te transform herself into Shui Ta; the effect is reminiscent of the Chinese theatrical convention in which characters change costume and become other characters before the eyes of the audience. In many interludes, Wang talks with the gods about Shen Te's tenacity in goodness or about the problems of being good. In each, the audience sees that the gods are deteriorating as a result of their contact with the real world of human problems. Their clothes become more and more ragged, they look increasingly haggard and travel worn, and intervention in human disputes earns one a black eye and another a crippled leg from the jaws of a trap. This is a strong visual statement that human problems must be solved by humans—gods are incapable of doing so.

The plot of the play is frequently interrupted by songs, poems, or characters speaking directly to the audience. The songs and poems are used to focus the attention of the audience on specific and critical philosophical issues. Shen Te sings "The Song of the Defenselessness of the Gods and the Good People," in which she questions why evil exists at all and why, if the gods are so powerful, they do not wage war against evil and win. The song forces the audience to consider that evil is not otherworldly, but purely human in its source, just as goodness is a purely human virtue.

Characters who speak directly to the audience confront the playgoers with the social and political messages of the play. They also narrate action that is about to take place, telling the audience what to expect. This telling all in advance encourages the audience to, rather than watching the play to see what happens, watch to see why and how things happen. This device renders audiences capable of solving the problems rather than simply accepting their presence in the human condition. For example, Mrs. Yang tells the audience that her son, Yang Sun, has risen high in Shui Ta's tobacco factory through a little bit of luck and hard work. Then she narrates each of the events that led to Sun becoming the foreman. As she does so, the scenes are enacted, complete with dialogue. The audience watches Sun make a coworker look lazy, a paymaster seem dishonest, and the assembly line workers appear incompetent until he takes over as their taskmaster. The spectator sees how he does this and understands that it is for his own advancement at the expense of others. There is no suspense over whether he will succeed, because his mother has already revealed that he does.

Bertolt Brecht sprinkles the play with tales and anecdotes that contribute to the sense of the exotic. They also provide an opportunity to preach directly to the audience. The spectator sees the contradictions inherent in accepted notions of good and evil in human behavior in Wang's tale of the trees who pay the penalty for usefulness by being chopped down in their prime instead of being able to live to a ripe age.

Critical Context

The first full text of *The Good Woman of Setzuan* was offered for production in 1942. The play came from a mature writer who was in his ninth year of exile from his homeland, Germany. During his nomadic travels to avoid Nazi rule and certain death, Brecht was constantly in need of money. By the time he settled in California in 1941, he hoped to create a play that would have some commercial success. *The Good Woman of Setzuan* is, for this reason, less strident in its revolutionary preaching and less concerned with the intricacies of Marxism than most of Brecht's earlier works.

Despite the softer approaches to revolutionary issues, this work raises the same economic question as earlier and later plays. In *The Good Woman of Setzuan*, as with his other plays, Brecht attacks the myth that human destiny is in the hands of gods. He replaces that myth with a call for human action to replace the social or political complacency that accepts things as they are rather than creating society as it should be.

The Good Woman of Setzuan is ranked as one of Brecht's greatest plays, along with *Leben des Galilei* (pr. 1943; *Life of Galileo*, 1947), *Der kaukasische Kreidekreis* (pb. 1949; *The Caucasian Chalk Circle*, 1948), and *Mutter Courage und ihre Kinder* (pr. 1940; *Mother Courage and Her Children*, 1941), all begun or completed in the difficult days of exile. Less political and not as obscure philosophically as his earlier works, these plays tend to be more accessible to theater artists and audiences steeped in the twentieth century Western dramatic tradition of domestic realism. All four are based on the premise that humankind is responsible for its own destiny and must structure society and the world in such a way as to dispense with the myths that contradict or discourage positive human action. In each play Brecht also confronts the moral issues involved in human action. Generosity in the face of poverty (versus the creation of more personal wealth), the containment and suppression of knowledge for what seems a greater good of society, the nurturing and use of resources, and personal responsibility in the advantageous economics of war are all strong themes in Brecht's great plays.

The sweep of *The Good Woman of Setzuan* is both typical and unique in Brecht's work. He chooses the large issues of the modern world for his works, expressing them in everyday terms but setting them in either distant times or places. Often he uses extraordinary people as his characters, but in having them do ordinary things he brings their efforts to a level that encourages audience contemplation and criticism. With *The Good Woman of Setzuan*, he creates a play of China that is really about Western ideas and problems. What might be expected to be an exotic fairy tale is a grim confrontation with the realities of labor and poverty and the philosophies that propound the problems.

Sources for Further Study

Benjamin, Walter. *Understanding Brecht.* Translated by Anna Bostock. London: Verso, 1983.

Bentley, Eric. *Bentley on Brecht.* New York: Applause, 1999.

_____. *The Brecht Commentaries.* 2d ed. New York: Grove Press, 1987.

Casabro, Tony. *Bertold Brecht's Art of Dissemblance.* Brookline, Mass.: Longwood Academic, 1990.

Esslin, Martin. *Brecht, a Choice of Evils: A Critical Study of the Man, His Work, and His Opinions.* 4th rev. ed. London: Methuen, 1984.

Ewen, Frederick. *Bertolt Brecht: His Life, His Art, and His Times.* New York: Citadel, 1967.

Fisher, James. Review of *The Good Woman of Setzuan. Theatre Journal* 52 (March, 2000): 20-21.

Becky B. Prophet

THE GOSPEL AT COLONUS

Author: Lee Breuer (1937-   )
Type of plot: Musical
Time of plot: Ancient Greece and the late twentieth century United States
Locale: Ancient Greece and a black Pentecostal church service
First produced: 1983, at the New Wave Festival, Brooklyn Academy of Music, New York
First published: 1989

> *Principal characters:*
> BLACK PREACHER, a contemporary religious figure who doubles as a Greek messenger
> OEDIPUS, the ancient Greek literary character who doubles as a gospel singer
> ANTIGONE and
> ISMENE, Oedipus's daughters, the princesses of Thebes
> CREON, king of Thebes
> THESEUS, king of Colonus
> POLYNEICES, Oedipus's son, the prince of Thebes

The Play

The Gospel at Colonus is a curious blend of the ancient Greek drama of Sophocles and a modern gospel musical. The text is an adaptation of Sophocles' *Oidipous epi Kolōnōi* (401 B.C.E.; *Oedipus at Colonus*, 1729), the second play in the cycle of the Theban Trilogy, although it makes references to certain occurrences in both *Oidipous Tyrannos* (c. 429 B.C.E.; *Oedipus Tyrannus*, 1715) and *Antigonē* (441 B.C.E.; *Antigone*, 1729). The immediate setting of *The Gospel at Colonus* is a black Pentecostal church service, where the play opens with the black preacher taking the text for his sermon from the "Book of Oedipus." Through flashback, musical performance, and dance, the audience is transported back in time to the suffering of Oedipus, the King of Thebes' self-imposed banishment from his home city, and his difficult journey in search of sanctuary. Oedipus's journey and his constant suffering are dramatized in the audience's imagination as the Pentecostal preacher re-creates the classic story of redemption through suffering.

The first scene shows Oedipus on the road, accompanied by his younger daughter, Antigone, as he approaches the gates of Colonus, the city in which he will ultimately be granted a resting place. Although the townspeople attempt to refuse his entry out of fear that his sins will infect them, Oedipus is granted entry to the city by King Theseus, himself a victim of angry gods and thus sympathetic to Oedipus's needs. Ismene, Oedipus's elder daughter, arrives from Thebes with the news that he is now welcome to return to Thebes, but Oedipus refuses. In the meantime, Creon, the present ruler of Thebes, who is also the brother-in-law and uncle of Oedipus, arrives to persuade Oedipus to return to his home city, fully aware that the Delphic oracle has prophesied that the city that grants Oedipus a final resting place will forever prosper. Oedipus refuses the invitation, and in an effort to force Oedipus to return to Thebes, Creon kidnaps Oedipus's daughters. Theseus speaks movingly of Oedipus's plight and vows not to rest until he restores Oedipus's daughters to him.

Shortly after Oedipus's arrival at Colonus, he is visited by Polyneices, one of his two warring sons. Polyneices has been driven from Thebes by his brother Eteocles and has traveled to Argos to raise an army to attack his home city. Polyneices asks for his father's blessing in battle, but Oedipus rebukes him for his foolish fighting and for his refusal to help his father when he had the chance. Shortly thereafter, Theseus keeps his promise and returns Antigone and Ismene to Oedipus and grants Oedipus official sanctuary in the city of Colonus. There Theseus presides over Oedipus's death, a siutation in which he is caught up in a whirlwind, a Pentecostal rapture. Thus Oedipus gains his final resting place in peace though he has suffered endlessly.

Flashbacks are interspersed with the contemporary preacher's sermon, and, as the sermon builds to its high point, it is augmented by gospel music. At the end of the play, a catharsis is experienced, and the shout—the Pentecostal "holy dance"—is performed as the audience's emotions are purged of pity and fear, as they were in ancient Greece upon Oedipus's rapturous death. Indeed, the audience—both that of the play and that of the preacher—understands that if there was a celebration of Oedipus's triumph over intense and long-term suffering, then it can happen for them as well.

Themes and Meanings

The principal themes in *The Gospel at Colonus* are redemption and reconciliation, both important themes in Sophocles' Theban Trilogy and a number of other plays from the classical Greek theater. In *The Gospel at Colonus*, these themes are viewed vicariously as the Pentecostal preacher creates vivid images of Oedipus's suffering for his congregation. Moreover, these images are experienced through the black Pentecostal ritual that becomes an integral part of the play's blending of ancient and contemporary theatrical forms. In the myth of Oedipus, a certain timelessness is explored in the matters of fate and individual responsibility, the respect for and adherence to both God-given and human-made laws (and the potential conflict therein), and in the possibility of grace and redemption through suffering. Other themes that are explored include family loyalty and family treachery, and the ultimate exaltation of good over evil, of light over darkness, and of spiritual sight over physical blindness. These themes are realized by Oedipus as he accomplishes his destiny and are witnessed and celebrated by the black Pentecostal congregation as they apply the themes to their everyday lives. The importance of these themes are demonstrated by the use of the Oedipus story and are underscored and given depth through the performative power of gospel music in the black Pentecostal tradition.

The title of the play is significant. In the Christian tradition, "gospel" typically refers to the sharing of good news about Jesus Christ. Thus, spreading the gospel means sharing that good news with others. In this curious theatrical blend of pagan and Christian traditions, Lee Brewer locates that kernel of good—truth—in the experiences of Oedipus and shares that truth with others, namely, contemporary black America, in a tremendous celebration of all that is good and right in the world.

Dramatic Devices

The most obvious dramatic device employed in *The Gospel at Colonus* is the use of flashback. Even as the preacher mounts the podium to begin his sermon, the impulse to "look back" is present. Thus, as the preacher introduces his text from the Book of Oedipus, he begins to draw the picture of the once mighty King of Thebes, who is brought down so that he might be exalted, or "saved" in the Christian context. At one juncture, obviously to impart to the congregation just how low Oedipus was brought, the preacher recounts how Oedipus blinded himself by plunging the golden brooches from his wife/mother's garments into his eyes so that he could look no more on the sins he had committed. The power of such imagery is palpable for the audiences—the one listening to the sermon within the play, as well as the one experiencing the play.

The Greek Chorus, represented in *The Gospel at Colonus* by two gospel-singing choruses, is also an important dramatic device in its function as the Aristotelian notion of the ideal spectator and in the role of a contemporary gospel chorus. In the former sense, the two groups often provide point-counterpoint or strophe-antistrophe in order to give the audience different views of the same incident and to advance the plot by illustrating the preacher's next point in the text. The fact that both choruses are singing the same song at the end of the play confirms and underscores the play's important theme of reconciliation. In the latter sense, the choruses keep the play moving and add resonance to the preacher's intonations, functioning in the same manner as a church choir does in the black religious tradition.

The amphitheater-style seating of the audiences replicate the ancient Greek outdoor amphitheater, which creates a sense of verisimilitude as the spectators view the action of the play down below. The similar seating arrangement of the church congregation in the play itself not only replicates the actual arrangement of the churchgoers as they view the dramatic performance of their preacher, but also suggests a connection between the form and content of the ancient and contemporary. This fact is underscored as the interior audience—the church congregation—interacts in a call-and-response manner with the preacher in the play, and as the exterior audience—the theatergoers—respond to Oedipus's plight as it is dramatized onstage. Moreover, because all elements, including the external audience, interact with one another in the grand finale of the musical—the catharsis and the exodus—the author's unique vision of reconciliation once again resonates with all who witness *The Gospel at Colonus*.

Critical Context

Even before its formal debut at the New Wave Festival at the Brooklyn Academy of Music in 1983, *The Gospel at Colonus* reached a number of enthusiastic workshop audiences in the United States and England. Its energy, its unique and intriguing blend of seemingly opposing traditions, and its moving conclusion offered audiences a fresh experience and drew rave reviews from the critics. Although many saw the play as one in a long line of gospel musicals, it is clear to the discerning reviewer that *The Gospel at Colonus* transcends that genre in accomplishing what interviewer Patrick Pacheco called "a song of joyous affirmation." In fact, Lee Breuer says of the play, "It's not a gospel show, but gospel music is used as an inspiration for re-creating a classic Greek experience, and I believe it is the correct metaphor for our time."

Audiences and critics alike agreed with Breuer. Among the praise offered by the critics, Alan Rich noted in *Newsweek* that the play was "a great theatrical exultation, a jiving, shouting, hand clapping celebration." Jack Kroll, also from *Newsweek*, observed that *The Gospel at Colonus* is "a triumph of reconciliation, bringing together black and white, pagan and Christian, ancient and modern in a sunburst of joy that seems to touch the secret heart of civilization itself." Awards for the play included the 1984 Obie Award for best musical, the ASCAP (American Society of Composers, Authors, and Publishers) Popular Music Award, and the United Gospel Association Award. When *The Gospel at Colonus* moved to Lunt-Fontanne Theater on Broadway for a two-month run in 1988, praise continued, although the play was less than a financial success. Perhaps the most penetrating critical viewpoint of *The Gospel at Colonus* was offered by Mimi Gisolfi D'Aponte, in *Black American Literature Forum*, who argued that "the most telling measurement (of the play's success) is of the psychic space opened up in American theater when the marriage of Black Pentecostal ritual and Greek ritual took place in a musical theater event."

Clearly, *The Gospel at Colonus* was a theater event in offering a fresh look on an old story; a story which is worth preserving, and a contemporary vision that is worth sharing. According to an anonymous reviewer of Atlanta's Alliance Theater production, "*The Gospel at Colonus* is galvanizing theater . . . both a gigantic theatrical experiment and a return to roots, a celebration and an affirmation of faith."

Sources for Further Study

D'Aponte, Mimi Gisolfi. "*The Gospel at Colonus* (And Other Black Morality Plays)." *Black American Literature Forum* 25 (Spring, 1991): 101-111.

DeVries, Hilary. "A Song in Search of Itself." *American Theater* 3, no. 10 (1987): 22-25.

Feingold, Michel. "Gospel Truth." *Village Voice*, November 22, 1983, p. 109.

Gussow, Mel. "*Colonus* Mixes Songs with Sophocles." *New York Times*, November 12, 1983, p. 12.

Kroll, Jack. "An Oedipal Jamboree." *Newsweek*, April 4, 1988, 75.

Rich, Alan. "Oedipus Jones." *Newsweek*, November 21, 1983, 105, 107.

Rich, Frank. "A Musical of Sophocles and Pentecostalism." *New York Times*, March, 25, 1988, p. C5.

Warren J. Carson

GRANIA

Author: Lady Augusta Gregory (Isabella Augusta Persse, 1852-1932)
Type of plot: Folk
Time of plot: Legendary prehistory
Locale: Ireland
First published: 1912, in *Irish Folk-History Plays, First Series*

> *Principal characters:*
> GRANIA, the daughter of the king of Ireland
> FINN, an aging chieftain
> DIARMUID, a young soldier, Finn's protégé

The Play

Grania meets Finn on the eve of their wedding. She tells Finn that she chose to marry him because she longs for the good life at Almhuin, Finn's home and the center of his soldier-community, famous for poets, heroes, and comradeship. Finn tells her that the man she will admire most in Almhuin is his kinsman, Diarmuid; then he asks if she has ever loved any man. Grania says there was a man once, a visitor to Tara, but she only saw him briefly and never heard his name. They are interrupted by Diarmuid's arrival with jewels and gifts for the wedding. Grania immediately recognizes Diarmuid as the man she had seen at Tara. Shocked, she shrinks back. Finn calls her forth and places a crown on her head, but, looking at Diarmuid, she feels the crown too heavy. She is suddenly tired and begs Finn to postpone their wedding. He refuses, and she withdraws.

Finn confides in Diarmuid that he finds himself falling in love with Grania. He wonders if love is appropriate at his age and looks to Diarmuid for reassurance. Finn says he fears love, because it unseats other loyalties. Diarmuid swears his loyalty to Finn but asks to be excused from attending the wedding and sent instead to fight the king of Foreign. Finn reluctantly agrees but orders Diarmuid to rest until dawn. Covering himself with a cloak, Finn watches over Diarmuid.

Grania enters, mistakes Finn for Diarmuid, and confesses she can no longer bear to marry Finn, for she knows her heart belongs to Diarmuid. As Finn reveals both his identity and his anger, Diarmuid wakes. Grania chooses a life in the wilderness alone, but Diarmuid vows to go with her and protect her, while respecting her as Finn's queen (that is, he will not have sexual intercourse with her). As proof of his faithfulness to Finn, Diarmuid pledges to send an unbroken cake of bread every full moon for as long as he and Grania are together.

When the second act begins, Grania and Diarmuid have been living in the woods, fugitives from Finn's wrath, for seven years; for the past month they have been living as husband and wife. Grania chides him, "It was not love that brought you to wed me in the end," but rather jealousy of the king of Foreign, who had found Grania gathering rushes and was about to carry her off when Diarmuid appeared, chased him off, and then kissed Grania. She lingers over the memory: "It was a long, long kiss."

Their month-long intimacy has led them to new longings—Diarmuid for an isolated home and an end to their fugitive life, Grania for company and the respect of others. They argue, and Diarmuid flings her from him. Finn appears, disguised as a beggar hired to discover why no cake of bread was delivered to Finn on the full moon. Grania breaks a loaf in pieces and fiercely tells the "beggar" that she is proud and pleased about the broken vow, and that she still turns her back on Finn. The "beggar" goads Diarmuid, chiding him for living on hares and killing birds when the army of the king of Foreign is invading Ireland. Diarmuid straps on his sword and goes out with the "beggar" to fight, abandoning Grania despite her plea for him to stay.

Act 3 begins on the afternoon of the same day as Finn, having doffed his disguise, discovers Grania alone. Finn and Grania unleash on each other the bitterness and longing of seven years. In a duel of tongues, in which words are their weapons, they end in a draw. He confesses to the vulnerability of his age and his love for her, and she describes the loneliness and hardship of her life with Diarmuid, who until this month gave her no more than duty. They reach a moment of mutual respect just as Diarmuid's body is brought it.

Finn thinks Diarmuid is dead and steps aside as Grania bends over him and commands his spirit to come back, keening and wailing her love. Diarmuid regains consciousness but ignores Grania and speaks only to Finn. As the two men recall their former affection and loyalty, Grania's cries and exclamations fail to penetrate the closed circle of their reunion. Finn forgives Diarmuid who, laughing in his moment of death, declares, "It would be a very foolish thing, any woman at all to have leave to come between yourself and myself."

Finn orders the army to mourn Diarmuid as a fallen hero, and Grania realizes that Diarmuid never loved her at all, that all his love was for Finn and the brotherhood of Almhuin; she was no more to him than the shadow of a flight of birds. She swears to return to Almhuin with Finn, there to stand between Finn and the ghost of Diarmuid. The play ends as Grania takes her crown from Finn, places it on her own head, and faces the mocking laughter of the army and of Diarmuid's ghost, declaring, "I am no way daunted or afraid." Transformed by the vision of her exclusion from the hearts of the two men, she achieves the dignity and loneliness of soul which befit a mythic queen.

Themes and Meanings

Grania is a coming-of-age play. It concerns Grania's passage from romantic adolescence to an adult awareness that men and women have different values and love differently. Though the play includes a fully developed characterization of the aging Finn and portrays his relationship with Diarmuid in depth, it is Grania's play. Grania drives the plot forward; she chooses Finn; she refuses to marry him and decides to leave Almhuin; she braves seven years in the wilderness with Diarmuid's indifference. She faces up to the king of Foreign, and she proudly consents to intercourse when Diarmuid is moved by jealousy to take her. It is Grania who names her truth in a climactic confrontation scene with Finn and who makes the final decision to return to Almhuin. The crown which was too heavy for her in act 1 becomes her own by the end of act 3, when she places it on her own head, speaks the play's last lines, and strides into a future she has determined for herself.

Grania is also a play about love and jealousy. In the first scene Grania is not sure what love is, but she has asked "the old people," and they say it is "a white blast of delight and a grey blast of discontent and a third blast of jealousy that is red." The play proves the old people right as love, discontent, and jealousy weave in and out of the characters' lives. The love that triumphs is that between male comrades. In Diarmuid's death scene Finn declares, "you are my son and my darling, and it is beyond the power of any woman to put us asunder." He and Diarmuid are reunited in heroic comradeship while Grania is excluded, and in her anguish she realizes that both men "had no love for me at any time." Love resurfaces in the last scene as Finn says to Grania, "it was the cruelty and the malice of love made its sport with us," and "it is certain I can never feel love or hatred for any other woman from this [moment] out, or you yourself for any other man."

Then Grania steps forward beyond love into a life of her own choosing, "no way daunted or afraid." Lady Gregory creates a universe in which love is both an unholy grail and a source of purification, a universe in which the heroine comes of age as she gains the vision to see beyond her dreams of love. Grania's coming-of-age is a loss of innocence in the classical sense, but Lady Gregory leaves the director, the actors, and the audience to conclude whether the final movements are transcendent or bitter.

Dramatic Devices

Grania is a play in which two dramatic devices predominate: characterization and the use of poetic language quite outside common English usage. These devices make possible the staging of a three-act play with only three speaking roles, little in the way of plot, a minimum of suspense (the legend and its outcome were known to Lady Gregory's audience), and relatively little action, which is nevertheless tense with dramatic conflict and stirring to the ear.

Each of the three characters is multidimensional and is transformed by the course of the action, though it is certainly Grania who changes most. In order to give her characters room to grow, Lady Gregory sets them up as models of simplicity at the start of act 1. Finn, far older and more courageous than Grania, is respectful of the power of love and jealousy but holds both at a distance. Grania, all innocence and directness, expects never to know what love is but to live in domestic harmony with Finn. Diarmuid, whose soldier-spirit is dauntless, has but one emotion: loyalty to Finn. Lady Gregory develops and exposes the complexity of her characters by introducing a rapid series of tests, inner conflicts, doubts, and disappointments for each one. Finn's vulnerability and self-doubt countermine his courage; Diarmuid's passion and jealousy undercut his loyalty; and Grania's innocence disappears as her self-determination grows. Every moment of the play reveals some new disillusionment, risk, or conflict that spirals among the three principals, influencing each, so that all three are constantly changing and contributing to the changes which take place in the other two.

Love triangles are common fare in dramatic literature, and depth of characterization alone would not account for the respect this play has garnered since its publication in 1912. Its distinctiveness comes from Lady Gregory's depiction of character through a poetic language that is exclusively hers. She wrote in a language she developed from listening to Irish people speak English, a dialect she called "Kiltartan." It employs an altered syntax, heavily rhythmic and larded with imagery, which conveys a flavor of Irish speech without using the odd and often clumsy phonetic spellings usually used to denote dialects of English. For example, in act 2, when Grania begins to be discontented with Diarmuid, she tells him, "it is hard to nourish pride in a house having two in it only." In act 3, Finn predicts Grania will return with him to Almhuin in words that evoke the very sound and color of remorse:

> I tell you, my love that was allotted and foreshadowed before the making of the world will drag you in spite of yourself, as the moon above drags the waves, and they grumbling through the pebbles as they come, and making their own little moaning of discontent.

A few minutes further into their argument Grania observes, "I have a great wrong done to you, surely, but it brings me no nearer to you now." The entire play is as tightly crafted as a poem, offering page after page of dialogue which resonates with mellifluous and hypnotizing rhythms unlike anything else in English except Lady Gregory's own other works.

Critical Context

All Lady Gregory's plays were written under the influence of Irish nationalism, in the era just before and after Ireland won independence from English rule. As one of the cofounders of the Abbey Theatre, established as a home for Irish drama and a center for nationalist expression, Lady Gregory (herself a member of the Anglo-Irish Protestant aristocracy) wrote numerous frothy one-act comedies. These feature Irish humor, Irish folklore, and Irish patriotism. A typical night at the Abbey in its early days would feature one or two Gregory one-acts, followed by the "serious" work of the evening, a Symbolist drama by William Butler Yeats or John Millington Synge. Calling herself "the charwoman of the Abbey," in part to diminish the appearance of privilege stemming from her aristocratic background, Lady Gregory posed as a hack writer, one who wrote to suit popular taste but was happy living in the shadow of two genuinely Irish men of greatness. It is true that her comedies were popular with Dublin audiences; it is also true that she supported and nourished Yeats and Synge. If *Grania* did not exist, it might even be possible to view her as she wished to be viewed—as a well-meaning hack.

Grania is a complete departure from comic folk-drama. Considered by most critics to be her masterpiece, *Grania* is her only full-length play. Its poetry, its dynamic shaping of myth, and its intense dramatic tension make it unrepresentative of her work as a whole. Lady Gregory based *Grania* on a body of ancient legend which she herself had translated from the original Irish; she wrote the play when she was fifty-eight years old, and she refused to allow it to be staged in her lifetime. Perhaps its power and its passion embarrassed the author, an eccentric woman reared amid Victorian values, a woman widowed at twenty-eight who wore black till her death at eighty—a woman who cultivated an image of herself as a nonartist, a functionary, a "woman of the house, that has to be minding the place, and listening to complaints, and dividing her share of food." In an age less hampered by ideals of womanly decorum, this play has emerged as the equal of any written in the Irish Renaissance. Since her death it has been translated into the Irish language and performed both in Irish and in the "Kiltartan" in which it was written.

Sources for Further Study

Coxhead, Elizabeth. *Lady Gregory: A Literary Portrait*. 2d ed. London: Secker & Warburg, 1966.

Kohfeldt, Mary Lou. *Lady Gregory: The Woman Behind the Irish Renaissance*. New York: Atheneum, 1985.

Malone, Andrew E. "The Folk Dramatists." In *The Irish Drama*. Reprint. New York: B. Blom, 1965.

Mikhail, E. K. *Lady Gregory: Annotated Bibliography of Criticism*. Troy, New York: Wilson, 1982.

_____. *Lady Gregory: Interviews and Recollections*. Totowa, N.J.: Rowman and Littlefield, 1977.

Saddlemyer, Ann. *In Defense of Lady Gregory, Playwright*. London: Oxford University Press, 1966.

Kendall

THE GRAPES OF WRATH

Author: Frank Galati (1943-   )
Type of plot: Social realism
Time of plot: The 1930's
Locale: Oklahoma and California
First produced: 1990, at the Cort Theatre, New York City
First published: 1990

Principal characters:
 TOM JOAD, a parolee from prison
 PA JOAD, his father, a dispossessed tenant farmer
 MA JOAD, his mother, the family's "citadel"
 ROSE OF SHARON, his sister, the pregnant wife of Connie Rivers
 GRANMA JOAD, his grandmother, a senile old lady
 GRAMPA JOAD, his grandfather, a senile old man
 RUTHIE, his younger sister
 UNCLE JOHN, his paternal uncle, another dispossessed tenant
  farmer
 NOAH, his oldest brother
 WINFIELD, his youngest brother
 CONNIE RIVERS, Rose of Sharon's husband
 AL JOAD, a mechanic
 JIM CASY, a former preacher

The Play

 The Grapes of Wrath opens during a dust-obscured dawn, depicting the Dust Bowl conditions of Oklahoma during the Great Depression. Two unidentified tenant farmers, one on each side of a worn barbed-wire fence, survey their ruined crops as their wives watch them anxiously. This general setting then shifts to a narrative of the Joad family, with the preacher Jim Casy singing "Yes, sir, that's my Saviour." Returning home after four years in McAlster Prison for a homicide committed in self-defense, Tom Joad enters the scene and renews his acquaintance with Casy, who decides to accompany Tom and visit the Joads. The two men find the Joad home destroyed and deserted. A man named Muley Graves tells them that the bank has tractored the family off the land, knocking their house itself off its foundations. Muley also tells how his own home was demolished and asserts his determination to stay on the land, even though the rest of his family has joined the migration of dispossessed tenant farmers to the promised land of California.

 Tom and Jim eventually find Tom's family at Uncle John's farm, where Pa Joad is pounding nails into the wooden sides of an old truck in preparation for a long trip to California. Pa surprises Ma by asking if she has enough food to feed two strangers, and she is startled when Tom walks in. The members of the family decide to leave the next day, and they make their preparations for the journey. When Grampa Joad decides he does not want to go, others give him a soothing tonic and hoist him up onto the truck.

Ma sorts through her personal belongings, burning those that she cannot take with her and pocketing her treasured gold earrings. When Al Joad tries to start the truck, it sputters and dies. After he finally gets it started, Uncle John's house vanishes in the distance as the family begins its westward migration. Along the way, Grampa dies, and the family buries him alongside the road.

Sitting together in the front seat of the truck, Ma and Al discuss their apprehensions about going to a new place. Ma assures Al that most of her attention must be focused on how she is going to feed the family. Leaving the others to set up camp for the night, Al, Tom, and Casy drive to a town to get the truck repaired. When they return, the proprietor of the camp refuses to let them stay unless they pay an additional fifty cents.

In the camp, the Joads meet a man returning from California who tells them that he could not find adequate work and that his wife and children have died of starvation. When Pa starts to tell the man's story to Ma, Tom intervenes, sparing her the knowledge of the bleak prospects they may be facing. Pa and Casy agree that the man may be telling the truth but he also might be a troublemaker.

When the Joads reach the Colorado River, Noah leaves the family, continuing down the river. Ma is dismayed by the prospect of the family's breakup, and Pa blames himself. Later, when the Joads prepare to cross a desert, state agricultural officers stop them to inspect their belongings; Ma insists that they cannot wait for an inspection because Granma is desperately ill. Not until they reach California does she reveal that Granma is dead; Ma has held the old woman in her arms all night. With only forty dollars left, the Joads set out to find a coroner.

The second act opens with the twang of a Jew's-harp and the Joads' arrival at a "Hooverville" camp, where the dispossessed gather on the edge of town. There, ragged, sick, and hungry people move about, with one man wrapping a baby in layers of fabric for burial and another grinding the valves on a decrepit old car. A man demented by abuse, whom the others call the "mayor" of Hooverville, greets them. Floyd, the man grinding valves, tells Tom about the dire nature of the migrant situation—the lack of jobs and the starvation wages paid for such work that is available. Tom decides to move on when their truck is repaired.

Accompanied by a deputy sheriff, a contractor arrives in the camp to offer jobs, but the ensuing scene reveals how bad the situation really is. When Floyd asks to see the man's license for hiring, inquires about wages, and insists on knowing exactly how many workers are needed, the sheriff tries to arrest Floyd for hanging around a used car lot that has been robbed. When Floyd starts to run away, the deputy raises his gun to shoot him, but Tom trips him, and a bullet hits a woman's hand. When the deputy starts to fire his gun again, Casy kicks him in the face and tells Tom to hide in the willows. As a prisoner parolee, Tom cannot risk being arrested, so Casy takes all the blame for assaulting the deputy himself.

In short succession, Uncle John goes off to get drunk, Connie deserts his pregnant wife, Rose of Sharon (Tom's sister), and the Joads must pack up and leave because of a rumor that the camp is about to be burned. The demented mayor of Hooverville remains behind—wandering about the deserted camp, looking for junk left behind, ignoring the sheriff's deputies.

The Joads' next stop is Weedpatch Camp, a clean, well-kept, government-operated site with a kindly and humane director. There, a religious fanatic, Elizabeth Sandry, frightens Rose of Sharon by telling her about a woman who lost her baby because she went hug-dancing and complains about the camp's Saturday night dances. Ma Joad furiously insists that the woman leave, pierces her daughter's ears, and gives her her cherished gold earrings. Meanwhile, Al leads a girl into the shadows, where they kiss, and promises to marry her. At the camp's Saturday night dance, Ma and Tom dance together and then move offstage, with Rose of Sharon following them.

As the narrator describes the migrant way of life, always on the move, Pa announces that the family must head north in search of work. The Joads stop next at the Hoover Ranch, where they work for starvation wages and again encounter Casy. In trouble with the law because he is now a strike leader, Casy is murdered by a deputy, whom Tom then kills, receiving a head injury in the process. When Ma insists that Tom go into hiding, Tom takes on Casy's mantle of advocacy for the downcast and promises Ma that in spirit he will be wherever his people are.

A narrator describes the boxcars that are the Joads' next place of shelter. As Pa reminisces about the past, Ma looks to the future, insisting that they keep on going. Al announces his engagement to Aggie Wainwright, daughter of the family in the other side of their boxcar. The two families celebrate with pancakes and syrup, but Ma urges Al to wait until spring before leaving the family.

The migrants worry because rising creek waters threaten to flood the boxcar. Rose of Sharon emits a terrified cry of terror as her labor pains begin. To the sounds of screams and thunder, the migrant men build a bank to hold back the rising floodwaters. Struck by lightning, a cottonwood tree falls and tears up the bank. The water rises as the men go into the boxcar to find a stillborn baby in an apple box. Pa turns the burial over to Uncle John, who sends the box downstream, mute testimony to their suffering.

Leaving Al behind with Aggie to watch over their belongings, the rest of the family head for higher ground to take shelter in a barn. There they find a young boy and his starving father. Telling them that Rose of Sharon needs to get out of her wet clothing, Ma asks if they have a blanket. The boy gives them a blanket and asks for help for his starving father. Ma and Rose of Sharon exchange a glance and reach a silent agreement. The family leaves the shed, and Rose of Sharon kneels beside the starving man, takes him into her arms, and begins to nurse him with her breast. She looks up with a mysterious smile.

Themes and Meanings

Dispossession is a key theme of *The Grapes of Wrath*. Cast out of their homes and off the land that they have farmed for generations, the migrants leave behind all that is most familiar to them. Like the vast Exodus of the Old Testament, the migrants go in search of a Promised Land, hoping to establish new homes, to bring up their children, and to dwell peaceably. Theirs is a universal longing, as all people sift through their pasts, leaving behind what they must, and journeying toward an unknown and unsure future.

A corresponding theme is that of desolation, for the migrants must leave land on which they had lived for generations. Lonely and alienated, Muley Graves epitomizes this desolation, for he stubbornly refuses to leave the land with the rest of his family. He does this partly because the land literally contains the blood of his father, who died in a barnyard after a bull gored him. Muley's lament that one's very identity is tied to the place where one lives captures the heart of the migrants' plight. Again, the sentiment is universal, for human beings tend to define themselves to some extent by where they live.

Dramatic Devices

Stage props are sparse, more suggestive than substantive, such as a barbed-wire fence, the shell of a truck, a water tank representing the Colorado River, a simple sign labeled "Weedpatch Camp."

Music is a primary dramatic device in this play. The whistled tune to "California, Here I Come" provides a scene shift from used car salesmen to Pa's thundering in nails as he puts wooden sides on the family's just-purchased Hudson sedan in preparation for their odyssey. Accompanied by a guitar waltz, Ma sorts through keepsakes, burning those that she cannot keep. When Al tries to start the vehicle, music captures its initial rumblings, as it sputters and dies. When he finally gets the vehicle going, a band plays, and a guitar player plaintively sings of Route 66 as Uncle John's house vanishes in the distance and the Joad truck slowly and ponderously begins its westward movement. They travel to a song of the Dust Bowl, a guitar churning out the noise of the engine, the twang of a Jew's-harp, a song about the growing wrath of the migrants as their situation worsens. Finally, a violin plays as Rose of Sharon nurses the starving stranger. Throughout the play, music contributes to the play's empathic appeal.

Another major device is the appearance of a narrator who describes the migrant way of life, always on the move—from Oklahoma to the boxcars where Rose of Sharon's baby is born. His depiction of a dust-obscured dawn captures briefly the essence of the Dust Bowl. Occasionally, the narrator's objective description mingles with the Joad narrative, as when Pa tells him that they are going to have to head north in search of work. The narrator serves to give the play depth and dimension, placing the Joads within the context of a larger migrant world.

Critical Context

Featured as one of the ten best plays of the season in *The Burns Mantle Theater Yearbook of 1989-1990*, Frank Galati's *The Grapes of Wrath* captures the essence of John Steinbeck's Pulitzer Prize-winning novel in a lyrical performance. For this production Galati won Tony Awards in 1990 for best play and best director. *The Grapes of Wrath* also won the Outer Critics' Circle Award for best play and the Drama Desk Award for best direction.

Galati has held myriad positions related to the theater: a professor of performance studies at Northwestern University, an associate director of the Goodman Theatre, and an ensemble member of the Steppenwolf Theatre Company. His other roles include screenwriter, for *The Accidental Tourist* (1988), and director, for such plays as *Ragtime* (1998), the Broadway revival of *The Glass Menagerie* (1994), and *Seussical* (2000).

Sources for Further Study

Dillon, John, and Thomas Connors. "The Paradoxical Professor." *American Theatre* 12 (October, 1995): 20.

Disch, Thomas. Review of *The Grapes of Wrath*. *The Nation*, April 30, 1990, 610.

Galati, Frank. *John Steinbeck's "The Grapes of Wrath."* New York: Dramatists Play Service, 1991.

Resnikova, Eva. "Theater: Sentimental Journey." *National Review* 42 (June 11, 1990): 58.

Steinbeck, John. *The Grapes of Wrath: Text and Criticism*, edited by Peter Lisca. New York: Penguin Books, 1977.

Weales, Gerald. "Stage: Vintage Production—Galati's *Grapes of Wrath*." *Commonweal* 117 (May 4, 1990): 294-297.

Barbara A. Heavilin

THE GREAT GOD BROWN

Author: Eugene O'Neill (1888-1953)
Type of plot: Expressionist
Time of plot: The early 1920's
Locale: The East Coast of the United States
First produced: 1926, at the Greenwich Village Theatre, New York City
First published: 1926, in *The Great God Brown, The Fountain, The Moon of the Caribbees, and Other Plays*

Principal characters:
WILLIAM "BILLY" A. BROWN, an architect
DION ANTHONY, an artist
MARGARET, Dion's wife and later William's
CYBEL, an earth mother-prostitute

The Play

The prologue to *The Great God Brown* takes place outside a high school during the annual commencement dance. Billy Brown's father, partner in a construction firm with Dion Anthony's father, anticipates that Billy will study architecture in college. Dion, wearing the mask of a reckless, sensual young man, is secretly extremely sensitive and anxious to create a self of his own unlike that of his stolid father. Margaret, adored by Billy, rejects him and is attracted instead to Dion's mask; when Dion takes it off, however, hoping to be loved for his essential self, she is confused and frightened. He replaces his mask, acknowledging that he needs her to be his "skin" even if she will never really know him.

Seven years later, in act 1, Dion and Margaret are married and have three nondescript sons. The Pan mask has become Mephistophelian and Dion's real face more ascetic. Because he has exhausted his father's inheritance, he allows Margaret to arrange with his rival Billy, now head of his own dead father's firm, to hire him as a draftsman. Billy's architectural designs are conventional and unimaginative. Envious of Dion's talent as well as of his marriage to Margaret, Billy hires him. Dion can reveal his spirituality and sadness only to Cybel, nominally a young prostitute but symbolically an earth-mother figure. When Billy finds Dion at Cybel's, Dion must put on his public mask again. Frustrated in his attempts to use art to see God, Dion resigns himself to serving the Great God Mr. Brown instead.

In act 2, seven years later, Brown, whose envy has made him a regular patron of Cybel, is puzzled by her summing up her preference for Dion by saying simply, "He's alive!" However, she suspects that she will never see Dion again, so close is he to collapse. Dion tries once more to show his real face to Margaret and is rejected as before. He goes to Billy, whom he accuses of having stolen his "creative life," knowing that Billy alone "couldn't design a cathedral without it looking like the First Supernatural

Bank!" Dion dies, having willed his mask to Billy, who wears it in order to have Margaret; she thinks that he is Dion grown younger.

In act 3, Billy has to pretend to his workmen that he has fired Dion, yet he wears Dion's mask when he is at home with Margaret. The terrible tension that results from this duplicity distorts his own inner face. The Dion part of his role makes him realize that he has only achieved "love by mistaken identity." Feeling "pursued by God, and by myself," he begins to talk to his mask as if Dion were still alive. He has made Margaret happy by giving her a rejuvenated Dion, but he himself can only suffer when she reminisces regarding her lifelong contempt for Billy Brown. Playing the role of Dion, he says cryptically to her, "Mr. Brown is now safely in hell."

In act 4, Billy's initial soliloquy reveals that he is nearing a breakdown. He has designed a state capitol that even he now recognizes "would do just as well for a Home for Criminal Imbeciles." He wishes that he had the strength to destroy the design but struggles for an honest reconciliation of, or an end to, his divided self. As Brown, he assures Margaret that, far from working Dion to death, it is he himself "who is to die." To a committee that has commissioned the capitol design, he admits that it is entirely Dion's but an insult to everyone's intelligence. He tears the plan into pieces; shortly thereafter, as Dion, he says that he will paste the parts together again: "Man is born broken. He lives by mending. The grace of God is glue!" When he tells them that Brown is dead, however, they think he has murdered Billy. Solemnly they lay the mask of Brown on the sofa.

Cybel comes to Billy in his home, recognizing that he is now Dion Brown, soulful sufferer though also an alleged murderer who must flee for his life. As he tries to leave, he is shot. Cybel comforts him in his last moments, assuring him of eternal peace: "Our Father Who Art!" When the police ask her his name, she replies, "Man!" The captain, uncomprehending, asks, "How d'yuh spell it?"

In an epilogue, Margaret, who "knows her life-purpose well accomplished" but feels at the same time "a bit empty and comfortless," releases her two grown sons to their own lives. They are about to become strangers to her. She kisses the mask of Dion whom she addresses as her lover, husband, and boy. She little realizes that she has never known the real Dion.

Themes and Meanings

The Great God Brown proceeds from the premise that selfhood is never singular but that, at the least, everyone has a public image as well as a private persona. Normally these, either by nature or by training, are compatible. A conflict can arise, however, when the extremely sensitive spirit of the inner person (an artist, for example) is very different from the ordinary people who surround him or her. If the person's responses are not allowed expression, then that inner self will feel isolated or even held in contempt, and an identity crisis can result. The person of integrity and independence has not only the normal problem of coping with changes that occur as one matures or as life's circumstances alter but also the problem of being understood in spite of the person's complexity and loved despite his or her differences.

In Eugene O'Neill's play, the struggle for self-determination and the right to fulfill one's dreams is most evident at first in the polarization of talented Dion Anthony and mediocre Billy Brown. A more subtle struggle takes place, however, between the dual natures of Dion Anthony himself: the sensual, ecstatic artist (Dion) and the ascetic, saintly mystic (Anthony). That particular division makes him ambivalent in his relationship with Margaret, who is both attracted to his life affirmation and puritanically repelled by its extremes. Sexual desire exists in her but is restrained. The role she prefers for herself is that of motherhood, not of passionate lover. Dion yearns to have his dual inner dimensions recognized, even as he suffers from their occasional friction within himself; he seeks Margaret's ordinariness to comfort and heal him, just as the nervous system needs the protective covering of skin. Dion seems to have nothing in common with the rigidity of his father, though he remembers his mother with some tenderness. Neither, however, is close enough to him to appreciate his need to grow into the fullness of his talent and to be encouraged to that end. Of all the characters in the play, only Cybel is the ideal mother who gives him unconditional birth.

O'Neill, in *The Great God Brown*, acknowledges a generational gap, a gender gap, a gap between the artist soul and the materialist body, a gap between seeming and being—all of which make confident self-identity excruciatingly difficult. Dion feels the urge and need to create; his creativity will define him and presumably mark his share in divinity. However, within his troubled psyche from time to time he questions whether divinity itself exists, or cares for him, or is willing to share the power of creation with him. The gap between God and humankind is the greatest distance of all, since its mystery is beyond measure. Cybel, the only truly compassionate character, tries to comfort both Dion and Billy in their dying by affirming the existence of a loving God, so that the suffering of these two men will not have been wasted. This is the ultimate dream, that of religious faith in the face of terrible doubt.

Dramatic Devices

Partly because scenes in *The Great God Brown* alternate so rapidly, returning to the same few places—office, home, Cybel's apartment—in a rhythm indicative of Dion and Billy's living harassed double lives, Eugene O'Neill's directions call for quick-change backdrops, rather than fixed or revolving scenery. The relative insignificance of place in the play also permits him to focus audience attention on the interior lives of his characters. To provide them with an experience of the sometimes dazzling complexities within each seemingly singular self, he developed the use of masks far beyond any earlier dependence on them. Not only Dion and Billy but also Margaret and even Cybel have masks, although in the case of the women the masks are simpler, less changeable. O'Neill was familiar with the use of masks among the ancient Greeks, but his purpose was not theirs. The Greeks were concerned with practical visibility in an amphitheater and with implied universality, when they put outsize masks on their performers. O'Neill's interest, by contrast, lay in dramatizing mass anonymity in *The Hairy Ape* (pr., pb. 1922) and conflicting layers of the inner man in *The Great God*

Brown, far beyond the triangle of ego-id-superego already introduced into psychological studies by Sigmund Freud.

O'Neill was determined to invent whole new ways of deepening theatrical commonplaces. His awareness of the actor as sacrificing personal identity to the role that he or she plays reinforced O'Neill's vision of inner-outer divisions in people in general. Similarly, dependence of the acting troupe on cosmetics as a form of conventional mask, to help establish this alternative identity, became an opportunity for O'Neill, in effect, to place masks beneath removable masks. The makeup used to delineate the progressive spiritual conflicts inside Dion and Billy differs from the external masks largely through the flexibility given to that makeup by facial expression. Never before and never again did O'Neill deploy dramatic masks so elaborately. Their use demanded much skillful handling on the part of the actor, since awkwardness would have brought laughter from an audience. Equally, they demanded a willingness on the part of audiences to submit to such unconventional devices in the name of greater intimacy and understanding of the characters.

Critical Context

After *The Great God Brown*, Eugene O'Neill turned his inventive mind to related experiments. In *Strange Interlude* (pr., pb. 1928) he tried what might be called "voice masks": Each character had a public voice that participated in normal dialogue and a private voice that gave the audience access to the inner thoughts of that character. The soliloquy, used for exactly this type of revelation, was a well-worn device, but it had never been used so extensively before. Despite the risk of prolonging his play by this added dimension, the device was necessary to satisfy O'Neill's desire to dramatize the conflict between every person's inner and outer worlds, as he already had managed to do with face masks in *The Great God Brown*. The "voice masks" were not so difficult for actors to manage as the face masks had been; the audience, too, could more easily accustom itself to the experimental device used in *Strange Interlude*.

In *Days Without End* (pr., pb. 1934) the playwright directs that one role be played by two actors, in order to convey the same division of worlds, though here they are finally resolved into one. In *More Stately Mansions* (pb. 1964), the "voice masks" appear briefly again, in act 2, with extensive soliloquies or asides given by a woman, her husband, and his mother, to expose unspoken dimensions of their fierce rivalry for domestic authority. The exhaustive use of masks in *The Great God Brown*, however, marked the climax of expressionistic experimentation for O'Neill.

Even as O'Neill turned to more surface realism in his later plays, his basic vision did not alter. Many of his works, early and late, are based on the supposition that it is humankind's ability to dream that separates it from animal life and offers some hope for an afterlife. Being no romantic, however, O'Neill understood the suffering imposed on humans by that very ability to dream and devoted his most important plays, therefore, to an attempt to distinguish among creative, destructive, and neutral protective dreaming. All these elements are discernible in *The Great God Brown*.

Sources for Further Study

Carpenter, Frederick I. *"The Great God Brown."* In *Eugene O'Neill*. Rev. ed. Boston: Twayne, 1979.

Engel, Edwin A. "Saint and Satan." In *The Haunted Heroes of Eugene O'Neill*. Cambridge, Mass.: Harvard University Press, 1953.

Estrin, Mark W., ed. *Conversations with Eugene O'Neill*. Jackson: University of Mississippi Press, 1990.

Falk, Doris V. *Eugene O'Neill and the Tragic Tension: An Interpretative Study of the Plays*. 2d ed. New York: Gordian Press, 1982.

Floyd, Virginia. *"The Great God Brown."* In *The Plays of Eugene O'Neill: A New Assessment*. New York: F. Ungar, 1985.

Frenz, Horst. "Desire, Masks, and 'Beautiful Philosophy.'" In *Eugene O'Neill*. Translated by Helen Sebba. New York: F. Ungar, 1971.

Houchin, John. *The Critical Response to Eugene O'Neill*. Westport, Conn.: Greenwood Press, 1993.

O'Neill, Eugene. "Memoranda on Masks." In *O'Neill and His Plays: Four Decades of Criticism*, edited by Oscar Cargill et al. New York: New York University Press, 1961.

Leonard Casper

THE GREAT WHITE HOPE

Author: Howard Sackler (1929-1982)
Type of plot: History
Time of plot: 1912-1914
Locale: United States, Europe, Mexico, and Cuba
First produced: 1967, at the Arena Stage, Washington, D.C.
First published: 1968

Principal characters:
JACK JEFFERSON, a black heavyweight champion
TICK, his trainer
GOLDIE, his manager
ELLIE BACHMAN, his lover
CAP'N DAN, a former heavyweight champion
SMITTY, a famous reporter

The Play

The Great White Hope opens at the Ohio farm of Frank Brady, the former heavyweight champion who is now being hailed as the Great White Hope—the fighter who will regain the title from the mocking black champion Jack Jefferson. After Brady is convinced by his manager Fred, Cap'n Dan, and Smitty to "stick a fist out to teach a loudmouth nigger" a lesson, Jack's manager, Goldie, agrees to hold the fight in Reno, Nevada, on July 4.

In a gymnasium in San Francisco, Jack shadowboxes and brags that he will destroy Brady, as he is watched by his trainer, Tick, and his white lover, Ellie Bachman, who will be the cause of his ensuing troubles. Although Goldie warns him about her, Jack refuses to hide their love, even after the reporters taunt them, and after Clara, who claims to be his common-law wife, attacks Ellie. At the Reno arena, Jack soundly defeats Brady and gains possession of his championship belt. At the end of this scene, Cap'n Dan explains that it is dangerous to have a black champion and vows to find another Great White Hope.

Scene 4 presents Jack's triumphal return to Chicago, where he is greeted by his well-wishers, who beat drums and cheer him and Ellie. The gaiety is threatened, however, by the arrival of the Salvation Army, which protests the immoral activities at Jack's Café de Champion. After Jack suavely prevents a potential riot, Mrs. Bachman enters with her lawyer, Donnelly, and demands to talk with Ellie, who refuses to see them. Donnelly warns Jack to send Ellie home, and the beating drums now begin to sound ominous.

Smitty, Donnelly, and Dixon, a shadowy federal agent, meet with Cameron, Chicago District Attorney, to discuss how to destroy Jack. When Ellie arrives, she is cross-examined about her sexual relationship with Jack. After she leaves, they agree to arrest Jack for transporting her across a state line for sexual purposes. Their plan is fulfilled at a small cabin in Wisconsin, where policemen break in to arrest Jack. Their forced entry represents the continuing intrusion of the establishment into the lovers' lives, which can never be private, given Jack's prominence and their interracial affair.

At the end of the first act, Jack arrives at his mother's house in Chicago and sets in motion his plan to escape his three-year sentence by going to England. As he changes places with his look-alike Rudy Sims, a Detroit Bluejays baseball player, Clara is prevented from revealing the plan to the officials in the street.

Act 2 has Jack in exile, wandering throughout Europe in search of boxing matches but encountering instead poverty, bitterness, exploitation, and growing estrangement from Ellie. After he is forced to leave England when a group of morally outraged people prevent him from boxing, Jack goes to France, where he savagely beats Klossowski, an arrogant Polish heavyweight. As the crowd grows ugly at the sight of the slaughter, Ellie is in the dressing room being questioned by Smitty, who wants to undermine her life with Jack.

Scene 4 moves to the darkened New York office of promoter Pop Weaver, who, along with Fred and Cap'n Dan, watches a film of the Kid, the new Great White Hope. Dixon promises to reduce Jack's sentence if he will agree to lose to the Kid. Like Cap'n Dan earlier, Dixon describes what it means to have a black champion who thwarts the establishment: "We cannot allow the image of this man to go on impressing and exciting these people."

In Berlin, Jack declines further as he engages in a series of pathetic tests of strength with four drunken German officers, who treat him as a curiosity. Ellie tries to persuade Jack to accept an entertainment contract with a sleazy Hungarian showman, Ragosy. Although Jack mocks her efforts, he is forced by economic necessity to appear as Uncle Tom in an ill-fated performance of *Uncle Tom's Cabin* in Budapest. Ironically, Jack is reduced to playing a role that he has steadfastly avoided in his own life. The second act ends as Jack refuses Smitty's offer to throw the projected bout with the Kid.

The third act presents the culmination of Jack's tragedy, as disruption, defeat, and death dominate his life. At the funeral of his mother, a riot breaks out when police attempt to repress the black preacher Scipio's separatist speech. After the Kid's backers meet again at Pop Weaver's office to discuss regaining the championship, Clara enters, clutching a bloodstained garment and crying for vengeance against Jack.

She receives her wish when Jack, reduced to training in an unused barn in Juarez, Mexico, finally tells Ellie that she must leave him. Distraught, she commits suicide by throwing herself down a well. The sight of her body compels Jack to accept the fixed bout with the Kid. The play ends in Havana with Jack, after punishing his opponent for a number of rounds, being "knocked out." The triumphant Great White Hope, with the championship belt around his neck, is carried aloft by his supporters like "the lifelike wooden saints in Catholic processions."

Themes and Meanings

In *The Great White Hope*, Howard Sackler presents the conflict between white power and black dissidence within the context of the struggle for the heavyweight championship in the years preceding World War I. Jack Jefferson antagonizes the boxing world by mocking and beating his white opponents and by having publicized affairs with white women. The play's themes, meanings, and conflicts emerge from its many perspectives on Jack's character. Jack appears to fulfill the stereotype of the black man lusting after white women, but he undercuts the public roles he adopts, with sarcasm and irony, to taunt his antagonists.

Although Jack himself reveals some aspects of his personality, he is more fully revealed by the views that others have of him. For Cap'n Dan, Jack is the "uppity" black who must be defeated by the Great White Hope. To Goldie, Jack is a fool to flaunt his relationship with Ellie. According to Clara and Scipio (but for different reasons), Jack betrays his race by loving a white woman. Finally, Ellie believes that Jack is a proud and loving man who is destroying himself by his futile attempts to defeat the establishment. As she says near the end of the play, when their resources have been exhausted, "How can you be your own man, they have you! They do and you know it, you're theirs. . . ."

Through the many perspectives on Jack's behavior, Sackler creates ambiguities about his motivations. Does he really love Ellie, or is he using her to taunt the white world? At the rural cabin in Wisconsin, Jack is very caring, but he grows increasingly bitter, particularly whenever she tries to influence his decisions. He may blame her for his exile, but he is the one who insists on flaunting their relationship. Jack drives the unstable Ellie to suicide by viciously rejecting her, but when he sees her broken body, he appears repentant and uses her death as the reason for his acceptance of the fixed fight.

In contrast to Jack's ambiguous behavior, the white power structure remains single-minded in its devotion to dethroning him. White people have power, money, and control over the legal system and public opinion. Jack has his talent, pride, integrity, and energy, all of which he loses as he attempts to escape through exile the destiny represented by the Great White Hope.

Ahead of his time in his rebellion against the establishment, Jack is forced to play only stereotypical roles which he infuses with a satirical edge, but which his antagonists use against him. He is a lone black champion in a white-dominated profession whose hierarchy crushes him.

Dramatic Devices

The Great White Hope is a sprawling play of nineteen rapid scenes that occur in eight countries and over two continents. Despite the range and speed of the scenes and the large cast, Howard Sackler infuses Jeffersons's tragic cycle of victory, exile, and defeat with unity through the use of parallel scenes, choral characters, and visual motifs such as the heavyweight championship belt.

Sackler employs parallelism effectively in the repetition of crowd scenes in which

Jack is at first applauded and then attacked and forced to escape. In Paris, when Jack savagely beats Klossowski, the cheering crowd turns ugly, and Jack and Ellie are forced to flee. Similarly, in Budapest the crowd, initially favorable to his performance as Uncle Tom, hoots Jack off the stage. These unpredictable crowds represent public opinion, a many-headed beast controlled by the forces that defeat Jack.

Another unifying device is the appearance throughout the play of five choral figures who provide different perspectives on Jack's complex personality. Cap'n Dan appears twice in a symmetrical fashion. After the third scene in act 1, when Jack beats Brady, Cap'n Dan vows to find a Great White Hope to defeat him, and at the end of the third scene in the last act he announces that everyone eagerly anticipates the Kid's victory. Cap'n Dan's prophecy joins with Clara's choral condemnation of Jack at the end of the preceding scene to lead inevitably to the destiny enacted at the Oriente Racetrack in Havana.

Sackler also uses the unifying visual device of the championship belt, which is emblematic of the theme and conflict of the play. In the first scene, Brady poses with the belt, which he promises to prevent Jack from winning. At Jack's victory celebration, however, Tick holds up the "gold belt in its plush-lined case." Finally, after the Kid defeats Jack, he wears the belt draped around his neck as he is carried by the crowd. The belt has passed from Brady to Jack and then to the Kid; it has served, along with the repetition of parallel scenes, to create structural unity in a series of diverse and rapid scenes.

Critical Context

Winner of the Pulitzer Prize, the New York Drama Critics Circle Award, and a Tony Award, *The Great White Hope* is an epic presentation of Jack Jefferson's tragedy, based on the history of Jack Johnson, the first black heavyweight champion. Howard Sackler endows the play with tragic magnitude through the poetic use of the American vernacular tradition. As a poet, screenwriter, and director of William Shakespeare's plays and T. S. Eliot's verse dramas, Sackler is able to fuse poetry, history, and popular culture into a classical yet modern drama in the tradition of Eugene O'Neill and Maxwell Anderson.

Jack Jefferson, the center of this hybrid drama, is at war with society and within himself as a result of his refusal to accept the roles that white and black people wish to impose upon him. Jack plays these various roles with equal parts of bitter glee, malice, condescension, and sadness, but he ends crushed by these demands and his inability to forge a powerful identity. Jack's tragedy is similar to that of the title characters in Sackler's long one-act verse drama *Uriel Acosta* (pr. 1954) and *Semmelweiss* (pr. 1977). Acosta flees the Spanish Inquisition to live in the Amsterdam Jewish community, but he soon learns that his prophetic spirituality is at odds with its crass materialism. In *Semmelweiss*, which also has an epic structure, the nineteenth century physician Ignaz Semmelweiss discovers the principle of antisepsis, which can prevent the spread of germs in hospitals, but the narrow-minded establishment refuses to accept his ideas. Eventually, he is driven to suicide by their continued ridicule. Sackler builds the conflicts in these plays around historical characters who represent the tragic fate of outstanding individuals attacked by societies determined to crush them for their superiority.

The Great White Hope is also significant for its relationship to the turbulent political and social context of the late 1960's, when the United States was engaged in the Vietnam War and African Americans continued their struggle for civil rights. Muhammad Ali, the black heavyweight champion who was stripped of his title for refusing to fight in the war, identified with Jack Jefferson's plight, which also paralleled the situation of many young men who escaped the war by going into exile. Thus for literary, social, and political reasons, *The Great White Hope* represents a distinguished achievement in American drama.

Sources for Further Study

Gilman, Richard. Review in *The New Republic* 159 (October 26, 1968): 36-39.

Paulin, Diana R. Review of *The Great White Hope*. *Theatre Journal* 53 (October, 2001): 506-508.

Trousdale, Marion. "Ritual Theatre: *The Great White Hope*." *Western Humanities Review* 23 (Autumn, 1969): 295-303.

Frank Ardolino

GREEN CARD

Author: JoAnne Akalaitis (1937-   )
Type of plot: Folk
Time of plot: The 1980's, with flashbacks to the late nineteenth century, the early twentieth century, and the 1960's
Locale: United States and a jungle
First produced: 1986, at the Mark Taper Forum, Los Angeles
First published: 1987, in *Theatre*

> *Principal characters:*
> RAYE, a white man, between forty and sixty years old
> JESSE, a young Latino man
> ROSALIND, a young Asian woman
> GEORGE, a Latino man, between twenty and forty years old
> JIM, an Asian man in his fifties
> DANA, an Asian man, between thirty and fifty years old
> ALMA, a Latino woman, between twenty and forty years old
> JESSICA, an Anglo woman, between twenty and forty years old
> JOSIE, a young Asian woman
> MIMI, a white woman, between thirty-five and fifty years old

The Play

    Green Card begins with a preshow tape loop lasting about twenty-five minutes. Voices, often speaking simultaneously, recite a litany of racist comments describing the supposed superiority of the Anglo-Saxon, Celtic race, and the alleged inferiority of Jews, Mediterraneans, Central and South Americans, Irishmen, and Japanese. A map of the United States appears, projected on a screen, while the scene in front shows a nineteenth century gentleman reading while a woman wearing a flag dress sleeps in the gallery. Amplified fragments of "primitive" music are heard from time to time.

    Gradually members of the company enter from all sides of the theater, some reciting simultaneously segments from the taped script, which describes how Anglo-Saxon men have mastered the world, while Jews are "in business." The nineteenth century man recites the Statue of Liberty poem, describing the "Mother of Exiles" who lifts her lamp to the "homeless, tempest-tossed." Meanwhile, another character claims that certain groups' inferiority is attested by their physiognomy, which he suggests is a kind of cruel joke of the Creator. The projection on the screen shifts to faces of the latest waves of immigrants to the United States.

    Jesse, a young Latino, appears as a stand-up comedian who delivers a series of insults and racial epithets. The projections constantly change, showing fragments of advertising, street signs, brand names, and other bits of Americana, while The Doors'

"L.A. Woman" plays in the background. Raye, as a Jewish man, speaks of the persecution in Lithuania which drove his family to emigrate. His almost sentimental description of their sacrifices is lightened by his account of receiving "nice sandwiches" and seeing his first banana. The women of the cast surround Raye and call out what he should beware of in this new land: swindlers, thieves, loan sharks, and people who make friends too easily.

In a communal letter home, the women recount the blessings of the United States, and Raye declares his love for his new homeland. Each of the players uses a different accent to describe the food, dress, or customs of another nation. Then Jessica, Rosalind, and Mimi insert their bourgeois comments about having a "theme party" or meeting an architect from France—an interesting contrast to Raye's description of his family's poverty. George speaks from a microphone in the audience, speaking in an "oily" voice of God's support for people making a living. Jessica, as a Jewish woman, goes through the audience offering pieces of cake, and then Dana, as Marshall Ky, speaks from the gallery, telling of all the luxury he gave up when he came to the United States.

In a section titled "English," slides of American signs and icons are projected as various cast members describe how they learned English. Jessica talks of the peculiarities of the differentiation in English between the imperfect and past perfect tenses, and then a taped voice asks them to tell the difference between such phrases as "burn up" and "burn down." Ellis Island becomes a game show, with participants given multiple-choice questions about fine points of the English language. Many of the questions focus on idiomatic usage; losers are sent back "to where they belong."

The issue of assimilation is viewed from two perspectives: that of immigrants, who are trying to become Americanized, and that of established Americans, who worry that their institutions are being undermined by "idol gods." Mimi appears as a newswoman interviewing cast members, who take on the exaggerated accents and mannerisms of stereotyped Vietnamese, Italians, and Japanese. The next section, called "Immigration," has cast members asking myriad questions typical of immigration service forms. What follows is a collage of words, names, and phrases derived not only from the culture of the United States but also from Spanish, German, and French culture; here again, various languages intermingle. Alma talks about her life as the cleaning woman for an affluent American family, and then the barrage of phrases continues at an accelerated pace until Jesse delivers a monologue recounting his experiences in El Centro after being detained for illegal immigration.

Act 2 has a pre-prologue, with the set changed to Southeast Asia and Central America. Under full houselights, George puts on an ethnic costume and tells of how the Spaniards came to conquer his people, how he tried life in the city and then returned to the country. With Asian music in the background, the actors perform a Vietnamese puppet dance. This segment also recounts the history of native people's resistance to colonial intervention.

In a section titled "Religion," Jesse, as a Jewish comedian, discusses how the Jews killed Christ. Then Dana, speaking as Marshal Ky, discusses the role which religion played in the politics of his region. The stage becomes a jungle with projections on the floor and a tape of locusts and jungle sounds playing throughout. In counterpoint to the taped description of the woods near Dvaravati, Mimi describes Asia from a caricatured tourist's perspective: She found Saigon "sexy," Phnom Penh "pure," and "little Pol Pot outfits" adorable.

In "History," various cast members tell of the atrocities of torture and oppression in various countries, while David Byrne and Brian Eno's "Mountain of Needles" plays in the background. Josie, Alma, Jessica, and Jesse tell of gang rape, cutting out tongues, and cigarette burnings; other cast members sew dolls and stuff them with red cloth. While film clips of the fall of Saigon and the battles in Nicaragua and El Salvador play, Sid Vicious sings his version of the Frank Sinatra song "My Way." The entire company recites the pledge of allegiance to the United States. The final segment, "Dying in Your Dreams," has the words "die" and "dream" alternating, as a taped woman's voice gives a coroner's report on an unspecified victim. The play closes as action freezes with the company of refugees and immigrants in line, waiting for a bus.

Themes and Meanings

Green Card is a play about the struggles of immigrants to the United States, but it goes beyond mere sympathy for their plight. It examines the connections between the policies and attitudes of the United States government and the responsibility of individuals in creating the bigoted atmosphere that greets most immigrants.

The form of the play, with its collage of voices and use of various media, is integral to its message. It re-creates the confusing welter of sounds and experiences that confront the refugee. The variety of characters and experiences also reproduces the variety of experiences of immigrants, from Latin American political refugees to such elite characters as Marshal Ky, who left powerful friends and expensive clothing behind him in his forced immigration. Attitudes range from that of the patriotic Jewish immigrant of the play's opening to that of the hardworking, bitter maid from Central America.

An important element of the play is the conflict between maintaining one's ethnic background and assimilating the customs and language of the United States. Certain voices, taken from such works as *In Their Place: White America Defines Her Minorities, 1850-1950*, depict the deeply entrenched xenophobia of those Americans who resent the influx of immigrants. Other voices are clearly critical of U.S. policies in Central America and in Southeast Asia. In several segments of the play, assimilation is portrayed as a form of cultural death for people with an ancient, proud heritage. However, while JoAnne Akalaitis criticizes United States government policies, particularly those of the Central Intelligence Agency, she does not neglect the injustices perpetrated by governments of other countries.

The play's deliberately overwhelming mix of opinion and fact demonstrates that there are no clear-cut boundaries in matters of acculturation. While the opportunity to learn English is viewed as a privilege by the immigrants, it is also shown to be an absurd exercise. This notion is underscored by the central image of the play, the game show *Green Card*. The multiple-choice questions have answers requiring such subtlety and sophistication that even native speakers would find themselves puzzled, yet these are the kinds of questions that determine the fate of people's lives. For example, Central Americans may be sent back to torture, prison, or death simply because they have an expression for money that differs from that of Mexicans—who, if they fail, are simply dumped out on the other side of the border. Akalaitis juxtaposes such scenes without comment, but her choice of details clearly indicates her political and ethical stance. She designs her play to make audience members consider their own place in the scheme of arrival and assimilation into American culture.

Dramatic Devices

Green Card has so many dramatic devices that one might describe the play itself as performance art, without the typical plot or development of scenes found in more traditional drama. Akalaitis's work is controversial because of her use of minimalist sets, onstage costume and character changes, and multimedia slide, film, and music shows. Some audience members find themselves frustrated by the bombardment of music, simultaneous monologues, ritual dances, and visual stimuli.

Akalaitis's purpose in presenting such cacophony and blurring of information is to force audiences to experience the play emotionally rather than regarding it with intellectual detachment. Viewers must choose the elements on which they focus; the theater is thereby more collaborative, active, and dynamic. Her method of completing a script is similarly unorthodox, with actors modifying the script, ad-libbing, and adding their own contributions to the final work. These devices lend spontaneity to the work of Akalaitis and to the acting styles of her company.

Versatility and concentrated focus are required of actors and audience alike, as actors change personae within single scenes. Aural cues dictate whether a character is a little old Jewish woman or a Vietnamese youth. Clothing changes sometimes aid the audience, but many alterations occur with no other clue than the shift in the actor's voice and mannerisms. This kind of shifting is designed to emphasize the universal nature of Akalaitis's subject. After a while, the blurring of characters created by constant changes underscores the point that this experience could happen to anyone.

The play has an equally flexible setting, with locales shifting from Los Angeles to Ellis Island, using just a hint of scenery to reinforce the change. Reminiscences of characters recall yet further reaches of place and time, from the shtetls of Russia to the jungles of Southeast Asia. Actors enter and exit from different parts of the theater, joining the audience at times to interact with them. This device again implicates the audience, calling upon it to consider its own responsibility and involvement in policies which might be creating new refugees.

Just as physical space is used to involve the audience, music provides ironic comment on the action of the play. For example, Sid Vicious's version of "My Way" plays simultaneously with documentary footage from Nicaragua, El Salvador, and the fall of Saigon, calling into question whose "way" created the political consequences shown on screen.

The closing scene is accompanied by haunting music from a bamboo flute. The play's ending has been considered by some to be a grim indictment of the United States, but other critics have seen in the image of immigrants waiting for a bus an element of hope. Despite the eeriness of the flute's death knell, the final taped words, "Will estrogen keep you young? Cooking in the West Coast Way," may humorously suggest that life, after all, continues.

Critical Context

JoAnne Akalaitis often combines in her work broad historical elements with highly personal experience, tragic events with absurdities, lofty concepts with homely sayings. In *Green Card*, she incorporates much of what she used in earlier work with Mabou Mines, the collaborative theater group with whom she formed her reputation as an avant-garde multimedia playwright. Her concern with social issues appears in *Dead End Kids: A History of Nuclear Power* (pr. 1980, pb. 1982), a play about nuclear power and weapons. Earlier works show less direct concern with contemporary issues. *Dressed Like an Egg* (pr. 1977, pb. 1984) is more obscure in its themes and topic, with information based loosely on the life of Colette and scenes dealing in some fashion with male and female relationships. *Southern Exposure* (pr. 1979), while more clearly dealing with an identifiable historical event, the first exploration of the Antarctic, is still similar to *Green Card* in its unconventional techniques and juxtaposition of dramatic elements.

Despite her desire to have her works experienced directly and spontaneously, much of Akalaitis's writing profits from close inspection. She researches her material quite thoroughly, and a number of references and quotations from other sources may be missed in a cursory viewing. This is as true of her earlier works as it is of *Green Card*, but *Green Card* may appear to be more accessible simply because of the subject matter of immigration, a topic with which most audiences are familiar. Her success may lie in her ability to combine timely subjects with unfamiliar approaches and information. *Dead End Kids* is her most popular work, and in this she confronts playgoers with a well-worn issue couched in a vast array of contexts, many of which are much clearer in the printed text than they are in performance.

Green Card, like the rest of Akalaitis's work as playwright and director, provoked mixed responses of outrage, irritation, and admiration. Much of her work makes for uncomfortable entertainment for playgoers, but perhaps her most vehement critic was playwright Samuel Beckett, who protested her direction of the American Repertory Theater production of *Fin de partie* (pr., pb. 1957; *Endgame*, 1958). She altered his stage directions, which call for an empty room with two small windows, changing the set to a subway station with a wrecked train in the background; other changes were made as well. Such tampering is an extension of the methods she uses in her own works, and her argument is that in order to keep plays vital, directors and actors must continue to alter sets, lines, and interpretations of plays, regardless of their source.

Some critics have seen much of the value of Akalaitis's work in her ability to challenge audiences and to stimulate discussion and controversy. *Green Card* certainly does this, but it does something more important as well. It combines disparate elements of culture, history, and media in a unified work whose structure is a carefully constructed dialectic. Just as the two large parts of the work show the contrast between the idealized view of the Horatio Alger-style immigrant and the oppressed, tortured political refugee, the individual scenes or tableaux provide counterpoints to one another. No single group or period receives special attention, and this evenhanded approach helps create a universal, timeless work. In addition, the selection of details demonstrates that playwright's wit and erudition, elements which may require second and third viewings or readings of her work. While *Green Card* may strike playgoers as confusing or disorienting, this organized chaos achieves the aims of JoAnne Akalaitis—to make her audience reconsider their values and their stand, as individuals and as citizens of the nation and the world.

Sources for Further Study
Cohen, Debra. "The Mabou Mines' *The Lost Ones*." *Drama Review* 20 (June, 1976): 83-87.
Kalb, Jonathan. "JoAnne Akalaitis." *Theater* 15 (May, 1984): 6-13.
Kramer, Mimi. Review in *The New Yorker* 114 (July 18, 1988): 66.
Marranca, Bonnie, ed. *The Theatre of Images*. New York: Drama Book Specialists, 1977.
Mehta, Xerxes. "Notes from the Avant-Garde." *Theatre Journal* 31 (March, 1979): 20-24.
Petzold, Roxana. "JoAnne Akalaitis." In *Contemporary Dramatists*. 6th ed. Detroit: St. James, 1999.

Rebecca Belle-Metereau

THE GREEN PASTURES
A Fable

Author: Marc Connelly (1890-1980)
Type of plot: Folk
Time of plot: 1929 and biblical times
Locale: Lower Louisiana and Heaven
First produced: 1930, at the Mansfield Theatre, New York City
First published: 1929

Principal characters:
MR. DESHEE, the preacher
GOD (DE LAWD)
GABRIEL, an archangel
ADAM and
EVE, the first human beings
CAIN, their son
NOAH, who built an ark to escape a great flood
ABRAHAM,
ISAAC, and
JACOB, the founders of the Israelite nation
MOSES, who led the Israelites out of bondage in Egypt
ZIPPORAH, his wife
AARON, his brother
PHARAOH, the ruler of the Egyptians
HEZDREL, who challenges de Lawd

The Play

Part 1 of *The Green Pastures* begins in a black church in lower Louisiana. An old preacher, Mr. Deshee, is teaching a Sunday school class of ten boys and girls. All the characters speak in the black dialect of Louisiana. Mr. Deshee begins the lesson by reciting the lineage of Adam. Expressing his belief that the Lord expects man to figure out a few things for himself, he replies to their questions by stating that before God made the earth, there was nothing but angels, who had a fish fry every week in Heaven and Sunday school for cherubs. The lights dim as Deshee reads, "In de beginnin', God created de heaven and de earth. . . ."

Scene 2 opens with the angelic singing of "Rise, Shine, Give God the Glory" to reveal a pre-Christian Heaven. Mammy angels wearing hats and men angels smoking cigars are enjoying a gala fish fry. After Gabriel awards diplomas to a class of cherubs, de Lawd enters, dressed in a white suit and Prince Albert coat of alpaca. Noticing that the custard needs more firmament, de Lawd passes a miracle and makes it rain. To provide a place for the firmament to drain, he also creates the earth. To dry off the cherubs' wings, he creates the sun. De Lawd then creates humankind because he agrees with Gabriel that it would be a shame to let the earth simply go to waste.

The promise with which de Lawd's creation begins in scene 2 changes to disillusionment by scene 7. Although Adam and Eve, represented by two farmhands, are the picture of confidence and health, the tree of knowledge at which they stare foreshadows Cain's murder of Abel in scene 4. Cain's attraction to a seductive girl in a tree in scene 5 causes de Lawd to return to Heaven. When de Lawd visits the earth again (in scene 7) after an absence of three or four years, his worst fears are realized. After witnessing a small boy gambling, he goes to Noah's house in the guise of a country preacher. Once he is convinced that Noah agrees with him that humankind is "goin' to the dogs," he reveals his true identity and instructs Noah to collect seeds of all the plants and two of every kind of animal.

Part 1 ends with a dramatization of the consequences of incurring the wrath of de Lawd. As Noah and his family are preparing the ark, they are mocked by a sinful crowd. Just before the ark sets sail, Cain the Sixth confirms de Lawd's harsh opinion of humankind by stabbing to death Flatfoot, his girlfriend's lover. In scene 10, with a drunken Noah at the helm, the ark finally makes it to dry land, prompting de Lawd to remark to Gabriel that his creation of the earth has turned out to be quite a proposition.

Part 2 begins in despair and ends in hope, a clear reversal of the pattern followed in part 1. Scene 1 of part 2 takes place in the office of de Lawd. Although frustrated by the seeming incorrigibility of humankind, he resists Gabriel's suggestion that he start all over again with another creature. Putting away the thunderbolts that he has been hurtling to earth, de Lawd summons Abraham, Isaac, and Jacob to his office and offers to turn over a valuable piece of property to their descendants. They choose the Land of Canaan and Moses as the overseer of the land. The scene ends with de Lawd voicing his intention to return to earth.

Scenes 2 through 4 chronicle God's efforts to save humankind through Moses. In scene 2, God reveals himself to Moses in a turkey-berry bush and provides him with a spokesman, Aaron, and the means for impressing Pharaoh: magic powers. Scene 4 depicts the attempts of Moses and Aaron to persuade Pharaoh to let their people go. When electrical shocks and swarms of gnats fail to change Pharaoh's mind, Moses asks de Lawd to kill the firstborn sons of all the Egyptians. As four men carry off his dead son, Pharaoh finally agrees to the Israelites' departure. While the Children of Israel are marching to Canaan, de Lawd promises Moses that he too will enter the Promised Land, though not Canaan, because he killed a man in Egypt. He also assures Moses that He will be with Moses' people even after Moses is gone. De Lawd offers proof in the form of Joshua's victory over Jericho, which is heard in the background. As the stage darkens, Mr. Deshee's voice is heard saying that the people "went to the dogs" again and returned to bondage, this time under the Babylonians.

Scenes 5 through 7 not only portray the Hebrews' rebellion against oppression but also depict humankind as being wiser than de Lawd. Scene 5 opens in a New Orleans nightclub, where the king of Babylon orders the execution of a prophet who has just forecast damnation for the sinners. The high priest prays to de Lawd for forgiveness, but de Lawd renounces the people, refusing to deliver them again. Even though de Lawd refuses the requests of Abraham, Isaac, and Jacob in scene 6 to let their people go, He is visibly moved by the puzzling voice of Hezdrel, which is heard while the prophet Hosea walks past his door. Scene 7 takes place in a shadowed corner beside the walls of the Temple of Israel. After a corporal informs Hezdrel that Herod plans to take the Temple in the morning, de Lawd appears, once again disguised as a preacher. Hezdrel informs de Lawd that he is not afraid of Herod because he has faith in the Lord God of Hosea, who is a God of Mercy, not a God of vengeance, as Moses' God was. He goes on to say that Hosea discovered the God of Mercy through suffering. Before leaving, de Lawd assures Hezdrel that there will be a place for him in Heaven.

Scene 8 duplicates the first scene in the play. God sits in an armchair near center stage, facing the audience. While eating custard, de Lawd tells Gabriel that he is thinking about what Hezdrel said about learning mercy through suffering. While he wonders out loud if Hezdrel meant that God too must suffer, someone points out that Christ is being made to carry the Cross and that he is to be crucified on a hill. The play ends with God murmuring "Yes." The angels begin to sing "Hallelujah, King Jesus." God smiles as the light fades and the singing becomes fortissimo.

Themes and Meanings

The Green Pastures provides a deceptively simple chronological summary of the first five chapters of Genesis. Marc Connelly's intention, on one level, was to demonstrate the importance of the Bible in the lives of rural African Americans. The types of questions that Mr. Deshee's Sunday school students ask make it clear to the discerning listener that they view the Bible as a practical guide for behavior. Thus, the little boy who wonders how long Adam and Eve were married before the birth of Cain is reflecting his people's concern for conventional morality. While the sins committed by the people in Mr. Deshee's narrative—gambling, drinking, murder—are social problems that plague society in general, de Lawd's concern with them makes it clear that they are especially prevalent in the black community.

By populating the Old Testament with African Americans instead of Hebrews, Connelly was able to make subtle comments on their social status at the same time that he was dramatizing the religious story. Connelly avoided making obvious social protest statements, choosing instead to imply that something is not quite right. For example, Mr. Deshee's Sunday school class in the very beginning of the play is impressed with the longevity of the central figures of Genesis because their experience dictates that most black people lead harsh, short lives. Connelly also attempted to neutralize the stereotyped notion of African Americans as being slovenly and immoral by balancing the incidents of gambling, drinking, and adultery in the play with such virtues as love for children, respect for authority, and hospitality. By the end of the play, when the courageous Hezdrel stands up to an unseen enemy, Connelly's message becomes somewhat more overt: that the Negro race, like the Hebrews, will deliver themselves from oppression, with the assistance and blessing of God.

Until the end of *The Green Pastures*, Connelly seemed to be saying that there are two types of black people—good but simple-minded ones such as Noah and bad, "uppity" ones such as Cain the Sixth—and that the bad ones could be reformed if they sought the benighted refuge of the heavenly fish fry or Mr. Deshee's Sunday school class. Beginning with the sixth scene, however, Connelly's emphasis shifts from the reformation of black people to the nature of humankind. Hezdrel is a black man, but he is also a complicated human being who knows more about the value of suffering than de Lawd does. Thus, the ending makes it clear that the subject of the play has been not merely the black race but indeed humankind itself. It becomes clear before the curtain falls that because they have become strong through suffering, black people are fitting representatives of the human race.

Dramatic Devices

Marc Connelly employed a variety of dramatic devices to add the dimensions of folk drama to his religious play. Although most of the play takes place in the Holy Land during biblical times, the costumes, dialect, and setting give the impression that the action occurs in the American antebellum South. The human beings are dressed as field hands and country preachers, and even the heavenly host smoke cigars and eat fried fish. Both the costumes and the rural setting recall the pre-Civil War days of the South, during which African Americans truly were oppressed people, much as the Israelites were in Egypt. By portraying God as a black country lawyer, however, the play transcends the stereotypes that it seems to be projecting and forces audiences to rethink some of their opinions regarding the status of African Americans. Connelly's replacing of the lofty language of the Old Testament with the black dialect of twentieth century Louisiana, with its connotations of illiteracy and ignorance, serves to add immediacy and relevance to the ancient stories of the Bible.

Although the play is firmly grounded in Judeo-Christianity and African American folklore, Connelly also relies heavily upon a device originated by the ancient Greeks: the chorus. Connelly eliminated the chorus leader and transformed the chorus into a choir, but he retained its primary function of commenting on the action of the play. For the most part, the choir foreshadows things to come, as it does in the end of scene 5 of part 2: The choir sings "Death's Gwinter Lay His Cold Hands on Me" just after de Lawd has renounced his people. The choir also comments on action while it is taking place. During the battle of Jericho in scene 4 of part 2, it sings "Joshua Fit de Battle of Jericho." At the end of scene 6 in part 2, however, when the choir sings "A Blind Man Stood in the Middle of the Road," the choir is actually criticizing de Lawd, who has just refused to help Hezdrel. Only once does the choir comment on both past and future occurrences. After Pharaoh agrees to let Moses' people go as a result of the death of Pharaoh's son, in scene 3 of part 2, the Choir sings "Mary Don't You Weep" and "I'm Noways Weary and Noways Tired."

Classical Greek drama also seems to be the source for the ironic twist that occurs at the end of the play. *The Green Pastures* is essentially a history of the "folk" until the reversal that occurs in the last few scenes, when de Lawd loses his superiority. The ironic evolution of humanity from the primal Cain and Flatfoot to the noble Hosea and Hezdrel dramatically brings into focus the primary theme of the play: that the "folk" are not only African Americans, they are human beings, and magnificent ones at that. Thus, Hosea and Hezdrel hold the same position that Tiresias holds against Oedipus and that Antigone holds against Creon.

Critical Context

The Green Pastures* derives its folk and religious origins from a book by Roark Bradford, *Ol' Man Adam and His Chillun: Being the Tales They Tell About the Time When the Lord Walked the Earth like a Natural Man* (1928). As he adapted the book for the stage, however, Marc Connelly's northern sensibility compelled him to make certain alterations. Though he preserved Bradford's image of long-suffering black people who spoke in black dialect, he transformed God from a white southern planter to a strong black figure. Connelly also departed drastically from Bradford's theme. At the end of *Ol' Man Adam and His Chillun*, Bradford implied that the African Americans' situation would stay the same; Connelly, on the other hand, boldly predicted a future of political activism for black people.

Even though *The Green Pastures* is Connelly's only religious folk drama, de Lawd's determination to resurrect the old virtues in the first part of the play brings to mind the characters of several of Connelly's previous plays. Like the African Americans of *The Green Pastures*, the characters of these early plays are underdogs who long for a better life. In *The Deep Tangled Wildwood* (pr. 1923; with George S. Kaufman), a New York playwright returns to his hometown in order to escape the fads of New York. By the end of *The Wisdom Tooth* (pr., pb. 1926), a timid clerk finds the courage to attack the superficial practices of his pragmatic coworkers. In *The Wild Man of Borneo* (pr. 1927; with Herman J. Mankiewicz), a con man who opposes conventional habits tries to rescue several people from the boring routines of their lives.

However, *The Green Pastures* represents a radical departure from Connelly's previous work in that part 2 takes up where most of his other plays end. While the characters of *The Wisdom Tooth*, for example, are on the verge of making a new beginning at the end of the play, humankind's attempt to rebuild the world destroyed by the flood in part 1 is the focus of the second half of *The Green Pastures*.

Despite charges that the theology behind *The Green Pastures* is too simple or that the characters reinforce unpleasant stereotypes, one must admit that *The Green Pastures* is an integral part of the cultural history of the 1930's. The awarding of the Pulitzer Prize to the play in 1930 reflects an awakening social consciousness in the United States, an awareness that was to permeate many of the great plays, films, and paintings of the 1930's. In fact, *The Green Pastures* is the most powerful expression of Connelly's lifelong preoccupation with the social outcast.

Sources for Further Study

Abramson, Doris E. *Negro Playwrights in the American Theatre, 1925-1959*. New York: Columbia University Press, 1969.

Connelly, Marc. "This Play's the Thing: *The Green Pastures.*" *Theatre Magazine*, May, 1930, 32-33, 66-70.

Ford, Aaron. "How Genuine Is *The Green Pastures?*" *Phylon*, Spring, 1960, 67-70.

Johnson, James Weldon. *Black Manhattan.* 1930. Reprint. New York: Da Capo Press, 1991.

Kelly, Marion. "Backstage: Marc Connelly Back with Prize Play." *Philadelphia Inquirer*, March 24, 1951, pp. 21, 24.

Mitchell, Loftin. *Black Drama: The Story of the American Negro in the Theater.* New York: Hawthorne Books, 1967.

Nolan, Paul T. *Marc Connelly.* New York: Twayne, 1969.

Alan Brown

THE HAM FUNERAL

Author: Patrick White (1912-1990)
Type of plot: Expressionist
Time of plot: 1919
Locale: London
First produced: 1961, at the Adelaide University Theatre Guild, Adelaide, Australia
First published: 1965, in *Four Plays*

Principal characters:
 THE YOUNG MAN, a would-be poet
 ALMA LUSTY, a landlady
 WILL LUSTY, a landlord
 THE GIRL (PHYLLIS PITHER), the Young Man's anima

The Play

Before the curtain rises on the stage, the Young Man delivers a prologue to the audience. Although the program notes specify London, 1919, as the setting of the play, the Young Man declares that time and place do not matter, that he could have been "born in Birmingham . . . or Brooklyn . . . or Murwillumbah." He explains that he is "alive" and therefore must "take part in the play, which . . . is a piece about eels." This produces his dilemma as a poet: He "must take part in the conflict of eels, and survive at the same time." In effect, he believes that he must live and yet maintain his artistic distance from life. The Young Man also warns the audience that "a number of you are wondering by now whether this is your kind of play"; he states that he cannot give them a "message."

When the curtain rises, the interior of a lodging house is disclosed, but only the basement is lighted. Will Lusty, the landlord, a "vast . . . swollen" man, sits immobile and silent, for the most part, listening to his wife, Alma, who is "in the dangerous forties, ripe and bursting." Before she asks the Young Man down for tea, she voices her discontent, her hunger for life, and her vanity (she repeatedly looks at herself in the imaginary mirror). Unconsciously, she reveals a tie between her dead son, Jack, and the Young Man, for she calls the latter Jack.

During the conversation in the Young Man's bedroom, which is connected with the basement by stairs, Alma and the Young Man reveal their antithetical values. While Alma "would like to devour the world, and keep it warm inside," the Young Man is withdrawn, lying down with his "cold," "dead" hands behind his head. Before they go down to tea, the Young Man asks about the tenant in the other front room, which mirrors his room, and Alma identifies her as Phyllis Pither, a "steady girl" who "most nights goes to bed with an aspirin and a cold." The Young Man, however, senses a presence, the touch of fingers on the other side of the wall where he rests his head.

Scene 4, in the basement, foreshadows Will's death (the Young Man describes the somber setting as a funeral). Alma is after "life," which is, according to Will, "wherever a man 'appens to be." The Young Man, suddenly aware that there is more to Will than he thought, wonders whether he is watching a tragedy or "two fat people in a basement, turning on each other." Jack, the dead son, is the focus of the conflict: Will was not his father. The Young Man, who speaks of himself as the chorus, not as an actor in the tragedy, leaves the darkened basement weary and disillusioned.

As he mounts the stairs, the Young Man speaks of his desire to be recognized for his brilliance, nobility, and generosity. His ensuing conversation with the Girl in the other front room, certainly not Phyllis Pither, shows him the futility of escape from what the basement represents. As the two, who are separated by a wall, speak to each other, they mirror each other's movements. The Young Man declares that if she remains on the other side of the wall, they can never "complete each other." However, if completion is not possible in life, as she points out, then discovery is. If the Young Man is to discover himself, he must not "overlook the landlord" in the basement; when he reaches the basement, however, he finds Will dead.

Alma and the Young Man do not handle Will's death well, either literally (they labor to deposit the heavy corpse on the bed but then discover that the feet have been placed on the pillow) or figuratively (the Young Man inadvertently refers to Will's "dead weight" and begins to hiccup). Their conversation consists of two monologues, Alma expressing determination to serve ham at the wake and the Young Man discovering that he must act to assemble Will's relatives.

In the street, the Young Man encounters two "ladies" who are rummaging through garbage cans. After he discovers a fetus in the trash, he concludes, "The landlord and the dead child are one," but he is less certain of his identity. He hopes to "retire again, into a corner, and dream," but he finally finds the relatives in a house that speaks, echoing his words. Although he invites four identical relatives to the ham funeral, only one accompanies him to the funeral; inexplicably all four attend the wake.

While the Young Man is in his room, the four relatives torment Alma, suggesting that she killed Will. Meanwhile, the Young Man and the Girl continue their conversation about a world that has "turned into a ball of mud," a world he cannot ignore. He returns, at the Girl's urging, to the basement wake.

After the Young Man dismisses the raucous, insulting relatives, he is left with Alma. Following is Alma's choreographed pursuit of the Young Man, whom she variously treats as Will, her husband; Fred, her lover; and Jack, her son. They fall on the bed, but the Young Man resists her, almost strangles her, and declares that "flesh . . . isn't the final answer." When he climbs the stairs again, he believes he is free, but the Girl informs him that he will again "wrestle with the figures in the basement . . . passion and compassion." The Young Man bursts through the door, but he does not find the Girl, who subsequently enters the house in the clothes of Phyllis Pither. He goes down to the basement, bids Alma good-bye, and walks "into the distance through a luminous night."

Themes and Meanings

The Ham Funeral portrays a young man's discovery of self and the resultant birth of a poet who had isolated himself from life. In the prologue he has just "woken," just become aware that he "must take part in the play" that focuses on him. Although he speaks of the "poet's tragedy"—"to know too much, and never enough," he is a poet only in theory, for his only poem has been discarded in the trash can. Before he can walk out into the "luminous night" at the end of the play, he must grapple with life, must hold the stage and participate.

Once the play proper begins, the audience first sees the Young Man in scene 3—in his bedroom, his hands behind his head, staring at the ceiling. He is physically and emotionally isolated from the vital if repellent reality in the basement. Alma's question, "Or am I speakin' to a dummy?" suggests not only that he cannot speak (and communication is another of White's themes) but also that he is not human. He is a fragmented personality, only partially developed. In Jungian terms, the Young Man, the animus, is the mind, the soul, incomplete without the Girl, the "anima" who directs his attention to the landlord and the basement, the world of the senses.

The Young Man must act in a play, not witness it, and must act in life, not retire from it. Action entails change and involvement in the cycle of birth, maturation, and death. Jack, who died as an infant, reappears—at least in Alma's eyes—as the Young Man and also as the abandoned dead fetus; Will dies, leaving the Young Man to "hold the stage," to replace him as lover to Alma. Alma's acceptance of such cyclical change is reflected in her comment, "Everything begins over and over again." The funeral is compared to a wedding.

Because she has "raped life," Alma is the true poet: "At least the landlady's poem speaks . . . after the fashion of imperfect flesh." The Young Man concludes that his own poetic attempts have been sterile "acts of self-abuse in an empty room." Before he can begin to be a poet, he must accept life. "This house is life," and it is also death.

To live is to communicate, however imperfectly or inadequately, and the Young Man's self-conscious verbal posturings are ironically less poetic than the words and actions of the Lustys. Alma distrusts the power of words: "All you get is words . . . good, bad, or doubtful. Or else it's silence." Only at the end of the play does the Young Man acknowledge that "words are bridges that won't bridge." Thus, he finally comes to know what he had stated in the prologue: "I can't give you a message."

Dramatic Devices

The house in which *The Ham Funeral* is set is a symbol of the Young Man's exposed soul or psyche. While the audience can see the conventional three walls, there is an invisible fourth wall against which there are dressing tables with mirrors: "Anybody making use of the mirror must expose themselves fully to the audience." Such exposure is essential to a play about self-discovery and about identity. Through lighting, the action alternates between foreground—the Lustys' basement room—and background—the two identical upstairs bedrooms, which the Young Man and Phyllis Pither occupy. The symbolic occupants, however, are the animus and the anima, the two separate parts of the Young Man's fragmented personality. The Girl asks rhetorically, "Am I your other self?" and adds that she will be with him in the basement "sitting on your right hand." Her choreographed movements mirror the Young Man's.

Urged by the Girl to descend to the basement, the Young Man must confront not only Alma's appeal to the senses but also Will's acceptance of life, his disbelief in the senses ("Bloody deluded!"), and his spiritual belief in inanimate objects ("This table is love . . . if you can get to know it"). Though they hold contrasting views of reality, Will and Alma embrace it, unlike the Young Man. In effect, before he can become an integrated (not "completed") personality, the Young Man must invade the other space in the set (the other bedroom and the basement) and identify with its inhabitants, other fragments of his psyche.

Critical Context

Although Patrick White was considered Australia's foremost novelist—he won the 1973 Nobel Prize in Literature—he was also an accomplished playwright who began writing plays in the early 1930's. Although none of his early dramatic works (drawing-room comedy, sketches, naturalistic plays) has survived, they do attest White's early interest in the theater. His novels reveal his gift for poetic dramatic dialogue. Written in 1946-1947, though not produced until 1961, *The Ham Funeral* marked a new direction for Australian drama when it was first produced (after having been rejected by the Elizabethan Theatre Trust and the Board of Governors of the Adelaide Festival) by the Adelaide University Theatre Guild.

White had new things to say in Australian drama, and naturalistic theater, then in vogue, was not an appropriate medium for him. Instead, he turned to expressionism and symbolism, which he also used in the three plays that he wrote and produced after *The Ham Funeral: The Season at Sarsaparilla* (pr. 1962), *A Cheery Soul* (pr. 1963), and *Night on Bald Mountain* (pr. 1963). In fact, the four plays, which were collectively published as *Four Plays* in 1965, are very much of a piece in technique and content. Their themes are consonant with the themes of his novels.

Though expressionism and symbolic sets were new to Australian theater, White's work does derive from an established tradition in Western drama. Henrik Ibsen and August Strindberg have been identified as influential, though White would also have been knowledgeable about the experimental efforts of W. H. Auden and Christopher Isherwood, which derive from the work of Bertolt Brecht. (The direct address to the audience in the prologue is blatantly Brechtian.) It is also possible that Tennessee Williams's *The Glass Menagerie* (pr. 1944, pb. 1945) was also a source; in that play Tom, also an autobiographical poet/narrator, addresses the audience, which watches a "memory play" enacted on a set similar to the one used in *The Ham Funeral*.

Regardless of its sources, *The Ham Funeral* did change the direction of Australian drama and established White's distinctive fusion of content and form. Not only were the other three early plays written in the same vein, but White's later play *Signal Driver* (pr. 1982, pb. 1983) closely resembles his earlier work.

Sources for Further Study

Argyle, Barry. *Patrick White*. New York: Barnes and Noble, 1967.

Beatson, Peter. *The Eye in the Mandala: Patrick White, a Vision of Man and God*. New York: Barnes and Noble, 1976.

Brissenden, R. F. "The Plays of Patrick White." *Meanjin Quarterly* 22 (September, 1964): 243-256.

Covell, Roger. "Patrick White's Plays." *Quadrant* 8 (April/May, 1964): 7-12.

Douglas, Dennis. "Influence and Individuality: The Indebtedness of Patrick White's *The Ham Funeral* and *The Season at Sarsaparilla* to Strindberg and the German Expressionist Movement." In *Bards, Bohemians, and Book Men: Essays in Australian Literature*, edited by Leon Cantrell. St. Lucia: University of Queensland Press, 1976.

During, Simon. *Patrick White*. Hyattsville, Md.: Oxford University Press, 1996.

Herring, Thelma. "Maenads and Goat Song: The Plays of Patrick White." *Southerly* 25 (1965): 219-233.

Loder, Elizabeth. "*The Ham Funeral:* Its Place in the Development of Patrick White." *Southerly* 23 (1963): 78-91.

Tacey, David J. *Patrick White: Fiction and the Unconscious*. Hyattsville, Md.: Oxford University Press, 1998.

Weigel, John A. *Patrick White*. Boston: Twayne, 1983.

White, Patrick. *Letters*. Chicago: University of Chicago Press, 1996.

Thomas L. Erskine

THE HAMLET OF STEPNEY GREEN
A Sad Comedy with Some Songs

Author: Bernard Kops (1926-   )
Type of plot: Folk; comedy
Time of plot: The 1950's
Locale: The East End of London
First produced: 1958, at the Oxford Playhouse, Oxford, England
First published: 1959, in *New English Dramatists*

> *Principal characters:*
> SAM LEVY, a seller of pickled herring
> BESSIE LEVY, his wife
> DAVID "DAVEY" LEVY, their son, a would-be crooner
> SOLLY SEGAL, a retired friend of the family
> HAVA SEGAL, his daughter
> MR. and MRS. STONE, middle-aged neighbors
> MR. WHITE,
> MR. BLACK, and
> MR. GREEN, young salesmen

The Play

The Hamlet of Stepney Green unfolds as Sam Levy, an invalid, has his bed pushed out into the garden by his old family friend Solly Segal and the latter's daughter, Hava. The lower-middle-class Jewish milieu is discernible in the dialogue. Two conflicts are immediately apparent: Sam believes himself to be dying, while the other characters, including his wife, Bessie, believe that he is exaggerating; and Hava (recently returned from an Israeli kibbutz) is interested in David, the Levys' son, but he ignores her. Sam's main worry is whether David (Davey, as Sam calls him) will settle down to take over his small pickled-herring business. David himself has ambitions to be a famous crooner. "I want to hear my voice blaring from the record shops as I whizz by in my Jaguar," he declares, and he appears to have no desire to satisfy his father in any way. This conflict emerges as the main issue in the first act, although the father and son are in no way antagonistic to each other. In fact, Sam's values are revealed to be ambivalent as the play proceeds, for he vacillates between urging David to settle down and urging him to be adventurous. Sam is also concerned that Davey marry for love and suggests that his own marriage was a second-best affair. He goes so far as to claim, "I've been poisoned by someone or something. What's the odds? By my life or by my wife . . . so my wife poisoned me." Davey does not understand the life/wife play of words and takes his father literally, especially when his father then suddenly collapses and dies.

Act 2 is divided into two scenes, both set in the living room of the Levy house, a week apart. Sam's funeral has just taken place, but Sam appears to David, who is sitting alone in the living room, waiting for the others to return from the service. Sam is now a ghost; he appears solid enough, but he tells David, "I live only in your mind and heart. No one else will see me; nobody else will want to." Parallels with William Shakespeare's *Hamlet, Prince of Denmark* (pr. c. 1600-1601), begin to manifest themselves, especially when David suggests the need for revenge. Sam, appearing not to realize that David has misunderstood his claim to have been poisoned by his life and wife, does not stop David's increasingly frantic talk.

They are interrupted in the debate by three salesmen coming in one after another, two apparently seeking to sell tombstones, the other to sort out Sam's life insurance. David continues to talk to Sam, and as the others cannot see him, they believe David to be mad. Consequently, it is not clear whether he can be paid any money from the insurance. The others return from the funeral and indulge in typical postfuneral talk. David reappears dressed as a teddy boy ("but the similarity to Hamlet must be stressed," Bernard Kops writes in his stage directions), makes a bizarre oration, and points a finger at his mother.

The second scene is set at the end of the week of mourning required by Jewish ritual; everyone is there as before. David now wants to put into motion a plan for revenge, but his behavior appears increasingly irrational. Sam's ghost reappears and tries to calm David down, telling Davey to treat his mother gently. David has noticed that Solly Segal is beginning to see Bessie as a future wife and that she is offering little resistance to the idea. Sam welcomes this turn of events, however, and sees a possible way to "take revenge." While the salesmen play cards, the women try to start a séance. Sam interferes, and the scene ends in total confusion, with Sam getting the message through that he is happy for Segal to marry Bessie.

Act 3 is set eight months later. It is early spring, and the scene shifts between living room and garden. The room is decorated for a festivity, apparently the wedding of Segal and Bessie. The three salesmen reenter, though they have now switched jobs. David and Sam also reenter. Sam sees that the only way to rid David of his fixation on revenge is to play along with it; he suggests that David concoct a poison to be drunk as part of the wedding toast. The concoction is, in fact, an aphrodisiac, and the incipient gloom of the wedding party is transformed into joy as the "poison" is drunk.

Only Hava and David do not drink. She goes into the garden, and David, encouraged by Sam, follows her. Suddenly, David realizes that he loves her. Sam's revenge is successful—if a Levy becomes a Segal, a Segal should become a Levy. The play ends happily on a note of celebration of David and Hava's love, echoed by their parents. Sam departs, his ghostly duty done.

Themes and Meanings

The title of *The Hamlet of Stepney Green* might suggest that it is a modern Jewish reworking of the Shakespearean tragedy. It features a father who claims to have been poisoned by his wife while lying in a garden, a need for revenge, a hasty remarriage of the mother, a sense of unease on the youthful hero's part, his bizarre behavior and the question of his insanity, and his rejection of the girl who loves him. The parallel plot details, however, are inexact; for example, Sam does not commission David to take revenge: David takes it upon himself. Also, Bessie marries after the ghost appears, and her marriage is sanctioned by the ghost.

Genre differences are much more significant than the plot differences. While Shakespeare's *Hamlet* may be seen as a subversion of the revenge tragedy, it remains a tragedy. Kops, however, turns everything into comic fantasy. In fact, his plot is a deliberate reversal of tragedy: Revenge gives way to a celebration of life. Kops called his autobiography *The World Is a Wedding* (1963), basing his title on a Jewish saying. This love of life is the central theme of this play in which funerals give way to weddings.

There is, in fact, a considerable amount of autobiography in the play, as might be expected from a first work. For example, Sam is a poor Jewish immigrant who left Russia at the beginning of the century; Kops's own family had similar origins. The conflict between Sam and David mirrors exactly the account Kops gives in *The World Is a Wedding* (1963) of his own father, even to his ambivalence, his realization that his own life had not really been fulfilled, and his paradoxical pushing of his son into the same pattern. The autobiography finishes with an account of Kops's second, very happy marriage, which clearly transformed him from a dropout to someone who embraced life fully. In the play, when David finally allows himself to love Hava, the audience senses that he will similarly be transformed. Thus, the "melancholy artist" in David is a sign not so much of *Weltschmerz* as simply of immaturity to be brought into maturity by allowing himself to love and be loved. David's search for meaning finds its goal in true love—a love that has been waiting for him. Ultimately, then, Kops's own life journey has imposed a much stronger pattern on the play than did his Shakespearean prototype.

Much of the background and stage matter reflect Kops's own Jewish background, as does the setting in the East End. Kops has made the play far more pastoral, however, than real life would allow; Stepney Green, including Kops's house, was bombed flat during World War II. In fact, the idealization may account for a certain thematic fuzziness in the play. Kops is writing intuitively and spontaneously, in the glow of good feelings about life, instead of allowing the depth and shape of his earlier rebellion to express itself. David's ambitions are typically adolescent and probably do not represent any sort of social or moral criticism of the lifestyles and values of his family or society in general.

Dramatic Devices

The parallels between *The Hamlet of Stepney Green* and Shakespeare's *Hamlet* are particularly noticeable in the dramatic devices employed. There is a ghost who can be seen by only David, a fact that leads to charges of insanity. However, David's behavior, like Hamlet's, really does appear bizarre anyway, and he seems out to shock his family. There is also the question of how seriously the audience should take the ghost. In this play, though, the incongruities do not matter; it is all part of the joke.

Revenge by poison is another parallel device, though there is no accompanying duel. The poison is turned into a love potion—an unexpected twist by the playwright and one of the more successful. The three salesmen could be seen as acting as Rosencrantz, Guildenstern, and Osric figures—petty courtiers now become salesmen. They are ordinary *hommes moyen sensuels*, ambitious in only a petty way, in contrast to David with his great dreams of glory. It could be equally well argued, though, that Kops simply enjoys crowding his stage—there seems to be little other reason for the Stones, a nondescript middle-aged couple. A final possible Shakespearean parallel is Bessie's remarriage; the device of a parent's remarriage features in other writings by Kops, for example, *The Dream of Peter Mann* (pr., pb. 1960) and *Yes from No-Man's Land* (1965). This common theme may reflect his own father's remarriage after his mother's death.

Kops appears to have consciously reworked an aristocratic hero into a lower-class one. The guise of a teddy boy (the proletariat youth's cult image of the 1950's) is intended to shock David's family, not to imitate Hamlet. In fact, Kops does not make it clear whether David himself is at all conscious of being a modern-day Hamlet. He is perhaps not aware of imitating, but occasionally he lets slip such phrases as "Prince of Herrings," which follows a takeoff of the "to be or not to be" speech.

Ultimately, however, the devices modeled on those of Shakespeare should not be seen as predominant. It has been suggested that the play stands in a long tradition of Jewish folk drama, especially popular in the nineteenth century, with songs frequently interspersed with dialogue. Children's games and songs open the play; later there are further songs sung by the children, as well as songs at the wedding feast and those David sings. This song device is used more systematically in *The Dream of Peter Mann*.

It could be argued that such devices show the great (and acknowledged) influence of Bertolt Brecht on Kops. While Kops has neither Brecht's political commitment nor his powers of social analysis, the mixture of comedy and tragedy, serious and bizarre, the disorientation, and even the antiheroic elements in Sam and David could be seen as Brechtian. They are also, however, typically Jewish. Jewish ritual is prominently featured; act 2, scene 1, ends with the Kaddish, the Jewish mourning ritual, but its mournful effect is lessened by both Sam's participation in it and David's bursting in wearing his teddy boy outfit and singing the song "My Yiddisher Father." The week's gap between scene 1 and scene 2 is also based on the Jewish ritual of family mourning, which Kops describes fully in his autobiography. Act 3 is based on a Jewish wedding. Kops himself evidently is not an Orthodox Jew, yet he sees his roots in the observation of such rituals and makes them a basic structural device for this play.

One other device that must be mentioned is the dividing of the stage between the interior of the house and its garden. Act 1 takes place in the garden, but the audience is aware of the house, act 2 reverses this situation, and act 3 strikes a sort of balance. Echoes of Arthur Miller's *Death of a Salesman* (pr., pb. 1949) might be intended, but Kops does not work the tension out systematically as Miller does. The garden becomes a pastoral motif and a fitting place to celebrate David's avowal of love to Hava. The gesture is too slight and too unsystematic, though, to have great impact on the play as a whole.

Critical Context

Penguin's publication of the play in the first volume of its New English Dramatists series shows the significance of *The Hamlet of Stepney Green* for the British theater in the late 1950's. After several decades of highly stylized upper-middle-class comedy, young British playwrights had revolted and set their plays in what they saw as the realities of working-class and lower-middle-class postwar Britain. John Osborne's *Look Back in Anger* (pr. 1956, pb. 1957) is generally seen as the first of such dramas.

The Hamlet of Stepney Green is perhaps more immediately to be compared to the plays of Arnold Wesker, especially *Chicken Soup with Barley* (pr. 1958, pb. 1959), which is also set in a Jewish milieu in the East End of London. Kops's mood is much more celebratory and optimistic than either Osborne's or Wesker's, and his bizarre humor avoids the grim absurdism of Harold Pinter, another Jewish dramatist of the period. Kops also lacks Wesker's political commitment, though his intuitive sympathies are not dissimilar.

The production of *The Hamlet of Stepney Green* soon moved from Oxford to London; the play was subsequently performed in Germany, the Netherlands, and the United States. It was generally hailed as the work of a promising dramatist, and on the strength of it, Kops was given an Arts Council bursary. Some critics believe that it is better than any of the more than two dozen others written since (which include some for television and radio). Other critics, however, see formal weaknesses and incoherences in *The Hamlet of Stepney Green* and prefer *Enter Solly Gold* (pb. 1961, pr. 1962), another Jewish tragicomedy, or *Ezra* (pb. 1980, pr. 1981), a play about Ezra Pound's last years.

Certainly, the play has had only intermittent revivals and has not been readily reprinted. Besides drama and his autobiography, Kops has written several volumes of poetry and more than a half dozen novels. He was classified as primarily a novelist in the late twentieth century, though it must be said that his reputation as a writer rests firmly on his drama, a reputation bolstered by plays in the 1990's that included *Sophie (The Last of the Red Hot Mamas)*, pr. 1990, *Playing Sinatra* (pr. 1991, pb. 1992), *Dreams of Anne Frank* (pr. 1992, pb. 1993), and *Call in the Night* (pr. 1995, pb. 2000).

Sources for Further Study

Dace, Tish. "Bernard Kops." In *Contemporary Dramatists*. 6th ed. Detroit: St. James Press, 1999.

Kops, Bernard. *Shalom Bomb: Scenes from My Life*. London: Oberon, 2000.

Lumley, Frederick. *New Trends in Twentieth Century Drama: A Survey Since Ibsen and Shaw*. 4th rev. ed. New York: Oxford University Press, 1972.

Taylor, John Russell. *The Angry Theatre: New British Drama*. Rev. ed. New York: Hill and Wang, 1969.

Wellwarth, George. *Theatre of Protest and Paradox*. London: MacGibbon & Kee, 1965.

David Barratt

HANDS AROUND

Author: Arthur Schnitzler (1862-1931)
Type of plot: Tragicomedy
Time of plot: The 1890's
Locale: Vienna, Austria
First produced: 1920, at the Kleines Schauspielhaus, Berlin
First published: Reigen, 1900 (English translation, as *Hands Around from La Ronde*, 1920)

Principal characters:
LEOCADIA, the prostitute
FRANZ, the soldier
MARIE, the maid
ALFRED, the young gentleman
FRAU EMMA, the young wife
KARL, the husband
THE SWEET GIRL, a naïve, lower-class woman
THE POET, a pompous young man
THE ACTRESS, a sophisticated, take-charge woman
THE COUNT, a hedonistic aristocrat

The Play

Hands Around consists of ten short scenes in the form of dialogues between a man and a woman. The central concern of each is conversation before and after sexual intercourse, which is itself not depicted onstage. The playwright's inspiration may have been William Hogarth's two 1736 engravings "Before" and "After."

The first partners are the prostitute and the soldier. Leocadia is so attracted to Franz that she offers herself to him free of charge. Since the swaggering soldier is not willing to accompany her to her room, they perch precariously on the banks of the Danube Canal while making love. Throughout this terse encounter, the brutish man prefers to remain faceless and anonymous.

The second instance of the recurring dialectic of persuasion and reluctance is the encounter between the soldier and the maid. Having met Marie at a dance in the Prater, Vienna's amusement park and pleasure ground, Franz takes the initiative and has his way with her on the grass. Afterward he agrees to take her home, but not until he has had some more fun dancing with another girl.

In the third scene, the maid is seduced by Alfred, the blasé, feckless young gentleman of the house, in his bedroom. After intercourse, eager to restore (or continue) the master-servant relationship, he orders her to answer the doorbell and rushes off to his favorite café.

The young gentleman is next shown with the young wife. This time Alfred does not improvise a seduction but carefully and aesthetically prepares for a visit from Frau

Emma, who arrives heavily veiled at the apartment he has rented for the assignation. After overcoming her scruples, he finds himself impotent, possibly because she is not his inferior but his socioeconomic equal. Alfred attempts to rationalize, intellectualize, and poetize his failure by recounting a Stendhal story in which some cavalry officers were unable to perform with the women they desired the most. One of them wept for joy with his lover for nights on end, presumably because their love was so pure. Frau Emma's attractiveness and experience finally enable the young gentleman to function after all, whereupon she remarks that this outcome is better than crying. After she leaves, he notes that he now has had an affair with a "respectable" woman.

The fifth scene presents the only sexual encounter sanctioned by society: conjugal love between the young wife and the husband. Placing his wife on a pedestal, the domineering philistine Karl priggishly preaches the virtues of morality and carefully rationed sex, with periods of friendship and continence to be followed by conjugal "affairs." As he smugly moralizes about the unhappiness of unfaithful wives, Emma, who desires to be his lover as well as his wife and wishes for a son in addition to her daughter, wistfully remembers their wedding night in Venice.

In an unabashed demonstration of the age-old double standard, the husband next takes up with the sweet girl in a cabinet particular (or *chambre separee*) of a restaurant. (Das susse Madel, a stock character in Arthur Schnitzler's plays, appears in various translations as the Sweet Young Lady, the Sweet Young Thing, the Sweet Young Miss, the Little Miss, and the Little Darling.) This earthy, naïve, pleasure-loving girl from the lower class is by turns prudish and promiscuous. Typifying a sort of realpolitik of love, she seems resigned to her fate of being loved and left. After their lovemaking, her hypocritical partner almost makes her apologize for his adultery.

In the next scene, the Sweet Girl is the foil of the pretentious, pompous Poet, who is fascinated by her "sacred simplicity" and "divine stupidity," attributes that serve to convince him of his own superiority, sophistication, and complexity. He vainly attempts to impress her with his nom de plume (she has never heard of the famous Biebitz), and he caresses her with one hand, as it were, while he jots down his poetic insights with the other.

At a country inn, the Poet gets his comeuppance from the Actress, a worldly, hardboiled, take-charge type who uses sex for her own enjoyment and prestige and to cement professional and social relationships. She does want sex from him but sees through and ridicules the fanciful vaporings of this poseur.

The Actress next receives the Count in her bedroom. The hedonistic but inhibited aristocrat does not believe in making love so early in the day, but on the morning after her triumph on the stage the capricious, strong-willed, and rather misanthropic woman manages to get him into bed with her.

In the tenth and last scene, which is a postlude only, the play comes full cycle with the Count and Leocadia. Having followed her to her shabby room in a drunken stupor, the Count awakens early in the morning without any recollection of the night. Once more a reluctant sex partner, he is disappointed to learn that he has done more than kiss the girl's eyes. A philosopher of sorts, he muses about the meaning of life, permanence, and happiness. Leocadia, who is this time emotionally uninvolved, is now more self-assured and "professional," speaking realistically and hopefully of her forthcoming move to a better district. She even gets the Count to give a tip to a servant, something that Franz had refused her in the first scene.

Themes and Meanings

Arthur Schnitzler had an early career as a physician, and though he was not a psychiatrist, he was admired by Sigmund Freud for his poetic anticipation of some of the psychoanalyst's clinical findings. A diagnostician rather than a therapist, he concerns himself more with the description of psychic structures than with a search for their origins. In *Hands Around*, Schnitzler presents a typology of amorous relationships, exploring the dark power of sexuality, which draws all characters into its vortex, and the sway of Eros, which levels all social and economic distinctions. Depicting a cross section of Viennese society at the turn of the twentieth century, the playwright questions the moral foundations of that decaying society and lays bare a psychological and social malaise within it as he exposes the exploitation of women by men, the weaker by the more powerful, and the failures by the successful. The notorious double standard has led to a socially sanctioned differentiation between love and lust. Schnitzler excoriates a society that regards its empty, mendacious rituals as normal and inevitable. The ancient Roman adage *Penis erectus non habet conscientiam* applies here: A lustful man will stoop to almost any strategy of seduction.

Eschewing any plot or character development in the conventional sense, Schnitzler is less interested in the sex act as such than in what leads up to it and what transpires in its aftermath. Intercourse is not discussed; this socially conditioned taboo and the Victorian denial that women also have sexual needs and appetites produce a series of linguistic and mimetic surrogates that often appear as banter and bluster, badinage and bathos. The spectator or reader is made aware of the ultimate futility of transient relationships and empty, impersonal hedonism.

Recurring motifs in the play are the man as hunter and the woman as his quarry, concern about the lateness of the hour, the fear of light and of discovery by an intruder, and the irruption of life into a hothouse atmosphere. Franz is the only man in a hurry; all the others without enough time are women. Only Frau Emma rushes to get home after intercourse; when their initial coyness has been overcome and they have surrendered, all the other women are frustrated in their desire for continued closeness and tenderness, a deeper gratification. Sham, hypocrisy, and mendacity are shown to pervade even the most intimate of interpersonal relationships, and seeming intimacy camouflages actual alienation. Another ancient Latin insight is pertinent here: *Post coitus omne animal triste est*. Coitus denotes a coming together or union, but after the brief sexual encounter the partners inevitably and quickly drift apart again. Each sexual climax is followed by an anticlimax. Rapture is replaced by melancholy, sadness, and even despair, and men and women seemed doomed to live and die in loneliness. The dance of life often seems like a dance of death of the medieval variety.

Dramatic Devices

The story is told (in Yiddish) about a man who attends his first play and then sums up his impression of the theater in these words: "First he wants to and she doesn't. Then she wants to and he doesn't. When they both want to, the curtain falls." In print, Arthur Schnitzler discreetly indicated sexual intercourse by a series of dashes or asterisks, and he thought that on the stage the conversational prelude and postlude might be separated by a brief curtain or blackout.

Schnitzler chose a circular structure for his play. *Reigen*, its title in the original German, denotes a round dance or roundelay; the word also means a sequence or series. In English it has been variously titled *La Ronde, Hands Around, Round Dance, Couples, Merry-Go-Round, Circle of Love* (in a film version), and *Dance of Love*. The last-named renders the playwright's working title, *Liebesreigen*, and *La Ronde* has prevailed since the film versions of Max Ophuls (1950) and Roger Vadim (1964).

Since each erotic encounter is so unsatisfying, the not-so-merry-go-round could be continued indefinitely. The sequence of scenes is determined by social possibilities, with a gradual progression up the socioeconomic ladder. The characters in the sexual rotation are not, however, interchangeable; an affair between the soldier and the young wife would be unthinkable. Schnitzler presents the figures as types, and their namelessness foreshadows the practice of expressionist playwrights, but his great theme of insecurity and evanescence places him in the mainstream of *fin de siècle* impressionism. The recurrent patterns of behavior and language serve to conceal rather than reveal. Only occasionally does a character have intimations of immorality or mortality. Thus the Count, who symbolizes the decline of the Austro-Hungarian aristocracy and its lifestyle, shows some interest in the life of Leocadia and attempts to ennoble her even as he, like the husband with the Sweet Girl, wonders about the risks of his lovemaking. An aggressiveness that precludes any more lasting relationship is the price the Actress pays for her escape from a patriarchally conditioned social and emotional bondage. The darkness on the stage during some of the dialogues symbolizes the feigned bashfulness of several of the women and also serves to obscure the identity and individuality of the partners. Schnitzler makes it evident that men regard the abstractness of sexual encounters as unsatisfying but convenient, whereas women seek not only sex but also more personal and enduring relationships.

Critical Context

Arthur Schnitzler wrote *Hands Around* between November, 1896, and February, 1897, and this tragicomedy bedeviled him for the rest of his life. In 1900 he had two hundred copies privately printed, and he distributed them to his friends. Three years later, a Viennese publisher brought out a commercial edition, which was either ignored or vilified by the press. Because of the controversial nature of the work, S. Fischer, Schnitzler's regular publisher, did not issue it under his imprint until the year of the playwright's death.

From the outset, Schnitzler was aware of the untimeliness and explosive nature of the play, and he had doubts about the advisability of staging it. For decades he referred to it in his letters, and in an unpublished note of 1922 he outlined some of its problematical points: The play does not communicate outrage at sex between casual acquaintances, and the sex act is marked by a short curtain at the midpoint of each scene, not its end. Seven years after an unauthorized Hungarian performance in Budapest in 1913, Schnitzler permitted Max Reinhardt to produce it in Berlin. Actually, Gertrud Eysoldt had already premiered the play there at her Kleines Schauspielhaus in December, 1920. In the inhospitable climate of the troubled early postwar years, *Hands Around* became a *cause célèbre*. There were demonstrations and riots. Far from viewing it as a critique of selfishness and lovelessness in a corrupt, doomed society, a hostile press and government officials chose to interpret it as smut, pornography, a celebration of promiscuity, and a lustful Jew's invitation to free sex. After a week-long trial the management and cast of the Berlin theater were acquitted. Numerous performances followed in Berlin and other German cities. Riots and scandals, however, led Schnitzler to prohibit further performances, and his son Heinrich did not lift the ban for the German-speaking stage until 1981.

Most critics have long regarded Schnitzler's play as a masterpiece and a modern classic. Though there is nothing to indicate that the author intended to highlight the dangers of sexual promiscuity, this comment by the Viennese-born psychoanalyst Theodor Reik is relevant in the age of acquired immunodeficiency syndrome:

> At any given moment in reading the *Reigen* one might wonder what would happen if one of the partners had a primary syphilitic infection. The picture of the merry-go-round would quickly be transformed into that of the danse macabre. . . . the dance of life becomes a whirlwind of spirochetes.

Sources for Further Study

Hannum, Hunter G. "Killing Time: Aspects of Schnitzler's *Reigen*." *Germanic Review* 37 (1962): 190-206.

Liptzin, Solomon. *Arthur Schnitzler.* Riverside, Calif.: Ariadne, 1995.

Reik, Theodor. "Hands Around." In *The Secret Self: Psychoanalytic Experiences in Life and Literature*. New York: Farrar, Straus, and Young, 1952.

Roberts, Adrian C. *Arthur Schnitzler and Politics.* Riverside, Calif.: Ariadne, 1989.

Sanders, Jon Barry. "Arthur Schnitzler's *Reigen:* Lost Romanticism." *Modern Austrian Literature* 1 (1968): 56-66.

Swales, Martin. *Arthur Schnitzler: A Critical Study.* Oxford, England: Clarendon Press, 1971.

Urbach, Reinhard. *Arthur Schnitzler.* New York: Ungar, 1973.

Weinberger, G. J. *Arthur Schnitzler's Late Plays: A Critical Study.* New York: Lang, 1997.

Wisely, Andrew C. *Arthur Schnitzler and the Discourse of Honor and Dueling.* New York: Lang, 1997.

Harry Zohn

HAPGOOD

Author: Tom Stoppard (Tomas Straussler, 1937-   )
Type of plot: Problem play; suspense
Time of plot: The 1980's
Locale: London
First produced: 1988, at the Aldwych Theatre, London
First published: 1988

> *Principal characters:*
> ELIZABETH HAPGOOD, the head of a British spy unit
> PAUL BLAIR, her immediate superior
> JOSEPH KERNER, a Russian-born physicist and double agent
>   working for the British
> BEN WATES, an operative with the Central Intelligence Agency
> ERNEST RIDLEY, one of Hapgood's agents
> JOE HAPGOOD, the eleven-year-old son of Hapgood

The Play

Hapgood opens with a mostly silent scene in the men's changing room of an old-fashioned indoor swimming pool in London. As a black man dressed like a bum shaves, voices are heard speaking on a shortwave radio. Men, some carrying briefcases, pass back and forth between the lobby, the changing cubicles, and the swimming pool. The briefcases are dropped off and picked up at various cubicles. After all but the black man leave, a woman carrying an umbrella and one of the briefcases emerges from the shower. Elizabeth Hapgood, of British intelligence, and Ben Wates, an American agent, discuss certain events as one of the men, Ernest Ridley, returns to say he was surprised that the two Russian agents in the previous maneuver are twins. He and another British agent, Merryweather, address Hapgood as "Mother." There is confusion about who ended up with what briefcase, and Hapgood orders the Russian twins arrested. After she leaves and Paul Blair, another British agent, arrives, Wates says, "She blew it."

In the following scene, Blair is at a zoo to meet one of the protagonists in the opening charade, Joseph Kerner, a Russian-born physicist. Kerner was sent to England years before as a "sleeper," but he is now a double agent working for the British. Blair tells him that his career as a spy is over and demands, "Joseph—I want to know if you're ours or theirs." Blair is upset because, in addition to the phony information Kerner has been passing, real secrets about his work on the Strategic Defense Initiative have turned up in Moscow. Another problem is that the tracking device in Kerner's briefcase disappeared during the switch at the swimming pool. While watching Hapgood's eleven-year-old son, Joe, play rugby, Hapgood reveals to Blair her suspicions about Ridley, wondering how, if he was following one Russian, he noticed that there were two of them. Blair would rather the traitor be Kerner, because "the real secrets are about intentions and deployment."

In Hapgood's office, Blair tells Wates that Hapgood, the only woman on the Defence Liaison Committee, is called "Mother" because she is always the one who serves the tea, and though she is also called Mrs. Hapgood, she has never been married. He refuses to identify the father of her son. Wates has traced the missing bleeper to Hapgood's office and had her followed. Hapgood arrives to disclose that she knows she has been trailed and that the bleeper is there because Merryweather drained the pool and found it. She threatens to have the Americans removed from this operation if Wates does not stop having her followed. Wates concludes that as long as the Russians are certain that Ridley is working for them, they do not care what side Kerner is on.

Hapgood informs Ridley that they are suspected of using Kerner to pass real secrets but that Blair is convinced of Kerner's being a triple agent. A conversation between Kerner and Hapgood reveals that the Russian is the father of her son. She wants him to meet Joe and marry her. He says that she does not love him and that he is considering returning to Russia.

In act 2, Hapgood insists to Blair that Kerner has no motive for treachery, but her former lover reveals that the Russians know about Joe: "They said I had lied, broken the bargain, they said it was an ultimatum now, or they would take my son." After Blair discloses that they prevented the Soviets from receiving Kerner's latest delivery, they discover that the boy has apparently been kidnapped. Ridley argues that they should give the Russians what they want since the military applications of Kerner's antimatter research are at least ten years away. After assuring Blair that she will abide by his decisions, Hapgood plots with Ridley to get back her son. Joe has not, however, been taken; Hapgood, Kerner, and Blair have laid a trap for Ridley.

In a photographer's studio, Ridley meets someone who looks exactly like Hapgood; he assumes that she is Celia Newton, the twin sister of his boss. On Hapgood's orders, he is paying Celia two thousand pounds to impersonate her sister. Blair, meanwhile, knows that, as with the Russian twins, there are two Ridleys. Ridley takes Celia to Hapgood's office so that she may receive a telephone message from Joe's kidnappers. He strikes her hand to ensure that she sound suitably upset during the conversation. After he leaves, Hapgood drops her pretense and assumes her own identity. In a cheap hotel room, Ridley unleashes a diatribe against Hapgood to her supposed twin, and "Celia" tells him that he must be in love with her sister. They begin kissing.

Back at the swimming pool, the British agents carry out another charade to snare the two Ridleys. First, Joe arrives as if just freed. After they catch Ridley picking up what Hapgood has ostensibly left to the Russians in exchange for her son, the double agent tries to convince Hapgood that she is fooling herself, that the British, particularly Blair, merely exploit her: "He's had enough out of you and you're getting nothing back, he's dry and you're the juice." As he draws his gun to kill her, she shoots him. Ridley's twin has been arrested, and Hapgood is angry at Blair for lying to her about making Joe appear in the Ridley stratagem.

The final scene occurs at Joe's rugby field, as Kerner bids Hapgood farewell before leaving for the Soviet Union. She accuses him of telling the truth about the Russians finding out about Joe, of actually being a triple agent. He does not deny her charges but finally meets his son. Turning to leave, he becomes caught up in the action of the game. The play ends with Hapgood cheering her son's team.

Themes and Meanings

Hapgood explores duplicity, the impossibility of knowing anything for certain, and the role of women in a masculine world. With double agents, a triple agent, two sets of twins, and Hapgood pretending to be twins, Tom Stoppard emphasizes how difficult the question of identity can be. Kerner is supposed to be spying on the British for the Russians but has been "turned" so that he can provide false information to the Soviets; however, if he can be made to betray one side, he can betray both. As Ridley points out, "Every double is a possible triple." According to Kerner, "A double agent is . . . like a trick of the light."

Even people certain that they are on the same side fool themselves about one another. Hapgood trusts Blair, perhaps even loves him, but he uses her son without her knowledge. He tries to justify his actions: "there was an either-or and we can't afford to lose. . . . It's them or us, isn't it?" After all the deception she has seen, Hapgood cannot easily distinguish between right and wrong in the game of espionage.

The difficulty of determining truth from lies is reiterated throughout *Hapgood*. Kerner's statements about the Russians' learning of the existence of his son and turning him into a triple agent are supposed to be the truth to Ridley and lies to Hapgood and Blair but turn out to be the real truth. The cynical Ridley expects everyone to be lying but admits, "you never know, now and again someone is telling the truth." Kerner, the scientist, perceives truth as a matter of interpretation: "The act of observing determines the reality." Kerner, who discusses physics, mathematics, and philosophy more than spying, is Stoppard's spokesman on the nature of reality.

In choosing an epigraph from the writings of American physicist Richard P. Feynman dealing with the absolute impossibility of explaining certain phenomena, Stoppard draws a parallel between scientific knowledge and human understanding. Kerner is describing physics, espionage, and human behavior at the same time as he explains that the movements of an electron "cannot be anticipated because it has no reasons. It defeats surveillance because when you know what it's doing you can't be certain where it is, and when you know where it is you can't be certain what it's doing." In discussing waves and particles, Kerner attempts to illuminate both the human capacity for rationalization and the unlikelihood of attaining absolute knowledge. According to Kerner, analysis of this world is only "your bet on reality."

However, Kerner is perhaps too rational, too aloof from human endeavors. He attempts to shut out the possibility of love until he sees the son he has kept himself from knowing. Hapgood is Kerner's intellectual equal but is willing to take chances on people, to have faith, even at the risk of being betrayed. Although the other characters always see her as a woman first, Hapgood shows that she is their equal if not their superior in all matters. Her powers of concentration are exceptional. As Wates confronts her over the bleeper, she deals simultaneously with this problem, her daily paperwork, a key Joe has lost, and a transatlantic chess game she plays without a board. There is at least a triple irony in the men working for her calling her "Mother." It indicates that they see her primarily as a woman, but the name also shows their childishness. To them, espionage is only a game in which the rules can be changed to fit the current situation. The final irony is that Hapgood is maternal both in caring about her cohorts and in being in complete control of them. Appropriately, she can take care of herself as well, killing Ridley before the macho Wates can get off a shot.

Dramatic Devices

Hapgood's depiction of a turbulent world is heightened by the play's division into twelve scenes in seven locations. Tom Stoppard's stage directions suggest that *Hapgood* is to have an almost cinematic quality. The opening scene is meant to hook the audience's attention, with the repeated yet fluid entrances and exits of the characters, and to suggest that the proceedings will involve an element of farce. As some scenes change, a character often remains in place, as if the play were a film cutting from one shot to another. Stoppard once provides an "inter-scene" in which the actor playing Ridley becomes Ridley's twin; the stage direction reads, "It's like a quantum jump." At the beginning of the final confrontation at the swimming pool, the stage is dark as one Ridley enters carrying a flashlight; the stage darkens further, obliterating all but the light into whose beam the other Ridley walks, moving to embrace his twin. Such techniques underscore the play's theatricality while commenting on its concern with identity and truth.

Hapgood is full of the jargon of espionage. For the Russians, Kerner is a "sleeper," an undercover agent slowly establishing his "cover" before beginning to reap the information his masters desire. To Hapgood, he is her "joe," an agent outside her service working directly for her. Language is used to make other points in the play. It separates the British characters from the American Wates, whose response to anything he finds surprising in the way his colleagues operate is the succinct "You guys." Blair admits, "I like the way they talk, the Americans . . . so direct, descriptive, demotic." He occasionally finds it confusing, as when he and Kerner debate whether Wates has used the term "ballroom," "ballgame," or "ballpark." Hapgood reprimands Kerner for refusing to perfect his English, as when he says "honeypot" when he means "honeytrap." She prides herself on her mastery of the language yet errs when she tells Blair the score in Joe's rugby match is "sixteen love" rather than sixteen nil. Given her feelings for her son and his father, the error can be seen as a Freudian slip. The ways the characters use language reveal how they see themselves and others and show the barriers separating them.

Stoppard also employs frequent puns. Of the KGB twins, Blair says, "Now that's what I call a double agent." Ridley calls Hapgood's hiring her twin "sibling bribery." There is also the pun on joe, Joseph and Joe. The protagonist's name seems to be a pun on the random morality of the modern world, the spy business in particular. Typical of the other humor in *Hapgood* is Hapgood's knowing that Wates takes lemon with his tea and going to Fortnum and Mason, trailed by Wates's men, to buy a lemon for their boss.

Critical Context

All Tom Stoppard's plays are examinations of philosophical issues. *Rosencrantz and Guildenstern Are Dead* (pr. 1966, pb. 1967) employs minor characters from William Shakespeare's *Hamlet, Prince of Denmark* (pr. 1600-1601) to depict the role of human beings in a drama over which they have little control. In *Jumpers* (pr., pb. 1972), a team of philosophers combine their intellectual acumen with gymnastics. *Travesties* (pr. 1974, pb. 1975) brings together novelist James Joyce, revolutionary Vladimir Lenin, and Dadaist Tristan Tzara to debate the role of art and the nature of reality. *Hapgood* resembles these and other Stoppard plays in examining the relativity of truth and the use of language to attempt to construct a cogent system of meaning, and it combines these intellectual concerns with the scrutiny of the nature of love from *The Real Thing* (pr., pb. 1982). Although the ending of *Hapgood* is more ambiguous than that of *The Real Thing*, it also implies that love is capable of conquering all.

Stoppard always draws upon the conventions of other literary and show-business forms, from vaudeville and melodrama to mysteries and drawing-room comedies. In *Hapgood*, he examines and parodies the literature of espionage. The byzantine twists of plot owe a considerable debt to the complex machinations of John le Carre's spy novels (though a few reviewers observed that Stoppard also borrows from the more mundane whodunit world of Agatha Christie). Stoppard delights in the clichés of espionage, even to having Kerner, an avid reader of spy fiction, comment on them. While recognizing that the moral ambiguity of this milieu allows him to create a new approach to the traditional philosophical concerns of his plays, Stoppard also sees that spying has the farcical elements necessary to making *Hapgood* as entertaining as it is intellectually stimulating.

Sources for Further Study

Billington, Michael. *Stoppard the Playwright*. London: Methuen, 1988.

Nightingale, Benedict. "The Latest from Stoppard: A Quark-and-Dagger Thriller." *New York Times*, March 27, 1988, p. B5.

Oorballis, Richard. "Tom Stoppard." In *British Playwrights, 1956-1995: A Research and Production Sourcebook*, edited by William W. Demastes. Westport, Conn.: Greenwood Press, 1996.

Radin, Victoria. "Whodunnit? Whocares?" *New Statesman* 115 (March 18, 1988): 29-30.

Schleuter, June. *Dramatic Closure: Reaching the End*. Teaneck, N.J.: Fairleigh Dickinson University Press, 1995.

Michael Adams

HAPPY DAYS

Author: Samuel Beckett (1906-1989)
Type of plot: Absurdist
Time of plot: Unspecified
Locale: A barren plain of scorched grass
First produced: 1961, at the Cherry Lane Theatre, New York City
First published: 1961

> *Principal characters:*
> WINNIE, a woman about fifty years old
> WILLIE, her sixty-year-old husband

The Play

Happy Days opens on a stark, barren scene that is bathed in intense light. A low mound, which slopes gently toward the front, is center stage. Scorched grass extends across an unbroken plain to the distant horizon. The simplicity, the symmetry, and the blazing light draw attention to the only visible character, Winnie, a well-preserved woman of about fifty, who is buried in the mound to her waist. She is plump, buxom, and wears a low-cut dress. On one side of her, a large black shopping bag lies on the mound; on the other side rests a folded parasol. As the play begins, Winnie is leaning forward, asleep on her arms. Willie lies asleep on the ground, hidden from the audience's view by the mound.

After a long pause, a piercing bell rings continuously for many seconds, but Winnie does not move. After another pause, the bell rings again, even more sharply than the first time, and Winnie awakes. She stares at the sky for a long time and then proclaims that it is "another heavenly day." Winnie mumbles her prayers and then commands herself to begin the day.

Throughout the first act, Winnie removes a variety of objects from her bag. The first is her toothbrush. As she brushes her teeth, she tries to wake Willie, noting that his ability to sleep through the bell is a "marvelous gift." While intermittently trying to decipher some small print that she notices on the handle of her toothbrush, Winnie cleans her glasses, awakens Willie by striking him with the parasol, kisses her revolver named Brownie, drinks a bottle of red medicine, and tosses the emptied bottle behind the mound. The bottle apparently strikes Willie, for the top of his bloodied, bald head appears behind the mound.

Awake, but only partially visible, Willie interjects phrases from newspaper headlines, obituaries, and want ads into Winnie's rambling memories of their youth. With the help of her magnifying glass, Winnie finally deciphers the words on her toothbrush handle—"Fully guaranteed . . . genuine pure . . . hog's setae"—and happily proclaims that "not a day goes by . . . without some addition to one's knowledge," then thoughtfully adds that even if such were no longer the case, one could "just close the eyes . . . and wait for . . . the happy day to come when flesh melts at so many degrees." Winnie is distracted from this somber thought by the appearance of Willie's arm. He is holding a postcard and evidently examining it from a variety of angles. Winnie takes the card, and despite her shock at discovering that it is pornographic, examines it minutely, even using her magnifying glass.

Winnie discusses the importance of Willie's companionship, expressing the fear that she could not continue in silence and total isolation. She recognizes that Willie rarely listens or speaks himself. She is, therefore, particularly pleased when he responds to her question regarding the appropriate pronoun to use in reference to one's hair with the monosyllable "it." "Oh you are going to talk to me today, this is going to be a happy day!" she exclaims with joy.

Winnie remembers her parasol but worries about putting it up too soon. The bell's arbitrary division of time and the unchanging light leave her with a dilemma. If she acts too soon, she could be left "with hours still to run, before the bell for sleep, and nothing more to say, nothing more to do." If she waits too long, the bell for sleep could go off with "little or nothing done." Winnie decides to unfold her parasol, but it soon bursts into flames spontaneously, and she tosses it onto the back of the mound.

As the first act nears its end, Willie speaks his longest line in the play. Winnie, still thinking about the message on the toothbrush, wonders what a hog is, and Willie says, "Castrated male swine. Reared for slaughter." Excited by Willie's communicativeness, Winnie implores herself to sing or pray, but finds that she is unable to do either.

Act 2 opens with the same set, but Winnie is now buried up to her neck, wearing the same hat, her head completely immobile. Beside her on the mound are her bag, the revolver, and her parasol. Once again the painful ring of the bell signals the start of the action. Winnie enumerates the shortening list of sense experiences that remain for her, the experiences that make existence "so wonderful." Cut off from the manipulation of objects that occupied her in the first act, she notes the items she can still see, the sounds she can still hear, and the memories that well up within her mind. She wishes that she could free herself from the authority of the bell, but she consoles herself by thinking that "there is my story of course, when all else fails." She tells of young Mildred being frightened by a mouse, and she screams in sympathy with the little girl's fright.

The play ends with an "unexpected pleasure." Willie crawls from behind the mound, dressed in full formal attire, and positions himself at the front where Winnie can see him. He attempts to crawl up the mound toward Winnie or the revolver, as she cheers him on and wonders about his motives. He fails in his effort and slides back down the mound, but looks at her and speaks her name. In joy, she bursts into song— the waltz from Franz Lehar's *The Merry Widow* (1905). The play ends with Winnie and Willie gazing at each other.

Themes and Meanings

As its title suggests, *Happy Days* focuses on the persistent human desire to believe that humankind's cruelly limited and meaningless existence can be seen as "happy."

Winnie, the play's central character, is obviously and comically limited. Buried in an earthen mound set in the midst of a barren and unchanging plain, she struggles to survive in a cultural and spiritual void. Even her waking and sleeping are conditioned by a Pavlovian bell that rings unpredictably and irresistibly. Condemned to a timeless and uneventful purgatory of unchanging light and unvarying landscape in which even the basic temporal sequence of day and night is no longer available, Winnie is deprived of the external patterns that give human existence a comforting semblance of order. With no prospect of meaningful action short of suicide, Winnie works to fill this arbitrarily divided time by performing routine personal tasks, examining her mundane possessions, cherishing each insignificant bit of new information, and talking. She uses the slightest occurrence to maintain her illusion that she is living another "happy day."

The desperate need to communicate, no matter how imperfectly, is central to Winnie's condition. Her speech is a clutter of partially remembered bits of poetry, a cultural montage that she creates in an effort to link herself to the "old time" when life seemed to offer greater meaning. To continue, she must believe that human communication exists. Thus, she is ecstatic when Willie responds to her, even if his response is monosyllabic or random, disconnected "titbits from *Reynolds' News*." She is even satisfied if she can convince herself that he is listening, or if not actually listening at least hearing. Meanwhile, she talks on and on, trying to forestall the silence that she fears more than anything. In the second act, when her opportunities to fill time are even more limited, she reassures herself that "someone is looking at me still," as though communication need only be the awareness of some other, not necessarily the sharing of meaning.

Willie's abortive attempt to reach Winnie at the end of the play rekindles Winnie's hope although, since Willie is dressed for either a wedding or a funeral, it is unclear whether he means to kiss her or kill her. Perhaps it does not matter to Winnie. When Willie fails to climb the mound and weakly calls her name, panting on all fours at the base of the mound, Winnie is inspired to sing of love.

The play displays the comic persistence of hope. Despite the glaring light that makes it impossible to ignore the horror of Winnie's situation, she resists using Brownie or expressing blasphemous anger. Instead, she exhausts herself with efforts to find something praiseworthy. She uses her diminishing energy to construct illusory fictions from the paltry array of objects and memories available to her.

Dramatic Devices

The set of *Happy Days* is carefully designed with a "maximum of simplicity and symmetry" that forces the audience's attention toward Winnie, buried at center stage. There are no other visual distractions; the intense light, coupled with the bright, heat-connoting colors of the backdrop, make Winnie an appealing visual alternative for the audience.

Many of Samuel Beckett's plays use darkness to express his characters' isolation, but in *Happy Days* he uses intense, unchanging light to counterpoint his central character's blindness. The unforgiving light compels the audience to face the bleakness of Winnie's condition while alluding to the proverbial heat of Hell.

The mound is the focus of the set. It physically represents Winnie's confinement, but it also serves as a barrier that prevents the audience from fully observing Willie throughout most of the play. Their obstructed view parallels Winnie's restricted perception, allowing them to share some of her discomfort and forcing them to adjust to limitations, as she must. The mound represents Winnie's entombment, her death-in-life, but the play suggests that she has created this situation herself. At least she confesses to a fear of floating away and a need to cling to the earth. As Winnie sinks deeper into the mound in the second act, it becomes the insurmountable obstacle that separates Winnie and Willie.

The bell is the goad of the play. Its harsh, extremely elongated ring forces the audience to share in Winnie's discomfort and helps them understand the Pavlovian manner in which she is controlled. Winnie dreams of being able to ignore the bell, but such freedom seems impossible within the context of *Happy Days*.

The various articles that Winnie pulls from her bag speak voicelessly of the manner in which humans attempt to define themselves through possessions. Winnie busies herself with removing, using, and examining these things. In the first act this is her primary way of filling the arbitrarily divided time in which she exists. In the second act these objects lie about her, but since her arms are buried and she is unable to move even her head, Winnie can no longer fill her time with them—nor can she escape from time by using Brownie, her revolver. In this state, she must resort to her mental faculties to fill time.

Critical Context

Although he considered himself a novelist who turned to drama when he reached an impasse in his prose, Samuel Beckett was best known for his plays. Indeed, starting in the 1960's he spent much of his creative energy supervising productions of his plays in several countries.

Happy Days marks a midpoint in the inexorable progression of Beckett's drama toward immobility and silence. In many ways more austere than Beckett's earliest dramatic work, *Happy Days* is clearly more traditional and direct than his later works.

Beckett's literary reputation was made by the success of his play *En attendant Godot* (pb. 1952; *Waiting for Godot*, 1954), a work that alone has sold more copies than all of his other drama and fiction combined. Along with his second important play *Fin de partie* (pr., pb. 1957; *Endgame*, 1958), *Waiting for Godot* established Beckett as the central figure in the Theater of the Absurd. Although each of these early plays presents a world of severely limited possibilities in which mortals have no effective control over their physical condition, each also portrays mobile characters who interact with one another.

In contrast, Beckett's next two important plays, *Krapp's Last Tape* (pr., pb. 1958) and *Happy Days*, focus on individuals who are almost completely isolated. The lone character in *Krapp's Last Tape* sits in his room listening to his own tape-recorded reminiscences, carrying on a dialogue of sorts with his own temporarily distant self. Winnie of *Happy Days* speaks to Willie, but most of her speech is a rambling monologue to which Willie rarely responds. Thus, *Happy Days* moved Beckett's drama toward the solipsism that characterizes his later work.

These two plays are also the first dramatic works that Beckett wrote in English. Beckett wrote in French because he believed that the acquired language made his work more disciplined, but he was sensitive to the accusation that he wrote in French to hide himself. He also chose to write these plays in English because he was eager for a commercial success. The subject matter of *Happy Days*, which in its early versions contained much harsh criticism of the Anglican Church and British policies toward Ireland, also made English an appropriate language choice.

Beckett's subsequent drama became much more austere. *Play* (pr., pb. 1963; English translation, 1964), which was first produced in a German translation (*Spiel*, 1963), portrays three characters entombed in urns, in some after-death state. Each is completely unaware of the others and speaks only of self, with no hope of communication. *Not I* (1972), a teleplay, speaks through a disembodied mouth suspended in total darkness at mid-stage; *Footfalls* (pr., pb. 1976) shows only a strip of light through which the feet of an old woman can be seen passing as she speaks in the darkness; *That Time* (pr., pb. 1976) offers the white-bearded head of an old man suspended in air and darkness.

Sources for Further Study

Andonian, Cathleen. *The Critical Response to Samuel Beckett.* Westport, Conn.: Greenwood Press, 1998.

Cohn, Ruby. *Just Play: Beckett's Theater.* Princeton. N.J.: Princeton University Press, 1980.

Doherty, Francis. "Theater of Suffering." In *Samuel Beckett.* London: Hutchinson, 1971.

Eastman, Richard M. "Samuel Beckett and *Happy Days.*" *Modern Drama* 6 (February, 1964): 417-424.

Fletcher, John, and John Spurling. *Beckett: A Study of His Plays.* London: Eyre Methuen, 1972.

Gontarski, S. E. "Literary Allusions in *Happy Days.*" In *On Beckett: Essays and Criticism.* New York: Grove Press, 1986.

Gordon, Lois. *The World of Samuel Beckett.* New Haven: Yale University Press, 1996.

Gussow, Mel. *Conversations with and About Beckett.* New York: Grove-Atlantic, 1996.

Kenner, Hugh. *A Reader's Guide to Samuel Beckett.* Syracuse, N.Y.: Syracuse University Press, 1996.

Worth, Katharine, ed. *Beckett the Shape Changer.* Boston: K. Paul, 1975.

Carl Brucker

HARPERS FERRY

Author: Barrie Stavis (1906-   )
Type of plot: History
Time of plot: 1859
Locale: Harpers Ferry, Virginia (now in West Virginia) and a nearby farmhouse in Maryland
First produced: 1967, at the Tyrone Guthrie Theater, Minneapolis, Minnesota; pr. 1962 as *Banners of Steel* at Southern Illinois University, Carbondale, Illinois
First published: 1967

Principal characters:
JOHN BROWN, the leader of the abolitionist guerrilla band
MARY BROWN, his wife
OLIVER and
WATSON BROWN, his sons
MARTHA BROWN, Oliver's wife
MRS. HUFFMASTER, a neighbor across the road from the farmhouse in Maryland
FREDERICK DOUGLASS, an unindicted co-conspirator
COLONEL ROBERT E. LEE, the commander of the federal forces
LIEUTENANT J. E. B. STUART, the leader of the final assault on the guerrillas
HENRY A. WISE, the governor of Virginia
COLONEL LEWIS WASHINGTON, his military aide
JUDGE PARKER, the presiding judge at the treason trial of John Brown
ANDREW HUNTER, the prosecuting attorney at John Brown's trial

The Play

This two-act play chronicles the assault led by John Brown in 1859 on the United States armory and arsenal at the small river town of Harpers Ferry in what was then part of the state of Virginia. The attack shook the slave-holding South to its foundations and is considered by many to be the actual beginning of the American Civil War.

The first act is set in an ordinary farmhouse in Maryland, five miles away from Harpers Ferry. The nucleus of the abolitionist guerrilla band, formed with both African American and white members, has assembled there, and the men, accompanied by Mary and Martha Brown, are awaiting reinforcement. They are expecting fifty fighters from Canada, organized by the famous abolitionist, Harriet Tubman. They are hoping to be joined by a number of volunteers from the West, many of them veterans of the battles fought over slavery in Kansas.

Too much time has passed, however, and the tedium of inaction and being confined in such close quarters is taking its toll on the band's morale. Mrs. Huffmaster, a neighbor from across the road, has acquired the habit of dropping in without warning a couple of times every day. When she arrives, the men have to stop their formal debates on theology and their games of cards and checkers. They must flee up the ladder and hide in the attic, which also serves as their bedroom. Mrs. Huffmaster is bribed with favors and gifts when she visits so that she will not divulge the strange activity at the farmhouse, but everyone knows that it is just a matter of time before she gives them away.

After Mrs. Huffmaster leaves at one point, the guerrilla band undergoes a crisis of confidence. Dangerfield Newby, a member of the African American guerrilla band, has received a letter from his wife, who is a slave. The letter tells him that she and his children are about to be sold. This information serves to focus the frustrations of Newby and many of the others: They demand action from their captain John Brown. He reacts to this leadership challenge by calling for a vote to select a new captain. The guerrillas vote, but John Brown once again wins by a unanimous decision.

Unfortunately, he receives bad news in letters of his own. Harriet Tubman has fallen ill and the fifty fighters will not be coming from Canada. In addition, he learns that most of the men expected from the West will not be coming either. Finally, he arranges a last-ditch meeting with the great abolitionist Frederick Douglass, to try to win his participation in the raid. Despite their agreement in principle, Douglass has tactical differences with John Brown and decides not to take part in the raid. Even with these setbacks, and with a much smaller group than originally planned, the guerrillas move to attack.

The second act of *Harpers Ferry* is devoted to the battle and to John Brown's trial for treason, which followed the battle a few weeks later. Taking advantage of the element of surprise, the small force is successful initially. They have cut telegraph wires to isolate the military installation from outside communications, overpowered sentries to take the bridges, seized important buildings, and established a command center near the Engine House. The alert spreads quickly, however, and soon Harpers Ferry is swarming with volunteer defenders. In a matter of hours a detachment of federal troops led by Colonel Robert E. Lee arrives to reestablish control. Two of John Brown's sons are killed in the operation, and he is seriously wounded when a detachment of marines led by Lieutenant J. E. B. Stuart storms the Engine House to put an end to the insurrection.

John Brown is severely depressed by the failure of his raid on Harpers Ferry, but another way to carry on the fight is soon revealed to him. When reporters appear at his interrogation, he realizes that he can take advantage of his status as a famous defendant. The "sword" has been taken from his hand, but now he has a platform from which to use the "word" even more effectively in the fight against slavery. He becomes a passionate and eloquent spokesman during the final few weeks of his life. Historically, his trial and execution for treason ignited a political storm that eventually contributed to the election of Abraham Lincoln as the American president and subsequently the end of slavery in the United States.

Themes and Meanings

The central theme in this play illustrates the evil of slavery and the role of important figures in dismantling it. John Brown saw the detriments of slavery with great clarity, and his vision is dramatized effectively in *Harpers Ferry.* He was an ordinary man, who, forged by historical forces, struck at the heart of slavery's inhumanity. The attack on Harpers Ferry was the culminating act of his life, and it transformed him into a legend. He would neither be deterred by compromise nor be intimidated by the violence mobilized by slave owners to defend the billions of dollars they had invested in human property. He saw slavery as a perpetual state of war being waged against the slaves in order to keep them trapped in their subservient positions. The Fugitive Slave Act and other federal laws enacted in the 1850's had the effect of spreading slavery into the northern states, and in response to this encroachment, John Brown felt it was his duty to join the battle with a direct attack.

An important secondary theme focuses on the deep Christian faith that was integral to John Brown's character. It justified his abolitionist commitment and motivated his political and military action. His example served to reawaken the ambitious, stubborn Puritan spirit of the seventeenth and early eighteenth centuries in the United States and to mobilize the forces required to eradicate slavery and rededicate the country to its original conception of liberty for all.

A possible contradiction arises, however, between the love and forgiveness exemplified in the Christian tradition and the murderous resolve deemed necessary by the guerrillas to stop any military campaign. John Brown believed that education was the best way to defeat slavery, at least for the first four decades of his life. He nonetheless advocated a violent rebellion to enact change. The question remains at the end of *Harpers Ferry:* Could there be another way to bring forth reform? Does the path to a better society necessarily have to ford a river of blood?

Dramatic Devices

Staging battle scenes is very difficult because only talented actors can keep a physical fight from lapsing into slapstick humor onstage. There are no second takes in the theater, so Barrie Stavis followed the example of William Shakespeare. Just as Shakespeare left the battle of Agincourt out of *Henry V,* Stavis also leaves most of the actual fighting out of *Harpers Ferry.* Most of the play's action takes place during preparation for the raid and during the aftermath. Even the scenes of the battle concentrate on the verbal and emotional interaction among the participants.

Stavis manages to keep the drama at an intense level, however, by adapting Elizabethan and classical staging techniques. He calls his approach the "Time-Space Stage," in which both time and space can be used with maximum fluidity. His stage directions for *Harpers Ferry* call for an austere set design to match the mentality of the protagonist and require specific lighting on different levels of the stage. Actors in one scene typically freeze in place as action stops and the lights are cut in that space. Instantaneously, another part of the stage comes alive. In this way the actors in a production of *Harpers Ferry* are not required to reenact physical battles with every performance, but to convey the right message, the right pace of action, and the right impact, the lighting director needs an expert crew and the best equipment.

Critical Context

Harpers Ferry is a revision of an earlier play about John Brown by Stavis titled *Banners of Steel*, which was first produced in Carbondale, Illinois, in 1962. It became part of a tetrology of plays, each dealing with pivotal historical figures. The other three are *Lamp at Midnight: A Play About Galileo* (pr. 1947, pb. 1948), which centers on the revolutionary astronomer Galileo Galilei; *The Man Who Never Died: A Play About Joe Hill* (pb. 1954, pr. 1955), which focuses on the early twentieth century labor leader; and *Coat of Many Colors: A Play About Joseph in Egypt* (pr. 1966, pb. 1968), which takes the Old Testament figure as its subject. Stavis attempts to capture the exact points in history when the world is ripe for change and a person steps up to enact that change.

His interest in critical figures in history puts Stavis fundamentally at odds with the post-World War II fascination with the antihero. Stavis believes that postmodern theater is obsessed with frustration and defeat, personality maladjustment, and sexual dysfunction. To survive the nuclear age, he feels it is necessary to maintain a positive attitude, to make an ethical commitment, and to follow the light of reason. His focus on theater as a vehicle for promoting social awareness by appealing to the critical faculties of the audience is reminiscent of the approach of the German playwright, Bertolt Brecht. Like Brecht, Stavis does not want members of his audience to lose themselves in emotional catharsis during his productions. He wants people to realistically analyze the issues being dealt with in dramatic form onstage. *Harpers Ferry* was probably better appreciated in Europe than in the United States, where the emotional intensity of the turbulent 1960's made rational reflection on such sensitive issues especially difficult.

Sources for Further Study

Boyer, Richard Owen. *The Legend of John Brown*. New York: Knopf, 1973.

Quarles, Benjamin, ed. *Blacks on John Brown*. Urbana: University of Illinois Press, 1972.

Shore, Herbert. "Barrie Stavis: The Epic Vision." *Educational Theatre Journal*, October, 1973.

Stavis, Barrie. *John Brown: The Sword and the Word*. South Brunswick, N.J.: A. S. Barnes, 1970.

Villard, Oswald Garrison. *John Brown: A Biography Fifty Years After.* Gloucester, Mass.: Peter Smith, 1965.

Steven Lehman

HARVEY

Author: Mary Chase (1907-1981)
Type of plot: Comedy; fantasy
Time of plot: c. 1945
Locale: A city in the "far west"
First produced: 1944, at the Forty-eighth Street Theatre, New York City
First published: 1944

Principal characters:
MYRTLE MAE SIMMONS, a debutante
VETA LOUISE SIMMONS, a society matron
ELWOOD P. DOWD, an idle eccentric
RUTH KELLY, a nurse at the sanatorium
DUANE WILSON, an orderly at the sanatorium
LYMAN SANDERSON, a young doctor at the sanatorium
WILLIAM R. CHUMLEY, the director of the sanatorium

The Play

This three-act comedy follows the frustrated attempts of society matron Veta Louise Simmons to keep the eccentricities of her brother, Elwood P. Dowd, from public view. Elwood drinks and keeps introducing strangers to a companion whom no one else can see: a six-foot-one-and-a-half-inch-tall rabbit named Harvey. Veta's daughter Myrtle Mae worries that her Uncle Elwood's preoccupation with Harvey will scare away any marriage prospects for her. In the opening scene the guest of honor at a piano recital hosted by Veta is frightened away when Elwood tries to introduce her to Harvey. This incident is the last straw for Veta. In the next scene she visits Chumley's Rest, a sanatorium for mental patients, and asks to have her brother Elwood committed. As Veta gives the information to the head nurse, Ruth Kelly, it becomes clear that Kelly is interested in Dr. Sanderson, the new assistant to Dr. Chumley. As Veta becomes more and more agitated in describing the effect that "living with Harvey" has had on her nerves, Dr. Sanderson begins to suspect that Veta's attempt to commit Elwood is just a cover-up for her own psychosis. He orders Veta restrained and apologizes to Elwood for what he now thinks is his blunder. The fact that Elwood really does claim to see Harvey is comically suspended, as his attempts to introduce the rabbit to the psychiatrist are continually interrupted.

When Elwood leaves, Kelly's romantic interest in Dr. Sanderson begins to unravel. Elwood's charm and polite attention to her contrast sharply with Sanderson's professional aloofness. In retaliation, Kelly disavows any interest in Sanderson. When Dr. Chumley arrives and finds a hat left behind from Elwood's visit, he notices two holes cut in the hat—just the right size and position to accommodate rabbit ears. He concludes that Elwood is the madman after all and berates Sanderson for misdiagnosing Veta. In an emotional reaction, and in fear of possible lawsuits, he fires Sanderson.

Act 2 returns the action to Elwood's home, where Myrtle Mae is conferring with Judge Gaffney in the attempt to have Elwood declared insane. The popularity of Elwood in the community and his own personal affection for the man make the judge reluctant to commit Elwood to an institution. Suddenly Veta appears at the door, disheveled from her ordeal with the psychiatrists. Dr. Chumley arrives, with his strong-arm orderly Wilson, looking for Elwood. While Veta threatens to sue Dr. Chumley, Wilson flirts with Myrtle Mae. When everyone leaves the room on various errands, Elwood arrives and replaces the portrait of his mother, the focal point of the room, with one of himself and a giant rabbit—obviously Harvey. Elwood leaves and Veta returns. When she notices the painting, she knows Elwood has been there.

The scene returns to Chumley's Rest, four hours later. Dr. Sanderson is packing to leave; Kelly attempts to express her true feelings about him, but Sanderson's brusqueness makes it impossible. When Elwood arrives, it is clear that Wilson thinks he has harmed Dr. Chumley, but Elwood says that the psychiatrist is with Harvey. When Chumley appears in act 3, he asks for a private meeting with Elwood. When the two are alone, Chumley reveals that he, too, now sees Harvey, and sees Elwood as a true visionary rather than a crackpot. He is selfish enough, however, to pretend to agree with Dr. Sanderson's diagnosis, tricking Elwood into taking a serum that will "cure" him from the "hallucination" of seeing the giant rabbit. By doing so, Chumley hopes to "keep" Harvey for himself. Elwood agrees to the injection to please Veta, but at the last moment Veta realizes that making Elwood "normal" will erase his finest qualities: affability, generosity, magnanimity. When it comes down to it, she realizes that she will miss Harvey. Veta and Myrtle Mae, now reconciled to living with an eccentric uncle and a six-foot rabbit, leave to go home. Elwood follows, and the door to Chumley's office opens, presumably to accommodate Harvey. Elwood puts his arm around the invisible rabbit and the two exit together.

Themes and Meanings

Harvey is an exploration of the importance of human imagination and the way twentieth century American culture looks at the irrational. Some critics, particularly British reviewers, have seen the play as an indictment of the psychiatric profession. However, the focus of the play is not really Elwood's drinking or his hallucinations (if they *are* hallucinations; the staging implies that Harvey is real). Rather, the salient feature of Elwood's character is that he is eccentric and different. Mary Chase's inspiration for the character was neither a drunkard nor insane, so far as she knew. When Chase was a child, some boys were throwing snowballs at a poor old woman. The playwright's mother shooed away the hooligans and told her daughter never to be unkind to a person others say is crazy, because often they have a deep wisdom. That lesson stuck with young Mary, and she turned it into a Pulitzer Prize-winning comedy.

British critic Sandy Wilson, himself a successful writer for the comic stage, lamented what he saw as the play's glorification of dementia. It is nothing of the kind. If there is a national or ethnic element in Chase's fantasy, it is not American but Irish, or at least Irish American. Both of her parents were born in Ireland, and while the main character's name, "Dowd," sounds Anglo-Saxon, the play is peppered with Irish American names: Ruth Kelly, Verne McElhinney, Dr. McClure, and Ed Hickey. Thus, at the end of the first act, when Wilson reads in the encyclopedia that the *pooka*—the species of manifestation Harvey represents—is from old Celtic mythology, Elwood's irrationality, if it can be called that, becomes clear: It is of the Celtic variety, a frank acceptance of a reality beyond the material and the empirical. It is that, and not alcoholism or psychosis, that Elwood represents.

Elwood is not an escapist either. The giant rabbit is not his escape from reality: In act 3 he reveals to Dr. Chumley that Harvey can stop time and take Elwood anywhere he wants to go. However, Elwood is always happy wherever he is. Dr. Chumley, on the other hand, wants desperately to escape and describes an interlude in Akron with cool beer and a beautiful and sympathetic woman. Moreover, if there is any character who wants to avoid the realities of life, it is Veta. She wants to stop Elwood's drinking, all the while she is planning a high-society cocktail party. She thinks the psychiatrists are perverts because they talk about sex urges and warns Myrtle Mae to avoid the libidinous interests of men, while simultaneously trying to marry off Myrtle Mae. She objects to the notion of a Celtic superstition, yet she expresses a belief in astrology. By being such a mass of contradictions, Veta prepares the audience for the play's denouement, in which she acknowledges that, given a choice between Elwood's reality and the norm, she chooses Elwood's reality.

Dramatic Devices

The most central device in *Harvey* is the use of mime to create the illusion of an invisible giant rabbit. There are a few instances of related mechanical effects, such as doors opening without any visible human agency, but for the most part the illusion must be carried by gestures and looks: a friendly arm around the rabbit's waist, a wink at a shared private joke, endless attempts to introduce the giant *pooka* to acquaintances. This mime element is so crucial that amateur productions, of which there are hundreds each year, succeed or fail according to how well it is carried off. No matter how good the acting is, the production will fail if Harvey is not sufficiently realized through mime.

One of the ways in which Chase reinforces the effect of mime is with dialogue, and in turn, she reinforces the mime and dialogue with characterization. One example is the flirtatiousness of Dr. Chumley. At the end of act 2, scene 1, when he first meets Myrtle Mae, the stage direction instructs the actor to show a libidinous interest in her. Yet, in case the audience misses or misinterprets it, Wilson, shortly thereafter, makes a verbal reference to the effect of Myrtle's attractiveness on Chumley.

Chase's use of misdirection to focus suspenseful interest on a prop is used effectively with the large framed painting in act 2, scene 1. Myrtle Mae announces that she has an item that will prove conclusively that her uncle is crazy. When she returns with the painting, it is still wrapped in brown paper, so the audience cannot see what makes it so conclusive as evidence. She is distracted by the conversation and forgets about the painting, but leaves it in conspicuous view of the audience. Chase takes care to leave the room empty for a few beats after the family exits and Elwood enters, the mystery painting solely commanding attention. When Elwood sees it, he tears off the paper and a portrait of Elwood and a giant white rabbit appears—the unveiling all the more effective for the postponement.

Critical Context

The subgenre into which this comedy fits, fantasy, proved to be the most comfortable form for Mary Chase's creative imagination. Shortly after the success of *Harvey*, Chase tried writing in a more serious style with *The Next Half Hour* (pr. 1945), which failed on Broadway. Although the plot turned on the paranormal element of clairvoyance, the stylistic emphasis was on the realistic actions of the characters, not on the fantasy. She returned to fantasy, however, with two Broadway hits in the same year, *Mrs. McThing* (pr., pb. 1952) and *Bernardine* (pr. 1952, pb. 1953). The fantasy in *Mrs. McThing* involves not apparitions but a magic spell, which causes a wealthy dowager and her playboy son to lose all their money—and they turn out the happier for it. The fantasy in *Bernardine* is the hormone-induced dreamworld of male adolescence, as a group of teenage boys weave sexual fantasies about their dream girl. As different as these plots are, the surreal vision of the main characters is familiar to audiences who know *Harvey*.

Reviewers most often compare Chase's style with that of William Saroyan, perhaps because of similarities between Elwood P. Dowd in *Harvey* and the genial drunk Joe in *The Time of Your Life* (pr., pb. 1939). Yet the comparison is usually a disparaging one, as if her comedy were merely diluted from Saroyan. What these critics see in Saroyan and find missing in Chase is an edginess, a consciousness of the harsh realities, the struggle of human existence. A second common comparison with *Harvey* is Joseph O. Kesselring's *Arsenic and Old Lace* (pr. 1941, pb. 1944), a comparison natural to the reviewers of the first production of Chase's hit, because Josephine Hull, who originated the role of Veta Simmons, also created one of the eccentric Brewster sisters in Kesselring's comedy.

Sources for Further Study

Berger, Maurice Albert. *Mary Coyle Chase, Her Battle Field of Illusion*. Ann Arbor, Mich.: University Microfilms, 1970.

Kerr, Walter. *God on the Gymnasium Floor*. New York: Simon and Schuster, 1971.

Miller, Jordan Y. *American Dramatic Literature: Ten Modern Plays in Historical Perspective*. New York: McGraw-Hill, 1961.

Nathan, George Jean. *The Theatre Book of the Year, 1944-1945: A Record and Interpretation*. New York: Alfred A. Knopf, 1945.

Reef, Wallis M. "She Didn't Write It for Money, She Says." In *More Post Biographies*, edited by John E. Drewry. Athens: University of Georgia Press, 1947.

Sievers, W. David. *Freud on Broadway: A History of Psychoanalysis and the American Drama*. New York: Hermitage House, 1955.

John R. Holmes

THE HASTY HEART

Author: John Patrick (John Patrick Goggan, 1905-1995)
Type of plot: Comedy
Time of plot: The early 1940's
Locale: Assam/Burma border
First produced: 1945, at the Hudson Theatre, New York City
First published: 1945

Principal characters:
YANK, an American soldier
DIGGER, an Australian soldier
KIWI, a New Zealand soldier
BLOSSOM, an African Basuto soldier
TOMMY, a Cockney soldier
MARGARET, a British nurse
THE COLONEL, a British officer
LACHLEN "LACHIE," a Scottish soldier

The Play

The Hasty Heart takes place in the convalescent ward of a makeshift British hospital behind the lines of the Assam/Burmese front in World War II. The bamboo hut, surrounded by jungle, houses six hospital beds, five of which are occupied by wounded soldiers of different nationalities. As the play opens, it is morning, and the British orderly awakes the men. As the men eat their breakfast, Yank, the putative leader of the group, reveals that he has an intense hatred of Scotsmen.

Soon after breakfast, the Colonel enters to announce that he is transferring a new patient to the ward to fill the empty bed. He has picked this ward because of the men's reputation for friendliness and because the new patient is a sullen Scotsman with no family or friends. An operation has left the Scot with only one kidney, and this kidney will soon fail and cause his death. The Colonel has decided against telling the Scot of his fatal condition and asks the men of the ward to keep the man contented in his last days.

When Lachlen (or Lachie) arrives, he proves to be very unfriendly, refusing pleasantries, conversation, and even favors from Margaret and the men. He declares that he does not like to be indebted to anyone in any way and prefers to be left alone. Although the men attempt to be friendly, Lachie manages to insult them all. Only Margaret is able to break through some of his gruffness to discover one of his secrets—he has never had enough money to buy a kilt because he has been saving to buy land to farm after the war. When he confesses that in a couple of months he will have paid for his land, Margaret and the men realize that he will never get a chance to enjoy his farm. Lachie's unfriendliness, however, has tried the men's patience, and the first act ends with Yank angrily surrounding Lachie's bed with screens so the Scot can live in the private world he claims to prefer.

Act 2 opens two weeks later. Lachie's aggravating surliness has everyone on edge, but Margaret has one more plan for winning him over with kindness. This day is his birthday, and she has bought a kilt that the men will present to him. While Lachie is out of the ward, the men plan their presentation and raise a delicate issue: Does the kilt require underwear, or do Scots wear them *au naturel*? A lively round of betting on the question concludes just as Lachie returns.

The impromptu birthday party and presentation of the kilt has an unusual effect on Lachie. Genuinely moved, he thanks the men in his awkward way but wonders if he has a right to accept the gift. Lachie explains that taking it would obligate him to return a favor and that he has nothing to give back. He does not want to make a mistake, for "sorrow is born in the hasty heart." However, Margaret persuades him to accept the gift, saying "For once in your life be hasty and risk a mistake."

The only remaining problem is that Lachie does not intend to wear the kilt until he is called back to his regiment. The disappointed men still have not settled their bet about the underwear. As the first scene of act 2 closes, however, Lachie is trying to make conversation and is offering the other patients cigarettes in a genuine attempt to be friendly.

In the next scene, a few nights later, the audience learns that Lachie has become garrulous—he has been "talking steadily for a week"—and his wardmates have become a polite but wearied audience. He now confesses to Margaret that he regrets his misanthropy and unfriendliness toward the men; he wants to redeem himself by offering something in return, but he seems to have nothing to give. Since Yank is leaving the next day, Lachie agrees to wear his kilt in Yank's honor instead of saving it for his return to the regiment. In this more sensitive mood, Lachie also reveals to Margaret that he loves her.

Act 3 opens the next afternoon, with the men lined up around Lachie to have their photograph taken. After the photography session, Lachie corners Yank and asks him how a man knows when he is in love. Lachie confesses that he wants to ask Margaret to be his wife. After Yank leaves, Lachie proposes to Margaret and she accepts, complicated as the situation is. Delighted, he goes behind a screen to change out of his kilt. The men crowd around the screen, trying to get a peek and to settle their bet.

The Colonel enters the ward, catching the men in their comic position on hands and knees around the screen. He dismisses them so that he can talk to Lachie alone. The Colonel informs Lachie that he has been able to arrange for Lachie to be flown home, and he finally tells Lachie that his condition is fatal. Lachie's first response is anger at Margaret and the men, because he concludes that they have been nice to him only because they knew he was going to die soon. He then destroys the film from the camera and returns the kilt, retiring angrily behind the screen surrounding his bed.

The play's last scene begins the following morning, with the screen put away and Lachie packing his bags. However, when Yank wonders rhetorically "what makes a man want to die despised and friendless," Lachie meekly confesses that he does not want to die alone. He tells the men that he wants to stay with them rather than return to Scotland. They welcome him back, and he goes into Margaret's office to change back into his hospital clothes. When he emerges, however, he is wearing his kilt. As they all gather for another photograph, one of the men peeks under the kilt and proclaims that he has the answer to the bet.

Themes and Meanings

The central theme of *The Hasty Heart* is most succinctly expressed in the familiar phrase from the seventeenth century poet and clergyman John Donne, "No man is an island." The play contends that human beings are vitally interconnected with one another regardless of whether they want to admit it. Human beings must care for one another, accept and tolerate differences, and work to make community possible. The individual who tries to deny friendship, interdependence, and caring merely denies that better part of humanity that yearns for human intimacy.

John Patrick communicates this theme through Lachie's experience with the men in the hospital, but the effectiveness of the story is enhanced by Patrick's preparation for Lachie's initial entrance. Patrick uses well over half of the play's first act to introduce the individual men in the ward. They represent diverse, often normally antagonistic nationalities, and Patrick gives each man a distinctive character, a distinctive dialect, and a fierce nationalistic pride. However, the men's sniping at one another is good-natured and embodies Patrick's social ideal of harmony within diversity. Once this ideal is embedded in the audience's mind, even subconsciously, Patrick can introduce Lachie, who denies the ideal but then discovers his error.

Patrick also prepares his audience for his message by giving Yank, the leader of the men, a virulent hatred of Scots. Yank has the most animosity to overcome when Lachie joins the group and must change more than any of the men besides Lachie during the play. Yank's change of heart is subtle but steady, so that the focus is kept on Lachie but the theme of interdependence is quietly reinforced.

Finally, Patrick communicates the theme by drawing the audience into the emotional maelstrom of the play. When Lachie first appears, he is genuinely unpleasant, a test of anyone's forbearance. Though audiences laugh at Lachie's brusque resistance to kindness, they also participate in the men's struggle to like him, and at the end of the play the audience must also evaluate Lachie's charge that the generous feelings toward him were only a shallow kind of pity.

Patrick's final comment on the theme is that brotherhood is understood by the heart and not the mind. Lachie's denial of brotherhood is seen as a psychological aberration, not as a rational choice. Through conversations with the men and Margaret, Lachie is revealed as desirous of friendship but pathologically afraid of rejection. He has covered up his fears of rejection by hardening himself against human intimacy. The convoluted mind with its fragile ego has misled him. The heart leads the way to the acceptance of brotherhood.

Dramatic Devices

The main device Patrick uses to communicate his message is dramatic irony. With the Colonel's entrance early in act 1, the audience is aware that Lachie has only six weeks to live. The men and Margaret know, the audience knows, but Lachie does not, so all the dialogue up until the Colonel's appearance contains this irony as a subtext. Lachie clearly assumes a long future for himself, but others' superior knowledge generates pathos for his plans to return to his regiment, his single-minded hoarding of money to purchase a farm, his love of his homeland, and his romantic attachment to Margaret. This pathos is a form of human concern, which exemplifies the theme of brotherhood.

The danger in the play, as Patrick seems well aware, is that the pathos might be construed as merely sentimental. Consequently, a very important complementary device in the play is the use of humor. Humor in the play is rich and consistent. Much of it is physical, as in the pursuit of the secret of the kilt, but the dialogue, too, is often quite amusing, especially when Lachie is abusing people verbally or when Yank is fighting to control his anger. Tommy has an especially humorous role, one written for a character actor who can communicate a Falstaffian zest for life. Humor, then, strikes a balance for the play, making the emotionalism seem more understated and less exaggerated.

Nevertheless, the pathos is an important dramatic device in itself, because a powerful emotional response to Lachie's situation will make the audience care about him and his relationship with his friends. In this regard, the most effective moment in the play is probably Lachie's climactic admission, "I dinna want tae die alone."

Critical Context

By his own admission, John Patrick was a commercial writer rather than a serious literary dramatist. A very prolific and relatively successful dramatist, Patrick worked as a writer for more than five decades, producing more than eleven hundred radio dramas, thirty-four plays, thirty screenplays, and one television play. His Hollywood scripts include such titles as *Look Out, Mr. Moto* (1937; with others), *Three Coins in the Fountain* (1954), *Les Girls* (1957), *The World of Suzie Wong* (1960), and *Gigot* (1962). *The Hasty Heart* was his second published play and his first commercial success, an Off-Broadway smash that was followed by several Broadway productions of his subsequent plays. The most successful of these was Patrick's best-known work, the Broadway hit *The Teahouse of the August Moon* (pr. 1953; film version, 1956; pb. 1954). This comical satire shows a military bureaucracy coming into conflict with a gentle Okinawan peasant village in the years following World War II. Like *The Hasty Heart*, *The Teahouse of the August Moon* succeeds artistically because it mixes serious thematic purposes with rich humor. This play won for Patrick several major New York critics' awards and the Pulitzer Prize in drama in 1954. Following this hit were several less successful plays, including *Everybody Loves Opal* (pr. 1961, pb. 1962), which continues to be popular in regional and community theaters.

The praise for Patrick's drama usually focuses on his theatrical craftsmanship. He can be depended on for effective plot structure, theatrically interesting characterization, and simple, crisp, often witty dialogue. He is generally considered a writer of gentle and compassionate comedy rather than of serious plays.

Sources for Further Study

Kienzle, Siegfried. *Modern World Theater: A Guide to Productions in Europe and the United States Since 1945*. New York: Ungar, 1970.

Leonard, William Torbert. "*The Hasty Heart.*" In *Theatre: Stage to Screen to Television*. Metuchen, N.J.: Scarecrow Press, 1981.

Moe, Christian H. "John Patrick." In *Contemporary Dramatists*. 4th ed. Chicago: St. James, 1988.

Rhodes, Russell, and Louis Kronenberger. "*The Hasty Heart.*" In *Selected Theatre Criticism*, edited by Anthony Slide. Vol. 3, 1931-1950. Metuchen, N.J.: Scarecrow Press, 1986.

Terry Nienhuis

HAVANA IS WAITING

Author: Eduardo Machado (1953-   )
Type of plot: Autobiographical
Time of plot: December, 1999
Locale: New York and Cuba
First produced: 2001, at the Actors Theatre of Louisville, as *When the Sea Drowns in Sand*, Louisville, Kentucky
First published: 2001

> *Principal characters:*
> FEDERICO, a Cuban American in his forties
> FRED, an Italian American in his early thirties
> ERNESTO, a cab driver
> THE PERCUSSIONIST, a nonspeaking drummer

The Play

Act 1 opens in December, 1999, in Federico's New York apartment. Federico, like Eduardo Machado himself, was one of the 14,048 children of Operation Pedro Pan, a secret operation administered by Roman Catholic charities with support from the U.S. government. Cuban parents sent unaccompanied children to Florida between 1960 and 1962, fearing that Cuban dictator Fidel Castro would take legal custody of them and indoctrinate them to be obedient communists.

Fred enters; they are going to visit Federico's native Cuba together, after thirty-eight years of exile since his parents sent him to the United States. Federico is reluctant and explains the angst of the exile: "Disoriented or unrequited? I do not know the answer to that. Was I thrown out or did I walk away from my country? Did I decide to leave or was I tricked?"

In Havana, Cuba, Federico is nervous as they ride in a cab driven by Ernesto, who provides political and historic context for their conversation. Ernesto asks, "So you went on the Peter Pan flights?" He explains to Fred, "So many kids, thirteen thousand. Sent to the U.S. Like cattle, all because of a CIA plot. . . . " Ernesto loves Cuba but not the American "imperialists," and he blames the Central Intelligence Agency (CIA) for the exodus of those children. Ernesto is pleased about the easing of travel restrictions that Castro calls "family reconciliation," but Federico replies that it is more like "dollar reconciliation."

They search for the house of Federico's early childhood. Federico and Fred play with a video camera, quoting the lines of the character Blanche Dubois in Tennessee Williams's play *A Streetcar Named Desire* (pr., pb. 1947). Federico blames his parents for not allowing him to grow up in the lovely city of Havana: "The money-grubbing sons of bitches. No wonder they are so bitter. . . . I am beginning to feel like I am someone. That I belong. That someone loves me." Fred and Federico often quarrel, while Ernesto remarks on the love that is evident between them. Ernesto is uneasy about Federico's open homosexuality, and though Fred repeatedly says he himself is straight, it is clear he is attracted to Federico.

They find Federico's childhood address, where there is now a school, but he is not allowed in. The three men join a neighborhood rally in which a crowd carries posters of Elián González, the little boy who was the subject of a custody battle between the United States and Cuba in 1999.

In act 2, Federico keeps trying to gain entrance into his old home. Fred reasons that Federico must see it for "the journey to be complete." Federico declares, "I never felt so much what class I come from. This country makes you feel that. I hate myself." Fred argues with him, but they agree that they both love Havana, and Ernesto tells Federico to listen to the drums: "They are saying the healing has begun."

Ernesto takes them to La Habana Airport. Federico muses, "Sometimes this seems like home sometimes it doesn't," and Ernesto says, "Sometimes you seem like family sometimes you don't." Ernesto finally shows some warmth to Federico, saying, "I am sorry that you never did get in." Federico replies, "I feel like I did. Why long for a building? The buildings have crumbled. The past does not exist. Does not, will not ever come back." Ernesto kisses Federico on the lips and Federico says, "The embargo is melting." Surprised, Ernesto says, "Not really," but Federico explains, "Between us."

As their plane takes off, Federico tells Ernesto to think "lovely thoughts," to imagine a "world where cold wars are not fought over children." Fred agrees, "Where a person can be a man a woman a boy a little girl. Whatever feels right inside." They fly back home, rhapsodizing about Cuba. Ernesto gets the last, brief, speech of the play. Holding the poster of Elián, he pleads of the United States, "You've kept us apart long enough. . . . Give them back. Give them back to us."

Themes and Meanings

Machado deals with the themes of loneliness, friendship, and self-identity. Federico is like Machado himself: a sensitive, intellectual, homosexual Cuban exile. Because Federico was exiled from Cuba, rather than voluntarily emigrating, he has always felt that part of him was amputated, that his childhood was stolen from him. Symbolizing Federico's divided self and the division between such dichotomies as capitalism and communism and heterosexuality and homosexuality, at the beginning Federico chants a fragmentary poem full of questions: "Can it be? Is this me?/ . . . Am I home?/ . . . Why am I not/ any good./ Why can't I hold/ on to you/ or it./ Or her./ Or me./ Or dreams."

His statements are incomplete but evocative: "When you've reached your/ promised land, Where the people often dance." Most of his lines are either questions or poetic, tortured expressions of his immediate emotional responses to his experiences.

An admirable part of Federico's characterization is that he is comfortable with and open about his homosexuality. Ernesto, the macho Latino, verbally abuses Federico at times, but he is won over by Federico's emotional honesty. Fred, meanwhile, finds himself converted to Cuba, speaks enthusiastically about the revolution, and says, "I'm not gay, but I feel like a woman." In a moment of passion, he weeps and asks

Federico to hold him. The name Fred is the Americanized version of Federico, suggesting not just friendship between them but, perhaps, two sides of the same person.

When Ernesto identifies Federico as a victim of the Peter Pan flights, Federico refers to the character Wendy in Sir James Barrie's 1904 novel *Peter Pan* because he, like Peter Pan, had trouble growing up. He alludes often to that novel, as when he says, "What I dreamt of all my life. Coming back to Never Land." Similar, but more complex, are Machado's allusions to *A Streetcar Named Desire*. Federico's dog in his New York home is named Stella, like the sister of Blanche Dubois in the play. Blanche herself is adult but, like Peter Pan, she refuses to face the realities necessary to maturation. Blanche represents loneliness and desire, tainted innocence, thwarted dreams, and the distance between the past and the present. It seems significant that Fred and Federico, quoting several lines from the Williams play, recite the lines of two women. Fred is discovering his feminine side; he tells Federico, "A man who can love like a woman. That's what I want to be. That's what this country is bringing out in me."

The three men each come to understand the other two better. Toward the end of the play, Fred tells Federico, "You can get inside my emotions whenever you want." Because Machado fervently hopes for a reconciliation between Cuba and the United States, he dramatizes an eventual pact of friendship between Ernesto and the two men who promise they will come again and bring goods to the starving island. Ernesto says with satisfaction, "At least you know what you're arguing about: The beauty of this land." When Federico and Ernesto finally shake hands, the moment is heartwarming.

Machado explained his change of title to an interviewer in 2001, saying that it

> refers to many things. First, Havana is waiting for a forty-year-old embargo to end. Havana means waiting, for the people who live there. Waiting interminably in lines for anything from a bus to ice cream, but more importantly Havana, or as they say in Cuba, La Habana, was waiting for me to return.

Dramatic Devices

Many drama reviewers noted that the characters in this play represent nations: Fred is the American, Ernesto is the Cuban, and Federico is the exile, belonging to both. However, they are not merely representative figures, because this is an autobiographical play. If it had been written in three acts, the characters would be more rounded, but Machado sought simplicity, a wise decision considering that the play is talky without any real action. Likewise, his setting is simple. The only props are Fred's video camera, a poster of Elián González, and the cigarettes that the men smoke. Fred's anxiety to videotape their journey provides the most delightful moments of the play; it allows us to see the friends laughing and enjoying each other's company, whereas most of *Havana Is Waiting* is ridden with angst.

Because the set is minimalistic, the audience focuses entirely on the three characters and the emotions they express. The fourth man of the dramatic production, the percussionist, never speaks. He is usually situated above the stage and provides accompaniment to the dialogue in the form of sensuous Latin drumbeats. Many plays use incidental music—music, that is, which complements the incidents—but Machado's choice of a single drummer was inspired.

To read the play is less satisfying than to see it staged live, because Machado forgoes the use of commas and complete sentences, and occasionally he breaks up a single sentence in two, as when Ernesto says, "Because in Marxism. Logic is God." A person must be talented at inventing voices in his or her own head to enjoy the experience of reading it, but with that talent will find a poetry and rhythm that match the drumbeats of the dramatized version. The characters occasionally speak in Spanish, but Federico translates most of these lines.

Critical Context

Machado, through his alter ego Federico, draws a parallel between himself and that other famous little "lost boy" (Peter Pan's friends in Never-Never-Land were called The Lost Boys), Elián González, who gave rise to a custody dispute between Cuba and the United States in December of 1999. Elián was a six-year-old Cuban boy whose mother took him from Cuba without the consent of his father and grandparents, but she and nine others died when their boat sank. Elián survived by floating on an inner tube for several hours in international waters until he was rescued off the coast of Florida. In Miami, Elián's relatives held onto the boy, refusing to return the child to his Cuban family (he finally went home in June, 2000). Mass protest demonstrations were held in Cuba—Federico and Fred witness one of these during their visit—and because Machado does not overemphasize the similarities between himself and Elián, the parallel is artistic and moving.

Contemporary critical reaction to *Havana Is Waiting* was mixed. Cubans and other exiles felt it to be a beautiful, passionate play, while others often found it self-absorbed and self-indulgent. Reviewers never missed the point, however. Many were impressed by the way that Machado articulated the difficult relationship between Cuba and the United States through the humanity of the three characters. Ernesto demonstrates how the Cubans can be proud, patriotic, and yearning, while his American guests are arrogant, expressive, and generous. Machado successfully shows the griefs and losses caused by the U.S. embargo against Cuba that began in 1961, after the 1959 revolution that installed Castro in power. His play argues that it is time for the two countries to reconcile and to discover what they have to offer each other.

Sources for Further Study

Brantley, Ben. "Eduardo Machado: Creator of a Paradise Lost." *New York Times Magazine*, October 23, 1994, 38.

Cox, Gordon. "Talk, Talk, Talk On a Trip to Cuba." *Newsday*, Oct 25, 2001, B8.

Machado, Eduardo. "Thirteen Commentaries." *American Theatre* 14, no. 5 (May 1, 1997): 14.

Spencer, Stuart. "Interview with Eduardo Machado." *BOMB* 30 (1990): 26-28.

Fiona Kelleghan

HOLY GHOSTS

Author: Romulus Linney (1930-   )
Type of plot: Psychological
Time of plot: An evening in early summer in the late twentieth century
Locale: The American rural South
First produced: 1974, at East Carolina University, Greenville, North Carolina
First published: 1977, in *Two Plays*

>   *Principal characters:*
>   NANCY SHEDMAN, a young woman
>   COLEMAN SHEDMAN, her husband
>   ROGERS CANFIELD, an elderly retired lawyer
>   THE REVEREND OBEDIAH BUCKHORN, SR., a Pentecostal preacher
>   OBEDIAH "OBY" BUCKHORN, JR., his son

The Play

As *Holy Ghosts* opens, a young woman, Nancy Shedman, sweeps out a sparsely furnished room in a ramshackle house that contains stacked folding chairs, benches, and an old piano. She has just fled her husband of one year to join a group of Pentecostal Christians offering her sanctuary in their farmhouse-church. Disillusioned by a childless marriage punctuated by beatings and drunkenly ineffectual lovemaking, Nancy has left home with her husband's furniture, possessions, and pickup truck. Aiding her in the move was Obediah Buckhorn, Jr. (called Oby), a passerby camper volunteering scriptural consolation who took her to his preacher father for counseling.

In act 1, Nancy is surprised by the entrance of her irate husband, Coleman, a redneck owner-manager of a fish farm. Hurt and humiliated, he accuses Nancy of infidelity and demands both the return of his chattels and a divorce. To facilitate the latter, Coleman has brought Rogers Canfield, an elderly alcoholic lawyer escaping a depressing retirement. The shabby but gentlemanly Canfield enforces a testimonial procedure for the angry couple to air grievances. Oby, a huge, childlike man, arrives and is reviled by Coleman for adulterous wife-stealing. Oby corroborates Nancy's story of the drunkenly abusive behavior that impelled her departure, Oby's celibate involvement, and his father's proposal of marriage—thereby astonishing Coleman, who thought Oby his rival. Agreeable to divorce but not to returning possessions claimed as her just due, Nancy hotly refutes Coleman's portrayal of himself as a caring husband betrayed by a perfidious wife.

As the Shedmans argue, a motley group of poor white southerners intermittently arrive, gathering for a religious service. One carefully carries in two large wooden boxes. The group is a strange collection of human flotsam, including a terminal cancer victim named Cancer Man, a grief-deranged owner of a dead bird dog, an expelled female Sunday school teacher, two hot-tempered but affectionate homosexual construction workers, a lady churchgoer made outcast for raising her skirts for any "good

Christian boy," a shotgun-wedded couple with baby, and the simple-minded Oby. The irrepressibly foul-mouthed Coleman overtly jeers at the oddness of the gathering.

The aging Reverend Obediah Buckhorn, Sr., enters, fondly kisses Nancy "with a gleam in his eye," calmly forestalls Coleman's rude queries, and announces the service to begin. The pastor's followers swiftly rearrange the room, placing the wooden boxes next to a makeshift altar. An erected sign reads, "Amalgamation Holiness Church of God with Signs Following." After hymns and prayers, Buckhorn welcomes Nancy to the fold. Impatiently, Coleman interrupts the service and, refusing to budge until his marital dispute is resolved, seats himself on the boxes. Kicking them in anger, he discovers them to contain deadly snakes and cries incredulously to the congregation, "My God. You're Pentecostal snakehandlers."

The audience learns that the sect's faith is based on a literal reading of Mark 16:17-18, which asserts the believers' salvation from damnation, signified when "in my name . . . they cast out devils. . . . They shall take up serpents. . . . " Should a follower be bitten and die, it is a sign of insufficiency of faith.

In act 2, Buckhorn responds to Coleman's accusation with the admission that their religion is illegal and dangerous, confessing that absent members do lie seriously ill or dead. Coleman entreats Nancy not to stay in this "insane asylum," but she refuses to leave. The congregation rallies around her and retaliates to Coleman's gibes with anger and supplication. Aware of the skeptic in their midst, the church members present self-revelatory testimonials illuminating their private torments and reasons for embracing a religion of acceptance, fellowship, and faith. Buckhorn's revelation that he has fathered seventeen children and buried five wives causes Nancy to reconsider his marriage proposal. He responds to Coleman's denunciation of the congregation as lunatics and fakers with an eloquently impassioned recital of the sect's creed and history, pleading with Nancy to choose between him and her husband.

As the followers sing to assuage their anger, Coleman asks Nancy not to marry "that old man" and to accompany him home, where he will change his ways. Slowly convincing Nancy of his good intentions, he notices that the congregation has stopped singing to listen to them. Enraged, he curses them for listening as he tries to talk with "my goddamn stupid wife"; losing control, he strikes Nancy. Despite his immediate contrition, she knows that he will never change, and she rejects him. Coleman sobs.

Stressing that only the Lord offers surcease from suffering, Buckhorn continues the service, now intensifying with Scripture reading and singing. Cancer Man takes out a snake and challenges Coleman to test God by doing the same. Wracked with as much pain and frustration as anyone present, Coleman takes up snakes with terror and, amazed that he is not bitten, cries out his conversion. The congregation erupts into spiritual frenzy. All shake with spasms, speak in tongues, and handle snakes—except for Nancy, who has distanced herself. Even the lawyer Canfield has now become a convert. Reaching a cathartic climax, the exhausted worshipers return the snakes to their boxes. Falling on his knees, Coleman begs to join the church, realizing who he is and where his salvation lies. Determined to go to business school and make her own way, Nancy announces her decision to leave. Bidding the congregation farewell, she departs in awareness that her salvation lies not with them but within herself. The congregation, renewed in faith, sings exultantly as the play ends.

Themes and Meanings

In an interview, Romulus Linney defined the point of the play as "the very unusual ways in which people find their . . . personal salvation . . . their adjustment to life, their . . . philosophy." *Holy Ghosts* incisively examines rural southern folk. Most of the characters are social or psychological misfits, rejected by a disapproving society.

Central characters Coleman and Nancy Shedman dramatically epitomize the struggle of tormented lives to cope with existence. Nancy undergoes a journey of self-discovery, as does her husband. Yearning for the respected role of wife and mother, she has entrapped herself in an unhappy marriage, from which she seeks to escape by seizing upon the communal comfort proffered by a bizarre religious sect. She discovers that neither a sect peopled by the desperate nor an equally desperate husband incapable of inner change can give her fulfillment; she must earn it herself. Consequently, she freely chooses to learn an independent livelihood in the outside world; in so doing, she displays great strength. Coleman has inherited a joyless view of life, which has led him to a joyless marriage. His scornful attitude toward the snakehandlers is reversed when he discovers that his frustration and self-loathing are equal to their own, and he experiences an emotional catharsis in the church's ophidian worship. Like the lawyer Canfield, another converted outsider, Coleman realizes a needed dependency on the sect's faith and fellowship.

Coleman's transformation takes place against the backdrop of the snakehandling sect's worship. Its followers represent a spectrum of the dispirited and dispossessed. Through their communal tolerance and their church's liturgy, these people have gained a relief and a hope they had never experienced in the outside world. Their dangerous ritual of snakehandling is therapeutic, for in worship they are transfigured by the conviction that they are in touch with a force, higher than the society that rejects them, that miraculously grants them the power to neutralize deadly serpents. The play points to people's need to find adjustment and personal salvation, however strange or unconventional the means. Themes of tolerance and freedom of choice are also made evident in the action of the play.

Linney neither ridicules his characters nor indicts their belief, but treats them with compassion. "People in the grip of religious experience interest me," Linney once said in discussing the play. "It affects them profoundly for the better." Presenting a convincingly realistic portrait of people in the midst of such experience, he effectively demonstrates his central themes. The audience is reminded that the snake (a familiar image in religion), while reviled in the Garden of Eden, also is entwined around the caduceus of Mercury, messenger of the gods, as a symbol of healing.

Dramatic Devices

The play's themes of personal salvation, self-realization, and tolerance are artfully highlighted by a conflict between a painfully frustrated husband and wife, who travel toward wholeness and end at opposite destinations. Dramatic changes in the Shedmans take place during a snakehandling sect's worship service. The implicit theatricality of the sect's bizarre and dangerous worship lends impact to both theme and action, in act 2 culminating in the frenzied climax of the snakehandlers' cathartic ritual, which effects Coleman's transformation. Around the Shedmans' contentious relationship, Romulus Linney creates a group portrait of dispirited Fundamentalists who have found a type of grace and the binding kinship of shared belief.

Exposition delineating the nature and motivations of the characters gives voice to Linney's thematic concerns in several ways. The initial confrontation between the Shedmans establishes their contentious personalities and is the first of many clashes that generate reactions from those around them. Further revelation of situation and character, which now extends to Oby and Canfield, is provided by the lawyer's insistence on a testimonial procedure in act 1. This procedure foreshadows the church members' self-revelatory testimonials. These testimonials expose the bleak past of the worshipers as well as exercising their communal protection of Nancy and one another and the defense of their faith against Coleman, the intolerant intruder. His insulting skepticism is contrasted with the patience, tolerance, and faith of the sect members and the soon-to-be-converted Canfield. The play's characters are effectively orchestrated to display their similarities and differences.

Linney regards his characters sympathetically, never satirizing them as country bumpkins or sentimentalizing them. His compassionate humor leads the audience to care for the characters. Human frailties and tattered souls are disclosed with strong lacings of comedy: For example, the slow-witted Oby, a former pinsetter, talks of "the religious nature of bowling"; Nancy describes explicitly the ludicrous sexual failure of her bibulous husband, who is prone to passing out during lovemaking; and the pastor's Bluebeard-like marital history is comedic in its extent. There are additional comic shadings given to characters. Even Coleman gathers audience sympathy as his confused anxieties increase and his inflexibilities are unmasked. Moreover, the language of the folk parishioners reveals a richness of imagery and metaphor, best exemplified in the Reverend Buckhorn's biblical eloquence.

Critical Context

Romulus Linney's most widely produced play, *Holy Ghosts*, is not a sociological document about Pentecostal snakehandling (a form of worship founded in Appalachia around 1909), yet it stands as the best-known dramatic work on the subject and doubtless owes much of its well-deserved popularity to curiosity about the practice. Beyond that, however, Linney's sensitive Pentecostal group portrait occupies a high rank in the canon of the author's works.

Reared in Tennessee and North Carolina, Linney has drawn upon his knowledge of the rural South for most of his plays. *Tennessee* (pr. 1979, pb. 1980) portrays an elderly Appalachian woman who recalls a frontier youth that restricted her own self-growth. *Sand Mountain* (pr., pb. 1985) encompasses two short folk plays: one about a discriminating young widow who rejects bragging men for a truth-telling widower, and a second about the visit to a mountaineer family of Saint Peter and a disguised Jesus. *A Woman Without a Name* (pr. 1985) concerns a turn-of-the-twentieth-century southern woman whose reenactment of past memories liberates her from despairing self-doubt and strengthens her sense of self-worth.

In another context, *Holy Ghosts* traces a pattern of action developed in many Linney dramas, in which his protagonists enter or mature in environments where they confront values foreign to or repressive of their individuality. Usually tempted or overcome by such values, these characters ultimately reach a decision to accept or reject them. Such a pattern is evident in at least three plays besides *Holy Ghosts*, *Tennessee*, and *A Woman Without a Name*. In *The Sorrows of Frederick* (pb. 1966, pr. 1967), Prussia's Frederick the Great emerges as a king who forsakes great artistic and intellectual gifts to pursue power. In *The Love Suicide at Schofield Barracks* (pr. 1972, pb. 1973), a military inquiry uncovers that a patriotic army general was so shattered by the Vietnam War that he undertook a ritualistic suicide to symbolize his despair. In *Democracy and Esther* (pb. 1973; revised as *Democracy*, pr. 1974), a combined dramatization of two Henry Adams novels, two intelligent women enter the Washington society of Ulysses S. Grant's corruption-ridden administration and renounce offers to marry two charming, influential men whose values they abhor.

Also a novelist and television scriptwriter, Linney is a distinctive writer of uncommon literateness and artistry whose dramatic writing has garnered awards—including an American Theatre Critics Association Award in 1990, an Obie for Sustained Excellence in 1992, and an American Academy of Arts and Letters Induction in 2002—and numerous productions. He ended the twentieth century with a host of plays, including *Shotgun* (pr. 1994), *Oscar over Here* (pr. 1995, pb. 2000), *True Crimes* (pr., pb. 1996), and *Mountain Memory: A Play About Appalachian Life*, (pb. 1997).

Sources for Further Study

DiGaetani, John L. "Romulus Linney." In *A Search for Postmodern Theatre: Interviews with Contemporary Playwrights*, edited by John L. DiGaetani. Westport, Conn.: Greenwood Press, 1991.

Disch, Thomas M. Review in *The Nation*, September 19, 1987, pp. 282-284.

Moe, Christian H. "Romulus Linney." In *Contemporary Dramatists*. 6th ed. Detroit: St. James, 1999.

Tedford, Harold. "Romulus Linney on 'Sublime Gossip'." *Southern Theatre* 38 (Spring, 1997): 26-32.

Wilmeth, Don B. "Romulus Linney." In *American Playwrights Since 1945: A Guide to Scholarship, Criticism, and Performance*, edited by Philip Kolin. New York: Greenwood Press, 1989.

_____. "Romulus Linney." In *Speaking on Stage: Interviews with Contemporary American Playwrights*. Tuscaloosa: University of Alabama Press, 1996.

Christian H. Moe

THE HOMECOMING

Author: Harold Pinter (1930-   )
Type of plot: Psychological
Time of plot: The 1960's
Locale: North London
First produced: 1965, at the Aldwych Theatre, London
First published: 1965

> *Principal characters:*
> MAX, a seventy-year-old retired butcher
> SAM, Max's brother, a chauffeur, sixty-three
> TEDDY, Max's eldest son, a philosophy professor in his middle thirties
> RUTH, Teddy's wife, a former model in her early thirties
> LENNY, Max's second son, a pimp in his early thirties
> JOEY, Max's youngest son, a boxer in his middle twenties

The Play

The Homecoming begins in the evening of an apparently normal working day. Max and Lenny are sitting in the large, slumlike living room in North London, which is the realistic setting for the entire action of the play; they are arguing. Sam returns from work, and Max verbally attacks him. Then Joey returns from his boxing gym, and Max also verbally abuses him. Later that night, after all three have gone to bed, Teddy and Ruth arrive from the United States, unannounced, and while Ruth goes out for a breath of air, Lenny enters and converses nonchalantly with Teddy. Teddy retires to his old bedroom upstairs, and Ruth returns, to be greeted by Lenny, who engages in provocative banter and storytelling. This leads to an incident with a glass of water that Ruth offers to Lenny with clear sexual implications. When Lenny recoils, she laughs, drinks the water, and retires upstairs to bed. Max, awakened by the conversations, comes down and abuses Lenny. The next morning, when Teddy and Ruth come downstairs, Max reacts violently, particularly against Ruth, and orders Joey to throw both of them out. Joey is unwilling, and Max hits him. Max then changes his mind; the act ends with Max about to embrace Teddy.

Act 2 begins sometime later, with all the characters around the lunch table, their meal completed. Max reminisces about his dead wife Jessie and his children's childhood years but soon reviles them; Sam leaves to do a taxi pickup, and Teddy talks in positive terms about his academic life in America as a professor and doctor of philosophy; Ruth, though, comments negatively on the life she leads in the United States. Teddy tries to persuade Ruth to return with him to America and their three children. Teddy goes upstairs to pack; Lenny puts on a slow jazz record and dances with Ruth. Teddy comes downstairs with the suitcases, and Joey and Max enter. Ruth allows Joey to lie on her but pushes him away and asks for whiskey, which Lenny brings to her. Teddy, prompted by Ruth, refuses to discuss his work as a philosopher.

The scene blacks out, and it is now evening. Max is talking to Teddy. Lenny enters, looking for a cheese roll he had prepared, but Teddy says that he has eaten it "deliberately." Lenny lectures him about his (Teddy's) role as a member of the family. Joey comes downstairs; he has been alone with Ruth in a bedroom but has not been "the whole hog"—one of a series of animal images used in the play. Lenny prompts Joey to tell Teddy a story about how they forced two women to have sex on a bomb site. Max and Sam return, and, with Teddy apparently passive, Max decides that Ruth shall stay with them in London. Lenny proposes to take her up to Greek Street to earn money to support herself, clearly suggesting that she become a prostitute, and they fantasize about the future income she will generate. Teddy warns them that she will "get old . . . very quickly." Ruth enters, and Teddy tells her that "the family have invited you to stay . . . as a kind of guest." Ruth discusses the offer, including the details of her proposed apartment, in practical business terms and appears to accept the proposal. Sam suddenly collapses while blurting out that the mysterious MacGregor "had" Jessie, Max's former wife, "in the back of my cab." Teddy leaves for the airport, and the play closes with Ruth sitting in the set's only chair, Joey's head in her lap. Max crawls around Sam (who has apparently suffered a heart attack and lies unconscious on the floor), begging her: "Kiss me." She makes no reply and while Lenny stands watching, the curtain falls.

Themes and Meanings

The Homecoming is a drama of human relationships—relationships conceived by Harold Pinter as continually under negotiation and expressed in language, silences, and the sudden eruption of actual violence. The many possible meanings of the play are to be found in the varied psychology of the characters and the history of their previous relationships with one another. The "facts" of those relationships, however, remain elusive to the audience. What is the truth of Max's relationship with his dead wife Jessie? Was she a whore? Are his three children really his or are they Mac-Gregor's? Whose "homecoming" is it—Teddy's or Ruth's? Perhaps it is a homecoming for them both, since Ruth lived in London, too, before her marriage.

Max is the patriarchal head of the London household, but his authority is constantly being undercut by Lenny, who taunts him with questions about his (Lenny's) own paternity and ignores him as he sees fit. Sam may be homosexual; Max purports to believe so, but this may be rather his method of attacking Sam—by focusing on Sam's ambiguous sexual identity. In any case, Sam has his revenge when he blurts out that the mysterious MacGregor "had Jessie in the back of my cab as I drove them along."

Pinter has said, "What goes on in my plays is realistic, but what I'm doing is not realism." He is a "hyperrealist" who presents a perfectly feasible surface of action and behavior beneath which there is a continual struggle by the characters to develop hegemony over one another. This may be said to be the theme of *The Homecoming*—but the meanings are many. The play presents in miniature the fragile and tenuous quality of human existence, conceived by Pinter to be forever irresolvable for the simple reason that meaning is never certain. As Tom says in another Pinter play, *Tea Party*, "I've often wondered what 'mean' means." *The Homecoming* has an apparently simple plot, yet it is a text which resists closure and elevates psychological ambiguity to the status of great art.

Dramatic Devices

The characters in *The Homecoming* are similar to those in Pinter's earlier plays— men (and, for the first time in a Pinter play, a powerful woman) of a common sort who live out their stage lives within the confines of a single room. The author creates an air of menace through threats conveyed both with language and silence, and acts of violence which suddenly erupt. The language Pinter uses for his characters seems to be that of everyday, colloquial speech typical of a London lower-middle-class family, but it is a crafted rhetoric which carefully, elaborately avoids the use of four-letter words. Regarding the play's silences, Peter Hall, the director of the original London and New York productions, commented that Pinter wrote in silences as much as he did in words, and the text of the play is specific about the length of time an actor should give to pauses in the language, depending on whether Pinter used either three ellipses, the word "pause," or the word "silence."

Another dramatic device is the use of everyday domestic objects as sites for verbal battles. The play opens with Lenny choosing horses from the newspaper and then asking and rejecting Max's advice over the likely winners. The glass of water used by Ruth in act 1 to tease Lenny sexually is used again when she orders whiskey from Lenny after teasing Joey. When Teddy "deliberately" eats Lenny's cheese roll, the scene demonstrates Teddy's ludicrous response to Lenny's appropriation of Ruth. The threatened violence becomes real when Max strikes Joey in the stomach at the end of act 1, and when Sam collapses of an apparent heart attack at the end of act 2.

Critical Context

Criticism on Pinter numbers thousands of pages, because there is a wide belief, as critic John Lahr has said, that "Pinter is the finest playwright to emerge in our technological society." Before 1965, there was comparatively little written on him. His first play, *The Room* (pr. 1957, pb. 1960), attracted mostly puzzled comment, as did *The Caretaker* (pr., pb. 1960). Both plays employed the device of presenting two people in a single room. In *The Homecoming*, Pinter's first major full-length work, there are six characters instead of two, but the claustrophobia of a single room is maintained— there is no change of set.

Lahr saw Pinter reinvesting people and objects with mystery. Some critics have focused on the comic grotesqueness of the characters, who hover between animal grossness and a veneer of culture, pointing out the frequency of animal metaphors in their language. Others see Ruth as a fertility goddess, with the men vying for her favors and the play a chilling version of the ritual renewal of life. Still others see the play as a parody of the comedy of manners. The two predominating modes of Pinter criticism in the late twentieth century were those based on either a cultural anthropological or a linguistic approach; earlier attempts in the 1960's by such critics as Martin Esslin to appropriate Pinter as a dramatist of the Theater of the Absurd came to be seen as too limiting. The play was Pinter's first American success, winning the Tony Award in 1967 for best play on Broadway. It was not until *Betrayal* (pr., pb. 1978) that Pinter experienced a greater commercial success in the United States.

Sources for Further Study

Billington, Michael. *The Life and Work of Harold Pinter.* London: Faber, 1996.

Dukore, Bernard F. *Harold Pinter.* 2d ed. London: Macmillan, 1982.

Esslin, Martin. *Pinter: A Study of His Plays.* 3d ed. London: Methuen, 1977.

Gale, Steven H. "Character and Motivation in Harold Pinter's *The Homecoming.*" *Journal of Evolutionary Psychology* 8 (1987): 278-288.

_____. *Harold Pinter: An Annotated Bibliography.* Boston: G. K. Hall, 1978.

Lahr, John, ed. *A Casebook on Harold Pinter's "The Homecoming."* New York: Grove Press, 1971.

_____. "Harold Pinter Retrospective." *The New Yorker* 34 (August 6, 2001): 76-77.

Quigley, Austin E. *The Pinter Problem.* Princeton, N.J.: Princeton University Press, 1975.

Scott, Michael, ed. *Harold Pinter—"The Birthday Party," "The Caretaker," and "The Homecoming": A Casebook.* London: Macmillan, 1986.

Silverstein, Marc. *Harold Pinter and the Language of Cultural Power.* Lewisburg, Pa.: Bucknell University Press, 1993.

Nicholas Ranson

THE HOSTAGE

Author: Brendan Behan (1923-1964)
Type of plot: Social realism
Time of plot: 1960
Locale: Dublin, Ireland
First produced: 1958, at the Theatre Royal, London
First published: 1958

Principal characters:
PAT, the caretaker of a Dublin lodging house
MEG DILLON, his partner
MONSEWER, the owner of the house
MR. MULLEADY, an elderly civil servant
LESLIE WILLIAMS, the hostage, a British soldier
TERESA, the maid-of-all-work, an Irish country girl
AN IRA OFFICER, a fanatical Irish patriot
FEARGUS O'CONNOR, an IRA volunteer

The Play

The Hostage opens with a scene of chaos and confusion in a lodging house in Dublin. The house is in fact used by many of its occupants as a brothel, with a floating population of male and female prostitutes, clients, and other visitors, mixed in with the regular staff and, later, the more sinister visitors from the Irish Republican Army (IRA). At the start of the play, though, this political theme is absent. The regular and irregular occupants of the house are engaged in dancing an Irish jig, from which Pat and Meg break off only to drink a glass of stout—the dark, bitter beer of Ireland.

Pat and Meg are, however, preparing the room they are in for a "guest." Who is this guest to be? The answer does not emerge for a considerable time, but slowly the picture becomes clearer. Pat, it emerges from his conversation with Meg, is an old soldier of the Irish War of Independence (approximately 1918-1921). In this war he lost a leg, though whether in glorious or discreditable circumstances remains uncertain. Pat holds his present job largely because of his status as a "veteran." The owner of the house, Monsewer, is meanwhile fanatically dedicated to the cause of Ireland, appearing throughout the play in a kilt (a most unusual garment in Ireland) and playing much of the time on his Irish bagpipes.

The tune he is playing at the start is a dead march. Monsewer is practicing this march so he can play it the next morning at eight o'clock, when a young Irishman is due to be hanged in Belfast jail for some unspecified terrorist offense. As for the guest for whom Pat and Meg are preparing the bed, he is an English soldier whom the IRA intends to kidnap and to hold hostage against the life of the man in Belfast jail, planning to execute their prisoner in reprisal if the British hanging is carried out.

None of this, however, appears at all serious in act 1. During this act, indeed, the audience realizes that Monsewer is almost mad, if amusing—he keeps on "inspecting" the occupants of the house as if they were not prostitutes but soldiers. Pat also is very possibly a fraud—the weapons he claims to have won from the English in the War of Independence were in fact bought from a British soldier in a pub; even the rebel songs sung by several characters are, to them, mere music, without serious political meaning. Monsewer is, despite his kilt, bagpipes, and nationalism, a member of the English upper class. The arguments about history that go on between the characters are presented as on much the same level as one prostitute's doubt over whether to accept a Russian sailor as a client (for she is a Catholic and he a communist) or the violent dispute over whether Mr. Mulleady is really praying or doing something else in his room with his girlfriend. At the end of the act the characters are once again dancing. Into the dance Leslie, the English soldier, is pushed, blindfolded, and the dancing stops.

Act 2 opens with another scene of near-farce, this time in the dark. The soft-hearted occupants of the lodging house are solidly on the side of the threatened English prisoner and try to show their sympathy by offering cups of tea, cigarettes, and stout. Feargus, the IRA volunteer, has been told to guard Leslie at gunpoint, however, and the continued movement in the house around him makes him nervous. It does not help matters that he is increasingly desperate to urinate, while the nameless IRA officer—the only teetotaler in the play—will not give him permission to leave his post.

Against this background of confusion several human relationships become prominent. Most important is that between Leslie and Teresa, the Irish skivvy. Both are nineteen, lonely, and confused, with much in common. Somewhere offstage between acts 2 and 3, their relationship, the audience is told, reaches physical consummation, but it can hardly be called a love affair; rather, it is a "sympathy affair." In spite of gaps of nationality and generation, something similar breeds between Leslie and Pat. When Pat talks of his bad experiences at the hands of the British military in prison, Leslie (completely ignorant of the historical past) assumes that he has suffered from the "redcaps," the military police, whom Leslie too regards as enemies. Though several characters try to remind Leslie of British atrocities in Ireland in the past, there is as usual doubt as to whether they really happened; in any case, he clearly had nothing to do with them. The identification between Englishman and Irish people reaches a peak when Leslie first "falls in" for one of Monsewer's ridiculous inspections, and then, when he is evicted from it, talks about cricket; this releases a flood of English nostalgia from Monsewer—who, as the others point out, is only pretending to be an Irishman, fanatic though he may be.

Sobriety is reintroduced at the end of the act by the realization that Leslie has been brought there to be shot. In act 3 this leads to increasing initiatives from Pat. He had been in the IRA during the wars of forty years before, but he has little sympathy for what his successor, the IRA officer—whom he despises as humorless and sober—intends to do now. At one point of unusual confusion, he almost gets Leslie away by the simple device of sending him off to buy a crate of stout. It seems very likely that someone in this ill-disciplined household will contact the Irish police, who will come to rescue Leslie; in the end it proves to be Mr. Mulleady who leads the police in their raid. In complete chaos, guns fire, bombs explode, Monsewer plays a lament on the pipes, Pat gives a running commentary, and Leslie looks for Teresa. As he finally makes a break to escape, though, he is shot dead—whether by the police or by the IRA is never explained. The IRA men are arrested while trying to escape in disguise. Teresa laments over Leslie's body and brushes aside Pat's attempts to derive a kind of justice from the event. In a coda, Leslie's ghost, and the cast, sing a parody of a Salvation Army hymn to the audience.

Themes and Meanings

The theme of *The Hostage* is unmistakable. It is the rejection of nationalism. Brendan Behan himself was a member of the IRA and was sentenced to three years' custody in an English reform school for possession of explosives in 1940, when he was only seventeen. He was released early and deported to Ireland, where, in 1942, he fired three shots at an Irish detective during the annual Easter Sunday commemoration of the 1916 Rising against the British government. It was an Irish court that sentenced him to fourteen years' imprisonment for this offense (he served less than five). Behan maintained his connections with the IRA and received further jail sentences in England and Ireland as a result. However, he was well placed to observe and to write about the internal contradictions of the Irish nationalist movement.

One of these is, simply, the close connection between England and Ireland, which nationalism attempts to deny. The Irish Republic refused, in the 1920's, to join the British Commonwealth under the Crown. However, many of the inhabitants of Pat's lodging house are devoted to the British royal family, which they regard as their own. When Teresa tries to make a nationalist point by asking Leslie what the English are doing in Northern Ireland, he replies with simple reversal by asking what the Irish are doing in London. The two nations, separate in theory, are irretrievably mixed in practice, by sentiment and often by blood.

By contrast, antipathies within Ireland, and within the nationalist movement itself, are strong, recent, and bitter. Pat is a veteran of the civil war that broke out in southern Ireland after the British left and was pursued (like Behan) by the Irish government itself. Even within the IRA there are factions. Pat recalls how the IRA evicted Kerry peasants from land they had taken from an exiled landlord, on grounds that the Six Counties in Ulster had to be freed first. However, these counties never were, and the only practical result was that the Kerrymen lost their land—not to the English, not to the Irish government, but to the IRA.

A final antipathy is over class. Almost everyone in the play is lower class. This means, in Dublin, that they cannot speak Irish, and have to have their "native" traditions taught to them by outsiders—in this case, by Monsewer, who learned his Irish at the University of Oxford.

The result of this host of ironies is that almost all the characters in the play decide in the end that politics has nothing to do with them. Leslie is no more a willing agent of the British government than is Teresa of the Irish. If the governments would leave

them alone there would be no killings and only comic hostilities. People could proceed with enjoying their lives instead. At the end Leslie is dead—and so, Pat points
out, is the Irish boy in Belfast jail. But the dead Englishman and dead Irishman have
nothing against each other. Perhaps, Leslie suggests before he dies, they will laugh
about it all on the other side of the gate of death.

Dramatic Devices

One obviously symbolic moment is the scene, near the end of act 2, when, after a
violent dance-cum-brawl, the flags of all the nations involved—Irish, British, and for
some reason Russian—are left lying on the ground. This, however, is only one of
many moments of something like choreography at work in the play: The jig and reel at
the start and end of act 1, the multiple movements in the dark at the start of act 2, the
melee (in the dark again) at the end of act 3. Behan suggests in his stage directions that
these scenes cannot be planned too carefully. They are to be part of the production, not
the play.

Another vital part of *The Hostage* is its music. Each act ends with a song from
Leslie, mocking or rueful. In addition, there are repeated renditions from Pat of the
rebel songs of Irish tradition, each counterpointed by derisive remarks from other
characters about their inaccuracy or incompatibility with real life. Monsewer also
sings his song of nostalgia for England, Harrow, and cricket, while Mr. Mulleady and
his girlfriend sing a kind of comic lament for the fate of the "respectable" middle
classes (themselves, that is), trapped by some mischance in a brothel. It is known that
Behan's view of the theater stressed its connection with the music hall, and that he
was convinced that any play should entertain first and carry meaning second. This
play takes that view almost to an extreme.

An associated point is the importance to *The Hostage*, despite (or perhaps because
of) its serious theme, of comedy. Several of the characters, especially Pat, approach
the well-known Irish image of "the blarney." They will talk about anything and will
continually divert their conversations in the direction of the unbelievable or bizarre. In
a way, telling a lie and persuading someone to believe it is the height of art; the characters test one another's limits all the time. The serious point behind all this is that very
little of what is accepted about Irish history can be relied on. There have been too few
historians and too many mythographers. Important to this level of the plot, too, is the
chorus of prostitutes, homosexuals, and sailors who form an audience to the central
characters but repeatedly threaten to burst out of their subordinate roles. The internal
politics of the lodging house, one may say, is good-tempered anarchy. Clearly, if tacitly, that is preferable to the bad-tempered oligarchies of nation-states, governments,
and movements.

Critical Context

The Hostage was preceded, in June, 1958, by a play by Behan in the Irish language
called *An Giall* (Irish for "the hostage"). The English play is, however, not a translation of the Irish one, but an adaptation, with many significant differences. In the En-

glish play, Leslie is shot; in the Irish one, he is suffocated by accident while being hidden. In *An Giall*, minor characters such as Rio Rita and the other prostitutes are absent, while the romance between Leslie and Teresa remains a chaste one. In it, too, the furious comedy about the Irish language of *The Hostage* is naturally absent, while even Monsewer's bagpipes are treated respectfully. The Irish play, in short, remained serious and careful, being presented to a totally Irish audience; in the English play, a mocking attitude has been allowed to run riot.

Did Behan then "sell out" in his later production? That has been one allegation; another has been the charge that he was totally dominated by his English producer. Neither view seems entirely well grounded. No one connected with the production but Behan himself would have known enough about the IRA and its inner dissensions to shift the play in that direction, nor can the energy and amusement of *The Hostage* have been entirely counterfeited. It seems more likely that Behan, not an Irish speaker himself, wrote a careful propagandist work within the insular movement of Irish-language writing and then felt the theme grow under his hand as he moved to his native language.

Politically speaking, *The Hostage* has since proved all too prophetic. Ireland began another stage of its "Troubles" in 1969; since that time, many British soldiers have been killed by Irishmen, and many Irishmen by British soldiers. Far outnumbering both figures, though, is the number of Irish people killed by one another, including casualties of the infighting between factions of the IRA itself. The problem of the "Six Counties" is no nearer settlement than it was in 1959 or in 1929. What has happened instead is that the sides have drawn further apart. It is hard to imagine a former member of the IRA now, with prison sentences behind him, writing such a fundamentally tolerant parable as Behan's; nor would it find ready production if one did. This, though, is the ill fortune of England and Ireland, not the mistake of Behan. *The Hostage* may be considered a significant warning, which its audiences, regrettably, were too proud, or too superficially amused, to take.

Sources for Further Study

Boyle, Ted E., ed. *Brendan Behan*. New York: Twayne, 1969.

Gerdes, Peter Rene. *The Major Works of Brendan Behan*. Frankfurt: Peter Lang, 1973.

Hendricks, Johan. "The 'Theatre of Fun': In Defense of Brendan Behan's *The Hostage*." *Anglo-Irish Studies* 3 (1977): 85-95.

Jeffs, Rae. *Brendan Behan: Man and Showman*. London: Hutchinson, 1965.

Kearney, Colbert. *The Writings of Brendan Behan*. London: Hutchinson, 1977.

Mikhail, E. H., ed. *The Art of Brendan Behan*. London: Vision Press, 1979.

Porter, Raymond J. *Brendan Behan*. New York: Columbia University Press, 1973.

Simpson, Alan. *Beckett and Behan and a Theatre in Dublin*. London: Routledge and Paul, 1962.

T. A. Shippey

THE HOT L BALTIMORE

Author: Lanford Wilson (1937-   )
Type of plot: Comedy
Time of plot: A Memorial Day during the early 1970's
Locale: Baltimore
First produced: 1973, at the Circle Theatre, New York City
First published: 1973

> *Principal characters:*
> BILL LEWIS, the night desk clerk
> GIRL, a talkative prostitute
> MILLIE, a retired waitress
> MRS. BELLOTTI, the mother of an evicted resident
> APRIL GREEN and
> SUZY, prostitutes
> MR. MORSE, an elderly man
> JACKIE and
> JAMIE, brother and sister, residents of the hotel
> MR. KATZ, the hotel's manager
> PAUL GRANGER, a student
> MRS. OXENHAM, the day desk clerk

The Play

The Hot l Baltimore opens in a hotel lobby with a front desk, a lounge, and a stairway. This set is the Hotel Baltimore of the title, a dilapidated establishment scheduled for demolition. All the play's action takes place here, as the various employees, residents, and visitors interact with one another and with various other groups that drift in and out of the lobby.

As the play opens, Paul Granger, waiting for Mr. Katz to appear, is asleep in a chair, and Bill is making several wake-up calls while the Girl talks with him. She has tried several names but finds none of them comfortable. As the morning advances, various people appear, beginning with Millie, who complains that she cannot sleep late and later talks about the ghosts that haunted the restaurant where she worked. Then Mrs. Bellotti enters and asks for Mr. Katz; he has evicted her son from the hotel, and she wants Katz to take him back. At that moment, the Girl discovers eviction notices for the hotel's residents. April enters to complain that the hotel has no hot water, followed shortly by Mr. Morse, whose window will not shut. Jackie, followed by Jamie, whom she constantly orders about, comes in to ask for a favor but then volunteers to shut Morse's window for him. She borrows his key and goes upstairs as Morse and Jamie begin to play checkers.

When Katz finally arrives, Jackie returns from upstairs and asks him to cosign her loan so she can get insurance for her new car. He refuses. As Suzy enters with a john,

Mrs. Bellotti pleads with Katz to let her son, Horse, stay at the hotel. Again, Katz refuses; he claims that Horse is insane and a thief. Mrs. Bellotti goes upstairs to clean out her son's room. Quietly, Jackie asks Millie when the pawnshop opens; other characters hear the question, a fact that later proves significant. Katz announces that all the hotel's residents must leave in a month, for the hotel is scheduled to be demolished. This proclamation precipitates an argument. Joining the melee is Suzy, wearing nothing but a towel, who has chased her john into the lobby. This commotion awakens Paul, who begins shouting that the hotel is nothing but a flophouse. When Jamie returns from upstairs and sees the now-naked Suzy, he drops the box he is carrying, revealing goods stolen from the hotel and neighborhood shops. All laugh at him.

Act 2 opens later the same day with Paul questioning Katz and Mrs. Oxenham about his grandfather, who was a guest at the hotel but has since disappeared. They are most unhelpful. Morse and Jamie are playing checkers, but their game soon erupts into a fight. The Girl reconciles the two by getting Jamie to pretend that Morse blackened Jamie's eye. Jackie enters and begins browbeating her brother again. Meanwhile, the Girl begins a conversation with Paul; she reveals that she has been all over the country, and he reveals that he spent time in a work farm. Having discovered that Paul's grandfather was a railroad engineer, the Girl, who loves railroads so much that she has memorized all the train schedules, offers to help him search through the hotel's records to find a clue to his grandfather's whereabouts. Jackie begins going through a stack of health-food magazines and then shows the Girl a deed to land in Utah that she bought through a radio advertisement. She and Jamie plan to move there and live outside in sleeping bags, growing their own food. Complaining that the country has deteriorated, she wishes to escape to a simpler existence.

Suddenly, almost unable to speak, Morse enters from upstairs to complain that his room was burglarized. Katz discovers the stolen items in Jackie's purse and orders her and Jamie to leave the hotel by evening. The Girl, who has been to Utah, tells Jackie that the plan to return to rustic simplicity is a failure, because the land is worthless and will grow nothing. Although she does not want to believe the Girl, Jackie knows the truth and runs out crying. The act ends when Millie tells Paul that, although she never met him, she knows that his grandfather is alive.

Act 3 opens at midnight, as Bill calls the Girl and invites her to come down and talk. Just then April enters and begins telling bawdy stories about her johns. The Girl enters and begins looking through boxes of records, trying to locate a clue that will help Paul find his grandfather. Jamie enters and asks if Jackie, who has gone to get gasoline for the car, has returned yet for him. It becomes apparent that she has left him. Suzy enters with her luggage and then returns upstairs to get a surprise. The Girl finds a dated receipt for Paul's grandfather and tells him about it, but he no longer cares. Suzy returns with her surprise—two bottles of champagne, which she shares with everyone in the lobby. She reveals that she is moving into an apartment with a pimp, whom April derisively calls "Billy Goldhole." Suzy reacts angrily and, since the cabdriver has just arrived, leaves. She returns a few moments later, however, to say that she knows they love her and she thinks of them all as a family. After Suzy goes, Paul and the Girl argue over what she sees as his failure to follow up on her discovery. Since he can now locate his grandfather in a particular place on a particular day, his search can have more focus. Saying that it is none of her business, he leaves. The Girl says that he lacks conviction and passion. Gradually, the residents drift off to bed, except for April and Jamie, who dance to radio music.

Themes and Meanings

The Hot l Baltimore explores the transitoriness of social institutions and human relationships and comments upon the ways that people try to maintain a sense of identity in a constantly changing world. The hotel itself represents this theme of transience. Built in the nineteenth century, this once-elegant hotel is now the home of prostitutes and the elderly. The *e* in its sign has burned out and been left unrepaired, a fact that represents the decay and dissolution of the neighborhood. Now the owners have decided to cast out its residents and demolish it.

The play is comic rather than tragic. The characters try to find something to hold on to; losing one dream, they try to grab another or to embrace chaos. The Girl, for example, abandons what little stability her own name provides and talks of having traveled around the country, abandoning place entirely. Millie, on the other hand, very much wants rootedness. She puts her faith in a kind of transcendence that enables her to see ghosts. Jackie tries to achieve a utopian dream of returning to nature, only to have it shattered. She talks of helping others and being helped but uses a close relationship only to steal and betray; ultimately, she abandons even her brother in a flight from responsibility. Bill, who clearly feels much affection for the Girl, is unable to express himself to her and thus comes to the end of the play with his emotional needs unsatisfied. To the derision of all, Suzy leaves to look after a new pimp; everyone knows that she will soon return.

Ultimately, what draws the characters together and gives them a sense of place—more than the hotel itself can—is the sense of family, and Lanford Wilson explores this concept in the feelings of his characters for one another. Several of them have family members whom they attempt to care for. For example, Mrs. Bellotti argues with Katz for the fair treatment of her son, Horse, although she does so unsuccessfully. Paul claims that he is the only one who cares about his grandfather and does try to find him throughout most of the play; yet when confronted with hotel records documenting his existence, Paul gives up his search and leaves. Wilson contrasts this lack of feeling with the far stronger familial relationship among the hotel's residents. When the group scorns Suzy and her new pimp, she first leaves angrily, but then she returns, crying, to hug them all and say, "I'm sorry. I know you love me. I can't leave like that. Mr. Morse. We been like a family, haven't we? My family. Baby. I'm not that horrible. I can't be mad. Bill. I'll always remember this." A family is not something received, but something worked for, something earned.

The play ends with an expression of this emotional investment when April, the most amusing and pragmatic of all the characters, forces the abandoned Jamie to dance with her. "Come on," she says; "you're so shy, if someone doesn't put a light under your tail, you're not going to have passions to need convictions for." Only by continuing to move can humanity avoid the decay confronting the Hotel Baltimore.

Dramatic Devices

The Hot l Baltimore achieves dramatic success not through its story but through the ways the characters interact with one another onstage and through the situations that grow out of their relationships and experiences. All the play's characters are very well defined and respond to situations accordingly, their voices mingling with the responses of the other characters, even if all the personalities represented are opposed. For example, when at the end of act 1 a scantily clad Suzy chases a fleeing john into the hotel's lobby early in the morning, April responds with bawdy good humor; her laughter feeds Suzy's anger. Katz, on the other hand, responds as a hotel manager would: He orders the luckless prostitute to return to her room until she is properly attired. Similarly, the domineering Jackie orders Suzy to leave the lobby, no doubt increasing the latter's desire to stay right where she is. Morse, conversely, is unconcerned by something that has nothing to do with him; he continues to exercise and sing to himself. The noise awakens the visitor Paul, who, unaccustomed to such antics, begins screaming. All are brought to silence by the sight of the young Jamie, coming down the stairs and gaping at the nude Suzy. This one incident, occupying fewer than two pages of text, demonstrates how the drama is staged based on the interaction of competing character types. The play's abundant humor thus arises from character and situation, not from the story itself or the lines the characters speak.

The dramatic device that provides the best indication of this interplay is the overlapping of voices, often speaking at cross-purposes, that occurs throughout the play. This technique is evident from the play's outset, when Bill, trying to speak into the telephone and make his wake-up calls, is also talking to the Girl. The device comes into fuller use later, when, for example, Jackie tries to borrow money from April while Morse is complaining to Bill, and anyone else who will listen, that his room's window will not shut and that he is getting a cold. The device is dramatic and visual, calling for careful staging and for the performers to pick up on their cues immediately. Staged, the play must move very quickly, with scenes flowing into one another as characters enter and exit the stage.

The sounds in the hotel are also important, such as the music from the cheap radio to which Bill, but not Mrs. Oxenham, listens. This music provides a link between the acts; April and Jamie dance to it at the play's conclusion. Also, the sound of the occasional train whistle prompts the Girl's demonstration of her knowledge of railroads and railroad schedules. The railroad itself represents another American institution in decay, like the city of Baltimore, and like the Hotel Baltimore.

Critical Context

The Hot l Baltimore is probably the first of Lanford Wilson's plays that can be called a comedy; it launched his series of optimistic plays throughout the 1970's and 1980's. Focusing on alienated, even psychotic characters, his earlier plays are far more dour. *No Trespassing* (pr. 1964) concerns a teenager who kills his father, *The Madness of Lady Bright* (pr. 1964, pb. 1967) focuses on the unhappy plight of an aging homosexual, and *Lemon Sky* (pr., pb. 1970) deals with a failed father-son relationship. Even a play following *The Hot l Baltimore*, *The Mound Builders* (pr. 1975, pb. 1976), is an unhappy story of unrequited love, failed dreams, murder, and suicide at a southern Illinois archaeological excavation. This play does, however, take up some of the same themes of the decay of American institutions and ideals as those in *The Hot l Baltimore*. By 1978, however, Wilson returned to comedy with his trilogy of plays about the Talley family of Lebanon, Missouri: *5th of July* (pr., pb. 1978), *Talley's Folly* (pr., pb. 1979), and *A Tale Told* (pr. 1981), later revised as *Talley and Son* (pr. 1985). Like *The Hot l Baltimore*, the Talley plays are concerned with relationships and the kinds of families that people form. The main "family" in *5th of July*, for example, is composed of the elderly widow Sally Friedman (née Talley), Ken Talley and his homosexual lover Ned, and the single mother June and her daughter Shirley.

   The Hot l Baltimore is an important play for Wilson because it brought him his first widespread critical and commercial success. It won the New York Drama Critics Circle and Obie Awards as the best play of 1972-1973. After moving to the Circle-in-the-Square Theatre, it ran for more than eleven hundred performances. In 1975, a television situation comedy, *The Hot l Baltimore*, based on the successful play, had its premiere and ran for five months. Wilson was not involved in its production. The play also brought critical attention to the Circle Repertory Company, where Wilson became resident writer. Although at times he has been snubbed by academic critics, Wilson has established himself as one of the best and best-known playwrights of his time.

Sources for Further Study

Barnett, Gene A. *Lanford Wilson*. Boston: Twayne, 1987.

Busby, Mark. *Lanford Wilson*. Boise, Idaho: Boise State University Press, 1987.

Dasgupta, Gautam. "Lanford Wilson." In *American Playwrights: A Critical Survey*, edited by Bonnie Marranca and Gautam Dasgupta. New York: Drama Book Specialists, 1981.

Dean, Anne. *Discovery and Invention: The Urban Plays of Lanford Wilson*. Rutherford, N.J.: Fairleigh Dickinson University Press, 1995.

DiGaetani, John. "Lanford Wilson." In *A Search for a Postmodern Theater: Interviews with Contemporary Playwrights*. Westport, Conn.: Greenwood Press, 1991.

Jacobi, Marten J. "The Comic Vision of Lanford Wilson." *Studies in the Literary Imagination*, Fall, 1988, 119-134.

Sainer, Arthur. "Lanford Wilson." In *Contemporary Dramatists*, edited by D. L. Kirkpatrick. 4th ed. Chicago: St. James, 1988.

Savran, David. "Lanford Wilson." In *In Their Own Words: Contemporary American Playwrights*. New York: Theatre Communications Group, 1988.

Robert Chamberlain

HOW I LEARNED TO DRIVE

Author: Paula Vogel (1951-   )
Type of plot: Coming of age; memory play
Time of plot: 1969-1997
Locale: Suburban Maryland
First produced: 1997, at the Vineyard Theatre, New York City
First published: 1997

Principal characters:

LI'L BIT, a woman who narrates her memories of her relationship with an uncle

PECK, her uncle by marriage

MALE GREEK CHORUS, in the roles of grandfather, waiter, and high school boys

FEMALE GREEK CHORUS, in the roles of mother, Aunt Mary, and high school girls

TEENAGE GREEK CHORUS, in the roles of grandmother, high school girls, and the voice of eleven-year-old Li'l Bit

The Play

How I Learned to Drive uses a series of nonlinear scenes from the memory of Li'l Bit, who reveals her complex emotional and sexual relationship with her Uncle Peck. The scenes jump instantaneously back and forth in time on a neutral stage with minimal props. Li'l Bit is portrayed at various ages.

A one-act play, *How I Learned to Drive* begins with a disembodied voice saying "Safety First—You and Driver Education." This technique is used throughout the play to indicate how and where each scene is located within the overall narrative. On a bare stage with only two chairs representing a Buick Riviera, Li'l Bit takes her place, in the present, speaking directly to the audience. She describes suburban Maryland in 1969 "before the malls took over." A young Li'l Bit then steps into the scene, now seventeen years old. She is sitting in a parked car on a summer night with an older, married man—her Uncle Peck. In what appears to be a not completely unpleasant experience, Peck fondles and kisses Li'l Bit's breasts.

Members of the Greek Chorus assume their roles as Li'l Bit's relatives at a typical family dinner, which consists of vulgar jokes and crude comments about Li'l Bit's well-endowed figure. A protective and gentle Uncle Peck shields Li'l Bit from the insults. The scene ends with Li'l Bit bartering a secret, late-night rendezvous with Peck in exchange for the keys to his car.

Li'l Bit informs the audience that, despite the many rumors as to why she was expelled from college, the real reason was most likely her excessive drinking and late-night road trips. Driving intoxicated on the Maryland beltway, she never received a ticket. Uncle Peck, she tells the audience, taught her well.

The action jumps backward to when Li'l Bit is sixteen and has just earned her driver's license and Peck brings her to an elegant inn to celebrate. Peck has Li'l Bit served several cocktails. As Li'l Bit becomes increasingly intoxicated, the Female Greek Chorus comes forward in the role of mother to deliver a guide to "social drinking" while getting quite drunk herself. Dinner ends, and Peck carries the drunken and dizzy Li'l Bit back to the car. She flirts, then shies away from Peck, finally passionately kissing him in a moment of drunken confusion. Li'l Bit then expresses worry that what they are doing is wrong and will cause harm. Peck convinces her that the relationship will not progress until she wants it to, confident in the expectation that at some point in the future Li'l Bit will want to fully consummate the affair. The scene ends with Li'l Bit passed out in the seat beside Peck.

Peck takes little Cousin Bobby fishing. During the fishing lesson Peck employs his strategies of deception and seduction on the young boy. A sexual encounter between the two is implied.

A revealing dialogue among Li'l Bit, her mother, and her grandmother follows. Li'l Bit is "instructed" in the nature of sex from her elders' point of view, which is crude, vulgar, and devoid of romance.

Li'l Bit steps out of the past and describes her seduction of a young man she meets on a bus ride in 1979. In this seduction Li'l Bit thinks of Uncle Peck and for the first time understands the allure that seducing children has for Peck.

As Peck instructs Li'l Bit in a driving lesson, erotic photographs of young women and cars flash upstage. Though Li'l Bit nervously flirts with Peck, he is all business, intent on teaching Li'l Bit to drive with confidence and aggression.

An adolescent Li'l Bit is featured in the next several scenes, which take place in ninth grade. Painfully self-conscious of her maturing figure, Li'l Bit is the target of jokes and tricks played on her by classmates.

"The photo shoot" scene takes place one year earlier in Peck's basement. The shoot begins in a tense, businesslike manner. Yet as Li'l Bit relaxes, her poses become more erotic and seductive. Peck unbuttons her blouse and arranges each shot in ever more sexually explicit poses. Peck reveals that he intends to submit the photographs to *Playboy* when Li'l Bit turns eighteen. She becomes upset, but Peck assures her that if she wishes, the photos will always remain a secret between them. The scene ends as Li'l Bit, reassured, begins to unbutton and open her blouse and the shooting resumes.

Aunt Mary reveals to the audience that she is aware, at least to some degree, of the relationship between Peck and Li'l Bit. Ironically she defends her husband and places the blame on the young girl.

The action jumps back in time to Li'l Bit's thirteenth Christmas. As she watches Peck cleaning the dinner dishes, they arrange to meet secretly every week to "talk." Peck explains that his heavy drinking is the result of his loneliness and passionate nature. Peck encourages Li'l Bit in the belief that only she can help him.

The Greek Chorus comes forward to read the notes Peck has sent to Li'l Bit while she is away at college. As the notes become more desperate, it is clear that Li'l Bit has not responded to his gifts and cards. Though she has asked him not to, Peck travels to Philadelphia to visit Li'l Bit for her eighteenth birthday. Li'l Bit explains to Peck that she is failing her courses. She is confused and conflicted and tells him that their relationship must end. Desperately he begs Li'l Bit to lie down on the bed with him and allow him to hold her. She lies down reluctantly and nearly gives in to his desperate attempt at seduction. Peck offers her a ring, asking her to marry him. This proposal is more than she can handle. She tells him good-bye, never to see him again.

She tells the audience that over the next seven years Peck descended into alcoholism, lost his job and his wife, and, finally, even lost his driver's license. He died in a drunken fall down the basement steps.

The play ends with Li'l Bit's very first driving lesson. She is eleven years old and steers the car while sitting on Uncle Peck's lap. She takes the wheel in both hands, leaving Peck free to fondle her breasts and press himself into her. The scene ends with his orgasmic moans.

In her final monologue Li'l Bit explains that at the age of thirty-five, and with the passage of time, she has come to understand, and perhaps even forgive, Uncle Peck.

Themes and Meanings

How I Learned to Drive is a memory play that deals with issues of victimization, sexual abuse, incest, and alcoholism. It is also a play about growth, acceptance, and forgiveness. Paula Vogel blends comedy, sadness, and pathos to examine a deeply dysfunctional family with a sexual predator in its midst. The humor allows Vogel to present disturbing scenes regarding the sexualization of children. This sexualization and exploitation are not only condoned but are also encouraged within the family.

The collision of tones complicates these issues and forces the audience to realize that the damaged characters are sympathetic and even deserving of forgiveness. Uncle Peck is not simply a pedophile. He is a mentor and teacher whose driving lessons give Li'l Bit the ability to realize her identity as an individual. Indeed, Peck gives her the strength, confidence, and power that will ultimately allow her to reject him. He gives her the power to bring about his ultimate destruction as well as the sense of kindness to forgive him.

Vogel has said that the play illustrates how people may receive great love from those who harm them. What makes the play controversial for some is Vogel's resistance to portraying Li'l Bit as a victim. Not only does Li'l Bit receive gifts from Peck along with the abuse; she at times encourages the sexual aspect of the relationship. She sets limits on her uncle's inappropriate behavior, but there are moments when she seems to invite such behavior. Eventually, she even follows in Peck's footsteps, seducing teenage boys. Vogel presents the characters in such a way that Li'l Bit's complicity is understandable and even forgivable.

Ultimately the play is more about the idea of growth and maturation than the destructive force of abuse. Li'l Bit does eventually become reconciled to her past and finds the ability to forgive her family, Uncle Peck, and most important, herself.

Dramatic Devices

How I Learned to Drive is staged in a style that is both presentational (includes the audience) and representational (excludes the audience). At times characters narrate action directly to the audience while other scenes are presented in almost cinematic realism. Told in a series of nonchronological cross-cuts, the actions of Li'l Bit, Uncle Peck, and the family are examined over a period of several years. This blurring of temporal chronology allows the audience to see into the deliberations and consequences of the characters' actions in a unique way. The play is a memory told in a series of flashbacks and flash-forwards. The audience sees the end of Li'l Bit's relationship with Uncle Peck before it has even begun. The audience also sees the effects of the abuse before they see the cause.

The title of the play derives from its main action: the driving lessons Uncle Peck gives to Li'l Bit. The lessons become a metaphor for two of the major rites of passage for American youth: earning one's driver's license as well as sexual initiation, an event that often occurs in a car. This metaphor is supported through the use of phrases and terminology from driving manuals. Images of traffic signs are seen and heard to guide Li'l Bit's navigation on the road of life. They also help her find her way through the sexual landscape of her relationship with Peck.

Complicating the presentation of the play is the use of a modern Greek chorus of three actors who perform the roles of several characters. They also help to frame the narrative by appearing as neutral characters spaced throughout the playing area and reciting the phrases from driving lectures and manuals, which allude to the time, place, or emotional tone of each scene. The Teenage Greek Chorus is used to fragment Li'l Bit's character. In one of the most disturbing scenes of the play, the Teenage Greek Chorus steps into the role of eleven-year-old Li'l Bit. Peck fondles her breasts and presses himself into her as the older Li'l Bit looks on and comments to the audience.

Humor is used as a device to further complicate the story and mediate the disturbing nature of the subject of the play. The humor helps the audience to disengage or step back from the action in order to contemplate the themes from a less emotional stance.

Music and advertising images from the 1960's are used to accentuate the sexualization of young girls and reinforce the theme of pedophilia. The "you're sixteen" genre hits, such as Gary Puckett and the Union Gap's "This Girl Is a Woman Now," support the sexualization-of-girls theme. Li'l Bit herself is further eroticized through the use of images projected on a screen upstage during the photo shoot scene.

Critical Context

In 1998, when it was awarded the Pulitzer Prize, *How I Learned to Drive* was one of the most often produced play in the United States. It is typical of Vogel's work in that, like most of her other plays, it deals with issues concerning families, domestic violence, and abuse. Vogel's plays often explore taboo subjects in startling new ways. *The Baltimore Waltz* (pb. 1996) deals with a brother's death from acquired immunodeficiency syndrome (AIDS). *Hot 'n' Throbbing* (pr. 1993, pb. 1996) presents themes concerning female pornography and domestic violence. Vogel often uses comedy and seemingly inappropriate moments of humor to dismantle her audiences' protective emotional shells.

Vogel's treatment of social issues often centers on the family in its social context. Her characters are complex and multidimensional, with complicated feelings and problems.

Often Vogel's female characters are presented as desiring, rather than desirable, subjects. *Desdemona: A Play About a Handkerchief* (pr. 1993, pb. 1994) explores the secret lives and sexual desires of the women in Shakespearean tragedy. In an ironic turnabout, male characters in Vogel's plays often become the objects of the desirous female gaze.

Sources for Further Study

Guare, John, ed. *Conjunctions 25: The New American Theatre.* Annandale-On-Hudson, N.Y.: Bard College, 1995.

Mead, Rebecca. "Drive-by Shooting." *New York* 30 (April 7, 1997): 46-47.

Savran, David. *The Playwright's Voice: American Dramatists on Memory, Writing, and the Politics of Culture.* New York: Theatre Communications Group, 1999.

Scanlan, Dick. "Say Uncle." *Advocate*, June 10, 1997, 61-63.

Rhona Justice-Malloy

HURLYBURLY

Author: David Rabe (1940-   )
Type of plot: Naturalistic; psychological
Time of plot: The 1980's
Locale: Hollywood
First produced: 1984, at the Goodman Theater, Chicago
First published: 1985

> *Principal characters:*
> EDDIE, the protagonist, a casting director
> PHIL, his friend
> MICKEY, his roommate
> ARTIE, his business acquaintance
> DARLENE, his girlfriend
> DONNA, a woman picked up by Artie
> BONNIE, Phil's date

The Play

As *Hurlyburly* opens, the half-dressed Eddie is asleep on the couch, and the television on the coffee table is droning out the morning news. Phil enters and wakes Eddie with the news that he and his wife had a big fight the night before, because he was stoned and she would not let him explain his plan "to save the world." Phil reports that he "whacked" her and left her for good.

Shortly after Mickey enters, Eddie and Phil snort some cocaine and smoke some marijuana; Phil tells Eddie about a part he might get in a film with a certain director, and Eddie gives him the inside story on the director. Phil then exits with one of the scripts on which Eddie and Mickey are working. Left alone, the roommates begin to discuss Darlene, a "dynamite lady" whom Eddie dated and then introduced to Mickey, who has just had dinner with her "in order to, you know, determine the nature of these vibes."

Artie shows up with Donna, whom he says he found in his elevator; he has brought her to be used however the roommates wish. Eddie says sarcastically that Mickey would not want to fool around with Donna, since he has the dynamite lady, Darlene. When Artie tells them that he has a meeting with a certain Herb Simon, Eddie tries to give him the lowdown on people such as Simon. After Artie exits, Donna returns from the bathroom; while she tells about her experiences in Artie's elevator, Mickey tries to caress and undress her. Phil reenters, and Eddie explains to him how Donna was brought as a care package "for people without serious relationships." Eddie takes Donna away from Mickey and into the bedroom; they are followed by Phil, who professes delight with "the bachelor's life."

Scene 2 opens on the evening of the same day. Darlene is seated at the kitchen counter when Eddie enters, and they begin to squabble over his tendency to create confusion with thoughts and words. Entering with groceries, Mickey proceeds to tell them that he was outside listening before he came in and that what he heard, underneath the squabbling, was real passion. Such honesty allows everyone to confess the truth: that Eddie does have feelings for Darlene, that she cares for him, and that Mickey will eventually return to his wife and kids. After Mickey exits, Eddie and Darlene try to express their feelings.

Scene 3 begins in the late afternoon of the next day; Donna is watching television and listening to the record player when Phil comes in. They get into a shouting match; it is clear that Phil is highly distraught. When Eddie enters, Phil complains about Donna being there when all he wanted was to talk to Eddie about his problems and watch the football game. After Eddie leaves the room, Donna tells Phil that she wants to watch the game too, but he roughhouses with her and causes her to cry. When Eddie reenters, Phil claims that he was showing her something about football; Donna exits, swearing. Phil tells Eddie that he might return to his wife, who wants to have a baby, but Eddie urges him not to do it thoughtlessly. Donna enters and announces that she is "taking a hike" as act 1 ends.

Act 2 opens in the same house a year later. It is evening, and Phil and Artie are telling Eddie and Mickey how Phil knocked a fellow unconscious in a bar. This story leads into a discussion of Phil's violent nature, which Eddie explains in reference to Phil's baby having been born and his divorce having been finalized in the same month. He decides that what Phil needs is a woman, and he sets him up with Bonnie. Everyone begins to share an assortment of "pharmaceutical experiments"— marijuana, cocaine, liquor, and beer—after which Bonnie and Phil leave together.

Artie then turns on Eddie, assuring him that he is deceiving himself about the kind of person Phil is. Mickey agrees and prepares to leave with Artie, who tells Eddie— who has switched to vodka and begun to get mean-spirited—that he has taken in too much chemical pollution.

Bonnie comes through the door, her clothing ripped and dirty and her body bruised. She is furious at Eddie for having introduced her to Phil, who almost killed her by pushing her out of the car while it was moving. Eddie continues to drink heavily, and soon Phil arrives, apologetic and self-deprecating. Eddie rambles drunkenly about how depressed he is, Phil rushes out to get something from the car, Artie and Mickey enter, and Bonnie leaves in disgust. Phil reenters with his baby, having taken it while his wife was asleep, and announces that he is going to beg his wife to take him back.

Act 3 begins several days later, in the early evening. Mickey and Darlene are engaged in a joking conversation when Eddie walks in. Mickey leaves, and Eddie begins to criticize Darlene for being unable to choose when she has two alternatives, whether the decision has to do with men or restaurants. The telephone rings; Eddie picks it up and hears that Phil has died in a car accident.

Scene 2 opens with Eddie, Mickey, and Artie returning from Phil's funeral. After a brief discussion of the funeral, Artie leaves. Eddie is startled to find a letter from Phil in his mail; he opens it to read, "The guy who dies in an accident understands the nature of destiny." Mickey tells Eddie to forget it, but Eddie, determined to find out what Phil meant, begins consulting a dictionary. As he deciphers it, the message means, "If you die in a happening that is not expected, foreseen or intended, you understand the inevitable or necessary succession of events."

Alone, and once again drugged, Eddie turns on the television set and carries on a dialogue with it until Donna enters. He tells Donna abut Phil's death, and she tries to comfort and reassure him. Finally, they lie down on the couch to go to sleep in each other's arms as the lights come down.

Themes and Meanings

To talk in terms of a single theme in *Hurlyburly* would be to ignore the density of the play's content. David Rabe himself, in an essay written for the Grove Press book club edition of 1985, explained that he thinks in terms of at least two levels of meaning, the psychological and the philosophical. In the early stages of rehearsal, without understanding completely what he was saying, Rabe told the actors, "Eddie, through the death of Phil, was saved from being Mickey." In time, Rabe says that he came to understand that the play deals with the psychological union of opposites.

The house represents a whole self, an individual. In this house, Mickey and Eddie are, in Rabe's terms, "king," two sides to the same individual personality. Phil is the shadow side of the same personality, the powerful forces of vitality and disorder of the unconscious. Mickey's way of dealing with the "Phil" part of the self is to mask it behind cynicism, rejection, and resentment—the socially accepted way of dealing with this side of the human personality. Eddie, drawn to the "Phil" force within himself, seeks to channel these powers before they can overwhelm large and essential quantities of himself. Rabe says that while Mickey might oppose the threat of Phil by means of rational condemnation and thus keep himself removed from any possible influence, Eddie is unable to maintain such a purely cerebral stance and is "drawn toward the dangers of conflict and disorientation as if spellbound." This theme, Rabe declares, is "the essence of the play itself." Mickey represents the conventional and rational way of dealing with the "inferior side of the inner man." Eddie, sympathetic and supportive of Phil, accepts the shadow self, has compassion for the "inferior inner man," and thus is able to accept "the Self."

On another level, the play has strong philosophical overtones. The note Phil sends to Eddie occurred to Rabe quite by surprise as he wrote; he insists that it contains another theme, which is that out of accidents destiny is hewn. What Phil's note says, ultimately, is that chance is destiny. This idea harks back to the nineteenth century naturalists such as Thomas Hardy and Stephen Crane. Rabe says that this idea was very much on his mind when he was writing this play.

On a third level, the play may also be seen as a parable of contemporary American life, of a society caught up in the hurlyburly of dehumanization and despair. The characters struggle with language and meanings, they dress often in tattered and patched clothing, suggesting their unraveled lives, and they resort to a wide variety of pharmaceutical experimentation, looking for tranquillity in a frenetic, disjointed world.

Dramatic Devices

Since *Hurlyburly* is basically a realistic play, nonrealistic or constructionist dramatic devices are inappropriate. However, Rabe still creates powerful dramatic effects, primarily through rich, evocative images, strong action, and visual tableaux.

From the opening scene, when Phil walks in on Eddie, who is asleep with the television on, to the last scene, when Eddie, left alone onstage, turns on the television and begins his dialogue with Johnny Carson, the television set is ever-present as an object of fascination and contempt. Ironically, whenever Eddie watches television, rather than listening and watching passively, he argues with and harangues it in a grotesque, surreal demonstration of failed communication: The television does not listen to him nor he to it, yet each roars on at the other. Another irony arises from the fact that while television provides careers for the characters, they—especially Eddie—are repulsed by it.

The ingestion of beer, marijuana, cocaine, vodka, and Valium, which recurs with dizzying frequency, constitutes a major motif. More than once, Eddie takes out his box of stash and, like a high priest ceremoniously holding up a holy object, begins the ritual of laying out vials, pills, and powders, sometimes in order to share it with friends, at other times to perform his religious ceremony alone. The ironic fulfillment of the drug motif occurs toward the end of the play in a painful and memorable tableau when Eddie, drinking himself into oblivion, crawls on the floor with his bottle of vodka and a trash can. As he hugs the trash can tightly, the audience becomes aware of the wasted, discarded life.

Another dramatic device comes with the arrival of Donna, who carries with her an album of romantic ballads by Willie Nelson. Donna's description of the album seems to merge the mythic West with the corrupt city: "It's like this cowboy on the plains . . . and the mountains are there but it's still the deep dark city streets." The song "Someone to Watch Over Me" fades in and out between some of the scenes, creating the awareness that these characters, lost in dark city streets, do indeed need someone to watch over them.

As the play moves toward its conclusion, Eddie discovers a letter that Phil had mailed to him before his death. The unraveling of the contents of Phil's letter, with the aid of the dictionary, creates a powerful stage device, as Eddie, always searching for meanings, comes to grips with Phil's last act by saying, "It makes sense."

Critical Context

In both style and content, *Hurlyburly* marks a new direction for David Rabe, although in some ways it is a continuation of his earlier work. Such plays as *Sticks and Bones* (pr. 1969, pb. 1972), *The Basic Training of Pavlo Hummel* (pr. 1971, pb. 1973), and *Streamers* (pr. 1976, pb. 1977) stamped Rabe as a playwright of the Vietnam War. Only in *In the Boom Boom Room* (pr. 1974, pb. 1975) had Rabe departed from the subject of the soldier and the Vietnam experience. The Vietnam plays tended to be somewhat abstract and nonrealistic, at least in terms of external stage appearances.

In his three Vietnam War plays, Rabe's focus is on the individual who, as seemingly helpless and unwitting victim, is caught up in a violent and chaotic situation created by a society that appears to be indifferent to the soldier's needs. Whether it is Pavlo, who must keep reliving bits and pieces of his life in attempting to arrive at some sense of meaning, or Rick, who, returning from the war, is disoriented and cannot reenter a society which had sent him off to war, or the paratroopers in *Streamers*, who see the image of the unopened parachute as a symbol of their helplessness, Rabe's characters, confused and frightened, appear helpless to control their own destinies.

If, as Rabe himself intimates, *Hurlyburly* takes up the question of the nature of one's destiny, then it is both a continuation and a break with his earlier plays. Set in the jungle of Hollywood rather than Vietnam, it features characters who seem a bit brighter and much more articulate; accordingly, they arrive at a more clearly defined answer: Destiny is shaped by chance.

Stylistically, *Hurlyburly* is unequivocally a departure. Rabe's early plays make use of a variety of nonrealistic stage practices, yet while planning *Hurlyburly*, he has said, he was drawn to attempt a realistic or "well-made" play. It is a measure of his talent as a playwright that he has not been content simply to repeat himself, as is the fate of so many writers who achieve early success.

Sources for Further Study

Kolin, Philip C. *David Rabe: A Stage History and a Primary and Secondary Bibliography*. New York: Garland, 1988.

_____. "Staging *Hurlyburly:* David Rabe's Parable for the 1980's." *Theatre Annual* 41 (1986): 63-78.

Leiter, Robert. Review in *Hudson Review* 38 (Summer, 1985): 297-299.

McDonough, Carla J. *Staging Masculinity: Male Identity in Contemporary American Drama*. Jefferson, Mo.: McFarland, 1996.

Radavich, David. "Collapsing Male Myths: Rabe's Tragic-comic *Hurlyburly*." *American Drama* (Fall, 1993): 1-16.

Savran, David. "David Rabe." In *In Their Own Words: Contemporary American Playwrights*. New York: Theatre Communications Group, 1988.

Weales, Gerald. "Theatre Watch." *Georgia Review* 39 (Fall, 1985): 620-621.

Zinman, Toby Silverman. *David Rabe: A Casebook*. New York: Garland, 1991.

Tony Stafford

"I DON'T HAVE TO SHOW YOU NO STINKING BADGES!"
A New American Play

Author: Luis Miguel Valdez (1940-   )
Type of plot: Satire
Time of plot: The late 1980's
Locale: Monterey Park, a suburb of Los Angeles, California
First produced: 1986, at the Los Angeles Theater Center, Los Angeles
First published: 1986

> *Principal characters:*
> BUDDY VILLA, a Chicano and a career bit-part actor in Hollywood
> CONNIE, his wife, also a bit-part player
> SONNY, their son, a law student
> ANITA, Sonny's friend, an Asian American

The Play

Buddy and Connie Villa are Chicanos who, after thirty years of marriage, have risen from the barrio of East Los Angeles to a comfortable middle-class life in Monterey Park, a suburban enclave once wholly Anglo-American but now populated by successful immigrants. Buddy and Connie have achieved the American Dream of material success through their careers as Hollywood bit-part actors, having played those stereotypical roles of maids, gardeners, and bandits which Spanish actors have rarely been able to transcend. Buddy and Connie have few complaints, however, for their careers have enabled them to put their daughter Lucy through medical school and to send their son Sonny to Harvard Law School. Indeed, Buddy proudly refers to himself and Connie as the Silent Bit King and Queen of Hollywood.

The den of their tract home, where the entire play is set, is fitted with all the modern equipment of the good life, most notably a large console television and video recorder. This could be the den of any American home, since the only sign of the family's ancestral heritage is an imitation Aztec calendar stone hanging above the fireplace. This artifact is less prominent than an old framed poster of the 1948 film *The Treasure of the Sierra Madre*, which starred Humphrey Bogart.

A short prologue introduces Buddy Villa and reveals the allusion of the title. It is late at night, and Buddy, who is fifty-seven with a slight paunch, is sitting asleep while the video recorder plays a scene from *The Treasure of the Sierra Madre*. It is the scene in which Bogart and his companions are trapped in the mountains of Mexico by bandits, who are trying to prevent their escape with the gold they have mined. When the bandits approach, pretending to be federal police, Bogart asks to see their badges, to which a bandit responds: "I don't have to show you no stinkin' badges!" The scene ends with a gun battle, but throughout Buddy has remained asleep in his easy chair. Later in the play, Buddy reveals that he had his first professional part as one of the bandits in the film.

The first scene of act 1 opens on an early morning that finds Connie, an attractive Chicana of forty-eight, talking on the telephone to a friend when Buddy enters from his morning jog. Though Connie banters good-naturedly with Buddy, several serious issues form the subtext of their conversation. Buddy once had a "drinking problem," and he continues to drink beer heavily, which may in part account for episodes of impotence. Buddy becomes annoyed when Connie rejects as unsalable his idea for a film script that would feature a Chicano spaceman. Buddy's annoyance manifests itself in several racist comments directed at his Mexican and Chinese neighbors. Clearly, he feels trapped. Connie, on the other hand, seems content with having achieved middle-class status, and now she has identified her own goal of seeking bigger acting parts. One opportunity that may be offered her would take her on location to Panama for her first speaking part and first job without Buddy. Buddy unequivocally refuses her permission to take the role, and a clash is avoided only when her agent calls to offer both of them parts in a soap opera. Buddy's attempt to defuse Connie's dream by reminding her they "haven't gotten this far" by fooling themselves is decidedly ironic, since the scene ends with Buddy referring again to his film idea.

In act 1, scene 2, Sonny arrives home in the evening of that same day with his new girlfriend, Anita, an Asian American who is intent on breaking into Hollywood. Buddy and Connie are out on a job. As Sonny and Anita settle in, it becomes clear that he loves her as a symbol "of everything beautiful in my life," though Anita does not return this love. When Anita goes to take a shower, Sonny reveals in dramatic monologues that he is tired of meeting his parents' expectations and that he sees that it is time to reach inside himself and grapple with the "white whale." Moments later, his parents return; Buddy is enthusing about yet another film idea, about a Chicano James Bond. After ridiculing his parents for taking roles as gardeners, Sonny reveals that he has dropped out of Harvard Law School to pursue a career as an actor, with the specific goal of "becoming the newest superstar in Hollywood." He has come to the realization that all the world is indeed a stage and that the most "real" work one can do is to act. Crushed by this decision, Buddy violently opposes his son. Anita enters at the end of this family fray, and Buddy begins to relent, perhaps because he charges Sonny's decision to his love for Anita. Anita's Asian heritage is significant for Buddy because he fathered a child as a soldier in the Korean War.

By act 2, scene 1, two weeks have passed, during which Sonny has experienced the bitter reality that Hollywood was not waiting for a Chicano superstar. Indeed, Sonny is dressed for a bit part as a *cholo* (a tough young gang member). If Sonny has become cynical about the "arrogant, preppy-ass, alligator shirt bastards" who run Hollywood, then Anita's experience serves as a counterpoint, for she has made progress toward her own dream. Sonny becomes so angry at his plight as a Mexican American who is "living on the hyphen" that he menaces her with his father's gun. Buddy and Connie arrive home from an awards banquet for Latino actors, only to have Sonny hold them all at bay with the gun while he vents his frustration at the death of his dream. At the heart of his protest is a feeling of isolation from his ancestral roots, the result of an American ethic in which all life becomes a crude imitation of images conveyed by television and films. Buddy, Connie, and Anita are in some doubt whether Sonny is acting, but when he shouts, "The white whale must die," it is clear that he is not acting and intends to kill himself. As he trains the gun on himself, the scene fades.

The play's final scene takes place six months later and serves more as a meta-dramatic epilogue or appendix than an extension of the play. Here the Villa den is presented as the set for a television production, a new situation comedy titled *Badges!* Buddy and Connie enter like characters in a conventional situation comedy, and they proceed to run through a series of tired routines greeted by canned laughter. Buddy and Connie reveal that Sonny is alive and well and being considered for a good part in a television series, *The New Advocates*. Sonny returns from his audition. He has not won a leading part, but Anita has. Sonny will take a lesser role in the same series. Anita enters, and there is general rejoicing, as at the end of many situation comedies. Then Sonny steps out of the play-within-a-play to protest to the show's director: "This sitcom ending is totally unbelievable." There ensues a debate between Sonny and the director, with the director winning the point that eliciting "lots of laughs" is more important than realism. Thereupon, Sonny announces that he is going back to Harvard to become a show-business lawyer, with the goal of establishing his own production company. For better or worse, he has realized that his identity rests in his role as son to Buddy and Connie. Sonny and Anita go out for dinner, leaving Buddy and Connie to savor this "happy ending." They head for the bedroom; the final words go to Buddy, who snarls to the audience, "I don't have to show you no stinking badges!"

Themes and Meanings

"*I Don't Have to Show You No Stinking Badges!*" dramatizes the conflict Mexican Americans (and by implication all Americans) suffer in their pursuit of the homogenizing American Dream: How does one achieve material success as American culture defines it without sacrificing one's ancestral heritage? This conflict is most acute in the play's protagonist, Sonny, who experiences a classic identity crisis. Sonny is trapped in a life "on the hyphen," the son of Chicano parents, at home neither in the Anglo culture of Harvard Law School nor in the indigenous Mexican culture to which even his parents pay little respect. In this sense, then, the play explores Sonny's longing to recover a sense of the past and to establish a historical consciousness as the foundation of an identity. However, for all Sonny's efforts, which have included a trip to the sacred grounds in the Mayan jungle, he can root his identity only as far back as a single generation. When his father asks him whether he has found out who he is, Sonny can only reply, "Your son—for whatever that's worth."

Sonny's failure to restore a history to his family forms the basis of the play's satiric indictment of both the "televisionized" American culture and people such as the members of the Villa family who yield to it. The ultimate responsibility, however, may be personal, for the ersatz Aztec calendar stone that hangs from the Villa fireplace symbolizes the family's numbness to their own heritage. Indeed, Buddy, Connie, and Sonny Villa can speak in little else except metaphors drawn from television and films.

Stasis permeates the play, so that at the end all arrive at the point where they began:

Buddy and Connie are still the Silent Bit King and Queen who believe in their own happy ending, and Sonny is returning to Harvard to renew his pursuit of material wealth and power. While Anita does make progress toward her goal, it serves dramatically to emphasize Sonny's regression. Even the flaunting of Anglo authority that is expressed in the play's title is presented as an empty—and purely fictional—gesture on Buddy's part. In the tradition of social satire, this play holds up the mirror to an element of American society not usually visible—the immigrant bourgeoisie—and in so doing reveals a culture whose values have been corroded as a result of accepting Hollywood's version of reality.

Dramatic Devices

It is difficult to overstate the importance of this play's primary dramatic device to the central themes of the play. This novel device is one of setting, for the play's opening note states, "The entire set sits within the confines of a TV studio." The intent is to draw an audience's attention to "the theatrical reality at hand in our story." In other words, this is a play—that is, a representation of life—that is inscribed within the unreality of a television situation comedy, and yet such comedies are themselves a constructed reality in which all too many American lives take place. The premise here is that life indeed imitates art, with the play continually calling attention to the theatricality and fictionality that underlies life.

This device is only a contemporary way of interpreting the Shakespearean metaphor that "all the world's a stage." Thus, near the end of act 2 Sonny rants that "Hollywood's just a metaphor. . . . We're locked into an image—HOLLYWOOD'S IMAGE—of us." The difference, however, is that William Shakespeare's metaphor implies a degree of volition granted to an actor free to choose a role, while Luis Valdez seems to deny that one can act anything but a predetermined role.

The crucial aspect of this device of the set as a television studio lies in the self-consciousness with which all the characters clearly see their lives, as determined by the fictional genres of Hollywood. At the end of act 1, after Sonny's confrontation with his parents, he remarks, "I'll keep the situation comedy from turning into a soap opera." Later, in act 2, Sonny complains to Anita, "I grew up in this low-rated situation comedy." This self-conscious attention to "theatrical reality" is a prelude to the play's final scene, in which the drama becomes a metadrama—that is, a play that comments on its own processes. Sonny's debate with the director over how *Badges!* should end is designed to destroy the illusion that real life is being represented on the same stage, at the same time that it points to the power of this illusion to shape people's lives. There can be little mistake that the happy ending of the play-within-a-play that is *"I Don't Have to Show You No Stinking Badges!"* is wholly ironic.

Critical Context

"I Don't Have to Show You No Stinking Badges!" can be viewed as a departure, if not an evolutionary step, in both the career of Luis Valdez and the development of American drama by and about ethnic minorities.

Since 1965, when he founded the Teatro Campesino, a California theater group that grew out of the United Farmworkers' struggle, most of Valdez's plays can be classified as social protests. His earliest plays were agitprop pieces that championed the economic causes of Chicanos. Such plays bear the tenor of such works as Clifford Odets's *Waiting for Lefty* (pr., pb. 1935). He followed these strident pieces with longer works that sought to present a fuller and deeper reality of the Chicano experience in America. In *The Shrunken Head of Pancho Villa* (pr. 1965, pb. 1967), Valdez depicts the conflict between two brothers, one an assimilationist and the other a *pachuco*. He attempts the construction of a personal Mexican mythology in *Bernabé* (pr. 1970, pb. 1976), and in his best-known play, *Zoot Suit* (pr. 1978, pb. 1992), he renders vital and visible the Chicano subculture. Each of Valdez's plays stand as part of a larger historical project in which the playwright seeks to force upon the American consciousness an awareness of the Chicano experience and in so doing to write an American history that is more "real."

"I Don't Have to Show You No Stinking Badges!" is also an ahistorical work that presents another cause of the historical invisibility and marginality of Chicanos: a televisionized American culture that acts as a maw into which all ethnic identity falls. Members of the Villa family are cut off from their ancestral heritage, and more than this, they have cut themselves off from their past by their tacit acceptance of Hollywood's images of them. Thus, the play becomes a complement to Valdez's historical project. Whereas before he sought to inscribe history in his plays, here he has advanced to a causal analysis of why such history has never been written. This play shows that the writing of history is first and foremost a personal responsibility, which the "New Americans" in the Villa family are yet incapable of discharging.

Sources for Further Study

Bigsby, C. W. E. "El Teatro Campesino." In *Beyond Broadway*. Vol. 3 in *A Critical Introduction to Twentieth-Century American Drama*. New York: Cambridge University Press, 1985.

Drake, Sylvie. "Valdez—A Life in the River of Humanity." *Los Angeles Times*, February 2, 1986, p. 36.

Elam, Harry J. *Taking It to the Streets: The Social Protest Theater of Luis Valdez and Amiri Baraka*. Ann Arbor: University of Michigan Press, 1977.

Herrara, Jaime. "Luis Miguel Valdez." In *Updating the Literary West*, edited by Max Westbrook and Dan Flores. Fort Worth: Texas Christian University Press, 1997.

Huerta, Jorge A. *Chicano Theater: Themes and Forms*. Ypsilanti, Mich.: Bilingual Press, 1982.

Savren, David. "Luis Valdez." In *In Their Own Words: Contemporary American Playwrights*. New York: Theatre Communications Group, 1988.

Mark William Rocha

I WILL MARRY WHEN I WANT

Authors: Ngugi wa Thiong'o (1938-   ) with Ngugi wa Mirii (1951-   )
Type of plot: Social realism; postcolonial
Time of plot: The 1970's
Locale: Kenya
First produced: 1977, at the Kamiriithu Community Education and Cultural Center, Limuru, Kenya
First published: Ngaahika Ndeenda, 1980 (English translation, 1982)

> *Principal characters:*
> KIGUUNDA, a farm laborer
> WANGECI, Kiguunda's wife
> GATHONI, the daughter of Kiguunda and Wangeci
> AHAB KIOI WA KANORU, a wealthy farmer and businessman
> JEZEBEL, Kioi's wife

The Play

The set of the opening scene in *I Will Marry When I Want* reveals the stark living conditions of Kiguunda, a common laborer, his wife, Wangeci, and their teenage daughter, Gathoni. The three of them share a one-room house that is sparsely furnished and decorated. It consists of a bed for Kiguunda and Wangeci, a broken folding chair, and a cooking pot that sits on three stones. A pile of rags on the floor establishes that "the floor is Gathoni's bed and the rags, her bedding." Prominently displayed on the wall is a framed title-deed for one and a half acres of land, a plot that was purchased after the Mau Mau Revolution of the 1950's, a guerrilla war waged by the Kikuyu, along with members of other tribal groups of Kenya, to reclaim the land from British settlers.

As the play opens, the family is making preparations for the arrival of important guests. Kiguunda is repairing the broken leg of a folding chair, while Wangeci is busy preparing a stew to serve to the guests. The makeshift nature of their accommodations reinforces the impression of the family's substandard living conditions. Wangeci, who has spent thirty cents on cooking oil and sugar, discovers that another important staple, salt, is missing and has to send the daughter, Gathoni, to borrow from the Gicaambas. During this bustling activity, the title-deed falls to the floor of the hut. Kiguunda picks it up gingerly and studies it carefully before returning it to the wall, his actions as well as his words identifying him as a proud landowner, despite the family's humble living conditions. In response to Wangeci, who asks why he gazes at the title-deed, Kiguunda explains that "these [one and a half acres] are worth more to me/ Than all the thousands that belong to Ahab Kioi wa Kanoru."

With the entrance of Kioi, a wealthy landowner, who is accompanied by another landowning couple, Samuel and Helen Ndugire, the framed title-deed again falls conspicuously to the floor of the hut. Literally, the crash is caused by the cramped living quarters; figuratively, it connotes the likelihood of land loss to the wealthy visitors, who deliberately seek to veil the true purpose of their visit.

The conflict in act 1 stems from the uncertainty surrounding the nature of Kioi's mission. Although prior to Kioi's visit Kiguunda had produced a letter from Ikuua wa Nditika, Kioi's partner, wherein Nditika had proposed purchasing Kiguunda's plot of land in order to construct an insecticide factory, Kioi makes no reference to the letter during the course of his visit. The confusion of Kiguunda and Wangeci is further compounded by their daughter's present involvement with John Muhuuni, the son of Kioi and Jezebel. Subsequently, when Kioi and Jezebel seek to persuade Kiguunda and Wangeci "to enter the church of God" and speak of a union of families, "your house and mine becoming one," Kiguunda and Wangeci are convinced that their aim is to ensure that their son marries into a Christian family. Acting upon that assumption, Kiguunda and Wangeci, in scene 2 of act 2, visit the home of Kioi and Jezebel to agree to consecrate their marriage in the traditional church wedding.

In order to finance the wedding, however, Kiguunda and Wangeci must mortgage their plot of land in order to secure a bank loan. Kioi does not offer to provide Kiguunda with a personal loan; he does offer, however, to become a guarantor for the loan, which is to be handled by the bank, for which he serves as director.

The duplicity of Kioi and his associates does not become apparent to the unsuspecting Kiguunda and Wangeci until act 3, the final act of the drama. In scene 1 of act 3, Kiguunda and Wangeci are absorbed in the plans for their impending wedding but are startled by the weeping of Gathoni, who has returned from an outing with John Muhuuni. When pressed by her parents, Gathoni reveals the ugly truth: She has been jilted by John Muhuuni after he has learned of her pregnancy. Upon hearing the news, Kiguunda and Wangeci shed their wedding attire, purchased with loan funds, and replace it with their old garb, indicative of their return to pauperism. At the end of the scene, they decide to pay an immediate visit to Kioi's home, convinced that Kioi will rectify matters.

In scene 2 of act 3, a confrontation ensues when Kioi denies any knowledge of a prospective wedding between the two families and challenges Kiguunda to seek redress through a legal suit, contending, "There are no laws to protect parents/ Who are unable to discipline their children,/ Who let their children become prostitutes." Kiguunda, enraged, draws his sword and threatens Kioi. Kioi is saved by his wife, Jezebel, from signing an agreement to make restitution to the family. Alerted by the watchman's whistle, she enters, armed with a pistol, and drives Kiguunda and Wangeci from the premises.

The duping of Gathoni by John Muhuuni had presaged the actions of Muhuuni's father. It was reported by Gathoni in act 1 that Muhuuni had invited her to travel with him to Mombasa, where he had been instructed by his father to survey some land that he had acquired with the intention of constructing a hotel for tourists. Gathoni, in defiance of her parents, had traveled with Muhuuni to the coast. In going against her parents' wishes, however, Gathoni gambled and lost. Deceived by Muhuuni into thinking that pregnancy would lead to marriage, since "he would never marry a girl/ Who had not conceived," Gathoni is discarded by Muhuuni in the same way that Kiguunda is discarded by Kioi after each has served the other's purpose.

The gullibility of Kiguunda and his family (because of their own social climbing aspirations), faced with the ruthlessness of Kioi and his associates, results in losses. The plot of land is possessed by the bank and is auctioned off to Kioi, purportedly to recover the bank's losses. The home of Kiguunda is described in the final scene as looking "very much like the way it was at the beginning of the play, except for the picture of Nebuchadnezzar and the board with the inscription 'Christ is the Head' which still hang from the walls as if in mockery."

Despite, however, the deterioration of the family's circumstances—Kiguunda is now a drunkard and Gathoni a barmaid—the drama's conclusion is one of hope as the neighbor, Gicaamba, identified as a former member of the Mau Mau revolutionary army, joins with Kiguunda and others in renewing their Mau Mau oaths to reclaim the land from foreign ownership.

Themes and Meanings

I Will Marry When I Want concerns itself mainly with the betrayal of the aspirations of the masses of people in Kenya by the postindependence African leadership. Contrary to the expectations of the people, following Kenya's independence from British rule, that the land would be restored to the indigenous population, independence seemed only to increase further the scramble for European investors. Illustrative of the country's economic policy are the frequent allusions to land acquisitions for the purpose of building additional factories, such as the insecticide factory, that specialize in exported goods. Kioi's and Nditika's wealth largely stems from their European alliance, which often results in their serving as figureheads for foreign industries based in the country. When Nditika proposes that Kioi consider serving as the local director for the insecticide project, he describes the responsibility as being no different from his present directorship of the local bank:

> It's not much work.
> It's just a matter of one or two board meetings.
> You become overseer.
> Just as you now oversee their banks.
> You and I will be like watchdogs.

The theme of betrayal is evident as well in reference to the "Homeguard," a quasi-military attachment of the British police force made up of African loyalists whose responsibility was to help restore calm after a series of Mau Mau raids and attacks. In effect, the Homeguard was to assist the British police by identifying and incarcerating suspected Mau Mau members. Such actions taken by the Homeguard against fellow Africans were perceived by Ngugi wa Thiong'o as treacherous. Ndugire, a nouveau riche farmer in *I Will Marry When I Want*, is identified as a member of the Homeguard who has profited materially from the European alliance, but at the price of his own humanity. He confesses that "I used to kill people,/ And to do many other terrible deeds/ As was the habit among the homeguards of those days."

Dramatic Devices

The betrayal of the African peoples, as well as the African culture, by the ruling elite is encapsulated in Ngugi's identification of their adoption of Christian names. Kioi's wife Jezebel is reminiscent of the biblical Jezebel, wife of the Israeli king Ahab, who forcibly appropriated the vineyard belonging to Naboth after he had refused to sell it. She accomplished this by sending letters in King Ahab's name to the community's elders with orders that Naboth be stoned to death for disobeying the king's orders. The Jezebel in *I Will Marry When I Want* is no less willful. It is she who surreptitiously produces a gun, thereby rescuing Kioi, also named Ahab, from a threat upon his life by Kiguunda. The weapon also shows the extent of Jezebel's assimilation of Western culture; Kiguunda, on the other hand, is armed only with a sword, a relic of the Mau Mau revolutionary war of the 1950's.

Ngugi perceives the conversion to Christianity as another form of treason, involving the disavowal of traditional customs and the acceptance of alien ones. This cultural treason is dramatized in scene 1 of act 3, when Kiguunda and Wangeci are transported to the site of their anticipated wedding. Vows are exchanged, or renewed, and Kiguunda and Wangeci are immediately given the Christian names "Winston Smith Kiguunda and Rosemary Magdalene Wangeci." The change of names, symbolizing a change of identity, is a dramatic device used by Ngugi to suggest the extent to which cultural imperialism penetrates the consciousness of its victims.

Critical Context

I Will Marry When I Want is a drama that celebrates, in a series of flashbacks, the events of the Mau Mau Revolution that quickened the pace of Kenya's march toward independence. References are made throughout the drama to the taking of oaths not to betray fellow members of the organization to British authorities or to sell land to the Europeans. After these vows are administered, the initiates pass in pairs through an "arch of banana leaves to the other side."

These allusions to the Mau Mau are also used as time markers. Kiguunda recalls his courtship of Wangeci as taking place "long before the state of Emergency," a period from 1952 to 1962 that saw the establishment of the Homeguard and the subsequent arrest and detention of suspected Mau Mau members. The frequent allusions to the martyred Mau Mau leader Dedan Kimaathi, who is praised in songs, contrast with references to the Homeguard, whose ascendancy to power is described as the result of crooked means. Hence, *I Will Marry When I Want* may be read as a tribute by Ngugi to Mau Mau leaders, those he considers the progenitors of Kenya's freedom and the rightful heirs of political leadership in postindependence Kenya.

Ngugi's criticism of the economic policy of Kenya's leaders in *I Will Marry When I Want* led to the banning of the play, and was in part the cause of his imprisonment from 1977 to 1979. Originally written in his native language, Gikuyu (or Kikuyu), as *Ngaahika Ndeenda*, the play was later translated by Ngugi and a fellow writer, Ngugi wa Mirii, into the English version, *I Will Marry When I Want*. Ngugi wa Thiong'o, in the chapter "Women in Cultural Work: The Fate of Kamiriithu People's Theater in Kenya," from his collection of essays *Barrel of a Pen* (1983), attributes his arrest to the unflattering depictions of the politicians in the drama: "Understandably, the wealthy who control the government did not like the stark realities of their own social origins enacted onstage by simple villagers. As a result, we were harassed, even some of us detained."

Although the banning of the play in Kenya has affected public exposure to the work and limited the available scholarship, if past criticism of Ngugi's work is a reliable indicator, the criticism of some reviewers of Ngugi's earlier work might also apply to *I Will Marry When I Want*. That criticism pertains to the stridency of tone which some attribute to the idealism prevalent following independence.

Sources for Further Study

Blishen, Edward. "Tumbled Traditions." *New York Times Literary Supplement*, January 28, 1983, p. 26.

Cook, David, and Michael Okenimkpe. *Ngugi wa Thiong'o: An Exploration of His Writings*. 2d ed. Portsmouth, N.H.: Heinemann, 1997.

Gikandi, Simon. *Ngugi wa Thiong'o*. Cambridge, England: Cambridge University Press, 2000.

Killam, Gordon Douglas. *An Introduction to the Writings of Ngugi*. Exeter, N.H.: Heinemann Educational, 1980.

_____, ed. *Critical Perspectives on Ngugi wa Thiong'o*. Washington, D.C.: Three Continents Press, 1984.

Ngugi wa Thiong'o. "Women in Cultural Work: The Fate of Kamiriithu People's Theater in Kenya." In *Barrel of a Pen: Resistance to Repression in Neo-Colonial Kenya*. London: New Beacon Books, 1983.

Robson, Clifford B. *Ngugi wa Thiong'o*. New York: St. Martin's Press, 1979.

Sicheraram, Carol. *Ngugi wa Thiong'o—the Making of a Rebel: A Source Book on Kenyan Literature and Resistance*. New York: H. Zell, 1990.

Tommie L. Jackson

IDIOT'S DELIGHT

Author: Robert E. Sherwood (1896-1955)
Type of plot: Comedy
Time of plot: 1935
Locale: The Italian Alps
First produced: 1936, at the National Theatre, Washington, D.C.
First published: 1936

> *Principal characters:*
> HARRY VAN, an American showman touring with a troupe of dancers
> CAPTAIN LOCICERO, an airfield commanding officer
> IRENE, an American of uncertain ancestry
> ACHILLE WEBER, a French munitions manufacturer
> QUILLERY, a French radical socialist
> DR. HUGO WALDERSEE, a German scientist
> MR. and MRS. CHERRY, English newlyweds on their honeymoon

The Play

Act 1 opens in the cocktail lounge of the Hotel Monte Gabriele overlooking Austria, Italy, Switzerland, and Bavaria. Captain Locicero, commanding officer of the nearby military airfield, enters, followed by Dr. Waldersee, demanding that the captain permit him to cross into Switzerland for his important cancer research demands. The captain explains that the threat of war has closed the borders. They are joined by an English couple on their honeymoon, Mr. and Mrs. Cherry, and a group of six exotic dancers from the United States and their leader, Harry Van. The radical socialist Quillery also joins the group; he is returning to France, where he hopes to unite all the workers of Europe against war. Finally, arms magnate Achille Weber enters with his companion Irene, who boasts a Russian ancestry. Weber describes himself as one without a nationality since he does business with all nations. As airplanes roar overhead, Captain Locicero announces that Germany has mobilized and that Italy and France are at war. Harry calls for music and dance.

As act 2 opens it is the evening of the same day. The Cherrys are declaring that they will remain superior to the war. Harry is again playing the piano and drinking. Quillery, ranting about the "dynamite of jingoism," attacks England, the "well-fed, pious hypocrite," and the arms manufacturers who have formed a "League of Death." He turns on Dr. Waldersee, who, as a German, represents the swastika, but the doctor declares that as a scientist he is not concerned with politics. Harry shifts the conversation, offering to put on a show for the other guests that evening. Irene continues telling of her escapes, hinting as the scene closes that she has seen Harry Van somewhere before.

Scene 2 opens later the same evening. Airplanes again drone overhead. Irene comments that war is a game that God plays called "Idiot's Delight." It "never means anything, and never ends." She blames Weber for the death and destruction caused by war, but he says that the greatest criminals are those he supplies with arms and that he merely furnishes them with "the illusion of power." Harry and his dancers perform for the guests, but they are interrupted when Quillery announces that Italian planes have bombed Paris. In a violent outburst, he blames the Fascists; the captain has him arrested and taken away to be executed. The scene ends with the guests dancing in the lurid lights of the color wheel. In scene 3, Harry and Irene are alone on stage, the others having gone to bed. Harry says that he dislikes Weber, who considers the "human race just so many clay pigeons," but Irene defends him as being necessary to "the kind of civilization that we have got." Harry reveals that he suspects her to be the woman he knew in Nebraska, but she coyly evades admitting the truth.

When act 3 opens, it is the following afternoon. Quillery has been executed by the Fascists. The captain announces that they all will be permitted to leave. The Cherrys are returning to England, where the husband will enlist and fight for "civilization." Dr. Waldersee has abandoned his scientific research to return to Germany and use his scientific knowledge to kill rather than to cure. Although her passport is not in order, Irene will be permitted to leave because Weber will vouch for her. He declines, however, forcing the captain to detain her. Harry learns of Weber's betrayal and offers to help her, but she declines his offer. Before he leaves, she admits that she knew him in Omaha. The others depart, but soon Harry returns. As he and Irene drink champagne and make plans for her to join his show and tour with him, bombs begin to fall around them and machine-gun fire can be heard. They stand together at the window singing "Onward, Christian Soldiers" as the curtain falls.

Themes and Meanings

All the characters and relationships in *Idiot's Delight* are defined or affected by the impending conflict between the Allied forces and Nazi Germany. The play's perspective broadens as the play advances, beginning with the narrow sphere of the cocktail lounge and ending with the air raid that symbolizes a conflict that envelops all of Europe. Thematically, the play develops the idea that humans are too fearful, narrow-minded, and patriotic to resist the urge to defend national honor. Morally, war is regarded as abhorrent and evil, but, the play suggests, humans are too emotional and too easily manipulated by "patriotic jingoism" to live up to their moral convictions.

Each of the major characters represents a specific point of view about war, its nature, and its consequences. Harry Van, the optimist, believes that the desire for peace and goodwill are fundamental to human nature and will eventually triumph. Achille Weber, the most morally depraved of the group, believes that humans are driven by self-interest, as he is, and by national honor, which he exploits for commercial gain; patriotism, he declares, is simply a mask for greed and mistrust.

Quillery betrays the passionate believer's weakness by succumbing to his own patriotic fervor, which turns into a ranting nationalism. His execution confirms the point that war is idiotic in part because it destroys harmless people like Quillery. The Cherrys represent the disruptive effects of international turmoil on young love and the allure of nationalism; they believe that their superiority and ability not to "give a damn" protects them against the war, but they too succumb to national fervor and abandon their aloofness. Dr. Waldersee also undergoes a complete reversal of spirit. In a fit of despair, he abandons his humanitarian research and dedicates himself to killing people, convinced by the outbreak of war that people are maniacs who do not want to be saved. If Weber is the complete cynic, Dr. Waldersee is the complete pessimist.

Irene shows the most development and is the most complex, hiding the secret of her past, confessing that her life has been a series of escapes, and ultimately seeing that Achille Weber is evil for his part in making war possible. She imagines the kind of horror for which Weber is responsible—the killing of babies, the destruction of cities—and at last, unable to accept his cynical opportunism and debased morality, she leaves him. Her decision ends a life in which she has always made escapes, she declares at one point, admitting that with Weber, she is a prisoner in an ivory tower. Ironically, her decision to escape that life leaves her confined to the hotel but free of the lies she has been living. Leaving him and deciding to face the future on her own demonstrate that she has at last found the courage to face the truth and the future.

Harry Van's loyalty to Irene and to his troupe of dancers—he makes sure they are safely on their way to Geneva before returning to Irene—offsets Weber's disloyalty and loveless nature. Harry's character and actions are the mirror opposite of Achille Weber's and contribute substantially to the play's uplifting finale. As the others shrink into nationalism, Harry becomes increasingly compassionate and selfless. Robert E. Sherwood suggests that war does not transform everyone into monsters; some, like Harry and Irene, become the better for it. Their final union is an affirmation of love, trust, and courage. They are the only characters who see clearly the insanity of war, who do not succumb to nationalistic fervor, and who do not take up arms against others.

Dramatic Devices

Sherwood depicts the horrors of war by employing a number of subtle and dramatic devices. Mainly, he relies on his characters to demonstrate war's "bestial frenzy" and its dangers. Quillery's frenzied outbursts are shown to destroy him, Dr. Waldersee's pessimism destroys his career, and patriotism lures the Cherrys from their honeymoon. The sound of machine-gun fire and the deafening roar of bombers create a vivid image of war's menace.

The play also relies on lighting to reinforce content. The darkening of the stage signals oncoming night but symbolizes the approaching darkness of war. The color wheel in the cabaret sequence sheds a lurid light on the dancing couples, suggesting the unnatural effects that war brings with it. Lighting therefore becomes a visual connection throughout the play that also symbolizes events offstage.

Onstage, the characters often speak in different languages simultaneously. This device reflects, on one hand, the difficulty of communication among nations—suggesting one of the causes of war; on the other hand, it dramatizes the human characteristic of not listening to or hearing others—not being interested enough in what they are saying to shut up long enough to hear them out. The discordant chorus of voices is an apt symbol of human self-centeredness and the jangle of failed communication that contrasts with the musical elements in the play.

The play's setting is important because it enables Sherwood realistically to bring together assorted characters representing not only a certain point of view but a certain nationality as well. The setting is also central to the antiwar theme and itself symbolizes the idealist's appeal for international accord and the ideal place to be when human affairs grow heated. When Irene exclaims in the end, "Here we are, on the top of the world," her meanings resonate throughout the play. High in the Alps she is indeed on top of the world, but morally she has ascended by embracing truth and love and by not succumbing to patriotic fervor. She has risen above the sordid horror of destruction and asks rhetorically, "Do you want to go in the cellar?" By placing the action on top of the world, Sherwood suggests that the best place to be is above it all.

Critical Context

In his early plays, Sherwood focused on relationships and individual concerns in a predominantly comic spirit, though antiwar sentiments are often evident. It has been said that all of his plays are about pacifism. In four plays his sharpest views on war may be traced. In *Waterloo Bridge* (pr., pb. 1930), the soldier finds love more attractive than war. *Idiot's Delight* takes the view that the individual cannot escape being caught up in war's consequences. *Abe Lincoln in Illinois* (pr. 1938, pb. 1939) shows a peace-loving man faced with the task of plunging the nation into war; and in *There Shall Be No Night* (pr., pb. 1940) a man who wins the Nobel Peace Prize is forced to fight for freedom and human dignity. Running throughout all of Sherwood's plays is the belief that personal sacrifice is often necessary to achieve the common good, and this sacrifice establishes the individual's worth and faith in human goodness.

The popularity of Sherwood's plays, beginning with *The Road to Rome* (pr., pb. 1927) and extending to *There Shall Be No Night*, and his work with the Playwrights' Company and the American National Theater helped to keep the American theater alive in times of great social change. When *Idiot's Delight* won the 1936 Pulitzer Prize, Sherwood was established as an important voice in prewar American drama. He believed that drama should entertain yet reflect the realities of the world outside the play, and his dramas embrace this dual purpose. His early plays reflected the light-hearted mood of the American 1920's, whereas by the 1930's the grim realities of the Depression and the rise of communism and Nazism cast a darker shadow over the plays. *Idiot's Delight* was written and produced when major nations were poised to start another war, so its plea for sanity and the preservation of peace is all the more effective for its timing.

During the war years, Sherwood became a speech writer for President Franklin Roosevelt, and by war's end, it is generally agreed, his artistic powers had declined, though he continued to write for the stage. On the whole, his plays gave audiences something positive to ponder while reflecting their hope for peace and faith in reason and human goodwill. The shifts in Sherwood's feelings and thinking, reflected in his popular plays, present a clear record of what most intelligent, liberal people were thinking and feeling as well. Without being overly preachy, *Idiot's Delight* accurately reflects the general moral climate of the 1930's and captures the sentiments and point of view of large groups of people in a time of national and international crisis.

Sources for Further Study

Brown, John Mason. *The Ordeal of a Playwright: Robert E. Sherwood and the Challenge of War.* New York: Harper and Row, 1968.

_____. *The Worlds of Robert E. Sherwood: Mirror to His Times, 1896-1939.* New York: Harper and Row, 1965.

Flexner, Eleanor. *American Playwrights, 1918-1938.* New York: Simon and Schuster, 1938.

Meserve, Walter J. *Robert E. Sherwood: Reluctant Moralist.* New York: Pegasus, 1970.

Sahu, N. S. *Theatre of Protest and Anger: Studies in Dramatic Works of Maxwell Anderson and Robert E. Sherwood.* Delhi, India: Amar Prakashan, 1988.

Shuman, Robert Baird. *Robert Emmet Sherwood.* New Haven, Conn.: College and University Press Publishers, 1964.

Bernard E. Morris

IN THE SHADOW OF THE GLEN

Author: John Millington Synge (1871-1909)
Type of plot: Comedy
Time of plot: 1900
Locale: County Wicklow, western Ireland
First produced: 1903, at the Molesworth Hall, Dublin, Ireland
First published: 1904, in *Samhain*; revised, 1905

> *Principal characters:*
> DAN BURKE, a farmer and shepherd
> NORA BURKE, his wife
> MICHEAL DARA, a young shepherd
> A TRAMP, a stranger who appears at Nora's door

The Play

 In the Shadow of the Glen opens on Nora Burke in the kitchen of her cottage. It is a typical Irish peasant cottage, with a turf fire and a table in the center of the room. A front door and a small door to a bedroom are upstage. On a bed against the back wall lies a body covered with a white sheet. The stage directions indicate there are cakes, glasses, and whiskey on the table, "as if for a wake."

 As Nora is clearing things and lighting candles, there is a knock at the door. Removing a sock of money from the table, she answers it. She is greeted by a stranger, who says that he is walking to the Aughrim fair and asks whether he may come out of the rain and stay the night. She consents readily. The stranger is startled by the sight of the corpse on the bed. Nora tells him that it is her husband and that he died only hours before. When he asks why she has not laid him out or arranged him formally, she tells him that he cursed her, or anybody else, who might touch his body if he were to die suddenly.

 As they talk, Nora describes her husband's sudden illness and the great melodrama of his death throes. She offers the tramp whiskey and one of her husband's tobacco pipes. When he asks why she is not afraid to let him in when no man is around and she is so far from neighbors, she says that she is not afraid of "beggar or bishop or any man of you at all." They discover that they have a friend in common, one Patch Darcy. The stranger tells of being frightened by weird noises as he walked alone among the hills. He later learned that they were caused by Darcy, who had gone mad and died of exposure in the hills. Nora says that Darcy had had the habit of stopping in for a visit when he passed her glen and that it had kept her from being lonely.

 The mention of loneliness reminds Nora to ask whether the tramp has seen anyone on the path. When he says that he did see a young man trying to control a herd of sheep, Nora quickly asks him to stay and watch the corpse while she finds him. She wants to ask him, she says, to spread the word that her husband has died. When the tramp offers to go, she declines, clearly wanting to see the young man herself.

Nora leaves. The tramp sits before the fire saying the De Profundis under his breath. Behind him, the sheet begins to move, and the corpse begins to rise. When he finally notices this, the tramp leaps up in terror. The "corpse," trying to calm him, reveals that he is not dead after all. He asks the tramp to get him some whiskey before his wife returns, and he complains of aches and pains from lying still so long. He tells him to get his walking stick, which he hides under the funeral sheet. He threatens the tramp with it if he says anything about his trick, explaining that he has done it to catch his wife, because "it's a bad wife she is—a bad wife for an old man, and I'm getting old, God help me."

Hearing voices on the path, he jumps back under the sheet, repeats his threat, and lies perfectly still. The tramp returns to the fire and begins mending his coat. Nora and the young shepherd, Micheal Dara, enter. Dara, described in the stage notes as a "tall, innocent young man," is clearly afraid of the corpse and is soon revealed to be a poor shepherd as well, hardly a match for the feisty, outspoken Nora. When he complains that Nora has too many men friends, she replies, "if it's a power of men I'm after knowing, they were fine men." It is clear that she is trying to get the tramp to go to the other room to sleep so she can be alone with Dara. Seeing the potential for an interesting situation and a good wake, the tramp determines to stay.

In conversation with Dara (which the "corpse" overhears), Nora admits that she married her husband only for his "bit of a farm, and cows on it, and sheep on the black hills." She now regrets her decision and would never repeat it. She feels that life has passed her by and confesses that she has been constantly lonely in her marriage, except for the visits from men friends such as Darcy and Dara. As they talk, they empty Dan Burke's sock of money and begin to count it. Dara reminds Nora that she can now marry him, but she dismisses this, saying that she does not want to marry him, because he will soon get old like her husband. She begins to describe Burke's decrepitude, his shaking face, falling teeth, and white hair sticking out around his head. As she does so, he rises from under the funeral sheet, looking just as she described. Meanwhile, Dara counters her arguments against marriage, saying that it will be different with him. The dialogue continues with the "risen" Burke upstage unnoticed until he suddenly sneezes.

After initial terror, Nora and Dara realize that Burke is not a ghost. Burke, infuriated by all he has overheard, opens the door and demands that Nora leave immediately. Nora, equally angered by her husband's treachery, says that she will go gladly. When she hesitates, wondering how she will live wandering the roads alone, the tramp suggests that she come with him. After a halfhearted attempt by Dara to stop her, she leaves with the vagabond for a life that, in his glowing romantic descriptions, sounds to her liking. As Micheal is about to go after them, Burke steps in, offering him a drink. The two sit down and drink to "a long life, and a quiet life."

Themes and Meanings

In the Shadow of the Glen, a one-act play based on a folktale John Millington Synge collected on his first trip to the Aran Islands, off the coast of Ireland, is deceptively simple; actually, it is complex enough to contain most of the themes the playwright would explore for the rest of his dramatic career. The most obvious is the tension between the basic human need for security and the equally basic urge for freedom. The play pits Nora's secure domestic existence against the tramp's freewheeling life. Nora's marriage to Burke for his farm, livestock, and sock of money was her bid for security, but it has caused her only unhappiness and loneliness. That she leaves with the tramp rather than reconciling with her old husband or accepting his young counterpart, Micheal Dara, makes freedom the clear winner in the play.

This rejection of security makes *In the Shadow of the Glen* a very unusual comedy. Classically, comedy is the dramatic mode that substantiates society's bonds and celebrates human connection, especially marriage and birth. Synge's play, however, depicts—and even applauds—Nora's rejection of a constricting bond and her joyful embrace of a free, if insecure, life. Thus, an issue related to the general freedom-versus-security question in the play is marriage and women's role in it. Freedom's conflict with security is a universal problem; other Synge plays give it to male characters (notably Christie Mahon in *The Playboy of the Western World* [pr., pb. 1907]), but here the problem is Nora's, and Nora is not only a person but also a wife. Like Henrik Ibsen's *Et dukkehjem* (pr., pb. 1879; *A Doll's House*, 1880), Synge's play is a direct attack, not on all marriage, but on the convention of marriage as an arrangement by which a woman may live securely, provided she is willing to relinquish her freedom and her self.

In the Shadow of the Glen is unquestionably a feminist work. However, it is no lifeless tract. The feminist theme of the play is embedded in the character of Nora Burke herself. She is its most developed and attractive character; she is feisty, tough, and fearless. The satirical portraits of the old cuckold faking death to catch his wife cheating and the dull young shepherd who cannot even control his herd provide quite a contrast to her. Moreover, the tramp, supposedly her equal, is hardly developed dramatically at all. Like the Nora in Ibsen's play, her character unfolds so that, by the end, she is believable when she makes the hard choice of leaving her secure nest. She even usurps the dramatic climax of the play by turning her husband's decision to throw her out into her own decision to leave.

A final theme to be noted is loneliness. Although it is not strongly stressed in *In the Shadow of the Glen*, it is present, and it is clearly connected to the freedom/security question. The equation the play reverses is this: Freedom equals being alone; being alone equals loneliness. In her marriage, Nora has learned that one can be with someone and still be very much alone; she learns from the tramp, however, that one can be alone and not be lonely. The crux of the difference is independence. Loneliness is a perceived effect only; it is overcome by the self-confidence freedom brings.

Dramatic Devices

The set of *In the Shadow of the Glen* was constructed to replicate a western Irish cottage. The loft, peat fireplace, and thatched roof were rendered in detail, and small touches, such as leather "pampooties" for the actors' feet and correct color detail in their folk costumes, were included. The overall stage effect was of a precise realism, almost to a "folklife museum" extent. John Millington Synge and the Abbey Theatre producers knew that they were presenting a picture of the Irish peasantry to a middle-class Dublin audience that held a somewhat romanticized and unrealistic view of its lower-class, rural counterpart. So they went to some trouble to make the set of their dramatic representation as authentic as possible.

Such was the case with the language of the play as well. Synge had recorded peculiar pronunciations of words, unusual phrases, and special syntactical quirks in his notebooks during his field trips among the Aran peasants, and he expended great effort incorporating this folk speech into his play. The combined effect of the realistic set and the precise dialect was to give the production a striking documentary authenticity.

This folklife realism provided a suitable context for a story that itself was a field-collected folk anecdote. The plot of *In the Shadow of the Glen* came to Synge directly from the lips of one Pat Diran. Diran was a teller of tales, lies, and legends whom Synge met in 1898 during his first stay on Inishmaan, the largest of the Aran Islands. These are a bleak and isolated cluster of granite islands thirty miles west of Galway Bay in the North Atlantic Sea. Synge had gone to this desolate region for the express purpose of living among the most isolated Irish peasants and discovering their actual lore and language, as opposed to the romanticized, bowdlerized, and expurgated material found in the published volumes of armchair Celtic antiquaries. He did find this material, and like Diran's tale of the old cuckold faking his death, much of it did not paint a very heroic picture of the Irish peasant, the supposed source of the Irish national character.

Nevertheless, Synge's play is not simply a slice of life in the naturalistic mode. Its dramatic ingenuity lies in the ironic tension it maintains between a de-romanticized presentation of the Irish peasantry and the fiery speech and romantic imagination of those same peasants. If the play's stark picture was meant to clash with that cherished by its Dublin audience, it is also meant to clash with the imagination and yearning of its central characters. The theme of the story is that very clash—the struggle of the self to transcend the mundane world with its obstacles to freedom and fulfillment.

Basing the play on field-collected folklore and staging it to emphasize this base allows the contest between necessity and invention to work organically. That the play's trappings and atmosphere represent the losing side in the contest simply adds another level of irony to an already deeply ironic dramatic work.

Critical Context

Riders to the Sea (pr. 1903, pb. 1904) and this play were Synge's first dramatic renderings of the folklore he had observed and recorded on the Aran Islands. While the former is widely considered to be one of the world's great masterpieces and the latter is usually called a minor work, *In the Shadow of the Glen* is actually more indicative of Synge's artistic temperament and more of a piece with the later works he would create out of the same Aran Island material. While *Riders to the Sea* has a constantly somber atmosphere and dwells in a concentrated way on the single theme of human mortality, *In the Shadow of the Glen* features both the archly ironic tone and the freedom-versus-security theme that are so closely associated with this playwright's work in general. It is the prototype of Synge's later "hymns to vagrancy"—a description applied by a reviewer to *The Playboy of the Western World*.

The play also presents the first of Synge's great, dynamic female characters. Nora's energy, vitality, and self-confidence presage later Synge heroines, from Mary Doud to Deirdre of the Sorrows. Thus, *In the Shadow of the Glen* is the first of Synge's works to stake out his distinctive dramatic and philosophical territory. However, it is not merely of scholarly interest; it is in itself an effective piece of theater and inevitably succeeds when staged.

Finally, the Dublin audience's reaction to the play's premiere ahould be noted. While it did not cause the riots that *The Playboy of the Western World* precipitated, it did manage to generate almost as much hissing and booing as applause, thus anticipating the swarm of controversy that marked the production of almost all Synge's later works.

Sources for Further Study
Casey, David J. *Critical Essays on John Millington Synge.* Boston: Twayne, 1994.
Flood, Jeanne A. "Synge's Ecstatic Dance and the Myth of the Undying Father." *American Imago* 33, no. 2 (1976): 174-196.
Gerstenberger, Donna. *John Millington Synge.* New York: Twayne, 1964.
Gonzalez, Alexander G., ed. *Assessing the Achievement of J. M. Synge.* Westport, Conn.: Greenwood Press, 1996.
Greene, Nicholas. *Synge: A Critical Study of the Plays.* London: Macmillan, 1975.
King, Mary C. "Towards the Antithetical Vision: Syntax and Imagery in *In the Shadow of the Glen.*" In *The Drama of J. M. Synge.* London: Fourth Estate, 1985.
Skelton, Robin. "*In the Shadow of the Glen.*" In *The Writings of J. M. Synge.* London: Thames and Hudson, 1971.
Yeats, William Butler. *Synge and the Ireland of His Time.* Spartanburg, S.C.: Reprint Services, 1992.

Thomas Barden

IN THE WINE TIME

Author: Ed Bullins (1935-   )
Type of plot: Naturalistic; domestic realism
Time of plot: The early 1950's
Locale: An unspecified industrial city in the northern United States
First produced: 1968, at the New Lafayette Theatre, New York City
First published: 1969, in *Five Plays by Ed Bullins*

Principal characters:
CLIFF DAWSON, an unemployed African American man
LOU DAWSON, Cliff's wife
RAY, Lou's nephew, fifteen years old
TINY, Cliff's current lover
SILLY WILLY CLARK, Cliff's friend
RED and
BAMA, street toughs
DORIS, Lou's sister
MISS MINNY GARRISON, a busybody neighbor

The Play

In the Wine Time begins with a poetic prologue, spoken by Ray, looking back on his encounters with the woman of his dreams—brief meetings when she passed the corner where he waited each evening of the summer of his "last wine time." The relationship, with the two never speaking because "we know all we want to find out," puzzled Ray's aunt and uncle, Lou and Cliff Dawson, and led to arguments. Ray was crushed when the girl failed to appear one night, but she reappeared the next evening and spoke to him for the first time, warning him to stop drinking wine and promising that she would be waiting "out in the world" when he was ready to come. Ray finishes his prologue, then goes back in time to the summer he began the search which the older Ray confesses he has not completed.

Act 1 opens with the voice of a radio disc jockey, which gives way to the rhythm and blues music that will continue through the play, sometimes competing with Miss Minny Garrison's gospel music. Lou, Cliff, and Ray, sitting on their doorstep, watch the evening ritual of their white neighbor, Mrs. Krump, trying unsuccessfully to get her son to bring his drunk father in from the street, where he is urinating on a pole. As Mr. Krump is menaced by Red and Bama, two toughs, Miss Minny intervenes, getting Ray to take Mr. Krump—over Cliff's objections. When Red kicks Ray as he is carrying Krump into the house, Cliff and Lou argue, first over Miss Minny's interference, then about problems Cliff perceives in the way Lou and her late sister have reared Ray. The argument covers old ground, going back to Miss Minny's petition to have Lou and Cliff run off Derby Street after they first moved there. Cliff blames it on the fact that he was going to school on the G.I. Bill and "not totin' a lunch pail like all those other asses." Lou reminds him that she was working and he was seeing a lot of other women, which added to the neighbors' feelings. Cliff tries to deny this, then switches the subject to Ray.

When Lou finally says that it was their wine drinking, laughing, and singing that caused the problems, Cliff uses that as an excuse to twist Lou's arm until she yields to his way of seeing things. They argue about whether Lou is "Ethiopian" or "Hottentot," then settle down comfortably as the scene shifts to "the Avenue," where Red, Bama, Lou's sister Doris, and Ray's current girl, Bunny Gillette, spar then pair off.

Back on Derby Street, Cliff and Lou tease Ray as he returns from the Krumps' house. The talk turns to Cliff's troubled stint in the Navy, during which he spent most of his time in the guardhouse. Discussion of Ray's drinking, which started at home before his alcoholic mother died, leads to long angry speeches from Cliff and Lou, delivered loudly and simultaneously. Ray expresses his desire to join the Navy, of which Cliff approves but Lou does not. Ray wants to enlist, as Cliff did, when he turns sixteen; his birthday is just a week away. The resulting argument continues in spite of Cliff's slapping Lou—an action repeated when the scene shifts to the Avenue as Red slaps Bunny in the middle of an argument that ends when Doris draws her knife.

The scene shifts back to the stoop, where Ray is apologizing to Lou for causing the fight with Cliff; however, discussion of Lou's pregnancy and Cliff's refusal to get a job make clear that Ray is not the cause of the Dawsons' problem. Lou defines a man as one like her father, who worked with his hands and "brought us up to take pride in ourselves and to fear God." Cliff rejects her definition: "I am not a beast . . . an animal to be used for the plows of the world. But if I am then I'll act like one." He will not be domesticated or allow Lou to tame Ray, who must have a chance at "the world." The act ends with Lou's repeated refusal to sign papers for Ray to join the Navy.

Act 2 focuses on Ray and Cliff discussing Derby Street women. Ray talks about his affair with Bunny and their love for each other, unaware that she is two-timing him with Red. Then Ray tells Cliff about the girl described in the prologue. His story is interrupted by a fantasy sequence on the Avenue: Red and Bama dance around the girl until Bunny and Doris interrupt with a dance of "symbolic castration." Ray and Cliff's talk turns to Lou, who is different, Cliff says, because she has character. The group grows with the entrance of Tiny, a girl with whom Cliff has been having an affair, and Silly Willy Clark. The men decide that it is time for serious drinking and go to buy another jug of wine.

When act 3 opens, forty-five minutes have passed and the Dawsons' stoop is crowded; Lou and Tiny have been joined by Doris, Bunny, Red, and Bama. Lou is trying to keep the party under control, without much success, and when she learns of Tiny and Cliff's affair, she gives up the effort in disgust. Cliff, Ray, and Silly Willy return with a half-empty jug of wine, and the arguments grow until Miss Minny calls the police. Bunny tells Ray she's Red's girl now, and Red hands Ray a wine bottle into which he has urinated, precipitating a fight. When Red pulls a knife, Ray grabs his arm and they fight their way into the alley, followed by Doris, then Cliff. The policeman called by Miss Minny arrives in time to see Ray and Doris emerge from the alley with blood on their clothes. Cliff enters and takes responsibility for killing Red, leaving Ray free; Cliff exhorts him to go claim the world that is his.

Themes and Meanings

In the Wine Time provides an uncompromising picture of life among the African Americans Ed Bullins knows best—the urban poor in the ghettos of Northeastern cities. Space in the play has a confined, claustrophobic quality, representing the narrow choices and lack of power of the characters, which is consistent with the naturalistic view of humans as animals shaped by environmental pressures that they cannot control and of which they are not fully aware. However, Bullins breaks from naturalism in portraying his characters as having certain limited choices. By contrasting various ways that African Americans react to living under pressure from the largely invisible white majority, Bullins makes a clear case for the reaction that he considers appropriate—refusing to play the game.

In this play as in others by Bullins, the women present obstacles to the black men who try to reject societal pressure. Miss Minny Garrison, for example, acts in the "approved" manner. Gospel music symbolizes her commitment to the religion of the whites, and she tries to function as moral arbiter of the neighborhood—initiating petitions to get rid of the "undesirable" Dawsons, trying to direct Ray's behavior, and, when the final party gets out of hand, calling in the white police.

Lou puts a different kind of pressure on her men. She tries to talk Cliff into taking the menial, low-paying jobs that are available to him so that he will be a "good" father for their unborn child; she refuses to sign the papers that would allow Ray his one means of escape—joining the Navy.

Cliff, who manages to resist these pressures, serves as a model and a mouthpiece for Bullins's black nationalist views. In response to Lou's comments about jobs and pride, he explodes, "I'm goin' ta get me part of that [big, rich] world or stare your God in the eye and scream *why*. I am not a beast . . . an animal to be used for the plows of the world. But if I am then I'll act like one, I'll be one and turn this . . . world of dreams and lies and fairy tales into a jungle or a desert."

Some critics have connected the themes and characters in Bullins's work to the blues music that runs through *In the Wine Time*, associated with Lou and Cliff. Like the blues, this play details the painful black experience as a way to transcend it and turn it into an affirmation of African American life. Bullins spares his audience little, focusing on the strong language, the violent relationships, the escape found in alcohol. However, through Cliff, he portrays rebellion against those who would control the black man, including the black women he loves, as positive, even transcendent.

Critics, who have noted that Bullins's plays do not have much plot and that his characters do not achieve their dreams, complain that the ending of *In the Wine Time* is too melodramatic, with too much action. The ending is contrived and violent, but it also offers a sense of hope. Cliff sacrifices his own future, taking responsibility for Red's murder so that Ray may have his chance to escape, to claim his part of the larger world. This finish is consistent with both the environment that Bullins has created and the message that Cliff has delivered throughout the play.

Dramatic Devices

In the Wine Time takes a naturalistic approach, presenting a slice of black life in the urban ghetto. The characters are indigenous to this ghetto, street-smart hustlers engaged in aimless activities—casual sex, serious drinking. The major characters are well developed. The language is realistic, slangy, and often scatological; Bullins has been praised by a wide variety of commentators for his ability to capture the language of the street. Both the vivid scenes and strong language are offered without apology.

The use of the radio for background music is realistic, but the blues and the disc jockey's patter also underscore themes in the play. It's "one of them [hot] nights fo' bein' wit' the one ya loves," the disc jockey comments. "Yeah, burnin' up this evenin'." As the blues are played, Bullins presents characters whose love stories could be taken from blues songs—the two-timing woman, the man trying to forget the limitations of his life with wine and other women.

In addition to the "blues people," some have observed that Bullins's characters have roots in the black oral folk tradition—the trickster and the "bad nigger." The women characters, while realistically developed, also symbolize various aspects of the dominant black matriarch. Miss Minny is closest to the stereotype, with her reliance on the Christian religion and her efforts to control events in her neighborhood, but Lou also fits the type when she tries to pressure Cliff and Ray to conform to her wishes.

Within this basically naturalistic play, Bullins uses devices that show the influence of expressionism. Ray's lyrical prologue, which flashes back to the last "wine time," reveals his inner feelings. Here the language is elevated and the rhythm flowing; it stands in stark contrast to the naturalistic dialogue that follows. In other places, the disjointed dialogue, which illustrates the characters' inability to communicate, approaches the expressionists' telegraphic style. The two long speeches that Lou and Cliff deliver simultaneously are like the arias of expressionistic or absurdist plays, reflecting the characters' inner feelings and demonstrating their lack of connectedness. The fantasy dance sequence in act 2, with its "symbolic castration," also owes much to expressionism, although it is not as well integrated into the script as are the speeches.

Critical Context

In the Wine Time is one of numerous plays in which Bullins portrays the lives of African Americans of the northern urban ghetto. The playwright envisioned a cycle of twenty plays—the "Twentieth-Century Cycle"—portraying a number of interrelated black families whose history will stretch from the days of Marcus Garvey in the first half of the century to the "present."

In the Wine Time was the first cycle play to be finished; Bullins has since written a number of others. *In New England Winter* (pb. 1969, pr. 1971) is a sequel to *In the Wine Time*. Bullins bridges the seven- or eight-year gap between the two plays with a conversation between Cliff and his half brother Steve that reveals that Lou left Cliff before he returned from prison because she had a baby by another man. The action of this play centers on a single incident, the robbery of a finance company that is planned primarily by Steve, aided by Cliff and two other friends. Steve masterminds the robbery to get enough money to return to Liz, a girl he loved in his "New England winter."

The Corner (pr. 1968) recounts events leading up to *In the Wine Time*. Cliff is the central presence in this play, although he does not appear until the second half. He dominates the other characters and brutalizes Stella, his current lover. The play ends with Cliff revealing to Bummie that he is rejecting his friends and current way of life for Lou, who is pregnant with his child.

Other plays in Bullins's cycle include *The Duplex* (pr. 1970, pb. 1971) and *The Fabulous Miss Marie* (pr. 1971, pb. 1974). The major link between *The Duplex* and the earlier plays is Steve, Cliff's half brother and the main character in *In New England Winter*. This "black love fable in four movements" centers on a love triangle between Steve, his landlady Velma Best, and her brutal husband, O.D. Steve tries to break the cycle of violence and rescue Velma, but when he finally confronts O.D., he is badly beaten and forced to understand that he can only leave Velma with her husband.

Marie Horton, who plays a minor role in *The Duplex*, is the central character of *The Fabulous Miss Marie*. Action in the play, set in the early 1960's, is minimal; it centers on a party at Marie's, which features good times, good Scotch, and good sex but ignores the world outside, including the emerging Civil Rights movement. In this play, Bullins's emphasis is on depicting the lifestyle of the black middle class.

Although Bullins has written a number of nonrealistic plays, more didactic and more obviously tied to black nationalism and the black aesthetic with which he has been closely associated, it is his naturalist plays that have been most favorably received. Regardless of whether critics approve of the picture of black life that he presents, they generally concede that Bullins's portrayals are striking and effective and that he has made a unique contribution to the theater.

Sources for Further Study

Andrews, W. D. E. "Theater of Black Reality: The Blues Drama of Ed Bullins." *Southwest Review* 65 (Spring, 1980): 178-190.

Bullins, Ed. "An Interview with Ed Bullins: Black Theater." Interview by Marvin X. *Negro Digest* 18 (April, 1969): 9-16.

DiGaetani, John L. "Ed Bullins." In *A Search for a Postmodern Theater: Interviews with Contemporary Playwrights*. Westport, Conn.: Greenwood Press, 1991.

Hay, Samuel A. *Ed Bullins: A Literary Biography*. Detroit: Wayne State University Press, 1997.

Smitherman, Geneva. "Ed Bullins/Stage One: Everybody Wants to Know Why I Sing the Blues." *Black World* 23 (April, 1974): 4-13.

True, Warren R. "Ed Bullins, Anton Chekhov, and the 'Drama of Mood.'" *College Language Association Journal* 20 (June, 1977): 531-532.

Elsie Galbreath Haley

IN WHITE AMERICA

Author: Martin B. Duberman (1930-   )
Type of plot: History; epic theater
Time of plot: The mid-eighteenth century to 1964
Locale: United States
First produced: 1963, at the Sheridan Square Playhouse, New York City
First published: 1964

Principal characters:

SHIP'S DOCTOR, a man who describes the horror of the Middle
    Passage in the slave trade
A QUAKER, a woman who condemns the slave trade in Congress
THOMAS JEFFERSON, the former president troubled by slavery and
    race issues
THE REVEREND SAMUEL MAY, a minister who describes racist
    treatment of free blacks in Connecticut
MARY CHESNUT, the wife of a South Carolina senator, who
    describes the onset of the Civil War
COLONEL THOMAS HIGGINSON, the commander of the Union
    Army's first former-slave regiment
ELIZABETH BOTHUNE, a schoolteacher for the Freedman's
    Bureau
ANDREW JOHNSON, Abraham Lincoln's presidential successor
FREDERICK DOUGLASS, a chief spokesman for liberated slaves
MRS. TUTSON, a victim of Ku Klux Klan violence
BEN TILLMAN, a South Carolina senator opposed to antilynching
    laws
BOOKER T. WASHINGTON, a black leader who advocates a
    gradualist civil rights approach
W. E. B. DU BOIS, a black leader opposed to conciliation and
    gradualism
MONROE TROTTER, a black leader who denounced Woodrow
    Wilson's policy of segregating federal employees
MARCUS GARVEY, a black nationalist leader during the 1920's
GIRL, a high school student who attempts to integrate Central
    High School in Little Rock, Arkansas

The Play

A two-act play, *In White America* is divided into the century prior to the American Civil War and the century that followed the war's end. In epic style, it depicts the struggles of pre-Civil War abolitionist movements, the era of Reconstruction, early twentieth century racism and segregation, and the Civil Rights movement. As the curtain opens a white man reads the date from a newspaper (January 12, 1964) as the pros and cons of racial integration are debated among three black and three white characters. The opening scene concludes with the white man predicting violence and a black woman singing "Oh Freedom."

The play then begins its chronological story, drawing its text and characters from historical documents that the playwright notes are paraphrased only "where a word or two was absolutely necessary for clarity or transition." The action starts with African American slaves aboard a slave vessel in the mid-eighteenth century as the ship's doctor describes the horrid conditions faced by slaves during the Middle Passage. The horrific conditions described prompt a late seventeenth century Quaker woman to call for the abolition of the trade, while two congressmen debate the pros and cons of the petition. Although the petition is tabled by Congress, the audience watches Thomas Jefferson reflect on the issues involved and the place of African Americans in American life. He predicts that the hour of emancipation is approaching but concludes that the inferiority of blacks makes it impossible to govern them in the same manner as whites.

The living conditions of African American slaves, along with their worldview and their aspirations, are revealed in a number of slave interviews and letter exchanges between escaped slaves and their former masters. A white minister from Canterbury, Connecticut, Samuel May, describes one racist treatment of free blacks in the North: They are denied any form of organized schooling. Court statements by Nat Turner and John Brown, two eighteenth century men who used violence to fight slavery, are included in act 1, as are the statements of Sojourner Truth, an illiterate former slave who, in 1851, tied the antislavery struggle to the struggle to emancipate women.

As the Civil War's beginning looms, the cast sings a spiritual, "God's Gonna Set This World on Fire." The war years are covered only by two short diary entries: one by the wife of a South Carolina senator, Mary Boykin Chesnut, who voices suspicion of her house slaves in 1861 and 1863, and one from Thomas Higginson, the commander of the first former slave regiment called into the Union Army. Higginson's entries reveal the freedom fighter motives of three black volunteers. Act 1 concludes with a loud chorus of "From every mountainside, let freedom ring!"

As act 2 begins, white reaction to the Reconstruction era is viewed positively by a teacher for the Freedman's Bureau, Elizabeth Bothune, while a southern woman voices her fears about Yankee and black dominance. The audience witnesses prominent black leader Frederick Douglass eloquently pleading for civil rights, words that subsequently fall on the deaf ears of President Andrew Johnson, who lobbied for the emigration of blacks after emancipation.

Jumping several decades ahead to the early twentieth century, the audience watches congressional hearings detailing the actions of the Ku Klux Klan (KKK) and hears the horrid details of one of the KKK's torture victims, Mrs. Tutson. The audience then hears South Carolina senator Ben Tillman advocate the lynching of blacks accused of raping white women.

Historically, the issue of what actions to take regarding post-Reconstruction racism became a major concern of black leaders. The audience witnesses this decades-long struggle via a number of scenes with prominent black figures. For example, the audience sees Booker T. Washington advocating conciliation and encouraging blacks to gradually work their way up from the bottom, only to see his gradualist view attacked by W. E. B. Du Bois. Morris Trotter is seen criticizing President Woodrow Wilson's decision to segregate the Federal Civil Service in 1914 and getting evicted from the White House for daring to question the president. In the 1920's frustration grows as Marcus Garvey, a black nationalist, decides to launch a "back to Africa" movement after World War I to reestablish black pride. In the early 1930's Father Divine launches a black church self-help movement in an effort to beat back the ravages of the Great Depression.

The last documents used in the play bring the action to the rural American South during the Great Depression, where a type of sharecropping borders on virtual slavery, and where an army preparing to fight World War II is as segregated as those who fought the Civil War. The last dramatic scene shows a teenage girl facing an angry white mob and nearly being lynched after attempting to integrate Central High School in Little Rock, Arkansas. The tearful teenager is saved by a white man who comforts her and puts her on a bus to escape the danger.

The play ends with the cast reflecting on centuries of struggle to achieve basic things in life such as a cup of coffee at a lunch counter, a decent job, and political rights. They agree that gradualism can be tolerated no more and the time for change is now. The play concludes with an actor reading an excerpt from the preamble to the Constitution, while a singer performs the last verse of "Oh Freedom."

Themes and Meanings

In White America is a historical play that provides a sweeping overview of how racism, directed against African Americans, affected both blacks and whites from colonial times to the immediate aftermath of the landmark *Brown v. Board of Education* decision of 1954. The play is a skillful blending of narration, documents, dialogue, and song designed to raise the historical consciousness of the audience. It is the story of individual black Americans throughout American history, who, as the author states, "managed to endure as men while being defined as property." In this, Martin Duberman achieves his stated objective of combining "the evocative power of the spoken word with the confirming power of the historical fact."

Clearly the hypocrisy of white America is a dominant theme running throughout the play. Lofty ideals of "unalienable rights" proclaimed at the nation's birth were in direct opposition to real conditions faced by African Americans first shackled by slavery and then lashed by Jim Crow laws and racial segregation in post-Civil War America. This hypocrisy is reflected not only by congressmen and senators but also by presidents like Thomas Jefferson, Andrew Johnson, and Woodrow Wilson.

However, the play's major theme is the quest for freedom and equality. Historically, slaves' aspirations for freedom expressed in spirituals were manifested by such "escape routes" as the Underground Railroad, Nat Turner's Revolt, and fighting in the Civil War. Aiding in this effort were abolitionist Quakers, northern journalists and schoolteachers, and militant abolitionists such as John Brown.

After slavery, freedom meant a long struggle against institutionalized racism in order to achieve equality. Leading African American figures developed different solutions over time to achieve real freedom, and black citizens struggled against Jim Crow laws, the slavelike conditions of sharecropping, KKK terrorism, and lynching mania. In all, the play shows the progress toward freedom to be very gradual and incomplete by the mid-twentieth century.

As the audience is drawn into the emotional cataclysm of one black teenager's experience in attempting to integrate a Little Rock high school, they are forced to confront the theme that gradual and token change in regard to civil rights, at least in the deep South, has not achieved a great deal. The entire cast reiterates the theme that change is long overdue and the time for action to bring about racial equality is now.

Dramatic Devices

The play is a carefully crafted synthesis of document excerpts, dialogue, background narration, and powerful spirituals designed to sensitize the audience to the two-hundred-year struggle of African Americans. Words spoken in the play are powerful because they draw from historical truth.

Dividing the cast along color lines is effective in showing, at the beginning of the play, differences in opinion, and at the play's conclusion, uniformity in the belief that racial equality is long overdue. The use of the cast in portraying longer scenes drawn from social history (for example, slave life, common soldier and sharecropper interviews, the integration of Central High School) reinforces the humanistic element. Historical documents provide the material for constructing more numerous but much shorter scenes.

While real historical figures fade rapidly into the background as the play zooms across the period of two centuries, the one figure who remains in the audience's mind is that brave and overwhelmed teenager caught in the midst of the school integration crisis. The innocence of youth, the law, and the impartial rationality of justice must be protected from the forces of irrational hatred, fear, and injustice. The audience is brought to the realization that they are at a historical turning point. There is no longer time to rationalize about gradual progress. They can either assist the hate-crazed mob or take action to change white America into an equally blended America.

Critical Context

In White America was an immediate success both nationally and internationally. It received rave reviews by critics and standing ovations from enthusiastic audiences. Clearly it was the right play at the right time. Duberman won the Vernon Rice Drama Desk Award for the play. The play also contributed to his winning of the National Academy of Arts and Letters special citation for contributions to literature in 1971.

A few critics found the play better as a piece of research than an act of creative playwriting. They pointed to its reading like the Federal Theater's *Living Newspaper* or like a term paper. Duberman considered updating the play but became disenchanted with the lack of openness to social change: There was no model he could follow to change the play. He soon found fiction to be a better medium in which to accelerate social change, and the promotion of gay rights to be of primary importance. The play has undergone numerous productions since 1963. Because it teaches an important overview of African American history in a memorable way, the play continues to be performed in both regional and academic theaters.

Sources for Further Study

Cain, Paul D. *Leading the Parade: Conversations with America's Most Influential Lesbians and Gay Men.* Lanham, Md.: Scarecrow Press, 2002.

Dawson, Gary Fisher. *Documentary Theatre in the United States: An Historical Survey and Analysis of Its Content, Form, and Stagecraft.* Westport, Conn.: Greenwood Press, 1999.

Duberman, Martin, ed. *The Antislavery Vanguard: New Essays on the Abolitionists.* Princeton, N.J.: Princeton University Press, 1965.

_____. *The Uncompleted Past.* New York: Random House, 1969.

Finkbine, Roy E., ed. *Sources of the African American Past.* Reading, Mass.: Addison Wesley, 1996.

Franklin, John H., and Alfred Moss, Jr. *From Slavery to Freedom: A History of African Americans.* New York: Knopf, 2000.

Robinson, Paul A. *Gay Lives: Homosexual Autobiography from John Addington Symonds to Paul Monette.* Chicago: University of Chicago Press, 1999.

Irwin Halfond

INADMISSIBLE EVIDENCE

Author: John Osborne (1929-1994)
Type of plot: Psychological; naturalistic
Time of plot: The 1960's
Locale: London
First produced: 1964, at the Royal Court Theatre, London
First published: 1965

> *Principal characters:*
> BILL MAITLAND, a solicitor
> HUDSON, his managing clerk
> JONES, his clerk
> LIZ, his mistress
> JANE, his daughter
> SHIRLEY and
> JOY, his secretaries
> MRS. ANDERSON,
> MRS. GARNSEY,
> MAPLES, and
> MRS. TONKS, his clients

The Play

Inadmissible Evidence begins as three characters—Bill Maitland, one of Her Majesty's judges, and a clerk of the court—"come to some sort of life out of the blur of dream." In this nightmarish dream prologue, Bill's law office is temporarily metamorphosed into a courtroom where Bill is a prisoner on trial "for having unlawfully and wickedly made known, and caused to be procured and made known a wicked, bawdy and scandalous object." Bill's own life is the depersonalized "object" that is being tried. Bill pleads "not guilty" and, when asked to swear and affirm, ironically states, in bureaucratic jargon, his belief in "the technological revolution" and its attendant benefits and ills.

Bill is asked to proceed to his defense before the prosecution has made its case. He provides a rather disjointed history of his law career, asserts that he is indecisive, and confesses that he has "depended almost entirely on other people's efforts." Bill states that he had hoped only "to have the good fortune of friendship" and the "love of women"; he believes, however, that he hardly succeeded with the first and that he inflicted "more pain than pleasure" with the second.

As the dream ends, Bill emerges into consciousness and enters his office, where he addresses sexual innuendoes to Shirley, his secretary, and is hostile to Jones, his clerk. As a perfunctory apology for being late, Bill explains that he could not get a taxi, the first of many references he makes to not being noticed. As he prepares for Mrs. Garnsey's visit, he tells Hudson about his private life with Liz, his mistress, and repeatedly asks him why he has foisted Mrs. Garnsey off on him. Hudson's answer: "I'd say divorce was *your* line." Act 2 will demonstrate the ties between Bill's own precarious marriage and the failed marriages of his clients.

Before his first appointment, Bill speaks on the telephone to Anna, his wife, and to Liz, his mistress, then learns from Shirley, who is pregnant, that she is giving her notice. As the morning continues to deteriorate, Bill asks Hudson to become his partner, only to learn that Hudson is himself thinking of leaving. Mrs. Garnsey's comments about leaving her husband also ironically intensify Bill's growing isolation, as the parallels between her husband and Bill are painfully obvious: "I know that nothing really works for him. Not at the office, not his friends, not even his girls." The comment paraphrases Bill's own earlier comments about friendship and love; when Mrs. Garnsey adds that her husband is being ignored, the audience is reminded of the taxi driver who ignored Bill. When he sees that Mrs. Garnsey is quite upset, he is himself paralyzed and has Joy remove his client from the office.

Act 2 begins with Bill again struggling frantically to wake up, and the stage directions describe his behavior as apprehensive and cautious as he answers the telephone—the most significant prop on the set. The stage directions describe the subsequent telephone conversations as ambiguous, some of them resembling the unreal dream at the beginning of act 1, some of them seeming more realistic. The telephone calls also punctuate Bill's meetings with his clients, most of whom are women seeking divorce—one actor plays Mrs. Garnsey, Mrs. Tonks, and Mrs. Anderson.

In the interval between the end of act 1 and the beginning of act 2, Bill has had Joy stay after work, and their sexual union has been interrupted by the appearance of his wife. When Hudson again postpones the partnership decision, and even the despised Jones is reluctant to make a commitment to Bill's firm, Bill learns that his situation has grown more desperate. As Mrs. Tonks reads her divorce petition, Bill associates himself with Mr. Tonks, "a man of excessive sexual appetite," and then proceeds to "read" his own petition, which criticizes his wife's behavior and justifies his own. Joy again removes the client, who is replaced by Mrs. Anderson, who details her husband's failures. Her criticism prompts Bill's defensiveness as he attempts to rationalize his gradual estrangement from his wife; Mrs. Anderson is also removed by Joy.

Bill then tries to contact Winters, a colleague, but he cannot reach him, which reinforces his growing paranoia (he suspects that Hudson is with Winters) and suspicion that he is being ignored. Although his daughter Jane arrives to see him, Bill meets first with his next client, Maples, who has been charged with homosexual acts. Though the parallels are more metaphoric than literal, Bill does identify with Maples: "I should think Sir Watkin Glover Q.C. is sure to apply the full rigor of the law and send the both of us down."

When Jane finally enters to listen to his lengthy attack on her, her generation, and himself, it is clear why Bill has kept her waiting. She embodies the amoral world of progress that he claimed to affirm in the dream scene of act 1; the "you" he addresses is plural, not singular. After Jane and Bill "elude" each other and she leaves, Joy enters, but only to inform Bill that she will be taking tomorrow off. The last person to appear is Liz, who tells him that she needs him even as she accepts the inevitability of their parting. As the play ends, Bill is speaking to his wife on the phone, asking her not to come to the office and telling her that he will stay there, where someone, perhaps the Law Society, will eventually come.

Themes and Meanings

Inadmissible Evidence provides "evidence" that could not come before a court in which a man was being charged with the "obscenity" of merely being. The play chronicles two days in the life of Bill Maitland, whose self-destructiveness and self-deprecation bring about his isolation from a society with which he is at odds. As the play progresses, Bill's personal and professional lives reach their nadir: His women desert him and his associates abandon him, leaving him alone to await the arrival of "someone"—perhaps the Law Society, which will prosecute him for legal improprieties. Thus, the ending of the play fulfills in part the dream beginning of the play.

John Osborne ties Bill's isolation and impending breakdown to a failure to relate and communicate, a recurrent theme in his plays. The society that Bill scorns is insensitive, bent on subduing the world and achieving technological progress and affluence without regard to human cost. Bill maintains that a "clattering brute of a computer" will replace lawyers: "There'll be no more laws' delays, just the insolence of somebody's office." By having Bill paraphrase part of Hamlet's famous soliloquy, Osborne suggests ties between the two tragic protagonists: both rail against corrupt societies, both seem afflicted with a malaise that prevents meaningful constructive action, and both alienate those whom they love. Though Bill demands love, he cannot give it or express it, even to those who declare their love for him; though he speaks most of the lines in the play, he says little that is not ironic, contradictory, or tangential.

Bill's compulsive outbursts, which often express Osborne's own social criticism, may be seen as a means of asserting his own identity, which he believes is threatened; his equally compulsive sexual activity may be read as his defense against a sense of increasing impotence. He tells Jane, "They're all pretending to ignore me. No they're not pretending, they are!" Though he is nominally in charge of the firm, Bill's ranting, his insulting remarks, and his sexual conquests are treated with quiet contempt by Hudson, and rather than being the head of his family, he is a man forgotten by his own parents.

Bill knows that he has brought about his own fate, and his self-awareness does in part redeem him. Although his evidence does not acquit him, it does explain his behavior, which pales in comparison to the collective evil perpetrated by a corrupt society. Despite his sexual immorality and shady legal practices, Bill engages the audience's empathy because he does experience guilt—something missing in Jane's generation. In fact, Bill's behavior with Jane and Liz seems more insensitive and callous than it in fact is. Knowing that he can go on hurting Jane, whom Liz says he loves most, Bill lets her "elude" him, allowing her to pursue a lifestyle he despises. Similarly, when he senses that Liz desires to end their relationship, he takes the initiative, leaving her with her illusions about her commitment. It is not these acts of questionable kindness, however, that elicit the audience's sympathy. It is rather the audience's sense that Bill's fears about identity, mediocrity, and isolation are their fears as well, that they also are powerless speculators in an impersonal technological society.

Dramatic Devices

Osborne's play is both naturalistic and experimental, both dream and reality. The play begins with a dream trial reminiscent of Franz Kafka's *Der Prozess* (1925; *The Trial*, 1937), becomes naturalistic as the office routine is dramatized, and then, in act 2, vacillates between naturalism and stylization as Bill interviews his clients. Osborne's stage directions concerning Bill's telephone conversations indicate that the play's ambiguity is deliberately contrived, that the audience cannot be sure what is real and what (or who) exists only in Bill's mind. The telephone itself is a symbol of communication, a link to the outside world, but Bill's ability to communicate lessens as the play unfolds. Anna, Bill's wife, never appears onstage; she exists only on the phone.

Osborne insists upon a similar ambiguity for the "duologues," the alternating monologues that replace dialogue as Bill interviews his clients. The stylization of the duologues is enhanced by the device of having the same actor play the three female clients and the same actor play Jones and Maples. Bill is forced to reenact his failed marriage, first with Mrs. Garnsey, then with Mrs. Tonks, and then with Mrs. Anderson; when he interviews Mrs. Anderson, there is no semblance of dialogue—the audience watches the two characters take turns speaking in a dramatic stream of consciousness. The clients are not important as characters, but as vehicles for prompting Bill's memories. As soon as Joy removes one of the women, an identical woman returns, reminding him again of his own marriage. There is, as Bill knows, no escape.

Having the same actor play Jones, whom Bill despises, and Maples, the homosexual, as well as the clerk in the dream trial, enables Osborne to reinforce the impossibility of Bill's escape and to demonstrate the ties between Bill's conduct and his trial. As Bill observes, Jones would make a good witness, primarily because he has experienced Bill's insensitive taunting. Hudson, the judge of the dream sequence, acts as the evaluator of Bill's actions during the play. In fact, Hudson's decision to leave Bill to take a position with Piffards suggests that he has "convicted" Bill of the charges.

Bill's uncharacteristic sensitivity and understanding in his interview with Maples serves to identify Bill with Maples. Both men are becoming increasingly isolated and both face impending persecution by an unsympathetic society. Osborne's stage directions call for Maples to give his evidence "like Bill himself." Thus, Bill and Maples are linked theatrically as well as psychologically, and Maples's defense also becomes Bill's. Bill understandably counsels Maples to plead guilty, as he has accepted his own guilt and conviction, a judgment that he actually desired. As the curtain falls, Bill waits to be punished for his crimes, and the audience waits with him.

Critical Context

Although Osborne's best-known play is *Look Back in Anger* (pr. 1956), the drama that epitomized the "angry young man" genre, that topical play remains rooted in the 1960's. Despite the popularity of *The Entertainer* (pr., pb. 1957) and the notoriety of *Luther* (pr., pb. 1961), the play most likely to be considered Osborne's best is *Inadmissible Evidence*, which transcends its 1960's social criticism and portrays the plight of the individual at odds with society. *Inadmissible Evidence* draws upon Osborne's previous plays, particularly *Look Back in Anger* and *The Entertainer:* Jimmy Porter is also critical of society and does ironically invite the abandonment he fears; Archie Rice also awaits his fate, the tax man—a counterpart of the Law Society. On the other hand, Bill is mature and mainstream, more akin to an audience which feels mediocre, alienated, and persecuted. For many critics, *Inadmissible Evidence* represents the culmination of Osborne's considerable talent and the perfect blending of naturalism and experimentation. Osborne excelled at probing the psychological depths of complex, somewhat unappealing characters caught at a crucial point in their lives; the stylized duologues and casting of *Inadmissible Evidence* permitted him to present an external drama that mirrors the action that occurs within his protagonist's mind.

Many critics regard Osborne's later plays as departures from the fusion of form and content of his masterpiece. *Inadmissible Evidence* was the last play in which one character dominated the action; the play has even been referred to as a "monodrama." The later plays have muted the anger and intensity of *Inadmissible Evidence*, and they have not been as successful at incorporating Osborne's gratuitous social criticism into the dramatic text. *Inadmissible Evidence*, despite the topicality of its specific criticism, remains a play thoroughly modern and universal in its protagonist and its conflict between the individual and an impersonal yet paradoxically hostile society.

Sources for Further Study

Anderson, Michael. *Anger and Detachment: A Study of Arden, Osborne, and Pinter.* London: Pitman, 1976.
Denison, Patricia D., ed. *John Osborne: A Casebook.* New York: Garland, 1997.
Ferrar, Harold. *John Osborne.* New York: Columbia University Press, 1973.
Gilleman, Lu. *The Hideous Honesty of John Osborne: The Politics of Vituperation.* New York: Garland, 2000.
Goldstone, Herbert. *Coping with Vulnerability: The Achievement of John Osborne.* Washington, D.C.: University Press of America, 1982.
Hayman, Ronald. *John Osborne.* New York: Ungar, 1972.
Hinchliffe, Arnold P. *John Osborne.* Boston: Twayne, 1984.
Page, Malcolm, and Simon Trussler. *File on Osborne.* London: Methuen, 1988.
Taylor, John Russell. "John Osborne." In *Contemporary Dramatists.* 6th ed. Detroit: St. James, 1999.
Trussler, Simon. *The Plays of John Osborne: An Assessment.* London: Gollancz, 1969.

Thomas L. Erskine

INCIDENT AT VICHY

Author: Arthur Miller (1915-   )
Type of plot: Social realism
Time of plot: 1942
Locale: Vichy, France
First produced: 1964, at the ANTA-Washington Square Theatre, New York City
First published: 1965

> *Principal characters:*
> LEBEAU, a painter
> BAYARD, an electrician
> MARCHAND, a businessman
> MONCEAU, an actor
> LEDUC, a psychoanalyst
> VON BERG, an Austrian prince

The Play

   Incident at Vichy is a one-act play that takes place in a detention room in Vichy, France, during the German Occupation. When the curtain opens, the stage reveals a grim setting with little furniture except for a long bench upon which sit six men and a young boy. In the playwright's words, these characters are "frozen there like members of a small orchestra at the moment before they begin to play." In the course of the drama, each man anticipates and experiences a dreaded event: his being called into the office of the Nazi captain who is conducting an interrogation and checking identification papers to determine whether the detainee is Jewish. Before each summons, the characters demonstrate their mounting terror, fearful that the interrogation will result in their slaughter.

   During the tense moments between interrogations, the detainees discuss their fears, their disbelief that their countrymen are detaining them, their alternating desire to flee and inability to escape for fear of being killed in the process. Each character reveals his own value system, from Marchand and his capitalistic businessman's attitude to Prince Von Berg, who had fled Austria and rejected Nazism because of its vulgarity. Marchand's and Von Berg's summonses produce the same result: a white pass that means freedom. The reasons for the passes and the uses of those passes, however, are radically different.

   Marchand's words and actions suggest that, just as he had lived by a mercenary, heartless value system, so he was able to save his life by resorting to that same system and purchasing his freedom. When he leaves the place of detention, displaying his white pass, he leaves behind detainees who, except for Von Berg, can neither buy their freedom nor talk their way out of their eventual destruction.

Von Berg, a nobleman who had been detained because of his accent, is different from Marchand and also from the other captives. He is neither a heartless individual nor a Jew; he is a person who is struggling with the question of guilt and responsibility. He is troubled by the comments of the psychiatrist Leduc, who challenges him to assume responsibility for the atrocities being perpetrated by the Nazis. Von Berg insists that he has never said a word against the Jewish people, but Leduc asserts that it is not only verbal abuse that leads to culpability; the very human condition, according to Leduc, requires all people to assume responsibility for human brutality.

When Von Berg emerges from his interrogation with a white pass in his hand, he gives the doctor his pass, thus sacrificing himself to free the psychiatrist. As he leaves, Leduc's gestures reveal that he is aware of his own guilt, indicating that both he and Von Berg recognize that human beings share responsibility and guilt for their actions and the actions of other human beings. In the last moment of the play, a new group of detainees arrives to occupy the bench and observe Von Berg silently staring into the eyes of his Nazi captor and murderer.

Themes and Meanings

Incident at Vichy is a morality play that questions the tendency among human beings to evade complexity and elude confrontations with evil and thus to avoid responsibility for that complexity and evil. The words and actions of each character reveal some aspect of this moral dilemma.

The businessman Marchand views the process of detention and interrogation not as a prelude to human destruction but as a simple procedure for identifying people with false papers. The painter Lebeau announces that the measuring of people's noses on the streets has to do with a labor shortage: The Occupied Forces need people to carry stones. The actor Monceau explains that trains carrying Jews are simply transporting volunteers to work in Germany. Even Prince Von Berg, who recognizes the vulgarity and brutality of the Nazis, does not see his cousin Baron Kessler as the person whom Leduc knows—a Nazi who helped remove all the Jewish doctors from a medical school. Collectively, the detainees represent those human beings who, for various reasons, refuse to see evil and destruction in the world around them and therefore avoid responsibility for that evil and destruction.

Blinded to this reality, the characters participate in a victimizer/victim syndrome in which the entrapped victim seeks out another person to entrap and victimize. Thus, two nameless characters—the Gypsy and the Old Jew—are victimized by their fellow detainees, and the Major who is guarding the detainees speaks of his own entrapment. Holding a revolver to the head of Leduc, the Major speaks to the loss of humanity when all people are simultaneously victims and victimizers: "Tell me how . . . how there can be persons any more. I have you at the end of this revolver—*indicates the Professor*—he has me—and somebody has him—and somebody has somebody else."

Part of the difficulty in destroying this syndrome of victim becoming victimizer is that the characters rely too heavily upon logic and rationality in their efforts to understand the nature of the syndrome and the presence of evil. Two characters whose professions force them to deal with intuition and the unconscious—the painter Lebeau and the psychiatrist Leduc—speak often of the need to recognize the absurd illogic of suffering and the limitations of reason and intellect. Lebeau compares the meaninglessness of suffering to the lack of logical meaning in his painting. Instead of asking what his paintings mean, he says, people should look at them. In other words, instead of seeking neat, reasonable explanations, they should see with the mind's eye that not all paintings have meanings, not all problems have solutions. Similarly, Leduc comments that logic can be immobilizing and warns his fellow detainees of that paralysis: "You cannot wager your life on a purely rational analysis of this situation. Listen to your feelings: you must certainly *feel* the danger here."

Prince Von Berg ultimately feels the danger and acts with nobility and idealism when he sacrifices his life for Leduc's. He announces his belief in ideals before he goes into the interrogation. He asserts this belief angrily: "There are people who would find it easier to die than stain one finger with this murder. They exist. I swear it to you. People for whom everything is *not* permitted, foolish people and ineffectual, but they do exist and will not dishonor their tradition."

Von Berg does not dishonor his tradition. He courageously identifies the need for idealism and the fact that this idealism is, in a tragic sense, both noble and "ineffectual." The nobility is clear: One man sacrifices his life for another. This sacrifice has no effect, however, upon the perpetual victim/victimizer syndrome that is dramatically represented by the final moments of *Incident at Vichy*. One man is saved through the sacrifice of another, but another line of detainees arrives, none of whom will likely have a Prince Von Berg who will die for them. Thus, this morality play both affirms and questions idealism, leaving its audience with sacrificial gain and sacrificial loss, with hope for a human race that produces a Prince Von Berg but despair over human beings who detain and destroy one another.

Dramatic Devices

Incident at Vichy is a modern morality play. Like a medieval morality play, Arthur Miller's drama has characters who are allegorical, embodying abstract virtues and vices. Thus, when Dr. Leduc acknowledges that he and his fellow detainees are "symbols," he is speaking about the qualities they embody and represent. This representation is presented most dramatically when the curtain falls, and good and evil, in the characters of the idealistic prince and the brutal Nazi, are staring at each other, symbolizing the confrontational duality of humankind.

In addition to these two characters—and others—who represent virtues and vices, *Incident at Vichy* includes the symbolic use of objects, not all of which have single explanations. The Gypsy and the Old Jew, themselves symbols of universal victims, refuse to divest themselves of, respectively, a pot and a bundle when they are called in for interrogation. Each object seems to be representative of a value that these oppressed detainees cherish: The Gypsy has fixed the pot, and so it is his, and the Old Jew has likely plucked the feathers from his own chickens, and so the bundle of feathers is similarly his. In a universe in which characters are displaced from their property and distanced from their family and friends, these objects represent futile efforts to cling to the familiar and the beloved. The pot is broken and the bundle of feathers is torn open by a Nazi, in one more demonstration of the destructive power of human force.

Critical Context

Incident at Vichy follows the pattern Arthur Miller established in his earlier and greatest play, *Death of a Salesman* (pr., pb. 1949), and developed in subsequent dramas such as *The Crucible* (pr., pb. 1953) and *A View from the Bridge* (pr., pb. 1955). In these plays, Miller takes up the theme of individual guilt and commitment within the tradition of Greek tragedy. Concerned with creating tragic drama in an age which appears to have no classical tragic heroes, Miller explored the possibilities of bourgeois tragedy. In an essay titled "Tragedy and the Common Man," he argued that the modern age called for a new kind of tragic drama, which he aimed to produce.

While *Incident at Vichy* may not be considered his best example of such modern tragedy, it is an excellent demonstration of Miller's ongoing attempt to redefine the classical genre in terms of contemporary issues. Thus, his effort to examine Nazi genocide through the actions of his tragic heroes and villains has an important place in his artistic canon.

Miller's plays and essays continually call attention to the moral dilemmas facing contemporary society. His essay "On Social Plays," his introduction to the 1955 version of *A View from the Bridge*, and his introduction to his *Collected Plays* (1957) all give voice to the clarion call to view drama as a public way to raise questions at the heart of twentieth century civilization.

Sources for Further Study

Bigsby, C. W. E., ed. *File on Miller.* London: Methuen, 1988.

Corrigan, Robert W., ed. *Arthur Miller: A Collection of Critical Essays.* Englewood Cliffs, N.J.: Prentice-Hall, 1969.

Martin, Robert, ed. *Arthur Miller: New Perspectives.* Englewood Cliffs, N.J.: Prentice-Hall, 1982.

Moss, Leonard. *Arthur Miller.* Rev. ed. Boston: G. K. Hall, 1980.

Murray, Edward. *Arthur Miller, Dramatist.* New York: Ungar, 1967.

Roudane, Matthew C., ed. *Conversations with Arthur Miller.* Jackson: University of Mississippi Press, 1987.

Schlueter, June, and James K. Flanagan. *Arthur Miller.* New York: Ungar, 1987.

Welland, Dennis Sydney Reginald. *Miller: The Playwright.* 3d rev. ed. London: Methuen, 1985.

Marjorie Smelstor

THE INCREASED DIFFICULTY OF CONCENTRATION

Author: Václav Havel (1936-   )
Type of plot: Comedy
Time of plot: The mid-twentieth century
Locale: A flat in Czechoslovakia
First produced: 1968, at the Balustrade Theatre, Prague
First published: Ztížená možnost soustředění, 1968 (English translation, 1969)

> *Principal characters:*
> DR. EDUARD HUML, a social scientist
> VLASTA HUML, his wife
> RENATA, his mistress
> BLANKA, his secretary
> ANNA BALCAR, a social scientist
> KAREL KRIEBL, a technician
> EMIL MACHAL, a surveyor
> MR. BECK, a supervisor

The Play

The Increased Difficulty of Concentration opens on an empty stage set of Dr. Huml's flat. Mrs. Huml enters carrying a tray with breakfast for two. She wears a dressing gown. Huml, in pajamas, asks for honey; she ignores him and accuses him of failing again. He replies that conditions were not right and asks again for honey. She says, "In the cupboard." When he complains from offstage that he cannot find it, she jumps up and runs offstage, presumably to locate the honey.

Almost immediately Huml backs in, fully dressed, from his study, tiptoes to the same rear door Mrs. Huml just walked through, and stealthily leads Renata to the front door, kissing her as he sneaks her out. He goes back to the study door and ushers in Anna Balcar and Karel Kriebl, wearing lab coats, carefully carrying Puzuk, a machine, between them. They explain that information on Huml has been fed into Puzuk, which is about to ask Huml his first question.

Kriebl fusses with the machine, working on its keyboard, turning its crank, peering into its eyepiece. Balcar calls for the first question. Puzuk rumbles. Machal enters and takes measurements of the room, then writes a measurement on a piece of paper, which Kriebl feeds to Puzuk. Machal exits. Then the same business with crank and buttons and rumbles and a call for silence—Puzuk's red button goes on. It is overheated and must be cooled in Huml's refrigerator. Then its siren goes off. Now it is cold, and Balcar and Kriebl run out the back door to Puzuk.

Huml starts toward them, but Renata, wearing Mrs. Huml's apron, enters from the same back door, carrying a tray with lunch, a stew. They argue because Huml has not told his wife that their marriage must end. She locks herself in the study. Then Blanka comes through the study door to continue taking dictation from Huml. He is dictating a pedantic work on values, specifically, man's needs and notions of happiness. Blanka goes to the kitchen; Huml follows her. Mr. and Mrs. Huml's offstage voices indicate that she has found the honey.

Back at the breakfast table, they discuss Huml's telling Renata that their affair must end. Mrs. Huml leaves for work, giving instructions about the lunch stew that the audience has already seen. Balcar and Kriebl return with Puzuk and go through the same business. This time Beck interrupts pointlessly; the red button goes on because Puzuk is cold; they take Puzuk to the oven to warm it.

Huml apologizes for some affront to Blanka. She goes to get her coat to leave; then he greets her as she arrives at the front door. He dictates until she goes to put on the kettle. Immediately Renata comes in wearing Mrs. Huml's apron; they go upstairs to the bedroom. Balcar, Kriebl, and Huml come in and discuss their anthropological studies. Offstage, Puzuk's siren wails (it is too hot). Huml returns half-dressed. At last Puzuk's first question: In an effeminate voice, Puzuk asks, "May I have a little rest?" This ends act 1.

Act 2 begins with Mr. and Mrs. Huml discussing his mistress. They exit. Then follows the scene for which Huml apologized earlier. He makes a grab at Blanka while dictating. Her exit melds into Renata's quarreling with Huml about asking his wife for a divorce. Then comes the previously omitted scene of Huml's first introduction to Balcar, Kriebl, Machal, and Beck. They go to get Puzuk. Huml whispers to Renata, who answers from offstage. Then the Humls have a domestic quarrel about telling Renata that he is through with her. As Renata leaves, Blanka again asks Huml not to make advances to her; they continue an earlier dictation scene until he attacks and then runs after her, to return with Renata, both dressing from their act 1 bedroom scene. He asks Renata to tell Mrs. Huml. She repeats her earlier exit, but this time Blanka sees them kissing. Huml offers Renata the same excuses, turned around, that he gave Mrs. Huml. Balcar and Kriebl ask Puzuk for a question. Puzuk asks to rest again, explaining that it is tired. Balcar explains to Huml that Puzuk eliminates all repeated and therefore predictable responses to its questions and uses the remaining "random" responses as keys to individual personality. Puzuk lights up red, then green, then asks Huml a series of questions, such as "What is your favorite tunnel?" and "Do you piss in public, or just now and then?"

All the characters, including Puzuk, appear onstage repeating their demands and questions to Huml. The action and sound become chaotic and surreal, until Puzuk's siren-wail quiets them.

Disputing Balcar's ideas about her work, Huml explains that the "fundamental key to man does not lie in his brain, but in his heart." She is undone, sobs, is embraced and comforted by Huml; they kiss passionately, then exchange love-talk. The audience is reminded of the earlier dinner scene when Mrs. Huml chided Huml for not telling Renata. They sit down to dinner; she looks at him expectantly, and says, "Well?" On this note, the play ends.

Themes and Meanings

Obviously, the difficulty of concentration increases for the author, characters, and audience as the play progresses. The playwright will not concentrate on a scene for much more than a page. Huml cannot keep his life, his romantic commitments, or his thoughts (dictation) in focus for long. The sociologists and their machine cannot concentrate either. The audience cannot follow any dramatic thread until it has been seen at least once occurring and once in flashback.

The meaninglessness of personal relationships, the interference of the state and its pseudosciences upon the individual, the mindlessness of official and scientific jargon, and the absurdity of even the concept of individuality in a mechanical and repetitive existence—all are satirized in this farcelike comedy. Since Huml is the point of focus (all events involve him at home), this chaos on a treadmill may be seen as an exploration of his personal disorientation. However, every scene is so cartoonlike in its simplicity and illogical chronology that the suggestion seems clear that the protagonist represents either all people or nobody. The audience is not permitted emotional involvement with any character.

The longest passages are Huml's dictations. They involve his theories on humankind's search for satisfaction as the basis for its system of values. As Huml admits and as the play demonstrates, happiness and satisfaction and values are seen from various angles and modified by observance in different time frames. In other words, humankind does not really know what it wants, and studies of humans degenerate into contradictory clichés. Huml admits that no one shall ever arrive at an understanding of people because their complexity is so individually irrational that it is beyond scientific (systematic) analysis. Rather, he insists that the proper study of humankind lies in human relationships. The values, satisfactions, emotional conflicts, and accords seen in personal relationships are, he says, the key to understanding what humankind is.

The play both illustrates and contradicts that notion. What the audience learns of these people and this society comes from interactions, mostly within couples. However, what is shown is repetitive, dishonest, manipulative, and even more confused than confusing. No doubt, Václav Havel's position as a dissident artist in a state-controlled Czech society was a key to this bleakly comic picture of life with consistent values or purpose, but the unreality of the caricatured treatment works as well to reveal a twentieth century society in any "developed" country.

Dramatic Devices

The Increased Difficulty of Concentration uses the physical appearance of farce (constant, slapdash action, mostly entrances and exits of couples hiding their actions from others) to provide a metaphor for disorientation. The feeling that one is not sure what is happening is compounded by the drama's skewed chronology. Huml exits with one person in a situation and time frame that will be contradicted by his next appearance onstage with another person in what is obviously a quite different scene. Then the scenes turn backward on themselves and much later repeat a detail or action or comment that clearly belongs to a previous scene, illustrating the title.

Huml's dialogues with his wife and with his mistress are so amusingly parallel that it becomes clear that, though his attitude toward each may vary, his method of dealing with them is identical: He puts off all that they ask of him to pursue his own, uneventful concerns. His treatment of Balcar and his secretary Blanka is similarly parallel: They have needs and even obsessions (Blanka trying to decide upon marriage to a suitor, Balcar trying to pursue her "scientific" study of human individuality) in which Huml is uninterested and toward which he is unsympathetic. He sees them ultimately as objects for his own gratification. The overall pattern is dehumanized and sterile.

The comic tone is maintained not only through these patterns of quirky time shifts and repeated parallel lines and actions but also through such conventional comic devices as slapstick stumbling, comic curtain lines, and stock comic characters. There is much fun in seeing the actors make startlingly swift costume changes, obviously having to run backstage from one door to another in order to appear confusingly in different garb from another scene. This device, however, also serves to emphasize the time-warped experience and thoughts of the characters. The central theatrical image of the comedy is much like a treadmill on which bits of similar and even the same scenes roll by and return to their starting point without seeming to achieve forward motion toward any resolution or sure conclusion.

Critical Context

The Increased Difficulty of Concentration is perhaps a more mainstream effort than Havel's earlier, more biting satires. It shares with his *Zahradní slavnost* (pr., pb. 1963; *The Garden Party*, 1969) and his *Vyrozumění* (pr. 1965, pb. 1966; *The Memorandum*, 1967) a satirical reflection of a society made almost unbearable by its "scientific" modern age. The encroachment of scientific methods upon human behavior in order to achieve efficiency and understanding is mocked in all of his plays as social and political inhumanity. In *The Increased Difficulty of Concentration*, however, the result is not so much persecution as absurd chaos. The tone is somewhat lighter; the bureaucracy-imposed technology is less of a problem than it is in the two earlier works.

The Memorandum, which takes place in a translation center in which an official new language is installed, focuses on the resulting havoc in the operation of the institute. The madness of bureaucracy and the intrusions of officialdom are satirized so brilliantly in *The Memorandum* that many took the play to be a microcosm of communist-run Czechoslovakia. It achieved worldwide popularity, though it caused Havel some political difficulty at home.

The Increased Difficulty of Concentration does suggest that the same disorders result from pseudoscientific attempts at management of one's fellow citizen. It reflects the Theater of the Absurd's central notions of the basic inability to communicate, the absurdity of humans' belief in and desire for individuality, and the jargon and gobbledygook that pass for contemporary language. It is more personal in its comic reflections on human selfishness and the inability to relate honestly to one another. As such, it seems more humane and less of a philosophical dead end than the absurdist drama, and less clearly on the attack than Havel's earlier plays.

Havel was clearly the best-known and most respected Czech playwright of the period from 1965 to 1990. During the 1980's, he was jailed for leading antigovernment protests in Czechoslovakia and became an international *cause célèbre*. In 1989 he became president of Czechoslovakia and retained his office when the Czech Republic split from Slovakia in 1993.

Sources for Further Study

Burian, Jarka M. "Post-War Drama in Czechoslovakia: *The Increased Difficulty of Concentration.*" *Educational Theatre Journal* 25 (October, 1973): 311-312.

Goetz-Stankiewicz, Markéta. "Mechanized Minds." *Times Literary Supplement*, March 10, 1972, p. 267.

_____. "Václav Havel." In *The Silenced Theatre: Czech Playwrights Without a Stage.* Buffalo, N.Y.: University of Toronto Press, 1979.

_____. "Václav Havel: A Writer of Today's Season." *World Literature Today* 55 (Summer, 1981): 388-393.

Goetz-Stankiewicz, Markéta, and Phyllis Carey, eds. *Critical Essays on Václav Havel.* New York: G. K. Hall, 1999.

Krisova, Eda. *Václav Havel: The Authorized Biography.* Collingdale, Pa.: Diane, 1998.

Schumschida, Walter. "Václav Havel: Between the Theatre of the Absurd and Engaged Theatre." In *Fiction and Drama in Eastern and Southeastern Europe: Evolution and Experiment in the Postwar Period*, edited by Henrik Birnbaum and Thomas Eckman. Columbus, Ohio: Slavica Publishers, 1980.

Herbert M. Simpson

THE INDIAN WANTS THE BRONX

Author: Israel Horovitz (1939-   )
Type of plot: Absurdist; Theater of Cruelty
Time of plot: The 1960's
Locale: A Fifth Avenue bus stop in New York City
First produced: 1968, at the Astor Place Theatre, New York City
First published: 1968

>   *Principal characters:*
>   GUPTA, an East Indian, in his early fifties
>   MURPH, a young city "tough" in his early twenties
>   JOEY, a young city "tough" in his early twenties

The Play

The Indian Wants the Bronx is a one-act play that opens with a bewildered East Indian, who speaks no English, attempting to negotiate the complexities of an American urban setting. As he attempts to decode the unfamiliar landscape and find his way to his son's Bronx apartment, two young street toughs, who epitomize self-absorbed ignorance, arrive on the scene and begin to taunt him. They enter singing a song that depicts the world as a lonely and indifferent place. As the play progresses, it becomes clear that they come from unstable families and have a social worker who is attempting to rehabilitate them. Israel Horovitz makes it clear, however, that the institutions that are supposed to be assisting them have failed to reach them and that they are, accordingly, loose cannons with no real direction in life. They seem to wander the streets because they lack better alternatives.

From their first appearance onstage, Murph and Joey engage in juvenile banter that makes them appear even younger than they are. Despite their ostensible friendship, they communicate on a relatively elementary level and punctuate their conversations with crude sexual innuendo and street slang. Their reactions to Gupta highlight their stereotypic thought patterns and their provincial perspectives. Both their words and their actions leave the audience with the impression that the boys are bored and frustrated and are randomly venting their rage, which is fueled by their own insignificance and conflicted sexual identities. They appear to have fallen through the proverbial cracks, lack role models, and have values that are situational at best.

Throughout the play, their violence escalates, advancing from playful "noogies" and feigned knife play to the sadistic spinning game, which literally makes Murph ill, and the stabbing of Gupta. Horovitz does not, however, characterize the boys as malicious; he portrays them as lost. They seem caught up in the moment and one senseless action leads to another, even more senseless action. A moment of hope comes while Murph is offstage and Joey and Gupta engage in an ambiguous set of interactions, but what little hope this scene inspires is quickly dashed when Murph returns. Despite his compassion for Gupta, Joey lacks the nerve or skill to transcend the language barrier and lacks the will to subject himself to Murph's ridicule. Accordingly, he tacitly sanctions Murph's cruelty, tackling Gupta to prevent him from interfering with Murph's verbal assault on Gupta's son. Ultimately, Murph's severing of the telephone cord and cutting of Gupta's hand negate any possibility for communication or cross-cultural understanding. Significantly, Joey leaves before Murph actually impales Gupta's hand with the knife.

The play's conclusion parallels the opening vignette with significant differences. While the audience again hears the boys singing after they leave the stage, the stage directions describe the second rendition of the song as choruslike, suggesting that Murph and Joey represent the veritable isolation and hopelessness of all marginal individuals in this society. Horovitz underscores the universal nature of the boys' plight by leaving Gupta alone onstage, with his confidence diminished, his hand cut, and a ringing phone that offers false hope. The play ends ironically with Gupta offering the phone to the audience as he speaks the only English words he remembers and thanks the audience.

Themes and Meanings

The Indian Wants the Bronx centers on the irrational and random violence that seemed to dominate society during the mid-twentieth century and became more pervasive as the century waned. While the play highlights language barriers, the senselessness that Horovitz attributes to postmodern society exacerbates the problems. Both Murph and Joey qualify as "lost boys," grappling for some semblance of meaning and purpose. In the absence of meaning, however, they engage in mock one-upmanship. To prove their own self-worth, they must diminish the self-worth of others. This is evident both in their interactions and in the almost confessional exchange between Joey and Gupta when Murph is offstage. The fear and misunderstanding that all the characters experience preclude anything but terrified and irrational reactions to others.

To emphasize this point, Horovitz relies on sparse dialogue, punctuated by significant gestures. While he presents Gupta as a responsible adult who believes in human compassion, he presents the boys as immature adolescents who, while capable of compassion, transform everything into a game without considering the consequences of their actions. The contrast works to Horovitz's advantage insofar as it allows him to distinguish the two mind-sets without casting judgments. Significantly, Horovitz demonstrates that Gupta, because of his fear and unfamiliarity with the language and environment, is equally capable of violent acts.

Initially, the audience has no preconceptions about any character. They can discount the horseplay of the boys and sympathize with Gupta, but once the interchanges become more violent, this comfort zone evaporates. Only belatedly does the audience realize that Gupta represents the father figure that Joey never had and that part of Joey's action constitutes a payback for abandonment by his own father. Gupta realizes none of this and is sincerely confused by Joey's conflicting signals. He is also unaware of the power of peer pressure and machismo, which seem to motivate much of the play's action.

Horovitz depicts Joey as an individual caught in an approach-avoidance conflict, wanting to befriend Gupta and, yet, afraid to do so. By creating this dynamic, Horovitz reinforces his point that intolerance and stereotypes are not only irrational but also a function of our own inner demons and insecurities. Were either of the boys more comfortable with himself, he would have eschewed the mindless viciousness and attempted to help Gupta.

Because Gupta (like the audience) is powerless, he has no defenses with which to repel the senseless aggression and no power to bridge the cultural divide. He becomes the consummate victim: a foreigner with no English language skills who must endure a series of ritualistic hazings. In this sense, Horovitz follows the lead and sets the tone for many other writers who focus on the outsider-newcomer theme. Despite the rhetoric of inclusion, American society can be very inhospitable to foreigners and erect barriers that spawn violence.

Horovitz seems to be describing a social breakdown that has broader implications. The inability of Gupta to communicate with the boys is symptomatic of the barriers that preclude honest interaction in many settings. While he creates an extreme situation and introduces other variables that retard communication further, he seems to be making a larger point about the alienation and breakdown of community in this society.

As Horovitz deals with this theme, he echoes naturalist playwrights in that he emphasizes the vulnerability of the individual in a hostile environment. In this case, however, Horovitz puts the emphasis on social displacement and the indifference of others to the plight of their brethren. Yet, even while doing so, Horovitz implies that there is a chance to break through these barriers and understand one another. While the characters do not make this transition, the play suggests that Joey and Gupta at least made a faltering attempt to do so.

Dramatic Devices

To bring his message home, Horovitz blends humor with violence. In the first part of the play he uses countless plays on words and oblique metaphors. The language is jocular and the atmosphere is nonthreatening. Midway through the play, however, Horovitz warns the audience that the tone is about to shift. Suddenly the action assumes a new significance and the audience becomes uncomfortable with the level of violence. This is Horovitz's intent. He is attempting to jolt the audience out of its lassitude. More important, he transforms humor into a vehicle for social criticism by forcing the audience to participate vicariously in the violence and disallows them any alternatives, much as he disallows Gupta alternatives.

The Indian Wants the Bronx blends techniques from the Theater of the Absurd with the Theatre of Cruelty to achieve its effect. Because of the language barrier, much of the dialogue and action borders on the surreal. By having Gupta speak virtually all of his lines in Hindi, Horovitz puts the audience at the same disadvantage with regard to understanding Gupta as Murph and Joey. This device reinforces the theme of the outsider that Horovitz introduces in the epigraph to the play.

However, Horovitz is not content to allow the play to focus on social displacement. Instead, he introduces a more sinister element that transforms the play into a vehicle for indicting the ways in which language skills (or the lack of them) can produce near-tragic results. To accomplish this end, he introduces an unspoken language of violence. Even when the words are nonviolent, the actions are provocative and, in many cases, chilling.

The use of *mise en scène*, or the physical staging of the scene, augments the effects he achieves when Gupta speaks Hindi. Because the scenery is sparse and the dialogue fractured, the audience must focus on the nonverbal interactions of the characters. By minimizing distractions, Horovitz involves the audience in the action and makes the members virtual participants who are powerless to stop the violence. He also involves the audience by having Murph address "Pussyface" at the beginning of the play by calling into the audience.

In addition to the boys' actions, Horovitz uses language to reveal character. Just as the language used to abuse Gupta is startling, so too are the references to the social worker, the mothers, and other unseen characters. The boys' graphic depictions of others speak to the character of the boys and their grasp of the larger context. For them, life is a competition on the basest terms. For Gupta, life revolves around family. The boys, however, having known no stable family, seem to discount the importance of family and view their call to Gupta's son as a prank rather than a provocative act of terrorism.

Critical Context

Critics applauded *The Indian Wants the Bronx* for a variety of reasons. Some compared Horovitz's play to the work of fellow absurdists Eugène Ionesco and Samuel Beckett because it negates rational assumptions about human interaction and emphasizes the inherent alienation of modern life. Others saw the play as conforming to Antonin Artaud's concept of Theater of Cruelty, which inverts the traditional importance of words and action, elevating gesture and sound so as to shock the audience. Given the inspiration for the play, both of these assessments have merit. The idea for the play, according to Horovitz, traces back to an incident he observed while studying at London's Royal Academy of Dramatic Arts in the early 1960's.

One morning while Horovitz was waiting in line for breakfast at the Commonwealth Institute, he noticed a young Hindu dressed in Indian garb, also waiting in line. The Indian's attire set him apart from the others, and when a car full of "teddy boys" drove by, they unleashed a virulent stream of epithets toward the Hindu. To the amazement of the others, the Hindu, who spoke no English, simply laughed and seemed to encourage his attackers. After the incident ended, Horovitz approached the victim and realized that the Hindu was a lonely newcomer who was pleased by any overtures, however cruel or absurd.

This theme of social dislocation intrigued Horovitz and led him to write *The Indian Wants the Bronx*, which earned him his first Obie Award in 1968. He was struck by both the comedy and tragedy of the scene and used these competing elements to fuel many of his subsequent works, including *The Primary English Class* (pr. 1975, pb. 1976) and *Morning* (pr. 1968, pb. 1969). While these plays used different dramatic contexts, they continued to explore the social dislocation and random social violence of contemporary society. For this reason, many have applauded Horovitz as a master student of "the psychology of terrorism," a theme that seems even more relevant in the early twenty-first century than when he wrote these works.

Sources for Further Study
DiGaetani, John L. *A Search for a Postmodern Theater: Interviews with Contemporary Playwrights*. Westport, Conn.: Greenwood Press, 1991.

Horovitz, Israel. *Sixteen Short Plays*. Lyme, N.H.: Smith and Kraus, 1994.

Kane, Leslie, ed. *Israel Horovitz: A Collection of Critical Essays*. Westport, Conn.: Greenwood Press, 1994.

Lahr, John, ed. *Showcase 1: Plays from the Eugene O'Neill Foundation*. New York: Grove Press, 1970.

Marowitz, Charles. *Off-Broadway Plays*. Vol. 1. New York: Penguin Press, 1970.

Wetzsteon, Ross, ed. *The Obie Winners: The Best of Off-Broadway*. Garden City, N.Y.: Doubleday, 1980.

C. Lynn Munro

INDIANS

Author: Arthur Kopit (1937-   )
Type of plot: Social realism
Time of plot: The late nineteenth century
Locale: The Wild West and Washington, D.C.
First produced: 1968, at the Aldwych Theatre, London
First published: 1969

> *Principal characters:*
> BUFFALO BILL CODY,
> WILD BILL HICKOK, and
> ANNIE OAKLEY, characters from the Old West
> SITTING BULL,
> JOHN GRASS,
> GERONIMO, and
> SPOTTED TAIL, Native Americans from the Old West
> SENATOR LOGAN,
> SENATOR DAWES, and
> SENATOR MORGAN, emissaries of the president
> OL' TIME PRESIDENT, a U.S. president of the late nineteenth
> century
> NED BUNTLINE, a newsman

The Play

In the opening scene of *Indians*, a buffalo skull, a bloodstained Indian shirt, and an old rifle serve to provide historical atmosphere as Buffalo Bill Cody enters, riding an artificial stallion. At once, the audience learns that it is seeing a rendition of Buffalo Bill's famous "Wild West Show." Indians, too, are present; Cody claims to them, to the audience, and to himself that "I believe I . . . am a . . . hero . . . A GODDAM HERO!"

The next scene is set outdoors in the winter, somewhere in the West. Sitting Bull and other chieftains greet Buffalo Bill in the company of three United States senators, emissaries of and substitutes for the president, who has not come to the Indian council to discuss shared problems, even though Cody promised to bring him. Cody calls the Native Americans his brothers, but his use of the word is shallow and hypocritical. In the following scene, Cody continues to discuss the Native Americans' plight with them, but the audience has seen him callously destroying the livelihood of the Native Americans, shooting one hundred buffalo. Ned Buntline, the reporter who first made Buffalo Bill a popular American hero, is oblivious to the import of this destruction. The Native Americans are depicted as victims and the white people as callous and unworthy adversaries and victors.

Scene 4, the shortest in the play, shows both the senators and Sitting Bull's Lakota community watching Buffalo Bill's Wild West Show. Scene 5 is this show itself, something of a play-within-the-play: Geronimo, by reputation the fiercest fighter against the coming of the white settlers, parades around the stage pitifully, a pale imitation of his former self, while boasting vainly about past atrocities against white people.

The next scene is the structural center of the play. Here, the three senators interview John Grass, a Native American spokesman who has some knowledge of the ways and thinking of the white people. Grass wants to know what happened to the money the federal government had used to purchase the Black Hills from the Native Americans. Senator Dawes's reply is that "the Great Father is worried that you've not been educated enough to spend it *wisely*. When he feels you have, you will receive every last penny of it. *Plus interest*." The senator explains that the money is in a "trust." Grass also lists other verbal promises that the whites have not kept, among them a promise to deliver a steamboat to the plains. The meeting ends with the native community reminding Cody that he has not brought the Great White Father himself, the president, to talk to them as he promised.

In the second half of the play the action shifts first to the White House and then back to the Old West. In scene 7, the longest one, Buffalo Bill, Buntline, and Wild Bill Hickok all play themselves in a performance wherein an indigenous princess is saved but a large number of braves (also playing themselves) die. The First Family finds the play exciting; indeed, the First Lady is attracted to Wild Bill, who is, in turn, attracted to the Italian woman playing the part of the princess. The scene ends with Hickok tearing at her clothes.

The next scene returns to the discussion between the senators and John Grass. Clearly, misunderstanding on the parts of the white people and Native Americans alike has been a key factor in the victimization of the "red man." Specific items of the treaty are discussed, as Arthur Kopit juxtaposes the two cultures: The two groups cannot communicate with each other about land ownership, farm life, self-sufficiency, and whiskey. The situation is hopeless at every turn.

When scene 9 opens, for the third time in *Indians* the audience sees bits and snatches of the Wild West Show. Annie Oakley has joined the performance and does trick shots with her gun; to the cast of Native Americans Chief Joseph is added, to give his famous speech which culminates with "I will fight no more, forever." At the end of the Wild West spectacular, Grass, having given up on conveying anything to the senators, appears to lead the Native Americans in a forbidden sun dance in which he sticks barbs into his chest muscles until the loss of blood causes him to collapse.

Scene 10 is a flashback to the meeting between Buffalo Bill and the Ol' Time President at which the president refused to travel to the West to meet with the indigenous leaders; the viewer now learns that this meeting followed the performance of scene 7, in which Buffalo Bill and others appeared before the First Family. Cody dramatically tells the president that without his help the Native Americans and their way of life will die. The president will not help, and he calls Cody a fool for promising Sitting Bull that he would go to the West and talk to them personally. Instead, the president will "send a committee," and the fate of the Native Americans is assured: Extinction is inevitable.

For the third time in the play, the audience sees the committee at work. Again, the helplessness of the native community in the face of impending death is emphasized. Viewers realize that each side considers the other stupid. Buffalo Bill acknowledges that "if *their* way o' seein' is hard for *us* t' follow, ours is just as hard for *them*." At the high point of this scene, Sitting Bull, with full dignity yet in total desperation, suggests, "Tell the Great Father that if he wishes us to live like white men, we will do so." His Lakota community is stunned, but he proceeds to request that the president send the Lakota food, since "I have never yet seen a white man starving." He requests cattle, mules, horses, buggies, oxen, and wagons too, "for that is the way the white man lives, and we want to please the Great Father and live the same way."

Jesse James, Billy the Kid, and Poncho make brief appearances in the next scene, playing themselves as villains and as replacements of the Native Americans. Ironically, Buffalo Bill would now try to help Sitting Bull's village, but he himself had led in destroying the buffalo. Too late, he realizes that in killing buffalo he was also killing Native Americans.

The next scene concludes the play. A reporter interviews Colonel Forsythe and other soldiers who have just defeated the Native Americans in a post-Custer skirmish. Entering for a final conversation, Sitting Bull tells Buffalo Bill that he cannot understand why he killed the buffalo while professing love for indigenous communities. Sitting Bull acknowledges that acting in the Wild West Show had been humiliating, an imitation of his glory, and Buffalo Bill himself reveals that one of his greatest fears is that he will die with his makeup (rather than boots) on. The play ends with a repentant Buffalo Bill talking of what he has done; as he does so, some ten Native Americans are brought in one by one to die onstage. The last among these is Chief Joseph, who concludes the play by repeating, "I will fight no more, forever."

Themes and Meanings

Indians has two overriding concerns. The first is the American character or national identity, and the second is the U.S. role in the Vietnam War. Although it never mentions the war, *Indians* clearly protests America's involvement in Vietnam.

America itself is embodied in Buffalo Bill, who is young, masculine, aggressive, charming, straightforward, and well intentioned. What is wrong with Buffalo Bill is his tendency to act without regard for long-term consequences: He kills the buffalo and in the process destroys the Native Americans' livelihood. He is left, then, an imitation of himself, playing himself (and therefore no longer really himself) in his Wild West Show. In imitation of itself, according to Arthur Kopit, the United States, with its involvement in Vietnam, repeated its great mistake of the past century in its effort to dominate and control another country. The play's application to Vietnam is at no point explicit. Kopit's method is to define America by examining Buffalo Bill, in whose life he finds a number of parallels to that of the nation.

What myths, then, does the American self-image encompass? Were Americans in 1968 too confident of always being right? Is there something in the American national character that dictates that the nation will proceed with force and efficacy even when wrong? *Indians* seeks to answer such questions through implication rather than with directness. The playwright's suggestion is that the United States has become, like Buffalo Bill, an imitation of itself, a self which, for all of its good intentions and past successes, was not particularly moral.

The play cannot be interpreted as a diatribe against the war in Vietnam. It does, however, legitimately raise the question whether, in Vietnam, the United States was repeating mistakes of the past. Most telling of all, perhaps, is the fact that Buffalo Bill, after realizing his mistake, is unable to reverse the momentum; the destruction cannot be stopped. Cody cannot get the president to act, even after he persuades him that he should. At the end Buffalo Bill is afraid not of dying but of dying with his makeup on. Death is not to catch him repeating the mistakes of the past, even if he is acting. The parallel to the United States is immediate and engaging. Kopit is suggesting that the country should rid itself of "makeup" and abandon the "Wild West Show" in Vietnam. On one hand, the United States seems doomed to win the war in Vietnam (the Native Americans of the last scene die one by one), but on the other it would learn that it was wrong for it to do so. Such was Kopit's perspective in 1968; writing then, he could not realize that the United States would withdraw from Vietnam without winning the war.

Dramatic Devices

Some critics have too quickly categorized *Indians* as an absurdist drama. Arthur Kopit's play does meet some of the requirements of the Theater of the Absurd. His perspective of the human condition probably meets this criterion; the form of the play is not very realistic; its events do not unfold in a direct, connected fashion; and finally, and most important, the characters seemingly exist in a meaningless universe.

Kopit's method, however, does not ultimately qualify the play as absurdist. The reality of what white individuals did to the buffalo and to the Native Americans was absurd, as Bill Cody comes to realize; the inability of the two races to communicate is absurd; for Cody to promise to bring the president to the Native Americans is absurd; and for the indigenous communities to demand a steamboat for the plains and mountains is absurd. These things show that life is absurd, but they do not make history into absurdist drama.

Similarly, the play's unusual form and the nonchronological order in which events are given do not make the play absurdist. While the bulk of the play is based on historical facts, in many places Kopit takes dramatic license by having characters who never actually met each other talk to and interact with each other; episodes are not rendered sequentially; and conversations can be somewhat bizarre and existential. These devices make the play different and unusual, but there is an overall order to the play.

Of *Indians'* other dramatic devices, the most prominent is that of the play-within-the-play. The various scenes of the Wild West Show are used to emphasize what Buffalo Bill, Sitting Bull, and others were reduced to: The Old West and the Native Americans were dead as people and as a way of life, long before these figures from history actually died. The playwright conveys the same point with Ned Buntline's play, which is presented by Buffalo Bill and his friends at the White House. The audience is thus three times removed from reality (once in Buntline's play, once in Kopit's, and once in their own chairs) and should thereby have enough distance to have a healthy perspective.

Critical Context

Indians was first produced in the summer of 1968, the year of the infamous Democratic National Convention in Chicago. Robert Kennedy and Martin Luther King, Jr., had recently been shot, the country had just experienced explosive racial tension in the wake of the Civil Rights movement, and the Vietnam War was in one of its bloodiest periods. Because of these social and political realities, Arthur Kopit took the play to London for its world premiere. Although early reviewers were not unanimous in their praise, it seems clear that *Indians* will survive (it is being reprinted in anthologies) not because of its implicit criticism of the Vietnam War but because it is so effective at raising questions about American identity and self-image. The play transcends its immediate political context. It is a haunting reminder that the United States, despite its many accomplishments, has faults at its core that have not yet been fully confronted in the national conscience. Whether American involvement in Vietnam was just or unjust is not now at issue. More important, and far more central to *Indians*, is the problem of American identity. The play succeeds because it pricks the collective conscience—and perhaps the collective guilt—about its subject matter.

Of other plays written by Kopit, *Indians* most closely resembles *End of the World* (pr., pb. 1984). The latter looks to the United States' future rather than its past; in this future, the playwright finds certain nuclear destruction. The nuclear arms race and the ineffectual treaties it occasions are shown to be as absurd as the American conquest of the West; as in *Indians*, there is a play-within-a-play; life is depicted as absurd and uncontrollable; and the main character, a private investigator-playwright, is much akin to Buffalo Bill. Other Kopit plays include *Oh Dad, Poor Dad, Mama's Hung You in the Closet and I'm Feelin' So Sad: A Pseudoclassical Tragifarce in a Bastard French Tradition* (pr., pb. 1960), *Wings* (pr., pb. 1978), *End of the World with Symposium to Follow* (pr., pb. 1984), *Success* (pr. 1991, pb. 1992), *Discovery of America* (pr. 1992), and *Y2K* (pr., pb. 1999; later retitled *BecauseHeCan*).

Sources for Further Study

Gross, Karl. "The Larger Perspective: Author Kopit's *Indians* and the Vietnam War." In *Modern War on Stage and Screen*. Lewiston, N.Y.: Mellen, 1997.

Jenkins, Linda Walsh. "A Gynocratic Feminist Perspective in the Case of Kopit's *Indians*." In *Theatre and Feminist Aesthetics*. Madison, N.J.: Fairleigh Dickinson University Press, 1995.

Jiji, Vera M. "*Indians:* A Mosaic of Memories and Methodologies." *Players* 47 (Summer, 1972): 230-236.

Jones, John B. "Impersonation and Authenticity: The Theatre as Metaphor in Kopit's *Indians.*" *Quarterly Journal of Speech* 59 (December, 1973): 443-451.

O'Neill, Michael C. "History as Dramatic Present: Arthur L. Kopit's *Indians.*" *Theatre Journal* 34 (December, 1982): 493-504.

Weales, Gerald. "Arthur Kopit." In *Contemporary Dramatists.* 6th ed. Detroit: St. James, 1999.

Weaver, Laura. "Arthur Kopit." In *American Playwrights Since 1945: A Guide to Scholarship, Criticism, and Performance.* New York: Greenwood Press, 1989.

Carl Singleton

THE INFERNAL MACHINE

Author: Jean Cocteau (1889-1963)
Type of plot: Allegory
Time of plot: Mythological era in ancient Greece
Locale: Ancient Thebes
First produced: 1934, at the Comédie des Champs-Élysées (Théâtre Louis Jouvet), Paris
First published: La Machine infernale, 1934 (English translation, 1936)

Principal characters:
OEDIPUS, a young man, later King of Thebes
ANUBIS, the Egyptian god of the dead
TIRESIAS, the high priest
THE GHOST OF KING LAIUS
JOCASTA, Queen of Thebes, the widow of Laius
CREON, Jocasta's brother
THE SPHINX, the goddess of vengeance
A THEBAN MOTHER
ANTIGONE, the daughter of Jocasta and Oedipus

The Play

Before the curtain rises on *The Infernal Machine*, a Voice tells the audience how Jocasta, Queen of Thebes, left her baby son, his feet mutilated, on a mountainside to die, in order to counter the prophecy that he would kill his father and marry his mother. The child was rescued and adopted by Polybus and Merope, king and queen of Corinth, who treated him as their own. As a young man, Oedipus consulted an oracle and learned the same prophecy. Believing himself the son of Polybus and Merope, he fled that city in order to counter the oracle. One day, during a dispute at a crossroads, he killed a man; unknown to Oedipus, the man was Laius, King of Thebes, his father. Soon after, he heard of the Sphinx, which was killing the young men of Thebes, having first asked a riddle they could not solve. Queen Jocasta had offered her hand in marriage and the crown of Thebes to the conqueror of the Sphinx. Oedipus was victorious, married Jocasta—his mother—and became King of Thebes. The years passed. A plague struck, and the gods blamed an unnamed criminal. Having determined to find him, Oedipus discovered the truth about himself. Jocasta hanged herself with her red scarf, and Oedipus blinded himself with her gold brooch. Now, says the Voice, let the audience watch how a perfect machine constructed by the infernal gods encompasses the mathematical annihilation of a mortal.

Each act in *The Infernal Machine* has its own title. Act 1, "The Ghost," takes place at night. The atmosphere is heavy and the sky riven with heat lightning. Two soldiers patrol the raised platform alongside the city wall, while the nearby sewers discharge a stench and the noisy rhythms of nightclubs are heard. Laius's death is still recent. His ghost has tried to communicate with Jocasta. The soldiers discuss the apparition with their officer, who is more concerned about the way in which the matter was reported over his head than with the substance of the report. Jocasta arrives with Tiresias, the high priest. He treads on the end of her long scarf, and she comments that it is always trying to strangle her. She evinces an impatient insensitivity to the condition of her people, preferring to flirt with the young soldier (who reminds her of the son who would have been his age) than to take seriously the report of the ghost. She reflects that if her son were alive he would be handsome and brave (like the young soldier) and would conquer the Sphinx. The ghost comes again, but no one can see or hear him. Now the young soldier who reminds Jocasta so strangely of her son steps on her scarf. Only when she has departed does the ghost succeed in communicating again with the soldiers, but he cannot complete his message before he is dragged away by invisible underworld forces.

Act 2, "Oedipus Meets the Sphinx," follows the shape of act 1 in that after much preparatory conversation, striking dramatic action occurs toward the end; again, there is a humorous element. The act begins at the same moment as act 1, but on a hill outside Thebes. The Sphinx (who has assumed the form of a young girl) and Anubis wait to catch young men. A mother with her children stops to converse and explains the domestic problems of Thebes, unaware that she is addressing the Sphinx. When Oedipus arrives, the Sphinx, in whom the form of the young girl has become dominant and who is tired of killing, falls in love with him and reveals in advance the answer to the riddle he must solve. Despite his initial bravado, Oedipus is a helpless coward in her hands, but he solves the riddle. He shows no gratitude but hurries off. After Anubis and the Sphinx discuss the fate that awaits him, he returns, seeking the body of the Sphinx as proof of his triumph, before going to Thebes to claim his reward.

Act 3, "The Wedding Night," again begins on a stifling, stormy night. The bridal bed is the bed of Jocasta and Laius, the cradle is beside it, and the room is blood-red. Oedipus and Jocasta, in their heavy ceremonial robes, are exhausted and move as if drugged. Tiresias comes to warn Oedipus of danger, but Oedipus thinks that the high priest is in league with Creon against him and fails totally to penetrate his meaning. During the night, he dreams of his encounter with the Sphinx. Jocasta's soothing response to his distress is quasi-maternal; this and many other hints of his real identity are placed before them, but they are ignored or explained away. A drunkard sings a satirical song about the difference in age between Jocasta and Oedipus, and while he is chased away by the young soldier with whom Jocasta had flirted in the first act, Oedipus sleeps with his head against the cradle, gently rocked by Jocasta.

Act 4, the shortest, is titled "Oedipus the King." Seventeen years have passed; Oedipus and Jocasta have two sons and two daughters. The prophecy has been fulfilled, and the consequences emerge. The action speeds up appreciably as the "infernal machine" completes its process. A plague has hit Thebes. A messenger from Corinth announces the death of Polybus but also reveals that Oedipus was not the natural son of Polybus and Merope. Oedipus determines to discover the truth, despite the warnings of Creon and Tiresias, who have known for a long time but have kept their knowledge secret. Jocasta, and then Oedipus, are brought to realize Oedipus's identity. Jocasta hangs herself with her scarf; Oedipus puts out his eyes with her brooch. As Creon begins to take over the reins of power, the ghost of Jocasta—Oedipus's mother rather than his wife—fusing with the person of their daughter Antigone, leads away the blind Oedipus, who accepts the blind Tiresias's stick and thus at last acknowledges the old man's integrity.

Themes and Meanings

The Infernal Machine is not merely a modernization of a Greek myth but also a twentieth century exploitation of themes and meanings left unexplored in its principal source, Sophocles' play *Oidipous Tyrannos* (pr. c. 429 B.C.E.; *Oedipus Tyrannus*), into which Jean Cocteau integrates an illumination of the playwright's relationship with his creation. On one level, Cocteau exposes the political and social dilemmas latent in the myth, to provide a commentary upon the problems of threatened national security, economic crises, and simmering social tensions confronting France in the turbulent international and domestic climate of the 1930's. In the play, ordinary people of low intellect, with their ordinary preoccupations, are powerless to influence events. Even when they could, they do not. The soldiers decide not to report Laius's final warning, which, though incomplete, might have alerted Jocasta to the danger. They are more concerned with problems of status and bureaucracy than with questions of national importance. The mother who converses with the Sphinx is an ignorant gossip, but she strikes a chillingly realistic note when she alleges that the Theban government is corrupt and incompetent and that it welcomes the threat posed by the Sphinx because it diverts attention from the bankruptcy of domestic policies. The analogy to the series of weak French governments in the early 1930's is inescapable, as is the sinister import of the mother's conclusion that only a dictator could run the nation properly. Such a sentiment, not uncommon in France in that period, was anathema to Cocteau, who thus distances himself from it.

Those in power, for example Jocasta in act 1, are insensitive; there is implicit condemnation of governments' lack of interest in short-term measures to improve conditions for ordinary people. Long-term policies, it seems, are irrelevant. One cannot predict the future, and those who interrogate oracles will be baffled by the experience, of which no good can come. The Sphinx thinks that she can thwart the gods' wishes by sparing Oedipus, but her gesture is vain; instead, she speeds him toward his fate. Vain, also, are the attempts by Jocasta and Oedipus to alter their predestined fates. One should not delve into the past: Oedipus's determination to attribute the blame for the plague and to discover the truth behind the message from Corinth only precipitates the final catastrophe. Cocteau knew his compatriots: Here indeed is a striking prefiguration of the sinister French readiness in the Philippe Pétain era to seek scapegoats, not so much for the defeat of 1940 as for the moral turpitude that was adjudged to have blighted the nation.

On the second level, Cocteau demonstrates a playwright's absolute control of his creation. Once more, there is an analogy from the original myth, wherein the gods manipulate human beings according to their whim; similarly, the characters in a play are powerless to alter the predetermined roles they must fulfill. Cocteau delights in placing into the mouths of Jocasta and Oedipus unwitting hints of the discoveries they will make and the fate that awaits them. The title, *The Infernal Machine*, thus relates both to the mechanism that the gods have invented to annihilate a mortal and to the theatrical experience, invented by the playwright for an analogous purpose.

Dramatic Devices

Jean Cocteau in *The Infernal Machine* parades his genius for combining elements from different genres, by unifying the bawdy hilarity of bedroom farce and the solemnity of classical Greek tragedy. To this he adds burlesque (not only Oedipus's mock-heroic triumph over the Sphinx, when the powerless youth is a craven coward and shows no generosity in victory, but also the affectionate parody of the ghost scenes in the first act of William Shakespeare's *Hamlet*, pr. c. 1600-1601), drawing-room comedy (Jocasta's flirtation with the soldier, Oedipus's outrageous misapprehension of Tiresias's motives), comedy of morals (the soldiers and their preoccupations, the garrulous mother), deft touches of characterization (the impatient Creon, straining to take the reins of power), and especially the striking irony of visual devices (the metaphor of the blood-red bedroom, the cradle, Jocasta's maternal response to the sleeping Oedipus as she tiptoes about the room so as not to wake him, the scarf that so often nearly strangles her, the brooch). Another aspect is the bathing of the entire action in lurid violet light from mercury lamps, a device achieved in the first performance and often re-created in modern performances. In addition, the unseen Voice is to some extent a modern-day realization of the classical Greek chorus, summarizing, pointing out the moral, and above all emphasizing the theatrical locus of the action.

All of this, together with the many verbal prefigurations of what is to come, constitutes what Cocteau regarded as "the poetry of the theater," by which he meant the process of making apparent the theater's very specificity as theater. This concept was something Cocteau emphatically contrasted to the mere employment of poetry in a play, a method left over from before World War I and one he condemned as jaded and inappropriate to the world of the 1930's. For him, playwrights were wrong to use the theater as a vehicle for what was poetic rather than dramatic. Cocteau believed that the visible (both static and active) was the essential part of the spectator's experience of theater—not simply as a decorative addendum but as a living part of the drama. Thus, for example, stage properties such as the scarf, the brooch, the bed, and the cradle (even the stairs) seem to take on a life of their own and are invested with sinister significance; at the end of act 3, Jocasta's mirror comes to be identified with the audience itself, which knows the hideous immoral act she has committed. Indeed, Cocteau is never satisfied with a verbal account when visible action can be presented. Just as the audience witnesses Oedipus's encounter with the Sphinx, so too, unlike Sophocles, who permits himself little more than a coy reference to the crime of incest, Cocteau takes the audience right into the bedchamber and almost confronts the spectator with the very act, at once challenging prudish responses and repudiating Freudian explanations, which might seek to foreground the purely symbolic aspect of the crime.

Critical Context

Jean Cocteau's earlier plays *Antigone* (pr. 1922, pb. 1928; English translation, 1961) and *Orphée* (pr. 1926, pb. 1927; *Orpheus*, 1933) had been among the first of the impressive series of dramas on classical themes produced by a dozen writers, including also Jean Giraudoux, Jean Anouilh, and Jean-Paul Sartre, over three decades and more of French theater history. It was *The Infernal Machine*, however, that both consolidated the success of the form and showed how classical drama could be adapted to reflect aspects of contemporary life. Indeed, as is well known, in the following decade covert political comment embedded in certain neoclassical plays of the Occupation was able to pass unchallenged by the German censors. However, although by its confrontation of the supernatural with the everyday *The Infernal Machine* reminds its audience of the indissoluble link between the petty concerns of people as individuals and the wider spectrum of the politics of power, the meanings of this play are all on the surface, and this is where Cocteau intends them to be. There is no profound philosophy of life, no latent social or political message that cannot be readily apprehended by anyone familiar with the critical and historical context. There is, rather, an ironic but somewhat helpless commentary on events, the work of an elegant intellectual skeptic whose first priority was always to dazzle with his versatility.

Cocteau's career also embraced poetry, novels, ballet (and collaborations with some of the great composers of his day), cinema, criticism, painting, and illustrating, and in all of these one is aware of the guiding hand of the consummate master of showmanship. Still, there is also a profundity, though not where one might first expect to find it. It lies in the commentary on the merits of live theater, so that even were there no other reason, *The Infernal Machine* must not be dismissed as superficial, merely sensational, or merely a modern reworking of an ancient theme. It is one of the handful of greatest examples of twentieth century French neo-Greek drama.

Sources for Further Study

Crosland, Margaret. "*The Infernal Machine.*" In *Jean Cocteau*. New York: Knopf, 1956.

Crowson, Lydia. *The Esthetic of Jean Cocteau*. Hanover, N.H.: University Press of New England, 1978.

Fifield, William. *Jean Cocteau*. New York: Columbia University Press, 1974.

Knapp, Bettina L. *Jean Cocteau*. Rev. ed. Boston: Twayne, 1989.

Mauriès, Patrick. *Jean Cocteau*. Translated by Jane Brenton. London: Thames and Hudson, 1998.

Oxenhandler, Neal. "Liberty and *The Infernal Machine.*" In *Scandal and Parade: The Theater of Jean Cocteau*. New Brunswick, N.J.: Rutgers University Press, 1957.

William S. Brooks

INHERIT THE WIND

Authors: Jerome Lawrence (1915-　　) and Robert E. Lee (1918-1994)
Type of plot: Social realism; history
Time of plot: The 1920's
Locale: Hillsboro, a small town in the American Bible Belt
First produced: 1955, at the Theatre '55, Dallas, Texas
First published: 1955

> *Principal characters:*
> MATTHEW HARRISON BRADY, a noted prosecuting attorney
> HENRY DRUMMOND, a noted defense attorney
> TOM DAVENPORT, the district attorney for Hillsboro
> E. K. HORNBECK, a cynical Baltimore *Herald* newspaper reporter
> BERTRAM CATES, a biology teacher accused of teaching evolution
> RACHEL BROWN, Cates's fiancé, a twenty-two-year-old
> 　　schoolteacher
> THE REVEREND JEREMIAH BROWN, Rachel's father, a minister

The Play

Based on the real-life trial of John Thomas Scopes, convicted in 1925 of teaching the theory of evolution in his classroom in a Dayton, Tennessee, high school, *Inherit the Wind* owes much to the transcripts of the trial, although the authors fictionalize their material and do not intend their play to depict accurately the "Monkey Trial," as this historical proceeding was called.

The play opens outside the Hillsboro courthouse, where the trial of Bertram Cates, the accused biology teacher, will be held. The prosecutor, Matthew Harrison Brady, is a renowned jurist who twice ran for the presidency of the United States. Henry Drummond is the firebrand defense attorney championing an unpopular cause.

The opening scene is circuslike. The ultraconservative townspeople, most Bible-thumping Christians, await Matthew Brady's arrival. The eyes of the nation are on this small, Bible Belt town, which stands to rake in considerable revenue as the town fills for the ignominious trial. One localite hawks Bibles to the faithful, one sells lemonade, and another vends palm fans to the sweltering hordes. A hotdog vendor's business is brisk, and an organ grinder with a chained monkey amuses the crowd. People bear signs vowing that they are not descended from monkeys, that Satan must be destroyed, that Charles Darwin must go, and that Bertram Cates must be punished. Strains of "Gimme That Old Time Religion" fill the humid air.

E. K. Hornbeck, the reporter from Baltimore's *Herald* covering the trial, wanders among the crowd, sharp and cynical. In the midst of all the hoopla, Brady arrives to applause and cheering. Hillsboro's mayor makes him an honorary colonel in the state militia. Ever the politician, Brady glad-hands everyone in sight.

The agnostic Henry Drummond (Clarence Darrow in the actual case) is Cates's defense attorney. The townsfolk are obviously in Brady's corner in this contest. Drummond is considered the outsider who threatens Hillsboro's value system and will use whatever legal tricks he can to derail the religious fervor of sanctimonious Hillsboro.

Scene 2 occurs in the sweltering courtroom, where a jury is being selected. Brady questions the faith of potential jurors. Drummond seeks to find out whether potential jurors have ever read Charles Darwin or understand anything about *On the Origin of Species by Means of Natural Selection* (1859).

In one amusing scene, Drummond objects to Brady's being referred to as "Colonel Brady," complaining that the title prejudices the case. In response, Drummond is made a "temporary honorary colonel" in the state militia. In this scene, the opposing lines are sharply drawn: Brady represents the conscience of a community that firmly believes in the literal truth of scripture, while Drummond supports the scientific stand.

Brady and Drummond are old friends. Drummond campaigned for Brady in his presidential runs. They are now at each other's throats. The heated bickering in which they engage is lively and revealing, highlighting the roots from which each comes. Act 1 ends with an evening prayer meeting outside the courthouse. Brady accuses Drummond of moving away from him over the years, but Drummond reminds him that motion is relative.

The second act takes place wholly inside the courtroom, with scene 1 occurring in the midst of the trial and including the anguished testimony for the prosecution of Rachel Brown, the Reverend Jeremiah Brown's daughter and Bertram Cates's fiancé. In this scene, Drummond attempts to call six scientists whom he has brought to Hillsboro as defense witnesses to testify about the status of Darwin's theories among scientists. The judge forbids such testimony, so, to everyone's astonishment, the only witness the defense calls is Matthew Brady, labeled an expert on the Bible.

In his withering examination of Brady, Drummond completely shatters Brady's attempts to prove literal interpretations of the Bible. The dialogue is rollicking, especially when Brady cites seventeenth century Irish theologian Bishop Ussher's "proof" that the Lord began to create the earth on October 23, 4004 B.C.E., at nine o'clock in the morning. Drummond asks whether this was eastern standard time or mountain standard time. Brady is undone by the questioning, but it does not matter because his self-righteousness is strongly supported by the townspeople. In the play's final scene, Bertram Cates is convicted and fined one hundred dollars, which Drummond, who plans an appeal to the state Supreme Court, announces Cates will not pay.

As the courtroom is cleared, Matthew Brady seeks to make a final statement, which he wants entered into the record but which the judge rules as inadmissible. As he reads his impassioned statement, he collapses and dies. The play ends with Cates and Rachel leaving town with Drummond, who reflects on life without Matthew Brady.

Themes and Meanings

Inherit the Wind examines stubborn adherence to a set of antiquated but long-held and cherished notions that have, in the course of time, been scientifically disproved.

The townsfolk represent what real-life Baltimore reporter H. L. Mencken, of whom Hornbeck is reminiscent, aptly described as the "boobocracy": Such people are in the majority so, in Hillsboro at least, they rule. Ultimately this majority also wins at the local level. The play concludes before an appeal to the Supreme Court is launched, and the audience is left with the impression that perhaps such an appeal will not be filed. Bertram Cates and his fiancé leave town once the trial is over, perhaps never to return and fight the conviction.

Henry Drummond is less impressed by faith than he is by Truth, with a capital *T*. He thinks that God, if indeed there is one, has given humans the ability to think, question, analyze, and reason. Religion, as manifested and practiced in Hillsboro, has little to do with a quest for Truth. The townspeople are sheeplike: They accept and venerate the status quo. Not only do they not think deeply but also they do all in their power to thwart those who do. The perfect example of this thwarting is the court's refusal to permit the testimony of the expert scientific witnesses whom the defense has brought in to attest to the standing of Charles Darwin and his evolutionary theories among scientists. This decision reflects the tenor of the town. The attitude of most of the people in Hillsboro is "Do not rock the boat."

The conflict in this play is not merely between Bertram Cates and the town in which he teaches. It is rather the conflict between ignorance and knowledge, between blind adherence to outmoded beliefs and the rationality that would explore the validity of such beliefs, changing them if change seems appropriate. Henry Drummond demonstrates that there is no means of defending a wholly literal interpretation of the Bible. His rational approach, however, falls on deaf ears. The emotionalism and supercharged rhetoric of Matthew Brady reinforce the untenable ideas of the townspeople, including members of the jury, who deliver a guilty verdict.

Dramatic Devices

The most salient dramatic device used in *Inherit the Wind* is the chorus. The townspeople, who attack both Cates and Drummond, serve as a chorus and convey more than any other device in the play. The chorus represents the sentiments and emotions of the citizenry of Hillsboro, as appalling as these sentiments and emotions may seem to many who see or read the play.

The singing of "Gimme That Old Time Religion" recurs as a leitmotif and serves as a rallying point for the townsfolk. The stifling atmosphere of the sweltering July courtroom hangs heavily over the entire production and is emphasized by the lazy ceiling fans that move the humid air only slightly, by the motion of the palm fans that people in the courtroom agitate, and by the loose collars and sweat-stained shirts of the participants. The oppressiveness of the psychological atmosphere is underscored by the heat that pervades almost every scene in the play.

The unities of time and place are well maintained throughout the production, adding vigor to the drama and intensifying the focus of the action. The dark colors of the woodwork in the courtroom serve to heighten the oppressive feeling the audience gleans from realizing that when the trial was conducted, courtroom temperatures neared one hundred degrees Fahrenheit.

Critical Context

More than anything else, *Inherit the Wind* was an attack on the anti-intellectualism of the late 1940's and early 1950's, when hysteria about the communist threat was reaching hysterical proportions. It was upon this hysteria that Republican Senator Joseph McCarthy grounded his notorious hearings after concluding, quite without proof, that the United States Department of State was peppered with communists and that the communist influence in the media was threatening the very fabric of American society.

Jerome Lawrence and Robert E. Lee, liberals appalled at what was happening as the McCarthy hearings chipped away at the constitutional rights of many notable Americans, particularly playwrights and others in the arts, wrote the play. They distanced its issues by a whole generation from that which was going on in the country as McCarthyism spread insidiously into all walks of American life. They specifically refused to assign a date to the play's action, saying that it might be today, yesterday, or sometime in the future.

A version of *Inherit the Wind* existed as early as 1951, well before the McCarthy hearings began, but Lawrence and Lee sensed an erosion of individual liberties and wrote their play in part to illustrate how mass hysteria among those who do not understand the intellectual underpinnings of society can lead to disastrous outcomes. By the time the play was first presented in 1955, the McCarthy hearings were well under way, and the United States was divided by them. Many naïve Americans were misled just as the townsfolk in *Inherit the Wind* had been.

The play, translated into more than one dozen foreign languages, has been performed worldwide. In 1957, when it ended its Broadway run, it was the longest-running drama based on a historical event. The much-heralded 1960 film version, written by Nathan E. Douglas and Harold Jacob Smith and directed by Stanley Kramer, is reasonably faithful to the original script.

Inherit the Wind was consistent with other notable plays produced during this period. Arthur Miller's *Death of a Salesman* (pr., pb. 1949) explored the futility of existence for a thwarted man nearing the end of his career as a shoe salesman. In *The Crucible* (pr., pb. 1953), which focused on the Salem witch trials and was spawned by the same sort of hysteria that caused Bertram Cates to be arrested and tried in *Inherit the Wind*, Miller again addressed the question of irrationality. Both plays are aimed at demonstrating that history indeed repeats itself, usually to the detriment of society. William Inge's *Picnic* (pr., pb. 1953) examined the prejudices and crippling fears of common people living in small-town America, building on the kind of social criticism that Tennessee Williams presented in *The Glass Menagerie* (pr. 1944, pb. 1945). The climate for such social criticism was ripe for a play like *Inherit the Wind* when it was finally produced in 1955.

Sources for Further Study

Corey, Michael Anthony. *Back to Darwin: The Scientific Case for Deistic Evolution.* Lanham, Md.: University Press of America, 1994.

Darrow, Clarence. *The Story of My Life.* New York: Charles Scribner's Sons, 1965.

De Camp, L. Sprague. *The Great Monkey Trial.* Garden City, N.Y.: Doubleday, 1968.

Iannone, Carol. "The Truth About *Inherit the Wind.*" *First Things* 70 (February, 1997): 28-33.

Menton, David. "*Inherit the Wind:* An Historical Analysis." *Creation: Ex Nihilo* 19 (December, 1996-February, 1997): 35-38.

Weales, Gerald. *American Drama Since World War II.* New York: Harcourt, Brace and World, 1962.

R. Baird Shuman

AN INSPECTOR CALLS

Author: J. B. Priestley (1894-1984)
Type of plot: Mystery and detective
Time of plot: April, 1912
Locale: Brumley, North Midlands, England
First produced: 1946, at the Opera House, Manchester, England
First published: 1947

Principal characters:
ARTHUR BIRLING, a prosperous manufacturer
SYBIL BIRLING, his wife
SHEILA BIRLING, their daughter
ERIC BIRLING, their son
GERALD CROFT, Sheila's fiancé
INSPECTOR GOOLE, a purported police inspector

The Play

An Inspector Calls is set in the dining room of a large suburban house in the industrial city of Brumley, North Midlands, England. The time is early April, 1912, shortly before the fateful voyage of the *Titanic*. The action is in three acts. Act 1 opens during a formal dinner party. Around the table sit the Birling family: Arthur, a heavy-set manufacturer, in his middle fifties; Sybil, Arthur's wife and social superior, a rather cold woman; Sheila, their pretty daughter, who is in her early twenties; and Eric, their son, about the same age as his sister but shy and not as vivacious as she is. With them is their guest, Sheila's fiancé Gerald Croft, heir of a business fortune, an attractive young man of about thirty. A maid, Edna, is clearing the table and setting out port and cigars as the dialogue begins.

Birling is clearly pleased with himself. The occasion, an engagement celebration, has allowed him to ingratiate himself with Gerald, whose marriage to Sheila he hopes will smooth the way for a merger between the Birling and Croft firms. Gerald good-humoredly obliges his host's fancy and behaves like a perfect suitor as he offers Sheila a ring—which she delightedly accepts. As the conversation continues, Birling complacently dismisses the "silly little war scares" of the time, predicting that there will be peace and prosperity for decades to come. After the ladies leave the room for their coffee, Birling lectures the young men about the need for self-reliance in the modern world. Suddenly, a sharp ring of the doorbell announces the arrival of Inspector Goole.

Goole is middle-aged, solidly built, and disconcerting in his direct manner of speech. He wastes no time in getting to the point of his visit: The body of a young woman lies in a local infirmary. She had committed suicide by swallowing a bottle of disinfectant. Further investigation revealed that she was formerly an employee of Birling's company. Goole says that the woman's name was Eva Smith and then shows Birling—only Birling—a photograph of her. Birling acknowledges that Eva Smith did indeed work for him, but that she had been discharged nearly two years before for helping to instigate a strike on the issue of a pay raise. Gerald commends the action Birling took, but Eric objects that the girl had every right to try to improve her wages. Sheila reenters the room and, learning of the affair, sides with Eric. Naturally, their father is not happy with their attitude, nor can he accept the idea that the inspector appears to be blaming him personally for the tragic death.

Goole does not, however, single out only Birling; he blames the whole household for what has happened. Remorselessly pursuing his investigation through the first and second acts, he asks each of the family to tell of his or her relationship with the deceased. Sheila confesses that she had been instrumental in getting Eva fired from her job as a clerk because she thought that the girl had smirked at her while she was trying on a dress. When told that Eva had later changed her name to Daisy Renton, Gerald is noticeably startled and then admits that she had been his mistress, after he rescued her from the attentions of a "notorious womanizer." For her part, Mrs. Birling is forced to tell how, as chairwoman of a charitable society, she had used her influence to disallow the claim of a pregnant and penniless Daisy.

As the third act begins, Eric acknowledges that it was he who had made Daisy pregnant and that she had sought charity rather than accept money he had stolen for her from his father's petty cash. All these revelations provoke family quarrels; more important, each bit of evidence forges a chain of coincidences that binds everyone, morally, to Eva/Daisy's fate. Moreover, hers is not an isolated case, as the inspector makes clear: "We don't live alone. We are members of one body. We are responsible for each other. And I tell you that the time will soon come when, if men will not learn that lesson, then they will be taught it in fire and blood and anguish." Then, with a curt "Good night," he leaves the house. The subdued family is left to ponder his words.

At first they try to salvage what little self-respect they can. Gradually, however, their attention turns from the sorry events to the identity of the inspector. How was it, Sheila wonders, that he had seemed to know beforehand what the involvement of each one actually was? Birling wants to dismiss Goole as a crank who stumbled fortuitously on damaging information, but Gerald is able to show the local constabulary has never heard of an Inspector Goole. Further checking reveals that there is no dead body at the infirmary and that there has not been a suicide reported in the district in months.

Suddenly, the telephone rings. Birling answers. He announces that the police have just found a girl, dead after swallowing disinfectant, while on her way to the infirmary; a police inspector is on his way to the Birling home to ask some questions. The curtain falls.

Themes and Meanings

J. B. Priestley once said that, as a dramatist, "I owe much to the influence of Chekhov." He came to maturity during World War I, and his vision of the bourgeois family was shaped by the incisive topical realism of the plays and short stories of Russian writer Anton Chekhov. In *An Inspector Calls*, the audience is made more aware of the family's weaknesses than of its strengths, as the foundation of modern society. However, the play is marked by a hortatory tone that is generally absent in the more subtle Chekhov. Still, it is a work of solid theatricality and has proved very popular in many countries since its first production.

The play has, perhaps, three main themes. First, it points to the need for each human being to accept his or her moral responsibility for the welfare of others, especially of those who are less privileged. Second, it explores the various kinds of evasion of which humans are capable—through indifference or rationalization—when they try to avoid this responsibility. Finally, it shows through a conflict of generations that young people are at least more conscious than their elders of the importance of altruistic belief and behavior.

These themes find their focal point in the character of the inspector. Goole, as the instigator of the action, constantly endeavors to remind the Birlings and Gerald of their complicity in a young woman's sad life and death. More like an inquisitor of souls than a police officer conducting a routine examination, his questioning leads the audience to see how snobbishness, spite, and prejudice blind people such as the older Birlings to the wrongs in their society. The parents' moral obtuseness is countered by a sense of guilt and an openness to correction in the hearts of their children. Thus, Priestley dramatizes both the failure and the hope of the empathic imagination.

This said, it must be stated that the weakest character in the play is the one never seen in the flesh: Eva Smith. She remains an abstraction, more sinned against than sinning, certainly; yet surely she bears some fault for her own destruction, a fault that is never shown convincingly. Nevertheless, it is on what Eva represents that the symbolic meaning of the play depends, for only if humankind overcomes its egotism can society become a genuine community of shared values, respect, and love.

Dramatic Devices

An Inspector Calls clearly belongs to the mystery and detective play genre. However, it is more than that: It contains elements of the problem play, the psychological thriller, and the medieval morality. As theater, it is a fascinating blend of forms.

To begin with, it is an odd example of the mystery play because Goole is no ordinary detective and because there is no murder or murderer in the usual sense. There is, though, an unraveling of clues, suspense, and a final plot twist—all features of the stage mystery, particularly in England. *An Inspector Calls* begins, however, as a problem play, and as one gets to know the family one can see how J. B. Priestley is preparing the way for the crisis. The mood of carefree happiness is cleverly undercut by Birling's ironic reference to the imminent sailing of the *Titanic*, which, in approximately a week, will become the symbol of an age's hubris. The same is true of his pompous assurance of the world's safe future when Europe is about to undergo the disaster of World War I. None of this would be lost on post-1945 audiences, who would be aware of these calamities and conscious of the fact that they had just survived another world war and were living through an era of possible nuclear war. The sources of these horrors are the minds of ordinary men and women who create conditions of social and economic injustice, Priestley implies. As Goole begins to extract the family's secrets, the initial lighting of the set, soft pink, becomes "brighter and harder," emphasizing the change to a dark mood. Here the elements of a psychological thriller are apparent, as viewers move inside the recesses of characters' experiences on a steadily descending path to ignobility and guilt.

The inspector's very name may give one momentary pause, for its sound suggests unhealthy associations with the world of the supernatural (ghoul). It is ironic, therefore, that he is actually one who brings forth good out of evil by insisting that truth be divulged and then draws the appropriate moral conclusions. In short, he is the antithesis of a ghoul: an angel of light.

Priestley's handling of the final scene, in which the family members discover that they have been duped into a recognition of their shared guilt, is masterly in execution. He shows how they all, with the exception of Eric and Sheila, seek to avoid the spur of conscience and remorse. However, can any of them avoid the consequences of a real detective's inquiry into a real death? The audience has sat in judgment on their past actions; it must now decide whether the family, being forewarned, is now forearmed against truth.

Critical Context

By the time J. B. Priestley wrote *An Inspector Calls*, he was midway through a highly successful and amazingly prolific career as a playwright. His total output numbered some fifty plays; he also produced scores of novels, essays, biographies, editions, and pieces of journalism. Because so much of his writing was associated with British society, he was sometimes derided as a "professional Englishman" who wrote too much and too thinly about too many subjects. In any case, he was a devoted man of letters and was granted the rare honor in 1977 of membership in Britain's Order of Merit, for his services to literature.

An Inspector Calls is often compared with some of his earlier dramas, such as *Eden End* (pr., pb. 1934), also a play about a family facing social change in Edwardian England in 1912. Other plays, notably *Time and the Conways* (pr., pb. 1937), reveal Priestley's enthusiasm for the idea of time as a dimension of space, a concept popularized by H. G. Wells in his science-fiction novella *The Time Machine* (1895). Some of this interest in foreshadowing events through precognition is central to the plot of *An Inspector Calls*.

Sources for Further Study

Cook, Judith. *Priestley*. London: Bloomsbury, 1997.
De Vitis, A. A., and Albert E. Kalson. *J. B. Priestley*. Boston: Twayne, 1980.

Evans, Gareth Lloyd. *J. B. Priestley: The Dramatist*. London: Heinemann, 1964.

Foot, Michael. *William Hazlitt, J. B. Priestley*. Plymouth, England: Northcote House, 1990.

Gray, Dulcie. *J. B. Priestley*. Stroud, England: Sutton, 2000.

Hughes, David. *J. B. Priestley: An Informal Study of His Work*. London: Hart Davis, 1958.

Klein, Holger. *J. B. Priestley's Plays*. Basingstoke, England: Macmillan, 1988.

Priestley, J. B. *The Art of the Dramatist*. London: Heinemann, 1957.

Eric Thompson

IVONA, PRINCESS OF BURGUNDIA

Author: Witold Gombrowicz (1904-1969)
Type of plot: Absurdist
Time of plot: Unspecified
Locale: Burgundia
First produced: 1957, at the Teatr Dramatyczny, Warsaw, Poland
First published: Iwona, księżniczka Burgunda, 1938 (English translation, 1969)

> *Principal characters:*
> IVONA, a repulsive and ugly woman
> PRINCE PHILIP, the heir to the throne
> KING IGNATIUS, Prince Philip's father
> QUEEN MARGARET, Prince Philip's mother
> LORD CHAMBERLAIN, the king's adviser
> ISOBEL, a lady in waiting
> SIMON, a friend of the prince

The Play

The first act of *Ivona, Princess of Burgundia* is set on a promenade, with the king, queen, prince, and their court gathered together in conversation. While the king and queen engage their court in conventional praises of the sunset, their son Philip sets himself aside, obviously bored with the routine. Clearly he is looking for a change and is impatient with his male companions, who engage in all too typical commentary on the good looks of any woman who interests them.

Ivona catches the prince's attention. Not only is she not attractive to men, but even her female relatives find her a trial, for she is virtually inert, rarely speaks, and has an offensive demeanor. Ivona's aunt goes so far as to say that her phlegmatic attitude is a constitutional defect. In other words, it is unlikely that anything can be done to make her more appealing. However, this unique behavior is exactly what Prince Philip says he likes about her: She is not the kind of woman a young man should love. He is determined to act like an original and not like every other young man out to find a beautiful, charming woman. He takes pride in adopting an attitude that checks his inclinations and that defies the constricting dictates of nature and society.

Act 2 opens in the prince's apartments, with him declaring that Ivona is the dragon he must slay, the challenge he must undertake to prove his heroic distinctiveness. His friends are appalled; his mother and father are dismayed. The court, however, tries to be agreeable by accommodating his choice of this repulsive woman. It is tough going for everyone, including Philip, who manages to extract only a few enigmatic sentences from Ivona. He has never met anyone so self-contained, so impervious to external influences. She is her own being and is virtually immune to every attempt to draw her out. At first, he finds this a remarkable, even fascinating quality, perhaps because he has resolved not to be like anyone else, too. Soon, though, a note of hysteria creeps into his speeches, which grow longer as he tries to gauge her responses.

In the third act, the prince begins to suspect that people are laughing at him. For all of his rejection of conventional social attitudes, he is beginning to weary of his idiosyncratic stance. In fact, he succumbs to the attractiveness of another woman and breaks his engagement to Ivona, even as his parents and the court have been pondering what to do about Ivona. She makes them all uneasy, including the king and queen, who begin to have feelings of inadequacy.

In the fourth and final act, everyone is plotting to get rid of Ivona. The queen loathes her, for somehow Ivona reminds her of the poetry she has kept secret from the court and from her husband. Something about Ivona makes the queen feel deeply ashamed of herself. The king is in a foul temper, saying outrageous things and plotting with his chamberlain to have Ivona killed. They start by planning a huge state dinner—just the kind of event at which Ivona (a commoner) will feel uneasy. They have noticed how out of place she seems to be in such gatherings, so they will surround her with dignitaries, disconcert her with constant attention, serve her a boney pike, and generally contrive a situation in which she chokes on a bone at the dinner.

The plot proves entirely successful, and everyone is relieved and pleased. "Ah, yes, a bone. I see," Philip remarks over Ivona's dead body. It is a perfect ending for the court because everything appears socially correct—a point that is emphasized when Philip joins the court in kneeling beside Ivona's lifeless body.

Themes and Meanings

Ivona, Princess of Burgundia is about the social natures of human beings. Prince Philip would like to believe that he can act on his own, that he can defy the expectations of his male companions, his parents, and the whole court. However, in order to do so, he must act perversely—act, that is, contrary to what he admits are his inclinations. He is really attracted to beautiful women, but he fights against his attraction to prove that he is his own man.

Ivona's fate reveals the consequence of being truly individual: isolation from society. There is no way to have a simple conversation without taking into consideration and to a great extent incorporating other people's points of view. The play begins, for example, with a talk about the sunset similar to the conversations about weather that all people find it necessary to engage in. Such conversations ratify the need for human intercourse, for one person to listen and respond to another, no matter how trivial the matter might be. When Ivona does speak, it is usually to say what she does not feel, to make clear that she is not the sum of what people say about her. She is unwilling, however, to define what she is. She refuses to help others place her in some kind of communal context. She is no help to those who want her at least to acknowledge their questions or to take part in a dialogue they have initiated. By refusing to do so, Ivona attacks the very nature of society.

Ivona makes the king and queen feel inadequate because they are the rulers of society. They, above all people, depend on the obedience of others, on a court that will be ingratiating and cater to royal opinions and wishes. To confront a subject who concedes nothing of herself is to deal with an equal. Ivona reminds the queen of her poetry, which is the most private, most individual part of herself, the part the queen has never been willing to make public; not even her husband knows about it. When Ivona's individuality, her absolute determination to keep her thoughts to herself, becomes the subject of public commentary, the very notion of a private, secret self is exposed, and it is this very notion that the queen has kept to herself until Ivona's appearance at court. Thus, the queen feels embarrassed and exposed. The queen, the king, and the prince each have a role that clothes and protects their egos. Ivona refuses to play a role (as the prince's fiancé, for example) and so forces people to consider who they really are. At first, the prince finds her exhilarating for precisely this reason: Loving her releases him from a role. In the end, however, trying to live as one's true self and not in some socially defined capacity is so alienating that it cannot be sustained. Therefore, a social event must be staged that removes Ivona from the scene. Society must find a way of protecting itself.

Dramatic Devices

The most important dramatic device of the play is Ivona herself. It is remarkable how the playwright has been able to use such a simple stratagem—a character who almost never speaks—to precipitate action. As the various characters address Ivona and try to get her to agree or disagree with their observations and advice, they reveal themselves more fully than any dialogue between characters could do. For each time Ivona does not speak, her interlocutor must speak longer and more pointedly. Not only does this device help to define the other characters sharply, but it also increases the tension in the play. Everyone wonders when Ivona will speak.

Except for act 1, the setting of the play is indoors, in various rooms of the castle. The playwright does not describe the rooms. Indeed, the play contains almost nothing in the way of stage or set descriptions, since Witold Gombrowicz is not interested in the period or in the specific social customs of the court. Rather, he presents interior scenes that are meant to raise questions about the structure of society itself and about how rigid role-playing within society must be. The court itself can be viewed as a dramatic device, as a way of emphasizing how fixed human beings are by their societal functions.

Critical Context

Ivona, Princess of Burgundia is very much of a piece with Witold Gombrowicz's other plays and novels. *Ferdydurke* (1938; English translation, 1961), a novel about a thirty-year-old man turning into an adolescent, is the author's fullest expression of a certain immaturity he finds in the human character. As his other novels *Pornografia* (1960; English translation, 1966) and *Kosmos* (1965; *Cosmos*, 1966) suggest, Gombrowicz has little faith in the wisdom of civilization. Rather than growing into responsible roles, many of his characters seem coerced into adopting guises.

Although the playwright's characters seem to speak nonsensically at times, and although his depiction of society is satirical, it is perhaps going too far to say that his dramas are absurdist in the sense that they imply that there is no meaning in existence. Gombrowicz was a skeptic and certainly saw the vacuity of social relationships, but he was not a nihilist. Indeed, many of his characters have a compulsion to put their world in order, even if that order is rather trivial or ridiculous.

It is perhaps inevitable that Gombrowicz, a Polish writer who left Poland in the 1930's and took up a life of exile in Argentina, should be suspected of writing allegory. His plays and novels are sometimes interpreted as elaborately indirect studies of the way his country has been oppressed by other nations, chiefly Germany and the former Soviet Union. There may be some point to this approach, especially if *Ivona, Princess of Burgundia* is taken as a drama about how individuality is crushed in a conformist, authoritarian society. Gombrowicz himself, though, denied such allegorical interpretations. What seems more certain is that his historical experience as a Pole made him skeptical of any form of social or political control. All forms of policing human behavior, he implied, are only rationalizations for society's compulsive need for each of its members to submit to authority.

There is much humor in Gombrowicz's work, which is accentuated in *Ivona, Princess of Burgundia* by making the royal figures behave so foolishly. Once they are caught in the grip of their scheme to kill Ivona, they cannot stop talking about it. They become possessed by their plan to such an extent that the king expresses his murderous feelings at the very moment when he should conceal them: "As we have said, we are giving this modest but elegant entertainment to celebrate the violent end . . . I mean, the happy betrothal of our future daughter-in-law." As Gombrowicz said in an autobiographical work, *Entretiens avec Gombrowicz* (1968; *A Kind of Testament*, 1973), in writing *Ivona, Princess of Burgundia* he was "assailed by the limitless anarchy of form, of human form, of its dissoluteness and licentiousness." He appears to have had in mind the utter unreliability of human beings who, like the king, rule and yet are overwhelmed by impulses they cannot control. In the very act of trying to reimpose stability at court, the king loses control of his tongue. A deeply ironic writer, Gombrowicz nearly always had a wry smile, if not outright laughter, for the human pretense of self-government.

Sources for Further Study

Gombrowicz, Witold. *Diary.* Vols. 1-3. Edited by Jan Kott. Evanston, Ill.: Northwestern University Press, 1994.

Jelenski, Constantin. *Gombrowicz.* Paris: Éditions de l'Herne, 1971.

Kott, Jan. *Theatre Notebook, 1947-1967.* Translated by Bodesław Taborski. Garden City, N.Y.: Doubleday, 1968.

Miłosz, Czesław. *The History of Polish Literature.* New York: Macmillan, 1969.

Thompson, Ewa M. *Witold Gombrowicz.* Boston: Twayne, 1979.

Ziarek, Eva. P. *Gombrowicz's Grimaces: Modernism, Gender, Nationality.* Albany: State University of New York Press, 1998.

Carl Rollyson

JOE TURNER'S COME AND GONE

Author: August Wilson (1945-   )
Type of plot: Social realism
Time of plot: August, 1911
Locale: A boardinghouse in Pittsburgh, Pennsylvania
First produced: 1986, at the Yale Repertory Theatre, New Haven, Connecticut
First published: 1988

> *Principal characters:*
> SETH HOLLY, an African American tinsmith and owner of a
>   boardinghouse
> BERTHA HOLLY, his wife
> BYNUM WALKER, a "rootworker," or "conjure man"
> RUTHERFORD SELIG, a white American peddler and "People
>   Finder"
> JEREMY FURLOW, a resident of the boardinghouse
> HERALD LOOMIS, a resident
> ZONIA LOOMIS, Herald's daughter
> MATTIE CAMPBELL, a resident
> MARTHA LOOMIS, Herald Loomis's wife

The Play

Joe Turner's Come and Gone opens on a Saturday morning in the kitchen of Seth Holly's Pittsburgh boardinghouse. A skilled black tinsmith, Seth works nights for a white manufacturer. During the day, he makes his own pots and pans on the side and runs the boardinghouse with his wife, Bertha, dreaming of the day he might have his own manufacturing business.

On this Saturday the only lodgers are longtime resident Bynum Walker and a newcomer, Jeremy Furlow, who arrived two weeks earlier from North Carolina. Bynum is a "conjure man" or "root doctor," who claims that with his roots and herbs he can "bind," or bring together people who are meant for each other. Jeremy is an irresponsible young man who has come North to find work in the prosperous, industrial city. His main interests are playing his guitar and flirting with pretty women.

Rutherford Selig makes his weekly stop, bringing Seth the raw materials for his pots and pans, which Selig will then sell with the rest of his wares. An itinerant white peddler, Selig keeps track of all the people he meets and claims to be a "People Finder." For a dollar, Selig will attempt to find any missing person, and when Selig arrives this morning he reports to Bynum that he has still not found Bynum's "shiny man."

In a mystical experience on a rural road Bynum once met a "shiny man" who showed him the meaning of life. Bynum has hired Selig to find this or any other "shiny man" because Bynum believes that if he sees another shiny man it will be an infallible sign that his life's work has been fulfilled.

After Selig leaves, a mysterious and brooding stranger arrives at the door with his eleven-year-old daughter. Herald Loomis is searching for his wife and takes temporary lodgings. When he hears about Rutherford Selig, the People Finder, Loomis is determined to stay until next Saturday and hire Selig to find his wife, Martha.

In act 2, the audience will learn that ten years before the action of the play began, Herald Loomis, his wife Martha, and their baby daughter Zonia were living on a farm outside Memphis, Tennessee, where Herald was a sharecropper and a deacon in the Abundant Life Church. One day Herald was abducted and enslaved by Joe Turner (a real person in American history) and forced to pick cotton for seven years. After he was released, Herald returned to his farm only to find that his wife had left their daughter with her mother and gone North. For more than three years Herald and his daughter have been searching for Martha.

The next Saturday arrives, Selig returns, and Herald hires him to find Martha. Herald's taciturn, brooding manner and his wild and savage look have unnerved Seth since Herald's arrival, but Seth's apprehensions turn to open hostility in the last scene of act 1, Sunday evening after dinner. The residents have gathered for a Juba, an African call and response dance that ends in a religious frenzy. Herald enters in the middle of the dance and in a rage attacks religion as an ineffectual crutch for black people. In a frenzy himself, Herald unzips his trousers, exposes himself, and begins chanting in tongues, dancing around the kitchen. He collapses, recalling a powerful visionary experience of haunting imagery, and Bynum questions him avidly while the rest of the residents sit in stunned silence. Seth is outraged and determined to evict Herald as the first act ends.

At the beginning of act 2, Herald counters Seth's demand by insisting that he has a right to stay until the next Saturday because he has paid in advance. Seth reluctantly agrees. On Monday Jeremy reports that he has been fired from his construction job because he would not pay protection money to a white man. He persuades Molly, another resident, to leave with him, and they depart from the boardinghouse to see the world and pursue a life of pleasure.

In the last scene of the play it is Saturday again, and Selig returns with Martha in tow. When Herald accuses Martha of abandoning him and their daughter, Martha explains that she has spent the last three years looking for them. Herald explains that he has searched for Martha because he wanted to give Zonia a mother and say his goodbye to Martha face to face: "Now that I see your face I can say my goodbye and make my own world." This ritualistic act has not eased Herald's mind, however; he still feels enormous anger and resentment because he continues to feel trapped by his past.

Bynum explains to Herald that he has trapped himself, that he has let Joe Turner take his "song," that all he needs to do to be free is to reclaim his song and sing it. As the play ends, Herald has come to realize that Bynum is right. He has rediscovered his song, the "song of self-sufficiency." He quietly says good-bye to Martha and exits, and Bynum realizes that he has just met his second "shiny man."

Themes and Meanings

Joe Turner's Come and Gone is a play about African Americans cut adrift by slavery from their African past. Now technically free, they wander aimlessly without roots, looking for solace but often mistaking or not knowing what they really need, which is a sense of self-esteem and personal identity.

Bynum is the one character who has this quality, and he attempts to help others find it. Bynum says that every person has a "song," a unique identity and purpose in life; some people, he says, cannot find their song, or forget it, or let someone else steal it. Bynum explains that in his vision on the rural road, he saw his Daddy, who showed him that Bynum's song was the "Binding Song," that his role in life was to bind people who belong together. Bynum's confidence in his identity and purpose in life is unshakable. From the first scene in the play, Seth is openly skeptical and scornful of Bynum's magical powers, but Bynum's response is a cheerful insistence that he will know his song has been accepted "and worked its full power in the world" when he sees his second "shiny man." Bynum's magic does indeed work, for it reunites Martha and Zonia and helps Herald discover his own song, binding him to it for life and freeing him from the indignity he feels over his enslavement by Joe Turner.

Until the end of the play, Loomis thinks that he is simply looking for his wife so that he can turn his daughter over to her and say his good-bye, but Bynum teaches Loomis that what he was really looking for was his "song," his unique identity, his own sense of dignity and self-esteem. This theme is strengthened as Loomis is contrasted with other black characters who look to the wrong remedies for their suffering. Seth Holly is looking for entrepreneurial freedom—the opportunity to compete equally with the white man for a fair share of the so-called good life. August Wilson suggests, however, that economic power is not the essential need for black people. When Jeremy quits his job rather than pay protection money, Seth ridicules Jeremy's choice, asserting that a job with some money is better than none at all. Seth's willingness to sacrifice dignity for money demonstrates an exaggerated respect for economic power.

Jeremy is similar to Seth in that he longs for a fair chance to compete with whites, but Jeremy's competitive arena is much more frivolous. He wants only a fair chance to win honky-tonk guitar contests. His shallow pursuit of gratification is further indicated when he leaves with Molly—Jeremy wants most simply to possess as many women and see as many places as possible. Loomis is the metaphorical herald of true black needs because, although he himself is unaware of it, he is looking for the real solution: a personal identity, his own "song." Bynum says that "people cling to each other out of the truth they find in themselves."

Dramatic Devices

In *Joe Turner's Come and Gone*, August Wilson's style is basically realistic. The action takes place almost exclusively in the boardinghouse setting, where ordinary characters face ordinary problems, and their black dialects are faithfully reproduced. This style is useful for examining the mistreatment of black Americans early in the twentieth century because the realism of the presentation mirrors and reinforces Wilson's insistence on the reality of the historical exploitation and suffering.

Most of the play's effect, however—its raw emotional power—comes from the nonrealistic elements that Wilson adds to his play. The focus of these elements is the characterization of Bynum Walker. He is portrayed as a man of essentially magical powers, able to work completely unrealistic effects out of roots and herbs, able to penetrate to the essence of a person's history and character in a way that surpasses ordinary human ability. The basis of these powers was a mystical experience in which he saw sparrows the size of eagles and talked with a man who had light pouring out of him—just before the man disappeared into thin air.

In the play's opening dialogue, Seth's disparaging attitude toward Bynum makes Bynum appear eccentric. The subsequent account of Bynum's mystical experience is very compelling, however, and when he uses such terms as "shiny man," "the secret of life," "song," "binding," and "the road," it seems quite possible that Bynum is no mere eccentric. The terms are clearly metaphorical and carry thematic import. Then, early in the first act, Mattie Campbell comes to Bynum and asks him to work his magic to return her husband to her. Bynum becomes a very believable part of the play because his response to Mattie is unusually sensible and not at all eccentric. The audience willingly suspends its disbelief, and Bynum's magical powers become an accepted part of an essentially realistic play.

The vision recounted by Herald Loomis when he interrupts the Juba is as mystical and metaphorical as Bynum's. Herald's is a vision of the history of slavery, the central experience of African Americans, and at the end of his description, Herald reports that in the vision and at that very moment he is not able to stand. This image is specifically echoed at the end of the play. In his frustration, Herald slashes himself with a knife. He then rubs himself with his own blood and is able to stand, say good-bye to Martha, and leave, whereupon Bynum ends the play with the prophetic words, "Herald Loomis, you shining! You shining like new money!" These nonrealistic elements give Wilson's basically realistic play a haunting and poetic quality that realism alone would not have been able to achieve.

Critical Context

August Wilson exploded onto the contemporary theater scene in 1984, when his first major play, *Ma Rainey's Black Bottom*, was produced on Broadway; it was a solid, if modest, success, winning a New York Drama Critics Circle Award as Broadway's best play (in a somewhat lackluster season). With *Fences* (pr., pb. 1985), Wilson left no doubt that he was to become a major theatrical force. With James Earl Jones taking the starring role on Broadway in 1987, *Fences* won numerous awards, including a Tony for best play and the Pulitzer Prize in drama. *The Piano Lesson*, Wilson's 1987 play (pb. 1990), won the 1990 Pulitzer Prize in drama, as well as a New York Drama Critics Award—an award he also earned for *Seven Guitars* (pr. 1995, pb. 1996). He received Tony Award nominations for *Seven Guitars* and, in 2001, for *King Hedley II* (pr. 2001).

The dramatic quality of Wilson's canon is unmistakable, but his importance in contemporary theater was also established early in his career when he announced that he intended to write a play for every decade of the twentieth century, focusing in each on a critical aspect of the black experience in America. This epic scope has in itself attracted much critical attention. Set in 1911, *Joe Turner's Come and Gone* is the play for the second decade of the century. *Ma Rainey's Black Bottom* is the play for the 1920's, *Fences* the play for the 1950's, and *The Piano Lesson* (pr. 1988) the play for the 1930's. *Two Trains Running* (pr. 1990, pb. 1992) and *Seven Guitars* were his late twentieth century additions to this epic. Plays written and produced before Wilson's meteoric fame fit into other decades, but they remain unheralded, and the cycle is defined by the plays since *Ma Rainey's Black Bottom*.

Few question Wilson's success in capturing the psychological and social travails of black Americans in the twentieth century. Each play examines the problems specific to its decade while making effective generalizations about the enduring problems of black Americans. Most striking is Wilson's observation that black Americans have often directed their frustrations and anger at one another rather than turning them directly toward the oppressive white power structure. For example, in *Ma Rainey's Black Bottom*, Levee is poorly paid for his music and cheated by a white entrepreneur, but he turns his rage against the fellow black musician who accidentally steps on his new shoes. In *Fences*, Troy Maxson feels cheated by a white establishment that would not permit him to play baseball, but he takes out his disappointment and hostility on his son, Cory, denying him an opportunity for a college football scholarship. Because the white enemy is so difficult to pinpoint, it is simpler and more immediately satisfying to strike out at one's own family and friends.

The critical response to Wilson's work has been enthusiastic, with *Fences* often being compared favorably with Arthur Miller's *Death of a Salesman* (pr., pb. 1949). Praise, however, is frequently tempered by charges that his plays can be clumsy in their structure and are sometimes melodramatic. Wilson's strengths lie most clearly in powerful characterization and in a strong ear for colloquial dialogue. The mystical quality of *Joe Turner's Come and Gone* may always limit its commercial success, but in this play Wilson's characteristic use of controlling metaphors is more natural and powerful than anywhere else in his canon, and here he perhaps captures most powerfully his main theme, the search of African Americans for a satisfactory and well-defined place in society.

Sources for Further Study

Bernstein, Richard. "August Wilson's Voices from the Past." *New York Times*, March 27, 1988, sec. 2, p. 1.

De Vries, Hilary. "A Song in Search of Itself." *American Theatre* 3 (January, 1987): 22-25.

Freedman, Samuel. "A Voice from the Streets." *New York Times Magazine*, March 15, 1987, p. 36.

Herrington, Joan. *I Ain't Sorry for Nothin' I Done: August Wilson's Process of Playwriting*. New York: Limelight, 1998.

Savran, David, ed. "August Wilson." In *In Their Own Words: Contemporary American Playwrights*. New York: Theatre Communications Group, 1988.

Shafer, Yvonne. *August Wilson: A Research and Production Sourcebook*. Westport, Conn.: Greenwood Press, 1998.

Shannon, Sandra Garrett. *The Dramatic Vision of August Wilson*. Washington, D.C.: Howard University Press, 1995.

Wilson, August. Interview by Kim Powers. *Theatre* 16 (Fall/Winter, 1984): 50-55.

Zoglin, Richard, and Jonathan Beaty. "Exorcising the Demons of Memory." *Time*, April 11, 1988, 77-78.

Terry Nienhuis

JOHN BULL'S OTHER ISLAND

Author: George Bernard Shaw (1856-1950)
Type of plot: Naturalistic; comedy
Time of plot: Summer, 1904
Locale: London, England, and Rosscullen, Ireland
First produced: 1904, at the Royal Court Theatre, London
First published: 1907

> *Principal characters:*
> TOM BROADBENT, a civil engineer and a cheerful, robust
>   Englishman
> LAURENCE DOYLE, his partner, an Irishman
> CORNELIUS DOYLE, Laurence's father, a land-agent
> FATHER KEEGAN, a defrocked priest
> NORA REILLY, the "heiress" of Rosscullen
> BARNEY DORAN, a stout miller
> MATT HAFFIGAN, a brutalized small farmer

The Play

Act one opens in the Westminster office-cum-bachelor rooms of Broadbent and Doyle, civil engineers. Tom Broadbent, very much the cheery, beef-fed John Bull, just back from a trip, instructs his valet, Hodson, to pack their bags for Ireland. He inquires whether anyone has called while he was away. Only an Irishman named Haffigan, replies Hodson, so disreputable that the punctilious valet showed him the door. However, Broadbent expresses an enthusiastic desire to see him. At that moment, fortuitously, Haffigan calls again.

Seedy, red-nosed, and possessed of a "rollicking stage brogue," Haffigan rapidly downs half a pint of Broadbent's whiskey, borrows five pounds, and arranges to accompany him to Rosscullen, Ireland, where Broadbent intends to develop an estate for the Land Development Syndicate. Convinced of the benefits of English efficiency, Broadbent is elated to think he will thereby also do some good for the downtrodden Irish. He wants Haffigan, as a typical Irishman (a role Haffigan is playing to the hilt), to promote the project among his countrymen.

Their tête-à-tête is interrupted by the arrival of Broadbent's friend and partner. With Haffigan gone, Laurence Doyle exposes Broadbent's folly in taking for the genuine article a Glasgow con artist with incipient delirium tremens—a folly entirely dependent on Broadbent's subscribing to all the myths about the improvident, genial, and melancholy Irish-Celtic character. That character, says Doyle, is an invention of the English music hall. The real Irish character is bred by Ireland's misty climate: The Irishman, says Doyle, himself in a "passionate dream," is a hopeless dreamer whose dreams condemn him to perpetual squalor. Hence Doyle's fear of returning; furthermore, Rosscullen is his birthplace, where Nora Reilly still waits for him. Broadbent nevertheless persuades him to come.

The scene changes to the open countryside of Rosscullen, at sunset: a lonely white road, heather, an ancient round tower in the distance, and an outcrop of granite in the foreground. On the granite, a man is conversing in mock seriousness with a grasshopper, causing terror in Patsy Farrell, who begs Father Keegan not to put a spell on him. Keegan can hardly shake him off, but the car arrives, and Patsy hurries off to carry the visitors' bags, passing Nora Reilly, Keegan's favorite. They talk; Nora is clearly preoccupied with the man who left her for the wide world eighteen years ago. Both leave before Broadbent enters, in company with the parish priest and Cornelius Doyle, Laurence Doyle's father. Laurence Doyle, it seems, has been delayed in his journey. Cornelius's sister comes down the hill to meet them and to arrange tea and accommodation (on the parlor sofa) for their guest. Bullying the overburdened Patsy and embarrassed by their poverty, the Doyles head homeward.

A little later, well fed and watered (he has sampled potcheen, the illicit moonshine of Irish lore), Broadbent strolls out for a cigar by the Round Tower. Here he surprises Nora, who had hoped to encounter Doyle in this romantic setting. She is proudly distant, but enchantment with everything Irish has induced in Broadbent a condition of extreme sentimentality: Within two minutes he proposes. She blames the potcheen and leads him home; he is mortified to think that he has disgraced himself.

Act 3 opens shortly after breakfast in the garden of the Doyle home. A new arrival at the gate is identified by Laurence Doyle, now safely arrived, as another Haffigan— Matt, an unprepossessing peasant whose wits have been extinguished by degrading toil. His tales of injustice and suffering predictably stir Broadbent's sympathy. Meanwhile, the Englishman also worries about the night before; his confession elicits howls of laughter from Doyle for his "blithering sentimentality."

Cornelius, Father Dempsey, Matt Haffigan, and Barney Doran (a redheaded miller with "an enormous capacity for derisive, obscene, blasphemous, or merely cruel and senseless fun") now appear. They have come to sound out Doyle on the possibility of his standing for Parliament; they want a member with his own money, who will leave them alone. Doyle, however, has become a citizen of the world and knows that he is not for them. His talk of a minimum wage for the Patsy Farrells of Ireland, of turning the land over to those who can make it prosper, and of breaking the stranglehold of the Roman Catholic Church rapidly frightens them. Instead, it seems, the ideal candidate is Broadbent, who now takes a turn at speechifying. The locals then confer and decide that they could easily control him. Meanwhile, quite pleased with himself, Broadbent leaves to fetch his motorcar. He has seen a way to a quick bit of campaigning—he will give a ride home to the pig that Cornelius has just sold Matt.

Between acts 3 and 4, the comic catastrophe the audience has anticipated occurs: The terrified pig has gone hog-wild in the motorcar, which in turn has run out of control through the streets on market day. Molly Ryan's china stall has been smashed and an old lady injured. All of this the audience learns from Doran, who tells the tale with relish to his cronies, Keegan, and the family in Cornelius's parlor. The Irish sense of

humor has been thoroughly tickled by the preposterous Englishman. When Broadbent enters, however, full of the seriousness of Molly's losses, the old lady's injuries,
the unfortunate pig's demise, and other consequences that might have ensued, the audience—like Doyle and the family—is led to question whether his version of the story
is the better one. Even Keegan now tells him he will win the seat, although he is, unconsciously, a hypocrite in the service of Mammon (the syndicate).

The party breaks up. Doyle and Nora are left alone for the first time. An awkward
interview leaves Nora in tears. Broadbent, returning, cannot stand seeing her unhappy; he takes her in his arms for comfort and clumsily but determinedly wins her
promise to marry him. He is elated: What better wife could a politician have? He persuades her to come on a walk, and genteel Nora finds that she now must degrade herself in her own eyes by shaking hands with all and sundry. However, as Doyle makes
her see, she has made the best match she can; Broadbent will make her happy, healthy,
and useful. At the play's end, he is planning to do much the same for all Rosscullen by
turning poor farmers into disciplined workers for the Syndicate and building a hotel
and golf course near the Round Tower, which will become a tourist attraction. Not
even a final encounter with the mysterious and spiritual Keegan dampens his faith in
his power to do good, or Irish Doyle's faith in his Englishness, which has "made a
man" of Doyle too.

Themes and Meanings

John Bull's Other Island is a satirical comedy about national character. The fact
that George Bernard Shaw's characters, as in so many of his plays, are not merely incessant talkers but indeed inveterate speech-makers helps elucidate Shaw's themes.

In his sixty-page "Preface for Politicians," Shaw sketches his view of the English
and Irish characters. In contradiction to the received national mythology, he argues for
the sentimentality of the English as against the more fastidious imaginativeness of the
Irish, who combine a greater sense of the real with a debilitating sense of futility. This
analysis is animated in the play, which presents the Union of England and Ireland as a
marriage between the kindly, if brutally efficient, English husband and his sensitive
Irish mate—in which role Doyle serves as much as Nora.

The presentation is evenhanded and unsentimental; Matt Haffigan, for example, is
an unpleasant specimen, for all of his sufferings. Nevertheless—in contradiction to
the critical charge that Shaw is incapable of portraying human pain—the play's sympathy extends even to Haffigan's Glaswegian relative, who sheds tears of joy at the
thought of how much drink can be bought with a five-pound note. Furthermore, Father Keegan represents an undigested lump of suffering in the play: Only the de-
frocked priest, with his despairing sense of this world as a living hell, operates entirely
outside its comic economy.

Dramatic Devices

John Bull's Other Island eschews the box set of the period, demanding some ambitious staging—the landscape of act 2 in particular. The play is interestingly structured

around a spatial theme of penetration: The audience sees the Doyle house interior only in act 4. The other and much more striking dramatic device of the play is its language; the fake Irishman of act 1 allows Shaw an opportunity to dispense with stage conventions about the Irish character and also the Irish idiom. For Haffigan's hackneyed "top of the morning" and "broth of a boy" and his fabricated brogue are substituted fine nuances (indicated in the published play by phonetic transcription) unsurpassed in the rest of Shaw's work, not excepting *Pygmalion* (pb. 1912, pr. 1914).

John Bull's Other Island is still a humorous play. The sources of its comedy include episodes of inspired zaniness, the motoring pig above all. The slapstick takes place offstage (though Patsy Farrell has some comical onstage business with a large salmon), but in any case the comic effect depends more on the stoking and fulfillment of audience expectations. There are also ironic turns of event; plot is not normally Shaw's strong point, but *John Bull's Other Island* is effectively constructed and makes ironic use of the clichés of theatrical plotting (the exile's return, the girl who waits behind, and the like). Ironic twists that push the humor to new levels of comedy include the cronies' willing acceptance of Broadbent as their parliamentary candidate after the episode with Matt's pig. The play's breathless pacing adds to the comic effect.

One of the most important sources of the play's comedy is its dialogue, which exploits the absurdities of the characters' positions. The well-meaning Broadbent, for example, declares with "intense earnestness": "Never despair, Larry. There are great possibilities for Ireland. Home Rule will work wonders under English guidance." His very indulgence is insulting and his blind seriousness grandly comic: "It will be quite delightful to drive with a pig in the car: I shall feel quite like an Irishman."

In Laurence Doyle's despairing assessment of the Irish national character Shaw provides a philosophical basis for the Irish sense of hilarity at the center of disaster:

> Oh, the dreaming! the dreaming! the torturing, heartscalding, never satisfying dreaming, dreaming, dreaming, dreaming! . . . And all the time you laugh, laugh, laugh! eternal derision, eternal envy, eternal folly, eternal fouling and staining and degrading, until, when you come at last to a country where men take a question seriously and give a serious answer to it, you deride them for having no sense of humor, and plume yourself on your own worthlessness. . . .

Keegan has the last word on the comic spirit that inspires the play, but which the play also disturbingly questions: "Every dream is a prophecy: every jest is an earnest in the womb of Time."

Critical Context

George Bernard Shaw wrote, as he said, to change the world: " 'For art's sake' alone I would not face the toil of a single sentence." He took full advantage of the opportunity that publishing the play offered (in 1907) for holding forth on the nasty contemporary complexities of Ireland under English rule. His preface was written to teach the English reader not only about Ireland but also about other aspects of English imperialism, such as mindless militarism and misrule in Egypt. The play itself was written for an Irish audience "at the request of Mr. William Butler Yeats, as a patriotic contribution to the repertory of the Irish Literary Theatre." "Mr. Yeats," he added, "got rather more than he bargained for." Not only was staging the play beyond the resources of the Abbey Theatre in Dublin, but also the play was "uncongenial" to the spirit of the neo-Gaelic movement. Staged instead in London, *John Bull's Other Island* was a commercial hit. The English audience responded well to Shaw's criticism of Ireland while conveniently ignoring the play's equally scorching criticisms of the English. One reviewer, Shaw noted, even "dwelt with much feeling on the pathos of Doyle's failure as an engineer (a circumstance not mentioned nor suggested in my play)."

There is unquestionably much of Shaw himself in the play: Doyle gives voice to the playwright's socialist, internationalist political views. *John Bull's Other Island* provides fascinating psychological material for those critics who want to pursue the outsider or exile theory of Shaw as the Irish nobody who (like Doyle) turned himself into a somebody by joining the winning (English) side. The play also offers a working demonstration of the optimistic creed of "Creative Evolution" and the "Life Force" that Shaw built for himself out of the miseries of his early life: Despair is a greater danger than Broadbent's bumptious efficiency in the service of the grasping Syndicate, and Nora Reilly *is* better off as his wife.

Sources for Further Study

Bertolini, John. *The Playwriting Self of George Bernard Shaw.* Carbondale: Southern Illinois University Press, 1991.

Davis, Tracy. *George Bernard Shaw and the Socialist Theatre.* Westport, Conn.: Greenwood Press, 1994.

Gibbs, A. M. "Bernard Shaw's Other Island." In *Irish Culture and Nationalism 1750-1950*, edited by Oliver MacDonagh, W. F. Mandle, and Pauric Travers. New York: St. Martin's Press, 1983.

Grene, Nicholas. "*John Bull's Other Island:* At Home and Abroad." *Shaw Review* 23 (1980): 11-16.

Hassett, Joseph M. "Climate and Character in *John Bull's Other Island.*" *Shaw: The Annual of Bernard Shaw Studies* 2 (1982): 17-26.

Jenckes, Norma. "The Political Function of Shaw's Destruction of Stage Irish Conventions in *John Bull's Other Island.*" *Essays in Theater* 5 (May, 1987): 115-126.

McDowell, Frederick P. W. "The Shavian World of *John Bull's Other Island.*" In *George Bernard Shaw,* edited by Harold Bloom. New York: Chelsea House, 1987.

Meisel, Martin. "*John Bull's Other Island* and Other Working Partnerships." *Shaw: The Annual of Bernard Shaw Studies* 7 (1987): 119-135.

Page, Malcolm, and Margery Morgan. *File on Shaw.* London: Methuen, 1989.

Sidnell, M. J. "*John Bull's Other Island:* Yeats and Shaw." *Modern Drama* 11 (1968): 245-251.

Joss Lutz Marsh

JUMPERS

Author: Tom Stoppard (Tomas Straussler, 1937-   )
Type of plot: Farce; problem play
Time of plot: The future
Locale: England
First produced: 1972, at the Old Vic Theatre, London
First published: 1972

> *Principal characters:*
> GEORGE MOORE, a professor of moral philosophy
> DOTTY, his wife, a retired music-hall performer
> ARCHIE, the chairman of the philosophy department
> INSPECTOR BONES, a detective
> CROUCH, the butler
> THE SECRETARY, who takes dictation from George
> THE JUMPERS, professors of philosophy in George's department,
>   who also perform acrobatics

The Play

Jumpers begins with a party given by Dorothy Moore (Dotty), a retired music-hall singer. At this party, Dotty attempts to sing several sentimental songs, all of which include the word "moon"; it becomes clear, however, that she is suffering from a mental breakdown. The Jumpers, a troupe of rather mediocre acrobats, upstage her confused performance with a demonstration of gymnastics. As they pose in a human pyramid, the Jumper at the bottom of the heap is suddenly shot and killed by an unknown murderer. Though it is unclear whether she had a part in the murder, Dotty is left holding the dead body.

George Moore, Dotty's husband, is now shown dictating to his secretary a lecture for a philosophical symposium titled "Man—Good, Bad or Indifferent?" George, a middle-aged professor of moral philosophy, launches into a long and rambling monologue expressing his doubts about the course of philosophy and telling of his own desire to find a moral absolute, to prove rationally the existence of God. Logical positivists, who are moral relativists, dominate the philosophy department; their position is represented by the Jumpers who performed earlier, philosophy professors who double as acrobats. George, unfortunately, does not "jump"; his insistence on standards of good and evil is at odds with the current philosophical tide. Consequently, he has not been promoted.

George's musings are interrupted by Dotty's cries for help. Annoyed at the disturbance, he confronts her in the bedroom. The ensuing exchange makes it clear that their marriage has deteriorated. George suspects Dotty of having an affair with Archie, the head of his department and a successful logical positivist; Dotty accuses George of neglect and tells him that her mental problems have recurred. These problems, she tries to tell him, stem from her sudden loss of idealism when the first man landed on the moon. For her the moon represented a perfect romantic ideal, attainable only through poetry and music. Her crisis is very much like the philosophical loss of faith in God, the moral absolute. However, George cannot grasp this parallel between her plight and his own trouble with logical positivism. He gives his attention instead to his small pets—a tortoise named Pat, a rabbit named Thumper, and a goldfish— which are missing.

After George leaves to resume dictating his lecture, he is interrupted by the arrival of Inspector Bones, investigating the murder of the Jumper. George, who knows nothing of the murder, assumes that Bones has come in response to a noise complaint that George had called in on the night of the party. Each is mystified by the behavior of the other. Bones is enamored of Dotty, who was formerly one of his favorite singers. Although he believes her to be the murderer, he is more interested in getting an autograph than in questioning her. When summoned, he eagerly goes in to see her, record in hand. When he arrives in her bedroom, the dead Jumper falls out on the floor.

George, meanwhile, continues working on his lecture. At the end of the first act, after he has reached some conclusions about the necessity of goodness, he meets Bones in the hall, and both exit. Dotty is left in the bedroom with the dead Jumper. Archie, impeccably dressed, now makes his first appearance. With the help of the other Jumpers, he places the dead body in a large plastic bag. The Jumpers carry it off, and Dotty and Archie are left alone.

The second act begins with a discussion between Bones and George. Bones describes the night of Dotty's retirement from the musical stage and tells George that she could be cleared of the murder charge on the grounds of psychiatric problems. George finally realizes that Bones is there to investigate a murder. Bones tells him that there is a body on the floor of Dotty's bedroom; the disbelieving George goes to see it for himself.

Upon opening the door to the bedroom, he finds not a dead body but Dotty and Archie, engaged in suspicious activity behind drapes. Archie claims that he is performing a dermatological examination; George leaves huffily for his study. Seeing a possible medical witness to attest Dotty's insanity, Bones takes Archie aside into the hall. Archie offers not medical evidence but an alternative alibi: that McFee, the dead Jumper, committed suicide in a large plastic bag. Archie offers Bones the ridiculous bribe of an academic position in philosophy—the very professorship that George covets. From her bedroom, Dotty cries out for help once again, and Bones rushes off to her assistance.

George resumes composing his lecture but is once again interrupted, this time by Archie. They discuss the question of religious faith, and George is shocked by Archie's news that McFee has committed suicide. He asserts that McFee's logical positivism was incongruous with such an extreme act of self-inflicted violence. Dotty again screams offstage, this time the word "rape"; both men rush to her bedroom, where they find her and an extremely disconcerted Bones. Archie finds this a perfect opportunity to blackmail Bones into not arresting Dotty.

George goes to his study to muse further on the death of McFee. His thoughts and his lecture finally come to some kind of conclusion, and he returns to the bedroom, where Archie and Dotty are having a cheerful lunch. He asks Archie for the Chair of Logic, McFee's old position, and is denied his request. He discovers that Dotty is indeed guilty of murdering his pet goldfish; he suspects that she also killed his pet rabbit. George leaves to answer the doorbell. Crouch the butler appears and tells George that McFee was murdered. George rushes back to question Dotty, who says that she thought Archie killed McFee. George, unable to get an answer, goes back into his study with Archie. Both his secretary and Crouch are there. Crouch mentions that philosophy is one of his hobbies; the late McFee, he says, was his mentor. He supplies a final confusing clue to the murder: George's secretary, he tells them, had been McFee's secret mistress; immediately prior to the murder McFee had informed her of his intention to leave her for the monastery. The silent, unsmiling secretary rises during this story to leave the room; as she exits, her coat is shown to have blood on it. George discovers, however, that the blood comes from the bookcase. The true killer of Thumper the rabbit proves to have been George himself, who shot his pet during an illustration of his lecture. In despair, George accidentally kills his tortoise Pat as well when he steps off the bookcase.

The play ends with a dreamlike coda in which George is pitted against Archie in the symposium. Each speaker is ranked by scorecards. Archie's lecture is pure nonsensical wordplay but receives a nearly perfect score. There is another murder, this time of the new archbishop of Canterbury, Sam Clegthorpe. When Clegthorpe contradicts Archie, he is shot in the same manner as was McFee. Dotty appears in a spotlight and sings. After George makes his final plea for the existence of God, Dotty bids the moon good-bye with a single musical line.

Themes and Meanings

In *Jumpers*, the philosophical crisis experienced by George Moore, the hero of the play, is reflected in all aspects of the plot and characterization. George attempts to prove the existence of God—"the Necessary Being, the First Cause, the Unmoved Mover!!"—in order to provide his own philosophical arguments with stability. However, he is never successful in proving this existence, only in describing his need to believe in God in the face of an increasingly popular logical positivism. "The truth to us philosophers," Archie tells Crouch, "is always an interim judgment." Logical positivism is but one manifestation of a more general loss of faith. A lack of a moral absolute affects all the diverse worlds of the play: the philosophical world, the musical stage, the murder mystery, and the world that exists around them.

In the first act of the play Tom Stoppard sets up the many examples of this moral and ethical instability. The Radical-Liberal Party has taken over the government and the media by force and rationalized the churches; Sam Clegthorpe, the Rad-Lib Spokesman for Agriculture, has been made archbishop of Canterbury. A two-man team has traveled to the moon; however, an equipment malfunction has made it possible for only one to return, and Captain Scott selfishly strands his crewmate to die.

Each of the main characters is affected by this loss of idealism. Dotty's inability to reconcile her romantic vision of the moon with the scientific lunar explorations leads to insanity: Unable to distinguish the different moon songs, she wanders from verse to verse aimlessly. George's lecture is never conclusive; he cannot prove the existence of God, any more than he can gain his promotion or keep his marriage together. Similarly, the detective Bones is unsuccessful in his attempts to find the Jumper's murderer.

This mystery is unsolvable not because there is not enough evidence but because there is too much. Each of the characters except for Archie seems to be trapped because he or she refuses to give up some vestige of faith in an absolute standard; characters such as George and Bones insist on finding some sort of truth. According to the play's logical positivists, alternative systems of morality and belief are all valid. Standards of behavior and judgment lose their potency and become a hazard to those who still insist on them. Even Clegthorpe is killed at the end because he starts to believe that he truly is the archbishop. Logical positivism itself, when defined as a rigid belief, becomes subject to relativism. The dead McFee had confessed to Crouch that his beliefs were threatened by the persistence of extreme instances of human faith, such as altruism; McFee, it is apparent, had begun to doubt logical positivism itself.

Only Archie, who is able to "jump" from position to position, can succeed in such a world. The play itself ends without a resolution to either the mystery or the philosophical questions. Archie is victorious in the symposium, yet George is clearly the most sympathetic character. He struggles to maintain some integrity and some faith, however irrational, in the face of the chaos that envelops all the worlds of the play.

Dramatic Devices

One of the most striking characteristics of *Jumpers* is its mixing of different theatrical worlds. Tom Stoppard combines a parody of philosophical language with music-hall songs, a detective story, and the acrobatics of the Jumpers. He has expressed his liking for what he calls "ambushes for the audience"; the mixing of genres enables him to create a variety of dramatic surprises. Each of the highly theatrical effects he creates is integral to plot and theme.

In the beginning sequence of the play, the secretary performs a striptease on a swinging chandelier, Dotty sings a confused medley of songs all containing the word "moon," and an acrobat is shot out of the bottom of a human pyramid. The collapsing pyramid becomes a dramatic metaphor for the collapse of stability in the philosophical, political, and private worlds of the characters.

Stoppard draws attention to the lack of answers to the philosophical dilemmas of the play by giving the audience a number of dramatic puzzles, each of which has various possible explanations, all of which, it seems, become equally valid and compelling. The murder of the dead Jumper is given many alternative explanations: Stoppard hints that the murderer could have been Dotty, Archie, the Secretary, or even McFee himself. George believes that Dotty is having an affair with Archie; however, Archie tells him that his interest is merely professional and that he spends his time examining her. The puzzles range from the large to the small; for example, George and Dotty play games of charades. Each character is engaged, on some level, in philosophical inquiry.

In the face of their dilemma of relativism, the main characters hopelessly try to construct things that have some stable significance, some evident value as truth: George's lectures, Dotty's songs, Bones's detective work. This effort to make meaning, in the face of the philosophical acrobatics of logical positivism, is nearly always impossible. Dotty mixes up the words of her songs and the lines of poems she quotes; George's long lecture fails as a rational proof. Still, it is this very failure of rationality that makes these characters so appealing. George spices up his lecture with dramatic climaxes, outlandish metaphors, sound effects, and live animals as props. Even Archie does not make a compelling argument for logical positivism; instead, he strings together a dazzling string of puns on philosophical expressions. Dramatically, it is "the irrational, the emotional, the whimsical" that make the play so appealing.

Critical Context

Jumpers demonstrates several strong affinities with Tom Stoppard's other work. In its combination of theatrical styles it reflects both the earlier *Rosencrantz and Guildenstern Are Dead* (pr. 1966, pb. 1967) and the later *Travesties* (pr. 1974, pb. 1975). *Rosencrantz and Guildenstern Are Dead* parodies the dialogue, situations, and characters of William Shakespeare, Samuel Beckett, and Luigi Pirandello; in it, the two minor figures from *Hamlet* (pr. c. 1600-1601) become heroes, trapped in a tragic script beyond their understanding, merely waiting, like the two tramps in Beckett's *En attendant Godot* (pb. 1952; *Waiting for Godot*, 1954), for their cues. In *Travesties* Stoppard depicts the dream world of Henry Carr, a character who fantasizes about his relationships with famous personages. Henry, like George Moore, has long, rambling, incoherent speeches; his thoughts appear as scenes that parody a variety of literary styles, including those of Oscar Wilde, Shakespeare, and James Joyce. Stoppard again uses a contrast of different dramatic worlds, as he does with the detective story, the music hall, and the philosophical discussions of *Jumpers*; in *Travesties* these dramatic worlds are strictly literary and historical, and the resulting discussion has to do with art's relationship to politics and history.

Stoppard delights in the use of the mystery plot, not only in *Jumpers* but also in the earlier *The Real Inspector Hound* (pr., pb. 1968) and *After Magritte* (pr. 1970, pb. 1971). The mystery seems a perfect vehicle for these verbally and visually complex plays, since both audience and characters are put in the position of figuring out explanations for events and discovering an elusive truth. In these shorter works, the mysteries are marked by their farfetched situations, bizarre clues, and outlandish alibis. *Jumpers* can be seen as the clearest instance of how the mystery plot may parallel a philosophical question—the human quest for truth. Stoppard's earlier mysteries have fragile resolutions; in *Jumpers* the mystery remains unsolved.

Sources for Further Study

Anchetta, Richard A. *Tom Stoppard: An Analytical Study of His Plays*. Chicago: Advent, 1991.

Bloom, Harold, ed. *Tom Stoppard*. New York: Chelsea House, 1986.

Corballis, Richard. *Stoppard: The Mystery and the Clockwork*. London: Methuen, 1984.

Harty, John. *Tom Stoppard: A Casebook*. New York: Garland, 1987.

Hunter, Jim. *Tom Stoppard: "Rosencrantz and Guildenstern Are Dead," "Jumpers," "Travesties," "Arcadia."* New York: Faber and Faber, 2000.

Jenkins, Anthony. *Tom Stoppard*. Boston: G. K. Hall, 1990.

Londré, Felicia Hardison. *Tom Stoppard*. New York: F. Ungar, 1981.

Rusinko, Susan. *Tom Stoppard*. Boston: Twayne, 1986.

Whitaker, Thomas. *Tom Stoppard*. New York: Grove Press, 1984.

Josephine Lee

THE KARL MARX PLAY

Author: Rochelle Owens (Rochelle Bass, 1936-   )
Type of plot: Expressionist; biographical
Time of plot: The 1860's
Locale: London
First produced: 1973, at The American Place Theatre, New York City
First published: 1971, in *The Best Short Plays 1971* (one-act version); 1973, revised
   full-length version

> *Principal characters:*
> KARL MARX, the famous political philosopher
> JENNY VON WESTPHALEN, his aristocratic wife
> FREDERICK ENGELS, his collaborator and financial supporter
> LEADBELLY, the black representative of emerging Africa and
>   modern America

The Play

   The Karl Marx Play begins with four visual images. Three photographs, each dis-
solving into the next, serve as a prologue: a formal family portrait of Karl Marx and
the rest of the characters of the play, the famous portrait of Marx in full beard, and an
"austere fourteenth century Gothic representation of Marx." The play itself opens
with the fourth image, Marx holding "a mass of entrails over his arm like a jacket,"
which some of the other characters investigate. As the images suggest, the Karl Marx
dissected in this play is a man of many faces. He is a family man, he is the author of a
revolutionary theory, and he is, above all, an exposed and vulnerable human unsure of
exactly who he is. The opening scene reveals further some of the ways in which the
needs and desires of the other characters create conflict in Marx. Frederick Engels
taunts Marx about his Jewish heritage, complains about paying his bills, and goads
Marx to write *Das Kapital* (1867) so that he can share in his fame. Jenny von
Westphalen, Marx's aristocratic wife, is more concerned with obtaining money to buy
food for the family and to provide dowries so her daughters can find rich husbands.
For his part, Marx seems less interested in dowries or *Das Kapital* than in Jenny's
breasts, at which he peeks through keyholes.
   Marx's principal antagonist is Leadbelly, a black representative of Africa and the
modern United States, who demands with violence and threats of violence the manifesto that will inspire revolution. Leadbelly's influence is pervasive enough to be felt
even when the play shifts to the past, as it does in two instances. As Engels piously
theorizes to Marx about the revolutionary potential of the problems faced by American "Negroes," Leadbelly seemingly materializes in the coffeehouse, where Engels
treats him condescendingly as an ignorant savage whom Engels will help to liberate.

The action quickly shifts back in time, showing Marx and Jenny as young lovers. Marx is the poet who has given up poetry for the truth of economics; Jenny is the aristocrat concerned about their differences in class and religion. When Marx professes his belief in cultural equality, Leadbelly again appears and delivers a long oration, envisioning a "real" revolution in which Africa, the source of communal living, violently destroys white European culture. Leadbelly's challenges appear to draw battle lines. Leadbelly vows to "wage the war of vengeance." Jenny laughs at Leadbelly's emotionalism and responds by dancing seductively. Marx defends the superiority of his German philosophy and of European culture and retreats in his mind to the pleasure he felt at the university when his theory was a philosophical issue discussed in coffeehouses.

However, Marx cannot escape his fears and anxieties. Contrasted with a song his daughters sing on the joy and wonder of life is his memory of the death of his first son by starvation. Marx recalls the child looking into his soul, absorbing his suffering and absolving him from his sins, but in his song of mourning, Marx recalls his failure to say "magic words" to his son as he watched him die. At work, Marx is beset by other imagined demons: images of a black child who he asserts is the future; visions of his Jewish grandfather whom he vows to eliminate through his "philosophical mind," Yahveh (God), who he claims does not exist, yet whom he vows nevertheless to destroy. The vacillations become wilder and more strained; a magazine that would give his theory prominence gives way to romantic and sexual thoughts about Jenny, which in turn give way to a restatement of his theory of the destruction of society in procreative terms. Just when Marx appears to have worked through his anxieties, the thought of his family's poverty returns to crush his hope.

Marx's torment in writing brings first Jenny and then Leadbelly to his study. Mutual antagonists, their need to have Marx write his book for their own very different reasons further torments Marx. Jenny is envisioned as the sexual temptress Salome, holding Marx's head and making him promise (without his seeing the irony) to write the book that will bring wealth and a bourgeois lifestyle to her family. Leadbelly counters Jenny's embodiment of the seductive power of women with a sexual and savage energy derived from American jazz and African rhythms that is frightening to her. Leadbelly needs Marx's book to destroy the wealthy, and in the longest speech of the play he becomes John D. Rockefeller to expose the parasitic activity of those with wealth and power. Leadbelly's Rockefeller is obsessed with sucking milk from the breasts of oppressed women and upholding his role as the "savior-profit" who controls religion and culture. The Rockefeller mask falling away, Leadbelly reveals that the poor are infected by dreams of a millionaire and pleads with Marx to liberate them from themselves and their oppressors. His plea apparently goes unheard, however, as the Marx family dreams of the wealth that Marx's book will bring and decides to have a party.

There is little enjoyment in the party which begins the second act. Marx stands against the wall eating pickled beets, looking happy only while he chews them; the rest of the household complain about the lack of food and about Marx's failure to write the book. Pressured, Marx again cannot control his thoughts. He speaks demoniacally of dethroning Yahveh, of clinging to Europe, of being Africa and Asia devouring Europe. He fears the Jews, the Russians, and the Chinese, has faith in the Germans, and condemns workers as a stupid mob. He exalts his theory, again imagining it as a vehicle that will bring wealth and food for his family and fame and power for him. Confronted with the poverty of his family, however, Marx's grandiose vision collapses. He retreats to a Greek statue of a nude man and begins to suck on its breast, painfully reciting fragments from the book he is yet to write. His boils inflamed from sucking the plaster of the statue, Marx turns to Jenny and his children to console him.

Leadbelly's "righteous anger," however, will not allow Marx to escape his destiny. He orders Marx and Engels to write the manifesto, and when Marx complains that his boils and his poverty have sapped him of the desire to write his book and suggests that the revolution will come without his intervention, Leadbelly throws Marx's entrails in his face. Hearing his family now singing that they lack faith and confidence in him, Marx goes to Jenny's breasts to give him sustenance and strength, but Leadbelly denies him this comfort as well. He then acts as the hand of fate and applies a torch to Marx's intestines, driving Marx off the stage to write *Das Kapital* and to become, as the cast sings in the final song, the man who "Will change the destiny/ Of the world!"

Themes and Meanings

The Karl Marx Play presents a human figure behind the political icon. By placing Marx's economic and political theory in the context of his life and the demands placed upon him by those in his household, the play presents a Marx who is, in his own words, "doubled and tripled and shattered into a hundred fractures of Karl Marx!" The action of *The Karl Marx Play*, appropriately, depends to a great extent upon oppositions which are internalized within Marx himself. For much of the play, these oppositions lead to stasis—writer's block. For Marx to write *Das Kapital*, he must be forced out of time, out of the oppositions fostered by the demands of his family and friends in Victorian England, to meet, in Leadbelly, the future and his destiny.

To a great extent, the characters and their concerns establish the oppositions in the play. Jenny has little interest in Marx's theory except insofar as it will provide bourgeois comforts for her family and aristocratic husbands for her daughters. Frederick Engels, Marx's "collaborator," is no less mercantile in his responses to Marx, providing money so that Marx will write the book that will in turn give him fame and philosophic prominence. Marx himself struggles with his religion. He proposes to destroy religion and to replace it with his philosophy, but he can never fully escape his own Jewishness; he prays to Yahveh for the strength he needs to mount an assault on religion. It falls upon Leadbelly, a symbol of the future, of racial struggle, of the revolutions to be engendered by *Das Kapital*, to lead Marx to his greatness. Leadbelly attacks Engels and Jenny for their myopic, bourgeois concerns; he adopts the persona of Rockefeller to expose the parasitic nature of established religion; he uses the force of revolution—violence and threats of violence—to compel Marx to write his master-work.

Also set in opposition are the mind and the body, the philosophical and the physical. Marx's physicality is made vividly evident in the play's opening moments, when his entrails are exposed and examined and when his heart, the "heart of a man" and not a heart emblematic of "poetic mysticism," is produced by Leadbelly. This physicality becomes a major impediment to his writing. The poverty of his family and the recollection of the starvation of his first son torment him. His boils make it painful for him to sit and write. The momentary delights of eating pickled beets provide a pleasant distraction. His sexual delight in his wife, particularly his obsession with her breasts, becomes a method of escaping the strain of his inability to write and the demands everyone places upon him. It is thus through both the denial and the exploitation of Marx's physicality that Leadbelly forces him to bring his theory to print. Leadbelly denies Marx "suck-titty from Jenny" and then ignites his exposed intestines to force him to action.

Perhaps the most important opposition is suggested by Marx's continual reference to his description of the class struggle as his "theory." It is, for him, an academic exercise created in philosophic coffeehouse discussions, and it is to this coffeehouse environment that Marx longs to return. He is a poet and a philosopher rather than a political activist. For Leadbelly, however, Marx's theory cannot remain theory. It must come to fruition to liberate Africa and provide African Americans with the means to escape oppression. Before the word can become flesh, the idea must first become the word; theory must become text so that action can follow. As a representative of the future and a man of action, Leadbelly can see, as Marx cannot, the implications and significance of the theory. Marx's poetic and philosophic genius and Leadbelly's demand for action become the dialectic which culminate in Marx's creation of *Das Kapital*. Marx's theory, calling for an upheaval of culture and society, must be born in violence. Leadbelly acts by literally lighting the fire in Marx's belly, and "with a surge of superhuman energy" Marx rushes offstage to write *Das Kapital*. As Rochelle Owens notes in a preface to the play: "They, Marx and Leadbelly are the synthesis time has held in the making these hundred years and more."

Dramatic Devices

As the opening moments demonstrate, *The Karl Marx Play* makes extensive use of highly theatrical and visual images. While the portraits reflect some of the identities and demands placed on Marx, his exposed entrails graphically suggest his physicality and immediately establish him as a human being rather than as a political symbol. Owens's return at the end of the play to the same visual image—to suggest the force required to bring Marx's theory into existence—indicates the flexibility of her use of image. The visual images are often accompanied by songs—Leadbelly singing a political spiritual as the last of the portraits is presented, Jenny singing and dancing seductively when she becomes Salome. The sound of jazz and a howling wolf are heard as Marx struggles to write. Owens's mixture of theatrical devices contributes to the presentation of a play that presents a central character who is at once splintered, human, and superhuman.

Rochelle Owens is an established poet as well as a playwright, and in *The Karl Marx Play* she works as a poet. She argues that the "story is told as much by its imagery and tonal 'meanings' as it is by its plot." It is through the juxtaposition of poetic images and themes rather than through a narrative sequence of action that the play is constructed. This approach to the dramatic action is evident in the larger structure of the play, in characterization, and in the use of language. The play is episodic, moving easily from the present to the past and back to the present, and shifting between dialogue, soliloquy, direct address to the audience, song, and dream sequences. While this structure achieves many of the goals associated with epic theater, it also serves in this play to present the "shattered" identity of Marx and to underscore the connection and disconnection of Marx's theory to the future.

Characterization is as malleable as dramatic structure, as characters often take on different identities and roles. In a dream sequence, Engels believes that he is dancing with his love, Mary Burns, only to discover at the end of the sequence that she has again become Lenchen, Marx's housekeeper. Jenny becomes Salome, envisioning Marx's Jewish head upon a silver platter and dancing seductively for Marx and Leadbelly. Leadbelly, however, may be Owens's most remarkable creation in the play. A man from the future, the voice of racial and political struggles, he is also, in Owens's words, "the burning motive inside Marx, the future generations calling him inexorably to release his greatness for their sake." He also takes on another character, becoming his antithesis in John D. Rockefeller, perversely glorifying the values of capitalistic power and oppression. These shifts in characterization not only enable Owens to introduce and dramatize many of the central issues of the play, but they also reflect and emphasize Marx's character. Marx is philosopher, poet, husband, father. His numerous vacillations and contradictions, and his difficulties fulfilling these roles provide the essence of his character.

Images are juxtaposed poetically throughout the play, producing complex and often contradictory effects. Breasts and the sucking of breasts make up a recurrent image complex suggestive of many different meanings. Marx's attitudes toward Jenny's breasts are at various points in the first act comic, poetic, and engagingly sexual. With Leadbelly's John D. Rockefeller and Marx's sucking at the statue's breast and attempt to suck Jenny's breast, however, the activity is suggestive of dominance and escapism, the perversion of healthy attitudes and behavior. The image complex leads less to simplistic symbolism than to a reinforcement of the oppositions within Marx and within the play. Another example of Owens's poetic use of language occurs when Marx is struggling to write. As his mind shifts between his theory and Jenny, he begins to think of his theory in procreative terms; "Force is the midwife of every society pregnant with a new one. . . . The midwife is approaching, the revolution of oppressed classes." It is thus in the language of the play rather than in its central character that Owens presents a unified vision, the shattered pieces joining into an artistic mosaic.

Critical Context

There are at least two contexts in which *The Karl Marx Play* can be examined. One is that of a subgenre: biographical plays focusing on the lives of pivotal historical figures. Other plays of this type, for example, would include Bertolt Brecht's *Galileo* (pr. 1943), John Osborne's *Luther* (pr., pb. 1961), and Robert Bolt's *A Man for All Seasons* (pr. 1960). One of the aims of all these plays, *The Karl Marx Play* included, is to put a human face on the political and social struggles faced by a protagonist whose persistence in the face of adversity changed world history. Common to all these plays is a concentration on the protagonist's internal struggle, his weaknesses and self-doubts, even as he challenges the authorities and dominant social structure. However, *The Karl Marx Play* differs from most plays of this sort. As the title suggests, Owens is more interested in presenting a "play" than in accurately depicting the life of a historic figure. Her play draws upon "the circumstances and events, factual and imaginary, of the life of Karl Marx." It is a biographic play that does not seem biographical. Marx's principal interactions are with his family and an imaginary person from the future.

While *The Karl Marx Play* does explore the struggle between the individual and society, society is a force within Marx rather than an external force opposing him. Finally, Marx's great contribution, his theory of dialectic materialism, is not a central element of the play. Marx talks about his theory often, but only in the most general terms, and rarely using the language that later appeared in his book. The Karl Marx whose writings spawned revolution is nearly absent from the play. In his place is a fallible, confused, and indecisive man whose personal struggles nearly obliterate his historical significance.

The use of a biographical structure enables Owens to explore and control many of the themes prevalent in her other plays. Sexuality and sexual attitudes often play a role in Owens's plays, both as healthy animal delight and as sadistic, exploitative domination. Conventionally, as in *Futz* (pb. 1961, pr. 1965) and *The String Game* (pr. 1965, pb. 1968), social and cultural forces attempt to repress the healthy, if nonconventional, sexual attitudes of others. In other plays, *Istanboul* (pr. 1965, pb. 1968) and especially *Beclch* (pr. 1966, pb. 1968), sexuality often becomes the violent and destructive imposition of power over others. *The Karl Marx Play* brings both of the attitudes together and unifies them in the character of Marx, who delights in Jenny and, like Leadbelly's Rockefeller, tries to gain strength from her through sexual dominance. Consolidated within the character of Marx, these contrary responses attain the complexity that makes them unmistakably human.

As is also evident in *The Karl Marx Play*, Owens explores the desire somehow to escape from or transcend the human. This, too, is a concern evident in her other plays. In *Kontraption* (pb. 1971, pr. 1978), the two central characters escape by creating visions which then materialize before them. In *He Wants Shih!* (pb. 1972, pr. 1975), the central character abdicates political and social responsibility to become both male and female, thus escaping the role determined for him by his sex. Marx, however, is reluctant to leave the world with which he is familiar and comfortable. He is finally transformed, but it is through supernatural intervention by Leadbelly, a vision embodying what is yet to come. Owens's play occurs in a timeless world, a world unaffected by the constraints imposed upon historical biographies, a world that can both celebrate sexuality and allow—even demand—that characters transcend this human desire to attain greatness.

Sources for Further Study

Berkman, Len. "Parnassus (NYC)." In *Modern American Drama, 1945-1990*, edited by C. W. E. Bigsby. Cambridge, Mass.: Cambridge University Press, 1992.

Goulianos, Joan. "Women and the Avant-Garde Theater." *Massachusetts Review* 13 (Winter/Spring, 1972): 257-267.

Marranca, Bonnie, and Gautam Dasgupta, eds. *American Playwrights: A Critical Survey*. New York: Drama Book Specialists, 1981.

Shragge, Elaine. "Rochelle Owens." In *Contemporary Dramatists*. 6th ed. Detroit: St. James, 1999.

Young, Karl, ed. "A Symposium on Rochelle Owens." *Margins* 24/26 (1975): 76-135.

Ralph M. Leary

KASPAR

Author: Peter Handke (1942-   )
Type of plot: Speech drama
Time of plot: Unspecified
Locale: Unspecified
First produced: 1968, at the Theater am Turm, Frankfurt, West Germany
First published: 1968 (English translation, 1969, in *Kaspar and Other Plays*)

> *Principal characters:*
> KASPAR, a young man
> KASPARS 1-5, clones of Kaspar
> THE PROMPTERS, three loudspeaker voices

The Play

According to the playwright's instructions, the first person to enter the theater where *Kaspar* is being staged should find the curtain open, with stage props (tables, a few chairs, a sofa, a rocking chair, a wardrobe) arranged randomly and out of context with one another. After the lights in the auditorium are dimmed, the spectators become aware of movement behind the backdrop which suggests that a person is trying to find the partition of the curtain for an entrance onto the stage. Finally, Kaspar, wearing a mask expressing astonishment and confusion, stumbles through the slit in the curtain. He walks with great difficulty and finally falls down. Sitting in the lotus position in the middle of the stage, he begins to repeat his one sentence over and over, varying pitch and intonation: "I want to be someone like somebody else was once."

As Kaspar addresses this sentence, the only speech of which he is capable, to various objects on the stage, the voices of the three Prompters begin to drone from loudspeakers on all sides of the stage. They bombard him with commentary about his sentence and what that single sentence means to him. The fact that he knows that one sentence, they insist, means that he can learn other sentences. Gradually and reluctantly, under strong pressure from the constant indoctrination of the Prompters, Kaspar abandons his precious sentence; his sentence has been "exorcised," and he stands mute for a few moments. Then, with increasing intensity, the prompters teach him new sentences and force him to adopt them by the sheer quantity of the speech material with which they assault him.

Kaspar, deprived of his own sentence, which might help him resist their brainwashing, learns "orderly sentences," but the process is painful and his head begins to hurt. The "orderly sentences" are not merely grammatically correct; they also teach him to "order" his world and to adapt himself to the social order. Consequently, he begins to arrange the stage props in a manner the audience would call "orderly": The random arrangement of tables, chair, and wardrobe is transformed into an inhabitable room. The process of language education turns into a process of forced socialization.

Kaspar's original wish to "be someone like somebody else was once" is now replaced by the defiant proclamation "I am the one I am," a grandiose but empty statement that fails to characterize him as an individual personality. Significantly, this new self-definition occurs at the turning point of the play, with Kaspar complacently sitting in a rocking chair.

Kaspar's apparent satisfaction with his linguistic progress is called into question when he abruptly asks, "Why are there so many black worms flying about?"—a sign that his confident "I am the one I am" is only bluster and an attempt to hide his doubts about his new existential position. These doubts are justified, because the Prompters triumphantly declare that Kaspar has now been "cracked open." This declaration is accompanied by the appearance of five additional Kaspars, dressed and masked identically. They confront the protagonist with the fact that he is no longer a unique creature; he is a clone, indistinguishable from the other Kaspars. As the intermission approaches, Kaspar makes an eloquent and elegant speech acknowledging his new status as a good citizen: He recognizes that a new part of his life has begun. From now on he, who detested all forms of rational order, will be rational. He no longer wants to be someone else.

Peter Handke provides a text which ideally would be piped into the theater foyer, the restrooms, the bars, and even into the streets during the intermission. The text begins as a random collection of sentences that contain many references to violence, but gradually changes to a discussion of good table manners. The connection between violence and table manners is not clear to the audience until the beginning of the second part of the play, during which the Prompters recite a rhythmic chant on the virtue of brutalizing people in order to make them behave like good citizens. Kaspar's mask and those of his clones now express contentment. Harassed by the Kaspar-clones' raucous noises, Kaspar glowingly praises the code of behavior which society imposes on its members; lecturing the theater audience, he uses the same loudspeakers that the Prompters had used to indoctrinate him.

Suddenly, as if exhausted by this verbal outpouring, Kaspar stops; he cannot remember what he has just said. The voices of the Prompters have already stopped, for Kaspar has learned their lessons so well that he is able to take over their function. Having learned and mastered language, thought, and social conventions, however, he can also look at himself critically. The conclusion he comes to is that "every sentence is for the birds," a radical revision of his recent optimism. In a long speech about the word "snow," he brings to question the relationship between a phenomenon and the word used to describe it. He now understands that he was trapped when he used his first sentence and that by having been made to speak, he has been "sentenced to reality," and the reality is that he is "usable." The only way out of his dilemma is to abandon everything he has learned and to return to the condition he was in even before he learned his very first sentence. Accompanied by the growing cacophony of the surrogate Kaspars, he quickly reduces his speech from elegant sentences to fragments to incoherent phrases until the curtain in closing knocks over all the Kaspars, while the protagonist repeats Othello's cryptic words "goats and monkeys" again and again.

Themes and Meanings

Kaspar is a play about the tyranny of language and implicitly about the tyranny of society: It deals with the way in which society builds a human being. This is fairly easy with a child, since there the process is almost unnoticeable. In Kaspar's case, in contrast, the protagonist not only has to be conditioned but first must be unconditioned. Kaspar's one sentence indicates a previous existence, however mysterious, that was not molded by the environment into which he stumbles through the slit in the curtain, an obvious symbol of birth. He tries to establish a foothold (Kaspar initially walks only with difficulty), but has very limited resources at his command (his sentence may stand for inherited traits). These limited resources also constitute his greatest freedom: He can define the world and his position in it on his own terms, unfettered by social and linguistic conventions.

This freedom is immediately seen as a handicap by the Prompters (society), who pity him for his limited linguistic ability, which prevents him from communicating with them. In order to become a respected and respectable member of society, he must be weaned of his sentence and taught to order his world with an ever-increasing arsenal of words and sentences. His formerly unified and simple view of the world is complicated and fragmented: He is no longer Kaspar but only one of many Kaspars. He has traded individuality and freedom for security and respectability. As soon as he reaches this stage he becomes an ardent Prompter himself, extolling the virtues of orderly speech and socially responsible behavior. In the end, his new cognitive-linguistic skills enable him to look critically at himself. Stunned, he realizes the "impossibility of *expressing* anything in language" and rejects what he has learned. Like Othello, driven to irrational speech and action by the constant taunting of Iago, he mutters "goats and monkeys" at the end of the play.

The text of *Kaspar* is preceded by a listing of Kaspar's sixteen developmental phases and a poem by Ernst Jandl that establishes a connection between the protagonist of Handke's play and the historic Kaspar Hauser, an autistic young man who appeared in Nuremberg in 1828. Hauser, who could only speak one sentence ("I want to become a horseman like my father once was"), had lived in complete solitude for as long as sixteen years. In an extensive introduction which includes elaborate staging instructions, Handke makes it clear that he is not presenting a play about how "IT REALLY IS OR REALLY WAS with Kaspar Hauser"; rather, the play shows "what IS POSSIBLE with someone." Handke also mentions that the play could have been titled "speech torture." He does not want the audience to think of the protagonist as a clown (as suggested by the German *Kaspar,* the main character in the German version of the Punch and Judy show) but that he should resemble Frankenstein's monster, another tragic example of arrogant social engineering.

Dramatic Devices

Kaspar is a play about language. In order to focus the audience's attention on this issue, Handke abandons plot—that is, the causal dramatic interaction of characters, and the creation of any illusion of reality as far as the language, the action, and the stage design are concerned. Like Handke's other *Sprechstücke* (speech drama), *Kaspar* is not divided into acts and scenes but into numbered paragraphs. The physical appearance of the stage does not attempt to create any verisimilitude but serves as a symbolic reflection of the progress of the morality play in which Kaspar assumes the role of Everyman. The stage directions make it clear that Kaspar bears a resemblance to the Arlecchino of the *commedia dell'arte*: He is a naïve, childlike fool who is seduced into believing that growing sophistication of language will allow him to cope better with his existential and social problems.

This seduction is carried out not by traditional dramatic characters but by disembodied loudspeaker voices—the German word *Einsager* is usually translated as "Prompters," but it has a strong connotation of "indoctrination" in addition to "prompting" in its theatrical frame of reference. The use of the loudspeaker voices reinforces the concept of an impersonal social force rather than of an individual villain. Like all children, Kaspar at first resists the attempts to educate him out of his simple, irrational, childlike existence, but the anonymous voices are too strong and persistent. Kaspar becomes proud of his accomplishments; the growing order of his sentences is reflected in the increasing symmetry of the stage props. Now, however, he is no longer unique; he becomes an interchangeable member of society, as evidenced by the appearance of five identical Kaspars.

Finally Kaspar realizes that all this linguistic education has only been for the benefit of society; it has not brought him any nearer to an understanding of his existential condition. What he needs to know is why there are so many black worms flying about, but no Prompter can help him. What gives *Kaspar* its unusual power is Handke's ability to dramatize this dilemma, making the acquisition of language the very action of the play.

Critical Context

"The use of the stage as a moral institution gets on my nerves," Peter Handke once confessed to an interviewer. *Kaspar* and Handke's other *Sprechstücke* share the aims of contemporary avant-garde theater that attempts to break with the traditional theatrical conventions, particularly with illusionism, and to approach the "pure" play— drama that has no characters and no plot in the conventional sense. Written and performed after Handke's other "speech dramas," notably *Publikumsbeschimpfung* (pr., pb. 1966; *Offending the Audience*, 1969) and *Selbstbezichtigung* (pr., pb. 1966; *Self-Accusation*, 1969), *Kaspar* received instant critical acclaim and prompted critics to rank Handke with Samuel Beckett and Eugène Ionesco, playwrights who are considered pioneers of the modern anti-illusionist theater and whose work deals with the difficulty of meaningful communication and with the tyranny of language.

This concern with language as a manipulative tool of society is even more vital for Handke than for Beckett and Ionesco. The post-World War II generation of Austrian writers is acutely conscious of the propagandistic manipulation which the German language underwent at the hands of the Nazi regime. An attempt to discredit language, to break it down and to create new meanings and structures, is a strong feature

of contemporary Austrian literature, much of which rejects any connection with traditional German literature.

Sources for Further Study
Firda, Richard A. *Peter Handke*. Boston: Twayne, 1993.
Handke, Peter. "Nauseated by Language: From an Interview with Arthur Joseph."
    Drama Review 15 (Fall, 1970): 56-61.
Hern, Nicholas. *Peter Handke*. New York: Ungar, 1972.
Klinkowitz, Jerome, and James Knowlton. *Peter Handke and the Postmodern Trans-
    formation: The Goalie's Journey Home*. Columbia: University of Missouri Press,
    1983.
Nägele, Rainer. "Peter Handke: The Staging of Language." *Modern Drama* 23 (Janu-
    ary, 1981): 327-338.
Ran-Mosely, Faye. *The Tragicomic Passion: Clowns, Fools, and Madmen in Drama,
    Film, and Literature*. New York: Peter Lang, 1994.
Schlueter, June. *The Plays and Novels of Peter Handke*. Pittsburgh: University of
    Pittsburgh Press, 1981.

Franz G. Blaha

KEELY AND DU

Author: Jane Martin (pen name of unknown author)
Type of plot: Social realism
Time of plot: 1993
Locale: Providence, Rhode Island
First produced: 1993, at the Actors Theatre of Louisville, Louisville, Kentucky
First published: 1993

> *Principal characters:*
> KEELY, a pregnant, divorced woman in her early thirties
> DU, a sixty-five year old registered nurse, female guard of Keely
> WALTER, a sanctimonious, self-righteous fanatical pastor
> COLE, Keely's alcoholic ex-husband

The Play

Written as a one-act play but with a possible intermission after the climactic thirteenth scene, Jane Martin's emotional *Keely and Du* chronicles the fate of Keely from the last preparations for her imprisonment through her eventual release. Set almost exclusively in a sparsely furnished basement that has been converted into a prison, the play focuses on Keely's developing and changing relationship with her adversary Du, the fundamentalist Christian who guards her to prevent her from terminating her unwanted pregnancy.

In the beginning, Du waits for two male orderlies to bring in the body of the unconscious, kidnapped Keely. She prepares the bed on which Keely will lie, handcuffed to its iron bedstead, and greets Walter, the organizer of the kidnapping. Walter is a sanctimonious pastor of fifty, who acts with the single-mindedness of a well-programmed robot. Du, on the other hand, betrays her underlying humanity through small acts of kindness toward their kidnap victim.

With Walter gone for four days, Du tends to Keely. At first, Keely fights with Du, throwing her breakfast on the floor. Du responds in a befuddled way, almost like a disoriented grandmother, telling of her own children and marriage, when all Keely cares about is to leave her prison. Du reveals her religious beliefs to Keely and tells her that she will not be released until it is too late to have an abortion.

Walter appears and begins his lectures to Keely. Self-righteously, he justifies his actions with his extreme religious beliefs and tells Keely that she will come to love her child once it is born. Keely rejects this attack on her liberty and freedom of choice. Du eventually pulls back Walter when he becomes too overbearing. Against the biblical passages quoted by Walter, Keely reveals that she was raped by her ex-husband and does not want his child, nor can she afford to raise it. Walter presents her with graphic antiabortion pamphlets, and Du gives her baby shoes, all in an effort to manipulate her soul.

Keely and Du develop a personal relationship. Du tells Keely of her own uneventful marriage to a man whom she found dull, and with whom she has three boys, while her baby girl had died. Du confesses that once her husband, who is seventy now, discovered religion, he set their marriage bed on fire. Keely responds with the story of how she met her husband, Cole. A working-class alcoholic with a nasty temperament, Keely married Cole to anger her policeman father. After she left him, Cole stalked her and used what Keely wanted to be their final meeting as an occasion to rape and impregnate her. Very upset, Keely tells Du that she must have an abortion.

Walter and Keely fight again, and Du joins Keely in laughing at Walter's monotonous, robotic speeches. After he is gone, Du brings Keely her birthday gifts: a dress to wear and a sixpack of beer. Keely is unshackled, and the two women bond over shared beers. Keely tells Du of the satisfaction she found in rock climbing, remembering a night spent alone in a sleeping bag off a sheer cliff. She yearns to be alone and free.

The next day, Walter reappears and Du confesses the birthday party. Walter produces a surprise visitor, Cole. The man argues that he has found God and has mended his errant ways. Cole slides over to Keely, who is handcuffed to the bed again, and asks her to forgive him and raise their child. When he puts his hand in Keely's mouth, begging her to come back to him, she bites him. Cole slaps her hard and leaves with Walter. Keely uses the wire hanger of her birthday dress to perform an abortion.

With Keely unconscious and covered in blood, Walter runs away while Du calls an ambulance. The last scene shows Keely visiting Du in jail. Du still disagrees with Keely's choice but appreciates her visit. Keely tells her that she is going out with a married man, hoping for his divorce and a better future.

Themes and Meanings

Keely and Du is designed to address the ongoing debate about the issue of abortion. Narrowing the focus, the playwright juxtaposes the positions of those who oppose abortion on religious grounds with the beliefs and needs of a pregnant rape victim. The play explores the extreme actions to which strong religious convictions may drive people, and it also focuses on a woman's myriad reasons for needing an abortion.

Drawing inspiration from the historic, real-life violence against abortion clinics, their medical staff, and their patients, the play imagines a similarly extreme form of illegal activism. Keely is kept against her will. The meaning of her imprisonment is clear: The fate of her pregnancy is not to be decided by her, but by others who have made themselves the rulers over her body and spirit.

The religious-based opposition to abortion is given voice through the characters of Walter and Du. Walter lectures Keely with arguments familiar from real-life arguments against abortion. He presents her with graphic pamphlets of aborted fetuses that are handed out by some anti-abortion activists. He quotes real passages from the Bible that can be interpreted to prohibit abortion.

Keely's arguments are exactly opposite to Walter's. She demands respect for the American law, which prohibits kidnapping and gives a woman the right to an abortion. In the climactic thirteenth scene, Keely lays out her ultimate reasons for needing to terminate the unwanted pregnancy that was violently forced upon her. She is afraid she may hurt the baby, whom she may see as a symbol of Cole's evil. She is worried she will feel utterly depressed if she gives up the baby for adoption. She also fears being stalked by Cole, who may harm her or the baby if she refuses to get back together with him.

In Du, the playwright works out the complexities of the theme to the fullest. She is a character caught in the conflict between strong religious beliefs and motivation, and a general feeling of human compassion. As a woman, Du can relate to the anguish Keely is feeling and has even considered setting her free. As a devout fundamentalist Christian with a mission, however, Du feels spiritually obligated to prevent what she believes is the killing of an unborn life. By the end of the play the two women have become friends, but they still disagree on the issue of abortion.

Dramatic Devices

Strong dramatic unity of space is created by confining the action of all but the last scene to the basement room that functions as Keely's jail. With its sparse props, the stage fully conveys a sense of imprisonment. Immobilized by the handcuffs to her left wrist, Keely is literally tied to her bed and limited in her range of actions. Her quest to get rid of her shackles, even for a moment, and to be able to stand up again, lends urgency to her verbal pleading with Du.

Walter is the one character who freely moves on and off stage, passing through the stage's world of the basement jail and the free world outside the theater. His mobility is related to his leadership role. He is instrumental in organizing Keely's imprisonment, and he stays in touch with outside events.

Du has voluntarily confined herself to share the prison space with Keely. Whenever the lights go on to illuminate the next scene of the play, she is already onstage with Keely. The one moment when Du does leave Keely alone is when she follows Walter and Cole to minister to Cole's bitten hand. Without Du's presence, Keely performs the drastic act of abortion.

To give this climactic act great symbolic power, the playwright lets Keely use the prop of the wire hanger that came with her birthday dress. When the audience sees Keely pulling the wire hanger from under the mattress where she has hidden it and move it under her blanket, the spectators understand what action is theatrically implied here. When the lights come back on for scene seventeen, Keely's bed is drenched in stage blood, and the actress lies as if unconscious. This sight drives Walter into a panicked flight, revealing his ultimate loss of control over the situation. Du stays behind to call an ambulance. Her concern for Keely overrides her impulse to save herself.

With the last scene taking place in a proper jail, where Du is visited by Keely, the audience never escapes the atmosphere of prison. It is almost as if the contentious philosophical and moral debate about abortion threatens to imprison all those who wish to tackle this difficult ethical subject. Now Keely and Du's roles are reversed. However, no matter who is imprisoned and who is free, the friendship of the two women has endured.

Critical Context

Keely and Du has been hailed as a major achievement signaling Jane Martin's dramatic development and portrayal of a challenging subject. It is the eleventh play of the dramatist, who, by 2002, had nearly two dozen plays to her credit. It is also her most well-known play. In 1993, it was nominated for the Pulitzer Prize in drama, and, in 1994, it won the American Theatre Critics Association Award for Best New Play. Because of its topical subject, it is frequently performed at colleges and universities throughout the United States.

The identity of the playwright is shrouded in mystery. Jane Martin has never made a public appearance or spoken about her work in any medium. Instead, she is represented by Jon Jory, the former director of the annual Humana Festival of New American Plays in Louisville, Kentucky, who also directed the premiere of *Keely and Du*. Jory's wife, Marcia Dixcy Jory, has also written the introduction to the first collection of Martin's plays. This situation has many critics and insiders speculate that "Jane Martin" is really the pseudonym of either Jon Jory alone, or the team of Jon and Marcia Dixcy Jory. The Jories have denied these speculations, stating instead that Martin prefers to work in private. However, because all of Martin's plays are written so clearly from a woman's perspective and, like *Keely and Du*, focus on issues vital to American women, critics have argued that maybe the male playwright Jon Jory is hiding behind a female pseudonym to avoid the unjustified but possible backlash by people who would not grant a man the moral right to write a play from a woman's viewpoint.

Sources for Further Study

Gussow, Mel. "Plays by Women, for Anyone and Mostly About Violence." *New York Times*, March 24, 1993, p. C15.

Henry, George. "Is Kidnapping for Jesus a Moral Right?" *Time* 142 (November 29, 1993): 71.

Kintz, Linda. "Chained to the Bed: Violence and Abortion in *Keely and Du*." In *Staging Resistance: Essays on Political Theatre*, edited by Jeanne Colleran and Jenny S. Spencer. Ann Arbor: University of Michigan Press, 1998.

Klein, Alvin. "*Keely and Du:* The Battle over Abortion." *New York Times*, October 16, 1994, p. NJ17.

Martin, Jane. *Jane Martin: Collected Plays, 1980-1995*. Manchester, N.H.: Smith and Kraus, 1996.

Solinger, Rickie, ed. *Abortion Wars: A Half Century of Struggle, 1950-2000*. Berkeley: University of California Press, 1998.

Stearns, David Patrick. "*Keely and Du:* When the Body Politic Is a Woman's." *USA Today*, February 11, 1994, p. D3.

R. C. Lutz

KEEP TIGHTLY CLOSED IN A COOL DRY PLACE

Author: Megan Terry (1932-   )
Type of plot: Absurdist
Time of plot: The 1960's
Locale: A jail cell
First produced: 1965, at the Open Theatre, New York City
First published: 1966

> *Principal characters:*
> JASPERS, an intelligent lawyer in his thirties
> MICHAELS, a heavily built man
> GREGORY, a handsome young man

The Play

Keep Tightly Closed in a Cool Dry Place begins in a jail cell that contains two bunks and a single bed. At the start of the play, Jaspers, Michaels, and Gregory face the audience, then combine to become a human machine. Soon they change from parts of the machine to prisoners in a cell by moving in a "military manner" to their bunks. It soon becomes clear that all three have been accused of the murder of Jaspers's wife. The audience does not know which one has committed the murder, nor is it clear whether a murder has actually taken place at all.

Jaspers's energies in the jail are focused on finding a way out; he is a planner. He tells Michaels (who is in low spirits) that they must not give up the struggle to escape and that they will make Gregory confess that he had lied earlier by implicating them in the crime. Gregory, who has been sleeping, is now awakened by Michaels to make the confession. The scene abruptly changes. Michaels is now a bluecoat, Jaspers General Custer, and Gregory an Indian chief who refuses to sign a treaty surrendering his lands.

Just as suddenly, the three men become themselves again. Jaspers is annoyed with Michaels for having hired an amateur such as Gregory to kill his wife. He is still keen, however, to execute his plan of making Gregory sign a confession pleading his sole involvement in the crime. Gregory, who is asleep and evidently in the middle of a sex dream, is again awakened by Michaels. In an attempt to humiliate him, both Jaspers and Michaels ask Gregory to share his dream with them. At first Gregory hesitates, but he soon proceeds to narrate it. The dream centers on his brutal rape of a girl in a telephone booth soon after she gets off a subway. As he narrates the dream, Gregory becomes sexually excited and is unable to complete his story. Annoyed, Jaspers and Michaels climb back into their bunks. The dream makes Gregory recall a childhood incident, which he narrates to the audience. The hissing of a snake in Gregory's story slowly merges with the noise of a machine, as Jaspers and Michaels join him to act again as a human machine.

With the three characters springing back to their beds, the scene changes. Jaspers soon leaps out and asks Gregory how he murdered his wife—a question that slowly acquires the tone of a court inquiry: Gregory, the accused, is being interrogated about the murder by Jaspers, the judge. Gregory says that he was paid by Michaels to commit the crime. The inquiry then becomes an attempt by Jaspers to force Gregory to sign a confession addressed to the governor; Gregory adamantly refuses. Several scene changes follow, showing Jaspers as a fifteen-year-old boy dying in the swamps of Jamestown, then Gregory as Captain John Smith, then all three locking arms, singing, and moving in a simple dance step, finally becoming drag queens and film gangsters.

As a gangster, Gregory describes in gory detail the murder of Jaspers's wife. This scene is followed by a reenactment of the murder. The scene takes place in the kitchen of Jaspers's house. Jaspers, who is acting as his wife, is baking a pie. Michaels takes the part of Richard, Jaspers's young son, who tells his mother that there is someone at the door. The mother tells the boy not to open the door to strangers, but the boy says that he has already opened it. Gregory has now entered the kitchen, and the murder is reenacted as he stalks Jaspers with a cord. The two move around in a circle, in a "slow tense dance."

Once again the scene changes, as the characters return to their beds and Jaspers explains why he wanted his wife murdered. By killing her, he claims, he succeeded in killing his "female self," which was stifling his "living space." Jaspers now asks Gregory to cooperate with him against Michaels. He tells Gregory that together they will make Michaels sign a paper stating that he committed the murder, then implicated the other two in order to avoid the electric chair. Gregory asks how Michaels might be persuaded to do that, and Jaspers proceeds to demonstrate.

Jaspers is now a preacher, speaking from a pulpit; Gregory and Michaels are altar boys. Jaspers delivers a sermon directed to both himself and his congregation. He mentions the murder of a woman and claims that the man guilty of that murder is in their midst. The keyword of the sermon is "embrace." It is the ecstasy of embrace, he says, that gives one the strength to overcome loss. Sounding increasingly like a prophet, Jaspers cries, "You will lose your life. You will lose." Exhausted, he collapses into the arms of Gregory and Michaels, who are now Jaspers's sons Richard and Mark—eight and ten years old, respectively. The two children console Jaspers by saying, "Mommie is in heaven, "and reminding him that he has them for his sons. They start chanting the Our Father. Jaspers joins in subsequently with "Father, widower, murderer, my sons." Once again, the three men join hands in a circle and move like a machine wheel. The play ends with them saying, "And Roller and Rocker." The wheel suddenly stops and Jaspers faces the audience, saying, "This side should face you."

Themes and Meanings

Keep Tightly Closed in a Cool Dry Place can be approached literally or as a fantasy. In her production notes, Megan Terry highlights the ambiguity surrounding her play.

The director should decide, she advises, whether an actual murder has been committed or whether there is merely a desire to commit the crime. Whichever way one approaches the play, its central message deals with imprisonment, alienation, and dependency.

At the outset of the play, all these themes are brilliantly encapsulated by the setting. The jail cell is not only literally a cell but also a metaphor for imprisonment. The three men can be perceived as being imprisoned by their own limitations. Their various attempts to transcend these limitations (by becoming drag queens or film gangsters) lead only to further imprisonment. Terry is urging that people accept their limitations instead of being overwhelmed by them.

The several episodes in the play could be viewed as various stages in Jaspers's journey toward an acceptance of his limitations, with the "Dearly Beloved" sermon as a culminating point in this development. In this context, all the characters become various aspects of Jaspers, who is the planner: Gregory embodies his sensualist side, while Michaels is that aspect of Jaspers's personality that needs to be goaded on to do anything. Again, the key word of the sermon is "embrace." If on the one hand the sermon could be interpreted as Jaspers's forgiveness of himself for the most heinous crime he could conceive of committing (the murder of his wife), on the other hand it refers to his acceptance of his limitations and the limitations of life. The mechanized aspects of life (symbolized by the scenes in which the men act like a machine) may be alienating, but one may transcend them through human contact and love. The fact that the play begins and ends with the three men holding hands to act like a machine expresses this. It shows their need for interdependency to transcend their limitations.

Dramatic Devices

Keep Tightly Closed in a Cool Dry Place is not a conventional play. Influenced by absurdist drama, it defies traditional notions of plot, characterization, and dramatic presentation. The central technique used by the author is "transformations," a technique that throws into question established realities by constantly changing identities and circumstances. In a sense, the entire play is a game played between the actors and the audience. Each time the audience becomes comfortable with a given reality or character, a change occurs, making audience members reassess their conceptions of reality.

Through the technique of transformations, Megan Terry suggests that it is illusory to assume that there is a completed, unified self. Each person encompasses several identities. This is reflected in the play's episodic structure. The actors jump in and out of roles—General Custer, drag queens, film gangsters, and the like. Character description is kept to a minimum in the play; it is left to the actor to interpret the character he is acting. Such an approach clearly places a greater emphasis on the performance text than on the written text. This emphasis on the performance text is in keeping with the basic tenets of the Open Theatre (where the play was first produced), which advocates a collaboration between playwright and actors in the staging of plays.

Unlike traditional plays, this play has no plot but instead a series of episodes. The scenes in which the three characters act as a machine are deliberately placed at strategic points. These scenes, besides giving the episodic structure of the play some unity, effectively communicate the mechanized aspects of the lives of the characters.

The play has no fixed style. Using camp, kitsch, vaudeville, and the grotesque, Terry juxtaposes naturalistic and nonnaturalistic scenes.

Critical Context

Megan Terry worked with the Open Theatre, which greatly inspired and influenced her works, from 1963 to 1968. Her plays incorporate the basic approach of the Open Theatre: cooperation among the playwright, actors, and audience. Her chief contribution to the theater has been her use of "transformations," a technique that defies any fixed notions of reality. *Keep Tightly Closed in a Cool Dry Place* uses this technique effectively. Terry's *Comings and Goings* (pr. 1966, pb. 1967), written during the same period, is in fact subtitled *A Theatre Game*. It contains thirty transformations.

Calm Down Mother (pr. 1965, pb. 1966) is in many ways a complementary piece to *Keep Tightly Closed in a Cool Dry Place*. It has three women characters; the piece has been hailed as a feminist play, showing the struggles of women to know themselves as "living minds." *Approaching Simone* (pr. 1970, pb. 1973), a play for which Terry won the Obie Award, is a continuation of this feminist focus. Basing this play on the life of the French writer Simone Weil, who at the age of thirty-four starved herself to death, Terry created a symbol of heroism for other women. *Babes in the Big House* (pr., pb. 1974) is actually a female version of *Keep Tightly Closed in a Cool Dry Place*. The play shows the terrible living conditions of women prisoners. Whereas in the earlier play Terry was ambiguous about the nature of the oppression of prisoners, in this play she blames patriarchy for it.

Terry uses a wide range of genres in her plays. *Hothouse* (pr., pb. 1974) is a realistic drama, while *The Gloaming, Oh My Darling* (pr. 1966, pb. 1967) is more of an absurdist play. *Viet Rock* (pr., pb. 1966) is a musical. Subtitled *A Folk War Movie*, it was one of the first plays to confront the Vietnam War. Terry's later plays tend to deal with social issues. *American King's English for Queens* (pr., pb. 1978) takes up sexism in American English. Her works of the 1990's and early twenty-first century include *India Plays* (pr. 1992), *Sound Fields: Are We Hear* (pr. 1992), *Star Path Moon Stop* (pr. 1995), and *No Kissing in the Hall* (pr. 2002). Megan Terry's significance as a dramatist lies in her foregrounding of feminism and her return to drama as performance rather than as a literary text.

Sources for Further Study

Keyssar, Helene. "Megan Terry: Mother of American Feminist Drama." In *Feminist Theatre: An Introduction to Plays of Contemporary British and American Women.* New York: Grove Press, 1985.

Kolin, P. C., ed. "Megan Terry." In *American Playwrights Since 1945.* New York: Greenwood Press, 1989.

Marranca, Bonnie, and Gautam Dasgupta. "Megan Terry." In *American Playwrights: A Critical Survey*. New York: Drama Book Specialists, 1981.

Olauson, Judith. "1960-1970: Lorraine Hansberry, Adrienne Kennedy, Rosalyn Drexler, Megan Terry, Rochelle Owens, Myrna Lamb." In *The American Woman Playwright: A View of Criticism and Characterization*. Troy, N.Y.: Whitston, 1981.

Savran, David. "Megan Terry." In *In Their Own Words: Contemporary American Playwrights*. New York: Theatre Communications Group, 1988.

Terry, Megan. Interview by Dinah L. Leavitt. In *Women in American Theater: Careers, Images, Movements. An Illustrated Anthology and Sourcebook*, edited by Helen Chinoy and Linda Jenkins. New York: Crown, 1981.

Wilmeth, Don, ed. "Megan Terry." In *Speaking on Stage: Interviews with Contemporary American Playwrights*. Tuscaloosa: University of Alabama Press, 1996.

Teresa Taisha Abraham

THE KENTUCKY CYCLE

Author: Robert Schenkkan (1953-   )
Type of plot: Epic theater; family
Time of plot: 1775-1975
Locale: Southeastern Kentucky
First produced: 1991, at the Intiman Theatre, Seattle, Washington
First published: 1993

> *Principal characters:*
> MICHAEL ROWEN, former Irish indentured servant
> MORNING STAR, his Cherokee wife
> PATRICK ROWEN, their son
> SALLIE BIGGS, their African American slave
> JOE TALBERT, their neighbor
> REBECCA TALBERT, Joe's daughter and Patrick's wife
> JEREMIAH TALBERT, Joe's son
> EZEKIEL ROWEN, Patrick's son
> RICHARD TALBERT, Jeremiah's son
> JED ROWEN, Ezekiel's son
> JAMES TALBERT WINSTON, owner of Blue Star Mining Company
> FRANKLIN BIGGS, owner of Biggs and Son Liquor

The Play

The Kentucky Cycle, as its title suggests, is actually a series of nine short plays dramatizing the interrelated history of three fictional southeastern Kentucky families over two hundred years. The plays are grouped in two parts that may be performed in all-day sessions (with lunch or dinner breaks) or on consecutive evenings. Part 1 consists of five short plays (with their times) titled "Masters of the Trade" (1775), "The Courtship of Morning Star" (1776), "The Homecoming" (1792), "Ties That Bind" (1819), and "God's Great Supper" (1861). Part Two consists of the four short plays titled "Tall Tales" (1885), "Fire in the Hole" (1920), "Which Side Are You On?" (1954), and "The War on Poverty" (1975).

The Kentucky Cycle begins when Kentucky is "a dark and bloody ground," a beautiful but uninhabited hunting ground and battleground for several American Indian tribes who do not believe the land can be owned. This American Indian belief looms like an ominous curse over the rest of the cycle, as whites claim, inhabit, and despoil the land. The belief literally fits the first three plays in which former Irish indentured servant Michael Rowen (who killed his Georgia master) viciously kills his way to ownership of some Kentucky land, subdues a surviving Cherokee maiden as his mate, and in turn is viciously killed by their son, Patrick. Patrick also kills the neighbor Joe Talbert, takes Talbert's daughter Rebecca as his bride, and consolidates their land.

These events precipitate a family feud that lasts for generations. In the fourth play,

"Ties That Bind," Jeremiah Talbert, Joe's son, uses land speculation to get revenge: He buys up Patrick Rowen's bank loans, forecloses on Patrick's land and property (including the slave family, the Biggses), and reduces Patrick and his sons to tenant farmers. Jeremiah builds a big house on the hill from which he can watch over and enjoy his domain, including his slaves and the Rowens.

However, in the next generation and the fifth play, "God's Great Supper," the Rowens get their revenge and take back the land. In the Civil War, Richard Talbert, Jeremiah's son, leads a contingent of Confederates, including Jed Rowen (Patrick's grandson), who in the confusion of battle pushes Richard into the Cumberland River, where he drowns. Jed then returns home and, with his father, the preacher Ezekiel Rowen, leads an attack of biblical ferocity on the Talberts: The Rowens massacre the Talberts and their slaves (except for two Talbert daughters and the Biggs family), burn the big house and barns, poison the well, and plow salt into the nearby fields.

Part 2 of *The Kentucky Cycle* takes the story into the coal-mining era, where the massive destruction of the land and its people makes poisoned wells and salted fields seem insignificant. In "Tall Tales" the Rowens sell the mineral rights to their land to a shyster posing as an Appalachian storyteller (the "broad-form" deeds in such transactions also allowed free access to the minerals, without regard for surface owners' rights). In "Fire in the Hole," coal mining is in full swing, with the land deforested, coal waste dumped everywhere, and the people working for the coal company, living in a squalid company camp, and being paid in company scrip. However, the deplorable conditions lead to union organizing and, after more bloodshed, the union's triumph. In these struggles, the Rowens generally represent the union and the Talberts (now Winstons), the management.

"Which Side Are You On?" shows the brief period of union power waning, with large layoffs occurring as demand for coal drops and new mining methods (stripping the land with huge machines) are employed. The climax takes place when owner James Talbert Winston's economizing on safety measures causes an enormous dust explosion at the Blue Star Mine, with much loss of life, including that of Scotty Rowen, son of the union's district president, Joshua Rowen. "The War on Poverty" shows the aftermath, with Joshua Rowen, James Talbert Winston, and Franklin Biggs (owner of the only prospering local business, a liquor store) standing on the devastated land and quarreling about whether to sell it for strip mining.

Themes and Meanings

Robert Schenkkan's *The Kentucky Cycle* depicts a Darwinian world in which natural selection prevails, the fittest survive, and human life is nasty, vicious, and short. In the battle of predators, the savage settlers wipe out the Native Americans, then settle scores among themselves in long-running blood feuds. The survivors then succumb to superior forces from outside, such as shysters, broad-form deeds, and coal companies. Finally they join outside forces in the shifting fight between union and management—until both union and management go down, victims of economic forces beyond their control.

However, Schenkkan does not seem to hold this grim naturalistic view of existence on general principle, or at least not with any conviction. He does not write so much about how things are as much as what they have become and why. In fact, in an "Author's Note" appended to the printed version of *The Kentucky Cycle* (1995), Schenkkan states that the play is not about southeastern Kentucky, or even Appalachia, but about the United States. Rather, he saw southeastern Kentucky only as an awful example of how the American myth of the frontier, with its submyths of infinite abundance and escape, has played out. In choosing southeastern Kentucky for this honor, he was influenced by a 1981 visit to the region and by Harry Caudill's book *Night Comes to the Cumberlands: A Biography of a Depressed Area* (1963).

It is certainly true that some awful acts have been committed on American soil and rationalized by myths, for example, of racial superiority or manifest destiny. Yet, in the end, Schenkkan's "Author's Note" seems vague, insufficient, and merely disingenuous. It does not fully account for the numerous instances of human greed, viciousness, and depravity that the play contains, nor does it reflect the outright attack on capitalism that the play seems to make, as seen in the emphasis on owning the land, exploiting the people on it, and extracting its resources. The "cycle" seems to suggest only a capitalistic pattern.

However one explains it, the destruction of the land is certainly an important theme in the play. In the beginning, Cherokee warriors scoff at the idea that anyone can own the land, and, at least initially, the early settlers who kill the Cherokees and each other for the land love it. At the beginning of Part 2, Mary Anne Rowen voices how the beauty of the land supports the human spirit. This beauty is lost quickly when the coal mines arrive, until at the end there is the prospect that the already devastated land will be strip-mined into a barren moonscape.

Dramatic Devices

The Kentucky Cycle poses tremendous challenges for producing and performing. Besides its epic length, numerous characters, and changes of scene, it has speeches in Cherokee, violent acts difficult to act convincingly, battles, a drowning in a river, a train spewing machine-gun fire, and explosions. The original production solved some of these problems in the style of Shakespearean theater. The stage, a large, bare oval shape with an earthen pit in the center, suggested various settings with the help of a few props. Changes to the basic costumes were also minimal. Twelve actors and a chorus of seven acted all of the roles and remained seated in view of the audience when they were not onstage.

The original production solved other problems in a modern way. A screen was used on which to project various backgrounds, such as the sky, crows fighting, or a coal tipple. Spot lighting was also used to shift scenes and single out actors. Electronic equipment was used to provide sounds, such as the sounds of the crows fighting (at the beginning of "God's Great Supper").

As the crows illustrate, the play also makes use of symbolism. Perhaps the best example of symbolism is in the play's last episode, "The War on Poverty," where the possibility of the land's regeneration appears in the broom sedge and pine sprouts growing out of the waste. The robbing of a grave containing American Indian artifacts (and Morning Star's remarkably preserved daughter) connects the end of the play with its beginning, and the corpses rising out of their graves recall the whole cycle. At the very end, a wolf appears for the first time in more than fifty years, as though Nature is reclaiming her own.

Critical Context

When *The Kentucky Cycle* was first produced, it offended some people in southeastern Kentucky and throughout Appalachia who did not like how the play portrayed their region. They considered the play just another instance of stereotyping of "hillbillies," another example of the media's obligatory tour of Appalachian poverty. The award of the 1992 Pulitzer Prize in drama to *The Kentucky Cycle* did not help matters, since it seemed to applaud such stereotyping and imply gross national ignorance about the region.

Yet many Appalachians would wholeheartedly subscribe to the play's environmental message, and it is this message that Schenkkan has said he meant to send. The play is a warning: Yesterday Appalachia, tomorrow Los Angeles. Although the play portrays a grim regional history, it forecasts a grim national future.

The epic nature of the text and the original staging of the play also indicate that *The Kentucky Cycle* is far from a realistic portrayal. There is not room in the play for extensive character development and for examining all sides of the play's complex questions. Rather, the mode of the play is like the drama of the German Marxist playwright Bertolt Brecht, who gave the world the term "epic drama" to describe the propagandistic works he wrote. Similar plays in the United States are the historical outdoor dramas and religious dramas, and reaching further back in time, one can see distant similarities of *The Kentucky Cycle* to the medieval mystery cycles.

Sources for Further Study

Billings, Dwight, Gurney Norman, and Katherine Ledford, eds. *Back Talk from Appalachia: Confronting Stereotypes*. Lexington: University Press of Kentucky, 2001.

Colakis, Marianthe. "Aeschlyean Elements in Robert Schenkkan's *The Kentucky Cycle*." *Text and Presentation: The Journal of the Comparative Drama Conference* 16 (1995): 19-23.

Kaufman, Warner. "Theater: *The Kentucky Cycle*." *Nation* 257 (December 13, 1993): 740-743.

Mason, Bobbie Ann. "Recycling Kentucky." *The New Yorker* 69 (November 1, 1993): 50.

May, Theresa J. "Frontiers: Environmental History, Ecocriticism, and *The Kentucky Cycle*." *Journal of Dramatic Theory and Criticism* 14 (Fall, 1999): 159-178.

Harold Branam

THE KILLDEER

Author: James Reaney (1926-)
Type of plot: Comedy; melodrama
Time of plot: The 1960's
Locale: A small town in southwestern Ontario, Canada
First produced: 1960, at the Coach House Theatre, Toronto, Canada
First published: 1962

> *Principal characters:*
> HARRY GARDNER, a bank clerk, later a lawyer
> MRS. VINNIE GARDNER, his mother
> MADAM FAY, a cosmetics saleswoman
> ELI FAY, her son
> REBECCA LORIMER, the egg-girl and later Eli's wife
> CLIFFORD HOPKINS, the hired hand on the Fay farm
> DR. BALLAD, formerly the village doctor, now a hermit

The Play

The opening scene of *The Killdeer* takes place in Mrs. Gardner's cottage, where Madam Fay is selling cosmetics to a reluctant Mrs. Gardner. As part of her sales pitch, Madam Fay casually relates the story of her scandalous past. She recounts the ghastly murders and suicide in which her family and Rebecca Lorimer, the egg-girl, have been involved. The audience learns that Madam Fay's son, Eli, a nineteen-year-old child-man, hates his mother. He was left on the farm when Madam Fay deserted her family and ran off with her adopted sister's husband to Buffalo for a weekend. Madam Fay's husband, Gilbert, prodded by the resentful hired man, Clifford Hopkins (who had an affair with Madam Fay), went to the Lorimer home and shot Lorimer's wife and two sons and then killed himself. Rebecca was the only one in that family to escape the slaughter; she stayed on the family farm and turned it into a successful venture. Eli, feeling abandoned and lost, attached himself to Clifford, who dominated him and encouraged his childlike dependency. Lorimer, Rebecca's father, was placed in a mental institution in London, Ontario. Madam Fay's spellbinding story holds Mrs. Gardner, who, to hear more of the melodramatic tale, buys some cosmetics.

When Madam Fay leaves, Mrs. Gardner's son, Harry, a bank clerk, comes to tell his mother that he cannot have supper with her because Mr. Coons, his employer, has invited him to his home for dinner. During this exchange, Harry's dislike of his mother's cluttered parlor, her condescending tone, and her domineering manner is evident—as is his acquiescence to her every wish. Mrs. Gardner immediately envisions a marriage between Mr. Coons's daughter Vernelle and Harry.

In the third scene, the comic element of the play surfaces as two gossips, Mrs. Gardner and Mrs. Budge, discuss Madam Fay and her sordid past. Rebecca enters, bringing surprising news: She is going to be married to Eli the next day, a marriage arranged by Clifford. When Mrs. Gardner expresses astonishment that Rebecca would marry the son of her family's killer, Rebecca explains that she wants to "untie the evil knot" and make a fresh start. Her generosity and optimism are not shared by Eli, who suffers from infantile regression and does not want to marry Rebecca.

When Harry learns from his mother of Rebecca's intention to marry Eli, he confesses his love for her, even though he has only met her twice and the only thing he knows about her is her love for the killdeer bird. When Harry tells his mother about Vernelle Coons's marriage proposal to him, Mrs. Gardner advises him to accept it. Act 1 ends with the crash of bells and the playing of the wedding march.

Act 2 opens on a somber note in a courthouse. Several years have elapsed and many changes have occurred, which are related by Mrs. Budge and Mrs. Delta, the cleaning women of the courthouse. Rebecca has been sentenced to death for the murder of Clifford. Mrs. Gardner is dead, and Harry, after attending Osgoode Hall Law School, is now a practicing lawyer with a failing marriage. In the second scene, there is a confrontation between him and Vernelle; he leaves Vernelle and returns to live in his mother's old cottage. Still in love with Rebecca, he sets himself the task of delaying the date of her hanging, so that he can prove her innocence. He persuades the jailer's wife to let him visit Rebecca's cell. The play takes a melodramatic turn when he and Rebecca spend their "wedding" night in the cell, and Rebecca conceives a child; her pregnancy earns her a stay of execution until the child is born. Eventually a new trial date is set. Rebecca tells Harry that she is innocent but fears Eli is guilty of the murder and pleads with Harry to save them both.

Act 3 relates Rebecca's second trial. In the final scene, Harry cross-examines Madam Fay. Having learned of her irrational aversion to the killdeer, he shows her one in court. She breaks down and reveals the surprising truth: Clifford was not murdered but died of a heart attack. Both Rebecca and Eli are exonerated, while Madam Fay is charged with mischief and mutilation of a dead body; she avoids justice by escaping in her pink coupe. The play ends on an optimistic note, with the presence of the mysterious Dr. Ballad, who has been a representative of love and charity during the courtroom scene, adding to the feeling of affirmation. Harry and Rebecca are free to start a life together with their baby, and Eli, shedding his infantile regression, gives the baby his toys. Dr. Ballad, like Prospero in William Shakespeare's *The Tempest* (pr. 1611), presides over this transformation and releases them all from the bondage of the past.

Themes and Meanings

The Killdeer focuses on the individual's struggle to free himself from the debilitating influence of domineering parents who deny him his own identity and destiny. The three most important characters, Harry, Rebecca, and Eli, are all victims of parental domination. At the beginning of the play, Harry, the youthful protagonist, has no will of his own in the presence of his mother. He marries Vernelle Coons, his mother's choice, not Rebecca, whom he loves. Young Eli fears his heartless mother, is haunted by his father's brutality, and is emotionally abused and exploited by Clifford. Rebecca, too, must contend with a past in which she was victimized by adults.

The play shows that such exploitation of youth by manipulating, selfish adults can be overcome by love and sympathy. Harry's love for Rebecca and his generous and sincere concern for Eli are responsible for the truth being revealed and the couple being saved from execution. Rebecca herself is forgiving, marrying Eli to untie "the evil knot." She faces the world bravely, making a success of the farm left to her, and, like the killdeer, tries to protect those dependent upon her. Her love enables both Harry and Eli to mature and find some measure of happiness.

The play celebrates the spirit of hope and redemption. Both Harry and Rebecca remain optimistic and resilient even at the darkest moment, when Rebecca faces death at the hands of the hangman. James Reaney conveys this theme through literal, symbolic, and mythical images. Mr. Manatee, the hangman, is portrayed as a destructive monster associated with death. Harry defeats him by creating life in his lovemaking with Rebecca, though this action ensures only the postponement of the trial, not Rebecca's acquittal. Acquittal comes only through the intervention of the mystical Dr. Ballad, the village doctor turned hermit. Dr. Ballad, his very name associated with creation and song, enters the courtroom and ensures the safety of the main characters. He defeats evil, brings about peace and harmony, and creates a world of love and optimism for Eli, Rebecca, Harry, and the baby. It is significant that Madam Fay escapes the law after the trial, for the play affirms not vengeance or retribution but selflessness and forgiveness.

The play evokes the regional ethos convincingly. It captures the local idiom and customs and provides fine details of rural Ontario life, with its social factions and rivalries. However, Reaney's treatment of the themes of childhood innocence and its exploitation by manipulating adults, of the human potential for violence, and of the power of love and hope enables the play to transcend the regional and national and to achieve mythic and universal significance.

In *The Killdeer*, as in his poems and short stories, Reaney celebrates and champions the creative imagination. He presents the child as capable of viewing the world imaginatively. Eli, in particular, is seen as a reflection of the creative writer who is capable of avoiding the world of reality by creating a fantasy world into which he can withdraw. His imagination gives him the ability to see the world as he would like it to be, not as it is, and this illusion sustains him and provides temporary relief from harsh reality.

Dramatic Devices

That James Reaney began his creative career as a poet is evident from the abundant use of poetic imagery in the play. *The Killdeer* is episodic, with numerous current incidents and many accounts of past events, all of which are given some cohesion by the recurring imagery. Many of the images function both literally and metaphorically. The image of the title, for example, is central to the play. Rebecca is identified with the killdeer: It is her favorite bird, and, like the killdeer, she attracts the enemy and leads him away from those whom she wishes to protect. The killdeer is also crucial in resolving the central conflict of the play. Madam Fay, as a girl, had killed her foster-sister's pet killdeer out of jealousy; this has led to her irrational fear of the bird—the play's symbol of caring and selflessness. Harry is able to use this fear to disconcert her during the second trial, thereby discovering the truth. At the end of the play, the caged killdeer is allowed to go free, signifying the deliverance of the three characters from the bondage of the past and signaling a fresh beginning for them all.

Other bird images in the play portray the adults who are shown to be predators of the young and the weak. The vulture is used to characterize Vernelle and the lawyers at Osgoode Hall. The old gossips, Mrs. Gardner and Mrs. Budge, see themselves as two old crows. The odious Mr. Manatee confesses that he wanted to be a carrion crow.

Reaney easily shifts between simple, natural dialogue and free verse. In many scenes he authentically employs the southwestern Ontario idiom. Some critics think that the poetic utterances heighten the dramatic effect; others have reservations, believing that such diction is self-indulgent and detracts from the authenticity of the rural speech.

Even his most admiring critics have noted Reaney's tendency to melodramatize and sentimentalize at times, as in the account of Henry and Rebecca's meeting in prison and in the portraits of Dr. Ballad and Madam Fay. Some have observed that his tone sometimes shifts uncomfortably between the comic and the pathetic, and that the occasional curious blend of fantasy, comedy, and melodrama appears incongruous and forced. Reaney, recognizing some of the flaws of this play, especially in the trial scene of the third act, revised the play in 1970, republishing it in 1972. The revised version has only two acts. The first remains the same; act 2 has several changes. For example, Reaney omits the imprisonment of Rebecca, though she is still a murder suspect; also omitted are the conception and birth of Rebecca and Harry's child, the appearance of Dr. Ballad, and the entire court scene from act 3. These omissions and changes keep the play focused on the main themes and characters and add cohesion and credibility. Nevertheless, the original version of the play is still an ambitious and impressive work.

Critical Context

The Killdeer, *The Sun and the Moon* (wr. 1959, pb. 1962, pr. 1965), and *The Easter Egg* (pr. 1962, pb. 1972) are considered apprenticeship pieces. In these works, Reaney was learning how to adapt his poetic gifts to the demands of dramatic form. *The Killdeer*, the most impressive of these early plays, won the Governor General's Award for the best Canadian drama published in 1962. There Reaney established many of the devices and themes that have reappeared in subsequent plays such as *Colours in the Dark* (pr. 1967, pb. 1969), his most innovative and multilayered play, and what is perhaps his most convincing dramatic achievement, the Donnelly trilogy: *Sticks & Stones* (pr. 1973, pb. 1975); *St. Nicholas Hotel, Wm Donnelly, Prop.* (pr. 1974, pb. 1976); and *Handcuffs* (pr. 1975, pb. 1977).

Colours in the Dark was Reaney's first play to explore extensively the rich possibilities of using multimedia devices to engage and expand the viewer's imagination; it was also his first play to abandon conventional plot and to provide cohesion through an intertwining and overlapping of times, places, and characters. Like *The Killdeer, Colours in the Dark* is embedded in Reaney's native southwestern Ontario, and it similarly, if more readily, transcends the regional and national through its grand design, encompassing the history of humankind as told in the Bible and probing humanity's collective past and ancestral memory.

In the Donnelly trilogy, based on the murder of a family in southwestern Ontario in 1880, Reaney again employs multiple forms—poetry, song, dance, mime, marionettes, and screens—but he more effectively integrates the poetic and the dramatic, the mythic and the historical, the symbolic and the realistic, the static and the suspenseful.

Reaney's subsequent plays, such as *Baldoon* (pr., pb. 1976), based on a poltergeist story, and *Wacousta!* (pr. 1978, pb. 1979), a melodramatic retelling of John Richardson's novel *Wacousta* (1832), have been less successful. In spite of this falling off, Reaney, who has won two other Governor General's Awards in addition to that for *The Killdeer*, has secured for himself a position as one of Canada's most innovative and outstanding playwrights.

Sources for Further Study

Benson, Eugene. "James Reaney." In *Contemporary Dramatists*. 6th ed. Detroit: St. James, 1999.

Benson, Eugene, and L. W. Conolly, eds. *Oxford Companion to the Canadian Theatre*. Oxford, England: Oxford University Press, 1989.

Dragland, Stan, ed. *Approaches to the Work of James Reaney*. Downsview, Ont.: ECW, 1983.

Parker, Gerald D. *How to Play: The Theatre of James Reaney*. Toronto, Ont.: ECW, 1991.

Reaney, J. Stewart. *James Reaney*. Agincourt, Ont.: Gage Educational, 1977.

Tait, Michael. "The Limits of Innocence." In *Dramatists in Canada: Selected Essays*, edited by W. H. New. Vancouver: University of British Columbia Press, 1972.

Warkentin, Germaine. "The Artist in Labour: James Reaney's Play." *Journal of Canadian Fiction* 2 (Winter, 1973): 88-91.

Wilson, Milton. "On Reviewing Reaney." *Tamarack Review* 26 (Winter, 1963): 71-78.

Woodman, Ross. *James Reaney*. Toronto, Ont.: McClelland and Stewart, 1975.

Victor J. Ramraj

THE KILLER

Author: Eugène Ionesco (1909-1994)
Type of plot: Absurdist
Time of plot: The twentieth century
Locale: A large city in France
First produced: 1958, at the Landestheater, Darmstadt, West Germany
First published: Tueur sans gages, 1958, in *Théâtre II* (English translation, 1960)

> *Principal characters:*
> BERENGER, an average, middle-aged citizen
> THE ARCHITECT, a civil servant
> DANY, a typist
> ÉDOUARD, Berenger's friend
> MOTHER PEEP, a fascist demagogue
> THE KILLER

The Play

    The Killer opens on an empty, bare stage. Suddenly the stage is brightly illuminated with blue and white lights, which gives an impression of silence and peace. This is the Radiant City, an enclave within the "dark and dismal" metropolis where Berenger lives.

    Berenger, an ordinary, middle-aged man, enters to see the Radiant City; he hopes to move here. He is accompanied by the Architect, who later turns out to have a variety of other civil servant duties. Berenger is enraptured by the City, whose climate is controlled by concealed ventilators; flowers always bloom, it never rains, and the residential villas are built of the finest materials. Berenger finds in the City an embodiment of earlier momentary experiences he has had, sudden euphoria of joy and conviction; at first his pleasure in this new environment is ecstatic, only occasionally punctuated by the dry comments of the Architect. Using a telephone that he carries in his pocket, the Architect becomes increasingly irate about the tardiness of his secretary, Dany. When Dany finally arrives, Berenger falls instantly in love with her and proposes. She pays little attention to him; berated by the Architect, she resigns and leaves.

    Berenger now realizes that the Radiant City is deserted. Stones from an invisible source are thrown at him and the Architect; the Architect explains that, in the ornamental pool in the City, one or more people, lured there by the Killer, drown each day. Disillusioned, the idealist Berenger leaves with the Architect; the lighting reverts to the gray of the surrounding city, and, now at a bistro, Berenger and the Architect have a glass of wine and a sandwich. The Architect, who—like other civil servants—is safe from the Killer, explains how the Killer lures a victim to his death by pretending to be a beggar and offering to sell the victim a variety of objects from his basket, everything from artificial flowers to obscene drawings to a photograph of a colonel; finally, at the edge of the pool, the Killer gives the client a push so that he falls in and is drowned. The Architect reveals that his former employee, Dany, has just become the latest victim. Overcome, Berenger resolves to stop the Killer, and rushes off, leaving the indifferent Architect in the bistro.

Act 2 takes place in Berenger's squalid apartment. Outside, partially visible through the window, are various city people—Berenger's irritable concierge, truck and car drivers, a grocer, old men, a postman, and so on. Berenger returns from his visit to the City and discovers that, concealed in the dark of his apartment, his friend Édouard is awaiting him. Édouard is ill, has a withered arm, and is carefully guarding his briefcase. Berenger is still agitated about the death of Dany and about the Killer, but Édouard indifferently explains that everyone already knows about the Killer. As they prepare to depart for a walk, the briefcase opens and its contents are scattered. These objects turn out to be the same goods with which the Killer was attempting to interest his prospective victims. There is also an address book in which the Killer's victims are listed. Unconvincingly, Édouard explains that the Killer had wanted him to publish his diary in a literary journal. Berenger rushes out, with Édouard reluctantly accompanying him, to take the briefcase to the police; in their haste, however, they forget to take the briefcase with them.

Act 3 begins with a political rally conducted by a grotesque Fascist figure called Mother Peep; her followers are called "Mother Peep's Geese." She harangues them:

> We won't persecute, but we'll punish, and deal out justice. We won't colonize, we'll occupy the countries we liberate. We won't exploit men, we'll make them productive. We'll call compulsory work voluntary. War shall change its name to peace and everything will be altered, thanks to me and my geese.

Berenger, followed by the diffident Édouard, discovers that Édouard's briefcase has been forgotten, but several other briefcases appear, owned variously by an old man, a drunk man, and even Mother Peep herself. There are battles over the possession of the briefcases, but none of them contains the paraphernalia of the Killer. Mother Peep and her gang disappear, to be replaced by a hectic traffic jam directed by two giant policemen, who refuse to aid Berenger in finding the prefecture. Suddenly they, too, disappear, as do Édouard and the other characters, and Berenger is alone. It is twilight, and Berenger begins to walk toward the police station.

The final long scene of the play, an extended monologue by Berenger, now begins. The scene presents the encounter between Berenger and the Killer himself, a nondescript, one-eyed little man who does nothing but chuckle at each of Berenger's arguments, threats, and pleas to end his killings. All argument proves useless. Berenger takes out pistols, but he decides that they are powerless against the implacable will of his opponent. He lays down his weapons; the Killer, carrying a knife "with a large shining blade," and still chuckling, continues to advance toward Berenger, and the play ends.

Themes and Meanings

The Killer in the title of Eugène Ionesco's play is death itself. Here death is not ennobling, spiritual, or tragic; its occurrence is as nondescript and arbitrary as the figure of the Killer himself. In the very long monologue which ends the play, Berenger offers dozens of arguments—humanistic, practical, existential—against the activities of the Killer, but comes to admit their futility. He sees, as Ionesco himself put it in his stage directions, "the vacuity of his own rather commonplace morality."

Death may be mundane, but life is not an attractive alternative. Berenger tells the Architect that he can remember experiencing, when he was young, rare moments of a transcendent rapture of joy and otherness. These moments have gone. The Architect, efficient and bored, only half listens, demonstrating the fact that other people are no help.

Any effort to achieve contact is a failure; when Berenger falls instantly in love with Dany and proclaims his highly romantic passion, she barely notices him. Berenger's one friend is Édouard, a whining, miserable, self-pitying wretch. In the play there are a few characters who are comic (like the old man searching for the banks of the Danube) or sympathetic (like the young soldier with a bouquet of carnations who is cruelly reprimanded by a policeman). Most people, however, are as choleric as Berenger's concierge or as hateful as Mother Peep, with her vicious political program, or as insensitive as the owner of the bistro. Most people are mindless, and these are the people whom Berenger, by tracking down the Killer, hopes to save. Any organization that people attempt to create, like the Radiant City, which superficially offers a positive alternative to the ugliness of daily life, is fatally flawed internally. There is a kind of heroism in Berenger's efforts to combat the Killer, but more than a little irony in the cynical indifference that his efforts evoke among those he is trying to save. Another of Ionesco's protagonists, the Berenger of *Rhinocéros* (pr., pb. 1959; *Rhinoceros*, 1959), says wearily at one point, "I just can't get used to life." Ionesco's heroes are driven to despair by their refusal to conform to the limits that life imposes; moreover, their efforts are useless because they all come to the same end.

Ionesco does not offer any ameliorations for the human condition, and his comedy, based on the preposterousness of people and institutions, only serves to emphasize the bleakness of the prospect. His pessimism was not austere and elegant like that of Samuel Beckett; it was marked instead by violence of action and by extravagance of verbal technique. Very little happens in Beckett; in Ionesco, much happens, but it all points to the same end. It leads to a twilit, featureless avenue where the Killer—who never answers any of Berenger's frantic questions, who only chuckles—waits.

Dramatic Devices

Throughout *The Killer* and other plays by Ionesco there is a contrast between, on one hand, light, evanescence, and energy, and, on the other, dark, heaviness, and fatigue. This ambiguous polarity between light and dark is a matter both of philosophy and of theatrical technique. The Radiant City, where the Killer drowns his victims, is brilliant with a sinister light, while the metropolis itself is oppressively heavy and earthbound. The play ends, when Berenger meets his inevitable fate, in twilight, a modulation which provides a sense of closure.

There is also a contrast between the individual and the masses, as there is between a bare stage and a stage full of people and objects. The setting is minimal in act 1, where almost the only visible objects are the chairs and table at the bistro, but in act 2 (in Berenger's squalid, overstuffed apartment) material objects crushingly abound. By the end of the play, setting and properties virtually disappear, as one by one Berenger's arguments against death become deflated and even silly, until there is nothing left. Berenger's increasing isolation in the play is emphasized by his inability to communicate with all the people to whom he speaks. In most of act 1 Berenger is alone with the Architect, but in most of acts 2 and 3 the stage swarms with dozens of vociferous people: passersby outside Berenger's apartment, throngs of the faithful in Mother Peep's audience, soldiers, and police. At the end, Berenger is once again alone with the Killer, and he meets his death in solitude—indeed, the chuckling, wordless Killer may be part of Berenger (who cannot stop talking) himself.

As in all Ionesco's plays, everything is exaggerated, dreamlike, surrealistic. The policemen are giants on stilts; the confusion of the crowds and the traffic is a Kafkaesque nightmare. One of the main inspirations for Ionesco's plays is the unsophisticated theater of vaudeville, music hall, circus, and Punch and Judy shows. The malevolent energy of Mother Peep recalls the last of these, while the nonsensical jokes and illogical insistence of other characters derive from the other forms of popular theater. Abrupt changes, pointless surprises, bizarre displacements of normal literary continuity make up the dreamlike texture of the play. It is, in fact, a nightmare play, and like a nightmare its apparent absurdity conveys basic, irrational fears.

Critical Context

Ionesco's two major plays are *Rhinoceros* and *The Killer.* In his earlier plays, beginning with *La Cantatrice chauve* (pr. 1950, pb. 1954; *The Bald Soprano,* 1956), pure absurdity reigns, while in his later plays, such as *La Soif et la faim* (pr. 1964, pb. 1966; *Hunger and Thirst,* 1968), Ionesco's obsession with death becomes almost too insistent and bald. In *Rhinoceros* and *The Killer* an effective balance between absurdity and death, or between art and obsession, is achieved.

Berenger, who is both ordinary and heroic, is an embodiment of Everyman, but, unlike Everyman, he is doomed from the outset. It may be a fault of this play that, despite its comedy, it is too relentlessly pessimistic. The hopelessness of Berenger's quest to confront death is apparent from the beginning, and Ionesco's brilliance of invention does not successfully palliate his profoundly negative vision. A more obvious defect is that some of the scenes are too long; Ionesco's belief that if he is faithful to his own fears he inevitably reflects universal experience has led him to transcribe his fears too literally and lengthily.

In Ionesco's best plays, however, there is a single dominant image around which the entire drama is organized, and nowhere more effectively than in *The Killer.* In *Amédée: Ou, Comment s'en débarrasser* (pr., pb. 1954; *Amédée: Or, How to Get Rid of It*, 1955), Ionesco's first full-length play, there are the ever-growing feet and legs which finally occupy the entire apartment of Amédée and Madeleine; in *Rhinoceros* the pachyderms finally take over, leaving only Berenger (in several of Ionesco's plays the chief character is named Berenger) as the last human being alive; in *Le Nouveau Locataire* (pr. 1955, pb. 1958; *The New Tenant*, 1956), the stage becomes jammed with furniture. The weight of the external world upon the individual is relentless; Ionesco's protagonists cannot escape. The Killer may well be Ionesco's most powerful and poetic image; chuckling, obscene, intransigent, he is the embodiment of death. The inhumanity of the state, as personified by the Architect, and the anti-individualism of political movements, as personified by Mother Peep, both fade into insignificance beside the triumphant and terrible figure of the Killer.

Sources for Further Study
Coe, Richard N. *Ionesco: A Study of His Plays*. Rev. ed. London: Methuen, 1971.
Hayman, Ronald. *Eugène Ionesco*. London: Heinemann, 1976.
Ionesco, Eugène. *Notes and Counter Notes*. Translated by Donald Watson. New York: Grove Press, 1964.
_____. *Present Past, Past Present: A Personal Memoir.* Cambridge, England: Da Capo, 1998.
Jacobsen, Josephine J., and William R. Mueller. *Ionesco and Genet: Playwrights of Silence*. New York: Hill and Wang, 1968.
Lamont, Rosette C. *Ionesco's Imperatives: The Politics of Culture*. Ann Arbor: University of Michigan Press, 1993.
_____, ed. *Ionesco: A Collection of Critical Essays*. Englewood Cliffs, N.J.: Prentice-Hall, 1973.
Lane, Nancy. *Understanding Ionesco*. Columbia: University of South Carolina Press, 1994.
Lewis, Allan. *Ionesco*. New York: Twayne, 1972.
Plimpton, George, ed. "Eugène Ionesco." In *Writers at Work: The Paris Review Interviews, Seventh Series*. New York: Viking, 1986.

Charles Burkhart

A KIND OF ALASKA

Author: Harold Pinter (1930-   )
Type of plot: Existential
Time of plot: The twentieth century
Locale: England
First produced: 1982, at the National Theatre, London
First published: 1982, in *Other Places*

> *Principal characters:*
> DEBORAH, a woman in her mid-forties
> HORNBY, her doctor, a man in his early sixties
> PAULINE, her sister, a woman in her early forties

The Play

This one-act drama opens with Deborah's awakening from a long sleep. A woman in her mid-forties, she is sitting up in a white bed looking around. Her gaze falls on Dr. Hornby, who wears a dark suit and is seated at a table in one of two chairs. As Deborah tries to assess what is happening, Hornby questions her, wondering if she knows him or can hear him. Believing that he is not listening to her, Deborah refuses to identify him as anyone. She talks about her sleeplessness and notes that she can speak French. Hornby informs her that she has been asleep for a long time, is much older than when she fell asleep, and is now awake.

Deborah seems unable to digest this information. When she finally looks at Hornby, she tries to grasp what he has told her but seems disoriented. Unsure of what language she is speaking, she is still not convinced that she is being heard, and she speaks as if she were still the young person who fell asleep years ago. When Hornby informs her that he is the one who woke her, she is only more confused, since she does not know him; she continues to ask for others who were there when she fell asleep as a younger person. Unsure of her age when asked, she settles on fifteen but begins to accuse the doctor of "touching" her; when he tells her that her parents brought her here, she wonders whether it was as a sacrifice, insisting that Hornby has seduced and "ruined" her.

Continuing to try to locate herself in time and space, Deborah wants to verify her age through her sisters, Pauline and Estelle. Pauline, she says, is too witty for her own good, and Estelle is deep and sensual. Deborah also continues to speculate about where she is, conjecturing that she may be in a seaside hotel or in a white tent in the Sahara Desert. Becoming defensive with the doctor about her long sleep, Deborah finally asks how long it has been; when the doctor informs her that it has been twenty-nine years, she is further confused about whether she has been or is dead. She asks about her boyfriend Jack and wonders what crime she may have committed to put her in this prison. When told that her sister Pauline is waiting to see her, she insists that she does not want to see any sisters or brothers, suggesting that her sisters are gluttons and confiding to Hornby that she once prayed she would never see any of them again.

Deborah continues to oscillate between the past and present. Learning from the doctor that he woke her with an injection, she tries to claim him as her Prince Charming, but he refuses. She then reverts to the past, saying that she will settle for Jack, but she is upset by the memory of Pauline's telling her that her father had a mistress. Switching back to the present, Deborah wants to know what is happening.

Hornby and Deborah exchange information about the experience. He tries to explain to Deborah that she fell into a kind of sleep in which she was very still, though she was taken on walks and she sometimes made some spasmodic movements. Attempting to get out of bed and stand, Deborah falls, refuses help, and begins to dance in slow motion. She then sits and asks about current events, wondering whether the war is over and telling Hornby about the nature of her dancing while she was asleep.

Deborah notices her younger sister, Pauline, who is standing in the room and who asks Deborah if she recognizes her. Pauline and Hornby have a brief argument about whether Pauline should be there, and Hornby advises her to tell Deborah a mixture of lies and truth. After alerting Hornby to his trembling hand, Pauline tells Deborah that her parents and other sister are on a world cruise, but she has informed them of Deborah's awakening and they all send love. She again asks Deborah whether she recognizes her.

Puzzled by her sister's changed condition, Deborah questions her about it, but Pauline insists that it was Deborah who at age sixteen changed. Apparently, Deborah was placing a vase on the table during dinner and suddenly froze, unfreezing briefly only to come to a total stop when trying to move the vase so she could see her father. Unable to take this in, Deborah speculates that Pauline must be an aunt she has not met, or a distant cousin. Then, noticing Pauline's breasts, Deborah notices her own and concludes that they are both women. When Deborah reverts to questions that suggest she is still sixteen, Hornby admonishes her that she is not listening, and Pauline describes herself as a widow. Hornby explains to Deborah that he has cared for her since she fell into her sleep, marrying Pauline but then leaving her to live with Deborah and awakening her when he came to possess the means to do so. Her mother, he says, is dead and her father blind. He insists that Deborah has been absent, suspended in "a kind of Alaska," while he and Pauline have been the ones to suffer, Pauline visiting regularly and he trying to chart Deborah's journey.

Deborah voices her desire to go home and asks about her forthcoming birthday. When they encourage her about it and her presents, she becomes further concerned about whether she will be able to keep them. Beginning to flick her cheek with her hand faster and faster, Deborah seems to go back into "a kind of Alaska." Complaining that walls are closing in on her, she becomes rigid and hysterical, but this passes and she becomes calm. She then explains the experience in terms of being in a large hall of mirrors, silent except for a dripping tap. Now, she says, she has no intention of looking into a mirror.

The play ends with Deborah making an assessment of some of the lies and truths she has been told. She thinks that she has things "in proportion" and thanks Hornby and Pauline.

Themes and Meanings

A Kind of Alaska is a modern, ironic version of the Sleeping Beauty fairy tale. While the fairy tale explores sexual awakening—the transition from girlhood to womanhood that allows for resolution in terms of a Prince Charming who awakens Sleeping Beauty—Harold Pinter comments wryly on such a resolution. He does so by focusing on Deborah's disorientation as she awakes from a sleep of twenty-nine years and by denying her a resolution through her Prince Charming, Dr. Hornby.

Not only does Pinter call attention to the dilemma Deborah faces as she attempts to adjust to what seems like suddenly acquired womanhood, but he also extends the theme from awakening to one's condition as a woman to being awake to the human condition. As Deborah questions her Prince Charming, Hornby, she seems to be questioning the patriarchy, and her questions provide a critique of society. Indeed, she makes the audience wonder to what extent either Hornby or Pauline is "awake." Hence, on a literal or realistic level, Deborah is the disoriented victim of a sleeping sickness, while on a symbolic, archetypal level, Deborah's disorientation suggests the fragmentation of the modern predicament.

Deborah's disorientation indicates both a condition of lostness and fragmentation and a possible progress toward a fundamental reorientation toward rebirth, a true awakening. Pinter focuses this idea in terms of Deborah's upcoming birthday, often referred to in the play in such a way as to suggest Deborah's struggle with rebirth. Her description of a womblike condition in her "sleep" state, where all is silent except for the dripping of a tap, and the use of water imagery to suggest rebirth—when Deborah says she plans "to run into the sea and fall into the waves . . . to rummage about in all the water"—contribute to this sense of the play's action as a struggle with rebirth.

Pinter conveys Hornby's and Pauline's investment in this action of rebirth by depicting Pauline as a widow; Hornby explains that he married Pauline after undertaking Deborah's care but then left her to chart the progress of Deborah's disease, which he designates as a journey to "a kind of Alaska." The metaphorical suggestion here is that Hornby is dead, that he too has inhabited "a kind of Alaska." By his obsessive dedication to charting Deborah's "itinerary" into "quite remote . . . utterly foreign . . . territories," Hornby would seem to be seeking a new awakening for himself as well as for Deborah.

Deborah's final acceptance of her new condition is enigmatic. Perhaps she has completed the rebirth process, and unlike Rose R., whose case history Pinter drew on for the play, she will adjust to being awake. Alternatively, Deborah's acceptance of the world offered her by Hornby may suggest a deeply ironic comment on the subjection of women. Pinter withholds a fairy-tale conclusion, but however one interprets the ending, the play dramatizes an archetypal struggle for a true awakening.

Dramatic Devices

Harold Pinter begins *A Kind of Alaska* in a realistic fashion; the audience learns with the awakening Deborah that she has been asleep for many years. By dwelling, however, on the difficulties Deborah has in digesting this information and by exploring her disoriented leaps back and forth in time, Pinter draws the audience into an experience of disorientation that leads to a questioning of the reality that this ostensibly realistic presentation depicts. By the end of the play, the audience may be wondering which is true, Deborah's perceptions or Hornby's.

These leaps in time—one minute Deborah questions Hornby about being her Prince Charming, only to call the next minute for her former boyfriend Jack—tend to give a conflated impression of time, in which past and present are equally present and alive. When Deborah asks Pauline whether she is really her sister and, if so, where she got "those breasts," Pinter continues in the tradition of absurdist playwrights, making the audience feel the strangeness of the commonplace. This kind of mixture of the tragic and comic is also an absurdist technique, and what seems entirely natural, the development of a girl into a woman, becomes somewhat monstrous, or at least extremely strange.

Absurdist techniques appear as well in terms of Hornby's insistence that his wife is a widow because he has dedicated himself to the care and observation of Deborah. If one were to read this play as complete realism, Hornby as well as Deborah would become a case history, because of his obsessive concern with Deborah. Part of Pinter's technique, however, is to allow the bizarre—this obsession—to be treated as something perfectly natural, a technique of understatement in which the audience is invited to look at the acceptance of the very strange. Pauline, for example, makes no objection whatsoever to being designated as a widow.

Silence as well as understatement is a technique Pinter uses to draw the audience into the subtext of his drama. After Hornby explains to Deborah, for example, that he has lived with her rather than his wife, Pinter's stage directions indicate a period of silence, after which Deborah responds, "I want to go home"; she pauses, then says, "I'm cold." Such use of silence and non sequiturs leads the audience to seek the hidden connections and to sense the meanings beneath what is being said. Deborah seems to feel lost in the light of the information she is receiving, although she never directly makes such a statement.

Another dramatic device that Pinter uses is doubling. Deborah sees herself doubled with her two sisters, noting that the three of them were called "the three bluebells." By designating Pauline as too witty for her own good and Estelle as deep and sensual, she is exploring aspects of herself that worry her. Pauline contributes to this sense of doubling when she tells Deborah that Estelle is on a world cruise with the family because she, too, is in need of a long break. One cannot help but relate this need to the long break that Deborah has taken. This doubling technique, then, is one of many that draw the audience into an experience of the play's subtextual levels.

Critical Context

A *Kind of Alaska* may appear to be more realistic than some of Harold Pinter's other work; indeed, it is based on an actual case history from Oliver Sacks's book *Awakenings* (1973). However, it has the same kind of mixture of the realistic and the bizarre that characterizes Pinter's work, from *The Room* (pr. 1957, pb. 1960) to the plays with which it is published, *Family Voices* (pr., pb. 1981) and *Victoria Station* (pr., pb. 1982). Unlike Samuel Beckett's dramas, which have been a major influence on the younger playwright and which begin with such strange images as that of a buried woman or a suspended pair of lips, Pinter characteristically begins with a realistic situation and room and only slowly evokes the strangeness or surreal aspect of the action.

Deborah's sense of displacement in time and place is another version of Pinter's concern with such displacement in plays such as *Old Times* (pr., pb. 1971), in which the main character confronts herself in a visit from a former roommate who evokes her past, or *The Homecoming* (pr., pb. 1965), in which Ruth's arrival in a household of men suggests the return of the lost mother/wife. A *Kind of Alaska* then, is related to Pinter's other work in terms of its surrealistic style and its psychological concern with the impact of the past in the present; it also takes up the political power struggles that inform all of his plays. Deborah does not easily submit to Hornby's attempts at orienting her to a patriarchal society.

Finally, however, the play resonates with that existential anguish that always informs Pinter's tragicomic dramas. The question of how individuals can be awake to their existence permeates Pinter's plays; hence, it is not surprising to find him using the Sleeping Beauty motif for its further exploration. That he focuses with such sympathy on a woman's dilemma is not new, but is part of what makes this minor masterpiece of one of the most important contemporary playwrights of particular interest.

Sources for Further Study

Billington, Michael. *The Life and Work of Harold Pinter.* London: Faber, 1996.

Dukore, Bernard F. "Alaskan Perspectives." In *Harold Pinter: You Never Heard Such Silence*, edited by Alan Bold. Totowa, N.J.: Barnes and Noble, 1984.

Gordon, Lois. *Harold Pinter: A Casebook.* New York: Garland, 1990.

Gussow, Mel. *Conversations with Pinter.* London: Nick Hem, 1994.

Regal, Martin S. *Harold Pinter: A Question of Timing.* New York: St. Martin's Press, 1995.

Sakellaridou, Elizabeth. *Pinter's Female Portraits: A Study of Female Characters in the Plays of Harold Pinter.* Totowa, N.J.: Barnes and Noble, 1988.

Silverstein, Marc. *Harold Pinter and the Language of Cultural Power.* Lewisburg, Pa.: Bucknell University Press, 1993.

Katherine H. Burkman

THE KITCHEN

Author: Arnold Wesker (1932-   )
Type of plot: Social realism
Time of plot: The 1950's
Locale: London
First produced: 1961, at the Royal Court Theatre, London
First published: 1961

> *Principal characters:*
> PETER, a German cook
> MONIQUE, a waitress
> GASTON, a Cypriot cook
> HANS, a German cook
> PAUL, a Jewish pastry-cook
> ANNE, an Irish kitchen worker
> KEVIN, a newcomer to the kitchen
> VIOLET, a new waitress
> THE CHEF, the kitchen chief
> MR. MARANGO, the restaurant proprietor

The Play

The Kitchen spans a day's work at a large London restaurant. At the beginning of part 1, the stage is in semidarkness (there are no curtains). It gradually comes into full light as Magi, the night porter, lights five ovens in succession. As each oven is lit, it emits a hum; the effect of all five ovens is a roar, which continues at varying levels throughout the play.

Members of the day staff, of many nationalities, enter in ones and twos, exchange greetings, and take up their allotted stations to start preparing food. Waitresses move in and out on their way to the dining room at the back, with trays of glasses or piles of plates.

The bantering repartee ranges over various personal issues, but the main topic is a fight that occurred between two of the cooks—Peter, a German, and Gaston, a Cypriot—the previous evening, when most of the staff had gone home. Several different versions are given, some with racial overtones. The men are mainly critical of Peter, but Anne, the Irish woman serving coffee and desserts, reminds them that Peter is in a difficult emotional state because he is in love with Monique, a married waitress. Monique enters and presents Peter's role in the fight in a rather heroic light.

Peter, a young, boisterous, but good-natured cook at the fish station, arrives late and tries to effect a reconciliation with Gaston, but Gaston, a forty-something cook at the grill, is still angry. Peter and Monique quarrel through much of the scene, but eventually she agrees to ask her husband for a divorce.

There are some calm periods and lighthearted moments, but as the pace of work increases in preparation for the midday meal, tension mounts between various members of the staff. It is heightened by the arrival of the elderly, work-obsessed proprietor, Mr. Marango. Hans, a sensitive young German at the frying station, has an accident in the steam room, and his face is scalded.

Part 1 reaches a dynamic climax with the serving of the midday meal. Waitresses gathering at the various stations shout their orders, and the cooks shout back in repetition. Plates are passed to and fro. Tempers flare. Movements become increasingly frenetic; Kevin, an Irish newcomer struggling to keep pace, asks, "Have you all gone barking-raving-bloody-mad?" The tempo mounts until the waitresses are going around in a frenzied circle; the noise of the ovens crescendos. Finally, the lights dim, and calls for orders continue in the darkness until the stage is clear.

The interlude covers the afternoon break. Some of the younger men have gone out. In a mood of quiet philosophizing among those who are left, the idea of the kitchen as a symbol for the world outside takes shape. At a key point in the discussion, Peter asks each man in turn to express his dreams. Dmitri, a Cypriot kitchen porter, thinks of a workshop where he could mend radios. Hans dreams of money; Raymond, an Italian pastry-cook, of women; Kevin, who is stretched out on a bench, completely exhausted, of sleep.

In an important speech, Paul, a Jewish pastry-cook, says that he wishes he could find people to be less like pigs and more like friends. When Peter is asked to express his own dreams, he refuses and leaves suddenly with Monique. Others follow. The four Cypriots who are left move into a leisurely Greek dance, bringing the interlude slowly to an end. The dance merges into part 2, which is quite short.

The younger men drift back and talk about how they have spent the afternoon. Peter enters in a bitter mood; he has quarreled with Monique again, and she tells him that she will not leave her husband after all.

The Chef catches Peter surreptitiously passing some meat cutlets to a tramp and threatens him with the sack. Paul and Kevin bait him further, reminding him that he was unable to think up a dream. "I can't dream in a kitchen," he retorts angrily. There is a disturbance at the back of the kitchen, and it emerges from the dialogue that Winnie, like several of the other women, including Monique, has been taking abortion pills. She is having a miscarriage and is rushed off to the hospital.

The waitresses begin to come in with their evening meal orders, and a queue of them forms by Peter's station, shouting their orders. Peter, already choking with resentment, refuses to serve them until he is ready, and Violet, a new waitress, tries to help herself. In the row that develops, Violet calls Peter a "bloody German."

For Peter, this is the last straw. He goes berserk. Breaking away from the restraining hands of his colleagues, he grabs a large chopper and smashes the main gas pipe under the serving counter. For the first time in the play, the ovens are silent. Peter continues to create mayhem, smashing crockery and glass; he is finally brought under control, covered in blood and in intense pain.

Mr. Marango, summoned by the Chef, cannot understand what has happened. "You have stopped my whole world," he cries out to Peter. He is genuinely baffled as to why anyone should be dissatisfied, since he gives them work and pays them well. "What more do you want?" he asks Peter, who sadly shakes his head. The play ends with Marango repeating again and again, "What is there more?"

Themes and Meanings

The kitchen, as the dialogue makes clear, is a metaphor for the workplace (offices and factories are specifically mentioned) and indeed for society itself—for a society corrupted or even driven mad by greed. The interplay of character, dialogue, and work routine in *The Kitchen* is very complex, but it is possible to pick out three major ways in which people's lives are shown to be affected—in their social relationships, their personal relationships, and their creative or spiritual needs.

The racism under the surface breaks out at every crisis point and is clearly shown to result from the kitchen's work tensions. People fight against one another instead of cooperating. They brand one another "dirty German" or "filthy Cypriot," although Peter points out that they are all brothers under the skin.

Small incidents, such as the ugly moment when Peter refuses to let Kevin use his chopping board, illustrate the selfishness operating at the peak of the work tension and are contrasted with the very relaxed and cooperative atmosphere in the calmer periods, especially in the interlude between the midday and evening mealtimes.

Love between man and woman also falls victim to the kitchen. The unsatisfactory and ultimately tragic affair between Peter and Monique is echoed by frequent and bitter references by Paul to his broken marriage and by the doomed sexuality of many of the waitresses. Paul's domestic bitterness spills over into his political attitudes when, in a key speech of political naïveté, he expresses the desire that everyone support everyone else in a spirit of mutual solidarity; he cannot understand why one of his neighbors, in particular, has not responded to this appeal.

Most of the kitchen staff display embryonic creative talents. Dmitri can construct radios; Hans sings and plays the guitar; Michael the pastry-cook has a way with motorcycles; Peter has his own song. It is in the interlude, when Peter urges his colleagues to state their dreams, that the frustrated yearnings of the kitchen staff (that is, of the working class) are most clearly expressed. Peter finds their stated ambitions— for girls, money, and sleep—less than inspiring. His own frenzied admission, "I can't dream in a kitchen," is the play's sharpest point of protest.

Clearly, Arnold Wesker sees the kitchen—the workplace—as the corrupting force, and not the individuals, whatever their relationship to it. The kitchen, Peter points out, would still be there if all the staff disappeared, and he fantasizes about what it would be like if he woke up one day and found it gone.

Marango, the somber, work-obsessed employer, is not depicted as a deliberately cruel man. For him, life is about eating, sleeping, and money. His repeated "What is there more?" at the end of the play represents Wesker's condemnation of the dehumanizing effect of a system that not only cannot offer creative fulfillment but cannot even recognize that such a thing exists.

Dramatic Devices

The setting of this play is its central metaphor. The kitchen is not merely a back-ground; it is the dominant force in the drama, controlling the lighting, the volume of sound, the pace of movement, the relationship between the characters, and all of their moods and actions. The fact that the ovens—the basic machinery of the workplace—govern the lighting and the background noise makes a strong political point. When Peter severs the mains, the sudden silence of the ovens has a striking dramatic impact.

From the moment the kitchen staff enter, they are working to strict routines, con-trolled by the jobs they have been trained to do, the specialties of their stations, and the orders given by the waitresses. In the production notes, every kitchen worker is as-signed to a specific part of the menu and to particular tasks related to it. The waitresses are under the same tight constraints.

Although the ovens, crockery, grills, chopping boards, plates, and knives are real, there is no actual food. All the work, from preparation to serving, is mimed. The con-trast between the play's overall naturalism and the stylization of the food processes produces an atmosphere of alienation.

Peter's frustrated creativity, which he cannot express in words, is represented visu-ally by an archlike edifice that he builds with kitchen utensils during the calm of the afternoon break. When he returns in the afternoon, it is broken, and he smashes it completely in the end. Peter's song, Hans's singing and guitar playing, and the Greek dance that links the interlude with part 2 are counterposed against the mounting inten-sity and violence during work periods.

The violence of Peter's final, desperate outburst is prepared for in stages, beginning with the account of the previous evening's fight, followed by Hans's accident in the steam room, and then by Winnie's agony through her self-induced abortion.

Critical Context

Arnold Wesker was one of the leading playwrights in the social protest movement that dominated British theater in the late 1950's and early 1960's. While some of the dramatists, notably John Osborne, were dubbed "angry young men," Wesker was sometimes referred to as "the angry angel" because of the idealism at the core of his plays, including *The Kitchen.*

The Kitchen was the first play he wrote; it was given a performance, in a one-act version without sets, at London's Royal Court Theatre, one of the centers of social protest drama. It was not until he had gained his reputation with his celebrated tril-ogy—*Chicken Soup with Barley* (pr. 1958, pb. 1959), *Roots* (pr., pb. 1959), and *I'm Talking About Jerusalem* (pr., pb. 1960)—that *The Kitchen* in its revised, full-length version was given a full production at the Royal Court, in 1961. The play was adapted to film the same year.

Unlike most of the "angry young men," Wesker came from a working-class back-ground. He gained firsthand knowledge of kitchen life through working as a pastry-cook in French and British restaurants. The character of Paul, the Jewish pastry-cook in the play, is partly based on himself. Paul's naïveté led some critics to describe the play itself as politically naïve; it has also been criticized as melodramatic. Critic Kenneth Tynan was one of those who profoundly admired it. It "achieves something that few playwrights have ever attempted," he wrote; "it dramatizes work." *The Kitchen* can be seen as the sharpest and purest statement of Wesker's concern for the working class and its need for creative fulfillment, a concern that he developed in subtler and more ruminative ways throughout the trilogy and his later works.

Sources for Further Study

Barker, Clive. "Arnold Wesker." In *Contemporary Dramatists*. 6th ed. Detroit: St. James, 1999.

Cohen, Mark. "The World of Wesker." *Jewish Quarterly*, Winter, 1960-1961, 45.

Leeming, Glenda. *Wesker on File*. London: Methuen, 1985.

Leeming, Glenda, and Simon Trussler. *The Plays of Arnold Wesker*. New York: Harper and Row, 1976.

Pritchett, V. S. "A World of Kitchens." *New Statesman* 62 (July 7, 1961): 24.

Ribalow, Harold U. *Arnold Wesker*. New York: Twayne, 1965.

_____. "The Plays of Arnold Wesker." *Chicago Jewish Forum*, Winter, 1962-1963, 127-131.

Taylor, John Russell. *Anger and After: A Guide to the New British Drama*. Rev. ed. London: Eyre Methuen, 1977.

Wilcher, Robert. *Understanding Arnold Wesker*. Columbia: University of South Carolina Press, 1991.

Woodrofe, K. S. "Mr. Wesker's Kitchen." *Hibbert Journal* 62 (1964): 148-151.

Nina Hibbin

THE LAST MEETING OF THE KNIGHTS
OF THE WHITE MAGNOLIA

Author: Preston Jones (1936-1979)
Type of plot: Comedy
Time of plot: 1962
Locale: Bradleyville, Texas, a fictional prairie town
First produced: 1973, at the Dallas Theater Center, Dallas, Texas
First published: 1976, in *A Texas Trilogy*

> *Principal characters:*
> RAMSEY-EYES BLANKENSHIP, a seventy-five-year-old African
>   American custodian
> RUFE PHELPS, a refinery worker
> OLIN POTTS, a cotton farmer
> RED GROVER, a bar owner
> L. D. ALEXANDER, a supermarket manager
> COLONEL J. C. KINKAID, the owner of the Cattleman's Hotel
> SKIP HAMPTON, a young service-station attendant
> LONNIE ROY MCNEIL, a pipe fitter
> MILO CRAWFORD, a feed-store clerk

The Play

The Last Meeting of the Knights of the White Magnolia opens in the meeting room of the Knights of the White Magnolia in the Cattleman's Hotel. Ramsey-Eyes sweeps in preparation for the evening's meeting, giving the audience time to take in the play's single setting. The room is run-down, with stained walls and shabby furnishings. At one end is a podium decorated with a grimy painting of a white magnolia. Behind it, flanked by Confederate and Texas flags, hangs a cross ornamented with light bulbs. Opposite is the doorway, with a coatrack and tattered banners on the upper wall.

Rufe Phelps and Olin Potts enter arguing, setting the tone for the meeting, which will be marked by petty bickering. They totally ignore Ramsey-Eyes' greeting and other pleasantries, as does Red Grover, who enters next. Ramsey-Eyes, snubbed, leaves to return to the hotel lobby and is thereupon accused of being "uppity."

L. D. Alexander enters, and, after some ribbing, the men plan a practical joke on Skip Hampton, the lodge lush. When Skip comes in, they hide the bourbon provided by Red, claiming that Skip was to bring the "refreshments." Skip is fooled only briefly, much to Red's irritation. When Rufe and Olin leave to fetch Colonel Kinkaid, the rest discuss Floyd Kinkaid, his son, venting their resentment because Floyd has never joined the lodge.

Rufe and Olin, followed by Ramsey-Eyes, carry in Colonel Kinkaid, an invalid, and set him in a wheelchair. Once Ramsey-Eyes is dismissed, L. D. administers the oath and announces that instead of playing dominoes and drinking, the usual activities, the

Knights are going to initiate a new member, one Lonnie Roy McNeil, from Silver City. The others manage to placate the Colonel, who damns all Silver City men as cowards, but Skip and Red break into a quarrel over Skip's desire for a drink. Their wrangling is interrupted by the comic arrival of Lonnie, who enters held by Ramsey-Eyes like a captured spy. Red, with characteristic intolerance, sends Ramsey-Eyes packing back to the lobby.

Once underway, the meeting is frequently interrupted with abrasive confrontations. The audience does manage, however, to get a brief history of the organization, which flourished during the 1920's and 1930's but has since come on hard times. The lodge in Bradleyville, clearly verging on extinction, is the very last. The momentary optimism prompted by the anticipated initiation is punctured by Skip, who calls the hope of restoring former glories "a damn-fool dream." A new round of arguments ensues, and Lonnie, beset with doubts, has to be drawn back by L. D., who assures him that the initiation will be the "high by-God point" of his life. Lonnie is then sent from the room for the vote but is soon ushered back by Milo Crawford, who, as Ramsey-Eyes had done, has accosted Lonnie as a spy. Finally, with Lonnie once more dismissed, the brethren vote affirmatively on his membership, only to discover that the new member is nowhere to be found.

In act 2, the action continues with no break in time. Learning that Lonnie has not left the hotel, the others are speculating as to his whereabouts when he returns. Relieved, they prepare for the initiation. At first they are stymied because the lodge book is missing, but when the mystery of its disappearance is solved, L. D. is able to begin the ceremony. The members don ritual costumes and take their positions. Then, after some grumbling, the maimed rites begin. Each member intones some brief lines counterpointed by Lonnie's choric "Stempco, Stempco, Stempco," Colonel Kinkaid's senile meandering, and various verbal gibes among the members. As a finale, the cross is lighted, but the bulbs, covered with grime, are barely visible. Rufe cleans them and for a moment they shine brilliantly, but then they sputter and go out.

As if on cue, the bickering starts again, becoming increasingly vehement. As L. D. tries to calm everybody down, the cross suddenly flares up again, then goes off, sputtering now and then through the remainder of the play. Colonel Kinkaid becomes catatonic, and when Red tries to revive him by pouring some bourbon down his throat, the old man spits liquor all over him. Angry again, Red starts another fight with Skip, who threatens him with what proves to be a tire gauge. Chaos ensues. Lonnie, frightened, backs into the Colonel, who grabs him and sends him screaming from the room. Red smashes Skip in the stomach with a whiskey bottle, and L. D. makes an obscene remark about Milo's mother. Insulted, Milo, refusing an apology, goes off, pursued by Red's invectives. Rufe and Olin, after searching for Lonnie, wheel Colonel Kinkaid out of the room.

With cynical amusement, Red announces that the brotherhood is finished, that "the sun's done set, the moon's gone down, and the west wind's got a big splotch on it." L. D. makes a feeble effort to argue with him, but even he must face reality. Red exits, as Olin and Rufe return to reveal that Floyd Kinkaid is shutting down the meeting room. Dejected and resigned, L. D. announces that the brotherhood is "adjourned." He takes the lodge book and walks out. Rufe, Skip and Olin, arguing to the end, soon follow, meeting Ramsey-Eyes on the way in.

Ramsey-Eyes, now alone, turns on the cross and under its brilliant light reads from a piece of paper he has found on the floor. The words, from the initiation rites, the last words in the play, are faultlessly read by an old black man assumed by Red Grover to be too ignorant to write his own name.

Themes and Meanings

The Last Meeting of the Knights of the White Magnolia has a bald, insistent theme: An organization rooted in past traditions, unable to adjust to change, can only degenerate and die. From their peak in 1939, marked by a convention in Tulsa, the Knights of the White Magnolia have been reduced to a ragtag remnant. With the exception of Colonel Kinkaid, the members are a sorry bunch of "good old boys," petty, mean-spirited, and ignorant. All are in some measure failures, clinging to an old lie because it offers them a barren dignity that in other circumstances would be merely pathetic but, because it is bigotry, is too vicious to engage much audience sympathy. These are men sorely lacking in human decency.

The worst of what they are is apparent in their arrogant treatment of Ramsey-Eyes, the amiable, obliging custodian who takes their abuse with admirable equanimity. The accommodation that once characterized race relations in the South, still evident in Colonel Kinkaid's kinder treatment, has given way to the feckless invective of Red Grover, who perceives Ramsey-Eyes as nearly subhuman. Colonel Kinkaid, his values and much of his mental growth arrested in World War I, views Ramsey-Eyes as a "good soldier." It is Ramsey-Eyes, not one of the lodge members, to whom the Colonel has entrusted the lodge's book.

The older values of the Colonel are a luxury affordable only to Bradleyville's elite citizens, those, like Floyd, who can insulate themselves from the Civil Rights movement by footing the initiation fee and monthly dues at private clubs. For Skip Hampton, a service-station attendant without prospects, there is only stupefying drink, dominoes, delusions of heroism, and racial bigotry.

Skip, Red, and the others are devoid of the residual values based in antebellum principles of noblesse oblige. Unlike the Colonel, they are without honor or respect not only for Ramsey-Eyes but also for one another and themselves. Racial myths aside, these men lack conviction and simple kindness. They fall to mocking one another with cruel indifference to the pain they inflict. Blind to the irony involved, Red, the bar and package-store owner, ribs Skip for his alcoholism. Skip, a Korean War veteran who never got near the front lines except in his imagination, is vicious toward Colonel Kinkaid, a legitimate veteran of trench warfare. Even L. D., who as the last of the true believers has the most at stake in keeping the lodge together, joins in the abuse of Milo, the long-suffering victim of an overbearing mother.

Paradoxically, then, even their racial bigotry is not strong enough to hold these men together. It has drained them of the trust and friendship essential to any fraternal order, so that their lodge's demise is as inevitable as death itself. They, too, are victims of their bigotry.

Dramatic Devices

The principal theme of *The Last Meeting of the Knights of the White Magnolia* is enhanced by visual symbols. Chief among these are the movement's emblems: the cross adorned with light bulbs and the painting of the white magnolia. The stains on the latter suggest the degeneration of the brotherhood's values, while the cross, the central symbol, suggests the movement's fate. It shines brilliantly for a brief moment, then dies out, to be relighted by Ramsey-Eyes, who, ironically, possesses a generosity of spirit the brethren sorely lack.

Other elements suggest decay. The floor is splintered and warped and the walls stained and faded, creating the impression that the Cattleman's Hotel is itself a relic, a shabby reminder of the agrarian myth. Symbolic motifs include the disappearance of the book and the degeneration of the initiation ritual into mere travesty. The book, finally carried off by L. D., is missing the scrap from which Ramsey-Eyes reads, with its "journey toward de truth" that the lodge members cannot make.

Although taking a tough if oblique look at racial bigotry, the play remains comic in perspective. The regional dialect of the characters is often amusing. Red's cynical gibes, for example, are very colorful. He says of Skip that he "wouldn't pass up a drink if he had to squeeze it out of an armadillo's ass," and that letting Skip have the key to his liquor store "would be like givin' old L. D. . . . a Charg-a-Plate to a whorehouse." The rancor and hostility soften some with such comic leavening.

The regional dialect also suits the play's serious purpose, reinforcing the ignorance of its users. These are men unaware of a world larger than their own, as is suggested by the flags flanking the cross. When Red observes that Floyd Kinkaid might turn the Cattleman's into a hotel "for Coloreds only," he and the others seem oblivious of the nation's angry mood toward the old separate-but-equal doctrine. Furthermore, the unlettered and uncultured speech rides roughshod over standard English syntax.

The narrow, provincial perspective of the characters is also revealed in what they say. Though Olin knows the history of local families, he and the others reveal an appalling ignorance of a larger world. Lonnie, the novice, is able to identity Adolf Hitler as being "on the German side in World's War II," a ridiculous understatement reflecting his deficient education. Colonel Kinkaid, out of touch with reality, perceives the Germans, threatening in "them spiky helmets," as enemies still, while Rufe, from reading a magazine in the local drugstore, asserts that "them Russians got old Hitler hid out in a little room over there in Moscow." These are men holding an insensitive, paralytic finger on the pulse of change, vegetating in a small town that progress, represented by the highway, has been busily bypassing.

Critical Context

The Last Meeting of the Knights of the White Magnolia is the first and best known play in *A Texas Trilogy*, the others being *Lu Ann Hampton Laverty Oberlander* (pr. 1974, pb. 1976) and *The Oldest Living Graduate* (pr. 1974, pb. 1976). All focus on Bradleyville characters, many of whom appear in more than one part. Colonel Kinkaid, for example, is the titular and main character of *The Oldest Living Graduate*, while Skip Hampton, Lu Ann's brother, is a major character in *Lu Ann Hampton Laverty Oberlander*.

In their regional focus, the plays have much in common with plays such as Thornton Wilder's *Our Town* (pr., pb. 1938) and narratives such as Sherwood Anderson's *Winesburg, Ohio* (1919), works that deal with the intersecting lives of several characters. Like Anderson's "grotesques," the characters of *A Texas Trilogy* are more than mere small-town types. In particular, Colonel Kinkaid, Red Grover, Skip, and Lu Ann are well delineated and memorable.

The Last Meeting of the Knights of the White Magnolia has the narrowest time frame, taking place on a single evening in 1962. *The Oldest Living Graduate* covers four days in the same year, and its action enfolds and relates to that of the former play. In the final scene, Colonel Kinkaid, who earlier in the evening had gone to the last lodge meeting, is brought home, ill and disoriented. Similarly, in its three-decade span, *Lu Ann Hampton Laverty Oberlander*, the only three-act play in the trilogy, enfolds the other two plays, with action taking place ten years before the meeting, a year after it, and ten years later. It is in that play, a year after the lodge breaks up and Colonel Kinkaid dies, that Skip tries to kill himself by slitting his throat with a broken beer bottle in Red Grover's bar.

Although each play is complete and whole, a fuller understanding of any one of them can be gained from the whole trilogy. Furthermore, the delineation of some characters is not complete in a single play, nor is the thematic foundation. Finally, *The Last Meeting of the Knights of the White Magnolia*, undoubtedly the tightest and most forceful of the three, is acerbic in tone. Balance is provided by the other two, which depict their main characters in a kinder light. Tonally, they are gentler, almost wistful, and in the character of Lu Ann Hampton Laverty Oberlander, the play named for her reveals that even in such a suffocating atmosphere as Bradleyville one can be compassionate and quietly heroic.

Sources for Further Study

Busby, Mark. *Preston Jones*. Boise, Idaho: Boise State University Press, 1983.

Clurman, Harold. "Theatre." *Nation*, October 9, 1976, 348-350.

Cook, Bruce. "Preston Jones: Playwright on the Range." *Saturday Review*, May 15, 1976, 40-42.

Marsh, Annemarie. *Preston Jones: An Interview*. London: New London Press, 1978.

Prideaux, Tom. "The Classic Family Drama Is Revived in *A Texas Trilogy*." *Smithsonian* 7 (October, 1976).

Thomas, Les. "A Star Rises in Dallas." *Southern Living* 13 (January, 1978): 60-63.

John W. Fiero

LAST OF THE RED HOT LOVERS

Author: Neil Simon (1927-   )
Type of plot: Comedy
Time of plot: 1969-1970
Locale: An apartment in New York City's East Thirties
First produced: 1969, at the Eugene O'Neill Theatre, New York City
First published: 1970

Principal characters:
BARNEY CASHMAN, the owner of a seafood restaurant
ELAINE NAVAZIO, one of his customers
BOBBI MICHELE, an unemployed entertainer
JEANETTE FISHER, an old family friend

The Play

Last of the Red Hot Lovers begins on a bright December afternoon as Barney Cashman, a forty-seven-year-old man who is conservatively dressed and carries an attache case, rings the doorbell and then uses his key to enter what turns out to be his mother's small apartment. He carefully hangs his overcoat in the closet, puts his rubbers on a piece of newspaper, closes the drapes, and lights the lamps. Next, he removes a bottle of scotch and two tumblers from his attache case, setting them on the table. Finally, he takes out a bottle of aftershave lotion and applies it lavishly to his face and hands, smelling his fingers when he has finished.

Next Barney moves the coffee table and opens the convertible bed. Then, somewhat nervously, he reverses his action, taking a drink as he telephones the cashier at his restaurant to say that he will not be in until later because he is Christmas shopping at Bloomingdale's. At this point, Barney speaks aloud, saying, "What the hell am I doing here?" and goes toward the closet as if to leave. He is stopped, however, by the doorbell announcing the arrival of Elaine Navazio.

Described by the playwright as "a somewhat attractive woman in her late thirties, having an air of desperation about her," Elaine has accepted an invitation from Barney, anticipating a routine sexual encounter. He, however, has something quite different in mind. He tries to explain to her that he considers his life to have been completely uneventful—just "nice"—and so he is seeking a romantic affair, the first in his twenty-three years of marriage. There is much comedy as Elaine becomes desperate for a cigarette—Barney is a nonsmoker—and also over his attempts to "communicate" with her while she continues to remind him that they are wasting precious time, for Barney's mother is due to return at five o'clock. Clearly, these two people are completely incompatible, and the act ends with a verbal battle. Barney tries in vain to explain his desire to "live a little" before he dies, but Elaine replies, "no one gives a good crap about you dying because a lot of people have discovered it ahead of you. We're all dying, Mr. Cashman. As a matter of fact, I myself passed away about six months ago."

As the act ends, Barney vows aloud never to repeat this experience, but the next act, which takes place eight months later, finds Barney again in his mother's apartment, awaiting Bobbi Michele. Determined not to repeat his failure, Barney now has two bottles, scotch and vodka, and three packs of cigarettes. He again closes the blinds and telephones the restaurant, this time saying that he is at the dentist's office. After spraying his fingers to be sure there is no fishy odor remaining from his restaurant work, he opens the door to a pretty girl of about twenty-seven.

Barney had met Bobbi in the park the day before and lent her, a complete stranger, twenty dollars to hire an accompanist for an audition; she has come to repay him. The comic tone is set when he reluctantly agrees to accept the money, only to have her say that he may have to wait until she either gets a show in New York or does a series of concerts in New Zealand.

Barney is fascinated with Bobbi's bizarre stories about her many sexual adventures with such characters as the cabdriver who wanted to "make it with her" under the Manhattan Bridge, an unknown Mexican who beat her in a motel room in Los Angeles, a man who had had his teeth sharpened to ensure her obedience to his weird requests. Finally, she telephones the lesbian Nazi with whom she is currently living and talks "made-up German," all the while paying almost no attention to Barney. Then she asks him whether he objects to her smoking, but his three-brand selection is not what she has in mind. She has "sticks" from a Beverly Hills doctor, to be taken instead of tranquilizers.

Afraid to seem unsophisticated, Barney pretends that he also smokes marijuana and is simply trying to "cut down," but Bobbi insists, and Barney does get "high." At the end of the act Bobbi is still babbling, and Barney, convinced that he is dying, says, "So many things I wanted to do . . . but I'll never do 'em. So many places I wanted to see . . . but I'll never see 'em. Trapped! We're all trapped. . . . Help! Help!"

Only one month has elapsed by the beginning of act 3, and for his third attempt Barney has brought champagne. His visitor is Jeanette Fisher, a thirty-nine-year-old woman, described by the playwright as having only one distinguishable quality: "She is probably the singularly most depressed woman on the face of the Western Hemisphere."

From the first, it is clear that these two people have known each other for a long time; Barney and Jeanette's husband, Mel, are close friends, and Thelma, Barney's wife, is an intimate friend of Jeanette. Jeanette asks, "Why am I here, Barney?" and remarks that she does not find him physically attractive. Barney, however, attempts to make the best of the situation, insisting that Jeanette "put down her pocketbook," a symbol of her insecurity.

The conversation, punctuated by requests for Jeanette to sit down, relax, and put down her pocketbook, revolves around the immorality she sees in the world, her assertion that life is not worth living, and her conviction that people are all rotten. When Barney disagrees, she dares him to name even three people who are decent, loving human beings. He suggests Thelma, John F. Kennedy, and Jesus Christ, and she agrees, but her statements about "being sure" of Thelma almost succeed in depressing Barney to her level. Then she tells him that the reason she has come today is to "get even" with her husband, Mel, who has been having an affair and insisted on telling her about it, because it is now the "new guiltless society" in which people can do anything they want to, as long as they are honest about it.

From this point to the end of the play, Barney is engaged in convincing Jeanette that he is a decent human being. There is rich comedy in his transition from mouse to lion when she contradicts him; he stalks her, demanding the "indecencies" that she believes are normal. Frightened of the changed Barney, she finally agrees that he is a decent, gentle, loving person. After Jeanette's exit, Barney calls his wife, and the curtain descends as he is trying without much success to persuade her to meet him at his mother's apartment.

Themes and Meanings

Last of the Red Hot Lovers, ostensibly a comedy, deals with mid-life crisis, brought on by the recognition of one's mortality, the generation gap, and drastic changes in accepted standards of morality; finally, there is an affirmation that through it all there is hope for decency.

Barney Cashman, the protagonist, finds himself at the close of the 1960's trying to behave as a member of the "now generation," but because he brings with him the mores of a former time, he fails. As Elaine Navazio points out, he is an incurable romantic, dreaming of a liaison based on genuine communication, perhaps even affection, with sex only as a sublime culmination. The notion of casual, recreational sex has never occurred to Barney, although he has unrealistically allotted only a few short hours in which to realize his fantasy.

With Bobbi Michele, the playwright stresses the generation gap in earnest. Twenty years his junior, Bobbi exhibits all the freewheeling attitudes of the period regarding language, sex, and the use of narcotics. Furthermore, she is completely self-absorbed and irresponsible. Attempting to deny his age, Barney listens to her, but Bobbi does not reciprocate. It is only after they both get "high" that they manage a duet of "What the World Needs Now Is Love."

In the third segment of the play, Neil Simon, while maintaining the comic tone, comes to grips with the question of whether radically changed social behavior patterns have affected basic human decency. By having the third object of Barney's attempted affair a woman of his own generation and social group, the playwright is able to make clear that there have been some negative effects.

Jeanette resents her husband's infidelity more because of his insistence on confession than because he has been unfaithful. She relies on a psychiatrist who has her measure her "happiness factor," promising that when it is low enough she will be able to commit suicide. Furthermore, Jeanette takes pills to alleviate her depression, telling Barney that she is only one of an estimated sixty million Americans who now rely on drugs to cope with their emotional problems. Although all of her conversation is amusing—the scene is played with emphasis on Barney's failure to attain his objective—there is more than a little truth in her assertions about the results of the "new morality."

Nevertheless, Simon concludes with the idea that human beings, despite their inept, foolish behavior, are capable of being gentle, loving, and decent. Barney's call to his wife, however, subverts expectations for a saccharine ending. Once again, his attempt to have an "adventure," to break the monotony of his "nice" life, fails.

Dramatic Devices

The physical setting of *Last of the Red Hot Lovers*, described as a small, modern apartment with paper-thin walls and "good furniture" from a past era, gives the audience a clear picture of the protagonist's background. Barney's attempts to obliterate all evidence of having been there, even to plumping up the sofa pillows, make clear his rather timid personality. Furthermore, his preference for this apartment, despite the perils of being overheard by the neighbors, illustrates his romanticism. He tells Elaine that a motel room "seemed too sordid."

The apartment itself contrasts sharply with the women who visit there, especially Elaine and Bobbi, and much comic dialogue is based on Barney's attempts to appear an experienced seducer in such a place.

Barney has chosen to attempt his affairs during a very brief period in which his mother is customarily out, doing charity work for a hospital. The short time span he has allowed makes for comedy, but it also points up Barney's unrealistic expectations. How can one dream of true interaction, culminating in a memorable relationship, when there is a two-hour time limit?

"Running gags," some of which are visual, are devices common to the comedy of Neil Simon. In fact, audiences are frequently so busy laughing that serious themes may go unrecognized. For example, Elaine's need for a cigarette continues to her exit line: "Oh, please, God, let there be a machine in the lobby." Bobbi's increasingly bizarre stories are such a device, as is Jeanette's reluctance to part with her handbag. The fishy smell that returns to Barney's hands each afternoon is symbolic of his repetitive, boring existence, a motivation for his attempt to "live a little before he dies."

Since this is a three-act play, Simon is able to show his protagonist in relation to three quite different women; however, Barney remains basically unchanged. Therefore, the audience is able to laugh at his ineptness while still remaining sympathetic to him. His inability to persuade Thelma to join him in what he hopes will be a romantic interlude makes a hilarious ending. However, it also serves to highlight the plight of those who, unable to deal with mid-life crisis, or change their standards of morality, must simply live out their decent, uneventful lives without realizing their romantic dreams.

Critical Context

Neil Simon's reputation has from his first effort, *Come Blow Your Horn* (pr. 1960, pb. 1961), been based on his ability to make audiences laugh. Camouflaged by the comedy, however, there is usually an idea worth deeper consideration.

In the years between his first play and *Last of the Red Hot Lovers*, this concern became increasingly apparent. For example, in *Plaza Suite* (pr. 1968, pb. 1969), one of the segments features Sam Nash, a middle-aged man who, unlike Barney Cashman, seems very satisfied with his life. In fact, he tells his wife of twenty-three years that he would like to "live it all again." What he really means is that he would like to be young again, and in his futile attempt to avoid the inevitable, Sam is having an extramarital affair with his young secretary. He resists his wife's plea not to leave her alone on the night of their wedding anniversary, and for the first time a Simon play ends unhappily.

The playwright cut twenty-five comic lines out of *Last of the Red Hot Lovers* before its Broadway opening and convinced at least some critics that he was serious about showing the human predicament in comic terms. Clive Barnes and Marilyn Stasio applauded the effort, and a reviewer for *Time* wrote:

> Behind the laughs lies Simon's most serious play. In some peculiar way, comedy is no laughing matter. It is remarkably moral. It hopes to reform by ridicule. While it may seem like a strange thing to say, the only proper forebear of Neil Simon would be someone like Molière.

In *The Gingerbread Lady* (pr. 1970, pb. 1971), the playwright continued to mask serious problems with comedy, but the original ending had the alcoholic protagonist return to her old ways. Simon was persuaded during out-of-town tryouts to alter the script so that the audience would leave the theater with light hearts.

By the time Simon wrote *California Suite* (pr. 1976, pb. 1977), he was ready to include two segments (out of four) that are more serious than comic, although his characters still elicit laughter through their sophisticated repartee. In the first segment, "Visitor from New York," a divorced couple compete for the loyalty of their seventeen-year-old daughter. The humor is based on the traditional rivalry between New Yorkers and Angelenos, but beneath the surface both Hannah and Bill Warren suffer genuine pain. In "Visitors from London" there are fewer light moments and much more pain as Diana Nichols, a British film star, and her husband, Sidney, face the reality of Sidney's homosexuality. In this play Simon empathically treats the theme of human need and psychological dependence; it was a significant signal of plays to come.

Four admittedly autobiographical plays, *Chapter Two* (pr. 1977, pb. 1979), *Brighton Beach Memoirs* (pr. 1982, pb. 1984), *Biloxi Blues* (pb. 1976, pr. 1984), and *Broadway Bound* (pr. 1986, pb. 1987), continue Simon's comic style, but serious themes are increasingly evident. Family conflicts, death and grief, and racial and religious prejudices are dealt with honestly in these plays. Another of his more serious plays, *Lost in Yonkers* (pr., pb. 1991) won for him his second Pulitzer Prize in drama as well as a Drama Desk Award.

Simon's work has been deepening and broadening, but his insistence on mixing comedy and tragedy has met with some critical resistance. There have been those critics who insist that plays as hilarious as Simon's are cannot deal with serious themes.

However, the consensus is overwhelmingly favorable, and both his plays and his films make him one of the most important playwrights of his generation.

Sources for Further Study
Henry, William A., III. "Reliving a Poignant Past." *Time*, December 15, 1986, 72-78.
Johnson, Robert K. *Neil Simon*. Boston: Twayne, 1983.
Konas, Gary, ed. *Neil Simon: A Casebook*. New York: Garland, 1997.
McGovern, Edythe M. *Neil Simon: A Critical Study*. New York: Ungar, 1978.
Simon, Neil. Interview by Lawrence Linderman. *Playboy* 26 (February, 1979): 58.
_____. *The Play Goes On*. New York: Simon and Schuster, 1999.
Woolf, Michael. "Neil Simon." In *American Drama*, edited by Clive Bloom. New York: St. Martin's Press, 1995.

Edythe M. McGovern

LAST SUMMER IN BLUEFISH COVE

Author: Jane Chambers (1937-1983)
Type of plot: Social realism
Time of plot: c. 1980
Locale: A beach resort
First produced: 1980, at the Shandol Theatre, New York City
First published: 1980

> *Principal characters:*
> LIL, a lesbian dying of ovarian cancer
> EVA, an upper-middle-class housewife
> DR. KITTY COCHRANE, a doctor and author
> RITA, Kitty's secretary and lover
> ANNIE, a sculptor and Lil's best friend
> RAE, Annie's lover
> SUE, a wealthy woman in her mid-forties
> DONNA, Sue's lover

The Play

In this two-act play, a group of lesbians who meet every summer at an isolated beach resort, Bluefish Cove, find their vacation unsettled by two events. First is the fact that Lil, a popular woman in the group of friends, is suffering from terminal cancer. Second is the arrival of Eva Margolis, a heterosexual woman who has just left her husband and is unaware that the cabin she has rented is intended for lesbians who value their privacy.

As act 1 opens, Lil stands on the beach in front of a one-room rustic cabin. She talks aloud to a bluefish she is trying to catch with bait and tackle, and her amusing monologue captures the attention of Eva, who approaches and listens, then strikes up a conversation. Lil is at once attracted to Eva, but Eva does not know that Lil is a lesbian, and the opening dialogue is a comedy of misunderstanding before Lil realizes Eva is heterosexual. By this time, Lil has already invited Eva to a party that night at her cabin, and though she warns Eva that she "might feel out of place," Eva insists on coming, believing that it will be a party of married couples.

Later, Kitty, Rita, Annie, and Rae prepare for the party and discuss the possible threat of Eva's arrival to their happy summer. Kitty, a medical doctor and recent author of a self-help book titled *The Female Sexual Imperative*, is alarmed that Eva will reveal to the outside world that Kitty is a lesbian, a fact which could make her lose her credibility and ruin her writing career. The others reassure her that everything will be fine. Annie steps outside to speak with Lil, who is cleaning the fish she has caught, and their conversation reveals that Lil has devoted little commitment to her past relationships, while Annie has been happily "married" to Rae for nine years. When Eva arrives for the party, everyone is nervous, but Eva at once says that she is reading one of Kitty's books and thinks it wonderful, and within minutes Kitty reveals her own identity. However, Eva's warm welcome among the friends is chilled when middle-aged Sue and her young girlfriend Donna show up, and Eva's naïve questions offend Donna, who replies insultingly. Lil takes Eva outside to show her the beach, while the others scold and tease each other. The party ends early, but Lil and Eva have become interested in each other.

Act 2 takes place weeks later in mid-summer. Eva and Lil are in love, and the others are a little jealous that their beloved Lil is spending so much time indoors with a stranger, although they are also happy that Lil has found love in her remaining days. Lil, however, has not told Eva about her illness, and her friends worry about this, while Eva innocently and joyously talks about plans to marry and live together forever. Lil, who often refers to herself as an "alley cat," warns Eva that she should not plan to tell her parents about her new lesbian relationship unless she enjoys "verbal flagellation and suicide threats." Lil tells Eva to tell her family she has a roommate and nothing more unless she is prepared to lose them.

They decide to hold a "one month anniversary" party with the others. The lights fade and return to show the women chattering as they prepare a meal. Lil keeps telling everyone that she feels great and insists on carrying a cooler filled with beer down to the beach. The exertion, however, causes her to crumple over with abdominal pains, and the party is canceled when Lil must go to the hospital, while Eva asks in bewilderment what is wrong with her. One week later, Lil returns to the cabin, and while the others argue that she should have remained in the hospital for surgery, Lil declares that she wants to die as a person and not a patient, that she wants to go "wanting to live, not wishing I were dead." Lil lies to Eva: "I feel fine. Alley cats recover very quickly." They speak together lovingly before the lights fade again.

In the last scene, set in the autumn, Lil has died and her friends talk together as they pack Lil's belongings from her cabin. Things have changed among them: Kitty has decided to return to medical practice, Sue has broken up her relationship with Donna, and Eva speaks of looking for office work in Europe, saying that she'd like to travel and have "some adventures."

Themes and Meanings

The most vivid character in *Last Summer at Bluefish Cove* is Lil, who dramatizes the play's various themes of love, friendship, the joys and difficulties of being lesbian, and courage in the face of death. Jane Chambers wrote the play in 1976 shortly after a friend's death from cancer. In 1982 she herself was diagnosed with cancer, and she died of a brain tumor in 1983. For this reason, some critics call the play autobiographical. In many ways, *Bluefish Cove* is also a play about family: Chambers wrote in the play's Introduction that it is an exploration of "coping with a death sentence in the prime of one's life and the strength of the homosexual family."

Lil's fishing in the opening scene is symbolic: She is alone, yet enjoying the activity and still in pursuit of the joys of life. The love she and Eva discover allows them many moments of self-discovery, and they come to grips with the mistakes each has made in the past for the sake of love. Lil is witty, cynical, brave, spirited, and not used to commitment, while Eva is passionate and determined to stay with her to the end, at all costs. Lil says that Kitty's books will be on library shelves for one hundred years and that Annie's sculptures will last indefinitely, adding, "That's a kind of immortality. [*Pause.*] Alley cats just come and go." Lil knows that she herself will last only as long as her friends will remember her. She feels the agony of knowing that she has finally met the one great love of her life but has only weeks left to live.

Chambers shows that friendship is the strongest bond between people and can create a sense of family among society's outsiders. The eight women in the play may gossip and argue but they also provide each other with comfort, love, and understanding. Lil, telling Eva what it is like to be a lesbian, says,

> It was Annie who showed me the gay bars and restaurants, the gay resort areas—we gays are kind of like the hobbits—no matter how repressive earthlings get, we continue to thrive in Middle Earth. We're survivors. We straddle both worlds and try to keep our balance.

This reference to J. R. R. Tolkien's *The Lord of the Rings* (1954-1955) shows Lil's humorous response to the widespread antagonism that lesbians face among narrow-minded, "repressive" members of society and her sense that, like Tolkien's Hobbits, lesbians have their own kind of toughness. The women casually refer to each other as "dykes" and other, more insulting terms. They are not all as dedicated to the feminist movement as Kitty is, and they respect one another's decisions to remain in the closet or to "out" themselves.

Because the play is about universal themes, it has an appeal to a wider audience than merely lesbians. Chambers's examination of big-hearted Lil contributes optimism to the tragic ending, because *Bluefish Cove* is not merely the story of two lesbians who fall in love. Instead, it investigates every kind of love. The seven friends demonstrate to Eva that "chosen family" is just as important as the family into which she was born. The play contains not only a powerful theme about gay pride but also timeless dramatizations of romance, independence, loyalty, and self-determination.

Dramatic Devices

Chambers's set design suggests both the organic comforts of an outdoor area that is not so wild as to be dangerous and the intimacy of a sheltered cove that is "near the city" yet wholly apart from it. Lil's cabin, which appears upstage, features "a flight of weathered wooden steps to a one-room rustic cabin," while in the foreground, "a jutting rock rears its head above the sea, speckled with seaweed and colonies of clutching mussels." The effect is one of privacy, safety, and natural beauty, and Lil speculates that the following summer, after she is dead, her friends will say to the stranger who has taken this cabin, "Beautiful sunset, huh? Lil loved that view. She thought God put that rock down there for her. When she stood on it with the surf pounding against it, spraying salt so high that she could taste it on her lips, she was Queen of Bluefish Cove."

As in many dramas, the scenes are separated by blackouts, usually between the beach and the cabin above. This allows a fluid movement between simultaneous events, such as the conversation between Sue and Donna as they walk to the party while it is in progress. Chambers makes little distinction, however, between conversations held outside on the beach or up in the cabin. The lesbian friends feel natural and at home whether they are inside or out, and the openness of the cabin suggests the lack of walls between them. The setting is attractive enough to draw the audience in at once so that viewers feel part of the "family" as they interact onstage.

Critical Context

Until 1970, lesbians in literature were usually portrayed negatively as mannish, "butch" stereotypes, or as "vampires" who control younger women and lead them to destruction. Beth Allen, Chambers's agent and life partner, named Chambers's 1974 drama *A Late Snow* (pr. 1974, pb. 1979) "the first out lesbian play, the first one affirmative of the lesbian lifestyle as a positive experience." *Last Summer at Bluefish Cove* won two awards: the Dramalogue Critic's Circle (1980) and the Villager Downtown Theatre Award (1981). More important, it won a wide audience and general acclaim.

Jane Chambers has been called the most distinguished lesbian dramatist of the late twentieth century. Actor, essayist, novelist, poet, and playwright, she was the recipient of numerous awards, including the Connecticut Educational Television Award, a Eugene O'Neill fellowship, and a Writers Guild of America award. Her work is taught both in women's studies programs and in writing programs in colleges throughout the United States. She was a founding member of the Interart Theatre in New York City. The Kennedy Center American College Theater Festival and The Women and Theatre Program of the Association for Theatre in Higher Education created the Jane Chambers Playwriting Award in 1983 to encourage the writing of new plays that address women's experiences and provide principal roles for women.

Sources for Further Study

Brown, Janet. *Taking Center Stage: Feminism in Contemporary U.S. Drama*. Metuchen, N.J.: Scarecrow Press, 1991.

Curb, Rosemary. *Amazon All Stars: Thirteen Lesbian Plays, with Essays and Interviews*. New York: Applause, 1996.

Helbing, Terry. Introduction to *Gay and Lesbian Plays Today*. Portsmouth, N.H.: Heinemann, 1993.

Landau, Penny M. "Jane Chambers: In Memoriam." *Women and Performance* 1, no. 2 (Winter, 1984): 55-57.

Wolcott, John R., and Michael L. Quinn. *Staging Diversity: Plays and Practice in American Theater*. Dubuque, Iowa: Kendall-Hunt, 1992.

Fiona Kelleghan

THE LAUNDROMAT

Author: Marsha Norman (1947-   )
Type of plot: Naturalistic
Time of plot: The late twentieth century
Locale: Ohio
First produced: 1978, at the Actor's Theatre of Louisville, Louisville, Kentucky
First published: 1980

> *Principal characters:*
> ALBERTA, a recent widow
> DEEDEE, a housewife

The Play

The Laundromat takes place at three o'clock in the morning in the dreary, familiar setting of its title. The houselights come up to the song "Stand By Your Man" on the radio, and the play opens with the sound of the disc jockey's voice signing off for the night. Alberta, a carefully dressed, rather meticulous middle-aged woman, enters with her laundry. Noticing that the attendant is asleep, she turns off the radio static and tacks a notice on the bulletin board before beginning her wash. Almost immediately, a younger woman enters, tripping over a wastebasket and scattering her bundle of clothes on the floor. The conversation that results from this casual encounter between two women, both doing their laundry in the middle of the night, provides the basis for the sketch.

Deedee, the more talkative and energetic of the two, initiates the dialogue by noting that she has already picked clothes off the floor once tonight for her husband, Joe, who "thinks hangers are for when you lock your keys in your car." From the beginning of the play, Deedee's joking banter and perky demeanor only thinly disguise her troubled emotions. Although she is aloof at first, Alberta's good manners force her to respond; however, Deedee is not the kind of person to take a hint. In the extended dialogue that follows, Alberta learns more about Deedee's life and marriage than she probably cares to know. Deedee's husband, Joe, supposedly works a double shift at the Ford plant, they live above the Old Mexico Taco Tavern visible through the window of the Laundromat, and she usually washes their clothes at her mother's house. Deedee wants to have children, but her life centers on Joe: On Saturdays, she watches him drag race his 1964 Chevy, and on Sundays she helps him work on it; with him, she looks forward to "winnin' a big race. . . ."

Although she loves her husband and admires his mechanical abilities, Deedee's dissatisfaction with their marriage is also evident. She is angry at being left alone but panicked at the thought of losing Joe; her attempts to make light of her situation quickly give way to expressions of anger and helplessness. Deedee presents herself as scatterbrained, overly talkative, and childlike, but she is not as naïve as she acts. Like

Nora in Henrik Ibsen's *Et dukkehjem* (pr., pb. 1879; *A Doll's House*, 1880), Deedee keeps the knowledge of her part-time job (addressing envelopes) from her husband, knowing he would disapprove, just as she keeps from him her own dissatisfaction, fearing he would leave her. Near the end of the play, Deedee confesses to her knowledge of Joe's affair with the "Weight Control" woman at the bowling alley. As she tells Alberta, "I used to think he just acted mean and stupid. Now I know he really is. . . ."

Although Alberta would prefer to be alone on this night, she gradually gives way to Deedee's persistent questions, incessant chatter, and obvious need to talk. Her apparent concern helps Deedee to acknowledge her real feelings about "bein' dumped" by Joe. In turn, Deedee's tactless questions push Alberta to confront her own reasons for doing laundry in the middle of the night. Alberta first claims that her washing machine is broken, that her husband Herb is on a business trip in Akron, and that she is selling Herb's garden tools because he gave up gardening. Early in the play, she grabs from Deedee's hands a cabbage-stained shirt, explaining with unusual emotion that "it needs to presoak" first. Although Alberta is clearly hiding something, it is close to the play's end before Deedee says to her, "You're either kidding yourself or lying to me." Finally the pieces fall together: Herb died last winter, the day before his birthday and its present of garden tools; Alberta has avoided washing his things, especially the cabbage-stained shirt in which he died. Not having cried for forty years, Alberta is quietly grieving, depressed, and unable to sleep. Once Deedee understands Alberta's situation, she seems genuinely concerned as well as embarrassed by her own self-centered behavior. Alberta not only recognizes Deedee's good intentions but appears relieved to have told the truth about her husband to someone.

Alberta and Deedee's point of connection is the experience they have shared as wives, a fact Marsha Norman emphasizes by giving them the same last name (Johnson). Although their husbands' insensitivity and irritating habits provide the recurrent theme of the anecdotes they share, both women admit to feeling desperately lonely without them. By the end of the play, nothing much has changed: Alberta has not yet washed Herb's shirt, nor has Deedee decided to return home; however, each helps the other to survive a difficult night. Indeed, the two characters come as close to friendship as their differences in age, social class, education, and personality will allow. The casual nature of the encounter is reinforced when Alberta leaves, tactfully ignoring Deedee's request for her telephone number. As the house lights go down, Deedee is left alone, soda in hand, silently staring out the window.

Themes and Meanings

A play about loneliness, grief, suffering, and survival, *The Laundromat* sensitively explores a wide range of human emotion within the context of everyday life. Doing laundry in the middle of the night can be understood as a strategy of survival as well as a rather bleak metaphor for the human condition. Marsha Norman's focus on female characters also indicates an interest in problems and emotional dynamics specific to women. Alberta and Deedee present images of women trapped by their own feelings of attachment to the men they love. As Deedee angrily comments, if their husbands "were home where they should be, we wouldn't have to be here in this crappy laundromat" washing shirts in the middle of the night. So much of the dialogue alludes to Herb and Joe that these two absent men, as different from each other as Deedee is from Alberta, play a central and determining role in the drama.

From the opening of the play, the two women speak of their own mothers with ease and emotion and relate to each other as a mother-daughter pair. Alberta remembers reading Emily Bronte's *Wuthering Heights* (1847) fifty times to her dying mother. Deedee, whose own silent and critical mother still does her wash, seems alternately delighted and infuriated by Alberta's realistic, well-intentioned, and motherly advice. This mother-daughter dynamic explains why Deedee's attraction to the black disc jockey who frequents the pool hall next door becomes a source of tension between the two.

While Norman offers no easy solutions for the problems of her characters, they do at least find some comfort in being able to talk. The play's positive message lies in the therapeutic dimension of the women's conversation. Thanks to Deedee, Alberta finally explains how her husband had a heart attack as he carried out the garbage; in a poignant moment of self-revelation, Alberta admits not letting the air out of an old beach ball because it is "his breath in there." While Deedee's thoughtless questions force Alberta to verbalize her emotions in a way that surprises even herself, Alberta's questions enable Deedee to begin thinking more rationally about her own unhappy situation.

As a naturalistic piece, *The Laundromat* presents a miniature slice of life that remains, like experience itself, open-ended. On one hand, the play can be read as a moving portrait of two lonely women who share a fleeting moment of sympathetic human contact before returning to their depressing, isolated lives. On the other hand, the play leaves open the possibility that this accidental and in many ways unlikely encounter may somehow change each woman's life for the better. Norman's realistic and humorous depiction allows the audience to understand and sympathize with Alberta and Deedee as gradually and tentatively as do the characters themselves.

Dramatic Devices

The Laundromat carefully adheres to the unities of time, place and action, and Marsha Norman maintains the illusion of reality in a variety of ways. An onstage clock is set to the time of the action and runs throughout the play, the conversation between the two women punctuated by the business of sorting, washing, drying, and folding clothes. The rhythm and routine of domestic work not only helps structure the dialogue but provides a ready-made social connection between the women. Moreover, a laundromat is one of the few public places women might be found in the middle of the night, and the chore that draws them there is as boring, repetitive, and unsatisfying as the rest of their lives.

The set, too, is both realistic and potentially emblematic. As Norman describes it, the laundromat is a "standard, dreary" one that might be found anywhere: Its "dirty ashtrays" and "ugly chairs littered with magazines" pay tribute to the meaningless waiting endured by earlier customers. Despite such depressing surroundings, however, the Laundromat provides these women a well-lit haven in the night—a place to escape, if only temporarily, the darker reality of their own solitary existence. It is important to note that the play begins with the song "Stand By Your Man" and the voice of a late-night radio disc jockey signing off for the night: "And the rest of you night owls gonna have to make it through the rest of this night by yourself, or with the help of your friends, if you know what I mean." Thus Norman subtly and economically introduces her subject matter before the characters arrive onstage. The women are indeed "night owls" whose very presence in the laundromat is related to their underlying desire to remain loyal to their men, almost to the point of absurdity.

The humor, dramatic tension, and emotional charge of *The Laundromat* ultimately depends on the stark contrast between the play's two characters. A former schoolteacher, Alberta is mature, quiet, kind, and self-contained; Deedee, whose education and experience are quite limited, is self-deprecating, chatty, and openly expressive. Alberta represses her emotions while Deedee's outbursts edge on hysteria. Differences in age and personality are further set off by subtle distinctions in social class: Alberta lives in a house with a garden, has traveled, and owns clothes that are "mostly hand wash." Deedee has no washing machine, lives in an apartment above a tavern, goes to drag races on the weekend, and has trouble naming seven presidents. As the evening progresses, both the misunderstandings and moments of connection take on serious overtones, but the characters' ability to laugh at themselves saves the play from becoming sentimental. Norman slowly exposes the emotional reality that motivates two potentially stereotypical characters.

Critical Context

With its suggestion of what it really means for women to "get out," *The Laundromat* develops the central image of Marsha Norman's first play, *Getting Out* (pr. 1977, pb. 1979), but in a more lighthearted, comic vein. Like Arlene, who finds her release from prison in *Getting Out* is to another kind of cell with a different set of limited options, the women in *The Laundromat* find that simply getting on with life is a difficult, sometimes overwhelming task. In Norman's later play, *'night, Mother* (pr. 1982, pb. 1983), Jessie does not even try: Suicide presents for her the most appropriate alternative to a meaningless, repetitive existence. With its mother-daughter dynamic, naturalistic style, and central focus on women, *The Laundromat* clearly looks forward to *'night, Mother*, whose Pulitzer Prize-winning status represented for many a major breakthrough for women's theater. Unlike those of many of her British contemporaries, however, Norman's plays are neither feminist nor directly political in nature. For some, Norman's use of traditional forms and conventional themes represented a betrayal of the more politicized community of American women playwrights and helped account for her swift critical and box office success.

That the emotions and concerns Norman explores in her plays are not limited to women is made clear in *The Laundromat*'s one-act companion piece *The Pool Hall* (pr. 1978). It is about the close relationship between two black men, Shooter (a popular disc jockey) and Willie (a sixty-year-old pool hall owner), who have had a falling-out after the suicide of the younger man's father and older man's best friend. As in *The Laundromat*, the father-son pair in *The Pool Hall* spend the night talking, and by doing so, begin to heal the rifts that their shared grief, fear, anger, and misunderstanding have caused. In *Traveler in the Dark* (pr. 1984, pb. 1988), Sam, a famous surgeon, works through the grief and remorse caused by the death of his head nurse through verbal confrontations involving his wife, son, and father on the afternoon of the funeral. Both plays have been criticized for incipient sentimentality, and neither enjoyed the immediate success of Norman's earlier, "women-centered" plays.

Because the suffering of Norman's characters, whether male or female, involves questions of identity, Norman's plays are usually grounded in a family context—either literally or metaphorically. Such a focus places her firmly in the tradition of American playwrights from Susan Glaspell and Eugene O'Neill to Tennessee Williams, Arthur Miller, and Edward Albee, all of whom elaborate their political and psychological themes within in a familial context; Norman herself has cited Thornton Wilder and Lanford Wilson from this tradition as possible sources of inspiration.

Although occasionally criticized for stage situations that seem contrived or gimmicky (for example, an accidental meeting in a laundromat, or a daughter's announcement to her mother of her intention to commit suicide), Norman has been lauded for her unsparing and direct confrontation of painful psychological realities, for her authentic dialogue, and for the creation of memorable characters. The fact that she is alternately praised for her realism and blamed for her lack of it illustrates how important the experiences and assumptions each viewer brings to the theater may be in determining a play's final effect. Most would agree, however, that Norman's perspective has provided a significant contribution to contemporary theater.

Sources for Further Study

Brown, Linda Gitner. *Marsha Norman: A Casebook*. New York: Garland, 1996.
Gross, Amy. "Marsha Norman." *Vogue*, June, 1983, 104.
Spencer, Jenny S. "Marsha Norman's *She-Tragedies*." In *Making a Spectacle: Feminist Essays on Contemporary Women's Theatre*, edited by Lynda Hart. Ann Arbor: University of Michigan Press, 1989.
Stout, Kate. "Marsha Norman: Writing for the Least of Our Brethren." *Saturday Review* 9 (September/October, 1983): 28-33.

Jenny S. Spencer

LAZARUS LAUGHED

Author: Eugene O'Neill (1888-1953)
Type of plot: Epic theater; biographical
Time of plot: c. 30 C.E.
Locale: Bethany, Athens, and Rome
First produced: 1928, at the Pasadena Playhouse, Pasadena, California
First published: 1927

> *Principal characters:*
> LAZARUS, a dead man resurrected by Jesus
> MIRIAM, his wife
> TIBERIUS CAESAR, a Roman ruler
> POMPEIA, Tiberius's mistress
> CALIGULA, Tiberius's assassin

The Play

   Lazarus Laughed is based on the biblical story of Jesus raising a man from the dead. Instead of concentrating on the figure of Jesus, however, Eugene O'Neill makes the story of Lazarus central to the play. In fact, Jesus serves merely as the instrument for awaking Lazarus. The drama begins with a huge crowd of people discussing, in great anticipation, the appearance of the resurrected man. He has not been merely revived, for he is in every sense of the word a new man, affirming the wonder of existence and exulting in the laughter that leads him to express repeatedly his "Yes!" to life itself.

   Lazarus's home in Bethany has become known as the House of Laughter, the place to which his followers flock to hear his messages of acceptance, all-embracing love, and the denial of death. In his past life, Lazarus confesses, he considered himself a failure. He did not distinguish himself; he was not a success in business and he did not make his mark. His death and resurrection have caused him to abandon his feelings of self-defeat and to realize that his well-being resides in his union with others, in the part everyone plays in the unity of existence.

   What Lazarus counsels is a rejection of the individual ego in favor of absorption in the very processes of existence. Human beings must learn to live as the products and extensions of nature, not as the outgrowths of their individual egos. It is not human psychology or history that governs life but rather the eternal cycles of death and rebirth. Death, he argues, is a release and a fulfillment, and in that sense there is no death, no final end to things. Human beings return to the elements from which they came, understanding that out of the elements they will return to life again. Great crowds are deeply moved by Lazarus's rhapsodic pantheism, by the laughter that somehow disperses their feelings of alienation and isolation. In the very unity of their response to Lazarus, these crowds prove his point: Humankind is one and indivisible.

Lazarus holds such sway over people that he is perceived as a threat to both the religiously orthodox and the Roman authorities. His parents and sisters are murdered in fanatical religious conflict, and Lazarus is taken prisoner by the Romans. Lazarus has only a momentary sadness for these deaths—which to him are only a phase in the cycle of eternal recurrence—and this peace of mind and exultation are the envy of the Romans, who cannot believe that he has truly transcended the selfishness of the human ego and the craving for self-preservation.

Pompeia, Tiberius's mistress, is attracted to Lazarus's dynamism and wishes to have him for herself. When he gently rejects her advances, she reacts angrily and has his wife, Miriam, put to death, thinking that in this terrible act she will make him react as merely a man, suffering the agony and the fear of death. Instead, he only feels compassion for Pompeia's tortured selfhood. Miriam, who has herself expressed a sad perplexity that is evocative of Lazarus's life before his rebirth, briefly comes back to life in the moment of her dying to affirm her husband's contention that, in truth, "there is only life."

Tiberius Caesar and Caligula, each of whom wishes to rule the world, are torn between their love and their loathing for Lazarus, who will not bow before their earthly power or acknowledge the worth of their ambitions. Tiberius thinks that Lazarus may be a magician who has used some kind of potion to bring himself back to life. Perhaps Lazarus knows the means by which Tiberius can prolong his own existence. However, Tiberius fails to intimidate Lazarus or to understand the spiritual power of his renewal. In the face of Tiberius's threats and imprecations, Lazarus laughs. His immunity to Roman terror is unnerving, particularly to Caligula, who writhes onstage, caught in the contradictions of a nature that would simultaneously embrace and repulse Lazarus.

Not understanding Lazarus and incapable of renouncing his desire for power, Caligula stabs Tiberius as the emperor is having Lazarus burned at the stake. The Romans think that Lazarus will finally succumb to a terror of death, yet precisely the opposite is true. The fire merely refines Lazarus's message that his flesh is no more than an envelope of life whose elements will reemerge in another form. Lazarus tells the crowd from his pyre, "Fear not life! You die—but there is no death for Man!"

Themes and Meanings

Lazarus Laughed is a play about the modern curse of consciousness. Greatly influenced by Sigmund Freud and Friedrich Nietzsche, Eugene O'Neill tries to combine their central concerns in this play. Freud's emphasis on the individual, on the unconscious wishes and drives that can wreck civilization if they are not controlled and repressed, is expressed in characters such as Caligula who verbalize the conflicts of the human psyche. Freud's deterministic psychology, which suggests that human beings are in the grip of drives they have trouble mastering, is reflected in all the characters who have not reached Lazarus's level of conscious acceptance. For Lazarus, however, death has put an end to self-absorption and worries over his own well-being.

Lazarus is, in other words, a Nietzschean man, one who has surmounted the question of individuality. Having returned from the dead, he knows that the entire world goes through the same cycle; that is, the world is constantly dying and being reborn, and human beings have their wonderful part to play in the drama of existence. Nietzsche attacked Christianity for its emphasis on the individual soul and personal salvation. Such a religion, he thought, made humans cringing, frightened beings who lacked the imagination to see their links with all life. Taking his inspiration from Nietzsche, O'Neill creates Lazarus as a spokesman for life as an eternal return, a series of rebirths rather than (as in Christianity) a single rebirth, a single salvation. In *Lazarus Laughed*, O'Neill rejects Christianity as a historical religion, as the story of a Redeemer who came once for all. Redemption, Lazarus argues, is occurring every moment of existence, as all things go through the cycle of birth, death, and rebirth.

The Roman setting of the play is important in understanding its theme, for the Romans were a historical people who believed that they had a unique place in history. In the play, the Romans epitomize a people who consider themselves in charge of history and believe that they can control matters of life and death and the fate of peoples all over the world. They are also neurotic in that they refuse to confront the fact of their individual deaths or the inevitable extinction of their empire. They believe, rather, that they can dominate nature and set the very terms of existence. This certitude motivates Tiberius's search for a secret potion to restore youth and also Caligula's sadism: Each operates under the illusion that he can become a god and attain some sort of immortality. Lazarus has the demeanor of one who has found eternal life, but his insistence to Tiberius and Caligula that he is not unique—that they are not unique—defies their deep desire to dominate everything. They do not want to hear his injunctions to submit to the cycles of nature.

Dramatic Devices

Eugene O'Neill's dramatic devices are absolutely essential to a successful production of his play. Of paramount importance is his use of crowds. In order to mount a full-scale production of *Lazarus Laughed*, almost four hundred actors would have to be employed. With large crowds of Romans, of Lazarus's followers, and of various religious factions, O'Neill tries to evoke a society in turmoil, tearing itself apart, mesmerized by Lazarus's lyrical speeches yet afraid to relinquish individual concerns. The volume of sound produced by these crowds is used for a variety of effects: to suggest moments of unity when Lazarus's message is actually embodied in the behavior of a society, to suggest the discord and clashing of egos he has been able to surmount, and to suggest the beauty—a kind of sealike calm—that pervades his chorus of followers. These followers engage in a churchlike call and response, a series of refrains that answer Lazarus's arias of laughter and exhortation.

O'Neill directed that these masses of actors wear masks. In his stage directions, the playwright is quite explicit about what the masks represent:

There are seven periods of life shown: Boyhood (or Girlhood), Youth, Young Manhood (or Womanhood), Manhood (or Womanhood), Middle Age, Maturity, and Old Age; and each of these periods is represented by seven different masks of general types of character as follows: The Simple, Ignorant; the Happy, Eager; the Self-Tortured, Introspective; the Proud, Self-Reliant; the Servile, Hypocritical; the Revengeful, Cruel; the Sorrowful, Resigned.

Thus, "forty-nine different combinations of period and type" with distinctive colors give the play a panoramic, pageantlike quality, as though O'Neill were encompassing the whole of civilization on a single stage. The masks are a brilliant device, allowing the playwright to achieve the unifying effects that a sea of individual faces could not accomplish. Lazarus has no mask, for he is the only truly free character in the play.

Critical Context

In many ways, *Lazarus Laughed* is the culmination of Eugene O'Neill's early life and work. As a young man, he had attempted suicide, considering himself a failure. He was arrogant, aloof, and doubtful about his life's work. However, in the very act of trying to take his life he seemed reborn and went on to create great plays and to work with tireless energy, becoming one of the titans of modern drama.

In *The Emperor Jones* (pr. 1920, pb. 1921), *The Hairy Ape* (pr., pb. 1922), *All God's Chillun Got Wings* (pr., pb. 1924), *Desire Under the Elms* (pr. 1924, pb. 1925) and *The Great God Brown* (pr., pb. 1926), the major plays that preceded *Lazarus Laughed*, characters feel a rootlessness and displacement that is reminiscent of O'Neill's own disaffected travels and sense of homelessness. His characters are alien selves looking for some way to merge with life, to feel fulfilled and acknowledged.

Lazarus Laughed has received only one full-scale production, in Pasadena, California. Critics have not been kind to the play; they have faulted it for verbosity and monotony and asserted that O'Neill's dramaturgy lacks development. However, the play has scenes of undeniable power and impressiveness, and O'Neill himself continued to think of innovative ways of staging it, including the use of film as a backdrop for some of the crowd scenes. He also recognized that only an actor of enormous power and resilience could render Lazarus's long speeches and prolonged laughter.

In *Lazarus Laughed*, the playwright made explicit his ambition to create a theater in which his audience would be moved by feelings akin to what might be experienced in a mystical or religious mode. The play's incantatory style, with its choruses composed of human types chanting a verse pared down to a few frequently repeated words, often reads poorly but might be exceptionally effective on a stage where the sound overlaps, so that the words could be appreciated as much for their sound and resonance as for their meaning.

O'Neill never attempted another play like *Lazarus Laughed*, sensing perhaps that it had a unique place not only in his repertoire but also in the history of modern drama.

Sources for Further Study

Bogard, Travis. *Contour in Time: The Plays of Eugene O'Neill.* Rev. ed. New York: Oxford University Press, 1988.

Cargill, Oscar, N. Bryllion Fagin, and William Fisher, eds. *O'Neill and His Plays: Four Decades of Criticism.* New York: New York University Press, 1961.

Estrin, Mark W., ed. *Conversations with Eugene O'Neill.* Jackson: University of Mississippi Press, 1990.

Gelb, Arthur, and Barbara Gelb. *O'Neill: Life with Monte Cristo.* New York: Applause, 2000.

Houchin, John H., ed. *The Critical Response to Eugene O'Neill.* Westport, Conn.: Greenwood Press, 1993.

Manheim, Michael. *Eugene O'Neill's New Language of Kinship.* Syracuse, N.Y.: Syracuse University Press, 1982.

Martine, James J., ed. *Critical Essays on Eugene O'Neill.* Boston: G. K. Hall, 1984.

Miller, Jordan Y., ed. *Eugene O'Neill and the American Critic: A Bibliographical Checklist.* Hamden, Conn.: Archon Books, 1973.

O'Neill, Eugene. *Selected Letters of Eugene O'Neill.* Edited by Travis Bogard and Jackson R. Bryer. New Haven, Conn.: Yale University Press, 1988.

Raleigh, John Henry. *The Plays of Eugene O'Neill.* Carbondale: Southern Illinois University Press, 1965.

Ranald, Margaret Loftus. *The Eugene O'Neill Companion.* Westport, Conn.: Greenwood Press, 1984.

Carl Rollyson

LEAR

Author: Edward Bond (1934-   )
Type of plot: Allegory; psychological
Time of plot: Unspecified
Locale: England
First produced: 1971, at the Royal Court Theatre, London
First published: 1972

> *Principal characters:*
> LEAR, the king of England
> BODICE and
> FONTANELLE, his daughters
> DUKE OF NORTH and
> DUKE OF CORNWALL, his enemies
> THE GRAVEDIGGER'S BOY, a farmer who befriends him
> CORDELIA, the wife of the Gravedigger's Boy
> JOHN, a carpenter in love with Cordelia

The Play

Lear is a powerful, complex, and violent study of how men and women are crushed by the society they have created. The play focuses on Lear, who, to compensate for the errors of his life, attempts to change his society. *Lear* can be divided into four distinct phases: Lear as king; Lear at the house of the Gravedigger's Boy; Lear in his former kingdom, now run by his daughters; and finally, Lear as outcast.

The first phase shows King Lear building a wall to prevent an attack by armies led by the Dukes of North and Cornwall. During an inspection of the wall, Lear uses the accidental death of a laborer to speed up the work. He falsely accuses another laborer of causing the accident and passes a death sentence on him. Bodice and Fontanelle, Lear's two daughters who accompany him, publicly denounce their father's actions and choose this moment to inform him of their intended marriages to the dukes. Such an action establishes Lear's daughters as enemies of the state. Provoked, and partly in order to prove his power, an angry Lear shoots the innocent worker.

Warrington, Lear's chief administrator, receives letters from Bodice and Fontanelle; each urges him to betray both the king and the other sister. In separate comic asides, Bodice and Fontanelle tell of their dissatisfaction with married life and reveal ambitions to destroy each other as well as their husbands, marry Warrington, and run the country through him.

Civil war follows, and although Lear's two daughters fail to destroy each other or their husbands, the army succeeds in overthrowing the king. Warrington survives the war but, with his knowledge of each sister's counterplot, needs to be silenced. Fontanelle has his tongue removed; the two women then watch while he is tortured. As a result of their military takeover, Lear is forced out of his kingdom and deserted. The play, having shown the destruction of Lear's power, now presents an alternative way of life.

The second phase of the play opens in the wilderness, where Lear is befriended by the Gravedigger's Boy. Together, they return to the man's farm. Lear is content here and, under the cloak of anonymity, is able to rest. As he sleeps, the Gravedigger's Boy, so named because he used to dig graves with his father, argues with his wife, Cordelia, over his rescue of Lear. The farmer is compassionate and has also taken pity on a "wild man" from the wars, the silenced Warrington, who roams the woods. The farmer leaves bread and water out for him. Cordelia is frightened of these "filthy old men" and cannot understand her husband's priorities. While they all sleep, Warrington appears. His attempt to stab Lear fails, and he must hide in the well.

After a long rest, Lear awakes to see the arrival of a local carpenter, in love with Cordelia; he brings a cradle for the child Cordelia is expecting. The farmer, having been told by his wife that the water from the well is unclean, discovers that Warrington has fallen in and broken his neck. The farmer attempts to bring the body to the surface, but as he does so, soldiers arrive to arrest Lear. In a horrific climax to the first act, the soldiers murder the farmer and rape Cordelia. The carpenter, John, who has been fetching tools to mend a broken door, returns and kills the soldiers.

The third phase of *Lear* begins with Lear returning to his former kingdom, where he stands trial before his daughters. His grasp of the world has deteriorated so much that the judge declares him insane and sentences him to imprisonment. Bodice and Fontanelle then turn their attention to an uprising against the state, led by Cordelia.

In prison, Lear is visited by the ghost of the Gravedigger's Boy. Together Lear and the ghost share their sufferings, along with the ghosts of Lear's daughters as they were when young. This moment in the play is important because it allows Lear to see and understand the forces that have made his children the way they are. Cordelia, her new husband John the carpenter, and the army continue in their fight against Bodice and Fontanelle, whose power is dwindling. In the final throes of their rule, the two sisters both arrest their husbands, the dukes, who have tried to escape, and sign Lear's death warrant.

Despite the sisters' efforts to maintain control, the state disintegrates. Fontanelle is caught by Cordelia's soldiers and imprisoned with a number of men, including her father, who fails to recognize her. The past still haunts the present as the decomposing ghost of the Gravedigger's Boy appears, forgives Lear for endangering his home, and embraces him as a father. In the same way that Lear used his authority in the first scene by killing the worker, Cordelia's husband now orders Fontanelle shot, and Lear watches her autopsy. Bodice is also arrested, and is bayoneted to death by soldiers. The prison doctor, wishing to gain advancement with the new administration, makes Lear "politically ineffective" by removing his eyes.

The final act returns to the Gravedigger Boy's farm, now occupied by Thomas, his pregnant wife Susan, and John. In their home they shelter Lear and, despite Susan's reluctance, a few prisoners from the war. Lear speaks in public, and large groups of people come to listen. Cordelia, who has ordered the reconstruction of the wall, sees his speeches as dangerous to state security and requests that these activities cease. Lear, recognizing his earlier mistake in thinking that the wall would bring peace, informs her that it is of no value in the creation of a society. Cordelia refuses to listen and tells Lear that he must stand trial. The ghost of the Gravedigger's Boy, whose vision of creating a new world within the old has failed, dies.

The final scene shows Lear climbing the wall, attempting to pull it down. A farmer's son whom he has met earlier, now a junior officer in the army, shoots Lear, who dies at the wall.

Themes and Meanings

Edward Bond has described *Lear* as "a very grim play." Its importance, however, does not lie in Lear's tragic vision but in the story of one man who, against all odds, takes action to change his world. On this journey toward enlightenment, Lear undergoes tremendous suffering. Bond has said that "we develop through our problems, not just solving them, but through clashing with them." In many of his plays, this friction manifests itself in violence. Some critics have charged that the violence in *Lear* is excessive and gratuitous. In response, Bond contends that the play accurately reflects the consequences of the abuse of power. His intention in *Lear* is to show how individual acts of violence and the large-scale violence of wars and power struggles alike reflect the sickness of an unjust society.

This theme is most vividly expressed in Fontanelle's autopsy. Lear watches the doctor's exploration of the corpse, asking, "Where is the beast?" He believes that there is a monster inside his daughter that is causing her to act violently. Like Oedipus, Lear begins to see only after his blinding. He realizes that violent impulses do not have their origin within the individual. The wall he was building to prevent others from invading his lands was pointless, then, because it did nothing to solve the basic problems of society.

Similarly, it becomes clear during the play, both to the audience and to Lear, that Bodice and Fontanelle are really manifestations of their culture. The sisters' schemes, manipulation, and love of power are all characteristics instilled in them unknowingly by Lear. When the ghosts of Bodice and Fontanelle appear to Lear in the play, they do so just as the coffins of soldiers are being returned home for burial. It is evident Lear's daughters have been weaned on death and a confirmation of the established order.

Cordelia wants to understand how the Gravedigger's Boy views life but cannot reconcile herself to his abundant charity. Cordelia's fears are apparently justified as she witnesses her husband's murder and through her own rape and miscarriage. She becomes a tough guerrilla leader in response to the actions of those around her. Cordelia believes that she can forcefully create a society that is fair and just.

The Gravedigger's Boy presents a different way of life. On their farm, he and his wife provide for themselves, living off the land. Such a peaceful existence appeals to Lear, and for a brief time he thinks that he can be part of it. Bond, however, does not permit Lear to hide here. The destruction of this way of life is the writer's way of demonstrating the impossibility of either Lear's or the Gravedigger's Boy's escaping from reality: a reality resulting from a society Lear has formed but can no longer control. Bond is not criticizing a pastoral way of life; he is simply saying that it cannot exist within the established structure. The ghost of the Gravedigger's Boy appears as Lear screams, "I must forget! I must forget!" The ghost acts as a reminder that Lear is part of a world that he must rejoin and destroy from within if he wants to help in establishing a new form of society.

Dramatic Devices

Lear uses as its central figure the character of King Lear, who, according to Raphael Holinshed, "lived about the year 3100 after the creation." William Shakespeare's play, *King Lear* (pr. c. 1605-1606), deals with an old man who, through his own rash deed and misjudgment of his daughters, is subjected to terrible suffering. *Lear* is not a rewriting of Shakespeare's play but an examination of certain aspects of a myth in the light of Edward Bond's own experience of the world. There are, however, numerous similarities with Shakespeare's play that illuminate Bond's version.

The Gravedigger's Boy is Bond's fool, able to indicate Lear's mistakes but not to solve them. Bodice and Fontanelle, like Goneril and Regan, are created and given license to act by their father but turn this power against him. Although in *Lear* Cordelia is not the king's daughter, Bond does make a connection between the two characters. Cordelia inherits Lear's position as head of state and carries out her duties with a similar self-righteousness. Bond dramatically explores this reinvention of the political wheel, showing that the same mistakes are inevitable. The impact Shakespeare's play makes on a theater audience is such that a reinterpretation of the legend, such as Bond is attempting, can create new tensions and challenge an audience into thinking afresh about the issues contained in the play.

Lear, despite shocking scenes which arrest an audience's attention, also provides splendid moments of comic relief. Much of this humor arises from a contrast between the grotesque and the ludicrous: Bodice knits while Warrington is tortured, and the doctor calms Lear, after the removal of his eyes, with pleasant, soothing words. Moments such as these provide one of the keys to Bond's success as a writer. He is able to capture his total experience of the world and convert it into theatrical metaphors that operate on many different levels simultaneously. For Bond, these metaphors must always be political.

Critical Context

Although Edward Bond had written other plays, *The Pope's Wedding* (pr. 1962, pb. 1971) was the first to receive a professional production at the Royal Court Theatre, London, in 1962. Other major plays that followed were *Saved* (pr. 1965, pb. 1966) and *Early Morning* (pr., pb. 1968), which were also produced at the Royal Court Theatre. *Lear* and *The Sea* (pr., pb. 1973) completed what Bond has described as his first cycle of plays.

In them, Bond poses questions about the workings of society and reveals the violence inherent in it; for example, Bond writes about the murder of an old hermit in *The Pope's Wedding*, the stoning of a baby to death in *Saved*, cannibalism in *Early Morning*, and mass infanticide in *Narrow Road to the Deep North* (pr., pb. 1968). He has made it clear that "people who do not want writers to write about violence want to stop them writing about us and our time."

The second stage of Bond's work includes *Bingo: Scenes of Money and Death* (pr. 1973, pb. 1974), *The Fool* (pr. 1975, pb. 1976), and *The Woman* (pr. 1978, pb. 1979). In these plays Bond examines society in three stages of cultural development. After *The Woman*, Bond went on to write a series of plays beginning with *The Bundle: Or, New Narrow Road to the Deep North* (pr., pb. 1978). These he calls "'answer plays,' in which I would like to say: I have stated the problems as clearly as I can—now let's try and look at what answers are applicable." In the 1980's, Bond turned to an exploration of nuclear holocaust (in *The War Plays: A Trilogy*, pb. 1985), which he maintains "is for our time the only subject—directly or by reflection—for art."

Sources for Further Study

Hay, Malcolm, and Philip Roberts. "*Lear*." In *Edward Bond: A Companion to the Plays*. London: TQ, 1978.

Hirst, David L. *Edward Bond*. New York: Grove Press, 1986.

Lappin, Lou. "*Lear* and the Reconstruction of Tragedy." In *The Art and Politics of Edward Bond*. New York: P. Lang, 1987.

Mangan, Michael. *Edward Bond*. London: British Council, 1998.

Oppel, Horst, and Sandra Christenson. *Edward Bond's "Lear" and Shakespeare's "King Lear."* Wiesbaden, Germany: Steiner, 1974.

Scharine, Richard. "*Lear:* 'Suffer the Little Children.'" In *The Plays of Edward Bond*. Lewisburg, Pa.: Bucknell University Press, 1976.

Smith, Leslie. "Edward Bond's *Lear*." *Comparative Drama* 13 (1979): 65-85.

Spencer, Jenny S. *Dramatic Strategies in the Plays of Edward Bond*. Cambridge, Mass.: Cambridge University Press, 1996.

Ian Stuart

LEND ME A TENOR

Author: Ken Ludwig (1950-   )
Type of plot: Farce; comedy
Time of plot: September, 1934
Locale: A hotel suite in Cleveland, Ohio
First produced: 1985, as *Opera Buffa* at the American Stage Festival, Milford, New Hampshire
First published: 1986

> *Principal characters:*
> SAUNDERS, a middle-aged authoritarian manager of the Cleveland Grand Opera
> MAX, a company gofer and assistant to Saunders
> MAGGIE, the pretty and quirky girlfriend of Max and daughter of Saunders
> TITO MERELLI, a world-famous Italian tenor
> MARIA, his lively Italian wife
> BELLHOP, an aspiring singer
> DIANA, a sexy soprano in her mid-thirties
> JULIA, a chair of the Opera Guild

The Play

The play opens in Tito Merelli's hotel suite on the night of his performance with the Cleveland Grand Opera's production of Guiseppi Verdi's *Otello* (1887). At stage right is a sitting room with a door to the hallway and a kitchen door off the right. At stage left is a bedroom with doors to a closet, bathroom, and hallway. Another door connects the two rooms. The living room is furnished minimally with a sofa, pouf, radio, telephone, and coffee table, and the bedroom with a bed and bureau.

When the lights come up, Maggie is revealed rapturously listening to a recording of Tito on the radio. Max enters in a panic, since Tito has not yet arrived. Maggie soon reveals to her longtime boyfriend that she has a need to have a "fling" before settling down into marriage, preferably with someone like Tito. Maggie's father, Saunders, arrives, also in a panic over the tenor's absence, and Maggie attempts to calm him with a phenobarbital pill, leaving the bottle out. When Saunders hears that Tito is downstairs, he ushers Maggie out, tells Max to keep Tito away from "liquor and women," and goes down to the lobby. Maggie sneaks back in through the bedroom door. Max discovers her too late to remove her before Saunders arrives with Tito, his wife Maria, and an eager-to-please Bellhop.

Tito refuses to obey Maria's request to take tranquilizers to calm him for the performance, so she storms into the bedroom. After Tito announces that he will skip the afternoon rehearsal, Saunders admonishes Max to make sure Tito gets some sleep and then exits. Max and Tito soon become friends, with Tito giving Max a singing lesson.

When Tito offers Max some wine, Max spikes Tito's drink with Saunders's tranquilizers after Tito, to placate Maria, has angrily finished off his own tranquilizers. Once Tito consumes his laced wine, he and Max sing a duet while Maria pens a vaguely worded "Dear John" letter. Tito discovers Maria's note and lays it next to the empty pill bottle before passing out.

In the next scene, Max goes to wake Tito and finds Maria's note next to the empty pill bottle, which now reads like a suicide note. Saunders enters to news of Tito's death and after much panic and anguish, cajoles Max into impersonating Tito so they do not have to refund the audience's ticket money. As Max changes into Tito's costume and makeup, the sitting room fills with Tito's fans. As confusion ensues, Max, disguised as Tito, ushers his guests off to the theater. Tito rolls off the bed just before blackout.

Act 2 takes place after a successful performance by Max. After Saunders congratulates him, he orders Max to change clothes. As Saunders exits, Tito appears in the bedroom and hides in the closet. On his way to the bathroom, Max discovers Tito's body is gone and exits to get Saunders. Tito crosses to the sitting room to find three seductresses in succession: Julia, Diana, and Maggie. Tito sends Julia away but hides Diana and Maggie. Saunders enters thinking Tito is really Max in disguise and sends him into the bedroom so he can answer the door. Finding Max at the door, Saunders realizes that Tito is alive. Saunders again orders Max to get changed and exits to find Tito, who has left the suite. While Max is ambushed by Diana in the bathroom, Maggie emerges from the closet and crosses to the sitting room. Max bursts out of the bathroom to find Maggie undressed. As she lays Max down on the sofa, Tito enters and is put to bed by Diana. The couples make love as the lights fade.

Fifteen minutes later, as the women exit the stage for a moment, Tito opens the connecting door, sees Max, and, convinced that he is losing his mind, flees into the hallway. Max suddenly finds himself alone with two angry women. After stammering out a few syllables, he locks himself in the bathroom. As the women get dressed, the rest of the cast converge at the bathroom door. Soon Max comes out as himself to greet everyone. They exit, leaving Max alone with Maggie, who figures it out. She kisses Max to the sound of wedding bells.

Themes and Meanings

One critic described *Lend Me a Tenor* as "an American farce in the classic French tradition." Like all good farces, the play celebrates human foibles with a focus on basic human drives—the pursuit of pleasure, money, glory, and above all, a particularly earthy and immediate expression of love. Also, like most farces, it has no deep symbolism or literary complexity in the thematic sense; rather, its focus is on basic character drives and their actions in pursuit of their desires: Max wants Maggie to marry him; Maggie lusts after Tito; Saunders is preoccupied with money; Diana uses her sexuality in pursuit of fame; and so on.

Although one critic found the play's 1934 setting to have a "museum-piece air" that seemed a "cop-out," there may be something more behind the period setting. In many scenes, the play exhibits the influence of the vaudevillian stand-up comedy duo of the period. For example, there are several moments of verbal banter between Saunders and Max that are reminiscent of Abbot and Costello routines. More important, the setting shares some elements with Ludwig's other works, which are mostly set in the past and also display a fascination with musical and dramatic performers and their works. In fact, Ludwig displays a penchant for a playful reexamination of the past. Even though he fictionalizes the performers, they are clearly based on typical performers of the period, if not actual persons.

On another level, this is also a romantic comedy focusing on the relationship between Max and Maggie. In fact, the play's opening scene belongs more to the genre of romantic comedy than to that of farce. The play then gradually accelerates to the farcical so that by act 2, it is in full force. Interestingly, each act ends with a romantic moment between Max and Maggie. In the first act, Max, disguised as Tito, kisses her palm in a manner she has previously described to him. At the end of the second act, Max, returned to himself, reveals his masquerade (and performance in that evening's opera) by singing Maggie an excerpt from *Otello*.

Dramatic Devices

The play employs a number of devices common to farces: mistaken identity, double entendres, a playful sense of rhythm generally delivered with alacrity and precision, intricate blocking and sight gags, and frequent entrances and exits utilizing the six doors onstage. There are several sections characterized by silent physical comedy unencumbered by dialogue. The most elaborate is a moment in act 1, when the Bellhop is attempting to place suitcases into a closet in which Maggie is hiding. Max, discovering her in the closet, attempts to extract her while preventing the Bellhop from seeing her. The action takes place in a nearly pantomime fashion, with Max and Maggie frenetically gesturing to each other and the Bellhop blithely going about the business of repeatedly opening the closet door that Max keeps shutting.

In an author's note, Ludwig suggests that in casting, acting ability is more important than singing ability. Far from being merely practical advice, this suggests a deeper connection with the genre and structure of the play. For some time, the audience is asked to believe that Maggie should not be capable of recognizing her fiancé in his disguise as Tito, and that others (such as Saunders) should also succumb to the mistaken identity. In this play, the audience is eager to suspend their disbelief in favor of the fun offered by the plot line.

This play may be distinguished from the classic farce by its metatheatrical features. A term coined in 1963 by critic Lionel Abel in his book of the same name, "metatheatre" signals such devices as the play-within-a-play or performance-within-a-performance (such as the opera duet in act 1). Certainly it includes masquerading, which forms the basis for the mistaken-identity device that drives the action of the second act. There are also a few moments in the first act during which, in order to make a point to Max, Saunders addresses the audience as if they were members of the opera audience.

In some of the play's early performances, notably on the American West Coast, there was some controversy over the use of blackface as part of the *Otello* makeup, a device whose purpose is to make the identity confusion between Max and Tito more plausible.

Critical Context

Besides writing plays, Ken Ludwig is also an entertainment lawyer in the Washington, D.C., area. Although only a part-time playwright, he established quite a repertory in little more than a decade. His body of work includes *Moon over Buffalo* (pr., pb. 1996), *Sullivan and Gilbert: A Play with Music* (pr. 1983, pb. 1988), and the books for two musicals: *The Adventures of Tom Sawyer* (pr. 2001) and *Crazy for You* (pr. 1991), the latter of which was conceived by him and won three Tony Awards for best musical, costume designer, and choreography. *Lend Me a Tenor* is commonly considered his best nonmusical work. Its 1986 London production was nominated for the Olivier Award, and its 1989 Broadway production was nominated for seven Tony Awards, including best play, and won two of the awards, one for best actor and the other for best director.

Ludwig has noted that he derives some inspiration from the classics, such as William Shakespeare's *Much Ado About Nothing* (pr. c. 1598-1599, pb. 1600), and is particularly interested in reinventing classic devices for a modern audience. This is not to say that he patterns his plays after specific works, rather that he uses the devices that are common to comedy and farce. In fact, Ludwig's works all seem to derive some inspiration from the past, from literary and musical genres and styles to performers and their reputations.

The play is particularly useful for teaching comical devices and farce for advanced acting students, who have access to functional doors in the classroom. It breaks down nicely into scenes with two to four people, which facilitates scene study.

Sources for Further Study

Dunn, Don. "Broadway's Brightest Lights." *Business Week*, June 19, 1989, 105.
Hodgson, Moira. "*Lend Me a Tenor.*" *Nation* 248 (April 17, 1989): 534-535.
Hoyle, Martin. "*Lend Me a Tenor.*" *Plays and Players* 392 (May, 1986): 22.
Oliver, Edith. "Zaks Rides Again." *The New Yorker* 65 (March 13, 1989): 74.
Wetzsteon, Ross. "Zaks Appeal: Lincoln Center's King of Comedy." *New York* 23 (May 28, 1990): 50-57.

Ken McCoy

THE LESSON

Author: Eugène Ionesco (1909-1994)
Type of plot: Absurdist
Time of plot: The 1930's
Locale: An apartment in Europe
First produced: 1951, at the Théâtre de Poche, Paris
First published: La Leçon, 1954 (English translation, 1955)

>   *Principal characters:*
>   THE PROFESSOR, a man in his fifties
>   THE PUPIL, a young girl of eighteen
>   MARIE, THE MAID, a woman in her mid- to late forties

The Play

   The Lesson is set entirely in the Professor's apartment office, which is also a dining room, with a provincial buffet standing on the right. At center stage is a table that doubles as a desk. The window, upstage, is not very large, and through it the roofs of a small town can be seen in the distance. When the curtain rises, the stage is empty. After a few moments, the doorbell rings.

   The stout Maid, wearing an apron and a peasant woman's cap, enters through a door upstage, to the right, from a corridor of the apartment. She opens the hall door at stage left and lets in the young Pupil, a girl wearing a gray student's smock with a small white collar and carrying a satchel. The Maid exits, calling the Professor to come down. While waiting, the Pupil takes a notebook from her satchel and looks through it as though she is reviewing a lesson. She is smiling, lively, and dynamic, with a self-assured manner. The Professor enters, a short, aging man wearing pince-nez (eyeglasses with a spring clip) and formal black clothes, with a white collar and a small white beard. He is very timid, polite, and proper, but a lewd gleam comes into his eyes occasionally and is quickly repressed.

   After a polite exchange, the Professor says that he has lived in this town for thirty years but would prefer to live in Paris, or at least Bordeaux, and then admits that he has never seen Bordeaux and does not know Paris either. When the Pupil guesses that Paris is the capital of France, he jumps to the conclusion that she is a master of French geography. She needs help in naming the four seasons, yet says that she already has diplomas in both science and arts. Now, she declares, she is at the Professor's disposal, whereupon the recurrent gleam reappears and is extinguished. The Maid enters, looks for something at the buffet, irritates the Professor by urging him to remain calm, and exits. When the Pupil is able to add one and one correctly, the Professor concludes that within only three weeks she "should easily achieve the total doctorate."

   Thereafter, the Pupil gives answers that are sensible to her but often do not make sense according to the Professor's mathematics. She solves a massive multiplication problem through memorization but cannot rely on reasoning, so that she will never be "able to perform correctly the functions of a polytechnician." Consequently, the Professor decides to prepare her only for a partial doctorate. As he prepares to move on to the subject of philology, or the meanings of language, he is interrupted again by the Maid, now called Marie, who pulls on his sleeve and warns him that philology leads to calamity. He warns Marie that she is going too far, that he is not a child, and orders her out. Stage directions indicate that his voice changes during the play, starting off thin and reedy but growing stronger and stronger, as he becomes ever more authoritarian, until at the end it is extremely powerful. His domination reduces the Pupil to passivity, until she becomes "almost a mute and inert object."

The Professor proceeds to give a vacuous lecture full of absurdity, circular reasoning, and double-talk on the philology of various "neo-Spanish languages," including references to jai alai, a game resembling handball. He reproaches the Pupil for parading her knowledge, then lectures her on articulation in a flight of clumsy metaphors and clichés. The Pupil now begins to complain of a toothache. She continues to do so for the rest of the play, while the Professor lectures, ignores her increasing pain, and tries to force her into obedience. He threatens to extract her teeth. Then he tries to silence her by threatening to bash in her skull. He twists her wrist and she cries out. In a rage, he continues to lecture on languages.

Finally, the Professor is exasperated by the Pupil and calls in the Maid to help, but she refuses, warns him that once again he is going too far, and exits. He goes to a drawer and finds a big knife, "invisible or real." The lewd gleam in his eyes becomes "a steady devouring flame." He brandishes the knife happily, says that it will serve for all the languages, and orders the Pupil to look at it while repeating after him the word "knife." When she finally yields and repeats after him, he stabs her. They both cry "Aaah!" at the same moment. She flops onto a chair by the window in "an immodest position." He then stabs her to death, convulses, and collapses into a chair. When he returns to his senses and realizes what he has done, he calls in the Maid again. Marie lectures him, saying that "every day it's the same thing," and this pupil makes his fortieth murder; she warns him that soon he will run out of pupils. The Professor tries to strike Marie with the knife, but she overpowers him. He apologizes, she slaps him, and he cowers like a child. Then she forgives him and says that he is a good boy in spite of being a murderer.

With forty coffins to bury, the Professor is afraid that someone will notice. The Maid assures him that the sight is so commonplace that people wll not ask questions. Around his arm she puts an armband with an insignia, "perhaps the Nazi swastika." If he wears this armband, she says, he has nothing to fear. They exit, carrying the corpse. After several moments, the doorbell rings. As at the beginning of the play, the Maid appears, goes to the door, and ushers in the next Pupil.

Themes and Meanings

The Lesson satirizes totalitarianism in education, politics, language, psychology, and sexuality. This play is typical of Eugène Ionesco in its parodies, irony, nonsense, and themes of contradiction, proliferation, repetition, circularity, interchangeability, and futility.

The Professor exhibits the tendencies of bourgeois consciousness, especially reductive reasoning, to oppress and destroy the best in human nature—the Pupil—based upon repression of instinct, represented by the Maid. However, this description is itself reductive, for the free, imaginative spirit of the play transcends its own conceptual structure, through absurdity. The absurd shatters the order of rational consciousness and shocks or seduces it into at least a momentary acceptance of a larger reality, as when the self-contradicting Professor accepts from his Pupil the answer that seven plus one is sometimes nine: "We can't be sure of anything, young lady, in this world."

Some critics see the Professor as modeled on Ionesco's father and some of his teachers in Romania who were Nazis. At the end of the play, the explicit reference to a Nazi swastika points to a historical case that exemplifies on a world scale the psychodynamics of the repressed, provincial teacher, the Professor. The way he teaches makes him deadly whatever political form his opinions may take, and he is killing pupils every day.

The other characters, also, are what Ionesco calls archetypes. The most resonant lesson of *The Lesson* is conveyed by its circular structure and embodied in the stout Maid, or instinct, who opens doors, is the strongest authority, and is on the stage both first and last. The cyclical structure of the play implies continual recurrence, an archetypal pattern of human behavior.

In his reductive, totalitarian lecture on philology, the Professor equates language with geography, making the lecture a metaphor of conquest that evokes the rise of Adolf Hitler. His language is out of control. The Maid, one of the common folk, does not altogether approve of what he does—he goes too far—yet she is loyal, forgives him, continues to serve him, and puts the armband around his arm. She hints that she might become his lover. Her relationship to him is subordinate in her social role as maid, dominant in her instinctive role as mother, and devoted in her sexual role as "little Marie." She reinforces the indications in stage directions that the Professor is sexually frustrated and perhaps inclined to impotence, for she refers to gossip that he is "something of a priest at times." The language of the play is frequently sexual, its rhythm is a movement to climax, and the lesson is a mock seduction culminating in a rape.

The Professor tries to compartmentalize his mind and exclude the Maid from the lesson, saying that it is not her department. He justifies himself as a force of disintegration necessary to progress and identifies integration with the Pupil, who can add but not subtract. Ironically the Pupil is the better teacher. They sit facing each other at the table as archetypal opposites in contradiction, like hemispheres of a polarized brain. The Professor cannot force the Pupil to submit to his notion of progress, his ideology, except by killing her. The difference between ideology and integrated reality, the Professor and the play, is the absurdist factor.

Dramatic Devices

The Professor says of a military friend, "He managed to conceal his fault so effectively that, thanks to the hats he wore, no one ever noticed it." The Professor wears a conventional black skullcap, and the absurdities in his dialogue expose his faults of the head in a way that no one can fail to notice. As the absurdities increasingly reveal truths, it is the conventional that comes to seem absurd. Many ironies in the play depend upon sustaining the illusion of the ordinary while subverting it. Absurdity contradicts expectation, and contradiction generates irony. *The Lesson* reverberates with multiple ironies from beginning to end, and this ironic tone is clarified if the Professor is played with emphasis upon his self-contradictions.

The one window of the set becomes significant at the climax of the play: Just before stabbing his pupil, the Professor changes his voice and says to her, "Pay attention . . . don't break my window. . . ." He has her where he wants her now in his lust to dominate, and the window is a metaphor of his outlook, which, like the literal window, is not very large. At the beginning of the play, when the Professor is proper, the window looks out upon the town, and the sky is a calm grayish blue. Later, when he stabs the Pupil, she flops into a chair that stage directions place near the window. The view out the window, in particular the color of the sky, may be changed by stage lighting to correlate with the changes in the Professor. Approaching the end, exaggerated shadows are also appropriate.

Early in the play the Professor uses imaginary matches to illustrate a math problem, then writes at comical length on an imaginary blackboard with an imaginary piece of chalk. The leap from the commonplace to the absurd capsulizes Eugène Ionesco's method as a dramatist: requiring the audience to respond in a figurative rather than merely a literal mode. Similarly, stage directions say that the big knife may be invisible or real, but two subsequent references are made to "the invisible knife," implying that the knife should be seen as a metaphor. The murder is spiritual. The Pupil is killed by the word, an instrument of ideology that deprives her of independent life.

At the end of the play, the insignia on the armband is "perhaps" a Nazi swastika, indicating that it represents more than a single political movement. Some critics object that this reference contradicts the otherwise antididactic tone of the play. Others say that a larger meaning is conveyed if the insignia used is not a Nazi swastika but resembles or evokes one, and that this play, like *Rhinocéros* (pr., pb. 1959; *Rhinoceros*, 1959), may be reduced by too literal an interpretation of its symbols.

Critical Context

The density of meaning in *The Lesson* is evidence to some that Eugène Ionesco was more complex than Samuel Beckett, his rival for leadership of the influential avant-garde movement of the 1950's, Theater of the Absurd. This play, though less well known than *La Cantatrice chauve* (pr. 1950; *The Bald Soprano*, 1956) or *Rhinoceros*, is a more concentrated, resonant, and powerful expression of artistic vision and makes an excellent introduction to Ionesco.

In his first play, *The Bald Soprano*, Ionesco wrote with comic effect about what he called "the tragedy of language." The characters are like mechanical puppets manipulated by their language, which consists mainly of platitudes and clichés. In *The Lesson*, the dangers of language are emphasized, as the spiritual murder of the Pupil points to the literal murder of millions in World War II and beyond them to the ongoing carnage that is human history. In Ionesco's fourth play, *Les Chaises* (pr. 1952, pb. 1954; *The Chairs*, 1957), the deaf-mute Orator is comparable in his pretentious role to the wordy Professor in *The Lesson*. While some critics see these and later plays as chaotic and anarchistic, others see preconscious, mythic, or archetypal meaning underlying the absurdity.

Ionesco's early plays dramatize an existential view of life and represent the beginning of his effort to create an abstract theater, transcending the limitations of realism and the explicit politics of "committed" theater as represented by Bertolt Brecht. *The Lesson* is especially ironic in the context of Ionesco's aesthetics. Some believe that it is too didactic, while others, of the political Left, condemn it as not didactic enough. Some see his later plays as efforts to be more politically relevant, while others see consistency. As an antitotalitarian drama, *The Lesson* is comparable to *Tueur sans gages* (pr., pb. 1958; *The Killer*, 1960) and to *Rhinoceros*, in which everyone except the protagonist turns into a monstrous conformist, a rhinoceros.

Ionesco's bizarre abstraction, often derived from his dreams, has been related to abstract expressionism in painting and, in particular, to Surrealism. The analogy to painting is especially apt in respect to plays that include characters with multiple noses and breasts, and plays that focus on objects: chairs, eggs, coffee cups, and mushrooms. Because of its intellectual richness and visceral power, *The Lesson* is perhaps the most comprehensive example of Ionesco's distinctive qualities.

Sources for Further Study

Coe, Richard N. *Ionesco: A Study of His Plays*. Rev. ed. London: Methuen, 1971.

Hayman, Ronald. *Eugène Ionesco*. London: Heinemann, 1976.

Ionesco, Eugène. *Notes and Counter Notes*. Translated by Donald Watson. New York: Grove Press, 1964.

_____. *Present Past, Past Present: A Personal Memoir*. Cambridge, Mass.: Da Capo, 1998.

Kluback, William, and Michael Finkenthal. *The Clown in the Agora: Conversations About Eugène Ionesco*. New York: Lang, 1998.

Lamont, Rosette C. *Ionesco's Imperatives: The Politics of Culture*. Ann Arbor: University of Michigan Press, 1993.

_____, ed. *Ionesco: A Collection of Critical Essays*. Englewood Cliffs, N.J.: Prentice-Hall, 1973.

Lamont, Rosette C., and Melvin J. Friedman, eds. *The Two Faces of Ionesco*. New York: Whitston, 1978.

Lane, Nancy. *Understanding Ionesco*. Columbia: University of South Carolina Press, 1994.

Michael Hollister

A LESSON FROM ALOES

Author: Athol Fugard (1932-   )
Type of plot: Domestic realism
Time of plot: Autumn, 1963
Locale: Port Elizabeth, South Africa
First produced: 1978, at the Market Theatre, Johannesburg, South Africa
First published: 1981

> *Principal characters:*
> PIET BEZUIDENHOUT, an Afrikaner in his mid-forties
> GLADYS BEZUIDENHOUT, his wife, the same age
> STEVE DANIELS, his friend, a "colored" man, the same age

The Play

Piet is in the backyard of his house with an aloe plant that he is trying to identify from a field book, for names are important to him. Other potted aloes are set across the yard. His wife sits quietly nearby. Piet and Gladys have invited Steve Daniels and his family for supper, and because both are apprehensive about the impending visit, the waiting time is passing slowly. Gladys, to relieve her tension, goes into the bedroom of the house (visible to the audience) to get her sun hat and while there hides her diary under the mattress.

She returns and continues to discuss her worries about the expected visitors. Piet, trying to reassure her, sets the table and compliments her festive idea of the brass candlesticks. It shortly comes out that these will be the first visitors they have had since Gladys has been back. Where she has been is not fully revealed until act 2.

Piet returns to identifying his aloe. Gladys expresses her dislike of the plants, but Piet sees them as part of his Afrikaner heritage. To him they are hardy South African natives, surviving long droughts for brief flowerings. "Is that the price of survival in this country? Thorns and bitterness," asks Gladys, who exclaims that conversations with Piet have become "a catalog of South African disasters. Is there nothing gentle in your world?" The aloes "are turgid with violence, like everything else in the country," she says, a quality she refuses to let affect her. Piet nervously changes the subject by saying it is time to dress for the party.

Scene 2 takes place in the bedroom. Piet knocks and enters after Gladys has protectively retrieved her diary from under the mattress and put it on the dressing table in front of her. In the seven months since she has been back, not one of their friends has been around to see them. Gladys wonders if she is the reason, but Piet says people are simply frightened and have crawled into their own shells. He even admits to being frightened, which surprises Gladys, who remembers Piet's strong sense of purpose to life.

Gladys would be lost without this diary for keeping all of her woman's secrets and reminds Piet that she did lose all of her old diaries once, when the police came and took them. This is a painful memory for Gladys, who believes that that invasion of her privacy amounted to rape. Piet is quite alarmed by Gladys's agitated state, but she manages to control herself. Scene 3 takes place in the backyard. Gladys comes out dressed for the evening and quite calm in contrast to the violence and hysteria just displayed. Piet tells the story of how he got involved in the protest movement with Steve, before finally announcing the news that his colored friend is about to leave the country on an exit permit, which means he can never return. Gladys envies Steve, for she does not feel at home in Africa even though she was born there. She asks Piet, who had been greatly surprised by Steve's news, if he knows who the informer was who got Steve imprisoned for breaking his Banning Order and whether the others think it was him. Piet admits that they do. And Steve? Piet thinks not, but as the act ends, their friends still have not arrived.

Act 2 occurs two hours later. Piet starts to clear the table, then hears Steve coming and quickly resets it. Steve arrives alone, making an excuse for the others. It is clear that this is a warm meeting of old friends, but a certain awkwardness is also apparent. They start to drink Steve's wine, remembering the good times past as well as telling some new stories about each other.

Gladys joins them and tells Steve that he is fortunate to be leaving the country. Steve launches into some long remarks about how hard it is to be leaving, but he realizes that most of his dreams have soured and that he would have no future if he stayed, only oppression. Also, as Gladys had earlier, he realizes that Piet could never leave, though he cannot fully understand why.

This is their last chance to talk, and much passes between these old friends. Suddenly, Gladys asks Steve if he also suspects Piet of being the informer who sent him to jail. Reluctantly, Steve admits his doubts. After telling the story of his interrogation by the police, he asks Piet if it is true. Piet has no reply. Then Gladys says, "Of course he didn't do it!"

She becomes increasingly violent and hysterical, and it is suddenly clear where Gladys has been as she makes her own painful explanation of how she tried to resist the doctor's shock treatments by concentrating on a lovely picture of the English countryside hung in the antechamber to the treatment room. She then goes into the bedroom, and Piet explains to Steve about the diaries, the police raids, and Gladys's eventual breakdown and stay in Fort England Clinic.

Steve is still puzzled about Piet's silence on being asked if he was the informer. "If you could have believed it, there was no point in denying it." Piet has no final quotation, even for old times' sake, preferring this to be another occasion when he did not know what to say. Steve leaves, and Piet enters the bedroom where Gladys is sitting with her diary. She finally reveals that its pages are blank. She has been unable to start her life again and in fact feels she must return to the clinic in the morning. The play closes with Piet going into the backyard and sitting with his unidentified aloe before him.

Themes and Meanings

A Lesson from Aloes is about survival in a forbidding environment. The survival of friendship, marital love, brotherhood, one's humanity, one's sanity, even South Africa, are parts of the lesson. The aloe, a plant of many species native to South Africa, is used as a subtle emblem of survival in the play and, by extension, as symbolic of South Africa's history of apartheid.

Gladys does not like aloes. To her, they are thorns and fat, fleshy leaves, plants with a bitter juice and no redeeming scent. Unlike either them or her husband Piet, she is not tough, and so has fallen victim to this hot, arid land of infertile soil and violent politics. She admires Piet and his strength for endurance but has none of it herself. She would like to have remained apart from the social involvement of Piet and Steve, but this proved impossible. Involvement came after Steve was arrested, when the police raided their house and confiscated her diaries. This caused her to suffer a breakdown and go to a mental home with the wonderfully ironic name of Fort England to recover.

Piet loves his South Africa, especially the arid Eastern Cape region of Port Elizabeth and the Karoo. An Afrikaner who found himself joining the social cause of the "colored" and "blacks" (official racial designations used by the apartheid-era South African government), he is as much confined by this situation as is Gladys and the rest of the country. However, Piet will survive like the aloes he has potted, whose roots will "crawl around inside this little tin and tie themselves into knots looking for the space creation intended for them."

Piet is in a drought stage of his life, but he will endure to bloom like the aloe when the rains come again. By extension, Athol Fugard suggests that South Africa must also be tied in knots before it can work through to its salvation, though not everyone may be able to endure the process involved.

Steve loses his country too, but it has emasculated him with its persecution, leaving him totally ineffective. The only way he can even work again to feed his family is to emigrate to England, although that means he can never return to South Africa. In terms of the aloe, he is a potted plant from whom the little water that would keep him alive has been withheld.

The play is based on factual incidents that can be read about in Fugard's *Notebooks, 1960-1977* (1984), yet it transcends their specificity, just as it also transcends its several autobiographical aspects. The implications for South Africa and its people are clear, yet the play never becomes a political tract. It is above all a very touching and convincing exploration of human survival under extreme conditions, crafted by a skillful artist of the theater. For all its bleakness, the play is also an affirmation of hope, and therein lies its greatest strength.

Dramatic Devices

A Lesson from Aloes is a realistic play, though its plot demands a set that allows action to be played in the bedroom of the house while the backyard set remains in place and even occupied by other characters. All the devices common to realism, such as careful exposition, strict cause-and-effect motivation, a building of suspense, a sense of real time equal to stage time, natural dialogue, and convincing character interaction, are present. The play has been called Chekhovian, because of its similarities to plays written by Anton Chekhov, and while too much can be made of that description, it is accurate in the sense that everything the characters do is believable, and the overall effect is carefully achieved by a tapestry of accumulated detail instead of by a strictly linear plot, though at one level that is there, too. Nothing is ever obvious or superficial.

The first act presents a challenge that Fugard has met well in his writing, for on the surface, it is all waiting for Steve to arrive, while beneath the surface it is much more. The characters of Piet and Gladys are fleshed out, and other matters of exposition, such as the story of how Piet came to know Steve, are handled in a naturalistic manner. By the second act and Steve's arrival, the ground has been skillfully prepared for the revelations and climaxes that follow.

For example, a masterful irony that is central to the play's theme emerges from the fact that Steve is about to emigrate to England. He has always thought of Gladys as being English, so he asks her to tell him what this new place he is going to will be like. She says that she has visited it several times, always in a pleasant summertime, but her description for Steve is purposely delayed by other revelations until almost the end of the play. When she does finally describe England, it is a picture on the wall at the mental clinic called Fort England that she recalls, and it becomes clear that this is as close as she has ever been to the real England. The irony involved is completed when Gladys tells Piet that she knows she will have to return to the clinic in the morning. Like Steve, whose pending emigration to England she envies, she will escape to her England. South Africa has beaten her, at least for the present. Of the three, only Piet is left in his beloved Africa to care for his aloes. In less skillful hands, this ending might seem contrived and obvious, but Fugard makes it all quite natural and believable.

Critical Context

Athol Fugard's first two full-length plays, *No-Good Friday* (pr. 1958, pb. 1977) and *Nongogo* (pr. 1959, pb. 1977), grew out of his experiences with Sophiatown, a multiracial area of Johannesburg that had just been rezoned as a white area when Fugard went to work as a clerk in the Native Commissioner's Court, where passbook law offenders were tried. He made his first black friends while there and gained at first hand an understanding of how the bureaucratic maze of apartheid in his country functioned. These early plays are largely naturalistic, and while well received at the time, Fugard now openly considers them to be rather naïve apprenticeship pieces. They did, however, begin Fugard's continuing exploration of the theme of human survival under extreme conditions.

The Blood Knot (pr. 1961, pb. 1963) is about the relationship between two brothers, one of whom can pass as white. This play established Fugard as an author of considerable promise. It is the first of many plays to be set in Port Elizabeth, a bleak home to the kind of people about whom Fugard writes. *Hello and Goodbye* (pr. 1965, pb. 1966), *People Are Living There* (pr. 1968, pb. 1969), and *Boesman and Lena* (pr., pb. 1969) all allow audiences to identify effectively with various other characters on the fringes of society.

Orestes: An Experiment in Theatre as Described in a Letter to an American Friend (pr. 1971, pb. 1978) was the first of several experiments inspired by Jerzy Grotowski's work, in which plays were developed through improvisations with actors. *Sizwe Bansi Is Dead* (pr. 1972, pb. 1973), *The Island* (pr. 1973, pb. 1974), and *Statements After an Arrest Under the Immorality Act* (pr. 1972, pb. 1974) are stronger plays produced by the same process, which was itself carried on in defiance of the authorities who tried to stifle its performances. These plays are considerably nonrealistic when compared to both earlier and later works.

Dimetos (pr. 1975, pb. 1977) and the film *The Guest* (1977) belong to a less effective and more withdrawn period of Fugard's work. Then, with the film *Marigolds in August* (1982) and the plays *A Lesson from Aloes* and *"MASTER HAROLD" . . . and the Boys* (pr., pb. 1982), Fugard returns to the Port Elizabeth setting with a matured and effectively realistic style containing strongly autobiographical overtones. *The Road to Mecca* (pr. 1984, pb. 1985) and *A Place with the Pigs* (pr. 1987, pb. 1989) continue to explore the theme of survival, but with subject matter that is not explicitly related to apartheid. In the late twentieth and early twenty-first centuries, Fugard produced several new plays, including *My Children! My Africa!* (pr., pb. 1990), *Playland* (pr., pb. 1992), *My Life* (pr. 1994, pb. 1996), *The Captain's Tiger* (pr., pb. 1997) and *Sorrows and Rejoicings* (pr., pb. 2001).

Sources for Further Study

Benson, Mary. *Athol Fugard and Barry Simon: Bare-Stage, a Few Props, Great Theatre*. Columbus: Ohio University Press, 1999.

Fugard, Athol. *Notebooks, 1960-1977*. New York: Knopf, 1984.

Gray, Stephen, ed. *Athol Fugard*. London: Methuen, 1991.

Hauptfleisch, Temple. *Athol Fugard: A Source Guide*. Johannesburg: Donker, 1982.

King, Kimball, and Albert Ertheim. *Athol Fugard: A Casebook*. New York: Garland, 1997.

Mshengu. "Political Theatre in South Africa and the Work of Athol Fugard." *Theatre Research International* 7 (Autumn, 1982): 160-179.

Vandenbroucke, Russell. *Truth the Hand Can Touch: The Theatre of Athol Fugard*. New York: Theatre Communications Group, 1985.

Walder, Dennis. *Athol Fugard*. New York: Twayne, 1985.

Peter B. Young

LES LIAISONS DANGEREUSES

Author: Christopher Hampton (1946-   )
Type of plot: Social realism
Time of plot: The 1780's
Locale: Mansions and châteaus in and around Paris and the Bois de Vincennes
First produced: 1985, at The Other Place, Stratford-upon-Avon, England
First published: 1985

Principal characters:
MARQUISE DE MERTEUIL, a respectable widow
MADAME DE VOLANGES, her cousin
CÉCILE DE VOLANGES, the cousin's fifteen-year-old, convent-
    educated daughter
VICOMTE DE VALMONT, the Marquise's former lover and current
    partner in intrigue
AZOLAN, his valet
MADAME DE ROSEMONDE, Valmont's eighty-one-year-old aunt
MADAME DE TOURVEL, Rosemonde's pious young friend, wife of
    a presiding judge
ÉMILIE, a courtesan
CHEVALIER DANCENY, a twenty-two-year-old knight of Malta in
    love with Cécile

The Play

The opening dialogue among Marquise de Merteuil, her cousin Madame de Volanges, and her cousin's daughter Cécile in the marquise's luxurious salon on a warm August evening establishes the marquise's spotless reputation and Cécile's naïveté. With Valmont's arrival and the Volanges' departure, the play begins its alternation between the conspiratorial encounters of the two libertines, Valmont and the marquise, and scenes of their reprehensible manipulation of those they victimize.

Scene 1 introduces a double intrigue: The marquise wishes to revenge herself on Gercourt, a former lover who left her for Valmont's mistress, by having Valmont seduce and debauch Gercourt's pure fiancé, Cécile; Valmont is intent on seducing an administrator's virtuous wife, Madame de Tourvel. Although Valmont refuses such easy game as Cécile, and the marquise scorns his seduction of a married woman, the marquise promises to renew their earlier liaison upon seeing written proof of his victory over Madame de Tourvel.

Scene 2 finds Valmont at his aunt's chateau in the country, with the Volanges and Madame de Tourvel as fellow guests. To benefit from a scene of reform staged with Azolan's collaboration, Valmont declares himself to Madame de Tourvel, only to be spurned despite her attraction to him; immediately after, scene 3 shows his cynical recourse to Émilie's bare back, in bed, as a desk for writing Madame de Tourvel a love letter full of witty double entendres.

Ten days later, again conspiring with the marquise, Valmont is eager to seduce Cécile for his own sake, since he now knows that her mother warned Madame de Tourvel against him. Fooling both Danceny, who is in love with and is loved by Cécile, and Madame de Volanges, who rejects Danceny as a suitor for her daughter, into trusting her advice, the marquise arranges for Valmont to become the young couple's mediator. The upshot comes in scene 6, when, having allowed Valmont to make a copy of the key to her bedroom, Cécile is helpless to denounce him when he forces himself upon her one night.

Meanwhile, thanks to their proximity in Madame de Rosemonde's home and Valmont's machinations, Madame de Tourvel's passion builds to a climactic confrontation in scene 9, during which Valmont insists that she "look" her love for him. Desperate and hysterical from self-restraint, she collapses, but Valmont, uncharacteristically, resists the opportunity to take advantage of her weakness. Act 1 ends with Madame de Rosemonde's condemnation of men's incapacity for devotion and her tolerant kindness to her young friend, who flees in the night to escape temptation.

By the opening of act 2, the shared revenge against Madame de Volanges is complete, with Cécile pregnant by Valmont. However, the marquise is not entirely satisfied. Jealous over Valmont's obvious involvement in his pursuit of Madame de Tourvel, she mocks his slow progress and refuses to tell him the identity of her new lover, revealed to the audience two scenes later as Danceny. In the three scenes in which Valmont hurries to her Paris mansion to report on his interactions with Madame de Tourvel (scenes 12, 14, and 16), she becomes increasingly hostile and scornful.

From scene 11, where Valmont enjoys Madame de Tourvel's surrender, the play moves rapidly to his humiliation (scene 13) and rejection (scene 15) of this new mistress as a sacrifice to the marquise. It is only in scene 16 that Valmont realizes what the audience has long understood: that the marquise has schemed against him as well as with him and that she has no intention of granting a sexual reward. Having already punished her coldness by encouraging Danceny to leave her for Cécile, Valmont now threatens the marquise, and the two allies declare war on each other.

Subsequently, in a duel in the Bois de Vincennes over Cécile's honor, Danceny fatally wounds a careless Valmont, hears Valmont's deathbed warning to beware the marquise, and promises to relay Valmont's message of undying love to Madame de Tourvel. On New Year's Eve, Mertueil sits playing cards with Madame de Volanges and Madame de Rosemonde, discussing the death of Madame de Tourvel, Cécile's withdrawal to a convent, and Danceny's departure for Malta. The marquise rallies her companions by invoking better days that lie ahead.

Themes and Meanings

Hampton's play is a dramatic adaptation of the sensationally successful novel with the same title, written in 1782 by Pierre Choderlos de Laclos, a French career soldier. The decadence of the prerevolutionary, aristocratic world in Laclos's fiction proved an ideal match for Hampton's thematic consistency in exploring individual and cultural corruption, abusive and self-destructive relationships, and the tensions between individual fulfillment and moral responsibility. In Laclos's libertines Hampton recognized, and then re-created, eighteenth century counterparts to the malicious, sexually exploitative protagonists in some of his own work, including the poet Arthur Rimbaud in *Total Eclipse* (pr. 1968, pb. 1969) and Dave in *Treats* (pr., pb. 1976). Indeed, *Les Liaisons Dangereuses* recalls both *Total Eclipse* and *Treats* in its focus on intimate relationships shaped by malice, verbal duels, and the deployment of sex as a weapon.

The marquise's and Valmont's power games in the original novel accorded marvelously with Hampton's interest in intelligent, cold-blooded people who approach life as a competition that they must win by besting and even destroying others. This theme comes across in the game metaphor running throughout the play, as in the stage direction: "There flashes momentarily across Valmont's face the expression of a chess champion who has just lost his queen," or the marquise's comment that once women yield sexually, men "hold every ace in the pack." Understandably, Hampton also used military metaphors for his protagonists' assaults on the mores of their society.

In *Les Liaisons Dangereuses*, as in other Hampton plays, language serves as one of the vehicles of corruption: His two schemers habitually rely on irony, puns, and perversely echoed expressions to exploit and deride others. For instance, Valmont refers to the marquise's seduction of Danceny as "lessons," callously calls Cécile's miscarriage a "refurbishment," and later breaks with Madame de Tourvel by brutally repeating the words whose emotionality originally displeased Mertueil: "It's beyond my control." In describing his exertions to get the play's dialogue just right, Hampton said that he aimed at "a kind of language, artificial but tied to the period, elaborate but direct, the object of which was to mirror the novel's difficult combination of scientific detachment and perilous emotional extremes."

Although Hampton has insisted that as "a strategy for dealing with the horrors of the world . . . [the theater] should not pretend to console for things for which there is no consolation," his shift of emphasis at the end of the play actually provides more hope than Laclos's conception. By having the dying Valmont send a message of true love to Madame de Tourvel instead of vindictively giving Danceny the marquise's letters for public exposure, Hampton virtually redeems Valmont and romantic love. In fact, there are no letters, since, unlike her epistolary predecessor, Hampton's marquise makes it a principle never to write to her lovers. Something is salvaged in a cold world of calculation, viciousness, and debauchery.

By thus diluting both Madame de Tourvel and the marquise's victimization by Valmont, Hampton loses some of his source's attack on patriarchal abuse of women. True, in scene 4, he adapts the marquise's famous account of how she invented herself to "dominate [Valmont's] sex and avenge [her] own," and in their last encounter, he has the marquise accuse Valmont of bullying women. But despite describing Laclos, in a note preceding the play, as a feminist, Hampton chooses to make their shared male villain in his last appearance less a representative of a misogynistic society than a man reformed by love.

Dramatic Devices

The play's opening and closing scenes mirror each other: Two and three women, respectively, sit playing cards. Through this parallel, Hampton not only preserves the balance that he admires in classical French literature but also emphasizes his protagonists' view of life itself as a game to win through strategy and trickery. In addition, he divides the play into two acts, each spanning more or less two months and comprising nine scenes. Further dividing these scenes into three units of three, Hampton condenses many of his source's letters for most of the scenes but ensures that each unit includes "one interlude-like scene (always in second or third position) covering a single event, often in a bedroom, always featuring some kind of single-combat."

The play's final moments feature a stage effect that changes the novel's ultimate punishment of the marquise (through loss of appearance and fortune): After her closing line, "Meanwhile, I suggest our best course is to continue with the game," the silhouette of the guillotine appears briefly before the lights fade entirely, investing her comment about "look[ing] forward to whatever the nineties may bring" with irony and implying a violent reprisal for her aristocratic decadence. At the same time, this line, coupled with her comment about being "more than halfway through the eighties already," is also one of the play's most obvious links to Hampton's own time and his criticism of the callousness toward the less privileged under British prime minister Margaret Thatcher's conservative government in the 1980's.

Interestingly, Hampton's decision to set all the scenes indoors—triggered by a problem with prop storage at the premiering theater—intensified the social containment and worldly removal from natural rhythms already evident in the novel.

Critical Context

Les Liaisons Dangereuses fits into and represents the peak of Hampton's career-long passion for classical French literature. Although his first drama, *When Did You Last See My Mother?* (pr. 1966, pb. 1967), owed something to John Osborne's *Look Back in Anger* (pr. 1956, pb. 1957), subsequent projects—original plays, translations and adaptations—testified to the paramount influence of French precedents on his work. Notably, in *Total Eclipse* he explored Rimbaud's relationship with French poet Paul Verlaine; conceived the comedy of manners *The Philanthropist* (pr. 1970, pb. 1971) as a response to Molière's *Le Misanthrope* (pr. 1666, pb. 1667; *The Misanthrope*, 1709); and adapted Molière's *Dom Juan: Ou, Le Festin de Pierre* (pr. 1665, pb. 1682; *Don Juan*, 1755) in his *Don Juan* (pr. 1972, pb. 1974) and *Tartuffe: Ou, L'Imposteur* (pr. 1664, pb. 1669; English translation, 1732) in his adaptation of the same play (pr. 1983). In *Total Eclipse*, Hampton signaled his interest in *Les Liaisons Dangereuses* by having Verlaine compare his marriage to Valmont's interactions with Cécile.

The world derived from classical French literature that Hampton redesigned for the play clearly relates to his own society as well. Hampton's epigraph for the play—from French novelist André Malraux—relays a social-conscience message equally appropriate for France in the 1780's and Tory England in the 1980's: "As with so many works of our time—not just literary ones—the reader of *Liaisons* might have said, 'It can't continue like this.'" In fact, in a 1989 interview, Hampton explicitly connected Laclos's connivers with the selfish, greedy people in power in modern England—noting, however, that his contemporaries lacked the charm to seduce others into appreciating their vile triumphs. Thus, eighteenth century authenticity combined smoothly with contemporary social criticism.

Although Hampton himself has claimed to see no connection among his plays' themes and to have "no particular style," his hallmark seems to be sophisticated analysis of complex, intellectual, and articulate protagonists, whose self-absorption and conflicts he presents with wit and implicit political awareness. Many of these characters are admirably ironic and clever, but their deceit, ruthlessness, and self-absorption ultimately cut them off from their fellow humans.

For his remarkable success in dramatizing events originally relayed in the epistolary form, Hampton received almost unanimously glowing reviews and numerous awards, including the *Time Out* magazine's best production award in 1986, the 1986 Olivier Award for best drama, and the 1987 New York Drama Critics Circle Award for best foreign play. In 1988, his revision of *Les Liaisons Dangereuses* for a film directed by countryman Stephen Frears (starring John Malkovich, Glenn Close, Michelle Pfeiffer, and Uma Thurman) won him both the American and the British Academy Award for Best Adapted Screenplay.

Sources for Further Study

Black, Sebastian. "Makers of Real Shapes: Christopher Hampton and His Story-Tellers." In *Contemporary British Drama, 1970-1990*, edited by Hersh Zeifman and Cynthia Zimmerman. Toronto, Ont.: University of Toronto Press, 1993.

Colby, Douglas. *As the Curtain Rises: On Contemporary British Drama, 1966-1976*. Rutherford, N.J.: Fairleigh Dickinson University Press, 1978.

DiGaetani, John L. "Christopher Hampton." In *A Search for a Postmodern Theater: Interviews with Contemporary Playwrights*, edited by John L. DiGaetani. New York: Greenwood Press, 1991.

Francis, Ben. *Christopher Hampton: Dramatic Ironist*. Oxford, England: Amber Lane Press, 1996.

Free, William J., and Dale Salwak. *Christopher Hampton: An Introduction to His Plays*. San Bernardino, Calif.: Borgo Press, 1994.

Gross, Robert, ed. *Christopher Hampton: A Casebook*. New York: Garland, 1990.

Kiebuzinska, Christine. "The Narcissist and the Mirror in *Les Liaisons Dangereuses*: Laclos, Hampton, Muller." *The Comparatist: Journal of the Southern Comparative Literature Association*, May, 1993, 81-100.

Wilcher, Robert. "Christopher Hampton: Dramatic Ironist." *Theater Research International* 22, no. 2 (Summer, 1997): 175-176.

Margaret Bozenna Goscilo